MY
INDECISION
IS
FINAL

Jake Eberts entered the movie industry by chance after a degree from Harvard Business School had launched him into a successful career in banking. His ability to raise film finance led to the founding of Goldcrest Films, of which he was chief executive. He is currently chief executive of Allied Filmmakers. He lives in London and Quebec with his wife and three children.

Terry Ilott is a journalist and writer. He was editing the UK's leading film trade paper, *Screen International*, during the Goldcrest era. He is currently writing a book on film finance in the 1980s and is consultant editor of the *Financial Times* newsletter, *Screen Finance*. He divides his time between London and Wiltshire.

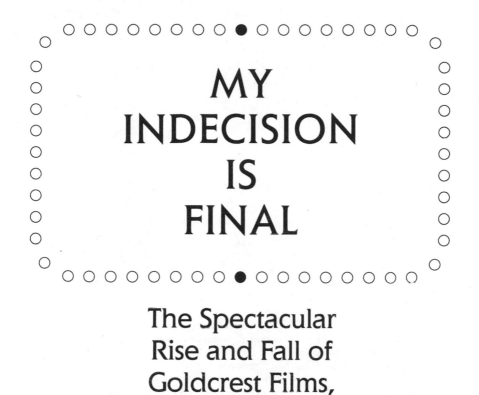

MY
INDECISION
IS
FINAL

The Spectacular
Rise and Fall of
Goldcrest Films,
the Independent Studio That
Challenged Hollywood

○ ● ○

Jake Eberts and Terry Ilott

THE ATLANTIC MONTHLY PRESS
NEW YORK

First published in Great Britain in 1990 by Faber and Faber Limited
First Atlantic Monthly Press edition, October 1990
Printed in the United States of America

First Edition

Library of Congress Cataloging-in-Publication Data

Eberts, Jake.
   My indecision is final: the spectacular rise and fall of
Goldcrest Films, the independent studio that challenged Hollywood /
Jake Eberts and Terry Ilott.—1st Atlantic Monthly Press ed.
   1. Goldcrest Films and Television—History. 2. Motion picture
industry—Great Britain—History. I. Ilott, Terry. II. Title.
PN1999.GC55E24   1990   384'.8'0941—dc20   90-1040

ISBN 0-87113-392-X

The Atlantic Monthly Press
19 Union Square West
New York, NY 10003

FIRST PRINTING

To my late father, who never saw any of the films I have been involved with, but who is nevertheless a daily influence on my life.

To my mother, who guarantees that at least *one* ticket will be sold to *any* film with which I have the remotest connection.

To the world's most honest critics, my wife Fiona and our children, Alexander, David and Lindsay, whose mere presence reminds me how lucky I am.

Jake Eberts

To my mother, Eileen, and in memory of my father, Jim; to my brother and sisters, Kevin, Ann and Francine; to Joe, Jon and Sarah; and to Emma, Kate, Lizzie and Katie.

Terry Ilott

Contents

List of Illustrations

Acknowledgements

The authors would like to thank the following former Goldcrest employees, film-makers, directors, executives and associates for consenting to be interviewed for this book: Sir Richard Attenborough, John Boorman, Chris Burt, Terry Clegg, Peter Coles, Don Cruickshank, Guy East, Bill Gavin, Fernando Ghia, Sam Goldwyn Jnr., Jerome Hellman, Hugh Hudson, Roland Joffe, James Joll, Paul Knight, James Lee, Sandy Lieberson, Jim Miller, David Norris, Andy Parsons, David Puttnam, Amanda Schiff, Terry Semel, Maureen Sheen, Iain Smith, Michael Stoddart, Garth Thomas, Steve Walsh, Alan Whitaker, Irwin Winkler, Mike Wooller and Steve Woolley. Thanks are also due to Frans Afman, Sue Austen, Anne Barson, Fiona Eberts, Diana Hawkins and Irene Lyons for their useful comments regarding various aspects of Goldcrest's history; to Ken Simson for assistance in preparing research materials; and to Esmee McConnell and Lucinda Sturgis for transcribing many hours of taped interviews.

The authors acknowledge with special gratitude the contribution made by John Chambers, whose assistance has been invaluable.

Preface

To most people outside the small world of the film industry, the name Goldcrest means nothing. But for ten years, 1977–86, it was a creative powerhouse, investing £65 million ($95 million) in feature films and £25 million ($38 million) in television movies, drama series and documentaries that between them received hundreds of awards, including no less than nineteen Oscars. Working with film-makers of the calibre of David Puttnam, John Boorman, Peter Yates, Richard Attenborough, Roland Joffe, Hugh Hudson and Bill Forsyth, investing in acclaimed productions such as *The Killing Fields, Chariots of Fire, Gandhi, The Dresser* and *Local Hero*, and backed by a host of respected financial institutions in the City of London, Goldcrest was the outstanding independent film company of the decade.

To the people who worked for Goldcrest, or whose films were financed by Goldcrest, the company was something even more than that: it was the centre of their universe. Its collapse left them stunned and bereft. Many are still trying to work out what went wrong.

Proof of their puzzlement and of their good faith is that they all co-operated fully in the preparation of this book, which thus serves not only as a record of events, but as a record of their various interpretations of those events and, inevitably, of their opinions of each other. The book, in other words, has become an intervention in the story itself. This is all the more true in that one of the key players in the saga, Goldcrest's founder and long-time chief executive Jake Eberts, is a co-author.

One of the main premises of this book, and the justification for co-authorship, is that the character of Eberts is the enigma at the heart of the story, at least in its earlier stages. Almost alone among the major figures associated with Goldcrest, Eberts did not have a grand plan. This speaks either for the modesty of his ambition or for the total identification, in his own mind, between the company and himself. The latter explanation is the more convincing, for the first seven years of Goldcrest's life revolved almost exclusively around his personality and interests. Indeed, it is no exaggeration to say that during that time the company was built in his image. When, in the autumn of 1983, he realized that others, especially James Lee, were shaping the company into something resembling their own likenesses, Eberts stepped down. No other reading makes sense of his decision to abandon the company when it was at the very pinnacle of its success.

Eberts's account of those first years is as objective as he can make it, but it remains unashamedly personal, and is all the more revealing for being so. It is his story that dominates the early part of this book. Goldcrest's crisis and collapse are then dealt with by Terry Ilott, who, having been an observer but not a participant in the events described, brings to the task a greater degree of detachment and objectivity. Eberts's personal narrative then brings the story to its conclusion.

It was the authors' intention that the two parts of the book should complement each other, Eberts's reminiscences being balanced by Ilott's account of the testimony of others and by the findings of his research in the archives. The value of the book depends largely upon the degree to which this balance has been achieved.

Other balances, however, have not even been attempted. For example, the documents that are reproduced in the text are invariably the work of the leading executives within the company, and it is their testimony which is most often quoted. Film-makers and junior staff do appear, and sometimes even the families of the leading players are mentioned, but only as seen by Eberts or Lee or their senior executive colleagues. This is, in other words, a boardroom book. As such, it runs the risk of taking at face value the documented record of the battles that preoccupied the Goldcrest managers and directors – battles that in many cases were the expression of personal rivalries rather than substantive arguments about the policies of the company. A different book could have been written from the point of view of the receptionist or office messenger. Another book again could have been written from the perspective of the film-makers who worked with the company. It was the authors' view at the outset, however, that it was beyond their competence to encompass all these books within one set of covers. Two books, Eberts's and Ilott's, presented difficulties enough.

The authors have told the story as plainly as they are able. By and large, they have avoided making broad judgements. A few comments at the outset, however, will help guide the reader through the many pages of analysis and anecdote that follow.

First, the executives who compete for space on these pages, much as they competed for power at board meetings, are all men. Indeed, they are all men of a certain type – white, middle-class professionals – and of a certain age – at the time of our story they were in their early forties. For many of them, working for Goldcrest was more than just a job: it was a chance for glory. In most cases, it was the first such chance that had come their way. To say this is not to make little of them or their ambitions. Most of us want to be better than we are – richer, more famous, more glorious, more powerful, more attractive or more virtuous – and we long for an opportunity that will enable us, or require us, to change. For the Goldcrest executives their jobs provided such an opportunity: the company, so successful, so glamorous and so exciting, enabled them to match their career moves with their dreams of personal fulfilment. This is not something that happens often, or to everybody, and there are still former Goldcrest executives and employees who have yet to get over the experience. For them, those were halcyon days.

Second, probably in no walk of life is there such confusion between reality and fantasy as in the world of the movies. It is a confusion that affects accountants and secretaries as much as actors and directors, for the glamour of film seems to rub off on everyone. Film studios are sometimes called fantasy factories not just because they produce fantasies but because they are themselves the subject of so much fantasy. So it was with Goldcrest. There were times, well documented in the latter half of this book, when the idea of Goldcrest was clearly a much more powerful factor in the minds of its decision-makers than was the reality. Unfortunately, each of them had in mind a different idea of the company, and each such idea reflected, however imperfectly, the idealized self-image of the executive in question. Hence the emergence of departmental fiefdoms – in business affairs, television, film production, finance and sales – which were engaged in continual feuding. Hence the constant stream of grandiose organizational plans and proposals that were presented to the monthly board meetings from the beginning of 1984 onwards. Hence, also, the obsessively overworked atmosphere that characterized the inner-life of Goldcrest, especially in its heyday.

Third, just as in the entire Goldcrest management team and board of directors there was found to be no place for a woman, so in Goldcrest's films there were few substantial parts for actresses. Indeed, it is striking how few parts there were for black people, bohemians, muscle-men, intellectuals – any kind of person, in fact, with whom the Goldcrest executives themselves could not strongly identify. Most of the pictures made by the company tell the same story, of an essentially middle-class man, whose honour, fortitude and decency enable him to triumph against the odds. *Chariots of Fire, The Killing Fields, The Mission* and *Revolution* all fit this pattern, as does the company's most successful, and in many ways most typical, product, *Gandhi,* the leading role in which was played by an Englishman. That Ben Kingsley was brilliant in the part, and that Sir Richard Attenborough cast him because he expected him to be brilliant, does not in any way invalidate the observation that, as far as the Goldcrest board and management were concerned, Kingsley, unlike Gandhi himself, was one of them.

Just as the enigma of Eberts's character holds a key to the origins and growth of the company, so the confusion between fantasy and reality, between the ideal Goldcrests and the real Goldcrest, between the heroics on screen and the heroic self-images of the Goldcrest executives, provides a key to its crisis and collapse. From May 1984 onwards, Goldcrest was led more by wishful thinking than by common sense. By early 1985, fantasy had run riot.

There are doubtless other ways of interpreting the story that follows. The characters who populate these pages are real people, after all, and they may see things differently. The authors do not expect, still less claim, to have had the last word.

London, January 1990

Cast List

(Many of those listed below have since moved on to other jobs with other companies. The job titles given here are those applicable at the time of our story.)

Frans Afman. Senior vice-president, Entertainment Business Division, Credit Lyonnais Bank Nederland. Important banker in the independent film business in the 1970s and 1980s. Would-be banker to Goldcrest in 1985.

Sir Richard Attenborough. Actor, producer and director. Credits include *A Bridge Too Far*, *Magic*, *Gandhi*, *A Chorus Line* and *Cry Freedom*. Influential director of Goldcrest Holdings (1981–7) and chairman of Goldcrest Films and Television Limited (1985–7). Close friend of Jake Eberts.

Roland Betts. American lawyer/financier. Senior executive of International Film Investors and founder of Silver Screen Partners.

Michael (Viscount) Blakenham. Chairman of Pearson, Goldcrest's principal shareholder. Responsible for the appointment of James Lee as chief executive after Eberts's departure in 1983.

John Boorman. Film producer and director. Credits include *Point Blank*, *Hell in the Pacific*, *Zardoz*, *Excalibur*, *The Emerald Forest*, *Hope and Glory* and *Where the Heart Is*. Executive producer of *Dream One*. Close friend of Jake Eberts.

Neil Braun. Senior executive of International Film Investors. Colleague of Roland Betts.

Roger Brooke. Chief executive of Pearson Longman until 1973. First investor, with Michael Stoddart of Electra Investment Trust, in *Watership Down* and the original Goldcrest development fund.

Christ Burt. Film and television producer. Associate producer of *Revolution*.

Michel Canny. Vice-chairman of Credit Lyonnais Nederland.

John Chambers. Financial director of Goldcrest (1982–7), then managing director (1987).

Jo Child. American financier. Co-founder, with Jake Eberts, of International Film Investors, which was a co-investor, with Goldcrest, in *The Killing Fields*, *Gandhi*, *Local Hero*, *Escape from New York*, *The Howling* and *Enigma*.

Terry Clegg. Production executive. Line producer of *Gandhi* and Goldcrest's executive in charge of production (1982–4).

Don Cruickshank. Deputy chief executive of Goldcrest (1984). Close associate of James Lee, with whom he had worked at Pearson Longman and McKinsey.

Guy East. Bill Gavin's successor as Goldcrest's head of sales (1984–7).

Jake Eberts. Goldcrest's founder and chief executive.

John Evangelides. Senior executive of Samuel Montagu, the merchant-banking division of Midland Bank. Goldcrest's would-be banker in 1985–6.

Bill Gavin. Film salesman. Set up Goldcrest's foreign-sales operation. Sales director (1982–4).

Fernando Ghia. Film producer. Credits include *Lady Caroline Lamb*, *Amarcord* and, with David Puttnam, *The Mission*.

Angus Grossart. Banker and financier. Principal officer of Edinburgh merchant bank Noble Grossart Ltd. Goldcrest shareholder and board member (1982–7).

Ted Harris. Corporate finance director of Midland Bank. Goldcrest's banker.

Jerome Hellman. Film producer. Credits include *Midnight Cowboy*, *Coming Home* and *Mosquito Coast*.

Hugh Hudson. Film director. Credits include *Chariots of Fire*, *Greystoke* and *Revolution*.

James Joll. Finance director of Pearson. Director of Goldcrest (1984–6).

Paul Knight. Television producer. Goldcrest 'satellite' producer (1981–6). Responsible for *Robin of Sherwood* series.

Norman Lear. American television producer and one-time co-owner, with Jerry Perenchio, of Embassy Communications.

James Lee. Chief executive of Pearson Longman (1980–3). Goldcrest chairman (1980–4). Goldcrest chief executive (1984–5). Close friend of David Puttnam.

Sandy Lieberson. Film producer and studio executive. Former colleague and long-time close friend of David Puttnam. Goldcrest's head of production (1984–5).

Earle Mack. American financier, businessman and patron of the arts. Would-be financial saviour of Goldcrest in 1987.

Alan Marshall. Film producer and former partner of director Alan Parker. Credits include *Birdy, Pink Floyd: The Wall* and *Another Country*.

Mike Massey. Midland Bank executive responsible for the Goldcrest account. Colleague of Ted Harris.

Peter Mayer. Managing director of Penguin Books. Non-executive director of Goldcrest (1982–7).

Bernie Myers. Banker. Senior executive at N. M. Rothschild and Sons. Responsible for the prospectus issued on behalf of Goldcrest Holdings in April 1984.

David Norris. Entertainment-industry lawyer. Goldcrest's director of business affairs (1982–5).

Andy Parsons. Accountant in charge of the day-to-day financial management of Goldcrest's film and television investments (1982–7).

Jerry Perenchio. American entrepreneur. One-time co-owner, with Norman Lear, of Embassy Communications.

David Puttnam. Film and television producer. Credits include *Midnight Express, Mahler, Chariots of Fire, The Killing Fields, Local Hero* and *The Mission*. Executive producer of the *First Love* series of low-budget television films. Influential director of Goldcrest (1980–6). Closely associated with James Lee and Sandy Lieberson.

Martin Rosen. Film producer. Credits include *Watership Down, The Plague Dogs* and *Smooth Talk*, the latter two part-financed by Goldcrest. Close friend of James Lee.

Terry Semel. President and chief operating officer of Warner Brothers.

Iain Smith. Associate producer of *The Killing Fields* and *The Mission*.

Michael Stoddart. Joint chief executive of Electra Investment Trust. First investor, with Roger Brooke of Pearson Longman, in *Watership Down* and the original Goldcrest development fund. Director (1977–84) and chairman (1984–7) of Goldcrest.

Julien Temple. Director of *Absolute Beginners*.

Garth Thomas. Goldcrest's executive in charge of production (1984–5), responsible for supervision of *Revolution, The Mission, A Room With a View* and *Absolute Beginners*.

Steve Walsh. Television salesman. In charge of Goldcrest's television sales and co-productions (1983–4).

Alan Whitaker. Executive director of Pearson and non-executive director of Goldcrest (1986–7).

Philip Whitehead. Television producer and politician. Non-executive director of Goldcrest (1984–7).

Paul Whitney. Senior executive of the National Coal Board Pension Fund. Major shareholder in Goldcrest and non-executive director (1985–7).

Irwin Winkler. American film producer. Credits include the *Rocky* series, *The Right Stuff, Raging Bull, Round Midnight* and *Revolution*.

Mike Wooller. Managing director of Goldcrest Television (1981–5).

Steve Woolley. Film producer. Credits include *Mona Lisa, Company of Wolves* and *Absolute Beginners*.

Key companies

Allied Filmmakers. Development and film packaging company founded by Jake Eberts after leaving Goldcrest.

Brent Walker. British company with interests in leisure, real-estate and entertainment industries. Bidder, via Masterman, for control of Goldcrest in 1987.

Credit Lyonnais. Major European bank, the Rotterdam office of which houses the Entertainment Business Division. This division, under the direction of Frans Afman, became the leading banker to the independent film business in the 1980s.

Deloitte Haskins and Sells. Major firm of London accountants. Audited Goldcrest's accounts and provided cash-flow reports in 1985–6.

E. F. Hutton. Major American stockbroker which handled the fund-raising for International Film Investors (IFI) in 1977–8. Subsequently acquired by Shearson Lehman.

Electra Investment Trust. One of London's biggest investment trusts. First investor, with Pearson Longman, in *Watership Down* and the original Goldcrest development fund. Major investor in Goldcrest from 1977–87. Joint chief executive of Electra, Michael Stoddart, was chairman of Goldcrest (1984–7).

Embassy Film Associates. Feature film fund raised on behalf of Embassy Pictures.

Embassy Pictures. American film and television company owned by Norman Lear and Jerry Perenchio.

Freshfields. Goldcrest's solicitors.

Goldcrest. There were three Goldcrest partnerships – Goldcrest Films International (GFI), Goldcrest Films and Television (GFT) and Goldcrest Film and Television Partners (GFTP) – as well as a myriad of subsidiary companies. All were merged into one company, Goldcrest Holdings Ltd, in 1984.

Hemdale. London- and Los Angeles-based film-production and distribution company. Bid for control of Goldcrest in 1987.

International Film Investors (IFI). American film-finance partnership founded by Jo Child and Jake Eberts. Linked to Goldcrest by a reciprocal investment agreement. Co-investor with Goldcrest in *The Killing Fields*, *Local Hero* and *Gandhi* among others.

Lazard Brothers. Merchant bank owned by Pearson. Monitored Goldcrest's weekly cash-flow forecasts in 1985–6.

Masterman. Company formed by Brent Walker and Ensign Trust to bid for controlling interest in Goldcrest in 1987.

Midland Bank. Major British bank. Goldcrest's banker.

Noble Grossart. Edinburgh-based merchant bank. Helped prepare prospectus for Goldcrest Holdings in 1984. Goldcrest shareholder.

Pearson. British holding company with interests in newspaper and book publishing, television, oil, engineering, merchant banking and property. Major shareholder in Goldcrest.

Pearson Longman. Part-owned subsidiary of Pearson until 1982 when it was absorbed into the parent company. Vehicle for Pearson's investment in Goldcrest.

Samuel Montagu. Merchant-banking division of Midland Bank. Goldcrest's would-be banker in 1985–6.

Solomon Finger and Newman. New York based firm of accountants and entertainment industry specialists. Valued Goldcrest's library and current investments in September 1983, prior to fund-raising in May 1984.

Prologues

1 – by Terry Ilott

Ilott: On 7 November 1983, just before the start of the winter season, the Fountainbleau, the biggest in the range of stuccoed hotels that crowd the narrow isthmus at the northern end of Miami Beach, prepared to play host to a convention of international television programme-makers and broadcasters. Crumple-suited European visitors observed the bikini-clad women on sunbeds around the pool and retreated to the interior gloom, where a handful of trade journalists gathered in the bar and talked about time zones and jet lag. In the ballroom, salesmen struggled to ready their exhibition stands for the opening. Video monitors were still in boxes; posters in tubes; notebooks, files, price lists, catalogues and brochures in bundles. In the lobby, the accreditation desk was besieged by delegates searching out their names on the pre-registration and room-allocation lists. Dealing with their inquiries were the convention's joint organizers, French and American, whose visible efforts to quell their mutual antipathy inspired neither order nor confidence.

By early evening, the hotel was packed with thousands of programme-planners, buyers, salesmen, syndicators and representatives of American cable, network, local and low-power television stations. All of them seemed to be acquainted. Among the greetings and back-slappings, the unbuttoned shirts, ill-matched blazers and pants, flapping lapels and suet complexions, the French – ultra-conservative, expensively tailored, chain-smoking, manicured and chic – moved fastidiously, searching out the handful of sellers, most of whom came from Europe.

This was the first, and last, American Market for International Programs, AMIP. It had been devised by an organization that for years had successfully mounted similar conventions in the south of France. AMIP, however, differed from those long-established events in one crucial respect: where their purpose was to showcase the latest American television output for the ever-eager buyers from Scandinavia, Italy, the UK, Hong Kong or Japan, AMIP's purpose was to enable the broadcasters from those same countries to sell their programmes to the far-from-eager buyers from the USA. All over the world, it seems, television producers are prey to a perennial pipedream: that somehow the very best of their output – prize-winning dramatizations of literary classics, ground-breaking documentaries, acclaimed recordings of ballets and opera, folk dance and song – will find an audience in the vast, rich and fragmented American market. It doesn't happen. Foreign-produced programmes account for less than 2 per cent of American viewing time, most of it on the non-profit Public Broadcasting Service (PBS). That AMIP was therefore doomed to failure was the unanimous opinion of the élite corps of foreign participants who had tried to sell to the US market before. Their pessimism was cheerfully endorsed by the majority of American 'buyers' themselves, who met the earnest and expectant looks on the faces of the inexperienced programme-makers from Europe with an amiable fallow-mindednes that all too clearly signalled that they were in town for a good time and not much more.

None of the naive Europeans had higher expectations than the hosts of the opening-night party. As the guests milled around tables laden with food, and waiters glided by with trays of drinks, on the lawn by the pool a large sign bore the name of the company that was footing the $15,000 bill: Goldcrest. Most of the Americans had never heard of it.

Amid the hubbub, an amplified voice asked for their attention. An unusually tall man in his early forties, slim, bespectacled and moustached, wearing a demure light-grey suit, stood before the microphone. His short speech, erratically punctuated by a severe stammer, welcomed the delegates to the convention and expressed confidence that it would prove a useful forum for business. The sub-text carefully stressed that Goldcrest, already an established force in feature films, would soon be a leading supplier of quality television – it was, in other words, a name to watch. The speaker was the company's founder and chief executive, Jake Eberts.

Accompanied by his head of sales, Bill Gavin, salesman Steve Walsh and head of television production, Mike Wooller, Eberts toured the party, shaking hands and making introductions. He was not one to spend $15,000 without working hard to make it pay.

His manner was pleasant, his comments well informed. In the intensely competitive and brittly paranoid atmosphere of industry gatherings such as this, he conveyed an air of robustness and reliability. To the qualities that lay at the heart of the company's expensively projected self-image – genial sophistication and vitality – he added an almost stateliness of bearing. His height, which forced him to stoop in conversation as if enrapt, had something to do with it. So, too, did his equanimity. Sober, as always, and burning neither with resentment nor with passion, this multi-lingual Canadian, long resident in London, was not as supercilious as the Brits – many of whom conveyed the impression that they had done the world a favour by coming to Miami Beach at all – nor as offensively (to European sensibilities) familiar as the Americans. He was a man with whom, in this context, everyone felt at ease.

Unbeknown to his colleagues, however, Eberts was finding it hard to concentrate on the matter in hand. While extolling Goldcrest's virtues to the American programme-planners and acquisitions executives, he was labouring under the unwelcome pressure of having to make a decision about his own position with the company. For six weeks he had been negotiating a new employment contract with Goldcrest's non-executive chairman, James Lee.

The renegotiation of this contract would have been a routine matter were it not for two things. First, Eberts could not persuade Lee to meet the terms that he was demanding. Second, he had been made an outstandingly generous offer by Norman Lear and Jerry Perenchio, joint owners of Embassy Pictures. In Eberts's mind, as he worked the room and mingled with the guests, these questions were resolving themselves into a simple choice: either Goldcrest or Embassy.

It was a choice he would rather not have had to make. While he was exceptionally able at the public, corporate duties that call for incisiveness and application, in handling his private affairs he fell prey to ordinary indecision and anxiety. During the three days of the Fountainbleau convention, he spent hours in his room on the telephone seeking advice from Goldcrest directors David Puttnam and Sir Richard Attenborough, Hollywood agent Marty Baum and leading showbiz lawyer Tom Lewyn, as well as discussing deal points with James Lee and probing the possibilities of the new role offered by Perenchio and Lear.

Salesman Steve Walsh noted Eberts's uncharacteristic absence of mind. A meeting to discuss a tour of the major American television stations, scheduled to start in New York on 5 December, was continually interrupted by calls which Eberts took in his bedroom, from where Walsh could hear him engaged in what sounded like contract negotiations.

On Thursday, 10 November, Eberts flew from Miami back to London. The following weekend he flew to his farm in Quebec, and on the morning of Monday, 21 November, he flew from there to Los Angeles. At each stop his time was taken up with further calls and conversations, negotiations, arguments and advice. The pressure on him to make the choice between Goldcrest and Embassy aggravated the asthma from which he has suffered, chronically at such times of stress, since the death of his father in 1977. His personal, domestic and business prospects waited upon his decision. Normal life was coming to a standstill. Goldcrest's affairs were beginning to be neglected.

His preoccupation did not escape the attention of other senior executives in the company. They knew that his contract was up for renewal, and most of them had heard about an offer from Embassy. But so strong was Eberts's identification with Goldcrest, and so solid appeared to be his commitment, that they presumed that the negotiations with Lee would be settled satisfactorily. As for Embassy, Eberts had been turning down offers from Hollywood for two years or more.

What they did not know was that this offer was different. Eberts had grown very close to Jerry Perenchio. The two had first met at the Cannes Film Festival in 1982 and had renewed their acquaintance at Cannes again in May. In the interim, Goldcrest had swept the board at the Oscars with *Gandhi*, the North American television rights to which had been acquired by Embassy. Through the summer months of 1983, Eberts had been an occasional guest at Perenchio's luxurious Malibu home. Together they had played tennis, gone out to restaurants and risen early to go running on the track at nearby Pepperdine University. As the burden of corporate affairs at the rapidly expanding Goldcrest had become increasingly unwelcome to Eberts, so the lavish hospitality offered by Perenchio seemed more than ever attractive. Likewise, the more intractable the negotiations with James Lee became, the more promising seemed the vast salary and congenial responsibilities offered by Perenchio's company.

The Embassy offer had first been made in June. Perenchio had mentioned it to Eberts now and then in the succeeding months, but had exerted no pressure; he knew that the negotiations with James Lee were dragging on without conclusion, and he knew that there would come a moment at which he would be able to force Eberts's hand. That moment had now arrived. Embassy was planning to raise $100 million for a film-production programme. A prospectus was being drafted to put before potential investors in early 1984, and Perenchio and his partner Norman Lear wanted Eberts's name to be in it. On this visit to LA, Eberts was again staying at Malibu and, over breakfast one day, Perenchio gave his house guest an ultimatum: he had until the end of the month to make a decision – after that, the offer would be withdrawn.

On Wednesday, 23 November, having concluded the business that had detained him in Hollywood (including a disastrous screening of a film called *Dream One* for the top executives of Columbia Pictures), Eberts flew back to London, and the following morning, Thanksgiving

Day, he went to the headquarters of Pearson Longman on the seventeenth floor of Millbank Tower, a glass-and-steel office block on the north
bank of the Thames, for a further round of negotiations with James Lee.
What Eberts wanted – a lot more than Goldcrest was currently paying
him, but less than he had been offered by Embassy – Lee couldn't give.
'Pearson won't accept it,' he said.

That night Eberts talked it through again with his wife, Fiona, and in
the morning he made his decision. He went to the office as usual,
attended to the urgent business on his desk and then took an afternoon
flight back to LA. By late afternoon the next day a deal had been agreed.
Eberts was to start with Embassy on 1 January.

Eberts's decision to leave Goldcrest startled, and for a while bewil-
dered, the company and the industry. He had built Goldcrest from
nothing. In six years it had become arguably the world's leading independent film company, picking up a dozen Oscars – and numberless plaudits
for single-handedly reviving the British film industry – along the way.
Films of the calibre of *Chariots of Fire*, *Gandhi*, *Local Hero*, *The Dresser*
and *Another Country* had achieved the elusive double of both pleasing
the critics and pulling in the crowds. On the strength of this record –
unmatched in the film business at that time – the company was in the
midst of a reorganization and a recapitalization that would virtually
double its investment capacity. Credit for the success was attributed
almost entirely to Eberts, the genial maestro. That he should quit just
at the point at which everything he had ever wanted seemed to be within
reach left observers puzzled, and suspicious. Two questions immediately
arose.

First, had Eberts been pushed? – and, if so, by whom and why? By
all accounts, he was admired by shareholders and film-makers, respected
by his peers in Hollywood, enjoyed good relations with his colleagues
and was well loved within the company. But success breeds rivalry, and
film people have long since learned that when any senior executive
unexpectedly resigns from a company, for whatever 'official' reason, it is
as well to look for the man, or men, holding the dagger. Suspicion
immediately, and naturally, fell on Eberts's successor – none other than
the very chairman, James Lee, who had failed to keep Eberts in the
company.

Second, with Eberts gone, what would happen to Goldcrest? Film is
a high-risk business in which success depends on luck and the astute
creative and commercial judgement, as well as extensive personal contacts, of a few top executives. Eberts was one of these; so much so that
he was a 'hot' property, for whose services Embassy was willing to pay

a lot of money. Lee, on the other hand, had no track record in films at all. He was a former high-flying management consultant whose business experience had embraced a wide range of studies for clients as varied as the Irish government, the Archdiocese of Malta and the Collins publishing empire. Pearson Longman, of which he was currently the chief executive, was a large holding company mainly involved in newspaper and book publishing. For three years, it is true, Lee had been Goldcrest's non-executive chairman, and it was this experience that made him, in the eyes of the shareholders, uniquely qualified to become the new chief executive. But when he took over from Eberts he was, as far as the film industry was concerned, no more than a knowledgeable novice. What guarantee was there that the whole house of cards would not now come crashing down around him?

In an attempt to answer both these questions, David Puttnam and Richard Attenborough, Goldcrest's best-known and most influential directors, aided to some extent by an amenable Eberts, mounted a hasty campaign of press management. The reasons given for Eberts's departure, that he was 'tired of administration' and that the Embassy offer was 'too good to refuse', were true as far as they went – there was no dagger – but they didn't get to the heart of the matter, and they didn't allay the suspicions in the minds of industry observers. Puttnam and Attenborough therefore shifted attention on to the golden future that lay ahead under Lee's leadership: the company was to raise new capital to make more and better films, and, perhaps two or three years down the road, it would be floated on the stock market, following which the horizons would be limitless. Puttnam even suggested to one reporter that, within this bigger picture, Lee, with his broader experience and proven skills as a corporate strategist, was in many ways to be preferred over Eberts as chief executive. In Puttnam's opinion, Eberts's abilities and interests had already been outstripped by the fast-expanding company.

Obediently, the trade press and the financial pages of the nationals played down the significance of Eberts's departure and emphasized the expansion planned by Lee. It was a mistake. Within eighteen months, and despite the injection of a large amount of new capital, the company had become enmeshed in financial difficulties, production scandals, runaway budgets and a string of unsuccessful releases, the most notable of which, Revolution, earned the worst American reviews of any major British film in recent times. The same newspapers that in 1983 had hailed Goldcrest as the 'saviour of the film industry' and had lionized Eberts, Puttnam, Attenborough and Lee as the leaders of the 'renaissance of British films' now trumpeted with even greater glee the company's precipitate decline into near-insolvency. By January 1986, just two years after Lee took command, more than £30 million of the company's total capitalization of £36.6 million had been written off. In September 1987, after a long-drawn-out death agony, what was left of the company was sold and Goldcrest's ten-year adventure was over. (The name still exists, but none of the original staff, nor anything of the original ambition, remains.)

This débâcle, one of the most dramatic corporate collapses in film history, began with Eberts's decision to leave in November 1983. Or did it? Just as Eberts has been given much of the credit for Goldcrest's glittering trail of success, so James Lee has been singled out to shoulder the blame for its subsequent ignominious demise. While it is true that catastrophic decisions were made by Lee – decisions that would probably have been enough to finish off the company in whatever circumstances – it is at least arguable that the company he inherited from Eberts was already incubating problems that would one day have to hatch. And even had Lee not sanctioned the budget increases on *Revolution*, or backed *Absolute Beginners*, or presided over a vast increase in overheads, he would at some point have come up against – as would Eberts if he had stayed – the inherent impracticability of a modestly capitalized British company trying to finance film and television productions without having any control over distribution in the US market, the major source of revenue. Goldcrest had beaten the system for more than six years, but it couldn't beat it for ever.

Thus, although November 1983 was undoubtedly a watershed – everything before that seemingly so successful, everything after that a failure – it is necessary to go back to the origins of the company to find out what really went wrong, and why.

Those origins are to be found in the person of Jake Eberts himself. Not only did he start the company, but for the first five years he was its sole executive. Even after joining Embassy in 1984, he remained, for the most part unwittingly, an off-screen player in the Goldcrest drama: the King Across the Water.

2 – by Jake Eberts

Eberts: I was born in 1941, the third child in a large, middle-class and English-speaking family in the predominantly French-speaking province of Quebec, Canada. I saw few films as a boy, preferring to spend most of my leisure time playing sports and exploring the lakes and mountains around my home town, Arvida. Nor did movies much interest me as I got older. In 1958 I was accepted by McGill University to study chemical engineering and for four years I was immersed in vapour–liquid equilibrium calculations, Young's modulus and integral calculus. Upon graduation, I took a job in Montreal with a French company, L'Air Liquide, but after only a few months I was transferred to France, where I worked on the design of new gas-liquefaction plants. Before I was twenty-one I had been promoted to start-up engineer, responsible for putting those new plants into service. This job, which took me to remote regions of France, Spain and Italy, was a challenge and it involved a lot of responsibility for a twenty-one-year-old. But the job was also repetitive and, frustrated by the narrowness and the limited earnings potential of engineering, I decided to re-train. I applied for admission to the Harvard Business School.

At Harvard I was captivated by the world of balance sheets, leverage, leasing and venture capital. Intellectually, it was much more satisfying than commissioning new chemical plants. I studied hard and graduated in 1966 with a good degree, but failed to land a longed-for job on Wall Street. Instead, I worked as a financial analyst for the diesel-engine manufacturer Cummins Engine Company, in Columbus, Indiana. I soon got over my disappointment at being stuck in the Midwest, for Cummins sent me back to Europe, first as an analyst, then as head of the company's European marketing operation. 1967 found me in Brussels, where I met my British-born wife, Fiona. At about the same time, I was at last offered a job on Wall Street. In March 1968 I arrived in New York, via a round-the-world honeymoon, with barely a cent to my name. I was twenty-seven.

Wall Street was then coming towards the end of one of its periodic booms. All sorts of investment-banking concepts were being tried out: leveraged buy-outs, venture-capital funds, contested takeovers, real-estate investment trusts, and oil and gas funds. New issues were commonplace and routinely sold at substantial premiums to their offer price. The company I worked for, Laird Inc., was in the vanguard of all this, and it was the perfect environment within which a young engineer-cum-analyst could learn about the world of high finance. For three years, I plunged into one transaction after another.

But New York was not a place in which Fiona and I wished to settle down. We wanted to be back in Europe. After unsuccessfully looking for jobs among the English merchant banks, I decided to move to London and set up on my own as a consultant. It was a rash move: at the outset I had neither clients nor contacts. But I was soon saved from the consequences of my folly by a chance meeting with Leon Levy, the chairman of Oppenheimer and Co., a well-established New York investment bank that was expanding its European business. Leon offered me a job in Oppenheimer's London office, where I was to work with a man by the name of Jimmy King.

Jimmy has what might be called a non-speaking, but none the less important, cameo role in the Goldcrest story. Born in China, he fled that country in 1948 and made his way to America. He studied modern languages at Yale and after college set himself up first as a stockbroker then as a private investor, making a fortune in various high-risk deals. At Oppenheimer, he took me under his wing and introduced me to the glamorous world of venture capital.

Unfortunately, our partnership was not a great success. A plan to buy the Marbella Hilton Hotel and turn it into Europe's first tennis village fell foul of the 1972-3 property crash. The acquisition of a very large vacant site in Frankfurt was followed by a long, unsuccessful struggle to secure a building permit. The land was eventually sold at a loss. Investment in a German company which started off as a mutual-fund sales force but eventually became involved in tax-shelter financing resulted in further losses, as did an insurance-broking venture.

From my point of view, matters were made worse in 1975, following the great upheaval in the equity markets that accompanied the abolition of fixed-rate commissions in the US, when it became clear that Oppenheimer's stockbroking business in London had been badly managed. The people responsible were removed from their posts and because there was no one else available I became managing director of the London office – a classic example of the Peter Principle (every employee tends to rise to his or her level of incompetence) at work. This just didn't fit in with my ambitions. For all its failures, my partnership with Jimmy King had given me a taste for venture capital. I wanted to take risks and make money. As managing director of Oppenheimer, by contrast, my business was primarily stockbroking – calling up clients and selling them shares in IBM – a business about which I knew little and cared less.

I stayed with Oppenheimer, but became more and more frustrated. Other things had gone wrong. I had taken out a big mortgage on our house in Holland Park when interest rates were very low, about 5 per cent. By 1974, the rate was 13 per cent and I could not afford the mortgage payments. The house had to be sold. We started again in rented accommodation. Furthermore, in order to finance my living expenses and various entrepreneurial ventures, I had borrowed heavily from Jimmy

King – by this time I owed him tens of thousands of dollars – and I had no immediate prospect of paying the money back.

There was a long period during which I was seriously depressed. For most people, it is true, being managing director of Oppenheimer's London office would not count as failure. But I come from a large family that I wanted to impress: I *had* to be a success in their eyes. Moreover, I had behind me not only a precociously successful academic career but the experience, at the age of twenty-one, of responsibilities that would have been uncommon even among engineers twice my age. To be now marooned at Oppenheimer was almost a humiliation. I remember feeling that my life was drifting in no particular direction. I was thirty-three years old, I had no money and all my ventures had been failures.

It was then that Dimitri de Gunzberg, one of the principals of Bankers Trust International, proposed that I undertake yet another highly speculative venture with only the remotest chance of success: raising money for an animated film based on the bestselling book *Watership Down*. This, at last, was to be a venture that worked, and I was to find my vocation in what was for me a most unlikely walk of life – the movie industry.

Chapter One

Beginner's Luck

Eberts: *Watership Down* had reviews like no other book I can remember. In every kind of publication – newspapers, literary journals, women's magazines, men's magazines, special-interest magazines – there were reviews of *Watership Down*, and they were all raves. It was these reviews that persuaded me to take seriously Dimitri de Gunzberg's proposal that I help him raise money for the film.

Bankers Trust had already invested in a number of film projects and had lost money on most of them. The experience, however, had enabled Dimitri to make a few contacts in the film world, among them the producer of *Watership Down*, Martin Rosen. Martin had taken the project to Dimitri, and he in turn, probably thinking that it was time someone else lost money on movies, brought it to me at Oppenheimer. Initially, the idea was just to raise the development finance. Development, of which we will be talking a lot in this book, is the process by which one takes a film idea to the stage where it has a script, a cast, a budget and a director. With that package you can then go off and find the money to put the film into production.

In banker's terms, development financing is a venture-capital investment, and for me as a financier it is the most exciting part of the movie business. Indeed, the *Watership Down* proposal was akin to the kind of venture-capital projects I had seen before at Oppenheimer. The degree of risk was greater, but the sums of money involved were much less: to develop *Watership Down* we needed $50,000, whereas, for example, when Jimmy King and I bought the option on the property in Germany we paid $1 million.

Partly persuaded by Dimitri's explanation of how film development worked and partly grasping at yet another straw, I agreed to try to raise the $50,000. I discussed it with my colleagues in London, but they were reluctant to get Oppenheimer involved and suggested that I take it to the chairman, Leon Levy. Leon was equally opposed. It transpired that he had made an investment in films some years before and the experience had been both frustrating and unprofitable. He had put up the entire budget, $250,000, for a film called *The Honeymoon Killers* – a critical success (it was said to be François Truffaut's favourite film) that took more than $11 million at the box office. But Leon never got his money back, let alone saw a profit.

Leon is an intellectual, a highly successful banker, a renowned stockmarket analyst, a man who can talk knowledgeably about the influence of taxation on world history and who has financed, out of his own pocket, archaeological digs in the Middle East. The fact that he had invested in a film that had cost very little and grossed relatively a great deal, but which still lost him money, was, for him, sufficient lesson not to meddle in a business that he clearly did not understand. When I took the *Watership Down* proposal to him, he turned me down flat. I don't know if I tried very hard to convince him. I was probably discouraged, having tried and failed in so many other areas. And I can't remember exactly how he handled it, although I do remember him saying it would be 'inappropriate' for Oppenheimer to get involved.

But Leon was very aware of my frustrations. I had spent a lot of time with him and had often told him of my sense of failure. I would say, 'Leon, I'm not happy in this job. I'm not successful. I feel as if I'm just not producing enough.' I wasn't being paid very much money at the time – the most I ever earned at Oppenheimer, including a substantial bonus, was $32,000 – so it wasn't as if I was a huge drain on the company, but I certainly wasn't producing the goods and I felt guilty about that. The Protestant work ethic kept telling me 'You've got to be more useful to your employer.'

So Leon gave his blessing to the idea, no doubt proposed by me in some desperation, that I should try to raise the development money for *Watership Down* on my own. It would not cost Oppenheimer a penny – I would look for outside investors – and Leon was happy for me to do that as long as it did not interfere with my Oppenheimer work. I knew absolutely nothing about the film business; I had never read about films, and still don't (I couldn't read a book about old movies now even if I had no other book in the house), so I clearly did not know what I was embarking on.

Fortunately, I had Martin Rosen. He *did* know about films and he *did* know something about the movie business. He had been an agent with the William Morris Agency and had been a producer on Ken Russell's *Women In Love*. He even looked right for the part: a classic Jewish entrepreneurial type, with a good sense of humour, very bright and very meticulous. As the producer, Martin was the man who was going to get the film made. I had nothing to do with the creative aspects, or the logistics, or the organization. I never even met the author of the book, Richard Adams. All I was going to do was raise the development money.

I sat down with a telephone and starting making calls. First I approached people I knew, like Jimmy King, who was given permission by Oppenheimer to put up some money as a private investor. Likewise Dimitri found some money through friends of his. The required amount was raised very quickly, from eight or ten people each investing, on average, $5,000. Not one of them had any connection with the film industry. I had prepared a short memorandum which set out what the film was about, how the money was going to be spent and what the likely risks were. It was only three pages long and, although the financial technicalities were all properly set down, I had to declare that I knew little or nothing about the film business. In the event, although the results didn't turn out to be quite as I had imagined, my little memo wasn't too far wrong.

The deal structure was devised, although I did not know it at the time – believing it to be Dimitri's work – by a very experienced entertainment-industry lawyer, David Norris, who was later to become a key figure in Goldcrest. According to his scheme, once the package had been developed – i.e. the rights secured, storyboard prepared (animation films have storyboards as well as scripts) and budget finalized – we would find the production money from a third party. We estimated that we would need $2.4 million. Part of that money would be used to pay back the $50,000, with interest, to the investors and to pay a small fee – $5,000 – to Dimitri and me. In addition, the development investors would get 10 per cent of the net profits of the film itself, and Dimitri and I would each get 10 per cent of their share – i.e. I would get 1 per cent, Dimitri would get 1 per cent, and the investors who put up the initial $50,000 would get 8 per cent.

However, raising the $2.4 million of production money proved to be more difficult than I had anticipated. Most private investors who have put money into movies have lost every penny, and the film industry is generally given a wide berth by the investment community.

Adding to my difficulties, although I did not then realize it, was the state of the British film industry at the time. In the mid-1970s a great deal of attention was focused on falling cinema admissions in the UK, the cut-back and closure of the UK production arms of the Hollywood studios, the reduction in British government subsidies to the National Film Finance Corporation (an agency that assisted the production of

British feature films) and the fall in profits of the handful of independent production companies then based in Britain. The conventional wisdom within the industry was that this was no time to put money into movies.

I had no idea of these problems. I would pick up the paper and read that in London four or five new films were released every Friday, Pinewood Studios was full, Shepperton was bursting at the seams and Twickenham was undertaking a rebuilding programme. It seemed to me, an uninformed investment banker, that the film business was in good shape. It never crossed my mind that raising film-production money was going to be difficult.

Fortunately, Martin Rosen, who had much more experience than I at this kind of thing, had already secured commitments from a couple of potential investors. Most importantly, he had received an indication of support from a company called Pearson, which at the time owned two thirds of Pearson Longman, which in turn owned Penguin Books, the publisher of *Watership Down*. Pearson Longman's then chief executive, Roger Brooke, who saw that there were potential spin-off benefits in the form of increased sales of the book, was prepared to put some money into the film. As Pearson also owned a controlling interest in the merchant bank Lazard, Martin and Roger had taken the idea to them. Clients of Lazard, as well as individual members of the Pearson family, together with the Pearson company, committed about $1 million, which was 40 per cent of the total required. We were thus able to say to other potential City investors, 'Here are some reputable investors who are prepared in principle to commit production finance to this film.' It was the most persuasive point in our sales pitch.

I had written a prospectus setting out the sum to be raised, how it would be used, how it would be recouped, the element of risk and so on. It was short and to the point, and I am sure it wouldn't withstand the scrutiny of a good lawyer. At the same time I had drawn up a list of City institutions that made venture-capital investments: merchant banks, investment trusts, life assurance companies and others. I was then greatly assisted by a friend, Powell Cabot, who was working for Oppenheimer as a stockbroker, selling shares to institutional investors, mainly in the UK. Powell became intrigued by the idea of raising film finance. He had a wide range of contacts and, thanks to his door-opening telephone calls, I was immediately put in touch with the key investment managers at the institutions on my list.

Dimitri was doing much the same thing, and between us we probably called around 100 potential investors. If they agreed to consider the idea, I would meet with them, give them the sales pitch and leave them a copy of the prospectus. But usually, at the mention of the word 'film', the answer would be no. They would not consider seriously an investment of this kind. Eventually, from all the names on our list, we were left with a mere handful of investors who had expressed a serious interest. Even then, people kept on dropping out, saying yes and then calling back to say no. Or saying yes, but . . . Or yes, if . . . Or they would suddenly reduce their interest from $500,000 to $250,000. It went on for weeks.

When I got close to selling the idea to someone, I would call in Martin Rosen. It wasn't my job to know about the film business; my job was to pitch the deal in terms that an investment manager would understand. If the investment manager was interested, he would naturally want to know more, and that's when Martin would come in. Martin was the expert, the man who could answer the detailed questions.

The $2.4 million budget figure had been arrived at after many months of analysis by Martin and the director of animation, John Hubley. As a rule, a full-length animated film takes two to three years to make, and the animators' wages represent about 80 per cent of the total budget, with the rest going on materials, rights, producer's fees, repayment of the development costs and miscellaneous expenses.

We made it clear in the prospectus that there was no guarantee that we would recoup the $2.4 million, for the film had not been promised a release in any market. Having no real idea what such a picture would sell for in, say, Japan, the United States or Germany, we sought advice from an experienced international film salesman, Charles Rosenblatt, and his associate, Arnold Kopelson (who was to win an Oscar in 1988 as the producer of *Platoon*). When the film was finished, Rosenblatt and Kopelson went to independent distributors around the world, showed them the picture and named a price. They closed deals in most of the important territories.

Distributors do not buy a film outright. They pay an advance against the revenues the film is likely to earn in their country. A distributor in Japan, for instance, might pay $1.5 million, for which he would acquire the rights to the film for a specified number of years. If the owners of the cinemas in which the film is to be shown keep, on average, 60 per cent of the box-office takings, and if the print and advertising costs (prints of the film that have to be struck in order to show it simultaneously in many cinemas, and advertisements that have to be placed announcing the opening of the film) represent a further 15 per cent of the takings, then the film has to generate $10 million at the box office in order for the distributor to recoup his $1.5 million advance. Thus:

Box office	$10,000,000
less cinema-owners' share	($ 6,000,000)
Rental	**$ 4,000,000**
less print and advertising costs	($ 1,500,000)
Distributor's gross	**$ 2,500,000**
less distribution fee	($ 1,000,000)
less advance to producer	($ 1,500,000)
Distributor's net profit	nil

In other words, in our example, in order for the distributor to break even, the box-office income has to be approximately seven times the advance.

While on this subject, it is as well to note that the money remaining after the cinema-owners (known as exhibitors) have taken their share is called the film rental. Rental figures tend to have wider use than do box-office figures in the film business, and they are the figures to which we most often refer in this book. The distribution fee, usually expressed as a percentage of film rental, covers the cost of the service provided by the distributor. In a typical distribution deal, the proportion of the takings returned to the producer increases as the film generates more income, so that the producer might receive, say, 30 per cent of the rentals up to a certain figure, 40 per cent of the next so many millions, and so on up to a maximum of, say, 60 per cent. The distributor negotiates a similar sliding scale of income distribution with the cinema-owners. The significance of this from the investor's point of view is that although it takes a long time for a film to reach break-even – and most don't get that far – there is a revenue threshold beyond which film investment can be very profitable. Hence, although most production finance comes from the established theatrical (i.e. cinema), television and video distributors – either directly, via their own production or co-production activities, or indirectly, via distribution advances and guarantees – there is always a steady, if small, stream of new money trickling into film production from outside. Investors are inspired by the example of such films as the independently financed and hugely profitable *Crocodile Dundee*.

I was later to learn that it is not necessary to have a finished product before selling a film to distributors. For example, producers can pre-sell a film on the basis of the script, the director, the budget and the cast. They might also have some artwork, either drawings or photographs, so that the distributor has a concept of the look and feel of the picture. If the distributor likes the proposal, he will guarantee to buy the film for a certain price, payable on delivery or by instalments during the course of production. That guarantee is sometimes backed up by a letter of credit from the distributor's bank which the producers then use to get their own bank to provide financing to make the movie.

Pre-selling, which in the 1980s was to become a major source of production finance throughout the film world, is naturally a more difficult way of doing things, because you are selling a concept, not a finished product. It takes far more salesmanship and much better relationships with the distributor – and, very importantly, a much better track record – to sell from a script than it does to sell a finished film. Also, since you are asking the distributor to take a much greater risk, the terms that you can command are likely to be less favourable. On the other hand, pre-selling does have advantages: you are dealing with a dream, by comparison with which the finished film is, almost invariably, a disappointment. In certain cases you can actually do better with pre-sales than you can with the finished product. Sometimes you are caught between the two: 'Do I try to pre-sell the picture? Do I wait until the picture is partly finished, then try to sell on the basis of thirty-five minutes of footage? Or do I wait until the picture is fully finished?' It mostly depends on how urgently you need the money.

In looking for investors, and later for distributors, for *Watership Down*, two of our earliest disappointments were with Rank and EMI Films in the UK. In those days the two companies, through the Odeon and ABC cinema circuits respectively, dominated theatrical exhibition in Britain. They were also involved in film production, EMI being particularly active, producing such films as *The Deer Hunter*, *Warlords of Atlantis*, *Death on the Nile* and *Convoy*. Furthermore, both EMI and Rank were major distributors, being able, through their control of the cinema circuits, to compete with the London branch offices of the Hollywood studios. They were thus by far the most important companies in the British film business, and if you wanted to raise finance from industry sources, they were the people to whom you went.

With this in mind, I prepared a proposal which, despite my inexperience, I knew would be very attractive to them. I was dismissed with ill-disguised contempt by both companies. After that, and despite considerable efforts on my part, I never succeeded in persuading either Rank or EMI Films (which ceased to exist as an independent company in 1986) to put any money into any project in which I was involved – at last count, nearly fifty movies.

When *Watership Down* was finally finished and released in 1978, it proved very successful: the investors who put up the $50,000 development finance got their money back with interest, plus an additional $450,000, making a total return of ten times their investment.

My financial reward was modest but gratifying. It was not as important to me, however, as the fact that, after a long string of failures, at last I had a success to my name.

Chapter Two
Bitten by the Bug

Eberts: It took more than three years to make *Watership Down*, from
raising the money to releasing the film, but long before we knew that it
was going to be a success I was captivated by the film business. It was
a world in which I, with my banking skills, had something special to
offer. It was different, and more interesting, than anything done by my
Harvard contemporaries. It was something that no one else in the venture-capital world would touch. It was creative: the end result was something to which I could be committed. In addition to all of that, it was fun.
I remember taking a telephone call from film producer Elliott Kastner, a
man to whom I had never previously spoken in my life. Like many
producers, Elliott would call anyone who was thought to be connected,
however remotely, with money. There were two or three other people
in my office at Oppenheimer as Elliott tried to convince me to help him
raise the money for a picture that was to star Richard Burton and Liz
Taylor. I repeated the words Burton and Taylor loudly enough for my
colleagues to hear, and I remember thinking, 'Boy, this sure beats all
that talk about p/e ratios, subordinated debt, equity finance and scrip
issues.'

But the way wasn't open to me simply to throw myself into the film
business. *Watership Down* was just a one-off. It taught me a lot, but it
didn't make me a movie mogul. I was still a banker, still managing
director of Oppenheimer.

I was, for example, very much involved with our German joint venture,
which, having started off as a mutual fund (i.e. unit trust) sales company,
had evolved into a tax-shelter financing operation.

Tax-shelter financing had a great impact on the movie business in the
1970s and early 1980s, and, as it was to play a significant part in the
Goldcrest story, it is worth explaining the principle of it here. It was a
system by which governments created special advantages for private,
corporate or institutional investors to encourage them to put money into

certain sectors of industry. In the UK it was known as the system of capital allowances, which permitted you to reduce your taxable income by the amount you invested in the targeted industries. For instance, if the government was trying to encourage the manufacture of diesel engines, for every £1 you invested in diesel-engine manufacturing you would be allowed to take £1 off your taxable income. Thus, if you were in the 50 per cent tax bracket, every £1 you invested would, in effect, cost you only 50 pence. Clearly the advantage to the investor could be very substantial. However, the advantages to the government and to the industries concerned were never conclusively demonstrated and, by the mid-1980s, tax incentives began to fall out of favour. One reason for this was that wherever they appeared – in Germany, Canada, Australia or the UK – these tax-shelter schemes attracted a class of investor more interested in the tax break than in the ostensible object of the investment. This development caused havoc in the affairs of some of the industries in question. The film industry was one.

In Germany, the tax incentives introduced by the government in the mid-1970s were initially very effective in attracting feature-film investment. It was an area in which I got involved, through Oppenheimer's German affiliate, in early 1974, at about the same time as we were raising money for *Watership Down*. Private German investors who were subject to very high personal income-tax rates were queueing up to put money into German feature films. Unfortunately, the tax breaks were so arranged that the investors could actually make more money if the film they backed was a failure than if it was a success. The German government, being exceptionally keen to promote the industry, gave investors a 240 per cent write-off for each Deutschmark invested, so that if an investor committed DM 1,000, and his tax rate was 50 per cent, then he could write off DM 2,400 against his other taxable income, thus saving DM 1,200. He then prayed that the film would not be a success because he was already guaranteed an effective net profit: for each DM 1,000 invested, he was getting DM 1,200. If, God forbid, the film was a success, then he would pay tax on his share of the profits at a rate which wiped out his initial advantage. Only if the film was a blockbuster would he move back into an overall profit position. This was a very odd set of circumstances, which, although it initially brought in welcome capital, was not at all a good thing for the film business: films were made for their tax-shelter value rather than for their intrinsic artistic or commercial value, and the result was a lot of forgettable films. The same thing happened in Australia, Canada and elsewhere.

Tax-shelter financing, although it was important to film-makers, was not a subject in which many of them were ever likely to become expert. They turned for assistance to people like me. I had already grasped, through my experience with *Watership Down*, that my main, indeed only, usefulness as far as the film business was concerned was that I was a banker. My sober blue suits and my familiarity with the jargon of capital and finance made me an acceptable emissary in the world of investment institutions and merchant banks. I was the kind of person who could raise money for the Martin Rosens of the world. And, because I was not myself a producer, I was an ally of Martin's, not a competitor; I raised the money, but I didn't interfere with the making of the film. This two-sided role – trusted by both the financial community and the film-maker – was to be my mainstay when eventually I moved into the film business full time. I have always been careful to present myself as a financier, not as a film-maker.

In the autumn of 1975 and through a large part of 1976, while carrying on with my regular Oppenheimer duties, I toyed with various schemes to get more involved in movies. Eventually, I pieced together a proposal for a film-development fund. Essentially, this was to be a small pool of capital with which I could provide development money for a range of film projects. I had not had great difficulty raising the $50,000 for *Watership Down*, but the idea of having to go through the same laborious procedure of telephone calls and sales pitches for every film thereafter did not appeal to me. Furthermore, it would mean that I could not actually commit to a film-maker until I had gone out and raised the money. All I could say to him was, 'I love your idea, I'd like to help, but you'll have to wait six months while I see if I can interest some investors.' And that would not be a very convincing way of getting the film-maker to do business with me. So, from my point of view, having a pool of capital would both save time and give me something credible to offer film-makers. More than that, I felt that since film development was a risky business, I really should spread the investment over a larger number of films. If each investor put up $50,000 and I spread that $50,000 over ten films, then on each film the investor had a $5,000 risk. Any one film going under would not mean catastrophe. Thus the portfolio approach would make it more attractive to the investor, which in turn would make it easier for me to raise the money.

Up to that time, there had been a number of film-production funds in the UK, most of them unsuccessful. However, no one had specialized in development financing alone. Development is an important part of a major studio's activity. Studios commission writers, producers and producer–directors to get projects going and get scripts written. For every ten or twenty such projects in development only one will be 'converted' into a movie, and in Hollywood it is possible, even commonplace, to make a good living as a writer or a producer developing projects that never go into production. Outside the studio system, however, development hardly exists. I chose development because it was different – I would in effect be the only game in town – and because it was the only thing that I knew about.

It was not until the end of 1976 that I had sufficient confidence in my development-financing scheme to approach Roger Brooke, the Pearson Longman chief executive who had been the first to commit funds to *Watership Down*. I liked Roger a lot. He was very enthusiastic and energetic and open to new ideas. Pearson Longman's main activities were in book publishing and newspapers, but Roger had already been persuaded by the example of *Watership Down* that film finance was not too distant from Pearson Longman's core business. To launch my scheme I needed £250,000. In those days, $50,000, the sum invested in the development of *Watership Down*, was worth roughly £20–25,000, and I reasoned that if we were to be involved seriously in this business we should be able to have ten projects going at once. I could not justify five or fifteen but ten, a nice round number, seemed about right. Roger was supportive, but also cautious: Pearson Longman did not want to go as high as £250,000 right away. Roger agreed that it was a sound level of investment, but he was prepared to put up only £100,000, and then only if Pearson Longman had a fifty–fifty partner. Later, perhaps, the investment could be increased.

At that time, Oppenheimer had just started what became a long and fruitful relationship with the newly installed managing director of Electra Investment Trust, Michael Stoddart, who was, coincidentally, also one of the investors in *Watership Down*. Most investment trusts have a vast number of holdings, spreading their risk across a wide portfolio. The shares in the trusts themselves are very often traded at a deep discount to the inherent aggregate value of these portfolios. In the case of Electra, one of the three or four largest investment trusts in the UK, because the discount was so great, the board had decided to jazz up the company's image and get involved in unquoted investment vehicles, including new companies. With luck, the higher return which could be generated from this sort of investment would increase the Electra share price and more accurately reflect the underlying value of its assets. Michael Stoddart, who had a long record of successful venture-capital investment, was brought in to do the job. Other investment trusts were doing the same thing; the National Coal Board Pension Fund (NCBPF), for example, was investing in art, antiques and even wine.

In my quest for an investor to join Pearson Longman in my new development fund, Michael was my first and last call. He is a very straight, direct businessman. He said: 'How much do you want? How much is it going to make? How long is it going to take? How are you going to run the business? How much are you taking out of it yourself?' It is very easy to deal with someone as direct as that, and, when I had answered his questions, he simply said, 'Yes.' Not only did my proposal fit, in however small a way, with his plans for Electra, but he knew that his management and his board would feel comfortable with such a blue-chip partner as Pearson Longman. Michael himself knew nothing about the film business, but he had invested in *Watership Down* and, although the film had not yet opened, the experience had given him confidence in my approach to business. I had been totally open in reporting the problems we had encountered on the project and Martin had been meticulous in controlling the expenses and explaining how the money was being spent at every stage.

A simple partnership agreement was drawn up, under which Pearson invested 51 per cent and Electra 49 per cent. Because of the possible spin-off benefits for their books, Pearson Longman were deemed to have the greater interest in building a film business and therefore should have control of the partnership. Electra, whose interest was solely to take an investment position and not get involved in building the business, were happy to let them do so.

I then informed Oppenheimer of my intention to resign, an announcement that came as no surprise to Leon Levy, although I am sure he expected me to be back looking for a job within six months. We agreed that my resignation would take effect on 31 December 1976. Oppenheimer, with whom I have always remained on excellent terms, agreed to provide me with an office and to make available the occasional consulting job in order to give me some income during the initial period of my new venture. (The deal with Pearson and Electra was that I would get no salary but that a trust that I had set up for my family would receive 10 per cent of the development fund's profits. In addition, the partnership would contribute $25,000 a year to cover the fund's overheads.)

My decision to leave Oppenheimer was as foolhardy in career terms as my decision to leave Laird back in 1971. I was starting from scratch in a business about which I knew almost nothing and which had an unmatched reputation for bankrupting interlopers like myself. I had no capital, no salary, a family and a large mortgage. What's more, I was intending to cover my cash-flow requirements by going back to consulting, a business in which I had already proved unsuccessful. But it never occurred to me that the venture would not work. I was convinced that the development business could be profitable, and I knew that no one else was in it.

Shortly before I was to leave Oppenheimer, I became involved in two projects that were to teach me some very basic lessons about the film business. The first, *Zulu Dawn*, plunged me into debt of such magnitude that it was to overshadow my domestic as well as my business life for several years. I will tell the *Zulu Dawn* story later in the book; for the present, I will simply record that it taught me rule number one: never risk your own money in the movies. The second project, *The Disappearance*, taught me rules number two and three: choose the people with whom you work with care, and never forget the extraordinary role that luck plays in this business.

A lawyer, James Mitchell, called me late one afternoon to explain that a film project on which he had been working for many months was facing serious difficulties. A significant piece of the financing had fallen through at the last minute. The film was called *The Disappearance* and was to star Donald Sutherland and Francine Racette. I had no idea how I might be able to help, but I agreed to meet with James and his colleagues. When I arrived at the meeting I was surprised to see Donald Sutherland in attendance. Apparently Donald was so keen to get the film made that he was proposing to invest some of his own money in it. He was the first star I had ever met and I was impressed both by his charisma and by his commitment to the project. In fact, it was mainly because of Donald's commitment that I agreed to make a few calls on the film's behalf. I got out my list of investors in *Watership Down* and the first one I rang was Anthony Gibbs, a secondary bank with a number of wealthy private clients. To my amazement, I was told that Anthony Gibbs did indeed have money available as they had recently raised $1 million for film investment which they had been unable to use. Within twenty-four hours a deal had been agreed, and Messrs Mitchell and Sutherland thought that I was a genius. I did nothing to disabuse them of this notion; of such strokes of luck are reputations made.

As part of the deal it was agreed that a packaging fee of $44,000 would be payable to Anthony Gibbs and Oppenheimer and Co., to be split fifty–fifty. It was the very end of my tenure at Oppenheimer and I wrote to Leon Levy asking if my new company could keep a part of the fee, as a gesture and as seed money for my new venture. Generous as always, he agreed to pay over the entire $22,000. It was to be the first, and last, easy fee I ever earned as a film packager.

However, the money was not paid over immediately and I had some trouble getting it at all. The film was being shot in Canada and, once the money had been raised, one of the Canadian producers authorized payment of the $44,000 packaging fee. I then had a telephone call from a person at Anthony Gibbs asking for Gibbs's 50 per cent share, $22,000, to be sent to his account in Switzerland. I asked whether this was an Anthony Gibbs account and why it was that Oppenheimer could not simply transfer the $22,000 to Anthony Gibbs in London. I was told that that wouldn't work, that because of an 'internal arrangement' which permitted bonuses to be paid directly to Anthony Gibbs executives it was better that the money went straight to Switzerland. I said, 'Well, I would rather pay the money to Anthony Gibbs in London. I can't send money over to a Swiss bank account. I just can't do that.'

The argument about where the money should go went on for several weeks. Finally, I simply refused to make the transfer as requested and Anthony Gibbs in London ended up with the $22,000 fee. I received a complaint from the Anthony Gibbs executive later on, and also from a third party who was supposed to share in that money. They were very unhappy that I had not agreed to make the pay-off.

Eventually I came to regret ever having got involved with *The Disappearance*. The film did just what its title suggests – it disappeared without a trace. However, the experience did have its uses. Not only did I have my first encounter with a request for a pay-off (part of the reason that the payment of the fee took so long was that I was too innocent to recognize what was being proposed), but it also taught me the difference between a packager and a producer.

A packager is someone who has little or no involvement with the production process but who, through some quirk of fate or maybe some small amount of talent, has got control of the rights to a project. He then goes about packaging the script, cast, budget, director and money. The packager steps out of the picture once the contracts have been signed and the money has been raised. To look after the actual manufacture of the film he finds someone, normally a line producer, who knows how to manage the production process. The line producer ensures that the picture does not go over budget, that the scenes are all shot and that the picture is delivered on schedule. For this he, or she, earns a fee. The packager re-enters the scene when the time comes to share out the profits, and the awards.

There are many more packagers in this business than there are producers. A packager is something which no one ever admits to being.

A true producer, as well as doing all the things that a packager does, has a far more intimate involvement with the actual production of the film, which he in effect controls. He is as familiar with the technicalities of production as a line producer, but has much greater authority and, as well as being responsible for the finances, legalities and logistics, he is often involved, with the director, in the creative aspects of the production.

In the case of *The Disappearance*, the packager who called himself a producer disappeared; once the deals had been done no one ever saw him again.

Before shooting started, I was asked what advice I, as a Canadian, could give about filming in Montreal in the middle of winter. Montreal in winter can be tough: your nose and ears freeze, your glasses continually fog up, engines fail to start and people do not function to full capacity. I thought that it would be folly to shoot exteriors there unless there was a lot of cover (indoor scenes you can shoot if the weather gets bad). My advice was ignored, with the result that when the camera equipment and most other moving parts – human as well as mechanical – started to freeze up in the −20° weather, the film got behind schedule. Costs quickly started to escalate and the film began to overrun its budget.

Going over budget is popularly regarded as some kind of mortal sin and directors who allow it to happen are depicted, in the press especially, as profligate and unreliable megalomaniacs who will sacrifice everything – especially the investors' money – in their quest for artistic perfection. This is very far from the truth. Budgeting is not an exact science and all budgets include a contingency, normally calculated at 10 per cent of the estimated cost of making the film, to take account of the unexpected. Most studio-financed films seem to go over budget. Most independently financed films do not, and, unlike studio films, they usually have a completion guarantee. The completion guarantor is paid a fee, much like an insurance premium, in exchange for which he undertakes to pay all the costs above the agreed budget in order to guarantee completion and delivery of the picture. The guarantor's fee is normally equal to about 6 per cent of the budget. Often a rebate clause is included, so that half of the fee is paid back to the producer if the guarantee is not called upon. Should the film at any time exceed the agreed budget, and the guarantee *is* called upon, production control passes from the producer to the guarantor, who is then obliged to finish the film in accordance with the script.

In fact, the system works best when the guarantor is not called upon for his most useful function is to act as a kind of policeman, forcing the producer and the director to be extremely careful about budgeting and shooting. It happens very rarely that the guarantor has to step in. It happened on *The Disappearance*.

The completion guarantee for *The Disappearance* was provided by a subsidiary of Anthony Gibbs, which seemed a good idea: the bank, as a major investor, would not wish to compromise the quality of the picture merely to satisfy its requirements as guarantor. However, Anthony Gibbs appointed as their production representative a man called Jack Abbott. Exactly how Jack came to be a production rep. I don't know. One story has it that he was originally a bus driver, who, while one day driving his bus down Park Lane, became intrigued by the posters on the backs of the buses in front of him. They all advertised films. He decided there and then to get into the film business. He eventually achieved his ambition and became recognized as a very efficient, if unorthodox, production supervisor. These traits made themselves felt during the production of *The Disappearance*. Upon learning that the film was over budget, but that the persons responsible had concealed this fact from him, he simply rented a van and drove one Sunday morning to Twickenham Studios, where the film was being edited, and took all the available cans of film away. He then announced that the cans would not be returned until the issue of the overcost had been settled. This proved to be a highly effective, if unusual, method of exercising his rights as the guarantor's representative.

While *The Disappearance* was shooting in Canada, I was working with Roger Brooke and Michael Stoddart to set up our new development-finance company. We agreed on the aims and structure, then set about finding a name. Roger suggested we use the name of a bird, as most of the Pearson Longman publishing subsidiaries were named after birds – Penguin, Puffin, Kestrel and so on. A list was drawn up with the help of Michael Hare (later Lord Blakenham), soon to be chairman of Pearson, who was a keen birdwatcher. My father, also an avid birdwatcher, was likewise consulted. Between us we settled on two names that we felt had a good ring to them: Goldcrest and Firecrest.

Goldcrest was to be the main operating company and Firecrest was to be a subsidiary, registered in the Channel Islands (under British tax law, Channel Island companies could achieve certain tax benefits as long as the money which they were spending was spent outside the UK). We decided on a logo – a stylized silhouette of a bird; and on the company colours – gold lettering on a green background.

We started business in January 1977.

Chapter Three

Looking For Projects

Eberts: Working from the office provided for us at Oppenheimer and Co. in the City, we started looking for properties that might be developed into films. An advisory group was set up, comprising Michael Walton of Electra House, Clive Gibson and Roger Brooke of Pearson Longman, Kaye Webb of Penguin, film director Robert Parrish and the lawyer Sam Lyons of Davenport Lyons, and we set about combing the Penguin backlist, the original idea being that we would choose film projects from properties to which Pearson Longman already owned rights. (This was to prove impractical as the Penguin library did not then have a lot of material that was suitable for contemporary audiences.) Apart from Robert Parrish, none of us knew the first thing about films, however, and it quickly became apparent that we didn't know what we were looking for. I also realized that not only is it hard to come up with ideas, but that ideas are not enough. There has to be passion: a real commitment to make an idea into a film. That kind of passion is the one thing that all good film-makers have in common. It is not much in evidence among bankers. I had, and have, lots of enthusiasm – boundless enthusiasm – but I do not have the artistic drive that compels a film-maker to make a motion picture. I rarely come up with a film idea of my own.

Clearly the thing to do was to marry my ability to raise money with the film-maker's passion to make pictures, making a clear distinction between the two functions. The first film-makers with whom I associated in this way were Tony Garnett and Ken Loach.

Garnett and Loach had achieved fame in Britain with their first full-length feature film, *Kes* (1969), as well as with a number of remarkable television plays, among them the celebrated production *Cathy Come Home* (1966). They were film-makers of proven ability, with a track record of bringing pictures in on budget (and small budgets at that), and whose work had a seriousness of purpose that was entirely admirable. They had acquired the film rights to a book called *Black Jack* by Leon Garfield.

As the exception that proved the rule, this happened to be a Penguin book. It was a children's adventure story set in eighteenth-century England which seemed to us to have wide appeal and we agreed to provide the funds for Ken Loach to write a script.

Our initial commitment was for the princely sum of £5,000, although this later rose to the giddy heights of £11,250. The film was eventually put into production, with funds supplied mainly by the National Film Finance Corporation, in September 1978. The budget was in the region of £500,000. Goldcrest got back its original investment, plus interest and a premium, making a total return of £14,600. We also had a 5 per cent share of the net profits. Unfortunately, this 5 per cent was to prove worthless. When the film was eventually released, in January 1980, it was a critical but not a commercial success. The film-makers had been unable to get distribution outside the UK because the story was seen to be too parochial – audiences in Germany, Japan or the US simply would not be interested. Also, Loach had shot it in such a realistic manner that the eighteenth-century regional accents were incomprehensible to anyone outside Britain (and to many inside Britain as well). Nevertheless, we had seen a positive return on our investment and we felt that we were doing pretty well.

I was never to work with Garnett and Loach again, but the next film-maker of my acquaintance, David Puttnam, was to become a long-term partner, and his importance to the Goldcrest story can scarcely be exaggerated. I had first met him briefly in late 1974, when we had completed the development financing for *Watership Down*. Two of his films, *Mahler* and *Stardust*, had been released that year and he was beginning to make a name for himself in the film industry. He was looking for production financing for *Bugsy Malone* and, hearing that I had successfully raised some money for a picture, came along to see me. Of course, at that time there was nothing I could do to help, as we were involved in development financing only, and, thanking me for my time, he went on his way. I didn't think much of it, but David has an extraordinary ability to keep in touch with people who might be useful to him, and in early 1977 he invited me to the première of the Ridley Scott film *The Duellists* in London. This time we had a more substantial conversation.

David Puttnam is a brilliant salesman and he is wonderfully perceptive: he knows what you want to hear. He sat there nervously fingering his beard, telling me that independent financing was crucial to the future of the business; that backing major directors and film-makers was the only way to achieve the kind of success ratio we had to have to survive as independent financiers; that I had been very astute in my handling of

Watership Down; and that it was an excellent idea that Goldcrest was to expand in this area. He said all the right things, in other words, and he said them in such a way that I didn't for one minute question his sincerity or his wisdom.

The film business is basically a business of selling ideas. Most often those ideas are impossible to put down in writing. They have to be described verbally and in a very persuasive, emotional style. David Puttnam can do that better than anyone else I have met. In addition, he has remarkably good instincts about talent. He can watch a poor film and identify the strengths of the writer or the director and say, 'This person has got something.' It is an ability that very few people have.

I did not know all this at the time, but I did appreciate that he stood out, far ahead of anyone else I had met in the industry. He was so clearly a man who knew what he was after, and was so obviously capable of achieving it, that he went to the top of the list of people with whom I wanted to do business. I plied him with questions, to educate myself, not to test him: how certain budget figures could be arrived at, how certain talent arrangements could be managed. On the details of how a film is made he was outstanding. But when I started talking about deals and financing, and about structuring profit participations and recoupment, and about selling off rights, he was not so experienced, maybe not even that interested. Naturally, I felt comfortable with that.

David's other remarkable ability is to make you feel that you are very important to him. Even though there are maybe twenty or thirty people around him at a reception or première, he is able to focus his attention on you without distraction – briefly, perhaps, but very convincingly. I remember on one occasion standing on the stairs of the theatre in which *Midnight Express* was being screened. David really was an important figure by this time and there were all sorts of people milling around congratulating him and vying for his attention. He was able to focus on me for just long enough – maybe fifteen or thirty seconds – for me to feel the impact, and to think, 'Well, David Puttnam knows who I am and what I do. He's interested, he's prepared to listen.' He did it very quickly, very effectively and then moved right on to the next person. That's a very important talent in the film business.

The downside with David is that you never feel intimate or completely at ease with him. You never feel that he's going to be a buddy. You find yourself very anxious to be in sync with him – it is a strange effect he has on almost everybody – but you know that you are not going to get close. He once told me, in an unusually intimate conversation, that he didn't really have any close friends; that, of all the film-makers with whom he has worked over the years, not one could be relied upon to come to his rescue in a crisis or to help him in an unselfish way.

He is a consummate politician, a loyal partner, a shrewd adversary, a man of strongly felt likes and dislikes, outspoken and sometimes opinionated. But to this day I never know what he is really thinking, nor have I ever been able to predict how he would react. He is a puzzle. As John Boorman observed in his book *Money Into Light*, it is no accident that Puttnam's company is called Enigma Films.

Shortly after the opening of *The Duellists* in April 1977, by which time we had just made our first investment in *Black Jack*, David went to Hollywood to join a company called Casablanca Film Works. Some weeks later, I called on him and was able to spend a few minutes with him, but I got the impression that he was seeing me only out of courtesy and that he had no real interest in Goldcrest's providing development financing for any of his projects. At that time, he had no use for me.

But I didn't give up and, as luck would have it, David's relationship with Casablanca quickly soured. In 1978 he came back to England and I was one of the first people to give him a call.

One afternoon in June 1978, partly as a response to my constant prodding, he outlined the basic story of *Chariots of Fire*. The following day he sent me a brief written summary of the project. I was impressed by both the storyline and the eloquence with which David had presented it, and, although he had not worked out in his own mind – still less with the proposed writer, Colin Welland – exactly how the film was going to be structured, I immediately agreed to provide development funds. I was delighted that Goldcrest was going to be associated with a producer of Puttnam's stature. I had no idea, however, that *Chariots of Fire* was to be the film that would change all our lives and set Goldcrest on its extraordinary trail of Oscar success.

We eventually invested £17,700 in *Chariots*, but the initial commitment was only £5,000 and I remember being somewhat concerned at sending David £500 to pay for Colin Welland's flight to the States (where he was to do research into the life of Jackson Scholz) because no documentation had been signed between us. I was used to that way of working in the investment-banking business and, as the supervisor of a number of stockbrokers who did millions of dollars' worth of trades every day without signed agreements, I was accustomed to being bound as much by my word as by my signature on a contract. But I wasn't sufficiently familiar with the film business to take this relaxed approach. David, however, proved to be completely reliable, and I came to realize that trust is a crucial element in the relationship between a financier and a film-maker.

Colin Welland got to work on the screenplay in June 1978 and worked with David for the next twelve months, producing a final draft at the end of 1979. What emerged was a very unusual project, one that was clearly going to be hard to finance through normal channels.

There is a body of conventional wisdom in the film business by which all of us are influenced to a greater or lesser degree. Two of its axioms are: first, that it is hard to finance a purely British picture – i.e. a picture whose subject matter can be understood only in the context of British society and culture; and second, that it is even harder to finance a period picture. With few exceptions, period pictures have proved disastrous at the box office. *Chariots* was both British and period. In addition, it had the kind of story which is very difficult to describe.

The chances of success in raising money for a film are in direct proportion to the ease with which you can tell its story. If it takes you half an hour, you have almost no hope of raising the money. If you can tell the whole story in a couple of lines, then you have a significantly better chance. In those days the terms 'high-concept' and 'low-concept' were not used, but today one would call a film whose story is easy to tell a 'high-concept' film, and a film whose story is difficult to tell a 'low-concept' film. High-concept films today are a lot higher in concept than their equivalents were ten or twelve years ago. Today a high-concept movie can be told in one sentence; for example *Lethal Weapon*: black/ white buddy police story, Mel Gibson, Danny Glover, drugs ring, boom. The terminology came in only a few years ago, as a way of describing the kind of films that studios were interested in doing. When a studio head was asked by a reporter, 'Now that you've just become the head of XYZ studios, what sort of films do you want to make?', he could reply, quick as a flash, 'I like high-concept films.' In the early 1980s it was 'event films'; everyone wanted to make 'event films'.

When I used to go regularly – once every month or six weeks – to New York or LA to knock on doors and try to get someone to listen to a pitch, I would often make the projects sound more high-concept than they really were. I remember on occasions being very glad the film-maker wasn't there to hear me as I distorted his complex vision with a few, simple, descriptive strokes. *Local Hero*, for example, became a quirky comedy about a giant American oil company, which, in trying to buy a small Scottish village, is confronted by the apparently principled opposition of the stalwart villagers, who, in reality, are only stalling to push up the price. Of course, it's a far more complicated film than that, but for the purposes of selling to Hollywood that's what you have to say. Years later this tendency became almost an art form with my pitch for *The Name of the Rose*, a movie based on one of the most complex, subtle and erudite books ever to be a bestseller: 'medieval murder mystery in a monastery, Sean Connery'. That's all I said.

Studio executives in Hollywood can't concentrate on anything for more than a couple of minutes, so you have to do it.

Critics tend to look down on high-concept movies, but, although most of the films with which I have been associated would most comfortably fit into the low-concept category, I have no particular preference either way. What I like are true stories. I feel comfortable raising money for a story which is based on historical fact. *Chariots, Gandhi, The Killing Fields, The Emerald Forest*: they were all true stories. I have a hard time really believing in made-up stories. Also, early on, I found that people often expressed a greater interest if I could hang my pitch on a query like, 'Did you read the article in so-and-so?', or if I could attach it to some real, historical event which they could be expected to know about, or at least be interested in. In other words, the true story – the man looking for his son in the Amazon (*The Emerald Forest*), the journalist searching for his colleague in Cambodia (*The Killing Fields*) – was as good a hook as a high concept.

Now it takes quite a long time to explain what *Chariots of Fire* is about. It's about class, it's about anti-Semitism, it's about achievement, it's about the Church of England, it's about growing up, it's about university life. It's about all sorts of things jumbled together which you cannot paraphrase in a few lines. By way of contrast, David Puttnam had at that time a second project for which I was trying to raise finance, *October Circle* – a story about a great cyclist who tries to escape from Eastern Europe. That's it – that's the whole story. Both projects were developed by David and both were earmarked for Hugh Hudson to direct, so when I went looking for money there was no doubt in my mind that *October Circle* was the main contender.

Early in 1978 we had put money into a project called *Breaking Glass*, the story of a New Wave singer's rise to stardom in London's music world. When the time came to look for production finance, we had gone, with producers Clive Parsons and Davina Belling, to Dodi Fayed, one of the principals of a company called Allied Stars, run at that time by producer Tim Burrill. Allied had agreed to finance the film and Goldcrest got back its original investment, £30,000, plus interest and a premium, making a total of £55,000. The transaction had been satisfactory for all parties and, when the *Chariots* script was nearly ready, towards the end of 1979, I went back to Allied Stars with both that and *October Circle*. I could tell Tim Burrill the story of *October Circle* in a couple of lines, but I had a terrible time explaining what *Chariots* was about. When I returned from the meeting, I said to David Puttnam, 'I think I did a lousy job on selling *Chariots*, but maybe I did a pretty good job on selling *October Circle* – I think we have a chance there.'

I had reckoned without David's powers of persuasion. David strongly favoured *Chariots* over *October Circle* and he immediately asked for a meeting with Tim Burrill. Soon after that meeting Allied indicated their interest in providing 50 per cent of the production finance. David then got in touch with his friend, and erstwhile partner, Sandy Lieberson, who was at that time head of production for 20th Century–Fox in Los Angeles. Sandy committed Fox to putting up the other 50 per cent. David Norris, the lawyer who had structured the first development finance deal on *Watership Down*, re-entered the story at this point, spending six months on behalf of Allied Stars, doggedly pursuing Fox to finalize the documentation and get the deal completed before shooting started in April 1980.

When the film went into production, Allied paid us back the £17,700 we had spent on development, with interest and a premium (making a total of £34,100) and we had a 7.5 per cent share of whatever net profits accrued to the finished film. In the event, this profit share was to be worth some £864,000 – a 5,000 per cent return on our investment. *Chariots of Fire*, more than any other project, vindicated my decision to quit Oppenheimer and move into development finance.

It is worth saying something more about the deal with Allied Stars, because originally we had a 10 per cent net profit participation and this was to be paid out of David Puttnam's share. If a film costs $10 million and grosses $80 million at the box office, after the deduction of the exhibitors' share, the distributors' fees and the print and advertising ('prints and ads.') costs, the revenue returned to the producer might be, say, $15 million. The investors will then get their money back ($10 million) with interest, leaving, say, $3 million net. That $3 million is normally referred to as the producer's share. It is the true profit accruing to the investment (see table opposite).

The producer's share is then split, typically 50 per cent to the people who put up the money in the first place, and 50 per cent to the producer and the rest of the people who made the picture, referred to as the talent. So of the $3 million, $1.5 million goes to the investors (i.e. they put up $10 million, which they have recouped with interest, and they have made a clear profit of $1.5 million). The other $1.5 million goes to

Box office	$80.0 million
Exhibitors' share	$44.0 million
Rental	**$36.0 million**
Distribution fee	$11.0 million
Prints and ads.	$10.0 million
Revenue returned to the producer	**$15.0 million**
Cost of the film	$10.0 million
Interest and other expenses	$ 2.0 million
Producer's share	**$ 3.0 million**

the producer and is divided up by him between, in most cases, the director, the writer and, where David Puttnam is concerned, a lot of the crew members. When an actor or director is said to have 'points' in a picture, it normally means that he or she is guaranteed a percentage of the producer's share.

In the case of *Chariots of Fire*, of the 50 per cent left to the producer, David Puttnam was already committed to giving Goldcrest 10 per cent, which left him with 40 per cent. He then paid out probably another 20–25 per cent to the writer, Colin Welland, the director, Hugh Hudson, and the trust fund he had set up for the crew, leaving himself in the end with between 15 and 20 per cent. This proved too great a sacrifice on his part. He came to me and said, 'Look, I've given away more than I had intended.' Could we, he asked, give him back a share of our 10 per cent? I agreed immediately. Of course, at that time we had no way of knowing what these percentages were going to be worth, but I felt that since he had been so generous with other people it would be unfair for us to hang on to the whole of our 10 per cent. We gave back 2.5 per cent, which, happily for David, proved to be worth nearly £280,000. It has to be said that, for a producer of his calibre and experience, David is very modest in his financial demands. Certainly, he regularly took less than half the fees he could get elsewhere when making films for Goldcrest.

(While on the subject of profit participation, I should point out that there is a difference between participating in the net, as outlined above, and participating in the gross. Gross participation is where certain profit shares are paid out before the investors have recouped their investment. If you have a superstar who is crucial to the film, and who is virtually going to guarantee a certain number of tickets – like Robert Redford or Clint Eastwood, or, in his Rambo character, Sylvester Stallone – then you offer him or her, in addition to a multi-million-dollar fee, a percentage of the gross. It is simply a further inducement to get the star to make the movie. Naturally, taking money off the top in this way can significantly reduce the prospect of net profits for everybody else down the line.)

The success of *Chariots*, following its release in 1981, was to be enormously important in raising the profile of the film industry in Britain and was to make it a lot easier for producers to secure funds from hitherto sceptical financial institutions. It also helped raise the profile of British films abroad, especially in the United States, and was to open many doors for us that had previously been closed. *Chariots* was a breakthrough – that much was not media hype.

In October 1978, while finance was being raised for *Chariots of Fire*, *Watership Down* opened in London to rave reviews and I had my first experience of what it was like to be associated with a winner. The results were sufficiently encouraging to persuade the investors to agree to provide development money for Martin Rosen's next animated film, again based on a book by Richard Adams, *The Plague Dogs*. This was to be my first disaster. It was made for all the wrong reasons: it was emotionally right but financially wrong.

In my view it was actually a better, and more straightforward, story than *Watership Down*; it wasn't so metaphysical. It was about two dogs who are captured and put into a research station. They escape and are chased across the country, ultimately to be saved through their own efforts by swimming out to sea. But the project had two fatal flaws.

The first was that Martin Rosen chose to make a very sombre, very downbeat film. What came across on the screen was a tragic and depressingly bleak story, whereas in the book it is uplifting: the dogs achieve heroic stature by escaping, meeting a fox, almost being captured and finally getting away. In the end they were going to live. In the film they clearly drowned.

Second, we made a crucial business error. We had a guaranteed advance from Embassy Pictures to distribute the film in the US, and, on seeing part of the film – the first five or ten minutes, which were great – we felt that they should pay more. We tried to renegotiate the deal, but all Embassy did was shrug and give us the chance to take it elsewhere – which, stupidly, we did. We never got an advance for the film from anybody.

While the film was eventually to prove unsuccessful, at the time – our first investment was made in the autumn of 1978 – it gave Goldcrest a semblance of continuity and fitted in with our desire to be perceived as a reliable source of development finance for a family of producers, of whom Martin Rosen and David Puttnam were the first members. This concept, to build up not only a portfolio of films but a portfolio of film-makers, was to be one of Goldcrest's basic building blocks. It arose partly because the film-makers I met all seemed to be anxious to have a home, a place to go, a company that understood them and looked after their interests. Since they were all very bright people – literate, intelligent and amusing – and had a touch of bohemianism which I found enjoyable and different from what I had had to deal with before, I was only too pleased to oblige. It also suited me because I wanted to be able one day to go to David Puttnam and say, 'David, we stick with our film-makers. If you do this film with us, then on the next one, which may be much more difficult, you know we'll be there to help you get the job done.' In other words, if we could cultivate loyalty amongst the film-makers we would stand a much better chance of having first look at all their new projects.

Although Goldcrest was not in the business of making or financing the production of films as such – our role was restricted to development only – finding such finance was obviously of central importance: unless the projects went into production we didn't get our money back. With their investments in *Breaking Glass* and *Chariots of Fire*, Allied Stars were becoming a major source of production finance, but we could not rely upon one company to finance everything. We had to look elsewhere. The studios don't have this problem; they have enormous revenues arising out of their distribution activities, and they are easily able to finance their own productions. For an independent company like our-selves, life is not so easy. Independent production finance comes from a wide variety of sources, and these sources keep changing, so that, for example, what was available in 1977–8 – say, tax-shelter finance – is not there now. Other avenues have opened up. The principal, and most reliable, sources are the independent distributors who advance money for the production of the film in return for the distribution rights in their territory. However, putting together a financial package from these sources is extremely complicated. Depending on the size of the film and the shortfall in your resources, you might have to put together two or three American distributors (a video distributor, a pay-cable distributor and a theatrical distributor) as well as fifteen or twenty distributors in the foreign markets. The more distributors you have, the more difficult it is to put the package together, because all the contracts have to be signed and sealed before you can start shooting. So on the one hand you are looking to raise as much money as you can and on the other you are trying to limit the number of participants, if only so that you can get the documentation done.

In those days the system of pre-selling was less developed than it is today. (At the three main film markets, Cannes, Milan and Los Angeles, tens of millions of dollars' worth of such deals are now routine, and virtually an entire banking system has grown up, complete with discounted contracts, advances, loans and guarantees, in what used to be the rather prosaic field of international sales.) Nor were there reliable alternative sources. We were left trying to raise the all-important production finance on a film-by-film basis – an even more complicated job than raising development finance project by project. For these reasons, and encouraged by the success of *Watership Down*, the Goldcrest investors and I began toying with the idea of moving Goldcrest itself into production financing.

This made more than just business sense. On a personal level, it had become apparent that there was no way for me to make a living if all we were doing was investing fairly small amounts of money and earning fees and premiums. I couldn't feed my family on that. I couldn't even run my business on the $25,000 contribution that Electra and Pearson were making to my overheads. As for my so-called consultancy work, it was a fiction: Goldcrest was now taking up all my time.

So, partly for business and partly for personal reasons, we started looking into the means by which we might secure our own production fund. At that point, I was introduced to a man who had a scheme of his own that looked as if it might achieve our objectives. His name was Jo Child.

Chapter Four

American Partners

Eberts: Depending on how you look at it, Van Galbraith should be either blamed or given credit for the next phase of Goldcrest's development. I had first met Van when I applied to him for a job when he and his colleague Dimitri de Gunzberg were setting up Bankers Trust International. While Dimitri was primarily responsible for introducing me to Martin Rosen and *Watership Down*, it was Van who, in the spring of 1977, had introduced me to Josiah H. Child Jnr., a man who was to have a singular impact on my life and on Goldcrest over the next few years.

Jo, who had a number of entrepreneurial credits to his name, notably in real-estate investment, is a Boston Brahmin. The Brahmins are old-line New England families whose history goes back to revolutionary times. They are very conscious of their historical role in the founding of the USA and to this day wield, or are thought to wield, considerable influence. Jo was from one of these families, and, even if he wasn't aware of it, he displayed all the characteristics of their idiosyncratic, even eccentric, style.

While looking into real-estate investment opportunities involving the US government's Small Business Administration (SBA), an agency set up specifically to encourage small businesses, Jo came up with the idea of forming a Small Business Investment Company (SBIC), which would invest in the movie industry with funds obtained from the SBA. As the SBA had never before provided funds for investment in films, Jo knew from the outset that his campaign to get it to do so would be time consuming and expensive, and, looking for ways to defray the costs, he had spoken to a number of investment bankers, finally persuading E. F. Hutton, and in particular its head of corporate finance, Paul Bagley, to provide some of the start-up financing. Bagley made it clear, however, that Jo had to have someone on his team who had film-industry experience, to add credibility to his application and to help him raise the capital. Jo had approached Van Galbraith and Van had sent him to me.

Jo is an imposing figure, very tall and invariably garbed in a well-cut, black double-breasted suit of the most expensive cloth, brown cordovan shoes and dark tie. He is more at home in the patrician atmosphere of the Knickerbocker Club in New York than he is in the Polo Lounge in Beverly Hills or the Carlton Hotel in Cannés, two important film-industry haunts that he was later forced to frequent. On first meeting him I was both fascinated and wary. He was undoubtedly brilliant, and, equally undoubtedly, he was quirky.

Jo gave a convincing account of how SBA money could be used to leverage private investment capital in the ratio 2.5:1, so that by raising $10 million from private investors we could obtain a further $25 million from the SBA. It seems astonishing, but the SBA was set up in order to provide just this kind of leverage; the kind of debt capital that you simply couldn't get from a responsible bank. (The theory behind it was that small risk-taking businesses, which have always had a hard time raising money, are good for America.) Applications for SBA funds have to come from businesses that fall within certain categories, primarily in manufacturing. Up until then no one had thought to extend the principle to the entertainment sector, but, even as Jo was formulating his plan, the SBA itself was shifting its policy: in an effort to keep up with the times, it was prepared to embrace certain kinds of non-manufacturing businesses, including films. If Jo didn't have the original idea, certainly he was one of the first to jump on the bandwagon when it was mooted by the SBA. He had a real talent for spotting that kind of opportunity.

I thought the scheme was very attractive and, being unaware of the difficulties of raising money from the American public, or of the endless negotiations required to get an SBIC licence, or indeed of the almost overwhelming frustration of working with Jo Child, I agreed to lend my energies and the Goldcrest name to the project. One attraction was the prospect of getting a substantial salary. If the SBIC ever got off the ground, Jo and I would be its principal officers and we would be paid for our services. Second, there was clearly a possibility of co-financing films between Goldcrest, or other partners, and the SBIC company (to be known as International Film Investors – IFI), thus going some way towards solving the problem of converting development projects into film productions. Third, I knew that we needed someone in America to choose projects and put together deals. Jo was clearly a very intelligent man and he seemed a good partner.

The fact that Jo had no film background didn't bother me because I hadn't either. But I became alarmed when I realized that he had some very unusual views about the film business. One of his theories was that if you put money into enough films, sooner or later one of them is going to be a big hit. He would say to a potential investor, 'Look, it makes no difference what film you put your money into, because the ones that you think are going to be great often don't sell a single ticket, and the ones that you think are going to be lousy are huge blockbusters. The important thing is to put money into lots of films and sooner or later something's going to work out.' I used to cringe as he said it. The Cannon Group, which built up a library of 900 titles in less than ten years and never had a major hit, proved that that theory simply does not stand up. It's like believing that you can beat the bank at roulette. Eventually you are bound to run out of money. My approach, then as now, was that you had to do both: put your money into a portfolio of films, but choose each film extremely carefully and make every effort you can to improve its chances of success.

Jo and I agreed to work together, and we embarked on an eighteen-month campaign, exploring ways to raise $10 million, which we would then take to the SBA to get an additional $25 million in debt capital. We finally came up with the idea of a limited-partnership offering, IFI, which would be sold by E. F. Hutton through its American branch offices.

A limited partnership is a financial structure which groups investors in a single pool of capital but within which they are each treated, for accounting and tax purposes, as if they are on their own. Such an investor personally owns a share of the cash flow, revenues and assets of the partnership and gets all the flow-through benefits of those (especially in terms of tax write-offs) as they arise. By contrast, if you own shares in an ordinary limited company, you do not actually own an individual part of that company's revenues, cash flow or assets, and you cannot use those to your own personal advantage. In particular, you cannot use the company's losses directly to reduce your own tax bill.

Our first task was to prepare a prospectus, setting out the opportunity, the risks and the possible rewards. This took many months and was finally finished in late 1977 by E. F. Hutton. Then I had to persuade the two partners in Goldcrest, Pearson and Electra, to invest $1 million in IFI. This was a considerable step up from their initial investment in Goldcrest Films and the fact that they were prepared to do it was proof of their good faith and of their confidence in the business. Like me, Pearson and Electra expected IFI to improve Goldcrest's trading position significantly, by giving us ready access to production finance. With these two respectable investors thus committed, Jo and I then set out to call upon E. F. Hutton offices across the United States.

Hutton is (or was then, having since been acquired by Shearson

Lehman) a huge stockbroking firm with hundreds of branch offices throughout the United States and overseas. In each of those offices are a number of salesmen, and each salesman has a number of clients. Naturally, Hutton has many corporate customers, but the majority of its clients are individuals with money to invest. The salesmen spend all day on the phone talking to these clients about investment ideas. Principally, the discussions revolve around stocks and bonds, but occasionally a new idea – a real-estate investment, say, or, in our case, a film investment – might be proposed by Hutton to its customers. The investors in IFI had to be fairly wealthy, as the minimum stake was $150,000. Each investor had to prove that he had a net worth of at least $1 million. They also had to sign a declaration saying that they recognized that IFI was a high-risk venture and that should their entire investment be lost it would not cause them hardship.

For months on end, Jo and I would go to the branch offices of E. F. Hutton, where we would be introduced to individual clients, either in groups or one to one, and make our pitch. I would start off by explaining what the film business was all about, how I got involved, what Goldcrest did and what IFI was going to be doing. I cited the example of *Watership Down* and generally painted an encouraging picture of the substantial earnings that could be made should an investment prove successful. I ended my spiel to the potential investors with, 'Gentlemen, of the $10 million we require, we have already got $1 million from my partners. That's how much faith we have in our business.'

I spent nearly a year on the road – the whole of 1978 – having already spent most of the previous year working on the SBIC application. I criss-crossed the United States, up and down, and back and forth. I came back home to London as often as I could, but I would be away for three or four weeks at a time, in Jacksonville, Florida; Birmingham, Alabama; Miami, Atlanta, Houston, Dallas, Fort Worth, Seattle, Portland, Los Angeles, Tulsa, Chicago and Detroit. I went to probably thirty or forty cities on my own account. Jo was doing the same. We soon discovered just how hard it is to get people to invest in the film business.

Worse, for me personally, was that I was doing all this without funds. I didn't have a penny, and I had to pay all the expenses myself. (I used to fly stand-by to cut the price of the air fare, which was a terrible risk because if I missed the flight, I would miss the meeting.) After nearly a year of travelling, my expenses totalled more than $75,000, most of it borrowed from my friend Jimmy King. If the deal hadn't come through, I would have been sunk: I would never have been able to pay off that debt. But not only did I believe in Jo's plan, I also had the incentive of knowing that, if we raised the money and were successful in our SBIC application, I would get a substantial salary for the first time in my life.

By December 1978, the $10 million was finally in place, and International Film Investors opened its first office, in New York. The biggest single shareholder was Goldcrest, with Pearson's and Electra's $1 million (an investment that was actually routed through our offshore company, Firecrest). Jo and I were the two general partners, which meant that we were not only responsible for running the company but were personally liable for any debts incurred in its operation. E. F. Hutton, who had provided the services of their branch offices and had paid some of the formation expenses, received a fee and a small profit share in the company.

Thus, at the beginning of 1979 I found myself running two film companies, Goldcrest in London and IFI in New York, and earning a substantial salary for the first time in my life. The two years that had elapsed since I left Oppenheimer had not been easy and I was still saddled with enormous debts. But my decision to quit banking had been vindicated and I could look forward to a steady improvement in my personal financial position from here on.

From the first day it was clear, however, that running IFI with Jo Child would not be easy. Jo and I argued over policy, strategy and specific investments. In essence, our disagreements arose because I was more cautious than he was. I objected strongly to his theory that we should put money into as many films as possible, no matter what they were, and I also disagreed with this view that we should do deals which enabled us to take a bigger risk in return for a bigger upside (i.e. a bigger share of the profits). His approach was: 'All right, here's a chance. Let's put a lot of money in. We won't give away any profit points unless we have to; we'll keep our fingers crossed that it's going to be a big blockbuster; if it is, we'll really score a home run.' That kind of attitude scared the pants off me. We were a small company and I felt we should be careful. We should cover ourselves as far as we could, and that meant taking on third-party investors and, inevitably, giving away part of the upside.

Jo was also happy to give money to anyone who he thought had a good idea, whether or not they had made films before. It was an extension of his law-of-averages approach: invest in enough people and one of them is bound to be a Spielberg. My approach was the opposite: since we didn't know anything about films, we had to back people who did, people who had made films before and had put all their mistakes behind them.

In my view, Jo had no concept of how difficult it is to make a film. He had never been on a set, for example, and he did not appreciate the skills and experience that go into making a good producer; nor did he have any idea why it is important to have a good producer. I would say, 'Jo, do you know what a producer does? Do you understand that a good producer is intimately involved in a creative way with the process of making a film? Do you know that he's the person who helps the editors? That he's the man who participates in choosing who's going to do the score? That he's the one who sits with the director and talks about music cues?' I am not sure that Jo even knew what a music cue was. It was the kind of argument we got involved in all the time. He had an extremely good intellect, but I could never make an impression on him, because he wouldn't listen.

However, whatever the frustrations we may have felt with each other, we were partners, and I was completely committed to IFI. (I was even more completely committed to the salary it was paying me.) Also, because Goldcrest was a major shareholder in IFI and because I was a senior executive of both companies, the destinies of IFI and Goldcrest were now inextricably linked.

All through the period of the formation of IFI, in 1977 and 1978, I had continued to explore development-investment opportunities on behalf of Goldcrest and to work on the production financing for Goldcrest-developed projects. By the time IFI was formed, the Goldcrest development fund had provided finance for five films – Black Jack, Breaking Glass, Chariots of Fire, The Plague Dogs and an East–West spy drama, Enigma – as well as for a couple of ideas that had not come to fruition.

The IFI relationship now gave us access to much-needed production finance. But it was soon clear that the money available was not, on its own, going to be enough, for, according to the SBA regulations, IFI was allowed to invest a maximum of $2 million or half the budget, whichever was less, in any one film. This meant that a production worthy of our consideration, which would almost certainly cost more than $4 million, could not be controlled by us. To solve this problem we agreed that Goldcrest should have its own source of production finance and be a co-investor with IFI. Throughout 1979, therefore, as IFI got into its stride with investments in Enigma, Plague Dogs and a John Belushi–Talia Shire film called Old Boyfriends, I spent most of my time in England putting together what was to become the first production fund for Goldcrest.

This was to take a further eighteen months. My first problem was that no self-respecting investment bank in London would put its name to a document that sought to raise finance for film production. Everyone I spoke to had at some time or other been burned by the film business, or they knew of some other banker who had. And one of the reasons they had been burned so often was that in London, unlike, say, in New York or Los Angeles, no one knew anything about the business. They still don't. If I go to an investment bank with an oil and gas deal, they have oil and gas experts, people who are very knowledgeable about those industries. Similarly, if I go along with a proposal about real estate, or airlines, or electronics, they have analysts with expertise in those areas. But none of them has any knowledge of the film business. So they could not begin to evaluate my proposal for a film-production fund. Nor were they about to spend the time and money acquiring the expertise; it wouldn't be worth their while. Not only does the independent film business have a bad reputation, but there is not enough revenue involved, the sums of money are too small. Making matters worse was the memory of a previous film-production fund, launched by Morgan Grenfell in 1971: by 1973 every penny in the fund had been lost.

Whereas in raising the $10 million for IFI in the States we had had the backing of E. F. Hutton, it was clear that in launching a similar exercise in the UK I would have backing from nobody. I had no choice but to do it myself. I wrote a prospectus in as much detail as I could and had it typed up by my secretary. I then drew up a list of possible sources of equity finance, sat down with a telephone and started making cold calls. I had four points in my favour. First, I had relationships with the existing investors in Goldcrest Films. Roger Brooke at Pearson Longman and Michael Stoddart at Electra House, showing remarkable faith in someone whom they knew perfectly well to have had no experience of film production, undertook to come in for an unspecified amount as long as I could get other investors. Second, as I was doing the rounds of the City financial institutions, photocopies of my do-it-yourself prospectus in hand, the results of *Watership Down*, which had been released in October 1978, began to trickle in. It was clear that we were going to make a substantial profit. Third, I could point to *Black Jack*, *Breaking Glass* and *The Plague Dogs*, all of which were now in production, as evidence of a good record of converting development projects into feature films. (Major studios convert about one project in twenty, a good independent development financier might expect to convert three or four in ten. We happened to have a higher rate than that, mainly because we worked with established film-makers for whom it is much easier to raise production finance. We had put development money into eight projects, three of which had already gone into production and two of which,

Chariots of Fire and *Enigma*, were certain to go ahead. Fourth, I could promise investors a well-capitalized, risk-sharing American partner in the form of IFI.

From the beginning of 1979 to the middle of 1980 I called on more than 150 potential investors: investment banks, trusts, pension funds and insurance companies. I made my pitch in Switzerland, France, Germany, England, Scotland, Hong Kong, Australia and Japan. I did not spend much time trying to raise money in the States because it was very hard to get an American investor in those days to consider making a sterling investment in the UK. In fact, it was hard to get anyone outside Britain to make a sterling investment in the UK, but at least the Swiss, French, Germans and Italians owned some shares on the London Stock Exchange, or had property investments in England, so they had some familiarity with sterling investments.

I was looking for £8–10 million. We had a minimum target of £5 million, but I was very careful to avoid strict commitments in the prospectus because I had no idea how much I would raise. Also, I wanted to have as few investors as possible. The fewer people you have to deal with, and get approval from, the better.

In the middle of my fund-raising preparations, towards the end of 1979, Roger Brooke resigned from Pearson Longman. His support had been crucial to me and I was naturally anxious not only that his successor should honour the commitment to invest alongside Electra in the new fund, but to be reassured that he was someone with whom I could establish a rapport. Roger and I had enjoyed a very close personal relationship; at the very least, his successor had to be someone with whom I felt at ease. The man appointed was a high-flying consultant from McKinsey, by the name of James Lee. He was to have a powerful and lasting impact on Goldcrest's affairs.

Chapter Five

The Pearson Connection

Ilott: Although much was to be made of the differences in temperament and business style between the two men, Jake Eberts and James Lee in fact have a lot in common.

Lee was born in Scotland in 1943. With his brother and sister he was brought up in a family which he describes as being of 'good, solid, Scottish, upper-middle-class stock, Presbyterian but not strongly religious'. His father was the chief executive of a large Clydeside ship-building firm and the Lee family, like the Eberts family, was accustomed to a prosperous life.

Lee and Eberts both believe that, of their parents, their fathers had the stronger influence. In fact, they describe their fathers in remarkably similar terms. 'A very, very fine man and a real gentleman in the old-fashioned sense of the word. If he was ambitious for me it was in the nicest sort of way. They [my parents] weren't strongly moralistic, but I would say my father had extremely strong principles and stood by them' (Lee). 'I was never put under pressure by my parents to perform or excel. We were under the pressure of expectations of a different kind; there was always a lot of attention paid to morality and integrity – it was a constant theme of my father's life' (Eberts). Messrs Lee and Eberts senior were successful businessmen who presided over thriving families. The sons, now in their late forties and successful businessmen both, play similar paternal roles within large, stable families of their own.

James Lee was sent to Glenalmond, the most academically orientated of Scotland's independent schools. Eberts, too, had a boarding-school education. Lee, like Eberts, was an above average student, especially in maths and science, and showed a particular interest in engineering. Mechanical engineering was thus the natural choice of subject when Lee went up to Glasgow University in 1962. There, at the age of nineteen, Lee met his future wife, Linn. Three years later they were married and they have remained together ever since.

Lee graduated with a good degree in 1966, but by that time had decided not to follow engineering as a career. Instead, he left Scotland to go to the Harvard Business School. His reasons for choosing Harvard were much the same as Eberts's ('it was the best'), who had been there, following more or less the same areas of study, three years before. From 1967 to 1969, Lee was immersed in the study of modern finance and business. Again, he was an outstanding student, a Baker Scholar, and on leaving Harvard at the age of twenty-six he was immediately offered, in his words, 'what seemed like an outrageously large amount of money' to work in the London office of leading management consultants McKinsey and Company. At McKinsey, the smooth progress of his career continued.

'I had had a rather privileged childhood, then I had a very privileged early career,' Lee observes. 'I joined this firm [McKinsey] and was immediately thrust into dealing with people at a very high level, and I got used to dealing with people at that level the whole way through my career, when most other people are working their way up through the organization . . . I had a very artificial progress, a very easy journey through life all the way . . .'

If one is looking for a point of contrast in the early careers of the two men, the most significant may be that Eberts, who had served his apprenticeship as an engineer, diesel-engine salesman and banker, had known professional failure, whereas Lee, who went straight from college to consulting, had not.

For ten years, Lee worked on a range of consulting projects, embracing both public-sector and commercial work. He helped reorganize the National Health Service in the UK, put order into the finances of the Catholic Archdiocese of Malta, contributed to a study of the separation of powers between brokers and jobbers for the Stock Exchange Council in London (ten years before Big Bang), investigated ways of boosting the agricultural sector of the Irish economy, assisted in drawing up a plan for the regeneration of Britain's inner-city areas, and was seconded to Lord Rothschild's think-tank, where he contributed to policy studies on social and economic questions for Prime Minister Edward Heath.

By the late 1970s, Lee had become something of a specialist in the media industries. In 1979, he advised Jan Collins in the spectacular boardroom battle for control of the Collins publishing empire. In the course of that struggle Lee not only learned a lot about publishing but picked up some very useful contacts, among them senior executives at Penguin.

Penguin was owned by media holding company Pearson Longman, which also owned the *Financial Times*, Westminster Press and Longman

Books. Longman and Penguin between them made Pearson Longman not only the biggest book-publishing concern in the UK, but, with Longman's extensive international interests, one of the biggest in the world. Westminster Press at the time owned 120 provincial newspapers. The *Financial Times*, as well as being a very profitable paper in its own right, had spin-off interests in *The Economist* and *Investors Chronicle*. With an annual turnover in excess of £300 million, Pearson Longman was one of Britain's largest media companies.

Towards the end of 1979, at the time when the Collins battle was drawing to a close (and as Eberts was putting the finishing touches to his production-fund prospectus), Pearson Longman's majority shareholder, Pearson, was looking for a replacement for the departing Roger Brooke. The managing director of one of Pearson Longman's constituent companies had been approached but had turned the job down, and there was no one else within the group considered suitable by the Pearson board. Head-hunters were appointed, and one of the first people they approached was James Lee.

Lee, by then thirty-six years old, was reckoned within McKinsey, of which he was now a partner, to be a high flyer. Nevertheless, he was surprised when the Pearson Longman job was first proposed.

'I was happily ensconced at McKinsey and I certainly wasn't in any mood to leave, when this head-hunter, who I didn't know from Adam, called me up one day and said, "Do you want to have lunch to discuss the prospect of running Pearson Longman?" ' he recalls. 'I said, "What do you mean, running Pearson Longman?" And he said, "They want to hire a chief executive." And here I am, thirty-six – this is fantastic. So I said, "I'll be right over." I think we had lunch the same day, or if not the next day, and I was thinking, "God, this is going to be a highly contested job – it's going to be extremely difficult to get." And much to my surprise this head-hunter said to me, "You're in a very good position to get this, because what Michael Hare [Viscount Blakenham, by then chairman of Pearson] wants is not somebody who is going to charge in there and run these companies in an interventionist way, but somebody to develop the long-term strategy for Pearson to acquire new companies and decide where to put the capital." '

Lee's years as a consultant, in other words, were seen to be appropriate qualifications for the job and to compensate adequately for his lack of line-management experience.

Viscount Blakenham runs a highly profitable but idiosyncratic business empire from the seventeenth floor of Millbank Tower, on the north bank of the Thames, not far from the Houses of Parliament. Two floors of this enormous office building are sufficient for the Pearson headquarters, and half of one of those floors is given over to the family department, which looks after the personal affairs of the company's president, Lord Cowdray, and his family. It is the family connection that makes Pearson idiosyncratic. On the one hand, it is a professionally managed industrial conglomerate with interests ranging from information and entertainment (Penguin, Longman, the *Financial Times*, Madame Tussaud's, Yorkshire Television), fine china (Royal Doulton, Crown Derby), oil and oil services (Whitehall Petroleum, Camco), merchant banking (Lazard Brothers) and engineering (Fairey) to pistachio farms in America and, until recently, vineyards in Bordeaux (Château-Latour). In 1987 these interests produced profits of £152 million on a turnover of £952.2 million. On the other hand, the company has its origins in the personal fortunes of the Pearson family, who owned it privately until 1969 and who are still significant shareholders. Many of the managers and directors of the various subsidiaries have been drawn from the family's ranks, including Lord Blakenham himself, the Duke of Atholl (Westminster Press), Lord Gibson (former chairman and board member) and Mark Burrell (Lazard).

The family connection appears to have had two consequences. First, what finance director James Joll calls Pearson's 'business culture' became fixed in an old-fashioned, masculine and patrician mode. While this undoubtedly appeared charming to some outsiders and suited the family and the rather upper-class directors with whom they surrounded themselves, it tended to exclude the new generation of business-school-trained professional managers, and by the mid-1970s Pearson was perceived, in financial circles, to be a rather sleepy empire, in danger of falling behind its rivals. The second consequence was that the centre, where the Pearson ethic was at its strongest, began to lag behind the periphery, where the operating companies, often run by hard-nosed and hard-working whiz kids (Peter Mayer at Penguin being probably the best known), increasingly became self-contained feudal domains. The Pearson board acquiesced in this, in rather aristocratic fashion, believing it to be a good thing that all these tough managers were getting on with the job and making them lots of money. There came a time, however, when some greater direction had to be given to the group as a whole, not least to ward off unwelcome predators. The process began when Lord Blakenham took over as chairman. Casting his eyes across his empire he focused his attention on Pearson Longman.

There he saw an immensely profitable business – at the time it contributed nearly half of Pearson group profits – which suffered, from his point of view, from two disadvantages. First, only 63 per cent of it was owned by Pearson. Not only did this mean that, although Pearson in effect had 100 per cent of the risk and responsibility, 37 per cent of the profits went elsewhere, but also that, as a separate public company with its own board of directors, Pearson Longman was outside Blakenham's full control: its management, also housed in the Millbank building, could resist Pearson's demands by citing the interests of the minority share-holders. Second, although Pearson Longman was cash rich (at the end of 1979 it had a turnover of more than £300 million, profits of about £30 million, and a cash balance of £30 million in the bank), as long as it remained a separate company none of that money could be moved into other, cash-hungry areas of Pearson's operations. Blakenham had failed in a previous bid to buy out the minority, but he planned to try again.

Blakenham had other reasons for wanting to bring Pearson Longman under his full control. At that time, many new investment opportunities were opening up in the area of media and communications, and Pearson Longman, although it was ideally placed, was failing to take advantage of them. The four principal divisions continued to develop in their own fashion but the company as a whole, so it was felt, was going nowhere. In addition, the advent of new technologies and changing work practices in the newspaper and publishing industries meant that support and direction had to be given to a major restructure of the Pearson Longman businesses, especially the *Financial Times* (which later opened a printing and distribution operation in Frankfurt) and Westminster Press (which had just embarked on a rationalization programme that involved closing down a number of unprofitable provincial newspapers).

It was with these considerations in mind that Blakenham sought a strategist rather than a manager to take over the company. After hearing the head-hunter's report, he arranged to have lunch with Lee.

High up in Millbank Tower there is a room of which the floor, ceiling and three walls are virtually a re-creation of a Georgian interior, decorated with Adam-style pastels and delicate plasterwork, tastefully carpeted, furnished with sofa, side-table and drinks cabinet, and decked out with oil paintings of English country scenes. The atmosphere would be that of a club or country house were it not for the expanse of plate glass, looking out on to Pimlico, Battersea and beyond, that constitutes the fourth wall. This is the antechamber to the Pearson directors' dining room. It was here, with the linen-draped table laid for two, the company's own second-growth claret, Les Forts de Latour, decanted on the side-table and the butler ready to serve drinks, that the interview began.

'Blakenham was absolutely charming,' Lee recalls. 'He didn't seem like the normal head of a big business at all; terribly relaxed, and, in the same way as I was saying about my father, very, very old-fashioned in his attitudes as to what business was all about. I liked the atmosphere he created, so I was also incredibly relaxed. There was only one interview, around that lunch table, just with Michael. And I was left with no real feeling at all whether I had done fantastically well or badly. I had no thought that he was going to hire me, nor that he thought I wasn't the right man.'

Ten days later, Lee was none the wiser. 'I eventually called up and said, "What happened?" "Oh," he [Blakenham] said, "I was just getting round to getting hold of you; if you want the job, you've got it."'

Lee started work as chief executive of Pearson Longman at the beginning of April 1980. He was perceived by the other Pearson directors to be 'an attractive, extremely clever and intelligent, very hard-working, very energetic sort of man' (former finance director Alan Whitaker), and 'a very open, bright and amusing fellow' (Whitaker's successor, James Joll). But he also soon proved to be, in Joll's words, 'a bit of a loner. He likes his own show. He doesn't fit in easily with colleagues. We saw he didn't have quite that collegiate approach that I think is the mark of most companies of this level.' Whitaker, too, was aware of Lee's maverick tendencies: 'He likes to have his own way . . . I don't think he took kindly to financial controls or other controls, or the need to carry colleagues along slowly.'

Don Cruickshank, one of Lee's closest colleagues at Pearson Longman, describes him as a 'very warm and friendly and cheerful guy', but adds that people 'divide into two groups with James'. Some, says Cruickshank, 'get the feeling that he just relates to them on the surface and that he's a bit manipulative. They don't feel a depth of relationship, so they're chary of him, which is why as a leader, as a manager of a large group of people, in difficult circumstances he's typically had problems. He has a tremendous tendency to go out on a limb and say, "If you guys don't follow me I'm going to cut myself off" – distancing himself from people so much that they can't follow him or even begin to try and influence him.'

Lee's energy and enthusiasm on the one hand, and his aloofness and insensitivity on the other, was a contradiction thus noted early on at Pearson. It was to become an important factor in the Goldcrest story.

By the time Lee was installed in his new role, Roger Brooke, a very *laissez-faire* chief executive and in many ways the antithesis of Lee in personality and style, had been gone for two months or more. There was thus no handover period and Lee was briefed by Blakenham, Whitaker and Joll, and Pearson Longman's finance director Reg West. His first decision – bearing in mind that Pearson Longman was very profitable, free of debts and had money in the bank – was to launch a review of the potential for new investment within the existing businesses. This review, he recalls, 'highlighted a number of things, like the *Financial Times* moving into Europe, and Longman getting into the United States. But it was jolly clear that we were short of opportunities.'

It was also clear that the four managing directors, Peter Mayer at Penguin, Tim Rix at Longman, the Duke of Atholl at Westminster Press and Alan Hare at the *Financial Times*, would resist any new initiatives that were imposed from the centre. The 'Red Barons', as Joll refers to them, were jealous of their independence and had become accustomed, under the Brooke regime, to being left to get on with things on their own.

Thwarted to a degree in his attempts to develop the existing businesses, Lee was soon to turn his attention to new areas of investment, such as broadcast and cable television, where there were not only real opportunities but also no entrenched opposition within Pearson. When he met Jake Eberts, and found in him a personality which complemented, rather than competed with, his own, and in Goldcrest came across a business that was in exactly such an area of new investment, he was intrigued.

That Goldcrest existed, however, at first came as something of a surprise.

'When I arrived, Michael Blakenham said to me, "One thing you'd better pick up on quickly is that Roger [Brooke] was interested in the film industry," ' recalls Lee. 'Now at no point during that early interview, or in the discussion with the head-hunter, or in any of the meetings about Pearson Longman, had there been any hint that Pearson Longman was going into the film industry. I thought it was a newspaper and book company.'

At that time, Pearson Longman's investment in Goldcrest amounted to the £100,000 committed to the development fund, Goldcrest Films, in 1977, and half the $1 million committed, via the offshore company Firecrest, to IFI in 1978. In the scale of things, these were insignificant sums, and it is not surprising that they had been overlooked in initial discussions with Lee.

Lee consulted Reg West to find out more about Goldcrest. Only three of Goldcrest's eight investments, *Black Jack*, *The Plague Dogs* and *Breaking Glass*, had by this time recouped their investments. Nevertheless, to have spread £100,000 across eight projects in three years, and to have five of those eight secure production finance, was a creditable performance.

Lee's Goldcrest inheritance was rounded off by Pearson Longman's commitment in principle to invest in Eberts's proposed film-production fund.

Thus briefed by West, Lee arranged a meeting with Eberts in April 1980. He remembers being impressed both by the man and by his plans for Goldcrest.

'It was very clear that he had thought through what he was trying to do,' says Lee. 'He seemed to have a good deal of knowledge about the industry, and although running an extremely small set-up – basically himself and Irene Lyons [Eberts's secretary] – he gave me the impression of being very well organized. He had some business plans. He had his figures all worked out. He was very financial in his outlook. The fact that he came from the Harvard Business School impressed me that he must be a good man.'

For his part, Eberts was relieved to find that Lee was pleasant mannered, enthusiastic and businesslike. He explained the production-fund proposal in detail and Lee gave it his full backing.

The prospectus for the new fund had been issued in February 1980. By July, when the offer was closed, £8.2 million had been raised, £3.6 million of which was put up by Pearson Longman, which consequently held 44 per cent of the stock, and £1.3 million by Electra. The two founding shareholders had a carried interest arising from their earlier funding of Goldcrest Films, which was now to be folded into the new company, Goldcrest Films International (GFI). The formation of GFI marked a qualitative leap in the development of Goldcrest, taking it from development investment into production investment and massively increasing the scale of its operations. The company was soon to be transformed from an interesting but minor player in the independent film industry to the celebrated, award-laden company of Wardour Street legend. Like IFI, GFI took the form of a limited partnership. The new shareholders included the National Coal Board Pension Fund (NCBPF), the Post Office Staff Superannuation Fund (POSS), Noble Grossart Investments Ltd, Thomas Tilling plc, investment trusts managed by Murray Johnstone Ltd and investment trusts managed by J. Henry Schroder Wagg and Co. Most importantly, 7.5 per cent of the new company was owned by IFI. This was intended to match the 9 per cent of IFI owned, via the $1 million investment routed through Firecrest, by Goldcrest. These cross-holdings were later to make life extremely complicated for both parties.

Chapter Six

The First Board Meeting

Eberts: From the outset, GFI was meant to be a co-investor with IFI in all IFI projects. Once the GFI money had been raised, however, we had to work out exactly what that would mean in practice. A very complicated document was drafted, which took months of work and many hundreds of thousands of dollars of legal fees, setting up a system whereby each company had the right to invest in the other's projects on an equal basis. This document was called the Reciprocal Investment Opportunity Agreement, referred to as the RIOA. The title was as convoluted as the deal. In fact, it was a classic example of how difficult it is to write a co-operation document free of conflicts of interest between two entities which are basically in the same business. (I should have learned my lesson from it, for the issue was to come up twice more, much later in my relationship with Goldcrest, and each time cause as much grief.) Not only did the respective sets of shareholders have different interests, but it was virtually impossible to reconcile the differences in overhead cost, fee agreements and business practices – IFI being in New York and GFI in London – of the two companies.

Since Goldcrest had virtually no personnel, just myself and my secretary Irene Lyons, and since my salary was being paid by IFI, there was a further agreement under which Goldcrest paid a management fee to IFI for the services of its staff: lawyers, accountants, secretaries, Jo and myself. The idea was that Goldcrest would thus avoid burdensome overheads. I had always done the Goldcrest accounts myself. Now, with £8.2 million in the bank, they were going to be too complicated and too time-consuming for me, so we arranged for Pearson to do the bookkeeping. For this, and for acting as company secretary, Pearson was paid a service fee of £25,000 a year. Goldcrest's overheads were therefore a fraction of what would normally be expected of a production company of its financial strength.

None of these arrangements would have been necessary if IFI and

GFI had simply merged, which at first sight would seem to have been the logical thing to do. But IFI was strictly regulated by the terms laid down by the Small Business Administration and could not easily join forces with a non-US entity. It would be in danger of losing the benefits of SBA leverage. Nevertheless, very soon after GFI was formed, the idea of a merger was proposed by Jo and over the succeeding months was to be avidly pursued by him, to the point where it became an obsession.

From the beginning, relations between GFI and IFI were complicated by a difference between Jo and me about what the role of each company was to be. Jo was unaware, for example, of the way in which a British board of directors works. In America the board doesn't exactly function as a rubber stamp, but it certainly doesn't involve itself very much with the detailed operations of the company. It deals with major corporate issues and strategy and has to approve transactions above a certain value, but other than that it pretty well leaves the management to get on with running the company. Furthermore, the chairman of the board of a US company is very often its chief executive, an arrangement that tends to tilt the balance of power decisively in favour of the management. In the UK, it is more common for the chairman to be a non-executive who formally participates only to the extent that he chairs the board meetings. In that position, nevertheless, he has a lot of power, and can become quite deeply involved in major strategic decisions, often acting as an arbitrator between the sometimes conflicting interests of the management and the shareholders, and even between one faction of the management and another. Most important, he is able to act as a brake on the chief executive.

Jo, wrongly perceiving Goldcrest to be a US-style company, thought that whatever IFI wanted to do GFI would happily endorse; that I, as the chief executive of GFI, would make the decisions; and that, as his partner, my decisions would always be in line with his. Of course, I never could make those decisions: I always had to go to the Goldcrest board to get approval for any course of action I might want to take. And, although I was chief executive, I was not chairman: I did not control the conduct, or even the agenda, of board meetings.

This misunderstanding, compounded by the antipathy that grew up between us – Jo, much to my annoyance, clearly saw himself as the boss, and IFI as senior to GFI – made relations very strained. (Throughout the period of raising the IFI money, I had tried to smooth over or ignore the differences between Jo and myself. I had very much wanted the venture to succeed, and I was desperately in need of the IFI salary. Once that had been accomplished, however, I could afford to be more assertive. I found Jo very hard to get on with and increasingly let my irritation show. Probably he found it just as hard to get on with me.)

By the time the GFI money was raised, Irene and I, having moved out of Oppenheimer's City offices, were installed in slightly larger and certainly more elegant premises in Mayfair, on the top floor of a building occupied by Dillon, Read (the New York-based merchant bank of which Van Galbraith, formerly of Bankers Trust, was now the London chairman). It was there, in the boardroom, that we convened the first meeting of the newly capitalized Goldcrest Films International in July 1980.

Ilott: The purpose of the first board meeting of GFI was to allocate all, or part, of its £8.2 million capital to film investments. Yet only one of the directors present, David Puttnam, had any film-making experience. The rest, among them Eberts, James Lee and Jo Child, Michael Stoddart and Michael Walton from Electra, Angus Grossart from Noble Grossart, Peter Mayer from Penguin Books, Clive Gibson and Michael Blakenham from Pearson, Michael Waterston from Murray Investment Trust, Richard Baker Wilbraham from Schroder, Lyn Hopkins from POSS, Doug Abbott from the NCBPF, and the chairman Teddy Barnes (at that time the corporate finance manager at Lazard), were all bankers, financiers or shareholders' representatives of one kind or another. At first sight, this would seem to be an odd collection of people to be sitting around a table making decisions about films, but in fact it underlines the original purpose of GFI. It was never intended to be a film-production company, merely a pool of venture capital, to be invested on strictly banker-like assessments of risk and return. There was no question of the board's having to make creative or commercial judgements about the projects themselves. That process was deemed to be the province of Eberts and Jo Child, the heads of GFI and IFI respectively. And even then, neither Eberts nor Child professed any particular expertise. They too were financiers, and they relied on the talent and probity of the film-makers with whom they chose to work. The obvious risks entailed in this hands-off approach were covered in typical mutual-fund fashion: the capital would be spread across a wide portfolio, there would be a ceiling on investment in any one picture, and GFI's exposure would, as far as possible, be laid off by pre-sales and third-party participation. Goldcrest, in other words, was an investment, not a film-making, enterprise. That, anyway, was the original intention. It was to change, and the seeds of the change were sown at this first board meeting.

David Puttnam had been invited to join the board partly to lend the voice of his experience, but partly also to cultivate him as a source of projects. (Of all the people Eberts had met, Puttnam was the most impressive and the one with whom Eberts most wanted to do business. What better way of forging a relationship than by inviting him to join the company?) But Puttnam's presence guaranteed that the discussion of film investments would include some consideration of creative and marketing questions, if only because his expertise was concentrated in those areas.

As effective as Puttnam in introducing film-making rather than investment criteria was Sir Richard (Dickie) Attenborough, who, although not yet a board member, had been invited to address the meeting. After the lunch adjournment, he was to make an impassioned, wholly un-banker-like – indeed tear-laden – speech about his long-cherished project, *Gandhi*, which, as James Lee remembers it, made a profound impression: 'We all thought, "What a wonderful human being" . . . We'd have got down and felt the hem of his jacket.' Thus, the bankers were drawn, from the outset, into areas of decision-making for which they were unsuited and ill prepared.

The meeting lasted through the day and took a wholly unexpected course. As well as attending to the main business of allocating funds, the discussion of which was conducted in a manner that alarmed Jo Child, the meeting formulated a policy of investing only in films that were both of high quality and identifiably British. This virtually guaranteed an immediate rift between GFI and IFI.

Eberts: As chairman, Teddy Barnes opened the meeting with the usual formalities and then handed over to me. I ran through more or less the same spiel I had given a hundred times when raising the money – that we would invest in proven talent, spread the risk and minimize our exposure – and I emphasized that the films in which we made investments should appeal to the international market and have a long shelf-life: topical subject matter, which dates very quickly, was out. Each of the investors' representatives then gave his view of the kinds of films we should invest in, and then we moved on to the specific projects being proposed.

IFI, which had been active for a year by this time, had committed to providing 50 per cent of the budget for both Joe Dante's *The Howling* and John Carpenter's *Escape from New York*. In line with the spirit of our Reciprocal Investment Opportunity Agreement, I had proposed that Goldcrest provide half of IFI's commitment, subject to the approval of the Goldcrest board. Teddy Barnes put the two films to the meeting but, far from being rubber-stamped, as Jo had expected, both proposals were subject to searching questions. The board expressed considerable misgivings, and Jo and I had our work cut out to persuade them that it was important for Goldcrest to be seen to be active straight away; that we should give a clear signal that we were interested in major films with international potential; and that these were two very good scripts and highly commercial projects in which there would be very little risk. On most of these points, the board, very much influenced by David Puttnam, took a different view, but, feeling bound to honour the verbal commitments already made by me, endorsed our proposals to invest £145,000 in The Howling and £720,000 in Escape from New York. Both were to prove highly successful and Goldcrest was to make substantial profits – £250,000 and £670,000 respectively – from these investments.

Jo did not hide the fact that he was very unhappy with the tone of the discussion. He was to like it even less when we discussed the next proposal, a film called Hopscotch. Billed as a comedy thriller, starring Walter Matthau, Glenda Jackson and Ned Beatty, and to be directed by Ronald Neame, it was put to the meeting by Jo, fully supported by me, only to be immediately savaged by David Puttnam, who forcefully expressed the view that Walter Matthau films appealed to a dwindling, if loyal, audience. His comments were couched in the most persuasive terms, referring to demographics and the box-office performance of a succession of comparable movies. In that company, his expertise was not far short of dazzling. Taking his cue, Teddy Barnes expressed the conviction that, not only was the film unlikely to appeal to large audiences, but that it was insufficiently British to be a suitable GFI investment. ('Insufficiently British' was to become a standard formula for turning down projects we did not want but could find no other respectable excuse for rejecting. It had the unlooked-for effect of promulgating the idea that Goldcrest was always to be a purveyor of quality British films, a notion that had never been mentioned in the GFI prospectus.) Hopscotch was put to a vote, and rejected.

Jo's ill-temper turned to fury. The scepticism with which the board received IFI's proposals was not at all what he had expected. That they should have turned down a project to which IFI was already committed, and which had been recommended by me, the chief executive of the company, was to him an outrage and led him to remark later that he 'should never have gone into business with Goldcrest'. Not only had he not expected all this talk about British films – SBA regulations prohibited IFI from investing in non-American productions – he had not expected any discussion of specific film investments at all.

He in turn managed to upset virtually everyone else at the meeting, in particular Electra's Michael Stoddart. Michael is not one to hide his feelings, and it was apparent from the start that there was going to be bad blood between him and Jo. (Some time later, after one of our periodic disagreements, Jo happened to write a letter to a third party which ended with the words 'the nettlesome Mr Stoddart'. Somehow a copy of the letter landed on Michael's desk, and that sealed Jo's fate as far as Michael was concerned.)

Jo has a very patrician way of speaking. If you can't see his point of view the first time, he really doesn't think you are worthy of hearing it a second. His greatest tribute is to say that somebody is bright. He would never say that somebody is enthusiastic, or energetic, or attractive or charismatic: you are either bright or you are not bright. As far as he was concerned the members of the Goldcrest board were 'not exactly a bright bunch of guys'. He hardly bothered to hide this opinion and the Goldcrest board, nearly all of them very astute individuals of proven achievement, did not take kindly to it.

The atmosphere of the meeting was tense, Jo was sulphurous with anger and there was still a long way to go on the agenda, when Teddy Barnes announced that we would adjourn for lunch.

Ilott: The first session of the GFI board meeting had two important consequences as far as James Lee's involvement in Goldcrest's affairs was concerned. First, Teddy Barnes, thoroughly alarmed both by the complexity of the subjects under discussion and by the passion with which opposing views on these subjects were held, quickly concluded that the chairmanship of Goldcrest was not for him. After the meeting he was to stand down, causing Lee, as the representative of the major shareholder (and the only volunteer), to take his place. Second, the breach that had opened up between Jo Child and the rest of the board, and especially the personal antagonism that was evident between Child and Eberts, was to draw Lee into taking a leading role as mediator between GFI and IFI. Both tasks led to his spending more time on Goldcrest than was warranted by its importance within the context of his overall Pearson Longman responsibilities. And the more he was to become involved, the more he was to like it. In James Joll's words, he was to become 'entranced' by the film business, 'fascinated by its immensely complicated financial structure . . . He began to fall in love with the business very early on.'

Eberts: During the board's luncheon break the talk was all about *Hop-*

scotch. As it happened, Teddy Barnes and David Puttnam were right: IFI never did make any money out of it. But the reasons had nothing to do with Walter Matthau's box-office appeal. The film, while neither a comedy nor a thriller, had sufficient elements of both to secure pre-sale guarantees from NBC (network television) and Viacom (television syndication) in the United States. IFI also had enough foreign distribution guarantees to make it look like a risk-free deal. It was to be the first of many 'risk-free' deals which somehow ended up losing money.

The film, which ironically had rather more in the way of British content than either *Escape from New York* or *The Howling* (the director of *Hopscotch*, Ronnie Neame, and the co-star, Glenda Jackson, were both British, and part of the film was shot in England), was eventually delivered on schedule and on budget, but IFI had great difficulty sorting out the US theatrical distribution. The producers, Ely and Edie Landau, were a husband-and-wife team with a reputation for unusual and innovative financing schemes, not all of them applied to successful films. One of the techniques they employed on *Hopscotch* was to get a number of American cinema chains to invest in the film prior to production, in return for exhibition rights on better than usual terms in their respective markets. Normally, negotiating with cinemas is one of the jobs done by the distributor, who organizes the booking of the film in theatres across the country, pays for the prints and advertising, ships the prints to the exhibitors and collects the receipts. For this the distributor earns a fee. The Landaus' plan was to bypass the distributor and keep the distribution fee.

On paper it sounds like a great idea. In practice, it doesn't work. First of all, you have a hell of a time finding cinema chains that are not in competition. If Mr Plitt, who owns a great string of theatres and wants the picture, happens to have a theatre in Westwood, Los Angeles, and Mr Smith at General Cinema, who also has a great string of theatres and wants the picture, happens to have a theatre in Westwood too, you are in trouble. Neither party will allow the other to show the film in Westwood, nor will they agree to split the audience by showing it side by side. Multiply that problem across the country and you very quickly realize how it is that the distributor earns his fee. (Distributors know the job and can fulfil the service – that's number one. Number two: they can get very good prices on prints and advertising, because, releasing dozens of films every year, they have real purchasing power. And number three: they can force the exhibitor to pay up quickly; if he doesn't, he might not get the next film, which, for all they know, could be a *Star Wars* or a James Bond.)

The distribution of *Hopscotch* quickly degenerated into a horrendous mess. Finally, IFI and the Landaus went to Bob Rehme, who ran the independent distribution company Embassy Pictures (which had handled the release of *Watership Down*), and pleaded with him to take it over. The film had already been sold to some exhibitors and Rehme had to do what he could with what remained. In the event, *Hopscotch* generated about $20 million at the box office, which translated into about $9 million rentals – good, but not enough to earn a profit for IFI. Later, when I talked to people like Charlie Bludhorn at Paramount and Terry Semel at Warner Bros., both of whom liked the film (it was a good movie and earned excellent reviews), they said: 'God, if we had had that picture from the beginning we could have easily done $20 million rentals.' This was the first time I had been exposed to the real power of the major studios, and I realized that, with the exception of a handful of art films, the box office receipts you can generate with a film distributed by a major studio are almost always more than can be generated by an independent. I have tried to stick with the majors in the US ever since.

After lunch the board meeting reconvened and we discussed, and committed to, a development investment in Sidney Schanberg's story, *The Killing Fields*.

The original idea for *The Killing Fields* was brought to us in February 1980 by Embassy's Bob Rehme, with whom we early on developed a very close relationship. Bob, in turn, had it from Lindsay Doran, who was working as a production executive at Embassy and had seen an article written by Schanberg in *Newsweek*. Rehme was very taken with the idea but was not authorized by his parent company, the AVCO Corporation, to invest money in development. He called Jo, outlined the story, and proposed that IFI develop it, on the understanding that later on Embassy would be very interested in putting up production finance in exchange for US or world rights. Jo was interested and sent a copy of the article to me.

The Killing Fields is about a Cambodian journalist's survival of a three-year period of incarceration during the Pol Pot era, and the attempts made throughout that time by his American colleague to find him. This unlikely partnership between a self-effacing Cambodian and a very difficult, domineering American is set against a background of enormous conflict: bombs and explosions, re-education camps and people fleeing to the countryside. It had obvious potential: the dramatic elements in the story were gripping; it was contemporary; and it was true.

I told Jo that, although I loved the idea, I would have no confidence in investing in the project unless we had a producer or director attached. Neither Jo nor I knew anything about making films, and clearly this story, with its paddy-field locations and battle scenes, was going to be a large-scale production: we needed a major film-maker to make it happen. I suggested to Jo that we approach David Puttnam, who at that time was just putting *Chariots of Fire* into production. Jo agreed.

Suggesting Puttnam's name was one thing; getting him to do it was another. I knew him well enough to give him a call, but I certainly didn't feel comfortable with the idea of giving him a sales pitch. In the relationship between financier and film-maker, it is usually the film-maker who does the talking and the financier who listens. David Puttnam, I knew, was the master of talking up a project. He had sold me the idea of developing *Chariots* over the phone. Hitherto, when talking to David, I had been the epitome of the upright, uncreative financier; I shied away from film talk and always deferred to his greater experience. So to put a project to him was not an easy thing for me to do. I called him from the Knickerbocker Club in New York, where Fiona and I happened to be staying, and, as I dialled his number, I was mentally rehearsing what I was going to say. When he answered, I stumbled and stuttered my way through the *Killing Fields* story. To my immense relief, he said, 'Oh yes, I know the story very well. I've been thinking about it myself.' It was quickly agreed that IFI would provide whatever development financing was required, subject to David's securing the rights from Sidney Schanberg and getting the full co-operation of the various State Department officials whose approval would be needed before the project could go ahead.

In fact, it was to take a long while to secure the rights and I very much doubt that Schanberg would have given permission to film the story to anyone less persuasive than David. The problem was that Schanberg had sold the book rights to Viking Press (owned by Penguin) for an advance of $48,000, but had not delivered a single page. I don't think he had even started work on the book. Viking would not let Schanberg co-operate with us until we repaid the advance, which we eventually did.

Even then David had to compromise in two areas. First, because of Schanberg's pending divorce, David had to change the original draft of the screenplay so that the break-up did not come across as unpleasant or antagonistic. In the end Schanberg's wife did not appear at all in the movie. Second, David had to change the portrayal of the American ambassador. In this matter he was under severe pressure from the US State Department, which had been very helpful in securing the co-operation of all the relevant American authorities. The ambassador eventually depicted in the film is a composite portrait of several ambassadors and no real blame for some of the things that happened in Cambodia is attached to him.

A further complication was that, as IFI could back only American films, David had to establish an American company into which we could make our investment. For reasons which remain obscure, his US company was set up in Nevada and was called Enigma Nevada.

All this had been settled by the time of the first GFI board meeting, at which the Goldcrest shareholders were offered a development investment in *The Killing Fields* under the terms of the reciprocal-investment arrangement. After some discussion, it was agreed that we would commit $350,000 to the development of the project, shared equally between Goldcrest and IFI. That money was to pay the $48,000 to get us off the hook with Viking; to pay Schanberg for the option on the rights; to pay Bruce Robinson to write the script; and to pay for research, which involved going back and forth between Thailand, New York, Washington and LA. Our eventual investment in *The Killing Fields* was to be an even greater sum because we put up part of the production finance, but as a development investment this was already a very substantial amount. It was a great deal more than we had committed to the combined development of, for example, *Watership Down, Chariots of Fire* and *The Plague Dogs*.

In fact, the first three films to which we committed expenditure at that meeting – production finance for *The Howling* and *Escape from New York* and development finance for *The Killing Fields* – represented a very considerable step up in the size of our investments. They were nothing, however, compared to the commitment made to the fourth film we discussed that day: *Gandhi*.

Chapter Seven
Backing *Gandhi*

'Gandhi was everything the voting membership of the Academy would like to be: moral, tan and thin' – Jan Morgenstern, Los Angeles Herald Examiner, April 1983

Eberts: I had first met Dickie Attenborough back in 1978. At the time – in the midst of arranging development financing for *Breaking Glass*, *Enigma*, *Chariots of Fire* and *The Plague Dogs* and running around America with Jo Child raising money for IFI – I was trying to put together a project on the life of ibn-Saud, the founder and first monarch of modern Saudi Arabia. The idea for the film had been brought to me by Rupert Chetwynd, whose wife Lucia Arrighi had done the production designs for *Watership Down*. Rupert was an ex-member of the SAS, Britain's equivalent of the Green Berets, and was a close associate of the regiment's founder, Colonel David Stirling. Stirling had served in the Middle East during the war and had become friendly with a Turk by the name of Kemal Adam, who, as well as being the head of the Saudi Arabian security services, happened to be married to King Feisal's sister. With Adam's support, Stirling and Chetwynd were putting together a feature film on the life of ibn-Saud. They brought on to their team a man called Henri Gebrier, an ex-member of the French Foreign Legion and very much an SAS type. (All these characters seem to have what I would consider right-wing sympathies and love to hang out together, reminiscing about parachute drops and undercover missions in this or that trouble-spot of the world.) Gebrier had been involved in the production of *Les Salaires de la Peur* (*The Wages Of Fear*), one of the very few non-English-language films even to come close to being a box-office hit in its subtitled version in the UK and US. It won the British Film Academy Award for Best Picture when it was released in 1953. This honour had given Henri the impression that he was an important film-maker.

From the start I had very severe doubts about Henri. Although he was a pleasant and colourful, if garrulous, individual, he did not impress me as being made of the right stuff to be a producer – a view that I made clear to Stirling and Chetwynd. I argued that what we needed was an altogether stronger and more experienced man at the helm. Although I did not know Richard Attenborough at the time, and had never seen any of his films, I had read many newspaper articles describing the complications and difficulties of making A Bridge Too Far, which he had produced and directed. In every case, the commentators had remarked on Attenborough's extraordinary organizational achievement: co-ordinating the planes, troops, bridges and tanks required to make this colossal film. It seemed to me that the ibn-Saud story would have similar logistical problems: Bedouin riding full speed across the desert, thousands of extras, battle scenes and remote locations. I suggested that, rather than rely on Henri, we should speak to Attenborough and see if he would be interested. Rupert and David agreed.

As far as I was aware, Dickie Attenborough had never heard of me before, and I was surprised by the alacrity with which he agreed to come round to my office and discuss the ibn-Saud proposal. He was then, as he is now, a very charismatic man with great presence. He wears very large sideburns that go two thirds of the way down his cheeks. These 'mutton chops' are somehow charming, as is his conservative mode of dress when he is on a selling mission: on the day he came to my office he was wearing a brown suit, brown tie and vividly striped shirt. We had scarcely exchanged two words before he was calling me 'darling', a common British stage-actors' form of address which has become Dickie's personal trademark. At that time he was editing a picture called Magic and was all enthusiasm and bonhomie, talking about film financing in general and British film financing in particular. But I don't think he had any intention whatever of talking about ibn-Saud.

Having spent fifteen or sixteen years looking for money to finance the greatest ambition of his life – the making of an epic film on the life of Mahatma Gandhi – he was quite prepared to go anywhere and speak to anybody who appeared to have access to film funds in the hope that some of his enthusiasm would rub off and start the cash flowing. Although he wasn't exactly talking about Gandhi as he walked in the door, it didn't take him long to get round to the subject. His enthusiasm was overwhelming: passion just poured out of him. (I have come to know that his passion, or the appearance of it, can be turned on at a moment's notice, and about damn near anything, as even he will admit; but in the case of Gandhi it was real: there was no acting, no pretending.) Of course,

I could not admit to him at the time that I had never seen a picture that he had acted in, or directed or produced. (Indeed, until *Gandhi*, I still hadn't. One day, years later, I admitted as much. He let it pass, but then sent me a birthday card which included a specially devised free ticket to every film he had ever acted in – fifty or sixty movies. I have kept the card and the ticket, but I still haven't seen any of the films.)

At that time, 1978, Goldcrest existed only to provide development finance, and it was immediately clear that the *Gandhi* project was out of our league. It sounded interesting, but expensive and uncommercial, and I said as much. Dickie then sat there twiddling his thumbs while I gave him the pitch on ibn-Saud. Had he been remotely interested, he would, I am sure, have taken up the opportunity. But of course he wasn't. All he was interested in was *Gandhi*, and there came a point when the conversation faltered: we both realized that his attempts to get me interested in his film were as fruitless as my attempts to get him interested in mine. Dickie went back to pursuing his dream and I went back to ibn-Saud. (The project was eventually shelved following the death of Henri Gebrier in a Paris hospital. The rumour was that he was murdered by unhappy associates for having failed to keep 'certain promises'.)

That was the end of *Gandhi* as far as I was concerned, until, two years later, in the early summer of 1980, the screenwriter Jack Briley, knowing that Goldcrest was on the verge of raising a significant amount of production finance, suggested to Dickie that he send me the script. Jack and I knew each other well. He had written the original screenplay for one of our development projects, *Enigma*, and we had worked together on an 'East-meets-West' project that brought an Arab hero together with an American heroine. He was now the latest in a long line of *Gandhi* scriptwriters. He gave me a call and persuaded me to read his screenplay.

The screenplay arrived within minutes, causing me to wonder whether Dickie had a car and driver standing by at all times to deliver copies to anyone who showed even a glimmer of interest. It was late in the afternoon as I settled down to read it – from the window of my attic office I could see the sun going down over the buildings of Mayfair. It took two hours, and when I got to the end I read it through again.

It is hard to describe one's reactions to a script. It is not a finished work like a novel; you have to read it with great concentration, visualizing every scene and trying to imagine the dialogue in the mouths of actors. In fact, few people can read a script successfully, and all of us have at some time or other, through our own failure of imagination, rejected scripts that have later made wonderful films. But sometimes the vision is so clear, the impact so powerful, that the effect on the reader is like that of a finished work. I was absolutely stunned by *Gandhi*. To this day, it is the only script I have ever read that has made me cry. Here was an outstanding project, one with which I would be proud to be associated. I called Jack in the morning to offer my congratulations and I vowed to do whatever I could to help the film. Jack immediately contacted Dickie, and within minutes Dickie was in my office, giving me what was to be the first of many brilliant and emotional performances, acting out every role and dancing around on his surprisingly nimble feet, re-creating scenes and events in the script – all with such enthusiasm and energy that, even if I had had any doubts, I would have been won over.

Exactly how I was going to help I wasn't sure. The project did not need development finance and we had not yet finished raising the money for our production fund. Dickie, however, was in desperate straits. He had to shoot the film during the cool season in India, starting in November and finishing the following April or May. (The summer would simply be too hot: a film crew could not function in the 110° heat.) But to start in November he had to be making preparations now, six months ahead: hiring the cast and crew, building the sets, sorting out the costumes, getting all the permissions needed to shoot in India, shipping the equipment and so on. These tasks, known as pre-production, are fairly straightforward if you are shooting in your own country, but are horrendously complicated when you are shooting overseas. To take a simple example, if you are going to fly in 125 people to make a movie, you have to book the hotel rooms and pay for them, or at least put down some sort of deposit, well in advance. That means knowing now exactly where you will want each of those 125 people to be on any given day over the four or six months that the film will be shooting.

The pre-production phase is crucial to any film. Months of meticulous preparation are rewarded by a smooth-running production that sticks to its schedule and budget. If the shoot is ill prepared, the result is usually chaos. But pre-production requires money, and Dickie needed that money immediately.

He had another problem. During all the fifteen or more years that he had been working on the project, with the help of Mountbatten, Nehru and other great personages, he had come very close to securing full, final, formal approval from the Indian government. But he had never quite got it. He was now on the verge of doing so. The Indians were in principle prepared not only to give the film their blessing, but to put up one third of the total cost, which represented the rupee portion of the financing (i.e. all the money that was going to be spent in local currency in India). All Dickie had to do was to show that he had access to the other two thirds of the financing. He had stalled on this requirement for some time, and if he prevaricated much longer, he would lose credibility, the Indians would withdraw and, having come so close, it was unlikely that the project would ever get started again. He needed to send some people out there, to start spending dollars in India, to get costumes made; above all, to show evidence of good faith to the Indian government.

This was not development money and, strictly speaking, it fell well outside Goldcrest's supposed area of activity, i.e. development financing. Nevertheless, I told Dickie that we would provide the funds.

The sum involved was $700,000, which I expected to split fifty–fifty between Goldcrest and IFI. For us this was an enormous commitment, especially as it was the kind of money that we might never see again, there being no guarantee that production finance would be forthcoming and that the film would actually get made. When I called Jo Child and explained the whole thing to him, he was naturally a little sceptical. I implored him not to turn me down until he had spoken to Dickie, who got on a plane that very evening and flew to New York. Within an hour or so of their meeting, Dickie had completely knocked Jo off his feet. Jo approved of the investment and in principle the deal was done: $700,000 pre-production money, half IFI and half Goldcrest, to be drawn down in stages.

It was this proposal that was put before the first board meeting of GFI for ratification. Dickie, who had patiently sat through the disagreeable events of the morning session and had heard all the arguments for and against investing in a large-scale production in a remote location (*The Killing Fields*), was now called upon to make the case for investing in an even larger-scale production in an even more remote location. But he judged the occasion and the audience beautifully and overwhelmed everyone with the force of his presentation. Approval was duly granted, and I was almost surprised that it wasn't accompanied by a vote of thanks to Dickie for allowing us to give him some of our money.

That being the final business on the agenda, the board meeting was brought to a close by Teddy Barnes. It had been an extraordinary day. Goldcrest, until then a minnow in the movie pond, had committed significant sums to two mainstream American films, *The Howling* and *Escape from New York*, and to two of the most ambitious films ever to be undertaken by a British film company, *The Killing Fields* and *Gandhi*. The rejection of *Hopscotch* meant that the relationship between GFI and IFI had suffered a setback. In my mind, this was more than compensated for by the fact that we were in business with film-makers of the calibre of David Puttnam and Dickie Attenborough.

Because Jo and I had stuck our necks out so far for *Gandhi*, Dickie, as a gesture of equal good faith, had volunteered to defer his salary. This meant that he wouldn't see a penny until, and unless, the film was in profit. It would be three years before that happened and, to keep himself going during the production and editing stages of the film, he mortgaged his very valuable art collection. (In the end, *Gandhi* was to be very profitable and Dickie made a lot of money, but the risk he took personally at the outset was at least equal to the risk that we were taking as a company.)

The budget had been worked out by the line producer, Terry Clegg, who was already on the payroll (paid by Dickie) and who had made a number of trips to India. Like the script, which was shot in exactly the form in which I had read it, the 'preliminary' budget was already a highly polished piece of work and proved to be very close to the final cost: $24 million. *Gandhi* was to be on a bigger scale than any film we had been involved with before. Approximately half the money was meant to be in the form of an advance from 20th Century–Fox, with whom Dickie had been engaged in discussions for a period of months; one third was meant to be in the form of cash from the Indian government to cover the rupee costs; and the difference, approximately $4 million, was to be put up by other sources, of which I hoped that Goldcrest and IFI would be a part. In return for their $12 million investment, Fox would get distribution rights in the English-speaking territories: North America, the UK, Australia and South Africa. The Indian government, through its film agency the National Film Development Corporation, would get the Indian rights and a substantial profit participation for its $8 million. The other investors would recoup from the rest of the world. Once each partner had recouped its investment, the worldwide profits were to go into a pot, which would be split 50 per cent to Dickie and the talent, and 50 per cent to the investors in proportion to their respective investments. Should IFI/Goldcrest invest, we would get a slightly bigger proportion of the profit for having taken the risk of putting up the $700,000 for pre-production.

That, anyway, was the plan. We never came even remotely close to it.

After his meeting with Jo in New York, Dickie had flown on to LA for meetings with Fox. At first, all went well and Dickie was highly optimistic: GFI/IFI had agreed to fund his immediate cash requirements, the Indian government were about to give their approval, and Fox was willing to put up half the production money. But a few days later Fox decided to turn down the film on the grounds that it was not sufficiently commercial. It wasn't an outright rejection, of course. They said, 'Not now, but come to us if you can structure it differently'; or 'Keep us informed'; or 'We just can't commit to the kind of deal that you're looking for, but we'd like to see the finished picture.' All that talk means nothing: everyone wants to see a finished picture. We had no choice but to find a replacement for the Fox part of the budget. But Dickie, without our help and prior to our getting involved, had been to every other studio, not once but a dozen times. In Hollywood, everyone had seen the script, had seen Dickie, had heard the story, had witnessed his spellbinding pitch. There was no way, with Fox dropping out, that the others were suddenly going to change their minds and come up with $12 million. Without the involvement of a major studio, we had no choice but to try to raise the money ourselves. (We also had to convince the Indians that we would succeed in this, because by that time we were asking them to start spending money on things like accommodation and transport.)

Throughout the third quarter of 1980, I called on over 100 potential investors. I went to Switzerland, France, New York and the City of London to talk to banks, pension funds, insurance companies and other investment houses. I went to independent film companies like EMI, Rank, ITC and PSO. I went to foreign distributors. Every week we would sit down and go through the list again to see who we had missed or who was worth another shot. But we got not the slightest show of interest from anyone. There wasn't even one close call.

The burden of keeping the show on the road fell increasingly on GFI, IFI and the Indian government. The pre-production phase was well advanced and we were getting ever closer to the November start date: it was like that old movie cliché where the pages of a calendar are torn off, one by one, faster and faster as the days fly by. We were now clearly in breach of both the letter and spirit of the SBA regulations, and we were similarly going against the founding principles of Goldcrest (i.e. that there should be a wide spread of investments, a ceiling on commitments to any one project and a reduction of exposure by laying off risks to third parties). We had already spent more than the $700,000 pre-production money we had pledged, simply to chase our investment. In fact, this was the beginning of a long period during which, at a number of points, the film could have bankrupted the company. During the course of 1980 and 1981 I was to go back to the board several times with the same plea: 'I need more money, more time, more understanding and more flexibility on your part to keep this thing going.' The board never let me down.

We revived the negotiations with Fox, and it was during one of Dickie's trips to Los Angeles to meet with them that, as he was checking into the Beverly Hills Hotel, a telegram arrived. Thinking that it was an offer of money from one of our many potential sources, he tore the envelope open anxiously, only to find that it was a message of good wishes to his wife, Sheila, from their children on the occasion of her birthday. Disgusted to find that the telegram was unrelated to the *Gandhi* financing, Dickie crumpled it up and threw it in the nearest waste-basket. Only later, when he realized that the message was for Sheila, did he apologize and try to make amends. He was part demented, part obsessed.

Towards the end of September, with shooting scheduled to start in November and with the vast bulk of the expenditure likely to fall in the three months to February 1981 – when the crowds were to be hired, the crew housed, all the flights back and forth paid for – the question of finance became critical. We had a couple of promising leads but they were a long way from realization and we had reached the point where either we found some money immediately or we called the whole thing off, saying goodbye to the $1 million plus that we had already invested. We knew we were putting a gun to their heads, but Jo and I could see no alternative but to go back to the boards of IFI and GFI and ask them to put up more money. We presented a proposal for each company to invest an additional $2 million production finance (the maximum allowed in IFI's rules), a good proportion of which had already been committed, or spent, without proper authorization. The boards agreed.

In doing so, they were encouraged by our account of the negotiations we had entered into with the two possible sources of investment. The first of these was Barclays Bank. Barclays at the time was earning enormous profits and, in order to reduce its tax bill, had set up a leasing subsidiary which would take advantage of certain tax allowances which were then available in the UK. For instance, if an airline wanted to buy a Boeing 747, Barclays Leasing would buy the plane and lease it to the airline, in return for which the airline would make regular monthly payments, eventually reimbursing Barclays the entire cost of the plane plus interest. As the owner of the plane, Barclays Leasing could also take advantage of the tax write-off associated with that particular piece of equipment and charge it against the parent bank's earnings. The bank thus saved taxes, and the airline acquired the equipment it needed without having to put up any capital. In effect, the UK Treasury was subsidizing both parties.

At the time, the British government was prepared to treat films in the same way as aircraft, and we set up an arrangement with Barclays Leasing whereby they would buy *Gandhi* and lease it back to us. They had the money, which we wanted, and we had the tax shelter, which they wanted. (As Goldcrest made no profits we didn't pay taxes, so the tax shelter was of no use to us.) We were thus able to strike a deal. It took a lot of time and effort, and vast amounts of documentation, but eventually we devised a scheme that appeared to throw up a cash benefit to us of about $8 million – in broad terms, our share of Barclays' tax benefit. This money was free: we did not have to pay it back and we did not have to pay interest on it. Even better, we did not have to give away any profit share to get it. Had we got the $12 million advance we had originally hoped for from Fox, we would have had to pay it back out of the revenues of the film, with interest and a distribution fee, and it would have borne a profit share. So the Barclays Leasing deal, a scheme cooked up by the ever-inventive Jo Child, far from being a desperate or makeshift arrangement, looked like being a bonanza.

The $8 million, however, still didn't fill the gap left by the withdrawal of Fox. We needed $4 million more, which is where the second major source of investment, an Indian family whom I shall call Patel, came in. In the course of my peregrinations around the world looking for money, I had called on every prominent Indian I could find, especially those who Dickie had told me were close to Mrs Gandhi. (Mrs Gandhi had been instrumental in getting the movie approved by the Indian Parliament, so anyone who was close to her, or wanted to be, was a target for me.) Somehow I got hold of the name Patel.

The Patel family consisted of four brothers, one of whom lived in London, one in Geneva, one in Bombay and one in New York. Govind Patel was the one I got to know best. He was a charming man and an extremely successful trader in all sorts of commodities. Over the course of about fifteen meetings in Bombay, London, Geneva and Paris, I managed to persuade Govind to put up the missing $4 million. The terms he demanded were tough, but acceptable. For example, he wanted a percentage of all the foreign sales – which was to be the area in which his investment would be recouped – off the top (i.e. out of the gross rental). This was unusual, but in the circumstances – we were only weeks away from the start of principal photography – I agreed. A deal memo was drawn up and circulated to the Goldcrest board.

The existence of these embryonic deals with Barclays Leasing and the Patels, supported by documentation in both cases, gave great comfort to the GFI and IFI boards and explains in part the apparent equanimity with which they responded to our request for more money.

By November 1980, all the negotiations had been satisfactorily concluded, the finance appeared to be in place and everything augured well. Dickie set up his cameras in Delhi and the first week or two of shooting went relatively smoothly. Then, on 13 December, less than two weeks before the Barclays Leasing deal had to be completed in order to fall within the tax year, Barclays pulled out. It was a bombshell: we could not abandon or postpone the film now, and there was no obvious alternative source of finance that could be brought in at such short notice.

In my opinion, Barclays behaved very badly. Other banks subsequently did deals of this type, and in fact we did a leasing deal on *Gandhi* two years later, although by that time the benefits were nowhere near as substantial because interest rates had changed and leasing deals had become less attractive. But Barclays did not even give us the courtesy of a letter of explanation. They simply pulled out and deprived us of cash when we needed it most.

The cameras were rolling, the cast, crew, support services, thousands of extras and costumes had all been committed, hotels were booked and transportation arranged. I had no choice but to go back to the Goldcrest board and say: 'Gentlemen, I'm sorry, but we're stuck. We're now up to our ears in this picture. Fortunately, we have the Patels in for $4 million, but we're $8 million short. The production looks fine – Dickie and Terry Clegg and their team have everything under control – and first reports of the filming are good. Are you prepared to make a further commitment?' GFI at that time had money in the bank, the unused part of the £8.2 million raised in July. Thanks to James Lee's solid support and skilful direction of the discussion (he was now chairman of the GFI board), it was agreed to increase our commitment to a total of £3 million. In those days the pound was still at $2.40, so expressed in dollars the GFI investment was now $7.2 million. IFI could not share in this because of the restrictions imposed on it by the SBA regulations.

I remember telling the board, 'Don't worry, this is the last amount of money we'll have to put up.' In fact, the cost statements coming back from the production showed that we were actually doing pretty well, and it looked as if the film was going to come in slightly under budget. If that were the case, GFI's additional investment, combined with the Patels' $4 million and a deal with the BBC for UK television rights, would cover most of the gap left by Barclays. Maybe. We re-did the numbers every day, hoping, praying, for interest rates to fall and currency rates to rise.

Jo and I and the two other senior executives at IFI, Roland Betts and Neil Braun, were working frantically, flying back and forth between India, London, LA and New York, trying to keep all the financing in place and making sure that Dickie got the cash flow he needed. I went to India seven times and to the United States eight times in a ten-month period. From October 1980 to April 1981 I was also embroiled in interminable negotiations with the Indian government on how the profits would be split: as the parties to the deal kept changing (Fox was out, Barclays was out, GFI was now in for a lot more than just a piece of the foreign sales), so the relative positions of each of the remaining partners shifted. These sessions were gruelling and, more often than not, fruitless. But they had to be endured, with courtesy and good humour, week after week.

The Indians kept up their cash flow as we kept up ours: neither of us ever missed a payment. There was no problem at all as far as the production was concerned, and the rushes looked terrific.

One Friday morning in February 1981, when Dickie was out shooting in some location so distant that we had almost lost track of him, I went down to the Patels' office to present them with the final contract for signature. Everything up to that point had been discussed, drafted, re-drafted and agreed. They had only to sign and we would have the money. They glanced over the contract, hummed and haa'd, and then said they weren't going to do it – or at least not on those terms. Instead they presented a list of new demands which were frankly outrageous. They wanted X per cent of this and Y per cent of that, and they wanted an override on world sales and approval of all foreign deals. The terms would have been unacceptable in any circumstances. The message was clear: they simply wanted to screw us to the wall, believing that we were too far in to do anything about it, or they didn't have the money. In any case they didn't want to honour their commitment.

I was in a state of near collapse by that stage. I was run ragged with travelling and fruitless negotiations with the Indian government. Now this. I left the Patels' office completely dejected. I had no idea how, or what, I was going to tell Dickie. I would have to speak to James Lee.

Ilott: From the Patels' offices, Eberts had to go straight to Pinewood Studios to see the fine cut of *Enigma*, which was then very close to its release date. He arrived just before lunch and immediately called James Lee. 'Look, you're not going to believe this,' he told him, 'but the Patels' $4 million has just fallen out.' After a brief explanation of what he considered to be the usurious and unacceptable new terms being demanded, Eberts gave Lee the number of the projection room and went to the screening. Lee knew as well as Eberts that, if the money wasn't in place by the Friday of the following week, GFI would default on payments in India and the production would come to a standstill. Given the delicacy of the relationship between Goldcrest and the Indian government, and the bitterly divided opinion about the merits of the project among the Indians themselves, many of whom were not reconciled to the idea of an Englishman making a film about their national hero, this would probably cause the film to be abandoned altogether. At the Patels' request, the Indian authorities had never been told the source of the $4 million; as far as they were concerned all the money was coming from GFI and IFI, who had constantly given assurances that everything was in order. Only on the basis of those assurances had the Indians gone ahead and funded $8 million worth of rupee expenditure. To default now would be to risk bringing the whole uncertain edifice of co-operation crashing down around Dickie Attenborough's ears.

When he took Eberts's call, Lee was about to join Lords Blakenham and Gibson in the Pearson dining room for lunch with the venerable Lord Cowdray. 'I was terrified,' Lee recalls, 'because I thought we were in a real bloody mess: we were either going to have to agree to these [the Patels'] terms or we were going to have to raise money from outside. It did not occur to me that there would be any stomach whatsoever to bail us out at Pearson: the sum of money involved in *Gandhi* was as much again as we had decided to put into GFI as a whole. But Lord Cowdray said, "James we will not be blackmailed. We will put up the funds. The only thing we must be sure about is that $4 million is actually what it's going to take to complete the project." I said, "To be perfectly honest, I cannot give you that assurance at this stage, because I am not close enough to the project to know." Then we talked about it over lunch, at the end of which I called my wife and said, "I'm going to India. Can you get my passport over to the office straight away?" '

Lee then called Eberts at Pinewood to say that Pearson was willing to replace the Patels and that he was going to fly out to make an on-the-spot inspection on Lord Cowdray's behalf. He left that night. Eberts's relief, and gratitude, that the crisis seemed to have been so quickly averted, was mixed with puzzlement about what Lee expected to achieve by going out to India in person. But as far as Lee was concerned, the purpose of the mission was 'quite clear'.

'I had to sit down with Terry Clegg, who was the executive in charge of production, and ascertain that $4 million was indeed the true requirement. We didn't want to get sucked in for more,' he explains.

'I flew to Bombay and from there I travelled down in this amazingly ropey old plane to Poona, where they were filming. That night I had dinner at a hotel called the Blue Lagoon, or something similar, next door to an ashram run by a very famous guru. Half the restaurant was full of the film crew, the other half was full of a lot of very prosperous-looking Westerners in saffron robes. At one table, James Callaghan was being entertained by Dickie and Sheila Attenborough.

'Terry Clegg made a very full presentation of the state of the film: he showed me what the expenses were; he showed me what had been completed. I asked him a few commonsense questions, explaining that if we put up the additional money this was all there was, and was he absolutely convinced that $4 million would do the job? He said yes.'

Attenborough remembers that he and Lee then had 'a two- or three-hour session. He cross-questioned me very minutely. He had obviously thought about it a great deal and examined it, and he knew the minutiae of it. And he said to me, "Dickie, if I go back and advocate putting these extra funds in, are you absolutely confident in your own mind that you really can finish on budget? Because if anything runs away there really is no more money, and I will be placing, on my say-so, Pearson in a hopeless position." And I remember saying, "Well, James, I can't swear because the skies may descend or something, but I promise you I will bring the picture in under budget, even if I have to compromise, unless the Lord God sends a thunderbolt." '

In Attenborough's opinion, there is no doubt that it was 'James's guts that got *Gandhi* completed'.

Lee continues his story: 'I spent the next night at the Taj Hotel in Bombay and the next day got on a plane back to London, where I made my report. What's very important to realize is that the reason I went to India was because most of the money was not to be put up by Goldcrest, nor even by Pearson Longman, but by Pearson.

'Now it may have been that [Patel] would have compromised when push came to shove, because when we told him that his $4 million wasn't needed, thank you very much, he was absolutely apoplectic that he'd been taken out.'

The Patel episode was only the most outstanding of many instances not only of Lee's personal support for Eberts, but of Pearson's and Pearson Longman's *ad hoc* financial support for Goldcrest.

'One of the things that never gets mentioned is just to what extent Pearson indirectly supported Goldcrest in its early years', notes Don Cruickshank, 'with guarantees of liabilities under leases and whatever, which never really got shown up in either the books or in a proper assessment of how much money it took actually to finance the company;

and which in the event took one hell of a lot of untangling. It explains to some extent why Jake had so much financial capacity to play with, seemingly from so little money.'

The episode also marked a pivotal change in Lee's attitude to Goldcrest. He had proved that he could grasp the details of film finances and that he could talk the film-makers' language. He had also demonstrated an ability to make clear, unequivocal decisions of great consequence in an operational environment. He found that he liked the feel of the film industry. From now on, he was to take a much closer interest in Goldcrest's affairs.

Eberts: The $4 million was actually underwritten by Pearson and then offered to the Goldcrest shareholders. But with the exception of Noble Grossart and Electra House, who put up $1 million between them, none of the other shareholders felt it was a risk they wanted to take. The money was invested on exactly the same terms as we had originally agreed with Patel, and it turned out to be an extremely good deal for the investors, because, although they didn't have any net profit share as such, they recouped their investment with interest and a premium in first position from foreign sales, on which, in addition, they had a 4 per cent override. Less than two years later, Goldcrest bought back that $4 million investment for $5 million, which already gave the investors a very substantial profit. And we in turn, on that $5 million, made another profit. The outcome makes it all the more puzzling that the Patels didn't come up with the money in the first place. I never found out what happened. We had shown them some rushes of the film in Delhi and maybe they didn't like it; or there may have been problems with the Indian government.

Throughout all these crises, my professional relationship with the board became pretty strained, but I was saved by James's attitude, which was very positive, and by my good personal standing with the shareholders. They regarded me as a fellow financier, a banker. I played by the rules and kept them very fully informed. If Barclays began to fade, the next day they would have a memo on their desks saying, 'Today I had a problem with Barclays.' Anything that was a possible cause for concern was relayed to them immediately and I sought approvals for everything.

Another relationship, though, was deteriorating badly: that between Jo Child and me.

Chapter Eight

Parting Companies

Eberts: Jo Child gave me asthma. His mere presence would start me stuttering and fighting for breath. I don't think Jo was ever reconciled to having me as his partner. He disliked having someone who could say no to him, and he disliked the fact that I knew more than he did about foreign markets, for example, or that I had my own relationships with people like Puttnam and Attenborough. Nor was Jo temperamentally suited to the film business. We used to go to the Cannes Film Festival together and he would just boil at the sight of what happened there. Cannes is a zoo: thousands of people milling about, rushing back and forth, eating and drinking too much, holding meetings every fifteen minutes; a lot of back-slapping, hand-shaking and false *bonhomie*; and dinners every night with people you can't stand but whose company you have to keep because they're going to buy your film. That sort of thing drove Jo mad. I used to say, 'Jo, you have to do it. It's just part of the game we're in.'

For my part, the more I knew him, the more I felt that he just wasn't cut out for this kind of work. For example, the ostensible reason that I, rather than Jo, did the Delhi trips was because London was closer to Delhi than was New York. But the real reason was that Dickie and I both knew that to get anywhere with the Indian government you had to have a very respectful approach and endless patience. Jo was disqualified on both counts. He knew that that was our opinion and he resented it deeply.

By the time Jo finally got to India, around Christmas 1980, our relationship had degenerated to the point where we were hardly speaking to each other. Increasingly, GFI's business with IFI was conducted between myself and either Roland Betts or Neil Braun, or between Jo and James Lee. Clearly matters could not continue in this fashion, and Jo took it upon himself to confront the problem on the morning that I arrived in Delhi, a couple of days after him, on an overnight flight from London.

All flights to India land in the middle of the night. They may leave Europe at a civilized hour and arrive in the Far East at a civilized hour, and vice versa, but India, being cock-in-the-middle, has to put up with virtually a night-time air service. Even at 3 or 4 a.m., however, Delhi airport is jam-packed: you can hardly move for people. Most of them have no need to be at the airport; it's just a place to go, to meet friends and be amused. Fiona and I made our way through the throng, found a cab and headed for the hotel.

No sooner had we checked into our room – this was now at about 5 a.m. – than I heard a rustle of paper and saw that a note had been pushed under the door. It didn't start with 'Dear Jake . . .' or any other such pleasantry. It simply said: 'There is a crisis in our relationship. We must meet at once. Please see me for breakfast at 7 a.m. – Jo'. But I couldn't meet Jo for breakfast, because I had agreed with Dickie that I would be on the set at 6 a.m. to go over with him what it was I was supposed to say to the Indian government, with whom I had a meeting at 9 a.m. The government meeting itself would take at least a couple of hours, so I would not get back to the hotel until around lunchtime. I just could not fit Jo into that schedule.

I had a shower and a quick change, got into the car and drove out to the set, where I found buses disgorging cast and crew, people running back and forth with tea, costumes, lights and cameras, and extras milling about everywhere. Dickie was in his element: enthusing, cajoling, encouraging and ordering people about. Few tasks are more gruelling than directing a movie, yet Dickie never appears to be under pressure. He is always relaxed, always smiling. I sauntered over. As usual, he gave me, as he gives everyone, the big embrace: 'Marvellous to see you, darling.' And so I was enveloped in Dickie and the project again, and completely forgot about Jo.

Dickie and I talked for a couple of hours. He would toddle off every now and then, look through the viewfinder, give a bit of instruction to the actors, and then come back. Eventually we got all our talking done and I went on to the Ministry, where I had one of probably 100 meetings in which we argued about who was going to get what profit share, and whether the markets in India were worth as much as the markets in North America, and what exchange rate we should use (the pound by that time had started to fall in value, meaning that the GFI investment cost less in dollar terms than before). And, like all those meetings, it went on and on and got nowhere. It was frustrating to have to listen to the government representatives endlessly reiterating a point of view that I had grasped, and to my own mind adequately answered, a dozen times.

It was even more frustrating to hear myself reiterating my point of view in return. But the rule when working in India seems to be: Don't Get Mad, Keep Your Cool, Be Relaxed and Press Your Point. It is negotiation by attrition: you press your point until you are sick of it, but you keep on doing it.

I finally got out of the meeting at about noon and returned to the hotel. Waiting for me was Jo. He was fuming. I had by that time taken to wearing Indian-style clothes, both because they are cool and because, when you are in negotiations with people in the government, they feel a lot more comfortable if you are wearing the same clothes as they are – just as we feel more comfortable in London or New York talking to an Indian businessman wearing a suit rather than a khaddar. After all the delays and misunderstandings, and the fact that I hadn't called him, and that he'd been waiting there in the heat for hours, the sight of me in a long shirt and baggy cotton trousers was probably too much to bear. Jo came storming out to meet me on the steps of the hotel, and, in front of all sorts of people, some of whom I knew, he screamed at me at the top of his voice. I had kept him waiting, I was disrespectful . . . What did I mean by going off, why hadn't I met him for breakfast, why hadn't I called him? There was no way we could carry on being partners, this was the end, this was the break, finish . . .

I walked through the lobby to the elevator. He followed me, shouting at me all the way. People stopped and stared at these two exceptionally tall Westerners, one in a black double-breasted suit and dark tie and one in cotton shirt and sandals, having a shouting match. (Actually I wasn't shouting. Scenes like that instantly produce in me chronic stuttering followed by an acute asthma attack, so I'm not one of the world's shouters.) I just carried on walking, all the while having abuse poured on me. Jo followed me into the elevator and, as the doors closed, he said, 'You're fired.'

I said to him, 'You can't fire me – I'm your partner.'

'I'll fire you if I want to fire you.'

I repeated: 'Jo, you can't fire me. I'm a general partner in the company.'

Finally I escaped, getting to my room before he could put his foot in the door. Fiona, who was trying to get some sleep after the long flight, had struggled out of bed to see what was causing the commotion.

'Nothing,' I said. 'I just h-h-h-h-had a meeting with Jo.'

As I went to the bathroom to get my asthma ventilator I resolved to get out of IFI as soon as I could.

A couple of days later, I watched some early footage – ten or twelve minutes of the approximately twenty minutes of script that Dickie had shot so far – outside on the roof of our hotel in Delhi. The hotel had no projection room, and Dickie had had to rig up a makeshift arrangement on the roof. With a single projector, some folding chairs and a large bedsheet, he was able to watch his rushes after dark, high above the teeming streets, under the canopy of a star-filled sky. It was an appropriate setting for what I was about to witness.

One of the first sequences to be assembled was the beginning of the Salt March, in which Gandhi leaves his ashram and walks out through the villages, picking up people as he goes. It is not a particularly emotional scene, but it has great cinematic power and there on the roof, with the white sheet lazily flapping in the evening breeze, its impact was profound and compelling. This was a beautiful, majestic piece of film-making.

Dominating it was Ben Kingsley. In Hollywood terms, Ben was an unknown, and casting an unknown to play the lead in a $24 million picture was thought by many in the industry to be a mistake. Indeed, it contributed to the difficulties we were having in securing a distribution deal with the studios. But Dickie understands acting and has a great eye for talent, and he had convinced us all that Ben was the right man for the part. We knew that he was an excellent actor, and naturally we hoped for great things, but his reputation had been made on the London stage, not in films, and I doubt if any of us had dared to expect a performance of quite this calibre: the intensity of his presence on screen was stunning.

Ben had gone out to India about six weeks before shooting started, to get a tan, lose weight and work himself into the part. He ate yoghurt and figs, took up yoga, learned how to spin, and adopted Gandhi's mannerisms: the way he sat, inclined his head, wore his clothes and so on. In the process, he acquired a kind of holy-divine feel. He became ascetic; he became religious; he was happy to fast. On the set people started to congregate around him, to catch something of the aura. It was quite a remarkable metamorphosis in life, and it was electrifying on the screen.

Many actors had been considered for the part. John Hurt, for example, was actually tested for it. John is a wonderful actor and his screen test was outstanding. But it wasn't Gandhi. Fortunately, on seeing the test, he had both the good judgement and the good grace to withdraw, saving Dickie the awful embarrassment of rejecting him. Dustin Hoffman wanted to do it. Again, he is a fine actor, but, no matter how cleverly he disguised himself, and no matter how brilliantly he immersed himself in the role, it would have been impossible to forget that it was Dustin Hoffman – no audience would have believed that he was Gandhi.

But they believed, the minute he came on the screen, that Ben was Gandhi. It wasn't an impersonation, and he isn't a lookalike; it was a re-creation of the presence of the man.

I returned to London convinced that we had not just a good, but a great movie in the making. I was also convinced that it would sell.

A few months previously, in October 1980, IFI and Goldcrest had jointly set up a company to handle the foreign sales of the pictures for which we had international distribution rights. *Gandhi* was our immediate concern, but we also had the rights to *Enigma* and had not yet decided what was to happen, for example, to *The Killing Fields*. I was supposed to be the expert in the international field, but in reality my experience and knowledge were limited: the international market is a specialized area calling for highly specialized skills. So Jo and I had agreed to set up a sales company and to find someone with appropriate qualifications to run it. Jo knew a leading entertainment-industry lawyer by the name of Tom Lewyn (who, incidentally, now acts on behalf of a number of the people associated with this story, including David Puttnam and myself). At that time, Tom was acting as special counsel to Paramount, and Paramount was a major shareholder in Cinema International Corporation (CIC), the biggest distribution company in the international market. CIC's chief executive, Pedro Teitelbaum, had just resigned, and Tom, being Pedro's friend, called up Jo and said, 'Look, Pedro is the number one foreign-sales guy in the world: after all, he ran the biggest international distribution company there is. Hire him to run your new sales company.'

Jo and I respected Tom Lewyn greatly and we were only too pleased to have his recommendation. There were two things, however, of which we were unaware. First, Pedro – and I say this as one who likes him and enjoys his company – is an unusual character, even by the standards of a business that teems with unusual characters, and he was very accustomed to the trappings of a large company. Second, there was no similarity whatsoever between what Pedro had been doing as the head of CIC and what we were intending to achieve with our sales company.

CIC had offices around the world in which local managers handled the distribution and marketing of films supplied by the three CIC partners, Paramount, Universal and MGM. Pedro had presided over this operation from his palatial head office, and, for all I know, he may have been very good at it. But his experience at CIC had sheltered him from the nitty-gritty of the independent distribution business: not only did he know nothing about the other distributors (he did not know the names of the companies, let alone the names of their leading executives), he had no insight into their work. For example, he had been accustomed to having on tap a constant stream (up to fifty movies a year) of high-quality films, whereas most distributors have to fight to get good movies from whatever sources they can, and when they don't get them they have to fight even harder to get the public to pay to see the not-so-good movies that they have had to take instead. The independent distribution business is a rough, highly competitive game, in which whom you know is a large part of what you know. Pedro, for so long cocooned within the world of the Hollywood majors, did not know the right people. Nor did he know how to sell to the independents. All he had had to do at CIC was to tell the distributor in Paris that next year he had X number of pictures, from which CIC was expecting Y amount of net revenue.

Thus Pedro was the wrong person for the job. But, inexperienced as we were, we hired him anyway.

The unusualness of his character made an impression from the start. He had insisted on the most extravagant terms in his contract, far more than IFI or GFI could bear as direct overheads, and, to keep the costs off our books, we jointly capitalized a new company, Filmcrest International, of which Pedro would be the president and out of the revenues of which his salary and operating expenses would be paid. Even before being hired, he had forced us to agree to a list of idiosyncratic personal requirements: we had to rent an apartment in New York for him; we had to redecorate his office in a certain way – i.e. very expensively; he insisted that he would stay only in a certain suite of a certain hotel in whatever town he was going to be in; he would sit only in a certain first-class seat on a certain flight to any destination; and his wife had to travel with him wherever he went, without exception. In the contract negotiations we had rejected or watered down his most excessive demands, but many of them stayed or crept back in later.

When the painting and decorating of his office had been done, the carpets laid and the curtains hung, the time at last came for Pedro to start work, and the first project he had to work on was *Gandhi*. It was immediately apparent that he did not have a clue what to do with it. He did not know how to approach independents such as AMLF in France, Neue Constantin in Germany, Roadshow in Australia or Toho Towa in Japan. These were people with whom he had never before dealt in his life. I ended up going with him, listening dumbfounded as he began to feel his way into what was all too clearly a new business for him. He did not know the correct form of negotiation, what prices to ask or what kind of deal structure to apply.

However, Pedro was on the payroll and we had to make use of him. Shortly after my return from my shouting match with Jo in Delhi, I called Pedro to say that the footage I had seen was so good that we should show it to Fox, who had left the door open after our last discussion. Pedro, who would fly anywhere at a moment's notice – favourite seat, wife, the whole thing – felt that it would be best to go first to Bombay, where the film was now based, see the footage there, talk to Dickie, and only then go to see Fox. I agreed, and telephoned Norman Levy, Fox's head of distribution. It turned out that Norman would be away for about two weeks at an international sales conference in Singapore, which is not a million miles from Bombay. So I said, 'Fine, we'll meet there. At least we'll have a captive audience.'

So Pedro, his wife and I flew out to Bombay, arriving, as usual, in the middle of the night. We went straight to meet Dickie on the set, where he was shooting a scene in which Gandhi, who is fasting and close to death, convinces some local thugs to throw down their weapons. It was very hot and the crew was exhausted, but Dickie was as relaxed and as good-humoured as ever, strolling around, getting the work done,

By this time, the editor, John Bloom, who was working feverishly in a London cutting room (film was flown back and forth every day), had assembled about fifty-five minutes of footage, and as soon as the night's work was over Dickie screened it for us. Pedro was as dumbstruck as I was: this was the most spectacular film we had ever seen.

The next day we took the four cans of film under our arms and headed for the airport. I was afraid that we were not going to be able to leave because Pedro couldn't get his lucky seat. After endless negotiations with the ticket agent, however, Pedro, at last got the right seat and we departed for Singapore, where we had difficulty locating anybody from Fox. Eventually we managed to track down Jean-Louis Rubin, Fox's head of foreign distribution, and I pleaded with him: 'This is crucially important to us. You've got to get your whole team together for a screening.' But Jean-Louis wasn't sure that he could organize it. Norman Levy had not been seen for days. We would just have to hang around and wait a little longer.

I spent the morning playing squash, taking in the sights and wondering what I was doing hanging around in Singapore when there was so much work to be done back in London. Then Norman surfaced and announced that he would see us with the Fox team at 3.30 that afternoon. He would leave it to us to make the screening arrangements. We made a few calls, found an out-of-town advertising agency with a screening room, rented a Volkswagen van, put the cans of film and the Fox distribution team in the back, and drove off. We arrived to find that the screen in question was hardly big enough for a home movie. My heart sank: here we were showing the greatest epic of all time, and all we had was a four-foot-square screen. The room itself was only about fifteen feet by twenty and we had trouble getting all the Fox people in.

Eventually everyone found a place, the lights were dimmed and the film started rolling. After a couple of minutes, we forgot about the size of the screen and the discomfort. The hustling and the bustling quietened down, and the shuffling stopped. I could tell they were interested. Fifteen minutes later, I heard sniffing, repressed sobbing, renewed shifting in seats, handkerchiefs coming out and the surreptitious blowing of noses. I thought; 'My God, this is Paradise. These guys will beseige me to get this movie.' When it was all finished and the lights went up, no one budged or said a word. They sat there, stunned and slightly embarrassed, wiping away their tears.

I said, 'Well, what do you think?'

Again there was a lot of shuffling. Film executives never want to say what they think until they hear what the boss thinks. They want to make sure that what they say is what the boss says. So they all turned and looked at Norman Levy, and Norman, who had been involved with these negotiations for a long time, didn't really want to say either. So he turned the question back to his pals and said, 'Well, what do you think guys?'

Finally someone had the guts to speak up. He said it was the most wonderful thing he had ever seen, but he didn't think the public would like it. A wave of relief washed around the room. They nodded sagely and said, 'Yes, it's wonderful, but it'll never sell.'

Here they were, crying, speechless, wiping away tears, and yet they could not bring themselves to believe that an audience would react in the same way. Surely, to be successful in any branch of the entertainment business, you have to do what you feel, in the belief that, because you are like most other people, their reaction will be like your reaction; that if you like it, they're going to like it. If you do not have that common touch, you are in the wrong business.

But these people didn't believe their own reactions, and because I couldn't persuade them that the audience would react just as they had reacted, there was no deal. Again, the door was left open; Norman, who is a great opportunist, did not want to lose it altogether.

I returned to London bitterly disappointed that we had again failed to secure distribution for the film. GFI and its shareholders had about $12 million invested in *Gandhi* by this time, and it was more than a little worrying that people as experienced as the Fox team, even after seeing nearly an hour's footage, had turned it down. I was also concerned about Pedro's inexperience: he had contributed very little to the discussion in Singapore, indeed had hardly even opened his mouth.

But looming over everything at that time was Jo's insistence that the differences between us had to be resolved. The working relationship between IFI and GFI had become paralysed by our mutual hostility. He had always been in favour of merging the two companies and, although I had initially gone along with that idea, I had become reluctant to do so the more I got to know him. After the episode in Delhi I was adamantly against it. Instead, I had come to the conclusion that the best thing would be to break up the relationship and let each company fend for itself.

Achieving that, however, would be no easy matter. Not only was I co-general partner in IFI and bound to it by contract, but Goldcrest was its single biggest shareholder: we had $1 million invested in the company. On top of that, we were bound by the Reciprocal Investment Opportunity Agreement, which had a number of years to run, and by numerous contracts with third parties – film-makers and distributors – that involved us equally and that would remain legally binding whatever our relationship. Furthermore, we were now joint owners of an international sales company, Filmcrest. The IFI/GFI relationship was no mere passing acquaintance; this was a tightly bound partnership.

I went to New York to discuss this matter several times in the early months of 1981. My view, that GFI and IFI should split, was vigorously opposed, not least by Bob Montgomery, a well-known lawyer and a board member of IFI, who was of the opinion that we could not undo all the contracts that had been signed on behalf of both companies; first, because to do so would be to IFI's material disadvantage, and, second, because the businesses were just too tightly intertwined and the contracts too complicated to make the attempt worthwhile. Montgomery supported Jo's view, that we should merge, as did Roland Betts and Neil Braun. But the merger proposal, too, had problems: the SBA and the respective investors would have to approve it, and there would be complications arising from the fact that the two companies were registered in different countries, subject to different laws and regulations. Roland and Neil, both of whom I liked and respected enormously, were very persuasive, but the more I heard, the more I began to appreciate that it would mean IFI taking over GFI and Jo Child effectively becoming the boss of the combined company. That was something I could not swallow. I didn't care how much money they offered me, how much I would get in the form of shares in IFI or how much more money I would have to play with when Goldcrest became part of a $35 million financing company; I just could not stand the idea of working under Jo. When it came to the crunch and they wanted an answer, I said; 'Gentlemen, I can't do it. I just can't do it.'

It was not entirely up to me, of course, but when I reported back to London, both James Lee and the GFI board seemed to be prepared to do whatever I wanted to do. They certainly were not in favour of merging with IFI. For one thing, among the GFI board members there was almost universal antipathy towards Jo Child; such a distaste for him that even if I had said yes, they would probably have said no.

In effect, having forced the issue, Jo had left us with no choice: we had to split.

Ilott: During the course of this dispute, James Lee became ever more involved in the affairs of the company. In the first place, Eberts turned to him for advice and support and got both in good measure: between them they were not only able to justify the split with IFI, but to formulate a plan whereby GFI, hitherto merely a passive pool of investment capital, would operate as a separate, independent corporate entity. Second, once the decision to end the partnership had been made, Lee became personally enmeshed in the complicated business of untangling the affairs of the two companies. For not only was the antagonism between Eberts and Child so acute that they found it hard to agree even on the means by which to end their relationship, but Child all along believed Eberts's behaviour was more than just personally reprehensible: it was, he maintained, in breach of Eberts's contractual obligations to IFI. This made matters, according to Lee, 'extremely complicated'.

'Jo Child argued that, as an employee of IFI, Jake was bloody well obliged to act under Jo's instructions and had a legal responsibility to act in the best interests of the IFI partners,' he recalls. 'Since we were setting out to make it clear that the interests of the GFI and IFI partners were different, and that we wanted Jake's services at GFI, Child cut up quite rough. At one point, Montgomery was threatening to sue Jake for breach of fiduciary responsibility, because Montgomery was convinced that Jake had led the IFI shareholders to believe that the GFI fund was going to be a parallel fund that would be used to leverage the bastion of IFI.'

According to Lee, Child's belief that Eberts had deceived him was perfectly sincere: 'He thought that Jake had taken the job with IFI, been paid a salary by IFI, with the specific responsibility for raising funds in London to match IFI's funds, and was therefore horrified when it became apparent that between Jake and myself we were taking Goldcrest down an independent route.'

The row that followed – what Lee calls the 'huge ruckus' – required him to fly to New York several times for long, and often tortured, meetings with Child and Montgomery. The already malign atmosphere of these discussions was made worse by Child's conviction that it was not Lee, but Eberts, who should have been on the other side of the table. But Eberts, who detests confrontation of any kind – a trait that was to have important consequences later – was only too relieved, indeed grateful, that Lee was both able and willing to shoulder this particular burden.

The negotiations went back and forth between London and New York from February until June 1981, and the documentation severing the connections between IFI and GFI was not completed until October, when IFI sold its 7.5 per cent holding in Goldcrest to the other GFI partners. Even then, GFI kept its 9 per cent holding in IFI and the RIOA remained in force. Eberts ceased to be an IFI employee, relinquished his shareholding and left Child in sole command. (Child's ascendancy was to be shortlived: within a year he was asked by the IFI board to resign. Pedro Teitelbaum's tenure was even shorter: he quit in November 1981 and Filmcrest International was subsequently wound up, at considerable cost to GFI.)

The solution that Eberts and Lee had arrived at to enable GFI – which had been designed as a simple fund, without overheads or staff – to lead an independent existence, was to set up a management company to run it. When this was eventually established it was to mark a significant step in the seemingly inevitable process whereby Goldcrest came under the control of its biggest shareholder, Pearson Longman, and Eberts became ever more beholden to Lee. The new management company was originally intended to take over only the secretarial functions and bookkeeping role that IFI and Pearson had between them handled for GFI. Most importantly, it was to be the vehicle that employed Eberts and his secretary Irene Lyons. It had therefore been devised, for simplicity's sake (it quickly became much more complicated), as a wholly owned subsidiary of Pearson Longman. One unlooked for consequence of this was that the Pearson Longman board found itself with 100 per cent of the responsibility, and hence risk, for a company in which it had only a 44 per cent stake. And while Goldcrest was a small enterprise of peripheral interest to Pearson Longman's, and later Pearson's, main businesses, it was, via the handcuffs of managerial obligation, to take up an increasing amount of those companies' time and attention. Another unlooked for consequence was that Lee, as both chairman and representative of the principal shareholder, was now to be directly, and solely, responsible for the management company that was to run GFI day by day. In particular, he was to be Eberts's employer. At the time, this was not thought to be significant, nor need it have become so were it not for the personalities of the two men involved. Lee, energetic and forceful, liked being a hands-on corporate manager: given overall responsibility for Goldcrest, he could not help but interfere in the details of its operation. And Eberts, while he did not mind answering to shareholders, had proved already in his career – most recently with Jo Child – that he disliked having to report to a boss.

It was to be a long time before either Lee or Eberts realized, let alone admitted, just how problematical their relationship was. As Lee became more involved in Goldcrest's affairs, so Eberts was to feel increasingly uncomfortable.

Detailed work on the plans for the management company was under-taken by Lee's deputy, Don Cruickshank, in the early months of 1981. When the company was eventually established, in July, it looked very different, and performed markedly different functions, from what had originally been intended, certainly by Eberts.

Eberts: One good thing that emerged from the otherwise unhappy IFI episode was a tremendous sense of commitment to Goldcrest, not only on my part, but on the part of leading members of the board, and especially James Lee. Our avowed ambition was now to build it into a viable British film company making quality films of the calibre of *Chariots of Fire* and *Gandhi*. In other words, out of the wreckage of our relation-ship with IFI, Goldcrest – the real operating company, not just the investment vehicle – was born.

Chapter Nine

Red Carpets in LA

Eberts: Fox's rejection of *Gandhi* in Singapore had shaken our confidence, and it was not until July 1981 that Dickie felt sufficiently comfortable to go back to the States with approximately two hours of footage to show to distributors. This time there was no way the studios could ignore the evidence on the screen; after nearly twenty years of showing Dickie the door, suddenly they were all laying out red carpets. Our first objective was to get a gross deal, which would give us a share in the revenues from the first dollar earned at the the box office. That way we did not have to worry about the studio raking off distribution fees and prints and advertising costs before we saw any money. If we could get such a deal we would be happy to take a low cash advance – the film was already shot and paid for, so we had no urgent need of cash – and push for the best possible back-end split (i.e. the division of revenues between the studio and us).

Our second objective was to retain the television rights. Normally a studio will buy all rights, giving each piece – theatrical, video, television, syndication, pay-TV, etc. – to an in-house division, or selling it on to another specialist company. Where the rights are sold on, the studio will take a 30 per cent distribution fee before sharing the revenue with the producer. In the case of *Gandhi*, television rights were the single most valuable asset we had. Here was a film that was good enough to be screened time and again, which had no sex or gratuitous violence, and which appealed to all age groups and audiences. In our view, it was like *Gone With the Wind*. At that time there was tremendous competition not only between the networks, but also between network television and pay television: they were all looking for the big, promotable television 'event'. *Gandhi* was certainly that. With these advantages, it seemed foolish to give away 30 per cent of the television sale price just for the privilege of having a studio handle the negotiation. We had a target television sale figure of $10 million, and I was confident that we could achieve that on our own.

As far as the international markets were concerned, initially we were undecided whether it would be best to include the foreign rights in a worldwide studio deal or sell them territory by territory through Film-crest. (*Gandhi*'s status as a joint venture between IFI, GFI and the Indian government was not affected by the IFI/GFI split. This explains why Dickie was so careful to remain neutral throughout the arguments between Jo and me.) The major studios have separate domestic and international divisions and it is common, especially in the case of films that might do well in one market but not the other (action pictures, for example, tend to do well in foreign markets, while light comedies do better in the States), to sell the rights separately.

Selling to the international independents is time consuming but often produces better prices – there being fierce competition for product among the distributors – and gives you more control. Also, the independent distributor will want to do well in the hope of acquiring product from you again. Selling to a major studio is easier (in theory, although, as in the case of *Gandhi*, the negotiations can drag on for years) and their power in the market is such that you are likely to get better distribution overall. But the studios are in so much stronger a position than you are that it is hard to get the best terms or to exercise any control over the distribution or the accounting.

A significant consideration in the mind of the producer is that in a typical worldwide studio distribution deal all the rights in all the territories are consolidated in a single package. On the one hand, this means that the studio will pay one advance for the whole lot: hopefully a large and attractive sum of money. On the other hand, the studio will similarly calculate the back-end terms over the package as a whole, so that, for example, if the film doesn't do well in Germany, the losses in that territory will be set against the profits in, say, Japan. A net-profit position, in which the producer and the original investors participate, will be reached only when the studio has recouped across the board, and taken its expenses and its fees in every territory and every market. This is called cross-collateralization and is often the source of bitter complaints on the part of producers who see their films do good business in this or that market but who never get a penny from the studios. If you go to the trouble of selling to independent distributors territory by territory, then, of course, there is no cross-collateralization: if the film makes money in Japan you get a share of that, regardless of the losses in Germany.

Occasionally, if you have a very hot property for which many of the studios are competing, you can force one of them – they hate doing it – into an uncrossed deal. This gives you the best of both worlds: the type of back-end terms that you would get from the independents and the worldwide distribution that you can get only from a major studio.

In the case of *Gandhi*, good distribution was of paramount importance. It was clearly going to become a phenomenon, one of those movies that is talked about in the gossip columns, written about by political commentators and referred to in editorials. Such a picture becomes news in its own right and quickly builds what in marketing circles is known as 'an awareness factor' amongst its potential audience. That awareness factor, with good handling, becomes the 'want-to-see', which is the starting-point for all ticket sales. But awareness and want-to-see are volatile ingredients: interest in any particular film reaches a peak and quickly dies, to be replaced by some other issue of the day or flavour of the month. If your timing is wrong – if the film doesn't open the week after the chat show or current-affairs programme has devoted minutes of priceless editorial time to it – then you've blown it: by the time the film does come to town, say five or more weeks later, people have the feeling that they have seen it already. This problem applies to the release by any distributor of almost any film in any country, but with an event picture like *Gandhi* the media interest can quickly spread around the world and the want-to-see becomes global. To take advantage of it you have to release the picture simultaneously in as many countries as you can. This costs a fortune and presents tremendous logistical problems. Director and stars, for example, have to attend premières and press conferences, and appear on chat shows, country by country, packing a huge amount of work and travel into a very short space of time. All the opening-night parties, with celebrities and press in attendance, have to be organized. The prints (thousands of them at $1,500–$2,000 a copy) have to be struck, and posters and advertisements have to be designed and paid for. The cinemas have to be booked and all the dates cleared. Magazine interviews and photo features have to be organized months in advance. All this has to be done in many languages and currencies. There was no way that we (myself and Irene in London, and Jo, the IFI team and Pedro Teitelbaum in New York) could ourselves co-ordinate the efforts of twenty or thirty independent distributors around the world for the purpose. Only a major studio could do it.

So our third objective, now that everyone was of the opinion that we had a great film and the studios were falling over themselves to get it, was to secure a worldwide, uncrossed deal with a major. That, plus gross terms and without television, is the best that any independent producer can look for in Hollywood.

Dickie and I arrived in Los Angeles with the two hours of film in July 1981. Contrary to appearances, Hollywood is a very small town: there are probably fewer than six or eight people there who can say yes to a deal like this. Screenwriter William Goldman once said of the movie business that 'no one knows anything'. That's true in terms of the ever elusive formula for making hit pictures. But in terms of deal points and properties, of what's around town and who is talking to whom, the opposite is true: everyone knows everything. The minute we appeared in Hollywood, everyone knew that at 10 o'clock we were screening at Universal, at 2 o'clock we were over at Paramount, and at 10 o'clock the following morning we were going to be at Columbia. Even the parking-lot attendant at Universal knew what we were there for. And it would have been extremely unusual for the impact of a screening at one studio not to be known at the others within minutes. Junior colleague No. 5 at studio X will call up junior colleague No. 5 at studio Y and say, 'Hey, the distribution guys just saw *Gandhi*. They were raving about it.' And that opinion goes straight up and down the grapevine in every studio in Hollywood, even as the projectionist is putting the print back in the can and the distribution executives are still locked in the post-screening meeting. By the afternoon of our first day, the word was that everyone liked the movie: we were hot. And even before we had opened nego-tiations with any of them, there was competition between the studios to get the picture.

The strongest bids looked like coming from Columbia, Warner Bros. and Paramount. Paramount's top executives at that time were Michael Eisner and Barry Diller, very astute men for whom I have a lot of respect. But, while they loved the picture, they made it clear that we would have a hard time convincing Charlie Bludhorn, president of Para-mount's parent company, Gulf & Western, to give us an uncrossed, gross deal unless we let them have the television rights. Paramount is very active in television and they knew precisely what *Gandhi* would be worth in that market. Similarly, at Warner Bros. Frank Wells would consider all our terms except the withholding of television. Frank Price at Colum-bia was prepared to accept the loss of television but, before committing to a worldwide deal, wanted his international division to give their opinion.

The negotiations continued in New York, where first of all we screened the footage for Patrick Williamson, Columbia's international-distribution chief, and his staff. Then, while they conferred with Frank Price and head of marketing Marvin Antonowsky in Los Angeles, we went off to see Charlie Bludhorn in his office at the top of the Gulf & Western building overlooking Central Park. Charlie, who had known Dickie since the mid-1970s, when Paramount had backed his first directorial effort, *Oh What a Lovely War!*, was adamant that he would not give up television. He was an unusually forceful man, and when he wanted something badly he made no secret of the fact. As the discussion went back and forth, and as we became more than ever stuck in an impasse on the television question, so he became increasingly impatient, to the point that he went over to the door and locked us in, refusing to let Dickie catch his plane to London until we had made a deal. I never knew whether or not he was serious. In any event, we stayed very late, but made little progress. At one point we did offer Charlie the television rights, but for the full $10 million that we thought we could get just by walking round the corner to NBC, ABC or CBS. Charlie dismissed the figure as outrageous and his impatience began to turn to anger: as far as he was concerned the terms he was offering were excellent, better than any independent producer would dare hope for. But we wouldn't budge. Then, in the middle of what had become a rather tense meeting, Frank Wells of Warner Bros., who knew that Dickie was leaving that night and who wanted to have a last shot at getting the picture, decided to give us a call. The secretary came through on the intercom in Charlie's office: 'Call from Los Angeles for Mr Eberts. Can you take the call?' Charlie went nuts. Here he was, tearing his hair out trying to get us to come to terms, and there was I discussing exactly the same deal on his phone with a rival company. I don't remember how we got out of the office, but we did, and we had not made a deal.

Ultimately the decision rested with Dickie, not with me. It was his property. Naturally he wanted to get as much money as possible, but he also wanted to go with the studio that would best distribute his film. On the former point, he was as confident as I was that we should do the television sale ourselves; on the latter, he was all along inclined to favour Columbia. In fact, we had left LA with Frank Price's entreaty ringing in our ears not to do a deal with anybody until he had had a chance to put together an offer. Sure enough, back in Pat Williamson's office, where we had just time for a quick meeting before Dickie's car took him to the airport, we received a call from Columbia's head of business affairs, Jonathan Dolgen. Gathered round the speaker phone – Dickie, Pat Williamson and me – we went over the structure of the deal: low advance, good back-end terms, gross participation, no television, no crossing. Dolgen agreed to our structure, Dickie and I agreed to his figures, and it was done. It had taken about two minutes (or, from Dickie's point of view, two minutes and twenty years).

After months of detailed contract documentation, done primarily by IFI's Roland Betts, Columbia acquired worldwide rights in all media, with the exception of India, US domestic television and UK television. Columbia paid an advance of $2 million against the domestic rights, but gave us 25 per cent of the gross rental from the first dollar. That percentage increased as the box-office receipts increased, to the point where we stood to take 65 per cent of the gross if the film was a smash hit. On the international side, the terms were similar, except that our share of the gross went up to a maximum of 80 per cent. There was to be no cross-collateralization. In addition, Columbia was committed to launch the movie with a promotional budget of not less than $12 million, covering prints, advertising, press receptions and promotional tours. (They spent nearly twice that.) Altogether, it was an unheard-of deal for an independent, and was made possible only by Frank Price's enthusiasm for the film and his conviction that it would both make money and be a strong contender for the Oscars, the prestige of which, should it win, would bring a much-needed injection of pride and self-confidence to the studio.

Dickie, who throughout the phone call had been squeezing my hand, partly as a gesture of encouragement and partly out of sheer excitement, was even more pleased with Frank Price and Marvin Antonowsky than he was with the terms of the deal. Although the money was important to him – he would not only get paid and be able to redeem his art collection, but would have to be extremely unlucky, given that it was a gross deal, not to make a lot of money from his profit share – what he really had, and cared about, were two men who were wild about the movie. And wild about Dickie.

Chapter Ten

The Second Front

Ilott: The sale of US distribution rights to Columbia was a vindication of the years of effort that Dickie Attenborough had put into the making of *Gandhi*. It was also a truimph for Eberts: the culmination of the dozens of trips he had made to California since 1977, assiduously wooing the Hollywood community. It was evidence, too, that GFI could live without an American partner. Following the break with Jo Child, Goldcrest had lost IFI's services, expertise and US contacts. While IFI's services and that part of the expertise relating to the back office (the legal, financial and administrative systems that kept the company machine running) were to be replaced by the new Goldcrest management company, the US contacts and front-office expertise (basically the skills required to make deals with film-makers, financiers and distributors) were in effect being replaced by Eberts himself. Liberated from the yoke of IFI, he revelled in the role.

Eberts: Our little attic office was buzzing. *Gandhi*, although it took up a lot of time and attention, was far from being the only project with which we were concerned. David Puttnam and Hugh Hudson had just delivered the final cut of *Chariots of Fire* to Fox and Allied Stars. It opened to sensational reviews and encouraging business, even though it was initially released in only a few theatres. At the same time, David was working with Bruce Robinson on the script of *The Killing Fields*; and he had just started work on another new project, *Local Hero*, which was again culled from the columns of a newspaper. This was to be the story of the long-drawn-out negotiations between a US oil company and the inhabitants of a Scottish fishing village. The oil company wants to buy the village and turn it into a storage depot. The villagers can hardly wait to sell, but in order to get the best possible price they feign opposition to the scheme. The story clearly offered opportunities for irony and humour as well as sharp observation of the two cultures. Whether it was this that made David think of director Bill Forsyth, or whether Forsyth was already involved, and maybe even suggested it to David, I don't know. But the combination of subject matter and film-maker was perfect. Forsyth had directed two very funny, understated comedies, *Gregory's Girl* and *That Sinking Feeling*, both of which were made on low budgets, and David, whose encouragement of young film-makers had already become a crusade, felt that Bill should be given a chance to tackle a bigger production. I liked the idea and, trusting in David's judgement, agreed to put up the development money. Forsyth himself wrote the script.

The Plague Dogs, in which we had invested £900,000, was still in production. *Breaking Glass*, which we had developed, had been released and flopped but, since we didn't have production funds invested, we didn't lose any money on it. *Escape from New York*, in which we had invested £720,000, was in the final stages of post-production and when it was released in June was to prove very successful: we made a profit of £670,000. *The Howling*, in which we had invested £145,000, had been released in February, making us a profit of £250,000. And *Enigma*, which we had developed, had gone into production in March. Written by Jack Briley, this told the story of a Soviet plan to assassinate five dissidents living in the West. We had put up the $58,000 development money, which we had recouped, and we now invested £985,000 of the $8.1 million budget, in exchange for which we had a 17.5 per cent net-profit share. It was to be one of Goldcrest's least successful investments, losing us just over £600,000.

Ilott: Overall, GFI had now invested in twelve development projects, of which five had been converted, three were still in development and four had yet to find a buyer or had been abandoned. Production finance had been committed to seven films, of which three had been finished and distributed, and four were still in production, pre-production or post-production. The record in profit-and-loss terms was still unproven, but the level of activity, the conversion rate of development into production and the success rate of those films that had been released gave the Goldcrest investors cause for satisfaction.

A notable feature in the Goldcrest lists was the output – *Chariots of Fire*, *The Killing Fields* and *Local Hero* – of David Puttnam, who had quickly become established as the most important producer associated with the company and whose influence extended far beyond the projects that he brought in himself. His was a powerful voice, both on the board, where, for example, he had been instrumental in the rejection of *Hopscotch*, and behind the scenes, where his advice was sought on projects where Eberts needed confirmation of a director's or a writer's talent. It was in this role that he got drawn into reversing Eberts's decision to reject a project called *An Unsuitable Job for a Woman*.

Eberts: This was not the first, but it was to be the last time that I made an investment decision against my own better judgement. The project had been submitted to us by the director, Chris Petit, and the producer, Don Boyd. I had originally turned it down because the script, in my opinion, was pedestrian.

The qualities that I look for in a script are, first, that it should be different. *Unsuitable Job* had nothing very different about it. It was a murder mystery but it had no particular catch or angle that had not been seen or heard before. Second, as I have explained, although there are exceptions like *Chariots of Fire*, I like to be able, having read the script, to express the essence of the drama in a couple of lines. If you try to tell the story of *Unsuitable Job* you just get wound up in who did what to whom, and how it happened, and what the sister was doing there, and how the girl faked her death. It just doesn't have anything to grab your attention. Third, it must have relevance to the interests of a sizeable audience. I don't think that the films that I get involved in have to have a message, but they do have to do something more than just entertainingly fill two hours of screen time. I like to think that at Goldcrest we made, in the words of a motto once used by Columbia, 'movies that mattered'. *Chariots* mattered, as did *Gandhi*, *The Killing Fields*, *The Emerald Forest* and, perhaps less obviously, *Local Hero*. I don't mean to be pompous about this, and I certainly don't believe that any views of mine are specifically worth propagating via movies that cost millions of dollars. It's just that, if you are going to spend millions of dollars, you might as well go for projects and ideas that matter. *Unsuitable Job* just didn't matter.

Also, I was not impressed by Chris Petit's track record. Track record is essential to me, because I have no way of judging raw talent. David Puttnam can do it. He can look at a television commercial and say that the director is terrific with the camera, the light, the design, the look, or with the way he moves the action. He can read something and say, 'It happens to be a terrible story, but the guy who wrote this knows what he's doing and, given the right kind of material, could write a good script.' I don't have that ability. I can't identify good directing unless it's a great movie. This is not as significant a failing as it may seem: I'm not the one who identifies the talent; my job is simply to convince proven talent to do the deal with me rather than with someone else. To me, therefore, track record is all important.

But even though I had already turned the project down, I changed my mind for two reasons. First, David Puttnam felt that Petit, as a young director, fully merited our support. I was swayed by David's opinion and thereby unwittingly put him in the uncomfortable position of judging his peers, who were competing with him for Goldcrest's money. The second reason was even more persuasive: the deal was good. I should have made the deal but not the movie.

Our investment was in the form of a guarantee – that we would pay £316,000, just under half the budget, on delivery of the picture – which Don Boyd was then able to take to the bank to raise the balance of the production funds that he needed. In exchange, we had the right to sell the film to distributors in the foreign markets, from which we would recoup our investment directly, charging, in addition, a sales commission of 15 per cent. On top of that we would have a 26 per cent share of the net profits. As part of the package, I undertook to try to do a tax deal from which we would take, in first position, any money still owed to us. *Unsuitable Job* was thus a pick-up rather than a genuine Goldcrest production – we guaranteed to pay the money only on delivery of the finished picture, the making of which had nothing to do with us at all. (We never did recover the guarantee, ending up instead with a loss of £120,000. We sold it, but not in enough territories and not for high enough advances. Independent distributors around the world felt much the same way about the film as I did.)

I had hitherto avoided getting involved in putting up guarantees, because when you do that you are really just a banker – last in, first out – and, because you are not at risk until the picture is delivered, you usually have no say in how it is made. I had always felt that it was preferable to put up an advance (i.e. take a much greater risk) and negotiate terms whereby you acquire some control – casting approvals and so on – over the production of the film. This is particularly important if your real interest is in net profits, as GFI's always was. Simply recouping an investment with a premium is normal, low risk/low return, banking business. It's not the kind of high risk/high yield, venture-capital investment for which Goldcrest was designed. Useful net profits to GFI could mean, on an outstandingly successful film like *Chariots of Fire* for example, a return of 5,000 per cent on our investment. And the only way to protect a profit position like that is to have some say in how the film is made and marketed.

However, although it was to lose money, *Unsuitable Job* did teach me a number of useful lessons and it contributed to a series of changes in the organization of Goldcrest which transformed it from a boutique financing operation into a fully fledged film-production and sales company. For, having put up the guarantee, I then had to consider how we were going to sell the foreign rights. We had been involved in a dozen or so films by this time, but our staff consisted of only myself, Irene Lyons, a secretary and Piers Gibson, who had recently been hired to read and, where appropriate, edit, the scripts that came through the door. GFI did not have the capacity, nor the expertise, to undertake foreign sales.

I had known, ever since the split with IFI was first mooted, that we would have to find a substitute for Pedro Teitelbaum, but I was so wrapped up in *Gandhi* and all the other projects that I had not given the matter a great deal of thought. I was now under greater pressure, not only so that we could recoup our £316,000, but because the other investors in *Unsuitable Job*, in particular Mamoun Hassan at the National Film Finance Corporation, were very concerned that the film should recover its costs. Clearly I had to find someone who was already experienced in foreign sales and distribution. The first person I approached was Bill Gavin.

I had met Bill at various Cannes Film Festivals. He had recently left Lew Grade's company, ITC, and was trying to build his own business as a film-sales consultant. He had the right experience, having been a salesman for Grade and, before that, general manager of one of Australia's leading independent distributors, Hoyts. He was highly regarded in the industry and he was the hard-driving, entrepreneurial type that I preferred to work with. He didn't want a full-time job, but he did agree to assist in the sales of *An Unsuitable Job for a Woman* on a consultancy basis, taking a 4 per cent commission (out of our 15 per cent) against which we paid him an advance. This arrangement suited me perfectly, for, at that stage, I did not want to get involved in building up a large organization. I wanted to keep things small and simple, and I was happy for Bill to be off the payroll.

My approach, however, was a little naive, and very quickly it had to change. First of all, Bill did a wonderful job and I realized that, if I wanted to keep him, I would have to make him an offer that was more attractive than just giving him an occasional project and letting him earn money on a commission basis. Second, we in any case needed a permanent arrangement to handle other films that we might want to sell. Up till then, the sales had been done, in the case of *Watership Down* and *The Plague Dogs*, by, or in association with, Charles Rosenblatt, who had been brought in by Martin Rosen back in 1975; in the case of *Chariots of Fire* by Fox; and in the case of *The Howling* and *Escape from New York* by Embassy. *Gandhi* was already sold to Columbia for the world, so that was taken care of. But we had *The Killing Fields* and *Local Hero* in development, neither of which had any distribution deals attached, and there were other projects in the pipeline. Third, the experience of *Unsuitable Job* had made me realize that foreign-sales guarantees for other people's films could be a useful means of spreading risk and generating cash flow. In particular, they could be used to reinforce our own rather thin catalogue of titles and thus support a permanent foreign-sales operation. To be able to offer such guarantees, however, we first had to have the foreign-sales machinery, which in practice meant that I had to persuade Bill to come on board full time.

With James Lee and his deputy at Pearson Longman, Don Cruickshank, I was already working on the plans for the management company that would replace the back-office services that had previously been provided by IFI. These plans were already much more complex than had at first been envisaged. We had decided, for example, that a financial director would have to be recruited, even if our legal affairs – the kind of work that had been done by Roland Betts – could for the present be handled by outside solicitors. My contribution to the further elaboration of the once simple management-company plan was the idea of adding a sales facility, existing semi-independently in association with our film-financing activities.

Ilott: The plans for the management company were to be subject to even greater elaboration, indeed transformation, as a result of discussions taking place at Millbank, where David Puttnam was making his influence felt with James Lee. Ever since the first GFI board meeting, at which Lee had been enormously impressed by Puttnam's presentation of the case against *Hopscotch*, the two had become close associates. According to Pearson's James Joll and Alan Whitaker, Puttnam was more often to be seen at Lee's office in the Millbank building than was Eberts.

'David had a considerable feel for the market,' says Lee. 'I had many long discussions with him about what we felt the audiences for films like *The Killing Fields* in different territories really were. Similarly we had discussions about the marketing of films and the Hollywood power structure and so on, which reflects the fact that he really understood the ins and outs of the way the industry worked as an industry. Jake just didn't think like that and he didn't talk like that, because he didn't think it was important. Jake's mentality – and I think he was bloody good at it – was to go out and make a deal. Dickie was more like Jake in a way: "I've got a project, I want to make it, let's do a deal."

'Puttnam seemed much more cerebral about the whole process. He talked about a longer flow of films than a single film. And that was actually more appealing to me because what I was interested in was how the hell we were going to develop the business and compete in that industry.

'Plus the fact that, as I got more experience with other producers, it became very clear to me that Puttnam was unusual. My view of what a producer should do, the role a producer should play, the responsibility a producer should be prepared to take and feel for his production, were all influenced by my impression of what Puttnam did. He could really cover all the bases, from the original negotiation of rights, to the packaging of the proposition, the negotiation of the money and the gestation of the final product, and then could get out there and promote the hell out of it – and remain clearly in charge and in control of the whole process from beginning to end. I thought that that was what we could depend on all our independent producers to do. But, other than Dickie Attenborough, none of them fulfilled that expectation. Puttnam was outstanding.'

As for Puttnam: 'I found him [James] wonderfully analytical . . . He didn't get caught up in the bullshit that goes on that has nothing to do with the job. He was about company structures and raising money, leverage, at what point to go public, etc.

'Did I have an influence over James? . . . In the early days I would say I did. I think it wasn't so much influence, more that we shared a vision of what could be done with the company.'

At that time, Puttnam was seriously of the opinion that there was no future for him in films. 'It started really before *Chariots*,' he explains. 'You have got to go back to the atmosphere of the time. If you look at [the] trade papers, there was some real sense that the film business was over in England. Even today, you cannot make a living as a feature-film producer in England. You really can't. Even I couldn't, and I was doing well. What it must have been like for other people, I shudder to think. That's why you find producers like Simon Perry [*White Mischief, 1984*] and Jeremy Thomas [*The Last Emperor, Merry Christmas Mr Lawrence*] drifting into a little bit of distribution, a little bit of exhibition. You have to. The French and Italians realized it years ago. We just took a long time to come to terms with it.

'You have to remember also that that was the year prior to the launch of Channel 4 [Britain's fourth television network, which, having no production facilities of its own, was committed to broadcasting the work of independent producers]. That was a revelation. I had a lot of conversations about that with Jeremy Isaacs [Channel 4's first chief executive], whom I had known for years. In a way I was responding, as a lot of other people were, to the opportunity for the first time in my life of being able to produce television. You couldn't do it before.

'You have to go back in history. As an independent film-maker, David Puttnam could not produce a film for the BBC. It didn't matter how friendly you were with Alasdair Milne, Brian Wenham or anyone else – as an independent you couldn't produce a film for the BBC. So the advent of Channel 4 was a phenomenally significant thing – suddenly you could produce television.'

Puttnam's discussions with Isaacs had led to the idea of doing a series of low-budget films, partly financed by Channel 4 (with the balance coming from sales to other territories), which would constitute 'really a manufacturing process – to try out directors and writers and use it as a test base'. This idea was to become the *First Love* series, which gave opportunities to such new talents as directors Pat O'Connor, Brian Gilbert and Gavin Millar and writers June Roberts, Noella Smith and Julie Welch. With this series in mind, Puttnam had set up his own television company, Enigma Television, but had no funds and no sales facilities – he needed to align himself with a properly capitalized production and distribution operation. He turned to his new friend, James Lee.

Just as Puttnam saw the new channel as a heaven-sent opportunity to rekindle his creative ambitions, so Lee saw it as a point of access to exactly those areas of new media investment that he had identified a year before as being essential for the further development of Pearson Longman. He had already made a successful investment in Yorkshire Television, of which he was now deputy chairman, and, in the first weeks of 1981, he had made a bid for the franchise to operate Britain's first independent breakfast-television station. For this he had secured the services of former *Times* editor Harold Evans, MP Christopher Chataway and one of British television's most experienced and respected producers, Mike Wooller, who was then controller of documentaries at Thames Television. The bid failed. Evans and Chataway returned to their other interests and Wooller went back to Thames. However, a few weeks later the plans for Channel 4 were announced, and Puttnam and Lee quickly sketched out a proposal for a television production fund. Lee phoned Wooller and again persuaded him to leave the security of network television to try his hand in the new independent sector. Pearson Longman would put £5 million into the venture, which was originally to be known as Pearson Longman Television. Wooller was to be managing director.

Eberts: James originally intended that Pearson Longman Television should operate completely separately from Pearson's 44 per cent interest in Goldcrest. But, at that time, in the summer of 1981, there was nowhere to put Mike Wooller, no physical space for him. Certainly there was no space at Pearson, the entire headquarters of which was crammed into two floors of Millbank Tower. Mike was hanging around, waiting for a place to put his desk. At about the same time, I was moving offices. I wanted Bill Gavin to be able to use our facilities; we were looking at the possibility of hiring someone to run the accounts; and I was thinking of a second secretary. Our small premises in Mayfair couldn't accommodate all that.

A friend of mine was running a company that was then going bankrupt. He had a wonderful office, which I had admired many times, in Holland Park Avenue, which is about five minutes' walk from my home. It had the great attraction of being adjacent to a tennis court, which, so I imagined, I could use at lunchtime. So I told James of my plans to move to this new office and he, of course, realized that it might be a good place to park Mike Wooller.

At first it was simply a question of putting Mike in the same building as me. But very soon after we moved, in the summer of 1981, it became evident that he had absolutely no idea how to run a television company. He was excellent at making programmes, but by his own admission he was no good at business; at Thames, and before that at the BBC, that side of things had always been handled by other people. So James came up with the scheme of aligning Pearson Longman Television with Goldcrest, hoping that I would be able to help Mike get established.

Ilott: In fact, Cruickshank and Lee had by this time revamped the management-company proposal in such a way as to make it a vehicle for all Pearson Longman's entertainment-media interests. What emerged was a £12 million wholly owned subsidiary of Pearson Longman called Goldcrest Films and Television Ltd (GFT), which had two divisions: Goldcrest Films, which was to look after Pearson Longman's 44 per cent shareholding in GFI, and Goldcrest Television (the name Pearson Longman Television having been dropped, and the new one adopted, with the approval of the GFI shareholders). Lee was to be chairman and Eberts chief executive of GFT, while Eberts was, in addition, to be managing director of Goldcrest Films, through which he would continue to run GFI, and Mike Wooller was to be managing director of Goldcrest Television. GFI transferred to the new company its $25,000-a-year contribution to Eberts's overheads and the service fee it had paid to Pearson Longman for looking after the books. As Wooller's costs were to be borne directly by Goldcrest Television, using the £5 million with which it was originally capitalized, the television and film arms of GFT were to be kept separate. The new company was launched in great style at a champagne reception in the fashionable Langan's Brasserie in London, in July 1981.

Its formation, and the attitude of the various participants towards it, had a number of consequences. First, of course, it extended Goldcrest's area of operations into television, the business side of which no one associated with the company – certainly not Puttnam, Lee, Eberts, or, as was quickly proved, Wooller – really understood. Second, it established an alternative line of command, between Lee, Puttnam and Wooller, parallel to the line of command between Lee and Eberts. The television operation had been the brainchild of Lee and Puttnam alone: it was they who had devised the plan; it was they who had held preliminary talks with Jeremy Isaacs; it was Lee who had hired Wooller; and it was all three of them – but not Eberts – who had flown out to the States in June of that year for a round of exploratory discussions with the US networks and cable companies. That the existence of this 'second front' (Lee's phrase) caused no immediate antagonism – all enjoyed good personal relationships and professed to hold each other in high esteem – belied the fact that a real confusion was being created over who was actually in charge of the company. On the films side there was no problem: Eberts was the boss, period. On the television side, responsibility fell between Eberts, who was the chief executive, Mike Wooller, who was the managing director but reported to Eberts, and Lee, who was the chairman, founder and, in a sense, proprietor, and to whom both Eberts and Wooller reported. On the corporate side – i.e. running the company as such – responsibility was Eberts's, but it was a role with which he never felt comfortable. In fact, from the outset he was in something of a false position: he was a deal-maker, never – as had been proved time and again in his career – a corporate executive. The relationships he understood and enjoyed best were those between banker and client, entrepreneur and investor, or financier and film-maker, not between manager and staff, chief executive and managers, or even chief executive and chairman. In the succeeding months, as the company grew, his reluctance to devote himself to management duties, and thereby properly to fulfil the role of chief executive, was to create a power vacuum that attracted both the soon-to-be-hired back-office executives, finance director John Chambers and head of business affairs David Norris, and James Lee.

Behind them all stood David Puttnam: off screen, perhaps, but a key element in the equations of power and responsibility in the new-look Goldcrest.

Puttnam's relationship with the company has been so often misunderstood that it is worth reiterating just how unusual his position was from the start. In the first place, he had developed *Chariots of Fire* with money from the Goldcrest development fund back in 1978. He had been appointed a non-executive director of GFI, which at its very first board meeting agreed to fund his next film, *The Killing Fields*. This was followed, in February 1981, with the commitment to develop *Local Hero*. The relationship was one of considerable mutual advantage: Puttnam needed Goldcrest's money, but no more than Goldcrest needed Puttnam's expertise (by 1981 he was arguably one of the top half-dozen producers in the world). Second, he had not only a good working relationship with Eberts, but at least as strong a relationship with James Lee, with whom he discussed all manner of plans and proposals for the company. When Lee later took over from Eberts as chief executive, Puttnam had already been, for three years, his most influential adviser. Third, as a television producer, through his company Enigma Television, he had a very favourable deal whereby Goldcrest contributed to his overheads, paid him producer's fees and undertook to finance his productions. The creative risks may have been his, but all the financial risks were Goldcrest's. And in television, as in films, his was to be by far the most significant individual contribution. Indeed, by 1984 Puttnam accounted for 44 per cent of Goldcrest's entire film and television investments.

This statistic not only testifies to Puttnam's extraordinary energy and ability, but bears witness to his hold over the company. As a power vacuum opened up between Eberts, Lee and Wooller, Puttnam became almost an icon; whether he wanted it or not – and probably he did want it – he acquired the power that they either surrendered or willingly invested in him. Later, when Eberts had gone, it became virtually official policy to give Puttnam what he wanted rather than court his displeasure. This recourse, what Lee calls the 'keep David happy' approach, was not as entirely wrong-headed as it seems: Puttnam's quality of output compares favourably with that of any other producer who worked for the company, and better than most, while the sheer quantity of his contribution made the relationship with him the cornerstone of Goldcrest's investment policy. But it led, as inevitably it would do, to a distortion of judgement on both sides. Goldcrest, for example, after Eberts's departure, invested £2.5 million in three medium-budget Puttnam films, *The Frog Prince*, *Mr Love* and *Knights and Emeralds*, which, in retrospect and by common consent (including Puttnam's), should never have been made – at least not in that way and not for that money. That they were made was described by one leading executive of the company as an act of 'corporate cowardice . . . we shirked saying no to David'.

Puttnam contributed more projects and received more funds, had a bigger say on the board and had more influence between meetings, from 1980 up until his resignation to take up his post at Columbia Pictures in 1986, than any other non-executive associated with the company. In Goldcrest's affairs, his influence was not far short of Eberts's and probably equal to that of James Lee. It is arguable that he played his part at least as honourably as they did and gave at least as much to the company as it gave to him. But the point, of course, is that not only was there an unavoidable conflict of interest between his being an influential – possibly the most influential – board member at the same time as being the major recipient of company funds, but that his power was not harnessed to a fixed responsibility: he could walk away at any time, as in 1986, when the company was at its lowest ebb, he did. (Interestingly, when he got to Hollywood he found himself up against a man who had exercised a similar kind of influence over Columbia's affairs, for a lot longer and to even greater effect, and who might almost have been his role model: Ray Stark. Saying no to Ray at Columbia was no easier than saying no to David at Goldcrest. Puttnam did say no. He lasted a year. At the time of writing, Stark is still there.)

Eberts: To be honest, I don't recall very clearly what my feelings were about all these developments, except that I was a bit surprised that James wanted me to be the chief executive of both sides of the operation: I knew nothing about television, and Mike Wooller was far too senior a person to take direction from me. Mike is an extremely able and very pleasant man. We had offices next door to each other and got on very well. However, the structure that had been set up, whereby I was notionally his boss, was uncomfortable for us both. Of course, I quickly allayed any fears that he had about the extent of his authority, and I made it clear to him that I was not about to start telling him how to make television programming, or who to make it with, or under what terms it should be made. Having said that, however, I quickly got dragged into his area.

Mike spent the first few months at Goldcrest Television putting together a list of projects for Channel 4. The channel had started life with nothing, and Jeremy Isaacs and his team were anxious to build up a store of programmes to see them through the first few months of their broadcasting life. They took one look at Mike's impressive, well-balanced list and said yes to virtually everything. But when Mike came back to the office he realized, as did James, that we had no idea what price to put on these things. Here were twenty or twenty-five projects, none of which we knew anything about in terms of financing or recoupment. The reason I became involved was that we decided to finance the television programmes in the same way that I had financed feature films. This, unfortunately, was a mistake.

In the feature-film business you can afford to have some form of deficit finance – i.e. the cash that you put up yourself to bridge the gap between what the film costs and what is already covered by pre-sales and guarantees. You can do that because you can estimate fairly accurately what you will get from the unsold markets when the film is finished. Also, in your calculation of risk there is the prospect of a very attractive upside if the film is a success: your profit share can yield a great deal of money. In television none of this is true. First, you cannot predict what the sales in the remaining markets might be, because in television you either sell a programme or you don't. There is very little middle ground. A wanted programme is sold, an unwanted programme is not sold – that's all there is to it. Because the business is all about scheduling, fulfilling statutory obligations, meeting the needs of a wide audience across the whole range of programmes and so on – because it is not about simple audience appeal in the way that film is – there is no way in which you can predict whether or not your programme will be wanted in any particular market. Nor, if it looks likely to be rejected, can you easily negotiate a deal by bringing down the price. If the broadcaster doesn't want the programme, no amount of price-cutting is going to persuade him to find a space for it in his schedules. It remains unsold. (Most programmes, in fact, are not sold at all. Documentaries, for instance, no matter how brilliant they are, are almost unsaleable in the international markets. You will very rarely see a foreign-made documentary on your television screen.) With a feature film, you almost always sell it, if only because the cinema system allows a distributor to take a chance, knowing that you, the producer, share the risk with him. It is only a question of agreeing on the size of the advance.

Second, a television programme has very limited upside potential. No matter how good it is, no matter how great its ratings, you don't get any more money for it. In fact, for the most part, the prices paid for television programmes are fixed by rate card: so much per hour. The only exceptions to this are long-running series, such as *The Cosby Show* or *M*A*S*H*, where there is an upside potential in the secondary syndication market in the States and, occasionally, in the foreign-sales field, where, if there is a big public following, the production company can try to push up the price of a second or third series.

Thus, to provide deficit financing in the television area – which is exactly what we started out doing – is not a wise move. If a programme costs £1 million, you might, at best, get £500,000 from the US, £300,000 from major foreign markets and maybe another £400,000 from the rest of the world. Thus, the most revenue you could generate would be £1.2 million, giving you a maximum profit potential of £200,000. If, going in, you have only £900,000 of those deals in place, then you would have to put up £100,000 risk capital, knowing that the maximum you could make was a return of £200,000, but with no guarantee that the sales required to achieve that will come through. That is a very big risk for a very small reward. In reality, it is almost impossible, even in the best case, to envisage a gross profit on any television production of more than 30–35 per cent, out of which you have to pay your overheads, sales commissions and other non-programme costs.

By comparison, if you had a £5 million film, and were risking, let's say, £2 million in deficit finance, not only are you better able to estimate the likelihood of recouping that £2 million from unsold markets, but you stand to make maybe £10 million on that £2 million if the film is a success. The risk is less, the reward is greater.

The high cost of quality programme-making and the inadvisability of deficit financing are the two basic reasons why so many prestige programmes are co-productions between broadcasters from several countries. They have agreed in advance on the cost and what proportion each of them is prepared to contribute towards it. Subsequent sales to other broadcasters are strictly icing on the cake.

I didn't know any of this at the time. In fact, I didn't know anything about television at all, and it became clear that, from a business point of view, no one else at Goldcrest did either. We went in completely blind. I remember at board meetings we used to talk about the problems in television and the general feeling was: 'We'll never break through in this market unless we take some sort of risk now – pay a tuition fee, buy a presence, buy a position – and the price we have to pay is several million pounds of investment which we may or may not get back.' Since we all thought that we were looking towards a golden age of independent television production, with the advent of cable, satellite, Channel 4, promises of deregulation and so on, that kind of reasoning seemed acceptable.

Similarly, and it sounds unbelievably casual now, the reason that Mike and I tacitly accepted that my title of chief executive was nominal as far as television was concerned was that initially we did not anticipate much need for me to make decisions or get involved. I rather expected to carry on running GFI, with Irene and a secretary, in the way I had always done; and for Mike to work independently of me, on his own projects with his own funds, in whatever way he wanted.

It was to prove a major miscalculation. From the outset I should have taken my role as chief executive more seriously. I should have insisted that I had the final authority to cancel, cut or shut down any project about which I had doubts. Indeed, I should have controlled the direction of television as a whole. I didn't. I relied entirely on Mike, and Mike wasn't up to it: it was a case of right man, wrong job. I don't blame him, because he was doing what he had always said he was good at, which was developing relationships with programme-makers. He never claimed to be good at running a business. But, because of my hands-off attitude, I didn't run it for him. In fact, from day one, no one was running television as a business. The only person with business ability who was interested in television was James, and he was chief executive of his own company with four or five other, much bigger, businesses to look after.

When I went down to Channel 4 with Mike to talk about the first Goldcrest–Channel 4 deal, I was in a complete fog. I had no idea what to ask for; I just went for the highest price that sounded reasonable. In fact, in the end, Channel 4 committed £5.4 million to sixty-eight hours of the programming that Mike had devised. That figure was quite an achievement and we came away very pleased with ourselves. When the details of the deal got out there were even mutterings in the industry that Channel 4 was favouring Goldcrest, was letting us become dominant in the independent production sector. But in fact, £5.4 million represented only 31 per cent of the cost of producing those sixty-eight hours, and we had no idea where the other 69 per cent was going to come from. That this didn't worry us at the time was only because we didn't know any better.

Ilott: The formation of GFT, and the grouping together of all Pearson Longman's film and television interests in one company, conclusively established Pearson's control over Goldcrest's affairs. Pearson Longman was not only the overwhelmingly dominant shareholder, and the employer of all the officers and staff of the company, but was the hub of its fairly complex pattern of partnerships and cross-holdings. The protection and support that Pearson had provided when Eberts was in effect part of a separate entity, GFI, were now augmented by an attitude that was both more proprietorial and more demanding, and, for a while, Goldcrest was to do whatever suited Pearson's wider corporate objectives, especially in the areas of television, cable and video. Also, whereas hitherto Eberts had managed things from his Mayfair office pretty much on his own, reporting to the GFI board as required, from now on James Lee controlled overall policy, had a veto over investment decisions, and played an active role in the recruitment of senior staff. He had, for example, been the person to appoint Mike Wooller, and he was soon to be involved personally in the recruitment of two key executives, John Chambers in finance and David Norris in business affairs.

It would be wrong, however, to overstate Lee's involvement in Goldcrest's day-to-day activities. He had other fish to fry. In 1981 and 1982, while, according to his own account, he held 'the policy strings of Goldcrest throughout', his role in fact was mainly advisory. 'I was probably not devoting a disproportionate amount of time to Goldcrest, because it was an extraordinarily energetic period for me altogether,' he says. 'I was doing a great deal of work down at the *Financial Times* on photocomposition and in Penguin looking at the diversification in the United States and coming to grips with Viking. We were buying professional publishing companies in Longman – we were trying to move the emphasis away from schoolbooks and into professional information. And we were closing down Westminster Press newspapers. Certainly one should not give the impression that, with a turnover of £300 million and pre-tax profits of nearly £30 million, the chief executive [of Pearson Longman] was playing at making films down at Goldcrest. There were periods when I became much more heavily involved . . . but other than those I wasn't more actively involved than elsewhere.'

Lee did nevertheless contribute ideas of his own, some of which were acted upon – for example the investment in a proposed cable-movie-channel consortium – and some of which weren't – for example his plan for a twenty-four-hour cable news channel.

Eberts: From my point of view, James's higher profile in the company was mostly welcome. So far he had been an ideal non-executive chairman. He never interfered in day-to-day decisions and he was very supportive, even through such murky episodes as the falling out of the Patel money and the disentanglement from IFI, in which he got rather more involved than I think he would have liked. At meetings, of which I am glad to say there were not too many in those days, he would ask very pertinent questions and quite properly demanded satisfactory answers. It was a good, friendly and businesslike relationship. Some people have accused me of being naive; of not realizing that a clash between James and me was inevitable. It is true that I was to experience some unease in our relationship and that at times we did not see eye to eye, but to this day I believe that James always acted in what he thought was an honourable and decent manner. I hope that he would say the same of me.

Where I do confess to having been naive was in having no concept of the sea-change in the affairs of Goldcrest that the formation of GFT was to bring about. From the days of *Black Jack* in 1977, I had run Goldcrest with an assistant and a secretary and, latterly, with a script editor. I was the sole executive. There was no need for any other decision-maker, since I could deal with all the film-makers myself. The only additional staff that I wanted to take on were someone in foreign sales, which was currently being handled out-of-house by Bill Gavin, and someone to take charge of the finances.

But Mike Wooller was starting something completely different. He was coming from a job at Thames Television where he had at his fingertips all the services that a major independent television company offers, and he now wanted to duplicate that at Goldcrest. He had to bring with him people who could generate ideas, who could come up with outlines, who could analyse scripts: who could do all the things, in other words, to which he had previously been accustomed. Also, Mike felt, and I think he was probably right, that he should have a number of producers around him who would be under contract to us. They would each get a retainer, in return for which they would submit their projects to us first. It was similar to my own policy of cultivating a family of film-makers. The difference was that, whereas I was talking about three or four feature films a year, Mike was looking at having twenty or twenty-five programmes in development at any one time. Again, he wasn't wrong: that's the way television works. But there was no way he could handle twenty-five projects by himself.

So, with the advent of Goldcrest Films and Television, we quickly went from a staff of four to a staff of ten, with the addition of a team of six satellite producers. That was just the start. Almost immediately, we realized that we didn't have the back-room resources – in accounts, administration and so on – to cope with the work that all these people would generate.

That's when I hired John Chambers. John, who started work as finance director on 1 January 1982, had had a lot of experience in the film business: we head-hunted him from EMI, and before that he had worked at British Lion. He therefore not only knew more about the detailed workings of the industry than did James or I, but he had experience of running a corporate machine. I am not a great administrator. I can do it if I have to (I had managed to get it done, one way or another, for five years while the company was starting out), but in those days, when we were so hard pressed, every minute I spent on administration took one minute away from working on film projects, and that, I believed, was an unproductive allocation of my time. So I was very pleased when John, an extremely capable, highly experienced back-room operator, came in to take over the administration, as well as the finances, of the company.

I was so busy that I did not stop to think where this was all going to end. I never thought about how many staff we should have. I didn't plan to employ twenty or thirty people. When I hired John Chambers, and he said that he would need two or three accounts clerks to do the bookkeeping, to me that was fine: he knew best how to do his job. I felt that by having John there, I could probably do two more pictures a year.

And from that point – the establishment of the television company and a proper accounts department – the snowball of Goldcrest's bureaucratic growth started to roll, gathering such momentum that within three years the company would have a staff of fifty-five. Overheads, a word I hadn't heard for years, began to be mentioned at meetings. The mentions became more frequent and got louder, to the point that 'Overheads!' was to become one of the rallying cries of the dissaffected at management meetings and on the board. They were right: bad investment decisions and a lack of production control may have killed Goldcrest in 1985–6, but excessive overheads had long since weakened it at the root.

Chapter Eleven

Goldcrest's Golden Age

Eberts: Life in our new offices in Holland Park Avenue was Paradise. We were in a beautiful Georgian house in a lovely London street. It was leafy, cool, green and intimate. We were all jammed into two floors, where we got along famously and worked very hard. If there was ever such a thing as the good old days of Goldcrest then this was it: there was just me, Irene Lyons, Mike Wooller, Bill Gavin, John Chambers and John's assistant Maureen Sheen. The offices were elegant only from the outside. Inside they were simple to the point of being spartan, and, from the first day, they were overcrowded; every morning we would ring round to see who wasn't coming in so that we could allocate the available desks. It took ages to get curtains put up, but we were working too hard to notice. We started early, finished late and were always in at weekends. The only disappointment was the tennis court: I played only twice in two years, once with Peter Mayer and once with Sam Goldwyn Jnr. I got the deal done both times.

The first six months of 1982 were, for me at least, more hectic than any time before or since. John Chambers set about putting the books in order, which was no small undertaking. Mike Wooller was wading through masses of ideas and scripts. The first of our television films, *Red Monarch*, produced by David Puttnam, went before the cameras in January, and the first documentary series, *The Body Machine*, started in March. And Bill Gavin was in and out, taking more projects into his sales portfolio, including *Local Hero*, which was to start production in April.

It had taken nearly a year to get the script of *Local Hero* ready, and in that time David Puttnam had signed an exclusive deal with Warner Bros. under the terms of which he had to offer them the opportunity to invest in, and acquire the distribution rights to, any film in which he was involved. Theoretically this was directly in conflict with David's obligations to us, since we had put up the development money for *Local Hero* and co-owned the project with him. Fortunately, we had a very good relationship with Warner boss Frank Wells and, when he left Warners at the end of 1981 (to climb Mount Everest), we had if anything an even better relationship with his successor, Terry Semel. Warners initially proposed that we go fifty–fifty on *Local Hero*. However, we had already made our own decision to commit the entire budget, £2.6 million, and wanted to keep both the control and as big a share of the profits as we could. So we proposed that Warner Bros., instead of co-producing it with us, pick up the US distribution rights for an advance of $1.5 million and give us a percentage of the gross in all media: 30 per cent of the first $10 million and rising in stages thereafter. To this they agreed.

A sensational script for *The Killing Fields* had been delivered by Bruce Robinson, and David Puttnam was now launching himself into a very lengthy pre-production process, involving scouting for locations in Thailand, sorting out the political problems in Washington, and finding someone to play the pivotal role of Dith Pran. The film was not actually ready to go into production until May 1983. Like *Local Hero*, this project was offered to Warner Bros. and we ended up financing it jointly.

In post-production in those early months of 1982 was *Pink Floyd: The Wall*, for which I had arranged a completion guarantee and put up a £4.3 million loan. In exchange, we got the completion fee, a 1.5 per cent arrangement fee and a 1.75 per cent override on the interest, as well as a share of net profits. This film, for which we acted as a kind of banker (we had no involvement at all in the making of it, nor did we retain any rights), brought me into contact with director Alan Parker and producer Alan Marshall, film-makers with whom I was to become very friendly in the following years.

Then in March we had our first taste of glory: *Chariots of Fire* won four Oscars, including Best Picture. Although Goldcrest had had nothing to do with the making or the marketing of the film, we had been in there at the beginning and we shared in some measure in the triumph. Over the years, the press increasingly bracketed Goldcrest's name with *Chariots of Fire*. This so incensed Dodi Fayed and Allied Stars, who had co-financed the picture with Fox, that they took out ads in the trade press stating that *Chariots* was their production and had nothing whatever to do with us. By that time, however, it was too late: 'Goldcrest's *Chariots of Fire*' had become a media label and was impossible to shake off. Naturally, we were delighted with the connection; it gave a tremendous boost to the company's image and gave the public, which had seen *Chariots* but which could not be expected to distinguish between one film company and another, something to know us by. This was actually to prove very useful, for at that time we were setting out yet again to raise money, and the boost to our profile opened a lot of doors.

Ilott: Since putting together the £8.2 million for GFI in July 1980, Eberts had made investments in thirteen feature projects, of which five were still in development, six had gone into production, but only three – *The Howling, Escape from New York* and *An Unsuitable Job for a Woman* – had so far been released. Most of these investments were thus still on the balance sheet. With only modest returns from pre-sale advances, tax-leasing deals, recoupment from the conversion of developed projects and early returns from the three new films that had gone into distribution, GFI's funds had not been significantly replenished. It was now fully invested – i.e. it had run out of money.

Goldcrest Television, too, had wasted no time in allocating its funds. Since the summer of 1981 Mike Wooller had made investments in eighteen projects, of which twelve were still in development, six were in production and none had so far been completed. In addition, just under £200,000 had been spent on retainers and overhead contributions for the six satellite-television producers (David Puttnam, John Gau, Barry Hanson, Paul Knight, Susan Richards and Kaye Webb).

In all, about £14 million had been spent on film and television projects since 1980. Overheads, with a staff that had increased from two to nearly twenty, were running at about £800,000 a year and, by mid-1982, Goldcrest's profit-and-loss account was showing an accumulated deficit of about £3 million. At the time, GFI also owed £1.8 million to its loan-stock holders (the original fund being in the form of subordinated loan capital on which interest was payable half-yearly). In addition, £125,000 of GFI's pre-1980 development investments had been written off.

However, with the risks spread across thirteen feature films and eighteen television projects, and with Goldcrest's exposure in any one of those kept to a minimum (in theory, anyway: the investment in *Gandhi* had broken all the rules and at one point GFI, IFI and Pearson had invested about £6 million in a project which had no pre-sales, no US distribution deal and no completion guarantee), there was good reason to believe that the returns on the £14 million, when eventually they began to come through, would show a healthy rate of profit overall. It was thus with some confidence that it was decided to raise fresh capital. The means chosen was to set up yet another partnership, to be called Goldcrest Film and Television Partners (GFTP).

Eberts: We had been thinking of a new fund ever since the summer of

1981, when we severed our relationship with IFI. Although the Reciprocal Investment Opportunity Agreement between IFI and GFI was still in force, we could hardly rely on Jo Child to continue to support our projects, and the loss of IFI's money was a significant setback, which, combined with the unexpectedly large drain on our resources caused by the financing of *Gandhi*, led to something of a cash crisis. In the short term, this was relieved by the promise of a loan of £1.5 million from the Midland Bank. However, because partnerships like GFI involve fixed sums of capital invested over a fixed period of time on fixed terms and conditions, we could not actually undertake such a loan without the authority of all the shareholders. Even having obtained the shareholders' approval, there was no way of collateralizing the loan to the satisfaction of the bank. All we had were investments of unknown value in films that were, in the main, yet to be released. Indeed, many of them were yet to be made. As always, James Lee helped us out. Together with Reg West, Pearson Longman's finance director, he gave assurances to the Midland that the loan would be repaid. In effect, Pearson Longman stood as guarantor (and, in fact, via GFT, loaned GFI £180,000 while the bank facility was put in place). It was all done slightly on a nod and a wink, but there was nothing untoward about it. There was nothing wrong with our business: the return on our investments would more than cover a loan of that size. And, while we urgently needed the cash to cover our outgoings, it was only for a short time until new capital had been raised. The loan was advanced on 7 July and the new capital was pledged on 23 July.

As well as wishing to replace the IFI money and to replenish our own exhausted reserves, there was another factor, arising out of the changing nature of the company, that made the new fund essential. It had become clear that, despite our intention of keeping Goldcrest Television and Goldcrest Films apart, there was going to be a spill-over between the two divisions. Already, time which I should have spent working for Goldcrest Films was instead being taken up with television affairs: in such a small office and with such a mountain of work to deal with, it was impossible to prevent it. I was acutely aware that this constituted a conflict between the interests of the smaller shareholders in GFI and the interests of Pearson Longman, which owned Goldcrest Television.

At the same time, however, the fact that there was now an in-house television capability opened up new avenues for investment. Had we so wished, GFI could have become involved in cross-over projects and in co-financing between films and television. So not only was there a problem of conflict of interest, but there was also an investment opportunity for the

GFI shareholders. I went to the GFI partners and said, 'I think that you should know that, one way or another, we're going to have some television programming here. Would you like to invest, or do you want to keep out of it altogether?'

I already had a project in hand, *The Far Pavilions*, which was going to be made as a mini-series for the cable channel Home Box Office (HBO) in the States and for Channel 4 in the UK, and as a feature film for the foreign markets. So I said, 'Here's an example. We're making a hybrid product. It's essentially made for television, but it also has a feature-film aspect to it and, strictly speaking, Goldcrest Films rather than Goldcrest Television should be putting money in. But, being television, it's perhaps not what you want.' Sure enough, most of the GFI shareholders said they did not want to be investors in television. They were putting venture capital at risk and they wanted the prospect of a big return.

Michael Waterston, for example, of Murray Johnstone Ltd, managed hundreds of millions of pounds of investments in less risky areas, but had only a very limited amount set aside for high-risk, venture-capital investment. He was quite happy to put some of that money into Goldcrest Films, because, although he might lose some, or even all, of it, he might also have a share in a blockbuster and make double or triple his investment. He could justify the high risk because of the high potential return. Television does not have that upside and Michael's view was, 'What the hell – even if I win, it's only going to be a 20 per cent or so profit. That's not what I'm interested in.' And he was right. He had different kinds of objectives. (Michael later caused me, and every other serious independent film financier, terrible grief by sinking $9 million into a disastrous and hugely expensive film called *Gunbus*. Everyone in the business knew that that film was going to be a failure, and all we could think of was the money that was going to waste. In fact, the failure of the film didn't just soak up money that could have been used elsewhere, but was to contribute to the total withdrawal of Scottish investment funds from film finance thereafter.)

Mike Wooller wasn't keen on *Far Pavilions*. It was too blatantly commercial, like a soap opera, and thus was not his kind of project. Also, there was no way that Goldcrest Television could undertake such a large single commitment. (Our investment eventually totalled £6.8 million, of which we got less than £5 million back, so Mike was right all along.) If I wanted to do it I would have to find additional money elsewhere. For this purpose, I decided to set up a partnership that would invest solely in television. The difference between this and what Mike was doing was really in the kind of projects and the kind of audience: I was thinking of television movies and features, for cable and possibly theatrical distribution in the foreign markets, whereas Mike was looking at documentaries and current affairs for network broadcasting. But, of course, as soon as I mentioned the idea of raising money for television, the potential investors would say, 'Yes, but we would like to have a chance to invest in your films as well.' They too were looking at the upside potential.

Which is why we ended up forming a hybrid, Goldcrest Films and Television Partners (GFTP). This was to be separate from Goldcrest Television, which was run by Mike, and separate from GFI, which was run by me but, like both of them, was to be managed by Goldcrest Films and Television Ltd. Like GFI, it would have no staff and no overheads, and would pay a fee to the management company for office services.

According to my plan, therefore, Goldcrest would have three pools of capital, raised from three separate sets of investors (although many invested in all three partnerships), all three of which would be managed by one company of which I was the chief executive. Each pool of capital would have its own board of directors and its own set of accounts. The only thing different about the design of the new partnership was that it would not actually do anything except invest – it would undertake no projects of its own – and it would do this by putting up half the money each time Goldcrest Television invested in a television project and half the money each time Goldcrest Films invested in a film project. That way we could keep the purity of Goldcrest Films, the purity of Goldcrest Television, and we would have no problems about conflicts of interest.

As can be imagined, this was to cause horribly complicated administrative problems for John Chambers. He would have to allocate costs and revenues across four sets of books: the three partnerships and the management company. That would be a nightmare enough in any industry, but in the film and television business the complexities of distribution deals, profit participations, amortization and valuation of assets, and currency fluctuations over the revenue-earning lifetime of a product, make it hard for even one set of books to meet the standards required by the auditors, let alone the Inland Revenue. John hired two or three more people to help, but still worked night and day.

To assist us in raising the money for the new partnership, we turned to Angus Grossart. Noble Grossart had been one of the institutions I had called on in 1980 when I was looking for investors for GFI. I had failed to get them to come in, but I was very impressed by Angus and marked him down as someone I would want to do business with in the future. (Coincidentally, one of his clients had been the bankrupt company in

whose offices we were now working.) The first two capital-raising exercises, in 1977 and 1980, had been done by me, more or less on my own.
However, I had made mistakes, especially in the documentation, and
anyway I did not savour the prospect of going through it all again. I
needed a merchant bank, much in the same way that Jo Child and I had
needed E. F. Hutton when we raised the capital for IFI. On previous
occasions I had not tried to involve a bank, because I was convinced that
it would have no interest in a new film-financing fund, but now that we
had a track record I thought it was worth a try. Lazard couldn't do it
because it was part-owned by our main shareholder, Pearson. And for
their own reasons other people I knew in the City, such as Warburg,
Schroder, and Hoare Govett, didn't want to do it – I think probably
because they were not familiar enough with the business. I then
approached Angus and, to my delight, he agreed.

When you are raising money, merchant banks can help you in three
ways: they bless the deal, give you access to investors and draw up the
documentation. As an independent, dispassionate and reliable observer
of the activities of the company, and as a financial institution of known
repute, a merchant bank is the investors' guarantee that their money is
not about to be squandered by the persons who are asking them to part
with it. If the bank does not like the look of the proposal or the people
involved, it will not put its name to the offering; potential investors draw
their own conclusions.

Given the kind of investors we were seeking, this wasn't such a great
advantage. I had, after all, been an investment banker myself for some
years. I knew my way around, and people knew me. Similarly, the second
function – of giving access to investors – proved to be of only marginal
value. I had been calling on all the available sources of equity finance
and risk capital for four or five years. Angus didn't come up with any
new ones. What he did do was set up meetings so that I could go back
and see people who had turned me down before. The Scottish Investment
Trust, for example, came in because of Angus.

But on the third point, the documentation, Noble Grossart's assistance
was invaluable. They knew how best to present our fund as a business
proposition and they were aware of all the pitfalls, the necessary disclos-
ures and the need for a clear statement of opportunities and objectives.
The resulting thirty-page prospectus was a much more polished piece of
work than my previous do-it-yourself efforts.

In it was a statement of Goldcrest's strategy.

It is a popular misconception, in Wardour Street at any rate, that
Goldcrest was carefully and quietly built up on the basis of a well-

conceived business plan. After all, both James and I, the chairman and the chief executive respectively, were well known to be Harvard Business School graduates. But, in fact, there was no plan. Things just happened, brought about more by our energy, enthusiasm and opportunism than by our far-sightedness. Plus, we had more than our share of luck: Channel 4 came along with production funds; *Chariots* won Oscars and was forever associated with us; the US cable business was going through a fiercely competitive phase and paid very high prices for our product; the major studios were looking for exactly our kind of pictures; and the exchange rate made our films very cheap for international, and especially American, distributors to buy.

I had a pretty clear idea of what I wanted to do with feature films: more of the same. That's about as far as my strategic thinking went. The long-term strategy about the television business, and integrating that with the film business, and getting into cable and satellite and new media, was created, as far as I was concerned, only to fulfil the requirements of the prospectus. I contributed to it, but mine was by no means the leading voice, certainly not by comparison with the voices of James Lee and Angus Grossart. James is very good at development strategy and that seemed to me to be a good thing. It made us complementary. I liked the idea of having a chairman who was a thinker. (Jo Child was also a thinker – it was one of the things which first attracted me to him – and if he had been content just to be that, and had restrained himself from getting involved with the film-makers and the deals, we might have got along better.)

Once the prospectus was finally approved, printed and despatched to our hit-list of potential investors, I took over and did what I am best at: selling. It was back to the telephone, thousands of calls, dozens of visits, talking myself hoarse with the sales pitch. The prospectus went out on 24 June 1982. By 23 July we had raised £9.4 million, bringing the total capital managed by Goldcrest Films and Television Ltd to £22.6 million: £8.2 million for Goldcrest Films, £5 million for Goldcrest Television and £9.4 million for Goldcrest Film and Television Partners (GFTP). Most of the new money came from existing shareholders. Pearson Longman invested £3.9 million, and Electra Investment Trust, Legal & General Assurance, London & Manchester Assurance and Coral Leisure all invested further funds. The handful of new investors were Scottish funds brought in by Angus Grossart.

Ilott: With the advent of Goldcrest Film and Television Partners, the structure of the company overall became even more complicated than before. As the GFTP prospectus put it, 'Goldcrest means GFT, GFT Investors, Goldcrest Films Ltd, Goldcrest Television, GFI, Goldcrest Films International Ltd [the general partner of GFI], and any other subsidiary and/or associate for the time being and from time to time of any of them.' Now, as well as GFTP, there was a general partner, Goldcrest Partnership Finance Ltd, to be owned by the GFTP shareholders. All these came together in a paper company, GFT Investors Ltd, the board of which was the means whereby shareholders in GFI and GFTP could participate with representatives of Pearson, Goldcrest Films and Goldcrest Television in formulating policy for the investment of their funds. The labyrinth of subsidiaries included further companies set up for the sole purpose of making this or that film, companies set up for the purpose of holding foreign currencies and companies set up as vehicles for particular areas of investment such as video and magazine publishing. At one time, there were thirty-two of these subsidiaries, including companies in Bermuda, Jersey and the United States.

The formation of the new fund hugely increased Goldcrest's capital and marked another quantum leap in its development. What had been a portfolio investment company, first in film development (Goldcrest Films) and then in film production (GFI), was now a fully functioning film and television production company in its own right. And what had hitherto been a matter of peripheral interest to the Pearson board began to assume altogether greater significance; the more so as, at about the same time, Lord Blakenham succeeded in buying out the minority shareholding in Pearson Longman, which as a result ceased to be a separate company and became an integral part of the Pearson group. Thus, in the summer of 1982, Pearson found itself with more than £12 million equity and loan capital invested in the various partnerships that constituted Goldcrest, which looked likely to become the fifth leg, alongside Penguin, the *Financial Times*, Longman and Westminster Press, in Pearson's media empire.

The formation of GFTP and the buy-out of the Pearson Longman minority also had important consequences for James Lee. First, as chairman and representative of the principal shareholder, he perforce became much more involved in Goldcrest's increasingly complex affairs, answering now not to Pearson Longman but directly to Pearson's main board. All investment decisions of over £500,000 were referred to him; he kept a close eye on adherence to investment criteria; he was involved in all senior appointments; and, most importantly, he chaired Goldcrest board meetings. The more involved he became, and the more knowledge of the film industry he acquired – especially from his discussions with Puttnam and Eberts – the more he liked it.

And his fondness for the film business increased in direct proportion to his growing disenchantment with his new role at Pearson. The buy-out of the Pearson Longman minority had been supported by Lee as being in Pearson's best interest, but it nevertheless robbed him of his cherished independence and freedom of action. Where before he had been the chief executive of an independent public company, with overall control of policy and with a headquarters staff answerable directly to him, he was now only one of the Pearson main-board members. He had responsibility for the conduct of the same businesses as before, but they were not his businesses now and he could not shelter behind the supposed interests of minority investors. Nor was he surrounded by his own executive staff: between Pearson and the management of Westminster Press or Penguin there was no longer to be the intermediary, Pearson Longman level of supervision. From being an officer in the field with his own battalions, he had become a member of the headquarters staff. He did not like it. He was, he says, 'less happy' with the 'bureaucratic life' at Pearson: 'I like to be my own man and it was very clear I wasn't going to be my own man after that.'

Not only did the lack of direct involvement not suit Lee's personality, neither did his personality suit his new role on the main-board team. His was not a 'collegiate' style, to use James Joll's expression.

Although Lee's disenchantment was not hidden from his colleagues, there was no boardroom hostility towards him. On the contrary, according to one of Pearson's directors, Lee was 'in good standing at Pearson . . . He was respected and liked . . . extremely diligent . . . very hard working . . . and full of ideas.'

Increasingly, however, Lee turned to Goldcrest, where his contribution was valued, where his skills were appreciated, and where – with the hectic and accelerating growth of the company and the increasing (although unconscious and at this time still hardly apparent) reluctance by Eberts to play the role of corporate chief executive – there was a real need for his services.

Finance director John Chambers spent most of the year trying to put some order into the rather haphazard bookkeeping that he had inherited ('I went back to basics, writing up books and sorting out petty-cash slips and so on'), while at the same time devising a system of accounting and reporting that would meet the requirements of the GFI shareholders, the GFTP shareholders and Pearson. David Norris, the lawyer who had devised the deal structure for the development and production of

Watership Down back in 1974, had been lured away from his law firm to become Goldcrest's head of business affairs. He joined the company in October 1982 and, like Chambers, was soon catching up on the documentation ('a miracle of patchwork – Jake had been very ingenious at cobbling these things together') for all thirty-one film and television projects, each of which involved contracts with co-financiers, writers and producers, sometimes with directors, artists and technicians, as well as with cinema, television, video and cable distributors around the world. In addition, Norris launched a programme of tax-leasing deals for as many of the projects – ten between October and Christmas – as he could.

Bill Gavin had now joined the company full time, as director of distribution and marketing, and Terry Clegg, the executive in charge of production on *Gandhi* and one of the most experienced line producers in the industry, had joined to oversee the physical production of Goldcrest films. (Clegg's advice to Eberts was sometimes a significant factor in deciding whether or not a project was given the green light, and after Eberts left it was Clegg's expert opinion that was to decide the fate of John Boorman's *The Emerald Forest*, the last major project on which Eberts had been working before he joined Embassy.)

Gavin, Clegg, Norris and Chambers – who together with Eberts and Wooller constituted Goldcrest's first executive team – brought into the company not only their own staff, thereby adding to the administrative burden against which Eberts was already beginning to rebel, but also whole new areas of technical discussion. Many of the questions they raised called for new policy guidelines. 'Whereas before it was very much a broking operation – an extension of the original seed-money idea – now it became much more directly a film-financing operation,' explains Norris. 'So there were actually quite a lot of policies that had to be sorted out, *vis-à-vis* the kinds of deal one would do with producers, in terms of what we would charge for financing, what would be the profit participation, what the overhead charge would be, what the distribution and sales arrangements would be, whether or not we would be our own completion guarantor . . . a number of things which nobody had put their mind to up to that point.'

All such policy questions came before the board, usually in the form of recommendations that had been formulated by Norris, Gavin or Chambers and discussed beforehand with Eberts or Wooller.

At the same time, there being a new tranche of capital available, the board was faced with a batch of investment decisions to approve: between August and November 1982, £5.6 million was committed to *Runners*,

The Ploughman's Lunch, The Emerald Forest, Dream One, The Dresser
and *Another Country.*

Thus Lee found himself involved both in very technical discussions of
policy and in key investment decisions, at just the time that his natural
inclinations and the changing circumstances at Pearson were leading him
anyway to wish to become more involved in Goldcrest's affairs.

Two incidents illustrate this increasing involvement.

In July, he committed Goldcrest to an investment in a video-publishing
venture, Catalyst Video. This decision involved Eberts to the extent that
he was a signatory to the heads of agreement, but the initiative all came
from Lee. Catalyst never thrived and eventually went under, taking
£500,000 of Goldcrest's money with it.

In November, Lee's continuing discussions with Puttnam led him to
the view that the feature-film side of Goldcrest needed a managing
director to carry out the same functions as those performed by Mike
Wooller in television. Like Wooller, the new person would report to
Eberts, who would thus be freed from part of the administrative burden
and some of the creative chores to fulfil more properly the role of overall
chief executive and principal deal-maker. Lee wrote to Eberts that,
'although our overheads are well ahead of plan, I don't think that cost
consideration should stop us from appointing a film head now if we think
such an appointment is needed. You are very badly overstretched and
will be even more so . . . if we go ahead with further fund-raising for
film and enter cable in a bigger way.'

A lunch attended by Lee, Puttnam and agent Anthony Jones – but not
by Eberts – on 10 November 1982 led to the drawing up of a short-list
of five possible candidates, all of them well-known figures in the British
film and television industries. The name most favoured by Lee and
Puttnam, and endorsed by Jones, was that of Sandy Lieberson, who
was then the London-based international vice-president of The Ladd
Company. Previously, and briefly, he had been president of worldwide
production for 20th Century–Fox, where he supervised and assisted in
the development of *Alien, Quest for Fire* and *Nosferatu.* Before joining
Fox he had been an independent producer and had worked on fifteen
films with Puttnam, who for many years had been his partner. Among
the pictures they made together were *Stardust, Bugsy Malone, Mahler*
and *Jabberwocky.* It was Lieberson who, while at Fox, had been instrumental in securing international distribution for *Chariots of Fire.* Later,
he arranged for his new employers, The Ladd Company, to take the film
for the US and Canada, where it was distributed via Warner Bros.

Eberts's response to this proposal, which Lee pressed upon him as a matter of some urgency (Lee's memo ended: 'If you want my personal opinion I think we should move *now*'), was lukewarm: he was only interested in films and not at all interested in being the corporate boss. He nevertheless agreed that Lieberson should be approached. Lieberson, who was anyway happy where he was, wisely perceived that 'Jake likes doing what I like doing' and the matter was allowed to drop.

The episode not only indicates Lee's increasing involvement in the management of the company and the closeness of his relationship with Puttnam, but it is also an early illustration of Eberts's tendency to acquiesce in matters over which he did not feel he had complete control. The idea of appointing a managing director of the films division, which was Eberts's real area of interest and in which he had proved immensely successful, was absurd, a view strongly held at the time by both John Chambers and Bill Gavin. Yet Eberts had allowed the matter to go so far as for Lieberson to be formally approached.

The new funds made available by GFTP triggered a wave of even more frenzied activity. At the start of August, the three companies, GFI, Goldcrest Television and GFTP, had fourteen film and television projects in development and thirty-three in production or distribution. They included feature films such as *Gandhi*, *Local Hero* and *The Killing Fields*; television productions such as *Red Monarch*, *The Body Machine*, *Gastank*, *Shakespeare's Sonnets*, *Bodyline*, *Robin of Sherwood* and *Rock Family Trees*; and hybrids such as *The Far Pavilions*, the *First Love* series, *Runners* and *The Ploughman's Lunch*. Between them, these projects had budgets totalling £23.5 million, a large part of which was covered by contracts secured by Bill Gavin from distributors and television companies around the world. To cope with all this work new staff were taken on: the number of employees rose to twenty-three and overheads climbed towards £1 million a year. It was a far cry from the 'small and simple' ideal that Eberts had so recently professed. The garret office in Mayfair, which had been run on the $25,000 overhead contribution from Pearson Longman and Electra, and which Eberts and Irene Lyons had left only a year before, was already a distant memory.

Chapter Twelve
Three Film-makers

Eberts: Among the film-makers with whom I became associated in this fresh burst of activity were Peter Yates, Alan Marshall and John Boorman. All three were people I had long wanted to be in business with, and all three had projects that they were trying to get off the ground.

Peter Yates is a very experienced director with an excellent track record: assistant director of *The Guns of Navarone* and director of *Bullitt, Murphy's War, The Friends of Eddie Coyle, The Deep, Breaking Away* and *Krull*, amongst many others. At that time, a director of Peter's stature could expect to earn $1 million per film working for a major studio in the United States. But every director who has worked in Hollywood has a terrible tale to tell about what happened to his share of the profits. I don't blame Hollywood for it. I blame the director's agent, or his lawyer, for not explaining exactly what the deal is. In Hollywood people don't cheat: all they do is live up to the terms of the contract, line by line, detail by detail. If you read a contract carefully, you will see that it is written in such a way that it overwhelmingly favours the studio. Distribution fees are deducted, expenses are deducted, certain costs are attributed which really have only a remote connection with the picture, profits made in this or that territory are set against losses elsewhere, and all kinds of premiums are added on. The whole thing is so complicated, and the studio is so much the master of the situation, that many film-makers have given up the idea of having profit points altogether. Instead they charge a very high fee and take that as their sole compensation for making the picture.

Goldcrest, by contrast, tried to offer film-makers a genuine partnership. We took lower fees, we offered participation in any benefits we could generate on the financing, and contracts were entered into as between friends with mutual interests. Indeed, since we were not ourselves distributors and did not rake off distribution fees and expenses, we usually stood at the same point in the line of recoupment as the producer and talent. If they didn't collect, we didn't collect. So when Peter Yates agreed to do *The Dresser* for no fee upfront, he did so because we guaranteed him a very substantial piece of our real profits. By real profits I mean profits of whatever kind, including any excess cash thrown up from doing a tax-leasing deal. (Benefits of that nature, which are nothing to do with the film as such, are rarely if ever shared with the film-maker by a studio.)

Very early in our conversations, Peter was much encouraged when I volunteered to send writer Ronnie Harwood $60,000 to write the first-draft screenplay. This was before we had agreed any other terms or signed any documents. I was experienced enough now to know the value of such a demonstration of trust: it creates a good atmosphere and gets the film off to a good start. Again, however, it is not typical of the way the film business works. In Hollywood no one trusts anyone and no money ever changes hands until every last detail of the contract has been agreed. It is a town dominated by lawyers and agents, and there are times when it seems that contracts and deals have become the central preoccupation of the film community, not movies. It is not uncommon for payments to be withheld by a Hollywood studio for months, sometimes even years, after they fall due, because of some minor contractual detail which has still to be ironed out.

At Goldcrest I took the opposite course. There was no risk involved: we were not talking about huge sums; we operated in a world which would abhor anyone who absconded with money; and we were dealing with people who were already successful. I did not for one minute think that Peter Yates, David Puttnam, Dickie Attenborough or John Boorman would take the money and run. They are all trustworthy people and they all have reputations to protect.

But while it didn't mean a lot to us, our relaxed attitude meant a lot to them, and the $60,000 cheque that I sent to Ronnie Harwood more than anything else put Peter firmly into the Goldcrest camp.

The amount you pay for a script varies widely. At the top end of the scale, Hollywood has been known to pay $750,000, maybe even $1 million, for a first-draft screenplay from a very well-known writer. That level might apply to William Goldman or Robert Towne, both of whom have a track record of writing successful screenplays. At the other end of the Hollywood scale, you can get a good first-time writer to do a first draft for as little as $35,000. Then getting down to the UK level, where the writer is not that experienced in features but has perhaps done quite a few television screenplays, you might get a first draft for as little as $15,000. Generally speaking, for mainstream commercial films, the first draft would cost in the range of $100,000 to $250,000. The second draft, if there is one, might cost another $125,000. Then when the film actually goes into production, you might pay a further $125,000. (Getting a production deal is the final confirmation that the script is acceptable, and the writer is duly rewarded.) So at that level you might end up paying between $400,000 and $450,000 for the final screenplay. In most cases the writer, if he is a good writer, will also have a small share of the profits, say 2.5 per cent of the net, which would come out of the 50 per cent allocated to the producer.

David Puttnam, who has this great ability to spot new talent, can pay much lower fees to less experienced, but often equally able, writers. Going back to *Chariots of Fire*, we put up £17,700 to cover all of Colin Welland's fee as well as a certain amount of research. Today Colin would probably command about $250,000. Proven writers can get that kind of money because, at this level of film-making, they are very few and far between. So few are they, compared to the number of outstanding directors around, that leading film-makers are now writing their own scripts. *Hope and Glory*, for example, was written, directed and produced by John Boorman. Roland Joffe, who made *The Killing Fields* and *The Mission*, wrote or co-wrote his next two films himself. It's not because these directors are megalomaniacs who want control of every aspect of their films; it's simply because they can't find writers to work with. At Goldcrest, producers and directors were always coming up with ideas, but we had great difficulty finding good writers to turn them into scripts.

Ronnie Harwood is a good writer. Within a very short time he had produced a first draft of *The Dresser* and within five months we were in principal photography. This proved to be the most pleasant production with which I have ever been associated. It was shot almost entirely at Pinewood, where Peter has been based for a number of years, and it was so lovingly made that it really didn't stand a chance of being a bad film. Ronnie Harwood was on the set every day, and Albert Finney, who adored being the star and the centre of attention, and Tom Courtenay, who played the Dresser, were in their element: they had so much acting to do.

It was a difficult film only in the sense that it had a hard time finding an audience. We knew that that was going to be the case from the outset, and the fact that we all made money (Ronnie, Albert and Tom Courtenay also had profit points) and the film got five Academy Award nominations vindicated our decision to go ahead with it. Goldcrest invested about £1.5 million in the picture, on which we made a profit of nearly £300,000.

At the same time as *The Dresser*, I was working on *Another Country*, which was also adapted from a successful stage play. It had been brought to me by Alan Marshall, who had impressed me enormously during the making of *Pink Floyd: The Wall*, for which I had arranged the finance. Marshall at that time was Alan Parker's partner. They had operated as a team for several years. Parker, as director, relied totally on Marshall, as producer, to perform all the mechanical functions required to get a film made: scheduling, organizing people, controlling the budget, sorting out logistical and other problems, and generally smoothing the way so that he had a clear run to make the picture without distractions. I don't think anyone in this business, except perhaps Terry Clegg, is as good at that job as Alan Marshall.

Pink Floyd: The Wall had been a difficult production, because the initial idea, which was based on a mere forty-page script, was to film a rock album; to have the songs connected by very limited dialogue but to have the visual aspects of the film so clearly defined that they made the story work. Parker and Marshall, both of whom always prefer to work on the basis of a highly polished script, had to draw very heavily on their stores of film-making expertise, and they worked out as best they could a shared vision of what the film was to be like. I don't think either of them enjoyed the experience.

In fact, Alan Parker was never meant to direct it. The original director found the problems insurmountable and was honest enough to admit as much, and Alan, who started out as the executive producer, took over two or three weeks into principal photography. Making matters worse were two extraordinarily talented men, Pink Floyd's Roger Waters and the designer Gerald Scarfe, who required Alan Parker's constant attention.

It was an exceptionally difficult experience for everybody. The one figure who strode like a colossus through all the mess and the monumental egos was Alan Marshall: a tough-talking, no-nonsense Cockney, whose greying beard makes him look many years older than he is and whose stern countenance frightens most people into doing what he tells them. He was rock solid.

When Alan came to me with *Another Country*, I was immediately enthusiastic. There were, however, two problems. First, he wanted Marek Kanievska to direct it. Marek had done a lot of television work but this would be his first feature film. I don't like working with what I consider to be untried talent, and it was only because Alan was attached to the production that I was prepared to take the risk. Marek is highly talented, very intelligent and difficult only in the sense that he has a tenacious grip on what it is he wants to do. He is thin, high-spirited and articulate, and he brought to the film an intensity and a clarity of expression that was extremely impressive. I knew, however, that all that concentration and pent-up energy needed someone like Alan Marshall to keep it under control.

The second problem was that we could put up only a limited budget. The film tells the story of a man whose homosexuality leads him to become a traitor; it is set in the milieu of English upper-class life in the middle decades of the century; and it deals with themes of honour, treachery, sexuality, alienation and repression. This was not a reliable recipe for a mass-audience picture. We invested £735,000, which compares, for example, with the £2.6 million invested in *Local Hero* and the £8.5 million invested in *The Killing Fields*, to both of which we committed production funds at much the same time. The total budget for the film was only £1.6 million, the balance being made up of £500,000 from the National Film Finance Corporation, the deferment of our fees and the proceeds of a tax-leasing deal with Eastern Counties Newspapers. This fairly complex financing structure, even for such a low-budget picture, was typical of the way we liked to work.

The potential for conflict between our low budget and Marek's ambition was all too obvious, but, thanks to Alan Marshall's iron hand, at the end of the day it worked very well: the film was spectacular, packing in a huge amount of value from the exteriors shot at Oxford University while maintaining the intensity and intimacy of the original stage-bound drama. It was finished on schedule and on budget.

The third film-maker I became close to at this time was John Boorman. Dickie Attenborough and David Puttnam had spoken highly of John and wanted Goldcrest to make films with him. David Norris, an old friend of Boorman's, arranged a meeting.

John has bright eyes and a permanent grin – not really a grin of amusement so much as a grin of wonderment. He lifts your spirits when he walks into the room because you never know what he is going to say: even to the most standard question you will get the most unexpected answer. When you first meet him, he can seem strangely incoherent. He has a halting way of speaking which almost amounts to a stutter. You sense that his brain is working well ahead of his mouth. It takes a while to get used to, but once you're in tune with it, and can catch the complexity and awkward precision of his thinking, he becomes a fascinating person to be with. I was captivated by him.

When he came to my office in July 1982, he had several projects in mind. One was called *Little Nemo* (later changed to *Dream One*), which he had developed with the young French film-maker Arnaud Selignac;

one was co-written with Neil Jordan and called *Broken Dreams*; and the third was *The Emerald Forest*. Ten years before, John had come across a short newspaper article, no more than a snippet, which he had cut out and put into his file of ideas. The article told the story of a Peruvian engineer whose seven-year-old son had been lost in the jungle. The father went to look for him every year for ten years. When finally he tracked him down he discovered that the boy was living happily with an Indian tribe and, believing that it was too late to bring him back to civilization, he chose to let him stay. John was interested in the human story; in the clash of cultures; in the destruction of the Indians' way of life; in the moral problems associated with commercial development; in the role primitive cultures have in the modern world; and in the ties of family and kinship. All these were thrown up by this deceptively simple story. In particular, he was committed to the idea of using the film to bring home to a wide audience the consequences of the appalling destruction of the rainforest in the Amazon. The story and the message appealed to me greatly.

As a show of good faith, and as an inducement to get John to bring *The Emerald Forest* to us, I also expressed interest in *Little Nemo*. But the third project, *Broken Dreams*, I found incomprehensible and turned down.

Our first encounter led to further meetings in Ireland and, in early November 1982, in California, where John and his co-writer Rospo Pallenberg went through the *Emerald Forest* story with me in much greater detail. We met in a hotel room. John had a blank yellow pad in front of him, and he and Rospo blocked out the sequences which would form the basic structure of the film. First there was the opening scene, in which the parents take the family out for a picnic and where you get the first impact of the rainforest. It ends when the boy is abducted by the Indians. That accounts for maybe six minutes of the picture. Then John would say, 'The next section will be the boy growing up, learning about the ways of the Indians. And the third section will be the father going about his life, building a dam. The fourth section will be . . .' And so he went on, building up the narrative and discussing with Rospo the characters of all the people involved. John would suggest one thing, Rospo would add another, and I would sit there, fairly silent most of the time. It is very intensive work and you cannot do it for hours on end: you have to break every now and then, let your mind freshen up a little, then go back to it. John and Rospo might spend four or five hours on it one day, and then the next they would go off and talk to a professor of ecology at the University of Southern California to get some ideas about what the rainforest really is; or they would look at Indian costumes; or they would consult an anthropologist. The process went on day after day until they had the whole picture sketched out and Rospo could go away and start writing. It was the first time I had ever been invited to sit in on this early stage in the life of a film. I had never sought the privilege before because I did not think that it was my business, but John is very open about ideas and is happy to have everyone's opinion.

The only area to which I made any contribution was in the discussion of language. How does the audience understand what the Indians are saying to each other? In what language are they going to be speaking? This problem dogged the film throughout the production, indeed right up until it opened. I could see from the outset that there would be tremendous commercial implications, as well as creative ones, arising out of our decision, for most audiences, especially in America, detest sub-titles. On the other hand, film-makers detest Indians who speak American English.

(We actually made two versions and, when the film was finished, we tested them simultaneously in the same multiplex cinema, with two identically chosen sample audiences. To John's great relief, we found from the test cards that it was much more believable for the Indians to be speaking their own language with subtitles than for them to be speaking English.)

Those few days working on *The Emerald Forest* were absolutely fasci-nating, but they were not the reason I was in LA. I was there, with Dickie, to assist Columbia in the preparations for the opening of *Gandhi*.

Chapter Thirteen
Crowned with Glory

Eberts: *Gandhi* opened on 30 November 1982. The documentation for the distribution deal with Columbia had been completed about a year before, and the film had actually been delivered, following a prolonged period of post-production, in May. Columbia decided, however, to delay the opening until all the youth pictures that traditionally dominate the summer season at the US box office were safely out of the way. This was a wise decision, as in that year they included *E.T.*, *Poltergeist* and *Raiders of the Lost Ark*. The delay also enabled Marvin Antonowsky's team plenty of time to prepare what was to be a complicated launch.

Columbia had fixed upon a two-part strategy: the film would be released at more or less the same time in as many territories as possible, to take the maximum advantage of the publicity that it was bound to attract, but within each territory it would open initially in only a small number of showcase cinemas. In order to translate public awareness into want-to-see, a film like *Gandhi* has to be handled very carefully. People may have heard of it and to some degree may be interested in it, but for them to want to go and see it there has to be something more: they have to be persuaded by radio, newspapers, television and, most of all, by word of mouth.

Word of mouth is a key concept in film marketing. If a film disappoints its audience they will speak badly of it, and within a week all their friends will have got the message that it's not worth spending money on. Such a movie – recent examples include mega-budget productions like *Howard the Duck* and *Ishtar* – can open in the States with more than 1,000 prints and huge amounts of advertising, take reasonable money from unsuspecting fans on the first weekend and then die. On the other hand, if a film satisfies its audience and the word of mouth is good – for example, *Chariots of Fire* – it can improve its takings over a period of weeks as more and more happy customers persuade their families and friends to give it a try. In the case of yet another category of films, of which *Gandhi* was one, the audience may have no expectations at all. Indeed, initially we didn't have an audience: *Gandhi* was not exactly a natural box-office draw for the American public and Ben Kingsley was an unknown. So Columbia's first job was to create an audience; then let the film work its magic; then have the first audiences go out and tell their friends about it; then, as demand increased, slowly widen the release, trying to keep the film's availability matched to its growing word-of-mouth. Eventually, if all went well, it would end up in the same place as a mainstream movie with well-known stars: a 1,000-print nationwide release. But it would have got there through astute marketing, which is relatively cheap, not by blanket advertising, which is very expensive. Indeed, had Columbia tried to open *Gandhi* across the nation from the start, the figures on the first weekend would probably have been so bad that the cinema-owners would have dropped it long before its audience had a chance to build.

To get the word of mouth going, Columbia used the summer months to screen the film to hundreds of invited audiences: journalists, religious leaders, students, athletes, politicians – anyone whose favourable response might carry some weight. They then opened it at only four cinemas, in New York, Washington, Los Angeles and Toronto. Then, as the good word began to get out, Dickie Attenborough, Ben Kingsley and Martin Sheen did radio chat shows, newspaper and magazine interviews, appearances on television and lectures at colleges and universities, all the while generating greater interest, as, at the same time, Columbia increased the number of prints and the film began to go wide. This release pattern, known as platforming, was followed in every major territory.

In most cases films are released territory by territory over a period of a year or so. It is not uncommon, for example, for fans in the UK to wait six, eight, or even twelve months for a film that has been a big success in the States to make it across the Atlantic. Not only do they have the frustration of waiting, but they often have to put up with prints that have already done the rounds of American cinemas and are consequently not in the best condition. But because *Gandhi* was a 'world event' (the phrase used by Columbia on the posters), we wanted it to open in all the major markets at the same time. This is not actually physically possible. What you can do is bunch all the openings into a few weeks, and even that takes considerable planning. Gala premières had been arranged in Delhi, London, Washington, New York, Toronto and LA, all within the space of seven days. Invited guests included local dignitaries, showbiz celebrities and leading figures from the industry. At the centre of each event was Dickie, and with him was a little gang of happy – if, for most of the time, exhausted – travellers that included Dickie's wife Sheila, myself and Fiona, Ben Kingsley and his wife, and, at various points in the proceedings, Martin Sheen, line producer Terry Clegg and other members of the cast and crew. There were probably eight or ten people in the core group and another eight or ten who joined us along the way.

The trip consumed a large amount of our personal energies and a small but significant proportion of the millions that Columbia was to spend on launching the film. By the time they had paid for the private planes, the first-class air fares, the Concordes, the hotel rooms, the taxis and limousines, the champagne receptions and the cocktail parties, they would not have seen much change out of $500,000. (There were times during the making of the film when I would have gone down on my knees for that kind of money.)

We left London for Delhi on Monday, 29 November, and that same evening attended a reception hosted by the British Ambassador at which Mrs Gandhi was guest of honour. I remember my feeling of pride on being introduced to her, only to have her stride right past me, after the briefest of acknowledging glimpses, to speak to a much more important, and no doubt useful, guest over my shoulder. The next day was filled with press interviews and a lunch given for us by the National Film Development Corporation of India. That evening saw the film's world première, in the presence of Mrs Gandhi, many Indian government ministers and an audience of about 2,000. This was a great moment for Dickie, but it was also an anxious one: most Indians had their doubts about the film and many had been very critical of the fact that a foreigner had been allowed to make it. Indeed, while the audience's reaction was enthusiastic, the next morning's press was decidedly mixed.

At 3 a.m. we got on a plane back to London, where, that same evening, we had the European première in Leicester Square, attended by the Prince and Princess of Wales. The British audience, like the Indian one, was very enthusiastic, but this time we had the added pleasure of getting rave reviews. The following morning we took the Concorde to Washington for another opening and another reception, held in one of the major museums and sponsored by Coca-Cola, which had recently bought Columbia Pictures. The next day we flew to New York in a private plane – no one would dream of flying commercial – for another opening. The next night we were in Toronto and the following day in Los Angeles. In seven days we had opened in six cities on three continents.

In each place the proceeds from the première went to charity. In India it was in aid of various causes including the Mountbatten Trust, an agency for the prevention and control of leprosy. In London the money went to the Nehru Memorial Trust, the Variety Club and UNICEF. In Toronto the proceeds were shared between the Muscular Dystrophy Association and the Canadian Diabetics Association. In Washington, New York and Los Angeles all the proceeds went to UNICEF. In each city the local UNICEF chapter organized a reception, somehow managing to transform dull hotel ballrooms into festive gatherings. In New York, Danny Kaye, UNICEF's ambassador-at-large, was the master of ceremonies and made the whole evening quite extraordinary: very funny, very generous-spirited and very uplifting. Altogether, these charity premières raised nearly £2 million.

The good reviews in London were echoed in Canada and the States, and I began to be a little less anxious about how the film would be received by the general public. You always worry, no matter how much faith you have in a picture, that, because you have so much riding on it, your judgement is impaired. With *Gandhi*, that suspicion was reinforced by the fact that, in the industry as a whole, while people applauded Dickie's tenacity in getting the film off the ground, they were overwhelmingly sceptical about its chances of finding an audience.

There are many films that have earned wonderful reviews, that have great casts, good scripts and fine direction, and that have simply flopped. There are several such examples every year. Just as frequently the opposite occurs: a terrible film, with a lousy script, poor acting and bad direction becomes a blockbuster. So you are never comfortable. You don't trust your own instincts. In fact, you actively distrust them. The anxiety gets worse as the opening night approaches, and is relieved only when you see the first box-office figures for yourself. We knew that *Gandhi* was not the sort of film immediately to attract the young people who account for 80 per cent of the cinema-going public. In fact, it was a film for an audience that no longer goes to the cinema very often. And it was a long film, which meant that it had fewer screenings per day, reducing the potential ticket sales. All we could do was promote it like mad and hope that an audience was sufficiently motivated by want-to-see to go down to the cinemas and buy their tickets.

Every day, every cinema in every major market provides its distributors with exact details of the money earned at the box office. In fact, most major cinemas in major cities can provide the figures for each performance. So we could ring up, say, the Ziegfeld in New York, where *Gandhi* was playing, talk to the manager and get the take for the first showing, the second showing and the third showing, as well as the daily, weekend and weekly totals. The studio distributing the picture does that every day, in every cinema, for every one of its films. Indeed, the numbers are exchanged between studios so that they can track each other's movies and get an idea of what's happening in the market overall. The head of each studio, on Saturday and Sunday mornings, gets shoved under his door at home a chart showing the previous night's box-office grosses, so that he knows how his pictures are doing even when he is not in the office. Those figures, or approximations of them, are printed in the trade papers every week, so there are no secrets about a film's performance.

The early returns are examined minutely, because experience has shown that certain patterns are followed from which you can tell very quickly if the picture is going to do well or badly. For example, you can compare your takings with the takings of another, similar film at the same cinema over the same period. Sometimes you are wrong: a film starts off slowly, then builds a head of steam and does better than you thought, or it has a terrific opening and then falls off very quickly. But generally speaking, you can make that kind of prediction fairly early on. We were both pleased and relieved to find that most of our early performances were playing to full houses. *Gandhi* was going to be OK.

By the beginning of 1983, Columbia, who were doing a terrific job (Dickie had been absolutely right in his estimation of Frank Price and Marvin Antonowsky), started to open *Gandhi* in more cinemas, gradually going wide as it became apparent that not only were we building a good audience but that we had a very strong chance of getting Oscar nominations. Newspapers, magazines, television shows and radio programmes were full of *Gandhi*, and every week the trades announced new house records in the cinemas where we were playing. It was a good time to get a television deal.

I started negotiations with Columbia themselves, since they were doing such a good job on the theatrical release and were very keen to get network and syndication rights. Our discussions proceeded slowly at first, partly because we had yet to establish what the asking price should be. We were not sure whether to stick with our original target of $10 million, or to come down to somewhere around $8 million. To test the market, I decided to make a number of calls to the networks. I was surprised to learn, when I called CBS, that Columbia had already offered them the film. I informed them, as calmly as I could, that Columbia did not own any television rights to *Gandhi* and had no authority to approach them. When I put the phone down I was, naturally, absolutely furious. Columbia were not only talking out of turn, but, by their approach to

CBS, could well have jeopardized our chances of making the best possible sale. I was particularly worried that they may have put *Gandhi* together with other films and offered them as a package, using *Gandhi* as the bell-cow. This is something that happens all the time: a studio will put three good films and ten duds together, using the good films as leverage to get a decent price overall. Naturally, since they have to share this income with the producers of the films in question – typically they take a 30 per cent fee, but it varies from contract to contract – they will apportion the revenue among all the films in whatever way enables them to retain the most profit. Since they will have been able to negotiate a higher commission on a dud than on a good film, where the producer would most likely have had a stronger hand, they will be inclined to allocate the highest possible price to the former and the lowest possible price to the latter, enabling them, as the seller of the combined package, to keep a bigger share. Not only is this unfair to the producer of the good film, but once the low figure has been mentioned it becomes the benchmark for all further negotiations.

I called Frank Price and Marvin Antonowsky and demanded an explanation. They shifted and squirmed and said that, in fact, they had not been actively negotiating, but had only implied to CBS that, should it happen that they did get the rights, they could then include *Gandhi* in the package they were currently offering. Their explanation certainly did not satisfy me: when you are in the early stages of a deal there is only a marginal difference between 'actively negotiating' and 'implying'. And as far as CBS was concerned there was no difference at all. When I called them, my asking price of $8–10 million was met with derisive laughter. The figures they had been considering for the Columbia package as a whole did not come anywhere near to justifying such a price for *Gandhi* on its own. From that point, CBS's interest was lukewarm at best.

Fortunately, no approach had been made by Columbia, at least not to my knowledge, to ABC or NBC. They were interested, but, again, not falling over themselves to pay the price I was asking. This was before the full results of the wider theatrical release were known, and they professed still to be unsure how much appeal *Gandhi* had. Also, at that time, the networks were beginning to realize that feature films were not getting the ratings that they had in the past. People who were really interested in a film now had a number of ways to see it long before it came on network television: in the cinema, on video, or on their pay-cable service. (In fact, the market for feature films on US network television has now virtually disappeared. The decline has been especially noticeable in the last four or five years, and it started at about the time that I was selling *Gandhi*.)

The biggest network interest I had was from ABC, who were considering $8 million for a virtually unlimited number of runs over a ten-year period. NBC were considering a price of about $6 million for one run, with an option to acquire a second run for $2 million. The network interest, tentative as it was, gave me a range of prices to work on. Our $10 million target included pay-cable and syndication, so ABC's figure for network rights alone was not far from the mark.

Matters improved considerably when I opened negotiations with the biggest American cable channel, HBO, whom I knew well from having done deals with them in the past. I was very friendly with their top executives, Michael Fuchs and Steve Schaffer. By that time, Neil Braun had joined them from IFI, where he had been involved with *Gandhi* from the beginning. So I had a lot of allies at the company and their first response was sufficiently encouraging for me to start revising the price upwards. A further boost came from Universal, who were very active in the television market. Gene Jaquinto, head of their cable-television division, and Mel Harris, head of the Universal television business overall, were very keen to get the rest of the competition out of the way and were inching up the price day by day. We quickly got into the range of $13 million. Emboldened by *Gandhi*'s ever-improving theatrical grosses, I told them that perhaps I might consider $15 million, but to settle for that I had to have a piece of the back end: a share of the future syndication revenue.

Then, in February, the Academy Award nominations were announced. *Gandhi* was named in an astonishing eleven categories. Once again we hit the headlines in the trades, and my phone rang even more insistently. Competition for the television rights was getting fierce and the price was going up. It was thus with an easy conscience that I left, with my wife and children, for a skiing holiday in the French Alps.

Every year we went to a small hotel in Courchevel, and every year for the previous seven years I had been pestered with telephone calls: from Goldcrest, from IFI, from the studios, from film-makers, from shareholders, the board or James Lee, with business that only I could deal with. It had become a family joke that there was never going to be an evening without interruptions – usually five or six such business calls a night. I spent my vacations jumping up from the dining table and disappearing into the little telephone booth in the hall of the hotel. There was a time when I didn't mind, when the interests of my career or the company were always paramount, but I had now reached the stage where

I did not want to have every evening, whether I was on holiday or not, destroyed by calls from America and London. So I was not in a particularly benevolent mood when I had a call from Jerry Perenchio, joint owner, with Norman Lear, of Embassy Pictures.

Jerry and Norman had been partners for years, primarily in television, where Norman had an unrivalled reputation as a producer of prime-time shows, including *Mary Hartman, Mary Hartman, The Jeffersons* and *All In the Family*. Jerry had started out as an agent and had become one of the most successful entrepreneurs in show business: promoting the first Ali–Frazier fight and founding the first subscription television company, On-TV. In 1981, Jerry and Norman had jointly purchased Embassy, the company that had distributed a number of our early feature films, with the intention of combining Embassy's feature-film operation with their television business to build a new major studio. However, they had not actually achieved much on the feature-film side in the two years since they had taken over, and this had hindered their efforts to establish a television-packaging operation that would sell films to the networks and to the syndication market.

Gandhi was a prestige film, a proven critical and commercial success, launched with a huge sum of money – it was by now being advertised all over America – and to which, most unusually, television rights were still available. It was just the kind of film they needed to head up a package and make a big impact in the television-distribution business in the States.

I had met Jerry a year or two before at the Cannes Film Festival, but I didn't know him well. Norman, on the other hand, had been very helpful to us and had been a great supporter of *Gandhi*. He had been invited to an early screening of the film and had been absolutely overwhelmed by it. Norman was thus already a confirmed *Gandhi* fan, and he and Jerry had no difficulty in agreeing that this was exactly the kind of lead title that they needed.

On the telephone, Jerry was very direct and very open. He said simply that they wanted to acquire the television rights to *Gandhi* in the United States, and he asked whether I was prepared to do a deal on the phone. I replied that I was already in advanced negotiations with two networks, as well as with HBO and Universal, and that unless he was very serious and was prepared to move extremely quickly, I felt it was probably wrong to get involved in fresh negotiations at this stage. He replied, 'What's your asking price?' Almost without thinking, I blurted out: 'Twenty million dollars.'

About an hour earlier, I had had a telephone call from IFI, our partners in *Gandhi*, pressing me very hard to accept the $13 million offer from Universal. The previous week, before leaving London, I had been instructed by the Goldcrest board to accept the first $15 million offer that I could get. Both parties, very nervous about having all those millions slip through our fingers, wanted a deal closed within a matter of days.

I knew that Jerry had the reputation of being a gambler; of being a man who did not take no for an answer; and of being a man who was prepared to follow instinct rather than what might appear to be good business judgement. And, of course, I knew that, with this combination of characteristics, he had been very successful. There was something in the way he talked on the phone that convinced me that he would go for it; that this was the man who was going to do the deal. When he heard the price he didn't flinch or pause. All he said was, 'I'll get back to you in half an hour.'

So I called IFI immediately (Goldcrest's London office being closed at that time of night) and said, 'I'm talking $20 million to Perenchio. I believe I can get the deal done. Don't ask me to accept the Universal offer just yet. Give me another day at least.' IFI, of course, were worried that Universal would go away. Lured, no doubt, by the prospect of all that money, they put caution ever so slightly to one side and said, 'Fine, one more day, but if you blow it, on your head be it.'

I returned to the dinner table, where I was severely criticized by Fiona, who by this time was at the end of her tether: this performance, back and forth between the table and the phone booth, had been going on for seven years. Indeed, my trips to the phone booth had very nearly become a marriage breaker. I had promised that this year it wouldn't happen.

Jerry called back in half an hour as promised. 'Give me twenty-four hours,' he said. 'I need to speak to Norman one more time.'

I said, 'Jerry you're putting me in a difficult position, because I have just told my people that I'm now in negotiation with you and they have pleaded with me not to lose the other offer. Can you get back to me in an hour?'

'I'll try.'

I knew now that Jerry definitely had a gut feel for the film and was determined to get it. Of course, he hadn't done the sums; there had been no time. He just wanted this picture as a leader for his package of films, and he wanted to get Embassy on the front page of the trades. I knew he would call Norman and, within an hour, it would be settled one way or the other.

I returned to the table and tried to make conversation with our guests, but my ear was cocked for that return call. Sure enough, as promised, Jerry was back within the hour: 'You have the $20 million. What are the terms?'

I said, 'I want telex confirmation by the time our office opens tomorrow morning; I want $5 million paid by the end of this week; and I want the other $15 million by the end of June.' This was all off the top of my head, made up as I was wiping the crumbs from my mouth with my napkin. Jerry just said, 'Fine, you've got it.'

I put down the phone and didn't know whether to call IFI immediately or go back to the table. It all seemed a little bizarre, and not entirely credible. I called New York and, once they had got over the thrill of hearing the magic number confirmed, they said, 'Well, if the telex is not there tomorrow morning at the opening of London business you've got to go ahead and close the deal at Universal'. They need not have worried: next morning the telex was there; by Friday we had the $5 million and by 30 June we had the other $15 million.

I went back to the table, thoroughly pleased with myself and intent on finishing my dinner. Of course, from that moment the phone didn't stop ringing: everybody – Goldcrest, IFI, Embassy, Universal, HBO, Dickie, James Lee – wanted to know what was going on. In fact, the phone didn't stop ringing for the rest of the holiday. Fiona was hardly speaking to me.

For their $20 million – an unheard-of sum for a single-picture deal – Embassy got all North American television rights: network, pay-cable and syndication. There appeared to be no way to recoup that money from those markets but, incredibly, within a couple of months Embassy sold all the television rights on, at a profit, to HBO. Unbeknown to me, and maybe to Jerry (although he is a hell of a smart operator), the two major pay-cable companies in the States, HBO and Showtime, were locked in a battle to sign up exclusive film deals with the major studios. Showtime had made a breakthrough, and astounded the industry, by signing a five-year deal with Paramount. This coup on the part of their smaller rival was a tremendous blow to HBO's pride. They panicked, and Embassy's pay-cable salesman, Hal Gaba, a very astute deal-maker, seized on their insecurity to sell them the package of *Gandhi* television rights for a whopping $23 million.

So Embassy made a profit on the film, even though they were then never able to use it for the purpose for which it was intended. I would find it hard to believe that HBO ever recouped. A network might have paid $6–8 million and HBO might have made $2–2.5 million in syndication, leaving them with up to $12 million to write off against their own pay-TV business. The top price we would ever have got out of pay-TV was maybe $6 million, so I can't see how they could have made the figures add up. They overpaid. Embassy had overpaid. We were ecstatic.

The Academy Award nominations are published at about 6 a.m. LA time. On that same day, the afternoon papers carry advertisements for whichever nominated films are currently on release, with the word 'Oscar' showing very prominently. Throughout February and March 1983 the legend 'winner of eleven Academy Award nominations' dominated the *Gandhi* posters. This in itself was a great boost to the film's box-office performance. If it then went on to win Oscars in the major categories, we could add maybe $25 million to the box office in the States and as much again in the international markets. (How much an Oscar is worth to a picture depends on the timing and pattern of the release: Columbia had all along been planning to make *Gandhi*'s widest release coincide with the awards in March.)

The Academy of Motion Picture Arts and Sciences is made up of around 5,000 members, all of whom are in some way involved in the film business. Within the Academy there are sections: the actors' section, the directors' section, the cinematographers' section, the production designers' section and so on, and it is from these sections that the nominations in each category are made. The nominations for Best Picture are voted on by all members.

During the period leading up to the nominations, the studios advertise like mad in the trade papers, trying to catch the attention of the Academy members, inviting them to free screenings and pointing out the virtues of this or that aspect of their film. After the nominations, the intensity of the advertising increases. The studios whose films have been nominated have six weeks to persuade the members of the Academy to vote in their favour for the awards themselves.

The impact of this kind of advertising, directly courting the Academy members, is probably over-estimated. Most Academicians, who after all are seasoned professionals, vote out of conviction and are not swayed by the advertisements. But the rewards of winning in a major category are potentially so great that the expenditure is always thought to be worthwhile. Columbia bombarded the trades with advertisements on *Gandhi*'s behalf.

The whole exercise may look like a circus from the outside, but within the industry, and especially within Hollywood, Oscars not only boost the box office, but carry great prestige. Cynics who know nothing about the business probably believe that it's all fixed. It is not. No one other than the auditors and a few essential members of the organizing committee has any idea, before they open those envelopes, who the winners are. The Oscars are a well-kept secret in a town which is not famous for keeping secrets.

As the awards night approaches you more or less lose consciousness. You become so enveloped in this miasma of advertising, promotion and excitement that you completely forget about the rest of the world. I probably did not even look at a newspaper in the final week – unless it was to read about the nominations.

Dickie and I had arrived in LA several days before the awards evening, partly because he had to make a lot of publicity appearances and partly because I was supposed to be attending to business on other films, including, for example, *The Emerald Forest*. But from the moment that we got there, our whole lives were completely taken up by rumours about who was likely to win, how the votes were going, what the buzz was around town and what the Academy's leanings were. All of which made not a whit of difference to what actually happened, but everyone, especially the nominees, gave everything credence; they had to have something to talk about, if only to relieve the tension.

Gandhi was already considered to be the front runner. But as our main competition we had *E.T.* and, although the Academy does not normally honour films which are clearly aimed at a mass audience, here was a case where such a film would be a worthy Oscar winner: it had a great script, it had a very unusual idea, it had a terrific director and it was beautifully made. The fact that it was the antithesis of *Gandhi*, appealing to a different audience, on a different level, by different means, generated a lot of animated debate and curiosity in the studio commissaries, fashionable restaurants and other meeting places of the Hollywood community. For me it generated a lot of anxiety.

The awards show goes out live all around the world: at 6 p.m. in LA, 9 p.m. on the East Coast, 2 a.m. in Europe, 10 a.m. in Australia and 9 a.m. in Japan. And people do actually stay up to watch it at all hours of the night. To meet those times, preparations for the ceremony start quite early in the afternoon, which means that your whole day is not only wired up with nerves and adrenalin but also weirdly out of sync. At 1 p.m. you put on your dinner jacket; at 2 p.m. you comb your hair for the eighth time. You leave the hotel at 3 p.m., invariably in a limousine – no self-respecting nominee would ever appear in a taxi or, God forbid, drive his own car. You make small talk as you head (in those days) for the Dorothy Chandler Pavilion, in the Los Angeles Music Center, seven or eight miles from Beverly Hills on the road to downtown Los Angeles.

From the small hill on which the Music Center is perched, thousands of limousines can be seen inching their way towards it through the traffic. The limos., like the dinner jackets, are of course rented.

Inside the building you are served either mineral water or a glass of warm Californian champagne. This you sip from a plastic beaker, which is in all too obvious contrast to the elegant surroundings and your style of dress. It also seems odd for the time of day. But so unreal is the atmosphere that you just go along with it. Nothing would have surprised me on that afternoon: if Gandhi himself had appeared swigging champagne from a bottle I would only have said how thrilled I was to meet him. That's what I was saying to everybody else.

You mingle in the foyer for about an hour, then suddenly you are shepherded to your seat. The show is about to start.

All the nominees and the really important people in the business – the major stars and the major players – sit in the first ten or fifteen rows, where the cameras can get a good look at them. The rest of us sit at the back.

The ceremonies have two curious features. First, no one walks up to collect an award: everyone runs, as if afraid that by walking they might hold up proceedings. Second, since it's a live show and since the camera is very often trained on the audience, the organizers go to great efforts to make sure that no seat is ever seen to be empty. If you leave to go to the toilet, as soon as you stand up someone else comes across and sits in your seat. That someone else is usually a college student, hired for the evening. Male students are given a dinner jacket, female students a gown, and their only job is to make sure that those seats are always filled. They stand in lines in the aisles, monitoring the rows, alert for gaps.

If you are the guest of a studio, you are bound to be seated with people you know. There will be a huddle of you together, with the head of the studio at the centre, so it is a very friendly as well as a very exciting evening. And, of course, it is very partisan too: you root noisily for your picture. (If your studio is involved with more than one nominated picture you have to be very careful not to be seen to be favouring one over the other. In 1983, Columbia had no other nominations, so we were all wildly in favour of *Gandhi*.)

It is a very long evening, not finishing until six hours or so after you arrive, and the major awards don't come until towards the end. Prior to that there are a host of technical awards, for sound effects, optical effects, costumes and so on. If a film collects a lot of these so-called minor awards – no award is minor as far as the recipients are concerned – it is likely to do very well when the major awards start being given out later on in the evening. So we got very nervous when *E.T.* won a spate of awards early on and *Gandhi* won none. For an hour and a half we were perspiring with anxiety. On so many occasions in the past a hot favourite has been passed over in favour of some other movie. Indeed, it had happened to Steven Spielberg himself and there was reason to think that this year the Academy members might decide at last to acknowledge his extraordinary contribution to motion-picture arts. At the back, my friends from Columbia and I were subdued and at the same time flushed with anticipation. At the front, Dickie, Ben Kingsley and the other *Gandhi* nominees were squirming.

Then we won our first award. Everyone leapt up, screaming with relief, hugging and kissing. Then another, and another. The one I wanted to have, from a selfish point of view, was Best Picture, since that was the only category that reflected my efforts as financier. But far more I wanted Dickie to win Best Director, as a reward for nearly twenty years of struggle, of good-humoured patience and of an unwavering commitment, not to mention the artistry that he put into the film. We won both. Indeed, the Best Picture award is the last to be announced, and by the time the envelope was opened we had already won Best Actor, Best Original Screenplay and Best Director. In those circumstances, it would have been extraordinary not to have won Best Picture as well. In the end, with further awards for cinematography, art direction, editing and costume design, we won a total of eight Oscars.

The exultation is great, but the relief is greater. I hadn't slept for two or three nights; I hadn't eaten properly; I hadn't been able to put my mind to anything else. Oddly enough, winning in itself is not so important. We could not pretend that *Gandhi* was better than *E.T.* They are both great films but so different that comparison is impossible. Nor did we think that by winning the awards we had beaten *E.T.* in any way. The pressure is not the pressure to win, but the pressure to have the whole thing done with, to find out.

Before the ceremony everyone has planned a victory party. Of course, only one can be a true victory party: the other four become simple celebrations. But at those four celebrations there is little sense of disappointment. For all that is said about Hollywood being a bitchy and cruel community, the fact is that people in the film business are by and large extremely generous in their praise for good work. Our triumph was a source of pleasure to everybody, not just to us.

Our victory party had been planned at a little restaurant between downtown Los Angeles and the Hilton Hotel in Beverly Hills, where, later in the evening, the Governor's Ball, to which we were all invited, was to be held. There was only one public telephone in the restaurant and we queued to place our calls back to England. Of course everyone already knew the good news, having sat up through the early hours of the morning watching it all on television.

A Channel 4 documentary crew had followed us throughout the shooting of *Gandhi* and had been at the openings in Delhi, London, Washington, Toronto and New York. Now here they were training their cameras on us at our celebration party. The big lights were on, people were being interviewed, champagne was being poured, and there was an extraordinary atmosphere that combined disbelief with I-told-you-so.

While our party, and the four almost-victory parties, were going on, there were other celebrations in Hollywood. Every year, for example, Irving Lazar throws a big party at Spago for celebrities who are not going to the awards ceremony, and that too is covered live on television. In fact, throughout the night, wherever you are, even in the back of the limo. taking you to the Governor's Ball, you can watch the Oscar celebrations on television – parties, clips from the awards, interviews with stars, and all the paraphernalia of the media circus that surrounds the event. On the way to the Hilton we saw pre-recorded interviews of ourselves which caused great hilarity. Dickie went from ebullient charm to tearful earnestness at the drop of a camera. He was just wonderful. When you think of the work he put into it, it can only have been the greatest moment of his professional life. Eight Oscars made an extraordinary, fairytale ending to a twenty-year saga.

The Governor's Ball was absolutely packed: a tuxedo'd version of Delhi airport. The tables were all squeezed together to make room for the dance floor and the band played so loudly you couldn't talk. The head of every studio was there, each displaying his power by the array of major stars at his table. Everyone I met would give me a big Hollywood embrace, congratulate me, make sure he knew what my name was and, equally important, make sure I knew what his name was.

Among the many people I bumped into that night was Jerry Perenchio, whom I had not seen since we did the *Gandhi* television deal on the telephone. He was obviously very happy with the eight Oscars. As we exchanged pleasantries, he nodded wisely, as if to emphasize that his judgement had been vindicated. Probably even as we were talking he was working out how much the Oscars would add to the price he was asking from HBO.

We stayed up until 6 a.m., drinking champagne, before crashing out in our hotels. The next day, we gathered for a special lunch at the Beverly

Hills Hotel, given by Dickie for some of the *Gandhi* crew and their families. Dickie wept his way through another emotional speech, and then we had a picture taken, with all the statuettes piled up on the table in front of us. That picture, and others like it, appeared on the front pages of newspapers everywhere. In the world at large Ben Kingsley was newly famous and Dickie was more famous than ever. In the smaller world of the film industry, Goldcrest, if it wasn't before, was now recognized as an important player.

Chapter Fourteen

Going Hollywood

'Everyone went bananas after Gandhi. *It was wonderful on the one hand, but it was fatal on the other. We should all have had dark glasses on when we looked at it.' – James Lee*

Ilott: The success of *Gandhi* changed everything. The eight Oscars, following the four for *Chariots of Fire* in 1982, delighted the British press, which seized upon Goldcrest as a patriotic flag to wave and fêted the company as the 'conquerer of Hollywood'. Exultant puffs and profiles of Dickie Attenborough, David Puttnam, James Lee and Jake Eberts appeared in every kind of publication every week in the early summer months of 1983. The company's public standing rose to extraordinary, and, in the eyes of rivals in Wardour Street, ludicrous, heights. From being merely a name in the shadows of celebrity, Goldcrest now, at least as far as the popular press was concerned, *was* the British film industry.

Naturally, a position of such pre-eminence could not be sustained for long. A few warning bells were sounded, for example, by finance director John Chambers, who had lived through the rise and fall of British Lion and the Deeley–Spikings regime at EMI (responsible for both the very successful *The Deer Hunter* and the disastrous *Honky Tonk Freeway*) and who voiced the opinion that 'in five years' time it won't be like it is now: we'll either be three times as big and taken over by someone else, or we'll be broke'. But the warnings were half-hearted and all but inaudible amidst the clamour of success. Indeed, the more that Attenborough, Puttnam, Lee and Eberts (the 'Gang of Four', in Lee's phrase) tried to curb the media adulation, and the greater the modesty with which they clothed each succeeding interview, the more they contributed to the myth of Goldcrest's invincibility.

For the awful thing was that, while the media hype was, as ever, full of exaggeration, its essence was all true. In Wardour Street, however much Britain's film community may have resented the fact, Goldcrest did stand head and shoulders above the rest. The calibre of its directors and staff, the reputation of the film-makers with which it was associated, the quality of its output, the energy that had driven its extraordinarily rapid growth, the acumen and self-confidence that had, for example, snatched the *Gandhi* television deal from the fist of the world's toughest marketplace, and the combination of nerve and financial sophistication that had not only sustained the production of *Gandhi* but had seen it turn a handsome profit, made the other British film companies, and especially the twin giants, EMI and Rank, look like plodders.

It was not only the cream of British film-makers who now submitted their work first to Goldcrest. In Hollywood the company was perceived, in the words of producer Jerome Hellman, to be 'a major motion-picture company, courageous lovers of film and backers of odd-ball projects if they had confidence that the people involved were good and serious'. Hellman, producer of *Midnight Cowboy*, *Coming Home* and *Mosquito Coast*, was one of a string of heavyweight independent American producers who now came knocking on the company's door. What they all admired was the apparent ease with which Goldcrest put before the public the kind of thoughtful, adult films – *Chariots*, *Gandhi*, *Local Hero* and soon *The Dresser* and *The Killing Fields* – that had become rare in a Hollywood in thrall to the teenage audience and obsessed with special effects. The studios, too, looked to Goldcrest as a possible partner for their difficult (i.e. less than sure-fire) projects. Scripts cascaded through the letter-box in Holland Park Avenue. Among them were *King David*, to be directed by Bruce Beresford and to star Richard Gere; *Mishima*, written and to be directed by Paul Schrader; *Falling in Love*, starring Meryl Streep and Robert De Niro; *Mosquito Coast*, to be produced by Jerry Hellman and directed by Peter Weir (at the time, Jack Nicholson was slated for the leading role, but it was later taken by Harrison Ford); *Birdy*, to be directed by Alan Parker and produced by Alan Marshall; *Legend*, to be directed by Ridley Scott; *Eleni*, to be directed by Peter Yates; *The Lightship*, starring Robert Duvall and Klaus Maria Brandauer; *Half Moon Street*, starring Michael Caine and Sigourney Weaver; and *Turtle Diary*, starring Ben Kingsley and Glenda Jackson. Goldcrest was no longer having to run to Hollywood, for Hollywood was beating its own path to the door at Holland Park Avenue.

(That most of these projects were turned down by Eberts, even though all were to find production finance elsewhere, is a good indicator of his caution in choosing projects. Don Cruickshank has remarked that it is hard to imagine how Eberts ever got away with the image of being 'the film-maker's friend', when, for every director he chose to back, there were at least a dozen he had rejected. That most films on the above list went on to lose money could also be taken as an indicator of Eberts's good judgement.)

At Holland Park Avenue the atmosphere was euphoric. Eberts, who is generally an easy man to get on with and whose policy was always to leave his lieutenants and their staff to do their work without interference, was variously respected, admired, loved or hero-worshipped, and at all levels in the company it was felt that under his leadership great things were in store. On Oscar night, whether with Dickie Attenborough in Hollywood or among Goldcrest's London staff, who gathered with James Lee in a wine bar around the corner from the office for a champagne celebration, or at Terry Clegg's house, where the rest of the *Gandhi* crew assembled for a party that went on through the night, the feeling was the same: that from now on anything was possible.

The shareholders, naturally, were mostly interested in the financial returns, and *Gandhi* was to be the first production to show the super profits that justify the high risk of film investment. Already, in the early summer of 1983, Chambers could predict a recoupment of about £11.5 million on GFI's and Pearson's £5 million outlay. This money, an altogether more serious sum – if a less spectacular rate of return – than the £844,000 recouped by *Chariots*, was to recapitalize GFI and sustain the company through the making of *The Killing Fields*. It was far and away the most successful investment – for all that it broke the risk-spreading, exposure-limiting criteria laid down in GFI's prospectus – that Goldcrest ever made.

'There was a sense of, yes, we really do have some rather talented people there and they do seem capable of judging the market, making the sort of films that we are pleased to see, rather proud of and that make money,' comments Pearson financial director, James Joll.

Nor were the shareholders entirely impervious to the choruses of praise that were being heaped upon the company. 'A lot of people say, what do you invest in, and you say, "Well, we invest in a widget manufacturer in South Devon and an engineering business in Halifax." Clearly it's a lot more interesting to say, "We invested in *Gandhi*." When Goldcrest was going well it wasn't a thing of which one was ashamed,' recalls Electra's Michael Stoddart.

However, there was, inevitably, a downside to all this. The Gang of Four may have been genuine in their self-deprecation, but they did not go so far as actually to refute the claims being made in the press on their behalf, for somewhere in there amongst the ballyhoo were more or less reflected the images they had of themselves, if not always of each other.

The danger, clearly, was that they, and the rest of the company, would start believing their own press. This may not have posed such a serious threat to Puttnam and Attenborough, who, with more than sixty years' experience in the business between them, had either (depending on your point of view) completely disappeared through the looking-glass of fame and now existed only as celebrities or, keeping an heroic grip on their true selves, had long since learned to turn media interest to their advantage without succumbing to its flattery. Either way, the fresh cascade of attention following the Oscars, whatever pleasure they may have derived from it, left them more or less unchanged. The same, however, could not be said of James Lee, nor, for different reasons, of Eberts.

The phenomenon of a person allowing his or her head to be turned by the glitz of the movies is so common that the industry has its own expression to describe it: 'going Hollywood'. It is arguable that, to a greater or lesser degree, everyone in the film business, however much they may deny it, has been seduced by its glamour. None, however, is as susceptible to going Hollywood as those whom the ballyhoo takes by surprise. They are outsiders mostly, people who have made their money or reputations in other fields and who arrive in the film business near the top rather than near the bottom of the heap. After years of anonymous toil they are easily seduced by the sheer pleasure, the apparently harmless fun, of being now and then illuminated by flashes of light from the media circus that surrounds the movies.

Unfortunately, the fun is far from harmless: if you are not completely in control of it – or immune, in the way that hardened professionals like Puttnam and Attenborough appear to be – it consumes you. As Lee now ruefully admits, it is 'the opposite of the Blarney Stone . . . when anybody touches it you are dead'. For outsiders – and there is a long, inglorious list of wealthy amateurs who have been attracted like moths to the glittering flames of showbiz only to retire, sooner rather than later, badly burned – are all too often firmly convinced that somehow they are more objective, more analytical, more businesslike, sharper, less inclined to self-delusion, than the average hyped-up and bullshitting Hollywood professional. Usually this is not true.

It wasn't true of James Lee. Puttnam, who admired Lee enormously (at one point even suggesting to Terry Semel that Lee could head up Warner Bros.' European operations) and saw in him exactly the kind of level-headed strategist and company-builder that he believed Goldcrest needed, and who held him to be of the type that is least vulnerable to the blandishments of filmbiz hype, was amazed to witness the change in him after *Gandhi*. 'James', he says, 'got show business like no one I have ever known in my life.'

Already less than thrilled with his new role at Pearson, Lee became besotted with Goldcrest.

As for Eberts, the success of *Gandhi* had a simpler and more obvious consequence: it led to a reappraisal, by himself and others, of his market value. He was being paid $120,000 a year at Goldcrest, with the opportunity, should the company do well, of earning additional bonuses of up to $60,000. His family trust also had 10 per cent shareholdings in both Goldcrest Films and Goldcrest Television. Even today this would be a substantial level of remuneration in Wardour Street. It paled, however, by comparison with the rates being paid in Hollywood. As Lee notes: 'Jake returned from the Oscars . . . and he had been wined and dined and been told that he was brilliant. He saw his value as a million dollars a year, and he believed that he could get it.'

A vast salary was not only something that Eberts believed he could now command, it was something that he desperately needed. Although he tended to keep his personal affairs to himself, it was no secret to either Puttnam or Lee that Eberts's earnings at Goldcrest were not enough to support both his enormous debts and his family. He had been in debt, without a break, since he first went to McGill University in 1958. College fees, mortgages, personal loans to help him get started first in New York and then in Europe, funds for his various unsuccessful entrepreneurial ventures at Oppenheimer – borrowed money had been an integral part of his entire adult life. In the early 1970s he was supporting debts totalling upwards of $100,000, much of it owed to his friend and Oppenheimer colleague Jimmy King. By 1974, as we have seen, this burden had become so onerous that Eberts had been forced to sell his Holland Park house and move into rented accommodation. That was a low point in the Eberts family fortunes. Worse was to come. Eberts had been badly caught over *Zulu Dawn*, one of the film deals in which he had acted as a financial consultant in 1978. It had left him with an awesome debt, which for five years had overshadowed his domestic as well as his business life and was now set to play a decisive role in his future.

Eberts: *Zulu Dawn* had been brought to me by British film financier Guy Collins, who had put a lot of his own money into the picture and had managed to persuade a number of banks in Geneva to do the same. Unfortunately, when shooting was about to start, he realized that, for one reason or another, the money he had was not enough. He came to me. I liked the script – I had very much admired the original film, *Zulu*, which had been a huge success – and I didn't see any great risk in what Guy proposed. I agreed to help find some finance.

At the time, Guy was finalizing the contractual arrangements with the film's stars, Burt Lancaster and Peter O'Toole. Burt's agent insisted on a letter of credit for the entire amount of his salary, without which he would not show up on the set. Such was the precarious state of the film's finances that a letter of credit could be furnished only if someone outside the production would underwrite it. Guy certainly couldn't do it and neither could I, so we ended up going to a bank in Geneva, the American Fletcher Bank, run by a fellow called Tipton Blish, who said he would act as underwriter as long as Guy and I would personally guarantee his note. God knows why I did it. It is easy to fall in love with your project. It was one of those situations where you put in so much time and effort, and you are so convinced that you are going to raise the money, that you feel there is no real risk, or that what little risk there is is worth taking to keep the show on the road. So I signed a personal guarantee that the funds would be available to honour the letter of credit. Strictly speaking, I was in no position to do this – my liabilities already outstripped my assets by a substantial margin – and I had to ask a friend of mine in New York, Fred Stein, if he would cover me. I showed Fred, on paper at least, how the risk involved was minimal, as the additional financing would soon be in place, and I reassured him that the picture could not go over budget as there was a completion guarantor attached to it. Fred duly forwarded the funds to cover Fletcher Bank's guarantee, which in turn enabled the production company's bank to issue the letter of credit for Burt Lancaster's salary.

I went back to Geneva to discover that the production was already in difficulty and that the completion-guarantee arrangements had fallen through. Furthermore, various financiers who were supposed to be investing in the production had either pulled out or simply failed to deliver. Realizing that I had obtained Fred's money under what were in effect false pretences, I made frantic phone calls – to Japan, Singapore and New York – and was eventually able to make complex, and personally risky, arrangements to replace him. The bank for some reason accepted my guarantee with alacrity, even though they knew that I did not have the assets to meet my obligations. Things then went from bad to worse. The picture went way over budget; key people in the production were either incompetent, dishonest or both; and my money, far from being a paper guarantee that would never need to be drawn down, began to look very much at risk. In fact, it was last in, last out money; the banks were miles ahead of us.

The finished film was not good enough to interest a distributor in the United States and it failed, dismally, to recoup its costs. Naturally, the bank which had underwritten the letter of credit for Burt's salary had had to pay up and, in turn, had called on Guy and me to honour our pledge.

But I had no money. I tried, feebly, to make a case for not paying, claiming that I, a person of insufficient means, had been coerced into signing a worthless guarantee by a bank that should have known better. My attempts inevitably failed, and in due course the bank instituted legal proceedings. These dragged on for months, until, in 1981, a date was set for a final court hearing, which I would undoubtedly lose and as a result of which I would very likely be forced into bankruptcy. In desperation, I again turned to Jimmy King. He was generous, as always, and, two days before the court action, I was able to settle with the bank.

The debt did not go away, but at least with Jimmy as the creditor I was safe from prosecution. I paid the interest as best I could, month by month, but by 1983 the sum involved had reached $475,000. Servicing that on my Goldcrest salary was barely possible and meant, for example, that my family enjoyed a standard of living well below what might have been expected given my apparent success. As for paying it off, there was no hope.

Ilott: That Eberts was burdened by some kind of crippling financial obligation was widely rumoured within Goldcrest and in Wardour Street, but only a few of his closest colleagues knew the details. One who did was David Puttnam, who, a few weeks after the Oscar ceremonies, at a dinner in Los Angeles, took Lee aside and advised him to try to find a way of alleviating Eberts's financial problems, 'because the guy is going to be offered a lot of jobs'.

'I said, I think he won't take the offers', Puttnam recalls, 'unless he continues to be in debt; because he's a human being and presumably at some point he is going to say, "To hell with this – I can get rid of all these debts now."'

Eberts: David was right. I was being approached with offers of jobs and I wasn't interested in any of them. But the financial pressure on me was intolerable and I could not withstand it for ever. The success of *Gandhi* at last gave me some leverage, although its beneficial effects would be bound to wear off. I didn't know what I was going to do – I certainly had no intention of leaving Goldcrest – but I knew that whatever it was, it would have to be done soon.

For the present, I had my hands full dealing with the upsurge of interest in Goldcrest that followed the Oscars. Doors that had previously been closed were now open. The studios, with whom we had vainly battled for more than two years to get a distribution deal for *Gandhi*, were vying with each other to have first look at our forthcoming projects. For example, for a period of several months, wherever I went – Tokyo, Paris, Sydney or New York – there waiting for me would be a message to call Paramount's Jeff Katzenberg. He was determined to get Goldcrest into a relationship with Paramount, and he especially wanted *The Killing Fields*. That picture had already been offered to Warner Bros., in accordance with the deal David Puttnam had with them, and Warners' boss, Terry Semel, had been so keen to come to terms that for a few days he gave it his highest priority. Knowing how tight my schedule was on my trips to Hollywood, on one occasion he even drove over to meet me at my hotel rather than have me go over to Burbank to meet him. When the head of a studio does that, you can rest assured that you've got something that he wants.

Terry and I had settled on a formula whereby Warner Bros. would put up a $4 million advance for *The Killing Fields* in exchange for distribution rights in all media in the States. IFI were co-investors in the film and, once again, Roland Betts negotiated very good recoupment terms for us. Nevertheless, we were still very exposed. Although we already had international theatrical pre-sales of $1.4 million and video sales of $1.2 million, this deal left us with an exposure of $6.5 million to be covered by sales in the remaining foreign markets. Later, after experiencing tremendous difficulties in these markets (the film was very downbeat and had no stars), we negotiated a further deal with Warners whereby they put up an additional $4.75 million for the unsold territories, leaving us with a deficit against budget of $2.75 million to be recovered from back-end returns, known in the industry as 'overages'. (To make things more complicated, we then agreed to do a swap whereby the $4.75 million was set against domestic rights and the original $4 million was set against foreign.)

The financing of *The Killing Fields* was therefore far from perfect, and it was made worse by the fact that we had no completion guarantee, a state of affairs that alarmed David Norris and John Chambers. On 6 April 1983, John sent me a memo, with copies to senior executives and members of the board, which questioned the wisdom of deficit financing a 'high-budget, long-schedule film to be shot in a difficult location' in a 'volatile political climate,' with a 'first-time director, and a team, which, though extremely talented and organized, has never had to handle a project of this size'. John strongly advised that we should 'pursue a full completion guarantee from a third party', as we did not have 'the resources to finance big overruns'.

I had decided, in fact, to dispense with a third-party guarantee, which would have cost us at least $700,000, and to make do instead with war insurance, which cost $50,000. This policy had been agreed between me and David Puttnam, who was incensed that John Chambers chose to interfere. He was especially upset that John's memo had gone to board level. It has to be said that, had *The Killing Fields* gone the same way as, say, *Revolution* was to go two years later, I would have been vilified for recklessly risking the company's money. But I had decided to go ahead in this way for much the same reason that I had gone ahead with *Gandhi*, which, if it hadn't worked, would have sunk the company without trace and no one would ever have heard of Jake Eberts again. I had complete faith in the film-makers, David Puttnam and his director Roland Joffe. There was no way that David would ever let the film get out of control and no chance, therefore, that it would go over budget. I can say this with complete confidence now, of course, because I know that the film did come in on schedule. But even then my confidence was absolute. It is hard to describe the great sense of purpose that we all had at Goldcrest in those days, and that we shared with film-makers like David Puttnam, Peter Yates, Dickie Attenborough and Alan Marshall. Those men would never let a Goldcrest film go over budget. Not only were they supremely competent, but they were proud of Goldcrest and what it was trying to do. They wanted the company to be a success. To a degree, their own futures depended on it. I think John Chambers understood this; he just did not have as much confidence as I had.

The most telling sign of the weight we now carried in Hollywood was the ease with which I secured distribution deals with Frank Price and Marvin Antonowsky at Columbia for *Dream One* and *The Dresser*. Normally I would have expected to go back and forth, having maybe half a dozen short meetings spread over several months with Columbia, and then to repeat the process with three or four other studios, before getting a deal. This time there was only one meeting and it lasted fifteen minutes. I came away from it with the entire budget of *The Dresser* covered by an advance, good back-end terms and a share of a tax deal. All we had to do was stay on budget and we were guaranteed a profit. I also got roughly the whole cost of *Dream One*, to which we kept the rights in the foreign markets. Again, all we had to do was keep on budget and all the foreign sales would go straight to the bottom line.

The speed with which these deals were done meant that *Dream One* – the production of which in the end got completely out of hand; the film went hugely over budget and actually lost money – was able to go into production in April. *The Dresser* – which came in on time and on budget, got five Academy Award nominations and made money, for Goldcrest and for our financing partners, World Film Services, if not for Columbia – was able to start in May. It amazed me how much easier it was to get things moving when we had eight Oscars and good grosses as our calling card. *Gandhi*, one of the great film projects of the decade, had been rejected by every studio, even when they had not only a script but more than an hour's footage on which to base a judgement. *The Dresser* and *Dream One*, by contrast, were much more modest in scope and yet were snapped up, almost without discussion, in fifteen minutes. It was proof of one of the oldest and truest sayings in Hollywood: that when you're hot, you're hot.

The two other projects that I took to California on that trip, *The Emerald Forest* and *Another Country*, were not sufficiently advanced for me to be able to show either scripts or budget details, and, while Columbia showed some interest, there was nothing really on which to structure a deal. I decided to leave them until Cannes in May.

Chapter Fifteen

A New Friend

Eberts: There are two sides to Cannes: the Festival and the Market. The Festival came first and has now been going for more than forty years. It is by far the most important film festival in the world and attracts about 30,000 visitors, of whom about half are accredited Festival participants. Of those, 4,000 or so are journalists. The Market grew like a parasite on the body of the Festival. With so many producers and distributors in Cannes for the fortnight, it was inevitable that they would talk business: setting up new projects, buying and selling films, reviewing the performance of pictures from the previous season and so on. The town's cinemas began to be taken over for the screening of non-Festival films that were available for distribution in the international markets. Distributors then started coming to Cannes to see these films and not to attend the Festival at all. This state of affairs was formally recognized about twenty years ago when the Marché International du Film was established as an event in its own right. By the early 1980s, the Marché was attracting about 4,000 industry professionals, amongst whom were all our most important clients.

A team of five or six people, including myself, Bill Gavin, his sales team and a couple of support staff, would represent Goldcrest in Cannes. In our suite in the Majestic Hotel, we would set up posters and sales material for our completed pictures and we would have scripts or outlines for the projects we wanted to pre-sell. Separate rooms were set aside for negotiations and contract work and we would have a video monitor for product reels and short screenings. Completed films would be screened during the day in cinemas in the town.

Next to our suite were the offices of the public-relations company, Dennis Davidson Associates (DDA), which was retained by a number of film companies, including Goldcrest, to make all the logistical arrangements – book cinemas and hotel rooms, chaperone stars and VIPs, and handle problems of protocol with the Festival and Market organizers and the municipal authorities – and handle the press. With so many journal-ists in attendance, Cannes is an exceptionally effective launching pad for new movies: reporters from the UK, Brazil, Italy or Australia can inter-view a director at the Festival and then use that interview to coincide with the opening of the film in their respective territories later in the year. If our office was always busy, DDA's was always frantic. In the three major hotels – the Majestic, the Carlton and the Martinez – in the vast Palais des Festivals and in offices and apartments along the Croisette, hundreds of film and PR companies were just as busy doing just the same kinds of things. The whole town is taken over by the movies.

In the course of the fortnight we would hold perhaps five or six major social functions – on the beach or in hotel ballrooms – to promote our latest productions, or to celebrate movies of ours that had been chosen for screening in the Festival. The guests of honour at these affairs would be the directors, producers or stars, whom we would introduce to the assembled distributors. In addition, we would host perhaps half a dozen select dinners, to which a few journalists would also be invited, and at which I would make short speeches designed to encourage our guests to feel very much at home – as if Goldcrest was a nice friendly place to be – and to emphasize the classy nature of Goldcrest's product and its personnel. With all these various functions, travel expenses, hotel bills and so on, attendance at the Festival could easily cost us $80,000. The Cannon Group used to boast of spending nearer $1 million: it is possible. There was a time when Alexander Salkind, producer of the *Superman* movies, would have a dozen planes circling the bay at lunchtime, trailing behind them the credits for his latest production. That kind of stunt doesn't come cheap.

I always saw my principal job at Goldcrest as being twofold: to make deals and to persuade film-makers to work with the company. Of the two, the latter was, in my opinion, the more important. Unfortunately, and despite all its other good points, Cannes is no place to meet film-makers. If they are there at all, it is because they have a film competing in the Festival or for sale in the Market: either way, their days will be booked solid with interviews, meetings, press conferences, distributor dinners and so on. I have often been at Cannes at the same time as close friends such as Alan Parker or John Boorman – we have even been staying in the same hotel – and have never found time to exchange more than a few words with them.

What Cannes was good for, from my point of view, was establishing a style and a reputation for the company. It is like a theatre that has two audiences: at the back, in the cheap seats, is the world's press, which is looking for stories, hot new talent and glamour; in the stalls at the front, closer to the action, is the film industry, which is looking to pick up deals, talent and money-making movies. On this stage you can perform in a way that attaches certain qualities to your name, by being seen to be highly selective about the kinds of films you have, the kinds of parties that you give and the kinds of people with whom you mix. Goldcrest didn't give the biggest parties; that wasn't our image. Nor were our films always sold for the highest advances. One heard of PSO or Cannon doing tens of millions of dollars of business each year at Cannes. If we did $5 million we were happy. More important to us was to attract the best independent distributors, in the hope that we would build reliable partnerships with them over a period of years so that when our films were successful they would do well, but when our films weren't successful they would still stand by us. Hitting them for big advances would not achieve that objective. It was far better to limit their downside risk, so that we went into a contract almost as partners, and take, in exchange, substantially better terms at the back end.

Calculations of this kind are at the heart of the business done in Cannes. If you are doing your job properly, your day will start with a working breakfast at 8 a.m. and won't finish until well after midnight. In those sixteen hours you will essentially have done nothing but hold meetings of one sort or another: appointments in the office, lunch with a producer on the beach, cocktail parties with distributors in hotel function rooms and suites, dinner in an out-of-town restaurant with a studio chief, late-night drinks in the bar of the Carlton or Majestic to catch up with people you've missed during the day, conferences with your own staff whenever they can be pencilled in, and phone calls to London in the morning, New York in the afternoon and Los Angeles in the evening. Even chance encounters in the hotel lobby or lift have a way of turning into business opportunities. While there is a lot of affable back-slapping and apparently jovial conversation, in fact industry professionals in Cannes are neither relaxed nor enjoying themselves. What they are doing is working. They return home utterly exhausted, having drunk too much, eaten too much, talked too much and slept too little. The only diversion that I have ever known in Cannes is tennis, and it was on the tennis court, in 1983, that I raised the subject of *The Emerald Forest* with Bob Rehme.

Bob was an old friend, who, when he was at Embassy, had distributed *Watership Down, Enigma, The Plague Dogs, The Howling* and *Escape from New York*, as well as helping out IFI on the distribution of *Hopscotch*. He was now head of Universal Pictures and, as we knocked the ball back and forth over the net very early one morning, both of us nursing sore heads and weary limbs, I told him the *Emerald Forest* story. He was immediately very keen, and almost seemed ready to do a deal there and then. In fact, he was so keen that I began to doubt that there was much chance of its ever happening: if the head of a studio wants your film, he's not going to be openly enthusiastic and thereby give you an advantage in negotiations. Rather, he'll express mild interest and put you under pressure to come to terms. Bob came on very strong, expressed a great deal of interest, and I was sceptical.

One problem was that he wanted worldwide rights, whereas we had only North America left to sell. Bill Gavin had already had great success with the project, securing more than $3 million in pre-sales in the foreign markets. At the time, we were working on a notional budget of $12 million, and our plan was to sell the American rights for at least $9 million, which, with the foreign sales, would put us in the clear. In addition, our head of business affairs, David Norris, was very confident that we could get a currency deal that would yield about $2.5 million. Thus, unlike, for example, *The Killing Fields*, this was a project that looked very healthy financially, even in its earliest stages.

Bob, though, was already talking about paying $13 million for the world. While this would give us an immediate profit of $1 million over our budgeted costs, the film would have to be a blockbuster for us to have a chance of further profits thereafter, for Universal would of course take the benefit of any tax-leasing deal and they would cross-collateralize. As far as I was concerned, there was no point in throwing away our foreign sales, currency deal and potential tax deal for the sake of a worldwide pick-up that would give us virtually no more than a fee for making the picture. But Bob remained very keen, going so far as to suggest that he might be able to persuade Universal to break with its usual practice and allow him to pick up North American rights only. We agreed to continue our discussions back in LA.

That same evening, John Boorman, who had come down to Cannes with his son Charley and other members of his family, as well as members of the cast and crew of *Dream One*, of which he was executive producer and which was then shooting in Paris, was the guest of honour at a dinner to which we invited leading distributors and journalists. At the dinner I made a short speech, introducing John and his troupe, and, as well as plugging *Dream One*, which had not generated much interest among the distributors, I managed to include a number of references to *The Emerald Forest*, to which most of them had that week committed advances. The

dinner was a typical Cannes event. It was expensive, but, with distributors from all over the world in attendance, it was also a very cost-effective
promotion.

After the dinner, I got a call from Mark Shanker, who worked for Bob
Rehme's old company Embassy. Mark had read the script of *The Emerald
Forest* and was anxious to see if there was some way for Embassy to be
involved. Where he got the script from I don't know; at that time we
weren't using it as a sales tool because it wasn't ready, and I was not
happy with people outside Goldcrest reading it. Mark was not a senior
figure at Embassy but I knew he was very friendly with Jerry Perenchio
and I assumed therefore that he was speaking with authority. Sure
enough, his interest led, a couple of days later, to a meeting with Jerry
himself. Jerry had just sold the *Gandhi* television rights to HBO and
consequently was of a mind to be very friendly. We met two or three
times during the remainder of the Festival. I discovered that he has a
great sense of humour and, on a personal level, I was very taken with
him. As for business, our conversation was restricted to the *Gandhi*
sale and Embassy's interest in *The Emerald Forest*. Mostly we drank
champagne: he had seemingly unrestricted supplies of Dom Perignon.

I did not think anything much about the time we spent together. In
the bedlam of Cannes, Jerry Perenchio was just one more person to be
nice to. Except that being nice to Jerry wasn't difficult: he seemed to be
a nice man.

After Cannes, you have to clean up. The sales team has to get all the
paperwork sorted out for the hundred or so deals that have been done,
and everybody else has to pursue the leads they picked up while they
were away. Also, of course, you have to try to make sense of whatever
has accumulated on your desk back in London. Complicating matters for
me was the fact that, immediately after Cannes that year, I became
involved with one of Dickie Attenborough's adopted charities, the Muscular Dystrophy Group. For twenty years Dickie had worked long and
hard for this charity, and he had now decided to form a new committee
to try to raise money from people in show business. He asked me to serve
as a co-chairman, along with Sydney Samuelson (head of Samuelson, the
big film-services company) and film producer Lord Romsey.

I decided that my contribution would be to organize a pro-celebrity
tennis tournament and, once I had dealt with my Cannes business, I
devoted virtually all my time to getting this project off the ground. It took
much longer than I had expected and, in the midst of the preparations, I
started getting calls from Jerry Perenchio. He phoned several times,

simply to say that he had very much enjoyed meeting me in Cannes and that next time I was in California I must be his guest. He added that if I had any difficulties with *The Emerald Forest* I shouldn't hesitate to pick up the phone and call him; and if there was any other product that Goldcrest thought would be good for Embassy, he would love to see it; and, incidentally, if ever I thought at all about living in California and working in the heart of the business, Embassy could be a home for me.

These conversations became more frequent as the tennis tournament drew closer. Jerry took an interest in that too, because, like me, he is a tennis freak. The fact that I had John McEnroe, Vijay Amritraj, Mats Wilander and other major names on the international tennis circuit coming to play in my tournament appealed to Jerry a lot. When he called we would talk about tennis almost as much as about the film business.

Then, on the night of the tournament itself, in the middle of one of the matches I got an urgent call. It was Jerry.

'Listen, I've just been talking to Norman Lear,' he said, 'and I want to come clean and tell you right now that we've decided that we would like to offer you a job and have you come and join us. We are going to greatly expand our feature-film business and we need someone like you to help us raise the money.'

Other people had made approaches after the Oscars but I had dismissed them all as being of no interest. I said, 'Jerry, I'm very flattered, but I just can't talk about it at this time. I'm completely tied up with this tournament and I have a desk full of work at Goldcrest . . .'

I didn't say yes, but I didn't say no either. I don't know why. There was something very attractive about Jerry and I wanted time to think about it before rejecting him.

The following week, John Boorman and I went off to LA on a sales trip. *The Emerald Forest* had by this time been turned down by Frank Price at Columbia, and we learned just after we got to LA that Bob Rehme had changed his mind: in his view it was going to compete with a film Universal was doing called *The River*. (They both had rivers in them, apparently. It didn't make any sense to me, but that's the reason he gave.) Warner Bros. turned us down without even asking for a meeting; we were turned down on the telephone by Paramount; and Fox took a passing interest but didn't pursue it. The only real possibility was MGM, whose boss, Freddie Fields, had indicated an interest in the film at Cannes.

We went to see Freddie in Culver City, but it turned out that he really wanted to talk to John about another film, not about *The Emerald Forest*. Much the same thing happened with Mike Medavoy at Orion, who wanted us to change the story and bring in the Rockefeller boy who had gone off to somewhere in South America, got lost in the jungle and is presumed to have been eaten by cannibals. So Embassy, which had been kept at arm's length while we hustled around the major studios, gradually began to take a front position. We quickly entered into serious negotiations with Jerry and agreed a deal in principle whereby they advanced $9 million against all domestic rights: television, video, pay-cable and theatrical. This was exactly what we had wanted. We would end up with about $16 million for a picture which was going to cost, according to our latest estimate, about $13 million, and we had good terms at the back end.

The only drawback was the one that had made us shy of Embassy in the first place. Being an independent, the company did not have the distribution machinery or the clout among cinema-owners that a major studio has, and they were to find it difficult to secure the best dates and the best cinemas for the picture. As a consequence, when it was eventually released in June 1985, it did not perform as well as it should have done.

On that trip I took up Jerry's offer and stayed with him at his house in Malibu Colony, an exclusive, movie-stars' enclave about forty minutes' drive from Beverly Hills. The houses there are neither big nor glamorous, just expensive. They are on the beach, which is constantly being washed away so that the houses are always in danger of falling into the ocean. After every storm their owners spend millions of dollars fixing them up, putting in new foundations and trying to protect them against the elements; and then another storm comes along and they have to start all over again.

Jerry has one large house right on the beach and three more near it at the back, so there is almost a Perenchio Colony within the Malibu Colony. This little empire of his is run like a hotel. He has a large staff to take care of his guests' every whim. Cars are always at your disposal. Everything you could possibly want, every kind of drink, every kind of food, is to hand.

I was to go to LA many times that summer and each time stayed with Jerry. He was a welcome relief from the chores of running the ever-expanding Goldcrest in London. For one thing, he wasn't all business. He was certainly very business-minded and he was an extremely successful entrepreneur, but he also loved to play tennis and go running, like I did;

and he loved to try new restaurants and drink champagne, which I loved; and he liked to screen movies, and to tell stories to which I could listen for hours. He had various girlfriends but he wasn't married and had no family to go home to at night, so when I was out in LA, away from my own family, he was an available pal. He always had a car and driver on hand: we could have a couple of drinks without worrying about driving, and we could go wherever we wanted.

If he knew I was coming over the next day, he would call me, in London or New York, and ask what I'd like for dinner the following night. I would say, 'Well, it'd be great to have some grilled swordfish.' Sure enough, the next night there would be the most impeccably cooked, barbecue-grilled swordfish.

He loved being the host. He even went to the trouble of building his own little pizza oven just so that he, personally, could make pizzas for his friends.

To me it was Paradise. We would get up at about 6 a.m. and go for a run on the track at Pepperdine College, which is less than a mile away. Then we would come back for a swim, followed by breakfast, usually with about ten different kinds of fruit. After that the driver would come and pick him up and I would get into my car and by 7.30 a.m. I would be on the road for my business meetings in Beverly Hills.

One day I was particularly flattered by Jerry. My family was back East, spending the summer as usual at our farm in Quebec. I was going to join them and was planning to catch an overnight plane to New York, a day flight from there up to Montreal, and then to drive from Montreal out to the farm. When he heard this, Jerry insisted that I take his private plane, which could fly me direct to the little airport at Newport, Vermont, which is only a short drive from my home. I felt very uncomfortable at the thought of using a private plane when I could easily get a commercial flight, but he was so persistent that finally I gave in. So there I was, flying across the country, the only passenger in a personal jet. I was impressed, and I was grateful.

I was also left in no doubt that Jerry was very keen to get me to come to Embassy. He was very patient. He didn't push me at all. He didn't insist I give him an answer by any particular time. But his offer was always there in the background, whatever we were doing.

He called a week or two after the flight to Vermont and said, 'We're still anxious to hear.' There was nothing I could say in reply. At that time a number of things were happening at Goldcrest that were not entirely to my liking, but I had no plans to leave the company. I had no plans, and yet . . .

Chapter Sixteen

Disenchantment

Ilott: Only with the benefit of hindsight is it possible to see that, by the summer of 1983, Eberts and Goldcrest were beginning to grow apart. Certainly it was not apparent at the time: Eberts continued to work all hours and within the company his prestige had never been higher. But his visits to LA became more frequent and his stays in Malibu more protracted, not simply because there was business there to detain him, but because he felt more comfortable there than he did in London, where the company that he had created was, like Frankenstein's monster, getting out of his control. The process had begun with the founding of Goldcrest Films and Television in 1981, which set the company on a path away from the original concept, of being merely an investment fund, towards becoming a fully staffed production and sales operation. Once started, that course followed its own logic, and the developments that were 'not entirely' to Eberts's liking were, for the most part, no more than the natural and inevitable consequences of Goldcrest's apparent success. Having spent most of the previous two years concentrating on film-makers and distribution deals, Eberts had given hardly a backwards glance to see what was actually being created in the London office; and, when he returned from Cannes in 1983, it was to discover that he was no longer comfortable with a company that had become, of necessity perhaps, increasingly bureaucratic. For the first time in seven years he began to distance himself, to distinguish between Goldcrest and Eberts.

Eberts: In the old days, when it was just me and Irene and a secretary, wherever I was there was Goldcrest. Now we had a whole office full of people, dealing with a much wider range of activities, and the company continued to function whether I was there or not. My leadership was never challenged or in doubt, but instead of being the sole authority I was now just the leading authority. As well as letting Mike Wooller do his own thing in television, I had a very high-profile head of sales, Bill

Gavin, and two expert back-office executives, John Chambers and David Norris. Each of them was perfectly able, and willing, to take the initiative and this, combined with my prolonged absences from the office, meant that I wasn't so clearly in control of Goldcrest as I had been in the past.

It had to happen, of course, if only because of the volume of work with which we were dealing. The development, financing, making and selling of a film were by no means our only involvement: in most cases there followed years of accounting and reporting, and, when the rights from the first round of sales reverted to us, of re-selling in the ancillary markets. Thus, our aggregate workload increased with each new addition to our film and television library. In the summer of 1983, we had *Dream One*, *The Dresser* and *The Killing Fields* in production; yet another David Puttnam project, *Cal*, soon to go before the cameras: *The Emerald Forest* and *Another Country* in development; and hundreds of hours of television programming in the pipeline. In addition, *Enigma, Local Hero* and *The Ploughman's Lunch* were in release and were soon to be followed by *Red Monarch* and *Runners*. Towards the end of May we signed a deal with the Samuel Goldwyn Company for the distribution of some of these smaller films in the States and, a few days later, largely as a result of James Lee's interest, we were one of the founder members of a consortium that was to provide a cable movie channel in the UK. It could never be said of Goldcrest that we lacked either energy or ambition.

And, of course, the company continued to grow. For more than four years, between January 1977 and the summer of 1981, Goldcrest had consisted of two, and sometimes three, people. In the latter part of 1981, with the addition of Goldcrest Television, our numbers had increased to eight. Then, from the beginning of 1982, when John Chambers came on board, to the summer of 1983, we employed a further thirty-six people, bringing the total up to forty-four. There were so many of us that in July we were forced to move from Holland Park Avenue to bigger, and inevitably more expensive, premises in nearby Holland Street. Of the total staff, eleven worked in television, eight in finance, nine in sales, five in legal and business affairs and six in administration and office services. But in the development and production of feature films there were still only five: myself and Irene, my new secretary Lucinda Sturgis, production executive Terry Clegg and his assistant Andy Parsons.

While it is true that much of John Chambers's work was on overall corporate finance, with probably as much emphasis on film as on television, and that the balance of work in sales was probably weighted towards films, by far the biggest factor in the increase in personnel was the volume of our television output. By mid-1983 Mike Wooller had twenty projects in hand, in which we had already directly invested over £9 million and to which we were committed to spend a further £3.4 million. But additional, indirect costs were incurred by the ever-increasing back-up services that this output entailed, for on most of our television projects we acted not only as the financier but as the producer, with responsibility for budgets, casting, crewing, scheduling, accounts, reporting, administrative services, contracts and documentation. Of all the staff listed above, in legal and business affairs, finance and administration, most spent most of their time dealing with the extra burden of work in television. Goldcrest's annual overhead increased from £250,000 in 1981, to £800,000 in 1982, to £1.7 million in 1983.

Although the sums directly invested in feature films were greater (we had spent over £22 million by this time), the indirect costs were less, for the simple reason that where films were concerned at that time we still acted essentially as a financier, not as producer. (This was to become less true as time went on, and ceased to be true at all soon after I left.) All our business was done by parcelling out chunks of money to film-makers and letting them deal with the production and administration themselves. In addition, of course, there were far fewer films than there were television productions, and therefore far fewer elements to be accounted for.

On my return from Cannes, at the end of May 1983, I had the first inklings of where all this was leading. Clearly, our overhead was getting too big for our level of capitalization. This was not only worrying from a business standpoint, but caused me some personal discomfort as I found myself at the head not of a tight and finely tuned film-investment company but of an army of administrators, accountants and lawyers. The machine was simply too big. Also, money was pouring into television, in which we had little business expertise and from which we had so far had only patchy returns: by September, those of our programmes which were already finished and distributed had cost us £3.6 million but had returned only £915,000, with the possibility of a further £2.3 million to come – i.e. we were even then forecasting losses. By comparison, our finished and distributed feature films, in which we had invested £10.5 million, had yielded revenues of £9 million with projections of a further £4 million to come.

I was the boss, and I could, and should, have done things differently. But when we launched GFT it had been originally no more than a marriage of convenience between Pearson Longman's television operation, which was separately capitalized, and my film-investment fund, and it had been understood, at least by me, that my day-to-day responsibility as chief executive was in practice limited to running Goldcrest

Films – 'and television' was in lower-case and was to be taken care of by
Mike. I am not trying to shirk responsibility by saying this. The fact is
that if you do not have initiative you cannot really take responsibility,
and the move into television was no initiative of mine, nor was the
running of it my particular task. In fact, I never really thought of television as being part of our business at all.

Ilott: Eberts's version of affairs is strongly contested by David Puttnam,
who maintains that 'he [Eberts] was hiring people, people were being
employed, the company had grown very rapidly. It's not true [that things
happened without Eberts's approval]. He was present at every single
board meeting. There is no question in my mind that if Jake as chief
executive had said, "No, I don't want to do this," it would never have
happened. No question.'

Eberts's perception of the kind of company Goldcrest should be was
in fact getting ever further away from the perception shared by Puttnam
and Lee, and his reluctance even to come to terms with the changes that
had already taken place were to them a source of some frustration.

'The company had grown significantly,' explains Puttnam, 'but Jake
wasn't prepared to be a chief executive. I remember him saying to me
bitterly, over and over again, "Look at all this bloody paperwork. Why
have I always got paperwork? I don't work well on paper." But if you
can't do the paperwork, you can't do the job. There was a genuine
management crisis, because – and Jake declared himself – Jake didn't
want to be management. He wanted to be freewheeling.'

Eberts's longing for a return to the days of the close-knit operation in
the garret office in Mayfair, where he read scripts by the evening light
and had neither administrative chores nor staff to look after, was something more than merely a matter of personal inclination: it had a certain
business logic. *Gandhi*, after all, was a GFI success. True, it was heavily
backed – even to an extent underwritten – by Pearson, but it owed
nothing whatever to the corporate growth that had followed the formation
of Goldcrest Films and Television in 1981. In fact, Eberts could argue
that the bigger and more complex the company became, the further it
seemed to drift from its original purpose, which was to make carefully
calculated investments across a wide portfolio of projects, covering its
risk while keeping significant profit positions that could, on occasion,
yield spectacular rates of return. Yet Puttnam and Lee were already
discussing a much grander vision, according to which Goldcrest would
become a powerhouse of film and television production, geared up in
preparation for the explosion of screen entertainment that would follow

the deregulation of European broadcasting and the introduction of new distribution systems, especially satellite and cable. Where Eberts looked for bonanza profits from the one project in ten that scored, Puttnam and Lee (and by this time most of the initiative came from Lee) were looking for a dominant position within the market – they wanted to build the company. From this perspective Eberts's reluctance to play the role of corporate boss was creating a leadership gap that was not only becoming obvious and unsettling within the existing structure, but was potentially an inhibiting factor in Puttnam's and Lee's plans for further growth. Indeed, one of the 'roots of [Goldcrest's] disaster' is identified by Puttnam as 'Jake's inability to manage an orderly transition of Goldcrest from a man-on-a-horse operation to a real company; his inability to raise his game.'

Already, in the summer of 1983, tensions were beginning to show, especially between Eberts and Lee, who, by now seriously engrossed in Goldcrest's day-to-day managerial affairs, was emerging as a rival figure of authority. On more than one occasion, Eberts was moved to remind his colleagues that he, not Lee, made the decisions, and that the management team, not the board, ran the company.

And it was not just Goldcrest that had changed. Eberts – his self-assurance bolstered by the Oscars, the open doors in Hollywood and the offer from Perenchio – had become a personage of considerable stature within the industry, and he knew it. He was conscious of his skills and he was more than ever convinced that administration and detailed company management were a waste of his time – an opinion he did nothing to hide in a series of interviews that appeared in trade, business and consumer publications on both sides of the Atlantic. The *Show Business Investment Newsletter*, which ran a verbatim question-and-answer interview with him, *Marketing Week* ('The High Hopes Riding on Film's New Wave'), *Toronto Star* ('The Canadian Who Put the Mahatma in Movies'), London's *Evening Standard* ('The Local Hero of UK Films'), the *Sunday Telegraph* ('How a Not So Local Hero Made Good'), *Screen International* ('The Man Putting Goldcrest in Front'), *The Business of Film* ('The Great White Hope of British Film'), and *Forbes* ('Goldcrest's Touch'), among many others (syndicated interviews appeared, for example, in the UK provincial press), combined to give Eberts, who is anything but a showman, a profile unknown among film financiers since the days of Joe Levine. Brimming with confidence in his ability to woo directors, identify viable projects and bring the two together in ingenious deals, his talk was all about films and film-makers, not about corporate strategies or company building. An unfortunate side-effect of this was that he unwittingly gave the impression that he alone was responsible for Goldcrest's success. The *Forbes* article in particular caused great resentment, especially within Pearson: in Millbank Tower, James Joll was, in Lee's phrase, 'spitting' at what he regarded as the brazen appropriation of credit that should have been more widely shared.

'I had this thing thrown at me saying, "What the flaming hell is all this about?" ' Lee recalls. ' "We've put up all this damn money and here he's being interviewed for two and a half pages and he's not even mentioned the fact that anybody's got anything to do with this damn thing other than himself." I was instructed to inform Jake that in future would he please be a little less egotistical in his publicity.'

Lee adds, in Eberts's defence: 'The interview was immediately post *Gandhi* awards. I had been with Jake in New York – we met for some reason, I don't know why – and he was off to the *Forbes* interview that day. And I remember the mood he was in. He was in such a state of excitement that he would have given that impression: that he was a film genius.'

Puttnam was on location in Thailand when he eventually read the piece and he was even more upset than Joll, for, as Bill Gavin explains, 'It finished up reading as if Jake had discovered the *Killing Fields* project, and it relegated Puttnam almost to the position of a line producer.' Gavin, who discussed the article with Puttnam as they were driving out to the set one morning, describes him as having been 'absolutely incensed'.

'He had written Jake this enormous letter saying how wrong he was and quoting times and dates and things on the *Killing Fields* thing. And then really, as I remember it, lecturing Jake, and saying, "This is the mistake that all the money men in the industry make: they suddenly think they're producers." A really tough letter. I read this, sweating quietly in the back of the car, and David turned to me and said, "Well, what do you think?" I said, "David, first of all I don't think you should send it. I can see your objection to what he's quoted as saying, but the chances are that he never said that. And even if he did, we're in a business where everybody makes every claim they can for themselves. And with the euphoria after *Gandhi* and so on – you know, it's probably only human that it should happen." He said, "No, no, he's getting too big for his boots." '

While on the surface relations between the Goldcrest principals were still good, the fact was that matters had to be resolved one way or another, and sooner rather than later, if the company was to build on its current success and move forward according to a coherent plan. Lee proposed a solution: instead of appointing a head of films below Eberts, a plan which, when first suggested with Sandy Lieberson's name attached, had been abandoned as unworkable, why not acknowledge Eberts's strengths – bringing film-makers and projects into the company – as well as his weaknesses – his dislike of paperwork and administration – by making him the *de facto* head of films and appointing someone above him to look after the proper administration of the office of chief executive? Naturally, Eberts couldn't be seen to be demoted, but such a change could be enacted by the simple expedient of bringing in James Lee himself as full-time executive chairman.

Few prospects could have been less congenial to Eberts than to have Lee, or, for that matter, anyone of Lee's seniority, working alongside, let alone above, him. But the proposal was only one of a number of changes that were discussed by Eberts, Lee, Puttnam and Attenborough at a series of meetings held in May and June 1983, and, for one reason or another, Eberts never made clear (perhaps himself never properly appreciated) his opposition to it. The discussions resulted in an elaborate proposal, presented by James Lee one Saturday morning in Puttnam's London mews house, for a complete overhaul of Goldcrest's complex and unwieldy corporate structure. His blueprint envisaged the amalgamation of the various Goldcrest companies in one corporate entity, which would be established independently of Pearson and run by a new management company, in which he, Puttnam, Eberts and Attenborough would be significant shareholders. Lee himself would be the full-time chairman, Eberts would be the chief executive (although there seems to have been a proposal at one time for Lee to have the titles of chairman *and* chief executive and for Eberts to become managing director), and Puttnam and Attenborough would be non-executive director–consultants with a considerable say over investment decisions and corporate policy.

For Lee, the prospect of working at Goldcrest offered all the excitement and challenge that his professional life now lacked. 'I saw the opportunity to really make a very considerable mark through running Goldcrest as an independent company,' he explains. 'It was certainly more attractive than what seemed to be a more and more bureaucratic life inside Pearson.'

In planning this move he was encouraged by what he believed to be the camaraderie that existed amongst the Gang of Four. He refers, for example, to a photograph that appeared in the *Sunday Times* 'of David Puttnam, Jake, myself and Dickie Attenborough, all standing arm in arm outside David Puttnam's Enigma office. [We had been] talking about the future of Goldcrest and how we were going to spin it off from Pearson and how we were going to develop it into, at long last, the company that the British film industry deserved, and all the rest of it. I thought we were all extremely close at that time.'

Lee's plan certainly had the enthusiastic support of Richard Attenborough, who saw in it the possibility of creating a film-makers' film company. Like Puttnam, Attenborough was never much interested in the rigidly commercial criteria that were supposed to govern Goldcrest's affairs. What did interest him was the possibility that Goldcrest might become the flagship, guide and protector of the film industry in Britain, a cause to which he had devoted considerable energies throughout his career.

'I have suffered, both as an actor and in large measure as a director–producer, from having to deal with, and cope with, and pound the beat for, people for whom I have next to no respect,' he explains. 'To give just one example, when we were trying to raise money for *Gandhi* the head of 20th Century–Fox literally said, "Who the hell do you think is interested in making a movie about a little brown man dressed in a sheet and carrying a beanpole?" Now that mentality is really soul-destroying. And so I fought for, and believed in, and saw in Goldcrest, the possibility of bringing, not only for myself but for other people, a board of management that would never place the creative people in the position that they had been placed in over and over again. And that, if somebody came with an idea, even if it wasn't viable for whatever reasons, at least it was treated with respect and understanding, and in a way kindness; that you knew what it meant to the person who brought it in.'

Puttnam's vision, less high-minded but no less ambitious, was of a Goldcrest that was strong enough, and stable enough, to enter into coproductions with the major American studios on an equal footing; not now and again, but as a matter of routine. He wanted to put an end to the debilitating and dispiriting practice, forced upon British producers for want of funds at home, of trailing from one studio to another, cap in hand, begging for the money needed to put each new film into production. His own contribution to the company, especially via his relationship with Warner Bros., had already done much to push it in this direction. Lee's proposal would give him the power to push it further.

Eberts professed to welcome the plan on the grounds that Lee's fulltime participation in Goldcrest would free him from some of his administrative chores.

But the proposal was not welcomed by other executives within Goldcrest, least of all by John Chambers, who, when he got wind of it, denounced it as a 'carve up'. Nor was it well received by the Pearson board.

'It was an absolutely ridiculous thing,' comments Pearson's James Joll. 'It was designed so that James Lee and Jake had all the equity and there were small amounts for Puttnam and Attenborough. It was . . . clearly not in the interests of the shareholders. It [created] a new series of relationships where they became highly profitably rewarded for doing in most cases jobs they were already doing. I strongly resisted it and said it wasn't something that we could possibly countenance.'

Pearson's veto was absolute.

But the plan did suggest ways in which Goldcrest might be reorganized to relieve Pearson of what was now becoming a burden. The Pearson top brass were alarmed, not only by the amount of their time taken up by the discussion of Goldcrest's affairs (since the buy-out of the Pearson Longman minority, Goldcrest had become a regular item at main-board meetings), but by the worryingly rapid growth of what was still an unproven business: in the seven years of its existence Goldcrest had yet to show a year-on-year profit.

Joll recalls a discussion at Pearson board level, 'about how many films you can make, what the cost of the average film was, and what was the average return on it', which proved, he says, that 'even if you made all the films and they were all highly successful, your return on capital was uninteresting'. As for television, which had been the main conduit of Pearson's investment in Goldcrest, and on the basis of which they had hoped to build an entertainment-media business to stand alongside their newspaper and book-publishing empires, it was already proving an expensive mistake: the upside just didn't exist.

As their confidence in the business waned, so Pearson became ever more uncomfortable with their leading role, not only as Goldcrest's principal shareholder and the 100 per cent owner of the management company, but as the putative general partner in every film and television investment, for each of which, it could be construed, they were wholly responsible. They had all the risks, in other words, but only 40 per cent or so of the rewards.

Thus, although the independent-management-company idea was dropped, other aspects of Lee's plan were developed further. After a long series of discussions, which took place throughout June and July 1983, it was agreed to form a new holding company which, much as Lee had envisaged, would acquire all the shares in all the existing Goldcrest partnerships and subsidiaries. Once established, this new company would raise new capital and negotiate a line of bank credit. It would thus start life with a simplified structure and substantial funds, as well as all Goldcrest's existing projects, staff, offices, trading relationships and so on. Initially, Pearson would continue to be the major shareholder, but it was expected that this would change, especially if the new company were ever publicly floated. Pearson's then finance director, Alan Whitaker, recalls that the board was looking towards an early reduction of Pearson's shareholding to something nearer 20 per cent.

As in the original proposal, Lee would resign from Pearson to become the full-time chairman of the new company, taking particular responsibility for corporate affairs and business strategy. He would bring with him, as his deputy, Don Cruickshank. Eberts would remain chief executive, but would concentrate on packaging film projects and doing deals. Attenborough and Puttnam, while remaining non-executive directors, would be brought much more closely into the day-to-day affairs of the company. The Gang of Four would have substantial share options, with a second layer of options being available for other managerial staff.

It is hard to see Lee's proposed move, from the highly remunerative comfort of the Pearson main board to the uncharted waters of an independent Goldcrest, as anything other than a bid for glory. 'I guess it was . . .' he admits. 'But [that summer] Peter Laister of Thorn EMI made a very hard effort to try and get me to take the job that he eventually gave to Gary Dartnall [heading up Thorn EMI Screen Entertainment, then the UK's biggest film company]. I tell you that not to boast about who did or did not offer me a job, but just to show you that at that time I had no wish to leave Pearson to go to Thorn EMI, which I regarded as a company of lesser quality than Pearson. What I was planning for Goldcrest seemed infinitely more attractive . . . I was terribly emotionally wrapped up in the whole Goldcrest thing. I saw it as something that could be spectacularly successful. I was absolutely convinced that our mission in life was to become the leading film-production, and ultimately distribution, company in the UK. Bigger than Rank and bigger than Thorn EMI. And possibly the biggest in Europe. I honestly thought that the original Goldcrest was going to be the building block of *the* leading film-entertainment company.'

Unfortunately, the challenge of building the leading film-entertainment company was not, and never had been, on Eberts's personal agenda. Indeed, from his point of view, the reorganization plan marked the beginning of the end of an era. Not only was the company, hitherto an agglomeration of investment funds that sheltered under the protective wing of Pearson, to stand on its own feet, but it was to develop along lines laid down by Lee and not by him. The baton of leadership, in other words, was being passed from one man to the other. Bizarrely, no one seems to have realized that this was what was happening; everyone went along with the idea, propounded by Lee, that Eberts's proven film skills and his own broad experience in corporate affairs and business strategy made the two together a very persuasive combination.

'The grand design was based on the notion that I would be the financial head of the organization and that Jake would be very much a hands-on executive producer and that the two of us would make an excellent – what is a two-person troika? – a doika perhaps,' confirms Lee. 'There was tension, because I obviously was the expansionist, I wanted to diversify; I was interested in things like cable programming, independent television production, and he wasn't. And therefore it seemed like a very suitable meeting of minds. He would retain his interest in a part of [the company] – the feature-film side, and the production–distribution end of film production – and I would act as the business head of the whole venture.'

Eberts: To be fair, the idea of James coming into the company suited me in a way. I was tired and fed up with administration; tired and fed up with television; tired and fed up with the number of people we had around the place; tired and fed up with what I regarded as the unproductive way I was spending my time, on administration and meetings, when what I really wanted to do was to develop screenplays with major directors and get deals done with major studios.

In other ways it didn't suit me, however. Having a full-time chairman in the next office is a very different thing from having a part-time chairman in an office across town – someone you see only every couple of weeks and whose function is basically to chair the board meetings. I didn't think that James was trying to muscle in on me or push me out, but I realized that if this plan came off I would have to convince him of the correctness of virtually every decision that I made. And I would have to respond to initiatives – and, given his energy and inventiveness there would be hundreds of them – made by him. As things stood, I had no worries about my status as the boss: I always got my own way. But as things were sketched out in this plan, my status was much less clear cut. The whole thing made me uncomfortable.

Ilott: Eberts never made his feelings known and the planning procedure gathered its own momentum. There were further discussions with Pearson and other leading shareholders, and an avalanche of detailed paperwork was prepared by Don Cruickshank. Without ever addressing the latent problem of Eberts's relationship with Lee, on the success of which much of the plan depended, the reorganization was formally agreed in principle in August 1983. Merchant bank N. M. Rothschild and Sons was appointed to draft the prospectus, to attend to the detailed, and immensely complex, work of unravelling the various partnership interests in all the GFI, GFT and GFTP film and television projects, and, with Noble Grossart, to lead the fund-raising effort. The reorganization, from which was to emerge Goldcrest in its latest incarnation, Goldcrest Films and Television (Holdings) Limited, and the share offering which followed, were to take eight months to complete and were to cost Goldcrest just over £1 million in fees and expenses.

Chapter Seventeen

Dinner at Michael's

Eberts: Meanwhile, John Boorman had spent several months travelling back and forth between the UK, the Amazon and Los Angeles working on *The Emerald Forest*: casting, location-finding, researching costumes and Indian customs, liaising with the Brazilian authorities and finalizing the budget and schedule. We were getting very tight for time, partly because John wanted to start shooting as early as possible in 1984 and partly because we were well into pre-production, spending money we didn't have building sets, making models and scouting locations. These things are expensive and it is not easy to stop them: once you start, like a roller-coaster you have to keep going. So it was important for us to finalize the deal with Embassy – which was still subject to casting and final script approval – and get some cash flowing.

In early September, I flew out to join John in LA, where I was to spend one day going over Embassy's observations on the final script, agreeing on the principal cast and, most important of all, getting signatures on the contract. As usual, Jerry offered me the use of one of his houses, but this time, the visit being so short, I turned him down. However, I did avail myself of his Century City apartment in order to shower, change my shirt and get ready for the dinner that Jerry was hosting for John and me at Michael's restaurant in Santa Monica that night. At the apartment I bumped into Jerry's assistant and general factotum. We chatted as I cleaned up and, at around 5 o'clock, Jerry offered us all a drink. I didn't have one – I have always been very wary of alcohol and in 1986 I gave it up entirely – but Jerry's assistant had an enormous martini. More drinks followed, so that by the time we drifted off to the restaurant, at about 6.30 p.m. the young man had already had a pretty good snootful of vodka.

Michael's is one of the best, as well as one of the most expensive, restaurants in LA. John and I were ushered to a big round table in the middle of the room, quite a long way from the entrance. There to meet us was script editor Lindsay Doran, the woman who had brought me the idea for *The Killing Fields* and who was now responsible, on Embassy's behalf, for work on *The Emerald Forest* script. John's business manager, Edgar Gross, was also there. After the introductions we sat down and, as usual, Jerry ordered Dom Perignon. We all had a glass. He ordered more.

The conversation started in the usual polite fashion and John, an old hand at these money-meets-talent affairs, began telling stories about his time in the Amazon jungle among the Xingu Indians. But early on things began to go awry. From their opening remarks, it was clear that the Embassy people had prepared some fairly detailed criticisms of the *Emerald Forest* script, and what was to have been a celebration looked set to become a script conference instead.

It is difficult to have a script conference with a group of people in a restaurant, because in a script conference the director is in the position of defending his vision against four or five people who are attacking it – a process that is not made easier by having to observe the pleasantries of dinner-party conversation. Also, most of the comments came from Lindsay Doran, whom John had never met before. He began to take offence that he was being subjected to criticism by someone who, from the evidence of her youth alone, could be only a very junior member of the Embassy staff. Not helping matters was the presence of Ed Gross, whose abrasiveness in defending John's interests cast a shadow across the table, even affecting the normally ebullient Jerry. And I was tense because we were trying to get them to commit: I needed to have the deal agreed that night, or the following day, so that I could get back to London, sort out the documentation and start the cash flow for the production. My attempts to be charming and relaxed were only too obviously laboured.

Lindsay Doran focused on Embassy's main point of concern in the script: the relationship between the mother and the son. She felt that the mother was not portrayed in a sufficiently positive light. John dismissed this criticism by saying that the story really was about the relationship between the father and the son, and that he felt that trying to build the character of the mother would distract the audience's attention. In any case, the picture would have to be a lot longer to give the required time for the mother's character to be developed in the way that Doran proposed. Why couldn't the mother go searching for the boy? Doran asked. John, I could see, was irritated by the question, but in what I thought was a good-natured and articulate, if stern, manner, he answered it conclusively: a film about the mother wasn't the film he wanted to make.

He finished off by saying, 'And after all, this is a story about the Amazon Indians,' at which point Jerry's assistant, aroused from the slouch into which he had declined after the third or fourth glass of champagne, said, in a very slurred voice, 'Well, who gives a shit about the Indians anyway?'

John was outraged. He rounded on the young man and said something to the effect that he hadn't realized he had come here for an inquisition, and that this was not the way he expected to be treated, least of all by a junior member of Embassy's script-reading department. At this, Jerry, deeply offended that John could be so dismissive of his staff, put his hand in his pocket and pulled out an envelope, on the back of which he had written some notes. He said, 'All right, if we're going to take off our gloves and start punching, I've got a few things I want to say about the script too.'

The evening degenerated from there. What we thought was going to be a pleasant dinner at a very fancy restaurant had become instead a really very unpleasant, difficult and highly volatile meeting which was going to break up at any moment with the deal cancelled. Across the table, Ed Gross was making moves to get up and stomp out. Whenever a gap appeared in the exchange of scarcely veiled insults, I tried to make conversation and introduce subjects which had nothing at all to do with *The Emerald Forest*. But, of course, I was up against it: Jerry had his notes in his hand; Lindsay Doran was deeply offended by John's dismissal of her comments about the relationship between the mother and son; Ed Gross was ready to leave the table; John was red-faced with anger – he has a temper that can just boil over like that; and, making matters worse by the minute, Jerry's assistant was growing bolder, throwing ever more barbed comments into the fray.

The unfortunate youth mumbled something like, 'You know, we don't need to have this kind of ego problem on one of Embassy's first pictures.' This remark, addressed by a novice to a man who had made a string of highly regarded and highly profitable films, and whose reputation for the tough management of his often very difficult productions had enabled him to raise finance as his own producer, was going too far, and Jerry realized it. Like me, he could see that we were coming close to losing the deal. He motioned to his assistant to keep his mouth shut, running his fingers over his lips in the 'seal your lips' gesture. The young man thought Jerry was pointing to some food that was stuck on his chin, so he wiped his mouth with his napkin and kept on talking. For several minutes Jerry, becoming increasingly annoyed, signalled, behind John's back, for his assistant to button his lip and the assistant, trying to oblige, continued to brush away non-existent crumbs, all the while talking about the film in the most insulting manner. I was sinking through the floor.

Jerry, seeing that John was pushing back his chair to get up and go, suddenly rose from the table saying that he had to visit the men's room. He walked down to the main entrance, got the head waiter and said, 'Go down to my table and tell the young fellow sitting on my right that there's a telephone call for him.'

John hadn't noticed this and was motioning to Ed Gross that as soon as Jerry returned they should leave.

The head waiter came down, tapped Jerry's assistant on the shoulder and said, 'Sir, there is a telephone call for you.' The young man said, 'Tell them I'll call them back,' and carried on berating John. The head waiter went back to Jerry, who was waiting out of sight at the entrance, and relayed the message. Jerry, furious, told the head waiter, 'Look, you go down again and you tell him that if he doesn't take this telephone call right now, he's fired.' So the waiter came down and very discreetly whispered in the young man's ear that Mr Perenchio wished to see him at the entrance. The youth, who began to show signs of realizing what was going on, sheepishly got out of his chair and staggered off, bumping into tables as he went. When the two returned to the table, the assistant did not open his mouth, not even to put food into it, for the rest of the evening. He sat there absolutely silent, desperately trying to sober up, for about two hours.

John, meanwhile, had been berating Lindsay Doran, demanding to know what films she had made and what experience she had had as a director. Naturally, and rightly, she regarded such questions as unfair, and the two of them were shaping up for some kind of irreparable showdown. Jerry, now in a peace-making role, tried to take the situation in hand. He had dealt with stars and directors all his life and he knew, or thought he knew, how to calm things down. He quietened Doran and made conciliatory gestures to John, but John would have nothing to do with it: if Embassy had any further comments about the script they could put them in writing and he would give them due consideration.

For form's sake, the dinner had to be endured to the end. All I wanted, and I know everyone else felt the same, was to get out of there. I was, of course, convinced that we had lost the deal.

However, the next morning, Jerry, to his great credit, retracted all the criticisms and said that he fully trusted John's judgement, and that, as far as Embassy was concerned, the picture could go ahead, subject only to final casting – in other words, the script had been approved. That afternoon I finally got the piece of paper I needed, committing Embassy's

$9 million. I was therefore able to fly back to London knowing that, with Bill Gavin's foreign sales and the prospect of a very attractive tax deal, we had a picture which was fully financed and already in profit. All we had to do was keep it on budget.

Chapter Eighteen
A Gulf of Misunderstanding

Eberts: I got back from Hollywood with more on my mind than the successfully completed Embassy deal for *The Emerald Forest*. I was now forty-two years old. Despite seven years of unremitting work, all the Oscars, the high profile and the track record, I was still in dire financial straits and I was being paid what was no longer, given the alternatives open to me in Los Angeles, a competitive salary. Naturally, Jerry's invitation to join Embassy had thrown me into some confusion about what to do next. On the one hand, Goldcrest Films, with *The Killing Fields*, *The Dresser* and *Another Country* in production and *The Emerald Forest* ready to go ahead, had never been in better shape; indeed, after *Gandhi* we seemed to have every major film-maker in the world knocking on our door with a project. The company was my creation: I had built it from nothing and I had surrounded myself with the best film-makers and an excellent, hand-picked executive team. Clearly, there were very persuasive reasons for staying on.

On the other hand, while I still enjoyed wooing film-makers and doing deals, I no longer enjoyed running the company and I wasn't really happy with the new direction it was taking. Jerry knew this, and the job that he was offering was specifically designed to leave me free from day-to-day administrative responsibility: I would, in effect, be a free agent, raising money for Embassy's production fund and bringing in films and film-makers to work with them. It would be like having to deal with only the best parts of my existing job. True, Embassy had little track record in feature films – certainly nothing to compare with Goldcrest – but Jerry and Norman, who between them had a wealth of experience in the entertainment business, had ambitious plans and considerable resources on which to draw. For me, especially as I was so friendly with Jerry, it was a very attractive prospect.

But it was not just a question of whether Goldcrest or Embassy was the more attractive. It was also, and above all, a question of money. I was aware that, with my personal stock standing high in Hollywood, now was the time to do something about my finances. Jerry had pitched his offer well above my current Goldcrest salary: I simply could not afford to reject that kind of money. So while in my heart I think I really wanted to stay at Goldcrest, I knew that I could afford to do so only if the company could go some way towards matching Embassy's offer. As my contract was due for renewal at the end of the year anyway, I went to James and proposed a new, much-improved employment package.

My opening proposal was that I should be able to earn, in a good year, the equivalent of about $300,000. This would comprise a new salary of $250,000, increased stock options in the newly capitalized company, a bonus scheme whereby I got a piece of end-of-year profits according to an agreed formula, and a personal participation in the net profits of every film we put into production. If we did exceptionally well, I would do exceptionally well, although there was a limit put on what I could earn. If we did so-so, I would do so-so. If we did badly, then my new package would amount to no more than an increase in salary, which I felt was more than justified by my record to date. In total, even by my best-case estimates, such a package added up to considerably less than I was being offered as a straight salary by Embassy, but it would be enough to keep me on board.

The first meeting with James to discuss my contract took place in the second week of September 1983. The subsequent meetings grew longer and more frequent throughout October and early November. We would convene at his office in Millbank Tower and the results of each session would be confirmed in writing: we quickly accumulated a fat file of correspondence on the subject. James led me to believe that everything we discussed was being reported back for consideration by the Pearson board, whose approval would have to be sought for any package that included options and performance-related incentives. However, I later came to believe that Pearson never discussed it at all.

This is something I cannot explain. I don't believe that James acted dishonestly, at least not in any conscious or calculating way. I think it is more likely that he felt that it was better for the two of us to hammer out a deal before he took it back to the board. It was, after all, his responsibility. He probably led me to believe that the board was respond-ing to my proposals because that seemed the simplest thing for him to do. Throughout our negotiations he was cordial and he tried to be constructive, but he never put forward a counter-proposal which met my requirements. His constant cry was, 'Pearson won't accept it.'

Ilott: Although Eberts and Lee had always been what Lee calls 'part-nerly', they had never been buddies. 'We saw each other socially occasionally, and we would go down to play tennis at my house in the country,' says Lee, 'but I wouldn't try to make out that we were close friends.'

In fact, one discerns, even now, a degree of unease in the way they talk about each other. Whether this is because they are, or were, in competition, or thought themselves to be so, or whether they are just temperamentally incompatible, are not questions that can be answered here. Suffice to say – and this is vouched for by everyone who worked for them both – there was considerable tension between them. This tension was forced into the open when Lee declared his intention to quit Pearson and move into what might be called the office next door. That was far too close for Eberts. While each has always professed to esteem the other's integrity – Lee describing Eberts as 'transparently honest', and Eberts, throughout this book for example, being at pains to exonerate Lee from charges of ill-intent – distrust began to creep in, especially, and inevitably, on Eberts's part. His distrust focused, of course, on the contract negotiation.

Lee insists that their talks were reported back, and discussed, at Pearson board level *'ad nauseam'*. But according to Alan Whitaker, 'He [James] would naturally have talked to Michael [Lord Blakenham] rather than to us.' To which James Joll adds, 'I think it was mentioned, but I can't recall any detail. I remember at some stage Jake saying, "Christ, you know all about this – it's been going on for months." And I said, "Well, it's certainly news to me." It might have been alluded to by James Lee. But it never came as a matter of decision to the board.'

Part of the reason for what was clearly a breakdown in communication between all concerned was that Eberts, unlike, say, Puttnam, was not well known in the Millbank building. According to Joll, he had 'hardly spoken to him', while Whitaker 'didn't know him well', adding, ruefully, 'perhaps we should have got to know him better'.

Not being well known, Eberts had no allies, other than Lee, on the Pearson board to whom he could appeal for assistance. And even if the subject had been raised at board level, it is quite likely that it was mentioned only obliquely and that, other than Blakenham, the board members did not give it close attention, preferring to leave such matters, as always, in Lee's hands.

Nevertheless, for all that they deny having discussed it formally, Joll and Whitaker did know enough of the details to have arrived at their own, unambiguous, opinions about Eberts's demands.

'When I heard of the actual money levels [required] to keep him, it was not a question of whether it was right or wrong, it was something that we couldn't really afford in such a small business,' says Joll. 'We were always aware that the [Embassy] offer was such that no one dared spell it out. It was a huge sum of money, enormous. So it may have been true that what he proposed to us would have meant that he would take a cut in what Embassy were offering, but it was still a sum of money that we just couldn't run to. I'm sure we were only too willing to contemplate options and interests, because, after all, success-related remuneration is on the whole much less painful: he may do very well, but he will only do well if the business and everyone else does well. What we weren't prepared to do was pay a whacking salary that was unrelated to the size of the company, or the job, or what could be afforded.'

The Pearson board was at that time engaged in discussions of a similar nature with Peter Mayer at Penguin Books. Mayer, already earning a huge salary by English, if not by American, standards, had transformed Penguin from being a crisis-ridden, loss-making and hidebound quasi-national institution into a profitable market leader. Whatever were the rewards he wanted for this, they were causing headaches in Millbank Tower, and Pearson was in no mood to consider similar demands from Eberts. It should also be borne in mind that the level of salaries proposed for both Mayer and Eberts was very much out of line with earnings elsewhere in the Pearson empire, including the main board itself.

Thus, whether or not he raised the matter formally at a board meeting, Lee was clearly aware that there were limits beyond which Pearson would not go. He was aware, too, that while Eberts may have been worth half a million dollars in Hollywood, 'just think about the realities back here at home. If there was one thing that was absolutely clear it was that poor little Goldcrest could not afford to pay an individual half a million dollars a year and have [the approval of] shareholders like the postmen's pension fund and the miners' pension fund.'

According to Don Cruickshank, Lee did nevertheless make his best efforts on Eberts's behalf: 'James argued very strongly with Pearson that they should support some such package. Whether it was precisely what Jake wanted or not, I don't know. But he [James] wasn't given the authority to go ahead.'

The question of whether or not the contract negotiations were properly conducted is a crucial one, for it is now agreed by almost all concerned, including Lee, that the failure to come to terms effectively forced Eberts out of the company, and that his loss was the beginning of the end for Goldcrest.

With hindsight, it seems improbable that Eberts and Pearson would ever have reached a settlement: the Embassy offer was just too strong. But within the company, where loyalty to Eberts was virtually unbounded, the shock of his departure was so great, and his own apparent regret at going so obvious, that it seemed that something must have gone terribly wrong. Almost inevitably, Lee was held responsible. He was even to be accused of stalling the negotiations in order to provoke Eberts's departure and thus give himself a free hand to run the company on his own. This is a charge that, naturally, he denies, pointing out that he had 'sold the Lee–Eberts, two-men-in-harness idea so strongly that when Jake announced he was going I had to immediately find a replacement for him. There was no way I could be arguing one month that it was essential that the business skills of Lee and the production contacts and knowledge of Jake should work together, and then suddenly say, "Oh, by the way, we don't have a problem. One of us is gone but I will do it all." From a personal point of view, the position I found myself in in the spring of 1984 was not the one I had planned for myself at all.'

Don Cruickshank, who had worked more closely with Lee than anybody at Goldcrest, defends him from the charge on other grounds: 'I think part of his lack of diplomacy is that he doesn't have that sort of ruthlessness. Diplomatists are essentially ruthless. None of them are nice guys. James is a nice guy. And there was a practical problem: to have done that consciously would be to have run a huge risk with the whole concept of setting up [the new] Goldcrest and raising new funds. It would have meant taking brinkmanship and ruthlessness to a degree that would be out of character with the way James is.'

At least part of the truth is that Lee, throughout the contract discussions, was wrong-footed. He had not realized how close Eberts had become to Jerry Perenchio and therefore was unaware of the seriousness with which Eberts was considering Embassy's offer.

'I certainly had no idea that Perenchio had actually been wooing him for quite a long time,' Lee remarks. 'When I read in John Boorman's book [*Money Into Light*] that Jake had been negotiating with Perenchio that autumn, I was shocked. Because at that precise point Jake was sitting down back here in London with Rothschilds and with Freshfields [Goldcrest's solicitors] and with myself and Don Cruickshank drafting this prospectus – you know, promoting the idea that the company was moving forward.'

Furthermore, Lee never realized that Eberts was unhappy with the proposed reorganization. Nor did he have any inkling that Eberts was uncomfortable with the prospect of his, Lee's, joining the company full time.

'When I first aired with him the idea that I would leave Pearson and become the full-time chairman of Goldcrest . . . Jake's reaction to that was nothing but positive: as far as the concept was concerned, "Great, that's the way to go," and as far as my involvement was concerned the impression he left me with was that he was sick and fed up with the administrative headaches of running the company,' says Lee. 'So it seemed like here was a real opportunity for two people who were very different, who had strong personalities, but who got on and shared a common view, to work together.'

It was thus in a state of blithe ignorance that Lee – assuming, like almost everyone else in the company, that Eberts's commitment to Goldcrest was unshakeable – approached the question of the new contract. It was, in his words, a 'heavy negotiation', but not until the very end, when he hastily, and belatedly, convened emergency meetings with Puttnam and Attenborough to try to find ways of keeping Eberts, did he realize that there was any cause for alarm.

For Eberts, on the other hand, the matter was altogether more serious from the outset. Perenchio had made his initial offer in June. It had been discussed and refined over the summer, and by the time Eberts opened contract negotiations with Lee in September, the question uppermost in his mind was already, and had been for some time, should he go or should he stay. He knew, in the way that Lee did not, that a momentous decision had to be made.

Thus, between Eberts's indecision and lack of candour and Lee's ignorance and lack of insight there emerged what Lee now recognizes to have been 'a ghastly lack of communication'. For this he accepts at least part of the blame.

'My wife, Linn, thinks that Jake simply was unable to voice his concerns. I mean I don't necessarily see it this way, but she sees me as a more domineering personality and therefore perhaps insensitive,' he says. 'I wouldn't say that she says that I bullied Jake into it, but I think she feels that perhaps if I had stopped for a while and maybe given him time, that he would have said that he did feel he was being muscled in on. He just couldn't get round to saying it. If that is the case, and if, as I think it turned out to be, it was to prove so central to some of the problems that emerged later, then it is a great tragedy. It would be ghastly if, in the history of the British film industry, a great opportunity collapsed on something as daft as that. Because there were certainly not only lots of ways we could have accommodated each other, but, if push came to shove, rather than lose him and end up the way we did, I would much rather have simply abandoned my plan and stayed on the Pearson side of the fence.'

Part of the blame must surely lie with Eberts, who simply did not make his feelings or his intentions plain.

This had happened before, for example in the matter of the true relationship between GFI and IFI. As Lee recalls, 'Jo Child in his own mind had heard Jake saying, "Yes, yes, yes," and the reason why IFI behaved the way they did at that first meeting, when *Hopscotch* was overruled, and why all the problems arose, was because Jo had been led to believe, rightly or wrongly, that Jake was happy for Goldcrest to act as a passive, sleeping partner to IFI.'

It had happened again, according to Eberts's own testimony, when he had silently disapproved of Goldcrest's move into television.

Eberts's unwillingness to deal with awkward or unpleasant situations is the negative character trait most commonly noted by his colleagues. Unfortunately, in the autumn of 1983, for all that the company was decked out in the garlands of success, from Eberts's point of view awkwardness and unpleasantness abounded at Goldcrest.

'It was in that period, between the decision to reorganize being made and mid-December . . . that Jake found himself facing a much more structured company, and probably found himself experiencing much more interference from James and Don Cruickshank,' comments David Norris. 'There was the beginning of a kind of discipline that Jake never liked and never wanted. It was becoming a rigid corporation. He could see which way it would go and probably didn't like it. And it happened to coincide with the offer from Perenchio. He had really had an offer he couldn't refuse and it was a question of steeling himself to leave his baby. It was his baby, whatever else it was; he had nurtured it ever since putting the first money into *Watership Down*.

'Had I been in his shoes I would probably have done the same. It's a career decision, and he was under all sorts of pressures. You can see yourself going into a corporate structure you don't like, pressured by people – not necessarily on the personality level – to do things you don't want to do, or in a way you don't want them done, for about a quarter of the money you can get somewhere else. I suppose the miracle is that he took as long as he did to make up his mind.'

Fiona Eberts was keenly aware of her husband's increasing frustration at Goldcrest. 'He hated the whole growth bit,' she says. 'It was his style to let other people in other departments do their own thing, but I don't think he ever wanted it to grow into a great sort of entertainment empire at all.'

Nor was Eberts at ease with the personal demands made of him as leader. He was enthusiastic and good-humoured, and he generated a positive spirit among the staff, most of whom held him in high regard. But he didn't like having to deal with personalities on a daily basis. According to one colleague, Eberts found it 'tiresome' to be looked to for emotional support; and, as his enthusiasm for the job waned, so he began to 'weary' of the people who depended on him.

He had never seen himself as a manager so much as a deal-maker, and when he was in the office he spent more time on the telephone than talking to his staff. Furthermore, he had identified his principal task as that of nurturing close relationships with film-makers. It was to them that he turned most of his personal attention. As for regular office life, he increasingly detached himself from its personal, emotional side, leaving that in the hands of Norris, Chambers and Wooller. His long absences from the office, especially his trips to Hollywood, were welcome rather than burdensome to him.

A further source of discomfort for Eberts was the restrictions which he felt were being imposed on him by the board. Whereas for seven years he had been more or less free of any kind of close supervision, he was now, especially since the decision to reorganize, increasingly made to mesh his actions and decisions with those of the directors – James Lee in particular. Just as he had been unable to stomach such an arrangement at the time of the link with the IFI, when we had had to coordinate his decisions with those of Jo Child, so he was unable to stomach it now with Lee.

And where before Eberts had been able, in running Goldcrest's affairs, to go from step A to step F without having to explain to anyone the logic of the steps between, now he had to justify laboriously not only his decisions but the logic that lay behind them. What galled him most of all, according to one colleague, was that 'he felt that the board no longer believed in him . . . that they didn't have faith in his track record, and didn't believe that, having done it before, he could do it again'. Instead, they wanted to impose new rules for debate and new criteria for decision-making. Neither the rules nor the criteria were to Eberts's liking.

Eberts's increasing irritability and impatience were becoming ever more obvious, even at home. Whereas in the early days, when the Goldcrest offices were in Holland Park Avenue, he had been bursting with energy and enthusiasm, he would now return to his Kensington apartment morose and depressed. It was reminiscent of the atmosphere in the bleak days before *Watership Down*.

He wasn't in control and he wasn't happy. Although Eberts would go to some lengths to avoid confrontation, it was not his style to knuckle down to the job in hand. Rather, he would allow the anxiety to build up.

The build-up carried on through September, October and November.

Chapter Nineteen

Ultimatum

'In the end I said to Jake, "This thing is not resolvable. Do yourself a favour and go." ' – David Puttnam

Eberts: A major factor in my discussions with James was my *Zulu Dawn* debt. With a $475,000 liability hanging around my neck, I was a potential bankrupt and therefore, under English law, not a suitable person to be the director of a limited company, which was what Goldcrest was now set to become. If I were to stay with the company, I could do so only if there was some provision in my new contract – profit participation in individual films or performance-related bonus – that gave me a chance of getting rid of this burden. I knew that the salary being offered by Embassy, plus the proceeds of the sale of my family trust's 10 per cent shareholding in Goldcrest, would probably be enough to see the money repaid within a reasonable period of time. It was up to Pearson, if they wanted me to stay at Goldcrest, to devise some means that would achieve the same end.

James and I toyed with all kinds of schemes that could be included in my remuneration package, but he wasn't hopeful. He argued, rightly, that my financial problems were not Goldcrest's responsibility and that there would be an outcry if the company were seen to rescue an executive from the consequences of his personal folly. It would be like using shareholders' money to pay off gambling debts.

Ilott: An attempt was made, nevertheless, to refinance Eberts's debt via a loan from Lazard, but it fell foul of the bank's house rule that all personal loans above a certain sum had to be secured against any property of the borrower, and that where that property is jointly owned the joint owner has to be informed of the debt. Since Eberts's Kensington apartment was owned jointly by himself and his wife, and since she did not know the details of his *Zulu Dawn* indebtedness, and since he was not willing for those details to be revealed to her, the attempt failed.

The negotiations between Eberts and Lee continued. The amount that Eberts needed, or wanted, was more than Lee, or Pearson, felt able to pay. According to Lee: 'There was a written offer made to him. My memory was that we eventually got up to $400,000. I know for a fact it was way above $250,000 because, believe it or not, when we hired Sandy [Lieberson] at $250,000 it seemed like a bargain after what Jake had been asking for. And he was going to have a not very big interest, uncross-collateralized net-profit participation, in each film.'

Eberts firmly denies these figures. The most he was asking for, he says, was $275,000, which included bonuses and profit shares. What Pearson was offering was less than that, and it was certainly not enough, given the benchmark set by Embassy, to keep him in the company. As the negotiations dragged on, the two men began to give conflicting accounts of progress.

'Jake used to tell us one thing,' recalls David Norris, 'and I used to believe Jake's story. Then James would tell us another version, completely different. I suspect the truth lay somewhere in between the two.'

'For about six weeks or two months it went backwards and forwards, backwards and forwards,' recalls David Puttnam. 'Things got a bit hysterical: "Jake Eberts was being greedy; Jake Eberts was being this; Jake Eberts was being that." Then a kind of war started. I said [to Jake], "You're going to lose this, and soon you will be nowhere. Go home, don't fuck around." Now somehow or other, not in Jake's mind, this has been interpreted as me encouraging him to go. I was not encouraging him to go. I was saying, "The reality is they are not, we cannot, give you what is sensible." It was clear that the company was being reduced to impotence while this fight was going on. For a six-week or two-month period the only discussion was Jake's deal. Everything else stopped. It became ridiculous. I mean, every phone call, everything, was Jake's deal.'

In fact, new film investments had already ground to a halt, the most recent commitment having been in May to Puttnam's *Cal*. Through the summer months of 1983, *The Killing Fields, The Dresser, Another Country* and *Cal* were put into production, and each drew a cash flow from the company, but no further production commitments were undertaken. There were, it is true, two major projects in the planning stage, *The Mosquito Coast* and *The Emerald Forest*, but neither had a start date and it was unlikely that both would get the green light. This drying up of new film investments was mainly a question of capacity, Goldcrest being again more or less fully invested. But partly, too, it reflected Eberts's preoccupation with his contract negotiations.

At the time, the hiatus in film investments after *Cal* was not thought to be a cause for concern. What no one could foresee was that Eberts would leave, and that the upheaval caused by his departure would so disrupt the planned reorganization and fund-raising that no new film of significant size, or in which Goldcrest had a significant stake, would go before the cameras for nearly a year. This was to have catastrophic consequences for the company's cash flow in 1985–6.

At the end of October, Eberts flew to Milan for the autumn film market, MIFED, where Bill Gavin was handling sales of *The Killing Fields*, *The Emerald Forest*, *Another Country*, *Dream One*, a clutch of low-budget *First Love* films and the theatrical version of *Far Pavilions*. From Milan, he flew straight to Miami Beach for the first, and last, American Market for International Programs (AMIP).

Eberts: AMIP was launched that year in an attempt to open up the American television market to foreign programme-makers. As this was a central plank in our own television strategy we decided to give the event a lot of support. Mike Wooller was there to talk about our programmes, Bill Gavin and Steve Walsh to handle any sales business that might arise, and I went along to shake hands and present our corporate face. On the opening night we gave an outdoor party at the Fountainbleau Hotel at which several thousand people showed up. I made a speech to welcome them all; I explained what Goldcrest was doing and what our aims and objectives were. We had by this time enough of a portfolio of television product, both completed and in the pipeline, to start talking seriously about the kind of package deals that you have to be able to put together to make an impact in the American market. Among the party guests were buyers, syndicators, network representatives, cable-company executives and other programme-makers like ourselves: a fairly representative cross-section of the American television industry. The more important ones among them were to be visited individually by Steve Walsh and me in a follow-up tour that we had scheduled to start in New York in early December.

After my speech I toured the party, introducing and being introduced to dozens of people whom I might never have reason to meet again, for, even as I worked the room, I was preoccupied by the choice I had to make between Goldcrest and Embassy.

Jerry Perenchio knew that I was getting nowhere with James, and he knew that there would soon come a point at which, if he demanded an unequivocal answer to his offer, I would almost certainly say yes. He is very good at timing. He hadn't badgered me at all when we had been together over the summer. He had raised the subject now and then but only in the most friendly, supportive, undemanding manner. He had often asked about the progress of my discussions with James, but, again, in such a way that he put no pressure on me. He was waiting for the time to be right, when he knew that James and I had reached a deadlock. Then he would become insistent.

In my hotel room at the Fountainbleau I spent hours on the phone to Jerry, James, David Puttnam, Dickie Attenborough (I begged them to put pressure on James to meet my terms) and Hollywood agent Marty Baum, who had become a friend and adviser. Marty, seeing it simply from the point of view of my career, recommended the move to Embassy: the money was better; the company was bigger and, just as importantly, Hollywood-based; I would get more experience and a fresh challenge; and I would be doing the kind of work I most enjoyed. But, like everyone else, he left me with the same parting words: 'It's up to you.'

I flew back to London on 10 November and had further talks with James. The refrain was the same: 'Pearson won't accept it.' The following Monday I had to be in Los Angeles to prepare for screenings of *Dream One* for Columbia, so on Friday I flew to Montreal to spend the weekend at our farm, where I could think things through on my own. I then flew on to LA, where, as was now customary, I stayed in Malibu. I spent most of the week with Bill Gavin and, on Sunday, 20 November, we endured some of the worst screenings either of us has ever had to sit through: *Dream One* did not go down well. The only age group that liked it was the under-twelves. I was due to fly back to London on Wednesday, 23 November, and at dinner on the Tuesday night Jerry delivered his ultimatum. He and his partner Norman Lear had finalized plans for a film fund similar to IFI, to be called Embassy Film Associates, and they intended to issue a prospectus to potential investors in the New Year. Their subscription target was $100 million, and they wanted me to raise a good part of it. When that was done, they wanted me to come up with some classy, Goldcrest-style projects, with classy Goldcrest-style film-makers attached. In exchange, they were not only prepared to pay me a lot of money, but they were happy for me to be based in London and to have no management responsibilities whatsoever: I would not be part of the Embassy hierarchy, but would report directly to Jerry and to the company's chief operating officer, Alan Horn. I had one week to give them an answer, after which the offer would be withdrawn.

As soon as I got back to London on 24 November, I met with James and told him that I was now under a lot of pressure from Jerry and that we had to settle the contract negotiation one way or another. We came no nearer to an agreement.

On Friday morning I woke up and it was as if the decision had been made in my sleep: I was going to go to Embassy. I flew back to LA that very day, only twenty-four hours after returning to London, met with Jerry, consulted my lawyer Tom Lewyn and Marty Baum, and by Saturday night it was all settled. I would start with Embassy officially on 1 January.

I flew back to London on Sunday night, arriving early on Monday morning, and went straight to Millbank Tower for a meeting with James. It was a very bright, sunny day and light flooded in through the windows. James and I exchanged the usual greetings and then he said, 'How did it go?' I said, 'Well, James, I'm here to tell you that I'm leaving.' He looked at me for a moment, as if perplexed, but I don't think he was really all that surprised. By that time, given all the problems we had had about my contract and the talks that he knew I was having with Jerry, it would have been extraordinary if he had not at some point contemplated the possibility of my going. I am sure that he was sorry about it. I am equally sure that he was very relieved to have already made his own decision to join Goldcrest full time; it meant not only that he was immediately available to take my place, but that, having already announced his intention of joining the company, he would not appear to be opportunistically jumping into my shoes. He expressed his regret and offered me his best wishes. We then spent some time working on a press release – James was naturally anxious to put the best possible gloss on my departure – and we talked about how we were going to make the announcement to the staff.

Ilott: A meeting was convened the following morning in the boardroom of Goldcrest's offices. Among those present were the old hands from the early days in Holland Park Avenue: Mike Wooller, John Chambers and his secretary Maureen Sheen, accounts staff Ken Simson and Ivy Garrett, Irene Lyons, secretary Amanda Barker and script editor Honor Borwick. Around them were the thirty or so staff who had joined the company in the past year. Absent from the meeting were Bill Gavin, who was in upstate New York spending Thanksgiving with friends; David Norris, who was in New York City doing a currency deal for *The Emerald Forest*; and Steve Walsh, who was also in New York preparing for the tour of American television companies that he was meant to be undertaking with Eberts.

Staff meetings were not a regular feature of life at Goldcrest, and it was particularly unusual to call one at such short notice. The problems surrounding Eberts's contract negotiations had been widely rumoured within the company, and the reportedly fabulous offer from Embassy had long been a talking-point. Expectations of a major announcement had, therefore, been running high for some time. Since Eberts's return from LA the previous day, he had, naturally, felt obliged to inform others of his decision: Chambers, Norris, Irene Lyons and Terry Clegg had been told in person. Eberts had left messages for Bill Gavin at the Drake Hotel in New York and had also, of course, telephoned Puttnam and Attenborough before leaving LA. Thus the word had already circulated that this meeting might be the occasion for an awful announcement.

When it came, it was still a shock. It is hard to convey what Goldcrest meant to its staff. It was more than just a company. It was more than just a job. Twelve-hour working days were commonplace at all levels. The *esprit de corps* was high, and stood in stark contrast to the truculence and cynicism prevalent elsewhere in Wardour Street. At Goldcrest, people were bound together by a sense of common purpose and, even more, by success. None of them expected that the whole house of cards would soon collapse around them. They all had reason to hope for great things from James Lee. But they knew that credit for the company's present success, even its very existence, was, no matter how much they may themselves have contributed to it, mostly due to Eberts.

Eberts: I stood in front of the meeting, James beside me, and said something like: 'I'm sure you're all wondering why we're here today. The reason is that, after much deliberation, I've decided that I'm going to leave Goldcrest and hand over the reins to James. I'm leaving because when I started the company I had in mind a small operation which was primarily to be involved with developing feature projects. Ultimately, perhaps, it would provide some production financing, but basically it was to have been a one- or two-man band. Look what's happened. It's succeeded beyond my wildest dreams – but at the same time it's grown beyond my worst nightmares. It's got to the point where it's just too big for me. I'm not an administrator, I don't operate well within big organizations, and I'm not happy when I have to compromise.

'In your best interests, as well as mine, I think it's better for a professional manager to take over and run the company in the way it needs to be run. James is available, and he's just the man for the job.'

It was only then that the full significance of my decision came home

1 Jake Eberts

2 Author Richard Adams watches as producer Martin Rosen introduces his wife, Betsy, to the Prince of Wales at the première of *Watership Down*.

3 Producer David Puttnam and director Hugh Hudson with the Best Picture
Oscar for *Chariots of Fire*.

4 Martin Sheen and Ben Kingsley in a scene from *Gandhi*.

5 Frank Price, head of Columbia Pictures, with Richard Attenborough.

9 (*top*) Director Peter Yates rehearses Albert Finney and Tom Courtenay on the set of *The Dresser*.

10 John Boorman at work.

11 (*top left*) James Lee.

12 (*top right*) Don Cruickshank, drafted in as Goldcrest's deputy chief executive.

13 Head of sales, Bill Gavin, television sales director, Steve Walsh, Jake Eberts and Goldcrest Television's managing director, Mike Wooller, at AMIP in November 1983.

14 Director of sales, Guy East.

15 Roland Joffe rehearses Haing S. Ngor and Sam Waterston while cameraman Chris Menges looks on, on *The Killing Fields'* location in Thailand.

to me: I was leaving the company I had founded, the one true success of my working life, and I was leaving people for whom I had even more respect and affection than perhaps I had realized. My speech faltered and I began to cry.

I said, somewhat fatuously, although I meant well by it, that 'the best, the nicest, thing you can do for me would be to keep it going and to respect its traditions and its values and its quality'. It was hard to say anything else. James stepped forward and said that of course nothing would change and that he was sure it would all work out for the best. Then he turned to me and thanked me for what I had done and, on behalf of the staff, wished me well in my new job.

And then we went back to our desks. It was all very British, very polite and very understated. It took about fifteen minutes. Simple as that. When it was over my only, and overwhelming, feeling was one of relief; as if the weight of the world had been lifted from my shoulders. I went back to my office and just sat there, saying, 'God, I've finally done it.'

Ilott: Then the phones started ringing. The trades, the business pages of the nationals, the Sundays, friends and rivals in the industry, shareholders, Rothschild and Freshfields: everyone wanted to know what was going on. Eberts, after all, was Goldcrest; and Goldcrest, after all, was the British film industry; and the British film industry, after all, had for the last two years been taking Hollywood by storm. It was a big story. The calls went the other way too, from Puttnam, Attenborough and Lee in particular, reassuring investors and presenting a coherent story to the press. For, at this delicate juncture in Goldcrest's planned reconstruction, it was crucial that press comment should be upbeat. At all costs, headlines of the order of 'Irreplaceable Founding Genius Quits Goldcrest, Says Company Is Too Big' (which would have been true), or 'Goldcrest Left Floundering as Eberts Quits for Embassy' (which would have proved to be true, eventually) had to be avoided: they would be guaranteed to cause uncertainty among potential investors.

Turning the story of Eberts's departure into something positive was not going to be easy when the press, which had for so long been in love with Goldcrest – had indeed raised it to the status of celebrity, and therefore treated it, as it does all its creations, as its own property and plaything – would be bound to look for evidence of skulduggery (e.g. 'Eberts Ousted'). The official press release didn't help. Instead of simply announcing the fact that Eberts was going and that James Lee was taking over, it started off:

202 / MY INDECISION IS FINAL

Pearson announces, after consultation with the board of Goldcrest and its institutional partners, a major reorganization and expansion of Goldcrest's film and television interests. As part of the arrangements, Mr James Lee, who is already non-executive chairman of Goldcrest, has assumed the role of chief executive. He will, therefore, be devoting all his time to Goldcrest and relinquishes his responsibilities for Pearson's other publishing interests. He will however remain as deputy chairman of Yorkshire Television in which Pearson has a 25 per cent shareholding.

Only then does it add, almost as an afterthought, 'Mr Jake Eberts, at present chief executive of Goldcrest, will be leaving at the end of the year.' There followed a quote from Lee, expressing his excitement, confidence in the bright future, etc., but none from Eberts. To any half-awake reporter such a form of words, and especially the absence of any quote from Eberts, clearly suggested that he had been kicked out.

Calls from *Screen International* elicited from Eberts that there was

nothing sinister about it at all. Doubt springs up when one leaves a company where things are going well, but now's the time to do it: not when things are bad. We are going into a reorganization and raising further money in the City and it would be offensive to go through with that if I was reconsidering my role. I feel great sadness to be going, but the company is much bigger now than I ever expected: I have a lot of administration and memoranda to deal with, which is not what I am built to do. James is wonderful at it and he has the full support of the management team and the board.

But to one who was unaware of the months of agonizing that had preceded Eberts's decision (and only the immediate circle of Lee, Puttnam, Attenborough, Perenchio and Co. were so aware), his professed dislike of paperwork did not sound like sufficient reason for leaving the world's most successful independent film company, especially not as he had created and built it himself. Eberts did admit to marginally more personal motives: 'In my heart I can't keep the level of energy and enthusiasm going, night and day, every day. Suddenly I'm not so keen to be at my desk at 7.30 every morning. I want to get back to what I'm best at: doing film projects and individual deals.' And he made an oblique reference to one area of Goldcrest's work with which he was clearly unhappy: 'At Embassy I do not intend to do any television at all, just British-based feature films, which is where my expertise lies. Television is not a bad business, but as far as I'm concerned it's not one that I want to be in.'

The reporter, on the look out for daggers sticking out of Eberts's back and knowing from experience that executives who have been sacked never admit it, was still not convinced. Eberts, however, was adamant:

I'm not just putting a brave face on what I'm doing. I know it's difficult for a journalist to understand. Goldcrest offered me a contract for three or five years, but I couldn't take it in good conscience. I concluded it would be better to go back to what I want to do. The combination of my desire and James's availability makes this a fortunate time for me to go. There's nothing more to it than that.

Eberts's story was confirmed by Lee. 'For myself, Jake's going is very upsetting, but the company has got a lot bigger and he found it a lot less fun,' he said, adding that, in his opinion, Jake 'hankers for the past'. He then offered, as a further, and clearly more convincing, explanation for Eberts's departure: 'Embassy have offered him a lot of money.'

Lee was sensitive to the possibility that press speculation, especially in the trades, would concentrate on Eberts's dazzling success and contrast it with his own inexperience. He therefore emphasized Goldcrest's 'competent and well-bedded-down' management, and he took great pains to outline the company's new prospects for growth.

We are set to raise additional capital and we hope, in three or four years' time, to launch it as a public company. Jake's leaving won't influence that at all, except perhaps to add a bit of a delay. We were to get final approval from shareholders on 4 December. That may be put back a month; at the most three months. What we're trying to do is to have a sufficiently large shareholders' capital to sustain a greater level of production and we will increasingly be able to take on productions without partners. Most of our films to date are co-productions because we don't have the cash to finance them ourselves. After the reconstruction we will have more films and a bigger Goldcrest share in those films.

Lee than went on to stress one significant difference between the policy of the new regime and that of the old.

We would at any rate have had to look at the project-development side. Jake's going just makes that more urgent. His way of working was to use established producers; we'd do the deals and we'd do the selling, but we were not in the business of developing new scripts and new people. Consequently we've relied very heavily on David Puttnam. The distinction between Enigma and Goldcrest has become blurred.

Goldcrest, it seemed, was to move away from Eberts's policy of relying on proven film-makers and to move towards the risky, and expensive, area of nurturing talent itself.

Puttnam took up this theme: 'Jake didn't ever develop projects and one thing that will now change stylistically is that at Goldcrest there will be less deal-making and more developing. When you have a low capital base you have to deal, but when you have a high capital base you don't need to.'

Stressing that 'you can't replace Jake; it's like someone whose wife has died', Puttnam further suggested that two new people might have to be brought on board, 'a developer and a deal-maker', and he predicted that Lee was 'going to have to learn very fast'.

Underlying many of the comments made by Lee, Attenborough and Puttnam, and curiously by Eberts himself, was that in the context of the new-look Goldcrest, Lee was in many ways better qualified than Eberts to be chief executive. All remarked on Eberts's distaste for corporate responsibility and his penchant for small-scale operations.

That week's edition of *Screen International* duly obliged with an upbeat interpretation of events, blandly, if accurately, headlined 'Eberts Leaves for Embassy – Founder and Chief Executive of Goldcrest Quits'. Taking its cue from Pearson's press release, the story gave as much emphasis to the planned reorganization and recapitalization as to the loss of Eberts, who was compensated by getting a side-bar story of his own concentrating on his new role at Embassy. It was much the same in the other trades and in the nationals. 'A Chariot Changes Drivers', proclaimed the (Pearson-owned) *Financial Times*, while *Variety* meekly let it be known that 'Eberts Moves to Embassy International'. The *Hollywood Reporter*, in a story filed by its London correspondent Chris Auty, did manage to raise an eyebrow with 'Goldcrest Films Loses Eberts in Surprise Move to Embassy'. But all of them took the line, fed by Puttnam and Attenborough, that, with Eberts staying in London and bringing lots of Embassy dollars to British projects, in effect there would now be two Goldcrests instead of one. *The Times* went so far as to run the story of Eberts's departure under the headline 'British Cinema Gets Hollywood Boost'. Even the normally astute *Financial Times*, having raised the question 'Has James Lee the sort of entrepreneurial flair that can spot winners?' let Eberts, of all people, answer it with the bland observation that 'he has a good nose for a deal and has been a very active chairman'.

It was left to film-maker Alan Parker, who regularly furnished topical cartoons for *Screen International*, to make the point that the loss of Eberts spelled catastrophe. In his cartoon that week, two film executives are pictured having drinks. One is reading the news of Eberts's departure from Goldcrest when the other leans across to inform him, 'They're renaming it Bronzecrest.' Parker, like Bill Gavin, John Boorman and Terry Clegg, did not believe in a Goldcrest without Eberts.

Eberts: I spent the next few days clearing up my desk and briefing James on the status of all the films and all the deals. He moved into my office almost immediately and the changeover took much less time than one would have expected. Of course, I was still going to be in London and I was always available for consultation. In fact, for the next two or three months I would get calls asking for information and clarification and I was always happy to oblige.

As soon as I was out of it, though, one thing immediately became clear: I had been burnt out with Goldcrest.

Burn-out is relative. There are many people who are much busier and much more successful in business than I have been who haven't been worn down by it. Carlo Benedetti, Rupert Murdoch, Robert Maxwell and Jimmy Goldsmith, for example, are people who have relentless drive and energy, who never let up and yet who never seem to suffer. But others, who maybe only work nine to five as clerks in insurance companies, doing repetitive calculations all day, can be destroyed by it. It's not the exclusive domain of people who run companies.

I think I suffered from burn-out because I never stopped thinking about the business: twenty-four hours a day, seven days a week, no matter what I was doing, where I was or whom I was with, I had Goldcrest on my mind, never anything else. I couldn't hold an intelligent conversation with my kids. I had nothing to say about the world or the people in it: it was always Goldcrest, Goldcrest, Goldcrest. I was totally obsessed. I knew it, but I couldn't stop. And, not being able to stop I grew resentful. It got to the point that I would get angry when the telephone rang at 8 o'clock at night, even if it was good news. I didn't want to hear *any* news. The person on the line would say, 'Great, the grosses are up', or 'The deal is done', or whatever it was, and I would be seething that I had had to take that call. But my anger was all inwardly directed. The obsession had become an ordeal.

I had been doing it for too long and too intensively, with never any kind of relief. It was my own fault, I know, but I had no idea how to deal with it. I took holidays. I used to go away every summer for a couple of weeks to Canada and I used to go skiing for a week every winter. But I couldn't relax. I couldn't get work off my mind.

By the autumn of 1983 it had got to the point where the thought of having to go to one more staff meeting, review one more legal document or discuss one more deal would send me into a depression. Looking back, I must have been on the brink of some sort of nervous breakdown. And that, as much as anything, is the reason that I quit. Jerry, you see, lavished attention on me and held out the promise of a golden, stress-free, debt-free life. When I did the deal with him I could hardly believe it: it was a wonderful, wonderful feeling – the anxiety was over.

On Friday, 9 December 1983, I walked out of the Goldcrest offices for the last time.

Or so I thought.

Chapter Twenty

An Uncertain Future

'The scene was set for disaster almost from the beginning' – James Lee

Ilott: When James Lee took over as chief executive of Goldcrest in December 1983, he did so in circumstances and in an atmosphere that were far from happy. From Eberts he had inherited many problems. Some were familiar – for example, the already urgent question of what to do about the unprofitable television division – and had been discussed at length by the two men before Eberts left. Others – the dearth of new projects in the pipeline, for example, or Columbia Pictures' decision not to pay for *Dream One* on the grounds that the picture was so bad that it was unreleasable – were soon to make themselves known.

But Lee's immediate, and most burdensome, inheritance was the ghost of Eberts himself. Eberts had created the company, and many senior executives owed a strong allegiance to him. Some, like Bill Gavin, lost heart the day that he left.

Gavin was then forty-six years old and had had a colourful as well as a chequered career. Born and bred in New Zealand, his first passion was for fast cars: he became a motor-racing journalist, wrote a biography of champion driver Jim Clark and was for a while manager of the Ferrari sports-car team. He walked away from motor racing in the early 1970s, and, at the age of thirty-seven, happened upon the film business, becoming managing director of GTO Film Distributors in London. In 1978 he was appointed general manager of one of Australia's leading cinema chains, Hoyts, whose business he extended into distribution. Two years later, he was back in London working as a salesman for Lew Grade's company, ITC. There he built up his all-important list of contacts and clients (as he recalls, in those days Lew Grade's name 'opened every door in the business'), and, early in 1982, after the demise of ITC, started working for Goldcrest.

By 1983 Gavin was in the top echelon of the world's film salesmen.

He was devoted to Goldcrest, but in particular he was devoted to Eberts, who was, as far as he was concerned, 'the leader, the guv'nor, no doubt about it . . . a really dedicated man . . . an original, really, in our business'. He could not conceive of Goldcrest's 'being run in any other way than as his [Eberts's] company'. He had been aware of Eberts's contract negotiations with Lee and the approaches made by Embassy, but he had been led to believe that matters had been satisfactorily resolved and that Eberts was staying. This impression had been reinforced during the week that they had spent together in LA preparing for the *Dream One* screenings, throughout which time, Gavin says, Eberts was 'one hundred per cent Goldcrest'.

After those screenings, Gavin spent Thanksgiving weekend with friends in upstate New York. He returned to the Drake Hotel in Manhattan without any inkling of what was to come. There he found, under the door of his room, a raft of messages, from Eberts and from Lee. He phoned Eberts first, and was stunned to hear that he was leaving the company.

He remembers the call: 'I said, "Jake you must do what's right for you. The company owes you everything and you owe it nothing." He was very appreciative of my comments at the time, because clearly other people were leaning on him. Don't forget, this was in the middle of the restructure, the refinancing and all of that.'

For all his words of encouragement, Gavin believed that Eberts's departure was 'a disaster for the company'. He called Lee, to be reassured that matters were in hand, that there would be a smooth transition and nothing, essentially, need change. But Gavin had no regard for Lee's film skills, and had little confidence that the management team would pull together once Eberts had gone.

The following day he met David Norris, who was in New York negotiating a currency deal for *The Emerald Forest*. In the course of their discussion, Gavin raised the matter of Lee's inexperience: while Lee might quickly pick up the reins of corporate affairs, he said, he clearly could not be entrusted with decisions about projects and scripts. Norris, in agreement, mentioned that Sandy Lieberson, Puttnam's erstwhile partner, had already been tipped to take over that side of the job. The mention of Lieberson was enough to convince Gavin that Eberts's departure and the takeover by Lee were the result of a conspiracy, 'a Lee–Puttnam–Norris plot'. Whether he was right or wrong – Norris, for one, took a lot of persuading that the appointment of Lieberson was a good idea – it was what Gavin believed, and it is what decided him, there and then, to tender his resignation as soon as he got back to London.

Similar thoughts occupied the mind of Terry Clegg. As far as the physical production of films was concerned – from budgeting to delivery of finished prints – Clegg, who had been in the movie business for nearly twenty years and had worked on films in every kind of production capacity, was by far the most experienced of the Goldcrest executives. It was his expertise, for example, that had cleared the obstacles from Dickie Attenborough's path when they were making *Gandhi* in India, and his advice had often been useful to Eberts.

'Jake's main skill,' notes Cruickshank, 'notwithstanding that he comes across as someone the film-makers can empathize with, is actually generating a view, and quite a wise view, as to whether a script at a certain budget has any chance of making money'. For a second opinion concerning the cost side of the equation, Eberts relied on Clegg. And when a project was lucky enough to be given the green light, it was Clegg who vetted the budget, supervised the pre-production and watched for warning signals should the film threaten to fall behind schedule. Clegg himself describes his role as that of 'an adviser, a court chamberlain to come in and tell him [Eberts] the facts of life'. It was not a creative contribution – 'that's not something I've had a lot of experience in,' he says – but more to do with 'the nuts and bolts' of making movies.

Just as Eberts's avoidance of unpleasantness is the weakness most often noted by his colleagues, so his ability to inspire and collaborate with experienced and respected figures like Clegg is his most often-remarked strength. Like Gavin, Clegg's loyalty to Goldcrest was outweighed by his personal loyalty to Eberts. 'Everybody believed in him,' he says. 'He has great magnetism. I couldn't believe it when I heard that he wasn't staying with the company. I was absolutely devastated. My instant reaction was that I was going to leave. I felt: "This is it, the company's finished for me. The company was Jake, and Jake's not here. I don't want to be part of a company with different people at the head, people I really don't know anything about." '

Steve Walsh, waiting in New York for Eberts to join him, was also 'absolutely shattered' when he learned of Eberts's resignation, 'I was taken by surprise. I really wasn't aware that things had got that bad,' he says. Like Gavin, Walsh 'had no doubt at all' that 'a number of people' had been anxious to get rid of Eberts: 'I've never been quite sure what Puttnam's position was, but I do know that afterwards Puttnam had a much easier time than he did before. Under James [Lee], some of the things that happened that were of benefit to Puttnam were really quite extraordinary.'

Again, it doesn't matter whether or not Walsh was right in his suspicions. (Puttnam appears to have lobbied hard on Eberts's behalf until he realized that the case was hopeless, at which point, in typically pragmatic fashion – 'I was very upset,' he says, 'but nothing could be done about it' – he hitched his horse firmly to the new wagon.) What matters is that such suspicions had arisen, and that Walsh, Gavin and to some extent Clegg – who found it 'bizarre . . . and a bit twisted somehow' that Lee, the agent representing Eberts's interests to the Pearson board, should end up taking Eberts's job – gave them credence.

The conspiracy theories were aired in the flurry of meetings that took place between Goldcrest's senior managers in the first days of December. Inevitably, they percolated down through the company. Film salesman Guy East vaguely remembers that 'there was a suspicion that there had been political manoeuvring around shareholders and other executives that had made him [Eberts] leave'. Accountant Andy Parsons talks of 'the pressure that had been unduly put on Jake by the coming of Messrs Cruickshank and Lee'.

Beyond the company, too, rumours circulated that Eberts had been ditched. John Boorman, who was particularly close to Eberts throughout this period and later was to have no reason to love Lee, still believes that 'there is no question that James Lee had been manoeuvring to get Jake out so that he could come in and take his place'. There was a lot of talk of that kind in Wardour Street at the time.

If Richard Attenborough is right, there is an awful irony in all this. According to him, had the original Gang of Four idea come off, and had Lee then had a free hand in running Goldcrest, he would 'almost certainly have found the money to keep Jake'. The problem, as Attenborough sees it, lay in the fact that 'James was constantly facing Blakenham's lieutenants, all of whom were very skilful, supposedly highly paid individuals, who at the end of the day were earning a quarter of what Jake had asked for'.

Eberts had not been the only skilled, and certainly not the most experienced, executive at Goldcrest. Nor was his record without blemish: *The Far Pavilions*, after all, which lost £2 million, had been his idea. But he was the only leader. Staff were stunned not only by the surprise of his departure but by the realization of the loss of his leadership. John Chambers remembers being 'flabbergasted' and 'absolutely dumbfounded'. It was, he says, 'an unmitigated disaster . . . How the hell were we going to make it work without Jake there?' Chambers's secretary,

Maureen Sheen, remembers being 'very upset . . . we all were', while in-house solicitor Peter Coles speaks of the 'general dismay' in the Holland Street offices. And in Millbank Tower, Pearson's director of finance, and newly elected Goldcrest board member, James Joll was 'aghast' when he heard the news.

Eberts had energy, enthusiasm and a great aptitude for the business, but more than that he had the confidence of everyone in the company. When he left, there was no equivalent figure, certainly not Lee, to whom that confidence could be transferred, and when the crises came in 1985, Goldcrest, by then faction-ridden and overburdened with leaders (real and would-be), found itself unexpectedly vulnerable. Individual efforts to keep the thing afloat were admirable, and James Lee was to be as indefatigable in the struggle as any, but the collective will of the managers, amongst whom, Lee says, there had been 'constant wrangling' from the start of his administration, was found to be missing. When the *Revolution* crisis hit the company, it was, in Lee's words, 'the inability of that group to coalesce as a team and to rally round' that destroyed Goldcrest.

It was a failure that had its roots in Lee's inability to establish the kind of hold over the company that Eberts had had. Indeed it could be said that, for all his dynamism and force of personality – and Lee is a much more assertive character than Eberts – he was never properly in control of the company at all. He wasn't Eberts, and that, in the eyes of some people in the company, was his problem.

The choice of a new chief executive was Pearson's, it being the major shareholder in Goldcrest and sole owner of the management company that employed the staff and ran the partnerships. Lee was the only candidate – having made himself available it would have been extraordinary for Pearson to have gone looking for somebody else – and his appointment was duly confirmed by Lord Blakenham. It was thus, in effect, a *fait accompli*. Reaction to the appointment was mixed.

First, there were Lee's supporters. Michael Stoddart, who had made the original investment in Goldcrest alongside Pearson in 1976, remembers that the prevailing wisdom among the shareholders was that Lee 'was perceived at the time to be a first-class chief executive, an ex-McKinsey man, thoroughly businesslike'. Joll, too, was greatly relieved that Lee was going to take over, Pearson's anxiety at the loss of Eberts being 'somewhat mollified at the fact that James was willing to do it . . . He was very competent and very confident and there was no reason to think that he wouldn't be able to deal with his lack of experience and so on – he had some very good people around him.' Joll's colleague, Alan

Whitaker, confirms that Lee's inexperience did not worry Pearson: Lee 'never lacked nerve', he says, adding, 'I have never known anyone as self-confident as James, never'. Mike Wooller, although 'very sad' that Eberts had left – 'because he was the man who had held it together; he was the man with the kind of charisma that people gather around' – nevertheless felt 'fine' at the thought of Lee taking his place. 'James was the man who had approached me in the first place and the man who had been, I suppose, the champion of television,' he says. And David Puttnam 'rightly or wrongly' had 'absolute' confidence in Lee, asserting, in addition, but without justification, that 'everyone did, not just me'.

Second, there were Lee's opponents, Gavin and Clegg, who, while they were never reconciled to his leadership, nevertheless speak highly of his personal qualities.

'I first met him when he came out to India and he virtually saved the movie [*Gandhi*],' recalls Clegg. 'I was quite impressed with him. I thought he was a nice man and I thought he was very together. Yes, I liked him. But to take over from Jake running a movie company – somebody who doesn't know anything about movies – I had very unhappy feelings about that. So many movie companies are run by people who don't really know anything about making movies. In the end it all comes down to the entrepreneurial figure at the top: do they have the little bit of magic that makes them great, or don't they?'

As far as Clegg was concerned, Eberts had it 'without a doubt', whereas what he had seen of Lee 'wasn't very encouraging . . . he was very much a businessman, not a creative person'.

Gavin, who claims to have 'never had a cross word' with Lee, was of the 'clear opinion' that 'James had no creative skills, no financial skills, no legal skills, no negotiating skills at all. I mean, I may be doing him a disservice, but I just didn't know what his value was to Goldcrest.'

And, third, there were the undecided; in particular, Dickie Attenborough, David Norris and John Chambers, and, behind them, the rest of the staff. Attenborough, who had become a very close friend of Eberts since the making of *Gandhi*, and who had had high hopes for what Goldcrest might become under his leadership, was greatly upset by his resignation. 'It was madness to let Jake go,' he says. 'Total madness. At the end of the day what do we all depend on? We depend on somebody's instinct. You can do all the calculations that you like, but at the end of the day you either go or you don't go. There's no other way of doing it. Of all the things you pay for in the movie business – forget the directors and producers – the thing that is of value is that somebody says, "I will back that", or "I will invest in that". And that know-how, that smell, that touch, that instinct – that can put the finger exactly on the public's pulse – that's what we pay for. It's that judgement that is worth tens of millions to any company. And that is what Jake has. That is what Mike Eisner has at Disney. That's what Frank Price had at Columbia.'

As far as Attenborough could discern, Lee didn't have it.

Nor, on a personal level, was their relationship an easy one. 'I was never totally relaxed with James, never felt completely at ease. I think it was on both sides to some measure, in that we are from very, very different worlds. We had difficulty finding common ground,' he says.

Attenborough thus greeted Lee's appointment with apprehension. Despite that, he was to play an important part in keeping the ship afloat in the early weeks of the Lee regime, persuading Clegg, in particular, to stay on board until matters had settled down.

The position of Norris and Chambers in the days after Eberts left is quite complex and, given the role that each was to play in the subsequent history of the company, is worth sketching here in some detail.

Norris, then forty-four, had been a partner in the leading law firm of Denton Hall and Burgin for thirteen years. He had specialized in entertainment law, had vast experience of distribution contracts – it was he who had devised the first deal structure for *Watership Down* – and had handled the personal legal affairs of a number of outstanding film clients, among them, for many years, John Boorman. By the time he joined Goldcrest in 1982 (incidentally at great personal financial cost; he made the move, he says, because he wanted the experience of being 'nearer the bows of the ship'), he was recognized as one of the most experienced and influential film and television lawyers in the UK. Indeed, he was one of the very few who could work on equal terms with the best in Los Angeles and New York.

John Chambers, then forty-five, is a seemingly down-to-earth accountant, whose bluff, north-country manner belies his considerable ambition. He entered the film industry in 1974 after six years in the oil business, and was head-hunted by Goldcrest from the position of finance director of EMI Films Group, where he had handled the finances of both one of the biggest successes, *The Deer Hunter*, and one of the biggest failures, *Honky Tonk Freeway*, in British film history. Familiar with the minutiae of distribution deals, tax and equity leasing, capitalization and amortization of assets, and all the other specialized financial paraphernalia of the film business, Chambers, like Norris, was an acknowledged expert in the field.

The two of them were the back-office executives, the real managers, of the company. Gavin and Clegg operated semi-autonomously, with few management responsibilities – which goes some way to explain the equanimity with which they contemplated resignation. Mike Wooller, although nominally managing director of Goldcrest Television, had all along confessed to having no particular business skills and operated mostly as a commissioning editor–executive producer, a role in television similar to that played by David Puttnam on his smaller feature films. It was left to Norris and Chambers, who at that time formed a very close alliance, to run the corporate machine: to ensure that contracts were signed, bills were paid, office systems worked and decisions were followed through. In carrying out these roles in Eberts's time they had had to shoulder more than the usual burden of managerial responsibility, and consequently had gained even greater authority in the eyes of the staff, by virtue of the fact that they had more industry experience than Eberts had and he would constantly turn to them for advice. Eberts was anyway a great delegator, not only letting them run their departments more or less as they wished, but passing on to them some of his own administrative chores.

Of the forty-one staff employed by Goldcrest at the end of 1983, the majority answered, directly or indirectly, to either Norris or Chambers. Even those who did not had become used to looking to them for guidance, if for no other reason than that they were often the only executives available. Through most of 1983, Eberts had spent days, even weeks, at a time out of the country; Gavin and his sales team had likewise been traipsing from market to market; Clegg had spent most of his time in studios or on locations; and Wooller had been buried beneath the considerable weight of the creative and other problems of the two dozen or so television projects that he had initiated. The staff thus came to regard the ever-present Norris and Chambers as virtually the joint managing directors of the company; and, by December, especially with Eberts gone, that was exactly how Norris and Chambers saw themselves. Indeed, it was they who had long since stepped forward, uninvited but also unopposed, to fill the management gap that had been identified by Puttnam and Lee, and acknowledged by Eberts, in the Gang of Four discussions in June. And it was into their world, much more than Bill Gavin's or Terry Clegg's, that Lee was now to venture. He did so in blithe ignorance of the facts, believing that the real power structure of the company conformed to the hierarchy set out in the staff chart: that Norris and Chambers were no more than departmental heads and would serve him as they had served Eberts.

When, within only a few days of his arrival at Holland Street, Lee became aware of Norris's and Chambers's claims, he was 'completely taken aback . . . blown out of the water'. They had seen themselves, he realized, 'clearly, as not just the joint number twos to Jake, but really as part of a three-man team'. And, from the minute that he grasped that fact, he knew that his hopes of quickly establishing himself as 'the strategist at the head of a smooth-running, sympathetic organization' were forlorn. For Norris and Chambers were far too senior, too experienced and too well established within both the company and the industry, meekly to accept Lee's inexpert generalship.

Indeed, they had already had to overcome considerable initial scepticism before being reconciled to the proposal that Lee should join the company at all, even alongside Eberts. Now that Eberts had gone, the idea of Lee's running the show on his own revived all their earlier objections.

'Although at that time I had great affection, and still do, for James, and also great respect for his intellect, I knew it was going to be a more difficult task in terms of working together,' observes Norris. 'I judged him to be very strong in his opinions . . . a lot of people from the world of external analysts are tremendously good at telling you what's wrong, but they haven't had any experience of running a business so they have to undergo a great learning curve to get to grips [with it].'

'He's a very bright guy,' adds Chambers. 'He's one of the few people at board meetings who, if you presented some financial data, would know what you were on about. He would ask very intelligent questions. I used to be very impressed with him . . . But he did not have much experience of hands-on running of a business. What he was doing [at Pearson Longman] was acting as chairman of all the businesses, at one remove from what was going on, which is very different from being involved day to day.'

Adding to their concerns was the unspecified role to be played by Don Cruickshank. Again, the proposal that Cruickshank, whom James Joll describes as 'an immensely sensible, head-screwed-on guy', should join the company had been discussed before Eberts's resignation, and Norris and Chambers had, albeit reluctantly, gone along with it (although interestingly, Eberts himself never seems to have given it his full sanction). Clearly, with Eberts gone, Cruickshank, Lee's right-hand man, would become, in one form or another, the deputy chief of Goldcrest. There would thus be two inexperienced executives at the head of a company that could not afford one, let alone two, such learning curves at that level.

Cruickshank, then forty, had worked alongside Lee at Pearson Longman and had spent many hours drawing up the reorganization and placing documents for both GFI and GFTP. At the time of Eberts's resignation, he was deeply immersed in the documentation for the new company, Goldcrest Holdings. He thus understood the structure and constitution of Goldcrest probably as well as anybody, but he did not know anything about the movie business. He had started out as an accountant, working for the Aluminium Company of Canada (of which, by coincidence, Eberts's father had once been vice-president and company secretary). He then went to Manchester Business School, where he took an MBA, and spent three years at McKinsey, which is where he first met Lee. In 1976 he joined Times Newspapers, of which he became, first of all, commercial director, and then general manager of the *Sunday Times*. He left the Times organization when Rupert Murdoch acquired it in 1981 and, at Lee's invitation, joined Pearson Longman as development director, investigating those areas of new investment that had so concerned Lee when he first took charge of the cash-rich company in 1980. Cruickshank was intimately involved in Pearson's acquisition of the 25 per cent stake in Yorkshire Television, the bid for the breakfast-television franchise and the building up and successive recapitalizations of Goldcrest. He was the man most responsible for Goldcrest's moves into cable television, via what was then known as the Television Entertainment Group, and video publishing, via Catalyst Video. While his corporate role at Pearson Longman was that of a combined finance director and business analyst, his personal importance to Lee was that, as James Joll puts it, he was his 'rock-solid partner . . . foil . . . anchor . . . brake'.

Cruickshank, personally, was held in high esteem and his skills were respected, but there was great scepticism within Goldcrest that he was actually needed in the company.

'We said, "Hang on a minute – Don's a nice guy but why do we need him as well?" ' recalls Chambers. 'And of course it had certain implications for David [Norris] and me. I said to James, "What exactly is he going to do? What is his relationship to me going to be?" It was all a bit unresolved. At least he was an accountant – although he'd done little accounting, more consulting – but when it came to business affairs there was a much bigger gap in expertise. David just said, "What do I need Don Cruickshank for?" '

Cruickshank himself was aware of, and made very uneasy by, this lack of enthusiasm for his appointment: 'The sort of role I might play was clear to people like John, and it really cut across his area of responsibility quite a bit, and indirectly would have meant him working to me. And I can understand why that wasn't particularly palatable. David Norris, to a certain extent, [felt] the same thing.'

Was there, in fact, ever a job for Cruickshank at Goldcrest?

'You bet there was,' asserts Lee. 'I mean, in the context of where we were going to go there was. Because I had great plans that we were going to develop further, raise more money, evolve into other things, and I saw him very much as my *alter ego* in new affairs.'

Yet Lee acknowledges that Cruickshank was bound to step on other people's toes, and even admits to having had a 'hidden agenda' (his words) according to which Cruickshank would police Chambers by 'trying to bring a little more control, financial control, into the company . . . Although we had lots and lots of information at Goldcrest – every month John would produce tomes of stuff . . . documents analysing everything . . . every single film, vast amounts of detail – it was never all pulled together into an overall context. And I saw Don doing that.'

How Chambers was supposed to interpret this, other than as a declaration of no confidence, is hard to imagine. Eberts had relied very heavily on Chambers; Lee, it seemed, was going to rely on Cruickshank, leaving Chambers with the role of glorified bookkeeper. However, Lee insists that opposition to Cruickshank was never voiced until after the decision had been made. 'There was no hint that he was unacceptable from either Jake, or from Chambers or Norris,' he says.

Cruickshank offers two reasons for leaving his promising position at Pearson in favour of a rather ill-defined role in a business about which he admits he knew nothing. The first is that, having spent a large part of the previous three months drawing up the prospectus for Goldcrest Holdings, he simply found himself sucked into the venture. 'Once you have put your name in a prospectus and you've been appointed a director, the whole weight of the machine rolls on and you find yourself deposited – as if you'd been a snowball and rolled down a mountain slope to the bottom, as it were – and you're not quite sure how you got there,' he says.

The second is that, having had experience of both financial management, at Times Newspapers and at Pearson Longman, and general management, at the *Sunday Times*, he was very keen to return to the general-management role, which is what he thought Goldcrest offered. This reasoning, of course, rather flies in the face of Lee's vision of him as a financial overlord, but it would not be inconsistent with the way things happened at that time for the two of them to have had quite different understandings of what his role actually was to be.

One key figure not quoted in the balance of forces outlined above, because he has not yet properly entered the story, is Sandy Lieberson. The hitherto relatively stable power structure of Goldcrest had already

been upset by the departure of Eberts and by the problems of accommo-
dating the claims of Norris, Chambers, Cruickshank and Lee alongside
the still senior figure of Mike Wooller. Now it looked as if Lieberson,
the only name seriously put forward to be the creative leader of the
company (a job that Lee knew he was not qualified to do himself), would
have to be added to the equation. In a film company, the man or woman
who makes the investment decisions – from which all the rest of the
company's business naturally flows – is, or should be, the leader, no
matter that he or she may answer to a president or chairman, and no
matter how many corporate managers sit at his or her right hand. Eberts
had been a typical example of this. But while it was now being proposed
that Lieberson, or someone like him, should make the investment
decisions, it was not being proposed, certainly not by Norris and Chambers and least of all by Lee, that he should be the leader of the company.
It was a contradiction that was never to be resolved.

The other key figure not quoted is Lee himself, who, while naturally
reluctant to sing his own praises, can presumably be counted as having
been on the side of his admirers. According to Mike Wooller, he had
'quite grand ideas that he was going to be the Messiah of the future
success of the British film industry . . . and, to a certain extent, at that
time one could see no reason why he shouldn't be.'

The situation then, in the first week of December 1983 – before Lee
had even lifted a finger or made an executive decision – was that Goldcrest, a genuinely happy, successful and settled company under Eberts,
was already enveloped in a cloud of confusion and anxiety. The ever-
ebullient Lee was delighted to be in command and he enjoyed the strong
support of the shareholders, none of whom had any idea either that he
was unsuitable for the job or that he was unwelcome to the management,
and nearly all of whom were gratified to see in him a man of their own
ilk. He was rejected by Gavin and Clegg, who also saw him as a man of
the shareholders' ilk, and who, on those grounds, regarded him as being
totally unsuited to run a film company. The non-executive and non-
investing board members, including Puttnam, Attenborough, Penguin
boss Peter Mayer and Longman's Tim Rix, were, by all accounts, divided
in their opinions. Of the management team, only Wooller really welcomed Lee, and then mainly because he looked to him to improve the
status of television within the company. Norris and Chambers, who in
many ways held the keys to the company's future, were sceptical and
unsettled, although in the end they set aside their doubts and agreed to
'suck it and see' (Norris) and 'give it a go' (Chambers). The rest of the
staff took much the same view. Lee had brought in Don Cruickshank,

for whom there was no obvious need, and he was proposing to bring in Sandy Lieberson, whose appointment, as we will see, was to be opposed by virtually the entire management team. Already there were three senior, and expensive, executives – Lee, Cruickshank and Lieberson – each of them accompanied by secretarial and back-up staff (and in Lieberson's case eventually by a whole script-development team), being squeezed into the space left by Eberts, the price for whose services, remember, had been rejected by Pearson as being too high. Where there had been an acknowledged management gap, mostly filled by Norris and Chambers, there was now to be a huge management surplus – with predictable, faction-forming consequences.

Chapter Twenty-one

A New Head of Production

Ilott: On Monday, 5 December, Bill Gavin returned from New York and informed James Lee that he was resigning. Lee asked him to give the matter further consideration.

'He said, "Look, let's not even discuss it now. Think about it for another twenty-four hours," ' recalls Gavin. 'So I got in the following morning and there was an offer from him on my desk – I mean a really substantial increase in salary. And so I thought about it for another day or two. I thought, "Well, it would not be all that great for the company if I left right now, and if they want me this badly I should give them the benefit of the doubt." So, I thir' not to my credit, I stayed on.'

Significantly, Gavin did not extend the benefit of the doubt so far as to sign the new contract of employment that he was offered.

Clegg, too, had announced his intention of leaving. His contract ran until the end of July 1984, but he could see no virtue in 'hanging on if I don't really have faith in the progress of the company'.

'But then, of course, lots of pressure was put on us not to rock the boat, because the company was at that point seeking to find additional capital for movies. Dickie Attenborough, who was also distressed at what had happened, came to me and said, "Whatever your personal feelings about what has happened here, if you guys leave this company is going to fall apart. We won't get the additional capital. There'll be a tremendous hoo-ha in the press about what is and what isn't happening in the company, and the company will be on the downward path. You've got to stick with it, see your contract out and give them the chance to find their feet. Give them the same sort of support that you gave Jake." '

Clegg, too, allowed himself to be persuaded.

For the moment, then, the management structure seemed to be settled – except for the problem of Lieberson. On 12 December the first management meeting under James Lee's leadership was held in the Holland

Street boardroom. Lieberson's proposed appointment as head of production was the major item on the agenda.

Although the ill-conceived plan to appoint Lieberson managing director of Goldcrest Films in 1982 had been abandoned, the door had been left open to him, and Puttnam and Lee had made intermittent soundings throughout the early part of 1983, again to no avail. (According to Lieberson, he 'wasn't interested' in any of their propositions.) Then, in the summer, the financially hard-pressed Ladd Company had indicated that it was going to close its London office and Lieberson was to be out of a job. He quickly made plans to set up in partnership with three of the most sought-after talents in British films, Alan Parker, Alan Marshall and Hugh Hudson. Eberts, who, a few years before, had arranged the financing for Parker and Marshall's *Pink Floyd: The Wall* and had provided development financing for Hudson's *Chariots of Fire*, had been keen to bring the new grouping into Goldcrest and had proposed a relationship along the lines of Goldcrest's deal with David Puttnam. But this proposal, too, had come to nothing, because the partnership never materialized (partly, according to an amused Lieberson, 'because Parker and Hudson ultimately couldn't agree about how not to agree').

Following Eberts's decision to quit, the soon-to-be-unemployed Lieberson was approached again, this time with the proposal that he take sole creative control of the company.

Lee, it should be said, was under considerable pressure to make an immediate appointment. Not only had Eberts's departure thrown the management team into turmoil, but, given Lee's inexperience in films, it had raised serious questions about the future direction of the company, especially in the minds of Goldcrest's customers among the independent distributors and Hollywood studios. More than that, preparations for Goldcrest's reorganization and recapitalization, which had started at the end of August and of which venture-capital fund managers in the City were already well aware, had had to be suspended. This state of affairs could not be allowed to continue for more than a few days. In placings of this kind, there comes a point at which form is all. With prestigious names like N. M. Rothschild giving their imprimatur to the prospectus, due process has to be observed, and be seen to be observed, for confidence – that mostly indefinable quality that is yet so highly valued by investors – to be maintained. For there to have been a change of top management at such a delicate stage in the proceedings was a grave embarrassment to all concerned and was bound to be interpreted as a vote of no confidence in the company by its erstwhile chief. The damage thus caused could be contained, but only by the immediate appointment of a very senior and respected production executive – someone who in film terms would be at least on a par with Eberts, and who, in purely business terms, could stand comfortably alongside James Lee – whose willingness to join the company could be presented to investors as evidence of its continued soundness and respectability.

But who, in London, was there? Puttnam recalls that only three names were ever proposed for the job – 'it wasn't as if we were looking at a great slew of people' – and that the outstanding candidate among them was Sandy Lieberson.

Lieberson, bearded, casually dressed and, in those days, often to be seen arriving at his office on a bicycle, was then forty-seven. He was a man of wide experience. An American, he had started out as an agent in Rome before producing his own pictures in London. He had good contacts among film-makers and independent distributors in most of the leading territories in the world. He had also worked in Hollywood and was known to, and respected by, the studios. Above all, he was a familiar and well liked – in Lee's phrase, 'almost godfatherly' – figure in the British creative community. It was the special esteem in which Lieberson was held by British film-makers that gave Puttnam and Lee reason to hope that he would nurture younger and newer talents where Eberts had relied on senior producers and directors of known ability.

Not the least consideration was that Lieberson had been Puttnam's partner for fifteen years and the two were the closest of friends. On the one hand, this would of course lead to accusations, such as were levelled by Steve Walsh and Bill Gavin, that Lieberson was Puttnam's puppet. On the other, it would guarantee some kind of continuity, as well as an especially close relationship between the company and its most important producer – no small advantage in the aftermath of Eberts's departure.

And Lieberson was, after all, Puttnam's choice. As Richard Attenborough has observed, it is part of Puttnam's 'massive skill' to 'choose the right people, creatively and organizationally'.

'He was absolutely sure about Sandy,' Attenborough says, 'not only in terms of instinct but in terms of track record. I didn't know anything about Sandy. I believed that there had to be a figure – no question – but whether he was the right man to handle Goldcrest or not I didn't know. But I accepted absolutely what David said.'

The management team, however, saw things differently. In the first place, they were not especially impressed by Lieberson.

'There was certainly some advantage in having somebody with a North American accent and access to the people at the top level in that marketplace,' says David Norris. 'And it's fair to say that when Jake went and one looked around to see who one could get, there weren't a great many candidates. There certainly weren't a great many candidates in the context of James being the new, self-elected chief executive. But I had no reason to think, much as I liked Sandy, that he could lead the company, in terms of creative decisions, any more than James could.'

'It was absolutely unanimous that Lieberson just seemed to be completely wrong,' recalls John Chambers. 'He was wrong personality-wise. He had always given the impression of being a bit laid-back, a bit idle, never really being in the swim of things. He seemed to us completely the wrong person for the job that was intended.'

'I have never subscribed to the "Sandy Lieberson, genius" theory, which a lot of independent producers and directors and creative people in this country believed for ten years,' adds Bill Gavin. 'And how it had been achieved, in my view, was that people would take along their projects to Sandy and he would say, "God, I love your script, I love your work, I love your other films. Woe is me – here I sit as the head of production for an American company and they just aren't interested in making this." And everybody thought, "What a very nice guy, and what sensible comments he's making about the project." '

Second, the Goldcrest management team resented the salary – at the time said to be in the region of $300,000 a year – that was to be offered to Lieberson, especially as it was well known that Eberts had been denied a sum which, they surmised, was approximately the same.

Third, although this they are less willing to admit, they were dismayed at the prospect of yet another interloper, along with Lee and Cruickshank, coming in above them (as Lieberson almost certainly would) in the company hierarchy.

And finally, they were afraid that the appointment of someone with Lieberson's background would set the company along a wrong course. 'We saw that he would introduce something that had not been present in Goldcrest before: a Hollywood-type development operation,' says John Chambers. 'All our development before had been done on a relatively small number of projects, with people we knew and wanted to work with . . . We didn't have people reading scripts and talking to agents – that wasn't our style . . . We let the producers do [all that]. Sandy would change that, with obvious consequences for our overheads.'

'Sandy is an American film-company executive, a major company executive,' echoes Bill Gavin. 'And the majors – it's really a different way of thinking. They all sit there turning over a billion dollars a year, or close to it, taking 30 per cent off the top . . . and they can afford to make the odd $20 or $30 million mistake. To them, it really doesn't matter. Sandy was of that mould.'

It is worth noting here that the identification of Lieberson as an executive from a different, and in their minds inappropriate, culture, should have been a warning to Lee that the management team was firmly wedded to the outlook and practices followed by Eberts. Because Eberts worked only with experienced film-makers, and then only on projects that they brought to him, he avoided undue development costs and maintained a very high rate of converting developed projects into actual productions. In the same vein, he had always been a project financier, not a company builder. By contrast, Puttnam's and Lee's efforts over the previous two years had been directed towards building Goldcrest itself, changing it from being, in Bill Gavin's description, a 'very specialized banking operation with a sales entity logically attached', towards being virtually a fully fledged studio in its own right, with interests embracing television, cable, video and even magazine publishing (Goldcrest was soon to be financing its own, ill-fated, movie publication, *Stills*). The appointment of Lieberson, with a brief to develop his own projects and nurture younger film-makers – in other words to bring into Goldcrest work that had previously been done by producers outside – would be a further costly addition to the burgeoning corporate structure.

Chambers, Norris and Gavin did not believe that building the company in this way was a sensible policy. As far as they could see, it just added to the overheads without either reducing the level of risk or enhancing the potential for profit. They were never to be reconciled to it and, just as there had always been an alternative strategy, formulated by Puttnam and Lee, in Eberts's day, so there was to be not so much an alternative as an opposition strategy, most cogently expressed by Norris and Chambers, from the outset of the Lee regime.

All this was discussed at the 12 December management meeting chaired by Lee. Accounts of the exact outcome vary – there may or may not have been a vote, and, if there was, it was either 5–1 or 4–2 against – but all, including Lee, are agreed that the majority feeling was very strongly, and unambiguously, against the appointment of Lieberson.

It made no difference, for Lee and Puttnam pressed ahead with the negotiations with Lieberson anyway. That they did so came as no surprise to the increasingly cynical Bill Gavin: 'I knew that, come hell or high water, if it's what Puttnam and Lee wanted, Sandy would be there.'

First, Lieberson had to be persuaded to come on board. Puttnam worked on him hard through the first fortnight of December, and Lieberson had a number of meetings with Lee and even with the now-departed Eberts. His initial reluctance stemmed from the fact that, after his spells of corporate responsibility at Fox and The Ladd Company, he really wanted to get back to producing his own films. Also, it was not entirely clear what was being offered: it was, he says, 'a bit amorphous in terms of the title and responsibilities at that stage'.

However, Puttnam painted a seductive picture of Goldcrest's golden future, while at the same time impressing on Lieberson that the company was desperate for his services.

'I was made to feel this company was floundering,' Lieberson recalls. 'Here was the hope of the British film industry and they needed a head of production. There was a lot of pressure on me, from David and Dickie and various other people, to take the job. You know, I was needed in effect.'

Lieberson eventually agreed to join Goldcrest if the company would meet his terms as regards salary and job description. Lieberson recalls that Goldcrest 'knew up front what my salary was from The Ladd Company, and I made it very clear that I wasn't interested in working as a studio executive, which ultimately is what I would be doing at Goldcrest, for anything less than my market value', which he describes as being 'by American standards very reasonable . . . [But] of course they had refused to give Jake exactly what I was asking for, and, as a British company, they weren't philosophically attuned to paying salaries commensurate with that kind of work.'

Lieberson notes that Goldcrest 'behaved very oddly over the negotiations, I must say: they were so begrudging about it that it gave me food for thought about what might be coming afterwards.'

Agreement was eventually reached on a deal that had two parts. First, there would be a three-year contract, according to which Lieberson would be paid $266,875 in the first year, $293,563 in the second and $320,250 in the third. In addition, he would receive 2 per cent – or, if Goldcrest's profit share exceeded 50 per cent, then up to 4 per cent – of the net profits of each film that went into production during the period of his contract. Should any film, or films, make a loss, then a maximum provision of £5,000 in any one year could be recovered from Lieberson's net-profit shares, but only if in that year these had already yielded him £20,000 or more. Second, Lieberson could terminate the contract, and become instead an independent producer for the company, provided that he gave six months' notice prior to the end of either the second or the third years of his employment. If he opted out in this way, he would be obliged to develop and produce films exclusively for Goldcrest, which would be similarly obliged to finance and distribute them, for an initial period of one year. For this privilege, Goldcrest would advance Lieberson $300,000, recoverable from his producer's fees (if any), and would contribute $150,000 to his overheads, recoverable from the budgets of films (if any) put into production. In addition, Lieberson was guaranteed not less than 15 per cent of the net profits of every such film included in the deal.

This agreement sounds remarkably similar to the terms asked by, and denied to, Eberts, and it far exceeded even the wilder guesses of the Goldcrest management team. To put matters in perspective, Lieberson's first-year salary, $266,875, was then worth £178,000. Following the massive fall in the value of the pound in the early months of 1985, his second-year salary was worth not far short of £250,000. On 1 January 1984, James Lee's salary as chief executive was £95,000; Cruickshank was brought in on £63,750; Norris was earning £60,000; Wooller £55,000; and Chambers £42,000. At the time, average annual earnings among Pearson's 23,000 UK employees were £8,300. James Lee agrees that Lieberson's deal was 'certainly a bad deal from the point of view of the shareholders', and he insists that 'it was fought all the way down the wire'. But, in the end, he says, Goldcrest had no choice, and Lieberson's lawyer, Frank Bloom, who 'knew precisely how important Sandy was to the fund-raising', pressed home his client's advantage.

The question of Lieberson's job description and his place in the hierarchy – 'who I reported to, what I had to report, what I could do, what I couldn't do, what authority I had and what I didn't have' – was more complicated and was never resolved in practice, only on paper, and then not satisfactorily. The problem was that for Lieberson to do his job properly, real power, which in a film company means the power to say yes or no to a project, had to be concentrated in his hands. This was not something that Lee was prepared to concede.

Lieberson was at first surprised at 'how adamant Lee was over the scope of his authority and responsibility', and it made him reflect that perhaps Eberts's departure had been 'not just over money'.

'I am only surmising,' he says. 'I mean, I don't know how Jake perceives it, or how he will describe it, but I think to a large extent he wanted an all-encompassing job and title. He wasn't objecting to James Lee being chairman, but he really wanted the ability to run the company. And of course he couldn't get that.

'So when negotiations over my contract took place it became pretty self-evident that James Lee wanted to retain ultimate authority over what films were made, and how, and to monitor it every step of the way.

There was a lot of negotiating and toing-and-froing, but ultimately I had to really accept the fact that I was reporting entirely to James Lee and he had final authority over almost everything. I had a small amount of discretion over development deals, but, aside from that, no real authority.'

Lee confirms that Lieberson had anything but a free hand. 'I appointed Sandy with the specific understanding that he was the head of production and would suggest production ideas, and that the decision-making process – in fact this was actually embodied in Sandy's contract because he insisted on it – was such that he would recommend production opportunities; that he and I would discuss them; that for major investments, which was most of them, the final decision would be taken by the board of the holding company; but that nothing could be recommended to the board unless I agreed. So in effect there was a decision structure set up that Sandy and I had to agree about everything, and if I didn't agree it wouldn't go ahead. And I had a side-agreement with him – this all sounds terribly formal but it wasn't, it was all hammered out quite amicably at the time – that I in turn would not recommend things to the board past him.'

This was a curious arrangement. Lieberson was to be head of production, but all his decisions were to be subject to Lee's veto. (As was the case in Eberts's time, such proposals would then be presented for approval to a board that included David Puttnam and Dickie Attenborough, two of the major recipients of company funds. This arrangement, with which Eberts had always been uncomfortable, was never satisfactory, not only because of the magnetic pull of Attenborough's and, more especially, Puttnam's own projects, but because Attenborough and Puttnam introduced non-commercial criteria into the discussion of new investments and thereby caused considerable confusion at board level.) The real curiosity, though, is Lee's reference to the side-agreement whereby he 'would not recommend things' to the board without Lieberson's approval. The implication that Lee was going to have a hand in production too was not lost on Lieberson, who notes that Lee had all along demonstrated 'a real desire to do the head of production job, to function in that area'. Indeed, while no Lieberson project was ever to go ahead without Lee's approval, there was to be one project proposed by Lee that was approved by the board and put into production specifically against Lieberson's advice. This was *Fifteen* (later titled *Smooth Talk*), a 'coming-of-age' film made by Lee's close personal friend, and Eberts's first collaborator, Martin Rosen. Lee remembers that on this proposal there was 'friction between Sandy and myself' but that while

Lieberson 'was not in agreement with it' and 'would not recommend it', he 'actually stood aside . . . saying that he was perfectly happy for it to be done if I wanted to do it'. In Norris's opinion, Lieberson had by that time – September 1984 – 'given up an unequal struggle'.

The formal relationship between Lieberson and Lee having thus been untidily resolved, there remained the matter of Lieberson's relationship with the rest of the management team. He believed – and in this he was strongly supported by David Puttnam – that, as the creative head of the company, it was his job not only to choose the projects and oversee their production, but to negotiate contracts with producers, directors and leading actors, handle the negotiation of major distribution deals and direct the work of the sales team. The only responsibilities that he did not want were for corporate strategy, which was a matter for Lee and the board, and administration, which was a matter for the back office. In other words, Clegg, Gavin and Wooller (since Lieberson insisted on having control over television as well) were to report to him.

In theory, Lieberson's position was perfectly reasonable: the equation of a movie is so complicated and its constituent parts, including contracts, distribution deals and so on, so variable, that to have more than one person in charge is to court confusion. What is needed is a chief. Every Hollywood studio has a chief, and Eberts himself had run Goldcrest that way. All that the system requires to work well is that the chief be surrounded by a good and supportive executive team.

But in practice, of course, there were to be two chiefs, Lieberson and Lee, whose roles, by virtue of Lee's veto, were bound to overlap. And far from the management team, so 'well bedded down' as Lee had emphasized to the trade press only three weeks before, being supportive of Lieberson, it had already voted, emphatically and unambiguously, against his appointment.

Lieberson could not have known what he was letting himself in for. He was very close to David Puttnam, but had no inside knowledge of the workings of the company and had had only a passing acquaintance with Norris, Chambers, Gavin, Clegg and Wooller. Lee, on the other hand, was perfectly aware of the management attitude towards Lieberson and must have foreseen what the reaction would be, not only to his appointment, but to his salary and to his designated place in the hier-archy. But, no doubt persuaded by Puttnam and by the absence of any other suitable candidate, Lee persisted with Lieberson nevertheless. In the third week of December, a memorandum was drawn up setting out the main terms of Lieberson's employment, which would start officially on 1 January 1984.

The news was announced at Lee's second management meeting, held on Monday, 19 December. The nearest anyone came to showing enthusiasm for the appointment was David Norris, who was prepared to 'give it a try'. Otherwise the reaction was wholly negative.

Chapter Twenty-two

The Changing Marketplace

Ilott: Three things impressed Lieberson when he started work at Goldcrest: the antipathy towards him on the part of the management; the inadequacy of the office space which he had been allocated; and, following the release of *The Dresser* in December 1983, the dearth of new projects in the pipeline. Goldcrest, he discovered, had four feature films (*Another Country, Cal, Dream One* and *The Killing Fields*) in various stages of post-production, all of them due for delivery in the first half of 1984. There were no films currently shooting and only one, *The Emerald Forest*, in pre-production. Another major project, *The Mosquito Coast*, was under consideration. In television, three films (*Arthur's Hallowed Ground, Forever Young* and *Sharma and Beyond*) were in post-production, as were two mini-series, *The Far Pavilions* and *Concealed Enemies*. All were due for delivery by April. Three big-budget documentary series (*The World: A Television History, The Body Machine* and *Assignment Adventure*) were in production, and one television film, *The Big Surprise* (also called *Winter Flight*), was in pre-production, ready to go before the cameras in March.

Of all these projects, in which Goldcrest had invested about £16 million, Lieberson could contribute only to *The Emerald Forest, The Big Surprise*, both of which had yet to start shooting, and *The Mosquito Coast* (should Goldcrest decide to finance it). On the rest, the important decisions had been made and the money had mostly been spent.

In development, there was only one feature film, *Mandrake the Magician*. This project, based on a popular cartoon strip, was to be directed by pop-promo specialist Julien Temple and to star Kevin Kline – a combination of elements that had been sufficiently attractive for Bill Gavin to have secured substantial pre-sales. However, since going into development in early 1982, *Mandrake* had been beset by seemingly intractable creative problems, and the prospects of its ever being successfully converted into a production were looking remote.

On the television side, Mike Wooller had about a dozen projects in development, in which Goldcrest had invested, in total, about £500,000. Among them were a drama series about the England cricket team's controversial 1930s tour of Australia, to be produced by David Puttnam, and an eight-part documentary series on the USSR.

As for new proposals for which development finance was being considered, there were only three (*A.W.O.L.*, *The Frog Prince* and *Summertime*), all of them low-budget feature-film projects put forward by David Puttnam.

Thus, when Lieberson began work he was really picking up the tail-end of Eberts's legacy. Once he had reviewed the handful of projects in development, he would, as he put it at the time, be 'starting with a clean sheet'. He promised, in doing so, to 'carry on what Jake had established'.

That he was unable to fulfil this promise was, according to James Lee, as much to do with changes in the marketplace as it was to do with Lieberson's own qualities as a film-maker.

In the first place, argues Lee, whereas for many years Goldcrest had enjoyed the advantage of being the only game in town, its very success had guaranteed that it would quickly attract rivals and imitators. By early 1984, HandMade Films, Virgin, a rejuvenated EMI, and the London office of Embassy, now that Eberts was there, were all fishing in the same pool of British talent. As for America, a host of independent production companies had suddenly grown up, among them PSO, the Samuel Goldwyn Company, Orion, Atlantic, Cinecom, Island/Alive and Hemdale, each of which was to compete with Goldcrest for talent, ideas and finance. All these companies were planning to put on to the market the same kind of films – appealing to a middle-brow, middle-class audience – as those made by Goldcrest. Even the studios were jumping on the bandwagon.

One result of all this was that, whereas in 1981 *Chariots of Fire* shared what Lee calls the 'yuppie market' with *Atlantic City* and *Four Seasons*, and in 1982 *Gandhi* was up against *Sophie's Choice*, by the time *The Killing Fields* was released, in 1984, there were ten films, including *Amadeus*, *Greystoke*, *Places in the Heart* and *Falling in Love*, all jostling for the attention of that market segment. By the time *The Mission* was released, in 1986, there were to be eleven such films, every one of them of outstanding quality: *Out of Africa*, *Hannah and Her Sisters*, *Kiss of the Spiderwoman*, *Ran*, *Children of a Lesser God*, *The Color Purple*, *A Room With a View*, *Crimes of the Heart*, *Mosquito Coast* and *Platoon*. According to Lee's research, the aggregate US box-office take for movies of this kind was $75 million in 1981 and $125 million by 1984 – i.e. in the space of three years twice as many films were chasing a market that had grown by only 60 per cent. As a result, average rentals per film decreased from $19 million in 1981 to less than $12 million in 1984.

To take the example of three major films produced by David Puttnam, *Chariots of Fire* took $31 million rentals in the US in 1981, *The Killing Fields* was to take $16 million in 1984, and *The Mission* was to take only $8 million in 1986. 'Was *The Killing Fields* only half as good as *Chariots of Fire*?' Lee asks, 'Was *The Mission* only half as good as *The Killing Fields* and a quarter as good as *Chariots of Fire*? I think you have got to say those relationships are not right.' The explanation, he says, is not to be found in a comparison of the films themselves, but in the marketplace.

Lee's thesis is, of course, debatable. So are his statistics. According to John Chambers there were twelve 'yuppie' films released in 1981, the year of *Chariots of Fire*. They took rentals of $222 million, making an average of $18.5 million. In 1982, the year of *Gandhi*, there were eleven such films, earning average rentals of $25 million. In 1983 there were six, earning average rentals of $18.6 million. In 1984, the year of *The Killing Fields*, there were again six, taking average rentals of $14.8 million. In 1985 there were only four, but as these included *Out Of Africa*, *Witness* and *The Color Purple* (Chambers dates the films from the day of release not from the length of the run as Lee seems to do), the average rental achieved was $31 million. In 1986, the year of *The Mission* and *A Room With a View*, there were seven such films, earning an average rental of $22 million; and in 1987 there were five, earning an average rental of $18 million. The conclusions to be drawn from Chambers's figures are that average rentals seem to bear no relation to the number of films released, and that, contrary to Lee's presentation, the number of such films declined from 1982 onwards.

The argument, of course, turns on the definition of 'yuppie' film. Chambers, for example, includes *Witness*, which Lee chooses to ignore. This is not a question that is worth going into here. What is worth going into, and what both men agree on, is that there was a significant increase in the number of films of all types distributed in the 1980s. And while it is probably not true to say, as Lee does, that films compete for audiences, it is true that they compete for play-dates and editorial space. Play-dates, in particular, are finite: if a cinema-owner sees no sure-fire hit in the pipeline, he will keep playing whatever picture will pay his costs. If he sees a blockbuster coming along, he will take off even a moderately successful movie to make space for it. Securing optimum play-dates is one of the arts of film marketing.

To give some idea of how great was the growth in film production in the 1980s, and how great was the consequent competition among distributors, one can look at the history of the American Film Marketing Association (AFMA), which was founded to represent the interests of independent, exporting American production companies (i.e. all those other than the major studios). Between 1981 and 1987, its membership roll increased from thirty-eight to eighty-five, and its members' aggregate world sales increased from less than $200 million to more than $700 million. In seven years, a leading AFMA member, the Cannon Group, built up a library of over 900 titles, and in 1986 had as many as forty-six films on its current production slate, making it the most prolific producer of films in the world. These independent companies, most of them new, brought with them substantial capital, derived from share offerings, junk bonds and, most importantly, lines of credit from such banks as First National Bank of Boston, Wells Fargo, Bank of America and, above all, Credit Lyonnais.

In addition, the pay-cable operators, notably HBO and Showtime in the United States, and the leading independent video labels, for example Vestron and Embassy Home Entertainment (EHE), in order to steal a march on their competitors, were offering not just advances but equity investment in films in exchange for distribution rights. This money gave a further boost to independent production.

In the financial community, too, there was renewed interest in film investment. Indeed, IFI had spawned a host of imitators: partnerships that would invest, often in a specified list of films, for a limited period. Among them were IFI's successor, Silver Screen Partners, and, of course, Embassy Film Associates, the fund for which Eberts was now raising money.

Between them, the new companies and the new funds – and a new distribution operation in the US called Tri-Star – pumped about $3 billion of new money into film production in the mid-1980s. Goldcrest thus became, as Lee argues, just one of the crowd, and its hitherto privileged relationship with distributors, both independents and the studios, was weakened.

With such an increase in the supply of product, prices, especially in the ancillary markets, where competition among distributors had until recently been so intense, had to come down. It didn't happen all at once and it didn't happen evenly. First, US pay-cable prices, which had accounted for one third to one half of the budget of television movies, mini-series and low-budget features, collapsed. Not only was there more product available, but the fledgling American cable business itself had settled down following its initial, highly competitive phase. Second, US network television quickly gave up trying to compete with the subscription-based, multiple-run movie channels and, after 1985, it virtually disappeared altogether as an outlet for feature films. Third, video, which, like cable, had experienced an initial boom during which the distributors fought to outbid each other for releasable titles, underwent, in the period 1983–5, a shake-out which saw most of the smaller labels go out of business and left the market dominated by the major studios, who were then able to control prices. And fourth, theatrical advances, with so many more films available, remained steady – i.e. they declined in real terms. Warner Bros., for example, which put up a $4.75 million advance for US rights to *The Killing Fields* in 1982, put up virtually the same sum for *The Mission* in 1985, even though the budget for the latter, in dollar terms, was twice that of the earlier film.

Another consequence of the phenomenal growth in film production was that technicians, writers, producers and directors found themselves in demand as never before. Inevitably, there was an explosion in production costs. *Chariots of Fire* had cost about £3 million; *Gandhi* had cost £9.5 million; *The Killing Fields* came in at about £10 million; and *The Mission* was to cost £17 million. One would be hard put to discern from the evidence on the screen what it was that made *The Mission*, beautiful film though it is, twice as expensive as *Gandhi*. Perhaps a truer comparison would be between *The Mission* and *The Killing Fields*: not only were they similar projects, in terms of scale and logistics, but they were made by exactly the same team of people. Indeed, all the preliminary calculations for *The Mission* assumed that it would not differ in any significant degree from *The Killing Fields*; the distribution deals, for example, were negotiated on that basis. Yet there was a difference in the below-the-line costs (the direct costs of making the film, not including the acquisition of rights or the fees paid to the director, producer and leading actors) of £3 million. Having made allowances for *The Mission*'s exceptional expenditures – additional set-building and the relocation of the entire crew from Colombia to Argentina mid-way through the production – 'the single biggest factor' in the difference in cost, according to James Lee, 'was the rates of the individuals. Not just the weekly rates for the same function, but in many cases they were precisely the same person. The cost had risen 30 per cent or so.'

More than that, the competition among producers engendered a revival of the star system, which had declined noticeably in the 1970s. Whereas Puttnam had done very well without stars in *Chariots of Fire*, and Attenborough's much-criticized casting of Ben Kingsley in *Gandhi* had been triumphantly vindicated, there was reason to believe that the casting of non-star Sam Waterston in *The Killing Fields* was a factor in the film's disappointing box-office performance. When eventually the time came for casting the major films of the Lieberson era, *The Mission* and *Revolution*, it was agreed that they could not compete in the over-crowded marketplace without attention-grabbing names. Goldcrest was to find itself paying huge fees, and giving away substantial chunks of its profit shares, to secure the services of Al Pacino, Donald Sutherland, Nastassia Kinski, Robert De Niro and Jeremy Irons. As a result, the already much-enhanced production costs were to be inflated further.

As if conditions in the film industry were not difficult enough, there was a further destabilizing factor: the fluctuating value of the pound against the dollar. It generally takes between eighteen months and two years to make a film, from the start of pre-production to the delivery of the finished print. And pre-production does not usually commence until some time, often a year, after the first development expenditures have been incurred. So as many as three years can elapse between making the first commitment and seeing the film go into distribution.

The costs of a film are incurred mostly during the relatively short production period. Where Goldcrest was concerned, these costs, with the exceptions of local expenses (in the case of films shot on foreign locations) and actors' fees (which might be in dollars), were paid in sterling. The distribution payments, however, the bulk of which were not payable until the finished films were delivered, were, with few exceptions, paid in dollars or calculated according to dollar equivalents.

Consequently, any movement in the pound–dollar exchange rate in the period between the signing of distribution contracts and the delivery of a film could have significant consequences for Goldcrest. In November 1980, when *Gandhi* went into production, the pound stood at $2.40. It then fell rapidly, reaching a low of $1.03 in April 1985. All the films that Goldcrest made and released in that period, including *The Killing Fields*, *Local Hero*, *Another Country* and *The Dresser* could be said to have benefited from the increasing value of their dollar contracts. (*Gandhi*, which would have benefited most of all, didn't secure any dollar contracts until well after it had finished shooting.) However, from April 1985 onwards, the pound began to recover, reaching $1.10 in early 1986, $1.50 in mid-1987 and $1.70 in the summer of 1988. All the films that were made and released in that period (*Revolution*, *Absolute Beginners* and *The Mission* started filming in March–April 1985 and were delivered, respectively, in December 1985, March 1986 and September 1986) were to suffer from the decreasing value of their dollar contracts. According to John Chambers, the worst consequences of such exchange-rate fluctu-

ations were avoided by setting dollar advances against dollar costs, and
by balancing exchange losses in one department against exchange gains
in another. Losses on exchange were nevertheless a constant source of
anxiety to the Goldcrest board, especially in 1985, when the pound was
at its most volatile and the company had more than £35 million invested
in production.

From all the above, one would be inclined to sympathize with Lee's
complaint that the deck which had been stacked relatively favourably
towards Eberts in the period 1977–83 was stacking up, from 1984
onwards, against Lieberson.

Not that this was apparent at the beginning of 1984, when Lieberson
first joined the company. His immediate problem, one with which Eberts
was all too familiar, was that Goldcrest was again short of cash. At the
start of the year, it had an excess of current assets (money in the bank
and payments due) over current liabilities (bills to pay and money owed
to shareholders) of only £596,000, which, with overheads now running
at £200,000 a month, and with considerable forward commitments to
the existing production slate (£3.4 million contracted, and £8.9 million
authorized but not contracted, for *The Emerald Forest*), meant that in
effect there were no funds for new investment. Lieberson, who, as he
says, was under 'tremendous pressure to get things rolling very quickly',
would thus have to wait until the new money was raised, which was then
expected to be sometime in March. In the meantime, he had nothing to
offer film-makers at all. He kicked his heels – and kicked up a fuss about
his office.

The arguments over Lieberson's office, niggling as they were, were
indicative of the perceived differences in attitude between his style of
work and that of the Goldcrest team. The Ladd Company office that
Lieberson had left behind was a stylish conversion of a Covent Garden
warehouse: a large open space, with wrought-iron columns, polished
wooden floors, painted brick walls, rugs, sofa, easy chairs, paintings,
discreet lighting and a big desk. The atmosphere within which Lieberson
worked was relaxed, informal and unhurried. The Goldcrest offices in
Holland Street, while they were a great improvement on the cramped
two floors of Holland Park Avenue, were plain, harshly lit, overcrowded
and hectic. The work ethic was all-pervasive: people were generally
good-humoured but nobody was ever relaxed. Lieberson, on seeing the
'tiny cubbyhole of an office' to which he was assigned, simply refused to
accept it. For six months, he says, he had to wait while another office
was prepared – 'an office where I could actually have somebody sit in it
with me'.

He found the situation, of being paid what was by English standards a king's ransom while at the same time being denied a decent office, 'bizarre', and he now interprets the delays and arguments over his accommodation as having been, at least in part, one of the many means by which Lee reminded him that 'he was the boss, that I worked for him'. Although this remark is probably unfair (apart from his penchant for doing Lieberson's job for him, Lee was very supportive of his new head of production, as he was – with the same reservation – of every other member of the management team), it does indicate the want of empathy between the two men.

Chapter Twenty-three

Inherited Problems

Ilott: In the interval between Eberts's resignation and Lieberson's appointment, Lee did his best to avoid production questions. There was one major investment decision, however, that could not be postponed: whether or not to back the production of a big-budget feature film based on Paul Theroux's *The Mosquito Coast*.

About four weeks before leaving Goldcrest, Eberts had received a letter from his friend Irvin Kershner recommending this project and its producer, Jerome Hellman. Hellman is one of that handful of independent film-makers whose tenacity, talent and track record make them bankable. His credits include *The World of Henry Orient, A Fine Madness, Midnight Cowboy, The Day of the Locust, Coming Home* and *Promises in the Dark*, the last of which he also directed. These films have between them received more than a dozen Academy Award nominations and they have made money: Hellman has become wealthy from that most elusive source of income, net profits. Bill Gavin describes him as 'a Puttnam, a little tiger, knowing what he wants and absolutely sure he's going to get it', and one has the impression, even after a single meeting, that the mix of wilfulness and obsession in his character – evident, for example, in his observance of a rigorous physical-fitness regime – while it makes him a formidable producer, could also make him a difficult colleague. In the autumn of 1983 he fell out with Warner Bros.

Warners' head of production, Bob Shapiro, had paid for the development of *The Mosquito Coast*. Paul Schrader was commissioned to write the screenplay, Australian director Peter Weir was lined up to direct and Jack Nicholson had been approached to play the lead role. Hellman, who owned the property, acknowledges that it was not a sure-fire winner: 'it was an offbeat film, and expensive – a difficult combination'. He was nevertheless disappointed to find, when the script was delivered, not only that Shapiro had left the company but that Warners' new production chief, Mark Canton, with whom neither Hellman nor Weir felt 'any kind of rapport', had, in Hellman's words, 'a mixed reaction' to the property. It was put into turnaround – i.e. Warner Bros. no longer wished to proceed with it and Hellman was free to take it elsewhere.

He went from studio to studio, but, Hollywood being at that time gripped by one of its frequent games of musical chairs, during which the heads of the studios change places and the lower executive levels are thrown into turmoil, he found that every person he talked to who showed even a glimmer of interest was 'out looking for work the next day'. It was then that Irvin Kershner interceded on his behalf with Eberts. Eberts asked to see the screenplay. 'I mailed off my script to Jake,' says Hellman, 'and my hopes went with it.'

Hellman then went to New York to try to raise production money on Wall Street. The trip was neither enjoyable nor successful. 'I was pretty depressed about it, and whenever I get depressed I escalate the level of my exercise programme,' Hellman recalls. 'So I was in a friend's apartment in New York doing sit-ups when the phone rang. I almost didn't answer it because I was in the middle of a set and I'd had nothing but bad news anyway. But I did pick it up and it was Jake. He said that he'd read the script, that he had some questions, but that he thought it was a very exciting project and felt that it was a picture Goldcrest should make. In a moment like that you fight the impulse to let your emotions soar, because you know that if you allow yourself to get too happy you're going to have your hopes dashed again. I knew from Kersh that Jake wasn't a guy who would be bullshitting, but still there must have been an element of uncertainty in my voice, because he laughed and said, "Look, I'm telling you I'm really seriously interested. What's your timetable?" '

By coincidence, Hellman lives only a few yards from Jerry Perenchio in Malibu Colony. By coincidence also, Eberts was due to be staying with Perenchio the following week. A meeting was thus easily arranged.

'It all seemed fortuitous,' says Hellman. 'But I've got to admit that always in the background of these things, even as you book your flight to California, there's a part of your brain that's saying he won't show up, or that his plans will change and he'll go to Marrakesh. That's the way this business works. And I didn't know Jake and I didn't allow myself to expect too much. But he and Bill Gavin and I met and we discussed the script. We discussed Jake's enthusiasms, his positive feelings about it. And we discussed his reservations and concerns, especially about the downbeat ending, several of which Peter [Weir] and I shared and subsequently worked on. But most importantly, as Kersh had predicted, I just felt that here was a guy I could really trust and talk to. I felt that he was a man who really was passionate in his feelings about film, who was coming from the same place as we were. He wanted to make films that were successful – we all do – but we all know that you don't always make films that are successful. And the one thing that we wanted to do, and I felt that Jake wanted to do, was to make films that we're proud of. You go in for the right reasons: you're not a bunch of guys trying to rip off the public and make a lot of money at the expense of things that are more important. So I felt a real affinity with him, a real kinship, a real sense of trust. And for the first time, my confidence was really reinforced.'

Further meetings during the course of the week – the same week in which Jerry Perenchio delivered his ultimatum to Eberts – resulted in an agreement to fund a reconnaisance of possible locations in Central America, on the basis of which Hellman would draw up a detailed budget and schedule. All being well, Goldcrest would then take over the project from Warner Bros.

Hellman, Weir and a Goldcrest-nominated production manager, Neville Thompson, flew down to scout locations in Belize on 23 November. They were to report back in the second week of December.

They arrived in London on the day of Lee's first management meeting. According to Hellman, 'everything was good: all of our information led us to believe that we could deliver'. The locations that they needed were, remarkably, all to be found within a mile radius of Belize City, and, given Weir's willingness to deal 'imaginatively' with some of the sequences (as Hellman says, ' "imaginative" is really just a substitute for dough, which is fine – there are many ways to make a film and you never know until you've made it which the best and rightest way is'), they were confident that they could deliver a budget, $16 million, that, in Hellman's words, 'we could stand behind'. The only cause for concern was that the seasonal weather conditions in Belize meant that filming would have to start no later than the first week of February, which left a very short pre-production period. But this did not worry Hellman unduly. It was thus in a very optimistic frame of mind that he called the Goldcrest offices, only to find, much to his surprise, not Eberts, but Lee in the chair.

'Once again Peter and I were in that funny situation: we'd gone out with one leader saying, "Good luck, I'll see you when you get back", and when we came back there was another guy sitting there,' Hellman recalls.

Within minutes of the start of what was to be their first, and last, encounter with James Lee, Hellman and Weir were horrified to discover that Lee was apparently not only unenthusiastic about the project, but openly, and in Hellman's view insultingly, unimpressed by them.

'It was a kind of arrogant disinterest: "Oh, you're the fellows who've been wandering around in the jungles . . ." – it was that kind of dismissal,' he says. 'Now, in fairness, it may be that he was uncomfortable or embarrassed or didn't know what the hell to say. It was probably a pretty tough situation to find himself in: Jake was the film-maker; Jake was the spearhead; Jake was the visible guy; Jake was the guy who, to the best of my knowledge, really made that company tick – and James Lee was suddenly without him. So to an extent that explains his behaviour, I'll give him that.

'But certainly there was no effort made by James Lee to encourage either Peter or myself to feel that he had a high regard for us as film-makers; that he knew our work; that whatever his final decision might be about *The Mosquito Coast* he came to it with a certain amount of respect, and, if not interest, at least curiosity.'

The truth is that Lee was in an almost impossible position. There was not much money left in the kitty and the company was in the middle of a major reorganization and fund-raising exercise that would not be completed until some time in the New Year. As yet, there was no creative head of the company and Lee was naturally reluctant, in his first week in the office, to take it upon himself to commit $16 million to a film that had to go into pre-production immediately. Mere prudence would anyway have advised him against having two big-budget films, *Mosquito Coast* and *The Emerald Forest*, shooting in the jungle at the same time. In effect, Eberts had landed him with the awkward and unpleasant, but in the circumstances unavoidable, task of saying no to Hellman.

Hellman was sympathetic – he had guessed that Lee was under pressure from shareholders to solve the problems caused by Eberts's departure – but still he complains bitterly at the way in which the matter was handled: 'I mean we're adults, James Lee could have said, "Look, fellows, come on in, let's really talk, let's pull our hair down. I'm in a really tough situation: Jake's gone; I've had the rug pulled out from under me; we're about to go to market, we're looking to raise money; I just don't know what I've got my hands on really. And here you are just back from ten days in the jungle, all filled with excitement. I know your work, I respect it and I respect your feelings about this picture, but I'm not in a position where, even if I loved this film – if after talking to you and reading the script it was the one picture in the world I wanted to make – I'm not sure that I could provide the financing right now. It could cripple us, sink the ship." Yes, we'd have been disappointed, but we would have had a lot of respect for him.'

Instead of which, Hellman felt, 'the whole sense of that meeting was one of dilletantism and a kind of thinly veiled disdain. It was awfully hard for us to hear. It was painful.' In the end, 'Peter and I went back to the hotel and said, "It's a write-off."'

Hellman was not to be the last American to find Lee's manner high-handed and off-putting. The health of Goldcrest's relationship with Warner Bros., for example, upon which so much of the company's success depended, was to be sapped by the antipathy that grew up between Lee and Warners' chief Terry Semel. But it is an interesting observation about Lee that those who know him best like him most. His apparent arrogance in fact masks a perfectly decent character. Immediately after making such a bad impression on Hellman, Lee was on the phone to Eberts to see if there wasn't something that could be done to save the project.

Eberts called Hellman. 'He said, "Listen, I know how you guys are feeling,"' recalls Hellman, ' "but things aren't as bad as they seem. I think I can bring Embassy into this in some kind of partnership arrangement, so that Embassy becomes the American outlet with Goldcrest." And he said, "Give me a day and let me talk to Perenchio and let's see what happens." The next day he called me and told me that, yes, Perenchio was interested in taking the American end of it and that he was now going to talk to James Lee about Goldcrest staying in the position it would have been in if he, Jake, had stayed.'

But Lee was uncertain about making even that commitment and quickly agreed to Eberts's suggestion that, subject to Perenchio's approval, Embassy should take over the project in its entirety. Eberts, who still harboured doubts about the script being too downbeat – he had warned Hellman that it would have to be changed – then pitched the idea to his Embassy overlords in LA and they duly gave the scheme their blessing. Hellman, when Eberts called him with the news, felt 'tremendous elation'.

For Lee, this was, at least, one inherited problem dealt with. But it was not the only such problem, nor was it the biggest.

Terry Clegg had flown down to Brazil to inspect the preparations for *The Emerald Forest* with John Boorman. Together with cameraman Philippe Rousselot, production designer Simon Holland, art director Marcos Flaksman and location manager Gerry Levy, they spent the weekend analysing, and arguing over, the logistics of the production. Clegg's inspection resulted, as far as Boorman knew, in 'only minor criticisms . . . He had gone through the budget with a toothcomb, gone round all the locations with me, and he pronounced himself satisfied –

more than that, very impressed – by the whole organization and the set-up. Of course, he had one or two criticisms to make. He thought we needed a transport manager, for instance, and we went along with that. But when he went back to report, I had no reason to think that there would be any problem.'

In fact, Clegg, although he was very enthusiastic about the project ('it was a good script and I thought the potential was marvellous'), had noted three major causes for concern. The first was the budget. Given the remoteness of the locations, the ambitious nature of the subject matter and Boorman's known, and for the most part much-admired, inventive-ness behind the camera, and given also that Goldcrest was putting together a prospectus for a share offering, the success of which would depend in part on the company's maintaining an image of competence and reliability, the board was more than usually anxious to be reassured that costs on this particular project would be kept on target. A further consideration was that the distribution deals for the film, with Embassy in the US and with independent distributors in the international markets, were all fixed: Goldcrest could do very well out of the picture, and so could Boorman, but only if it came in at less than $17 million (itself a considerable increase on the original estimate of $13 million). Clegg came to the conclusion that 'that script, with the plans and ideas that John had, couldn't be made for the money they said it could be made for; at the end of the day, I knew it could not be done'.

The second cause for concern was that, with filming due to start in February, there was still no actor set for the lead role. 'And it didn't look like they were finding somebody,' says Clegg. 'It looked like we were rolling to a point where the picture was going to kick off without having the major cast locked up.'

The *Emerald Forest* story – of an engineer's search for his kidnapped son in the jungles of the Amazon – can succeed only if the portrayal of the son, Tommy, is completely convincing, which is not easy as he is on the verge of adulthood, emerging, in the process, from the role of follower to the role of leader. Coming-of-age pictures are notoriously hard to play with a straight face, the solemnities and private agonies of adolescence being more easily milked for laughs. In *The Emerald Forest*, the potential embarrassment factor is racked up a good few notches by the physical necessities imposed by the tribal setting and the jungle locations: for most of the time, most of the actors and actresses are wearing few, if any, clothes. It is up to the actor playing the part of Tommy so to compel the audience's attention, so effectively to suspend their disbelief, that they will not be distracted from the drama by the titillating vision of naked youth cavorting in the sprays of jungle waterfalls. If it is so distracted, the point of the film is lost; it becomes merely another, if perhaps superior, version of *The Blue Lagoon*. Hence the importance of the casting and Clegg's anxiety that nothing much seemed to be being done about it.

The third cause for concern worried Clegg most. As he saw it, Boorman's deal with Goldcrest gave him 'absolute control' over the production. He was co-writer, producer and director. Goldcrest was providing not only the production finance but the completion guarantee. Should the film go over budget there would be nothing that the company could do: they couldn't fire Boorman, since without him there was no movie; they couldn't appeal to the producer, since Boorman was his own producer; and they couldn't refer the problem to an outside completion-bond company, since they were providing the completion guarantee themselves.

'He really had the company by the balls,' says Clegg. 'He wanted to be in a position of total control without somebody looking over his shoulder saying "You can't afford this", or "We can only afford that". I had no worries about the team: they were perfectly capable of doing the job. My worries were about John and John's determination. At what point would he draw in his horns? Would he say, "Well, OK, I'll accept that we don't want to spend more than this, so we'll trim that down and we'll remove a bit of this."? I don't think he was ever prepared to do that.' It was, continues Clegg – who has been a colleague and friend of Boorman's for many years and professes to be a great admirer of his talents – 'a bad deal, an open-ended deal. If he had wanted, he could have done whatever he liked.'

This deal had been offered by Eberts partly as an inducement to get Boorman into the Goldcrest camp, and partly because it fitted his philosophy of mutual trust between financier and film-maker. Boorman would receive fees, totalling very nearly $1 million, as director and producer; he would receive 52.5 per cent of the net profits, including an equivalent share of the proceeds of any tax deal; and he would have a completely free hand to do as he liked with the film.

Foremost among the 'several other people' who, according to Clegg's testimony, objected to these terms was David Puttnam. 'We were faced with the situation in which John was saying, "Fellas, you have got to trust me," ' he recalls. 'And we said, "We can't." On the basis that if we say yes to John Boorman on this, how can we ever turn anyone else down on anything? He was actually asking effectively for an open cheque.'

In part, the concerns expressed by Puttnam and others arose out of

Boorman's attitude to the débâcle of *Dream One*. From the outset, it is true, this project had been beset with problems that no one could have foreseen. But much of the blame for both its huge overcost and its subsequent ignominious failure, commercially and, in the opinion of most people who've seen it, creatively – David Norris describes it as 'the most disastrous piece of nonsense', and Bill Gavin calls it a 'non-film' based on a 'non-script' (Norris and Gavin, it should be said, were Boorman's staunchest supporters within the Goldcrest camp) – was that it was misconceived from the start and badly handled throughout. 'It was a real big fuck-up,' says Puttnam. 'From day one, not just a creative fuck-up, it was a horrendous financial fuck-up.'

Puttnam is not alone in believing that Boorman, *Dream One*'s executive producer, godfather and inspiration, should have stepped forward to accept some of the blame.

But Boorman did not accept any blame. He acknowledges in his book, *Money Into Light*, that at the Columbia screenings in November only the under-twelves seemed to like the film; the response of the twelve–fourteen and fifteen–thirty-four age groups was, he concedes, 'terribly disappointing'. But whatever his private feelings, he does not seem willing in public to accept that he is in some measure responsible for this failure. Instead he skirts around the problem, saying that 'people were just not ready to enter the film or accept it on its own terms', and shifts attention, and by implication blame, on to Hollywood's mania for market research (i.e. holding previews), which he calls a 'pseudo-science . . . behind which insecure executives can hide'.

The legal wrangling over whether or not the film was releasable, and hence whether or not Goldcrest had fulfilled the terms of its contract with Columbia, on which the payment of their $2.8 million advance depended, was to go on for months. The project in the end left the company with a net loss of more than £600,000. Boorman's attitude throughout what was a very unpleasant episode for the company angered some members of the board, at whose meetings, Puttnam remembers, 'the feeling was not benign towards John'. In particular, Lee, who, in his own words, 'had never been a fan of *The Emerald Forest*', was now something less than a fan of Boorman himself. 'John's attitude', he says, 'was that *Dream One* was Goldcrest's problem, not his.'

Lee therefore tended to believe that Boorman, without the restraint of a producer or completion guarantor looking over his shoulder, could not be relied upon to bring in *The Emerald Forest* on schedule. Clegg's report, when eventually it arrived on Lee's desk, was to reinforce that belief.

Chapter Twenty-four

Assets

Ilott: More important than either *The Mosquito Coast* or *The Emerald Forest*, indeed overshadowing everything at that time, were the preparations for the proposed reorganization and share offering. In their efforts to speed up the process, Lee and Cruickshank travelled back and forth between Goldcrest's offices in Holland Street, the Pearson headquarters in Millbank Tower and the offices of merchant bankers N. M. Rothschild and Noble Grossart in the City. The new company, Goldcrest Films and Television (Holdings) Limited, had been registered on 3 December. All the existing partnerships and their subsidiaries had now to be folded into this company before it, in turn, could go to the market and raise money. There were formidable obstacles in the way of both these tasks. Not the least of them was that Goldcrest's auditors, Deloitte Haskins and Sells, and its solicitors, Freshfields, were having great difficulty arriving at an acceptable formula for the presentation of the company's worth.

The problem, a familiar one in the movie business, was how to put a figure on the real, as opposed to the book, value of Goldcrest's film and television investments. When a company like Goldcrest finances a movie, putting in, let's say, £5 million, then the whole of that £5 million is, in the first year, written into the books as an asset of the company. In succeeding years, the figure is steadily reduced – amortized – according to a formula that seeks to match the writing down of the asset to its expected revenue-earning lifetime. For example, the £5 million might be reduced to £3 million in the second year, in anticipation of the distribution advances that would be payable in that period. In the third year, the asset value might be reduced to £2 million, as returns come in from television deals and the like. And so on, until, usually by the fifth year, the investment has been completely written off and ceases to appear on the balance sheet at all. It is a bit like spreading the purchase price of a motor car across the span of its anticipated useful life: at any point before the end it still has a resale value, and your estimate of that value is what you keep in your balance sheet.

The problem is that this method of valuing assets, as investments at cost less amortization, while it conforms to standard accounting procedures, does not allow for what those assets might be worth in the real world. Unlike a private car, which only depreciates, films are investments that can make money. Yet the book asset value of a film can never exceed its cost of production. *Gandhi*, for example, proved to be worth to Goldcrest about £11.5 million, whereas its maximum (i.e. first year) book value was only £5 million – the total sum invested by the company. Films can also lose money, of course. *The Far Pavilions*, in which Goldcrest invested £6.8 million, never came close to recouping its costs. It still went down in the books in the first year as an asset of £6.8 million, pending a decision about when provision would have to be made for the full writing down of its losses. (The general practice, naturally, is to do so as soon as possible. To do otherwise would be to invite charges of fraud.) A further complicating factor is that the revenue-earning lifetime of a product, especially with the advent of a new distribution systems like video and satellite, might be a great deal longer than five years, although most accountants are reluctant to extend amortization beyond that period. Three years is considered the norm in Hollywood.

So book asset value can be, indeed most always will be, at variance with the real or potential worth of a company's investments. To some degree, the same is true in all industries. What makes film more complicated than most is that film investments are inherently highly speculative: the value of the assets of a film company, comprising films and not much else, can only be guessed at until those films go into release.

Clearly, this element of uncertainty leaves plenty of scope for abuse. A film company, for example, may choose to extend the amortization period, so that a film which fails to perform and attracts very little revenue will nevertheless continue to appear as an asset on the balance sheet. Not only is the necessary provision for losses deferred, thereby improving the apparent current profitability of the company, but the artificial enhancement of its book asset value can be used to raise loans and lines of credit, or even to attract new investors. This happens, especially among companies that are doing badly, and it is the subject of much scrutiny by the Securities and Exchange Commission in the United States, where the balance sheet, rather than the profit-and-loss statement, is the main tool of corporate financial analysis.

Much the same ends can be achieved by massaging the income forecast from which the amortization rate is derived. Take the example of a film that costs £5 million but which the company in question knows is unlikely to earn more than £1.7 million in the first year (from, say, theatrical distribution advances) and £1.3 million in the second (from video or cable sales), making a total of £3 million – i.e. there will be a net loss on the investment of £2 million. The company, anxious to disguise this imminent loss, forecasts revenues of £400,000 in the first year, £600,000 in second, £2 million in the third, £2 million in the fourth and £5 million in the fifth, making a total of £10 million in all. It writes this income forecast into its books.

In the first year, the film duly earns £1.7 million. This is considerably more than the figure shown in the income forecast and, on that basis, the company can, if it wishes, declare the film a great success. The £1.7 million is amortized according to the formula:

$$\frac{\text{actual income} \times \text{cost}}{\text{total forecast income}} \quad \text{i.e.} \quad \frac{£1.7\text{m} \times £5\text{m}}{£10\text{m}} = £0.85\text{m}$$

Thus £850,000 is written off the book value of the film, leaving £4.15 million. At the end of the first year, then, the investment is, on paper, in profit: £1.7 million has been received in cash and an asset of £4.15 million remains on the books – £1.7 million + £4.15 million = £5.85 million.

In the second year, £1.3 million is received. Once again, the income is far in excess of the forecast and the film's 'success' can be trumpeted further. The £1.3 million is duly amortized:

$$\frac{£1.3\text{m} \times £5\text{m}}{£10\text{m}} = £0.65\text{m}$$

This time, therefore, £650,000 is written off the book value of the film, leaving £3.5 million. On paper, with cash receipts of £3 million (£1.7m + £1.3m) and a residual book value of £3.5 million, the film has moved even further into 'profit'.

Of course, thereafter, as no further income is received, the process goes into reverse, and, in the fourth year – the year in which the forecast income exceeds the actual income received – the film is revealed to be a flop. By the fifth year, the full £2 million provision will have to be made for the film to be written off.

Multiply this by the ten or twelve films that might be on the company's list, and add new titles every year, and you can see that it would be possible to continue to disguise the true performance of the company *as long as new money for investment was coming in.* Once the flow of money stopped, the game would be up.

Again, a company can attribute to a film's budget an unwarranted share of such things as its general overheads, interest charges or legal fees, thereby pushing up the film's apparent cost and increasing its book value. This has the effect, at the same time, of turning expenditures which should appear in the profit-and-loss account (reducing the profits) into balance-sheet items (adding to the assets). It also delays the break-even point after which the production company has to start sharing net profits with the talent and third-party investors. Indeed, inflating the stated, as opposed to the true, costs of a picture is endemic to the film industry, especially in the independent sector: a $1.3 million production is announced in the trade press as costing $2.5 million; a $6.5 million production is announced at $8 million; and so on. This practice not only leaves plenty of scope for creative accounting but serves to increase the value of the film in the eyes of the distributors who may buy it, thereby inflating its price.

Of course, at the end of the day the profit-and-loss account, the balance sheet and the bank statement all have to tally: creative bookkeeping alone cannot stave off disaster, but it can buy time, and it can disguise the true allocation of funds.

By and large, the matter of amortization and valuation of investments is decided by prevailing industry practice, company policy and the judgement of outside auditors, who, invariably and for obvious reasons, are suspicious of inflated valuations or extended periods of amortization. As a back-stop, every major industrial country has laws governing the presentation of accounts, which, in general, are expected to present a conservative rather than an optimistic assessment of a company's financial position.

None of this would matter in the normal course of things. As long as Goldcrest followed accepted procedures, which it always did, then the balance sheet could be taken for what it was worth: a necessary auditing tool, which was most useful when taken together with the profit-and-loss statement and the company's own estimate of future revenues. The matter became important only because of the reorganization and the proposed recapitalization. In the first place, an accurate figure had to be put on the value of every single Goldcrest investment in order to provide the basis for the allocation of shares in the new company between Pearson, owners of Goldcrest Films and Television Ltd, and the corporate partners in Goldcrest Films International and Goldcrest Film and Television Partners. Book value – i.e. cost less amortization – was clearly not enough. There had to be some assessment of the likely revenues accruing to the investments made by the respective parties. Otherwise, shareholders in GFI, for example, would find themselves subsidizing the losses of GFT. In the second place, the money-raising prospectus had to give a best estimate of the true aggregate worth of the company so that potential new investors could make a decision about whether or not to put money in.

Since 1977, £22.6 million had been invested by the shareholders in the various Goldcrest partnerships. Each year since then had shown an operating deficit (although the year-on-year performance had steadily improved, as more and more projects were completed and went into distribution). These accumulated deficits totalled £4.8 million at the end of 1982. The profit-and-loss account for the year 1983 showed a turnover of £12.4 million, of which £9 million was accounted for by the amortization of film and television investments, £275,000 by development investments that had been written off, £1.7 million by overheads, £190,000 by Goldcrest's share of the losses of associated companies (mainly the struggling cable-movie channel, the Television Entertainment Group) and £236,000 by interest payments to the bank. Income from distribution, sales commission, fees and leasing deals produced net revenue, before tax and before the payment of interest on loan stock, of £892,000, making 1983 the first year in which Goldcrest showed an operating profit. However, tax amounted to £662,000 and interest on loan stock totalled £1.06 million, making an overall loss of £830,000. When this figure was added to the inherited deficit at the start of the year, Goldcrest, in December 1983, had to report an accumulated loss to date of just over £5.8 million.

Thus, according to the books, the shareholders' funds of £22.6 million were, at the end of 1983, worth only £16.8 million: not, on the face of it, a great record with which to attract more money from the City, nor, indeed, a great legacy from Eberts's years of glory. However, three things have to be noted about these figures. First, half of the £5.8 million accumulated deficit was interest owed on loan stock, a large proportion of the investments made by the shareholders in GFI and GFTP being in the form of interest-bearing, fixed-term, convertible loans (GFI, for example, paid 10 per cent a year to its loan-stock holders, whose entire investment was due for redemption – i.e. the partnership was to be wound up – in 1987). Half of the deficit, in other words, was money owed by the shareholders to themselves. In the reorganization, they agreed to convert this debt into equity: a shareholder who was owed, say, £100,000 in unpaid interest on loan stock, accepted instead £100,000 worth of shares in the new company. Second, of the company's £16.8

million net assets, all but £300,000 represented the book value of current film and television investments, each of which, as we have seen above, could prove to be worth either a great deal more or a great deal less than the value shown. Naturally, as far as Goldcrest was concerned they were worth more, being mostly unfinished projects – one of them, for example, was *The Killing Fields* – from which the company hoped for great things. Third, the balance sheet did not show those film and television investments which had been fully amortized (i.e. their costs had been fully recouped, or they had been written off). Since 1977 Goldcrest had amortized some £18 million worth of its investments, and such films as *Black Jack, Chariots of Fire* and *The Plague Dogs* no longer appeared as assets on the balance sheet at all. These still generated income and therefore must be counted as having had some value.

So there was no question that the true financial position of the company was different and, in the minds of the Goldcrest management, likely to be better, than that shown in its consolidated balance sheet. The question was, how much better? In trying to answer this question, Goldcrest's advisers encountered all manner of technical and ethical problems. At all costs, the auditors, Deloitte Haskins and Sells, and the solicitors, Freshfields, had to avoid any computation of the company's worth, or of the worth of any individual project, that might leave them open to charges of misrepresentation. The solution at which they eventually arrived resulted in a set of figures which was to prove remarkably accurate in every respect except one: it seriously over-estimated the value of Goldcrest's television investments. Partly in consequence of this, the losses made by the television division were for a long time hidden from view – an oversight that was to cost the company dear.

On Tuesday, 20 December, John Boorman met James Lee for the first time and found him 'charming but a little cool'. In his diary he noted, 'Columbia's disappointment with *Dream One* and Jake's departure have certainly chilled the warm welcome I used to get in the corridors of Goldcrest. Mr Lee did not express any great enthusiasm for *The Emerald Forest*. Fortunately, things have gone much too far for him to pull out at this stage.'

The following day, at dinner at his home in Ireland, Boorman announced that his son Charley would join the crew in Brazil, 'initially just as a member of the family, with the possibility of playing Tommy'.

On Christmas Eve in Malibu Colony, the two Jerrys, Hellman and

Perenchio became involved in a disagreement as a result of which Embassy's offer to fund *The Mosquito Coast* was withdrawn.

Chapter Twenty-five

The Emerald Forest

Ilott: On Friday, 6 January 1984, Bill Gavin flew to LA to talk to Columbia Pictures about the release of *The Dresser*. (Peter Yates's film tends to be overlooked in accounts of the Goldcrest saga, partly because it was fully financed by Columbia and partly because it was such a trouble-free, and hence anecdote-free, production. In fact the film was well received and was to be awarded five Oscar nominations, including Best Picture.) Gavin's meetings, with Guy McElwaine, were scheduled for Monday morning. He spent the intervening weekend in Palm Springs, where Gray Frederickson, co-producer of many of Francis Ford Coppola's films, including *The Godfather – Part 2* and *Apocalypse Now*, told him the story of the Christmas Eve bust-up between Jerry Hellman and Jerry Perenchio. Gavin immediately called Eberts, who confirmed that, much to his own disappointment, Embassy was indeed no longer involved in *The Mosquito Coast*. Having ascertained that there would be no objection to his making an approach on Goldcrest's behalf, Gavin then called Hellman, who invited him out to his house for dinner. 'Jerry said, basically,' Gavin remembers, 'that Fox really wanted to do it, that they had a meeting with them arranged for the end of the week, but that Fox wanted a partner. And I said, "Well, that partner could very well be Goldcrest." '

Gavin calculated that, with Fox as the US partner, Lee might well consider the project again, especially as he now had Lieberson at his side. Gavin spoke to both Lieberson and Lee on Monday morning and, as he had hoped, they encouraged him to 'go after it'. He called Hellman with the news that Goldcrest was definitely interested, and then went off to his meetings with Guy McElwaine at Columbia. Lieberson, meanwhile, called Warner Bros. to find out why it was that *The Mosquito Coast* had been put into turnaround in the first place.

At Columbia, when the main business of the meeting was done, McElwaine enquired what Goldcrest was going to do next and Gavin told him that there was a chance that they would again be involved with *The Mosquito Coast*. McElwaine had earlier considered the project but had been deterred by Jack Nicholson's fee, $3.75 million, and by the budget, which at that time was about $15 million. However, in the interim he had seen *Terms of Endearment* and was sufficiently impressed by Nicholson's performance to regard the fee as not unreasonable. And if Goldcrest was going to share some of the cost, then Columbia, he said, was definitely interested in being involved. Gavin left the meeting cock-a-hoop. He walked across the lot to the Warner Bros. offices (Columbia and Warners in those days shared the Burbank Studios) where he was to have lunch with head of business affairs, Jim Miller.

'There was no business to talk about, it was just a social meeting,' Gavin recalls. 'And halfway through lunch – this is twelve o'clock Monday: at four o'clock the previous afternoon I hadn't even known that Embassy were out of it – Jim looks over and says, "I hear you people are thinking of getting back into *The Mosquito Coast*." I nearly choked. I said, "Jim, how the hell did you know that?" He said, "Well, I can't tell you, but, Bill, as you know, we had the thing in development here and let it go into turnaround, but, if Goldcrest is going to do it, we have to be your partners." '

Fox wanted it, now Columbia and Warners wanted it too. And they all wanted it with Goldcrest. 'I thought it would all be done by Friday,' says Gavin.

The following morning he called Goldcrest with the good news, only to find that Lieberson, who had now heard the story of the dispute between Hellman and Warner Bros. that had led to the project going into turnaround before Christmas, was no longer keen. (It was, of course, Lieberson's call, relayed through the Warner Bros. grapevine, that had alerted Jim Miller to Goldcrest's interest.) 'He said, "Jerome Hellman is an incredibly difficult man," ' recalls Gavin. 'And I said, "Sandy, I'm sure that's true, but Puttnam's an incredibly difficult man, no one knows that better than you." "No," he said, "really, if you can do a deal where you just put up money against foreign [sales], and it's just a pick-up for Goldcrest as a sales entity, then I'll go along with that, but I don't want to make this film." I said, "OK, fine." '

In fact, Lieberson's preferred arrangement was more or less what Fox wanted anyway, so Gavin chose not to inform Hellman of Lieberson's change of heart until after Hellman's meeting with Fox at the end of the week. He was to regret this decision, for, shortly before Hellman went into that meeting (with, as he thought, Goldcrest's commitment in his pocket), James Lee called Gavin and said that Goldcrest was not to be involved at all. Gavin was furious. As he saw it, Lieberson and Lee had authorized him to pursue negotiations with Hellman on Monday. This he had done, even lining up Columbia and Warner Bros. as possible replacements for Fox. Now, Thursday, Lieberson and Lee had changed their minds. This left Gavin with the extremely awkward, and personally embarrassing, task of explaining matters to a very disappointed and very emotional Jerry Hellman.

'I believe – I may be wrong – that you survive on your integrity in this business,' says Gavin, 'and the worst crime you can do to anybody is to waste their time – because it's finite. And Jerry obviously thought that I'd been wasting his time. He'd already had it turned around at Warners, turned around at Goldcrest, turned around at Embassy, now turned around at Goldcrest again – all in the space of six weeks. To this day he really thinks that I fucked him about and was acting beyond my authority. That pissed me off absolutely no end.'

Gavin, so recently persuaded to stay on board, thought again about leaving Goldcrest.

(Hellman was to spend a further two years looking for finance – even on two further occasions contemplating a Goldcrest involvement – before *The Mosquito Coast*, under the aegis of the Saul Zaentz Company, was able to go into production. By that time Jack Nicholson had dropped out, to be replaced by Harrison Ford, with whom director Peter Weir had worked, in the interim, on the much-praised thriller *Witness*.)

Terry Clegg, meanwhile, had returned to London and made his report on *The Emerald Forest*. His revised budget was now put at $17.5 million, well above the earlier estimates and $500,000 above the top limit set by Goldcrest. Even to reach the $17.5 million figure, Boorman had had to make cuts in the script and to agree to working six rather than five days a week: a major concession, since the rest days, as well as giving a certain amount of flexibility, are usually invaluable for reassessment, planning and rehearsal, not to mention rest. To Clegg's gloomy report, in which he also emphasized his concerns about the casting and about Boorman's reliability, was added the news that the chances of securing a tax-shelter deal, about which David Norris had been confident before Christmas, now looked remote.

None of this made Lee feel any more comfortable with a project on which he had never been keen. He called for an analysis of the cost increases from earlier drafts of the budget, asked Clegg to procure a detailed timing schedule, and emphasized the need for 'tight monitoring and control procedures' throughout the production. He also raised the possibility of looking for an outside completion guarantor. While this was certainly a sensible consideration, given Goldcrest's nervousness, it would be bound to have, at this stage, a profound – and from Boorman's point of view, unwelcome – impact on the production. The agreement as it stood was that Goldcrest would itself provide the guarantee, in exchange for a 4.5 per cent fee (i.e. $800,000) payable out of the budget. An outside guarantor would be unlikely to charge less than 6 per cent and would, in addition, require not only a contingency – an emergency fund to cover the first overcosts – of at least 10 per cent, but a detailed review of all the budget estimates before shooting would be allowed to start. In other words, additional costs and delay, as well as greater control, would be brought to bear on the production. This would be bound to be unacceptable to Boorman, who, it should be remembered, was first tempted into the Goldcrest camp by Eberts's espousal of a policy of mutual trust.

Boorman, at this time, was in Los Angeles, trying, with Rospo Pallenberg, to trim and polish the script. He was also auditioning actors to play Tommy. On 16 January he received a call from Terry Clegg informing him that, at a Goldcrest board meeting that day, it had been decided that $750,000 had to be cut from the *Emerald Forest* budget and that a third-party guarantor definitely had to be brought in. Boorman was at first shocked – he had assumed that Clegg had gone back to London to present a favourable report – and then hurt as he realized that fellow film-makers, and Goldcrest board members, Puttnam and Attenborough must have sided with Lee in making these decisions. (In fact, Attenborough did not participate in the discussion.)

For his part, Puttnam remembers being 'faced with the situation where the thing was about to go out. Terry Clegg came back to report that there was no schedule, there was no budget, no completion guarantee, no completed screenplay . . . Terry had done the numbers and we were tremendously influenced by his feeling that this was a completely out-of-control situation. Hopelessly out of control.'

The board's concern was not only about the budget. There was general, if lukewarm, support for the project as such, but many, including Puttnam, were not impressed by the script, which was felt to be sketchy and unresolved. Nor was Puttnam in favour of allowing one man to be both director and producer, on the grounds that in the event of a dispute the director always wins. (Attenborough, had he been at the meeting, would have raised an eyebrow at this.) Nor, in addition, could he have been pleased with the sums involved in Boorman's deal. No producer or director had ever been paid a fee in excess of $400,000 at Goldcrest, and no one had ever been granted more than 50 per cent of net profits. Boorman himself admits that his contract was, potentially, exceptionally lucrative: before the tax deal fell out, he was looking forward to making '$5 million or more' from the picture. (David Norris, who understood the contracts better than anybody, thinks that this estimate is wildly inflated.)

All these doubts would be put aside if it could be guaranteed that the production was under control: that what Goldcrest thought it was paying for was what it would get. For an answer to this question the meeting turned not to Lee or Lieberson, but to Clegg. 'The whole board was looking at me,' he recalls. ' "Can the cost be controlled?" I had to say with my hand on my heart, "I don't think so." '

From there it was a simple step to argue that Goldcrest was not just courting a *Dream One*-type disaster on a grand scale, but was placing the fund-raising in jeopardy: *The Emerald Forest* would be in production, and, it seemed, likely to be in trouble, at just the time that the prospectus was being issued. This argument quickly took hold among, in Norris's phrase, the 'doubting Thomases' (i.e. everyone except Norris and Gavin, both of whom strongly supported the picture). It was, of course, a self-fulfilling prophecy. For, if the management of the company believed that its one current major production was likely to go over budget, then it was bound to inform Rothschild of that fact, and Rothschild, in turn, would be bound to include the management's view in the fund-raising prospectus. Naturally, this was not something that the bank was prepared even to contemplate. As soon as Lee and Co. expressed their fears about *The Emerald Forest*, Rothschild insisted that the matter be dealt with: either guarantee that it would come in on time (which, given the power vested in Boorman, was impossible) or ditch the picture.

Clegg asked Boorman to return to London to talk the matter through. Boorman refused. He, in turn, tried to contact David Norris, his closest ally in the Goldcrest camp, but Norris, embarrassed by the turn of events, and caught between his loyalty to his friend and his obligation to argue the Goldcrest case, would not take his calls. An impasse was reached.

A few days later, Goldcrest informed Boorman that 'all expenditure other than that required to hold and maintain the production team, required prior Goldcrest approval' – in effect the picture was on hold. Boorman instructed his business manager, Ed Gross, to make discreet enquiries among the studios to see if anyone would take Goldcrest's place.

Eberts: Even before I left Goldcrest it had become apparent that James

Lee and the rest of the management team were getting cold feet about *The Emerald Forest*. The concerns about the budget did not just focus on whether John could, or would, stick to it, but also on the specific problems of how best to fund the location costs. The financing arrangements in Brazil involved Citibank acquiring cruzeiros (Brazil's unit of currency) for Goldcrest, to cover the set-building, accommodation, transport and local wages. But in Brazil, at that time, inflation was running at about 150 per cent a year, which meant that the currency was falling in value every day. Consequently, it was almost impossible to estimate the local costs of the picture over the four-month production period. This was one of the grey areas that made it very hard to agree on a final budget figure.

The sensible approach was to exchange small amounts of dollars or pounds at any one time and to assume that Citibank thereby always bought cruzeiros at the best available rate. In theory, inflation could not significantly exceed the rate of devaluation of the currency, so the production, as long as it delayed payment for a week or two on every invoice, would always be even. It is very hard to demonstrate conclusively that this approach works, but I, unlike others at Goldcrest, had been happy to proceed on that basis.

I had also been happy to trust John. We were very close friends and when he said to me that he would do something, and do it on time and on budget, I believed him. I could look him in the eye and say, 'If it starts going over you'll have to cut this, this and this', and he would give me his word that he'd do it. (This is again one of the reasons why I always work with experienced people I can trust: if David Puttnam, Dickie Attenborough or John Boorman is 12,000 miles away in the jungle, spending hundreds of thousands of dollars a week, no contract in the world is going to control him. Trust is the only way.)

Now James did not have that kind of relationship with John. Nor did Terry Clegg, even though he had worked with John a number of times over the years. So it was natural for them, on seeing so many imponderables in the budget and schedule, to take a negative – if you like, distrustful – view.

Also, I think there was a feeling within Goldcrest that this was my project, promoted and pushed by me. It is a common observation in the film business that new managements like to start with a clean slate, and although this leads to a lot of cynical comment, especially among filmmakers, the reasons for it are not necessarily sinister. Such is the risk involved in investing millions of dollars in what is only ever a vague idea or vision – even a completed script is open to widely differing interpretations – that it is natural to feel comfortable only with those projects and film-makers you have nurtured yourself. Other people's projects are just too hard to grasp. So it would not have been at all out of place for James Lee to say, 'Look, there's enough uncertainty here; it's really Jake's deal, his project – let's see if we can't get out of it somehow.' And the obvious person to take it over was me.

James and I had discussed the matter intermittently ever since I left Goldcrest, and we talked about it seriously and at length in the second and third weeks of January. I was familiar with all the pre-sales done by Bill Gavin. I knew that the costs of the picture were basically covered even before the cameras started rolling, and I could not see any difficulty in selling the idea to Jerry Perenchio. Embassy, remember, had already agreed to pay $9 million for the US rights. Goldcrest had only to indicate formally their willingness to let go of it and we could sit down and negotiate terms.

Ilott: On 23 January the Goldcrest management agreed that 'if other outstanding difficulties [with Boorman] were not resolved within the week' the *Emerald Forest* project would be offered to Embassy. In outline, Goldcrest's negotiating position would be that Embassy must use the cruzeiros that Goldcrest had already bought (the currency was of no use outside Brazil); that all foreign-sales contracts must be honoured; that Goldcrest must recover its development and pre-production costs, sales commissions, distribution fees and overheads; and that Goldcrest must retain a net-profit position. Should it prove impossible to meet these, or other acceptable conditions, then Goldcrest would carry on with the film: to abandon the project at that stage would have cost the company about $4 million.

Boorman, meanwhile, had flown from LA to Rio and was adamant that he would not return to England until the film was finished. His line producer, Michael Dryhurst, still in London, was therefore invited to a meeting to discuss the budget and the other 'outstanding difficulties'. At this meeting, held on 27 January, Dryhurst, like Boorman, was taken aback by Terry Clegg's lack of support. According to Boorman, Dryhurst described the encounter as 'rough' and James Lee's attitude as 'very hostile'. The outcome was that no further expenditure would be authorized until a completion bond was in place. Clearly, Goldcrest and *The Emerald Forest* had reached a parting of the ways.

Boorman called Ed Gross to discuss his next move, and then he called Eberts: if Embassy wanted to take over the picture then that would be fine by him.

Over the weekend of 28–9 January there was an exchange of telephone calls about *The Emerald Forest* between Lee, Eberts and Perenchio. Formal negotiations between Lee and Eberts commenced on Monday, 30 January. What Lee proposed was that Embassy should acquire all rights and obligations to the film, and that Goldcrest should, in effect, repurchase the foreign-sales rights for an advance of $5.5 million, all but $500,000 of which would be considered to be already covered by its cruzeiros costs and other expenditures to date. Goldcrest could recoup this advance, with interest and a 15 per cent distribution fee, from foreign-sales receipts. In addition, the company would keep 25 per cent of net profits. Embassy's acceptance of these terms would naturally be subject to a detailed review by their own production staff, but Lee pressed for a commitment in principle before the end of the week.

Should Lee fail to agree terms with Embassy, then Boorman would be asked to defer all but £250,000 of his fee, in order both to bring the budget down to within the set limits and to give Boorman an incentive to stick to the schedule. If that was not agreed, then the project, which was now believed to pose a serious threat to the fund-raising, would be abandoned altogether.

Eberts: Nothing was agreed that week other than that Embassy would definitely acquire *The Emerald Forest*. In fact, it was to take two months of haggling before contracts were exchanged. Nor did Goldcrest get anything like the terms they wanted. Embassy knew that Goldcrest was anxious to get out of the project and pressed for such a tough deal that I was embarrassed to sit across the table from my erstwhile colleagues and, in effect, hammer them into the ground. I asked to be relieved of the job. It wasn't just that Embassy were being tough; they were being unfair. They would pay no interest, no sales commission, no distribution fee, no profit share; Goldcrest was to get its money back, no more. Bill Gavin had done a lot of foreign sales and Goldcrest should have been given a fee for that – maybe not the full fee, but some kind of fee. Likewise, Goldcrest had invested money to get the film going and that should have been reimbursed with interest. And the company should have been given a small profit share for developing the project in the first place, say 5–10 per cent. That, to my mind, would have been a normal, equitable way of doing things, and one that would have guaranteed good relations in the future.

But Embassy, as I was soon to discover, was a true Hollywood company. Hollywood – the business side, not the creative side – likes victory more than anything else. And victory can be measured in the smallest things, like saving $25,000 of interest, or 2.5 profit points, or 10 per cent commission. Victory is worth far more than the actual amounts of money involved. And victory over Goldcrest is what Embassy wanted now. I handed over the negotiation to Embassy's head of business affairs Ron Beckman and was glad to have nothing more to do with it.

Ilott: Bill Gavin knew nothing of all this. He had been in New York trying to sell a package of *First Love* films to the cable channel Showtime. From New York, he had flown down to Rio to sell titles from the back catalogue. In the normal course of events, the lesser titles in the Goldcrest library would remain unsold in Brazil for want of dollars on the part of local distributors. But, since *The Emerald Forest* needed cruzeiros, Gavin could for once trade in the local currency. It was, he says, a 'wonderful opportunity to do deals'.

'So, I flew overnight down from New York. I checked into this hotel in Rio and, literally as I checked in, the phone went on the reception desk and the girl answering it said, "Oh, it's for you Mr Gavin." It was James, calling from London to say that we'd pulled out of *The Emerald Forest*. I was stunned more than anything else. I mean, here was a situation where we had delivered pre-sales of, I think at that point, $12 million, including the $9 million from Embassy. And they walked away from it.

'Out of sheer cussedness or professionalism or stupidity or whatever, I then stayed in Rio for a few days and did some dollar deals. I think I sold, for my sins, *Local Hero* and, believe it or not, *The Far Pavilions*. Then I went off and stayed with some very good friends in Colombia. I had about ten days' holiday and just completely relaxed. And I thought, "It is insane to work this hard for anybody other than yourself." There you are, busting your gut. You're staying in the Beverly Hills Hotel and it sounds lovely, but in fact at six in the morning you're up, you're awake, you're running the office in London. By the time you've made your breakfast appointment, at half past eight or nine, you've already been working for two or three hours. And it just goes on and on. You have dinner in a lovely restaurant but it's with somebody in the business, and, God help me, it's really work. It's just crazy. I'm burning myself out. And for what? – for people who not only don't appreciate you, but who will drop you right in it.'

Gavin decided to resign when he got back to London. Clegg, meanwhile, who could not really see a comfortable role for himself in the new order – Lieberson's skills overlapped too much with his own – informed Lee that he would not be staying beyond the expiry of his contract at the end of July. David Norris, who, as well as being bitterly disappointed about *The Emerald Forest*, had already had a number of clashes with Lee over their respective areas of responsibility, had lunch with a former client, Malcolm Wilde from the merchant bank Guinness Mahon. The purpose of the meeting was to discuss the setting up of a new film fund, what Norris calls 'Goldcrest 2', for which Guinness Mahon very much wanted Norris's services. And John Chambers had been invited to talk to his former British Lion and EMI boss, Michael Deeley, about the possibility of his and Norris's working with Deeley at Consolidated Productions. One by one, the Goldcrest executives – so 'well bedded down' as Lee had put it when he took over from Eberts, but in reality so discomfited by the importation into the company of Lee, Cruickshank and Lieberson – were looking for ways out.

On 12 February John Boorman cast his son Charley in the role of Tommy. Rospo Pallenberg, regarding the decision as absurd, remonstrated with him, but without success. He vowed never to speak to Boorman again.

On 13 February the first complete draft of the Goldcrest Film and Television Holdings prospectus was circulated to directors and senior staff. It was to provoke an immediate management revolt.

Chapter Twenty-six

Management in Revolt

Ilott: There had been earlier drafts of the prospectus, mostly setting out Goldcrest's financial record, an account of its current investments and details of the share offering. These early drafts, which were the most succinct and up-to-date summaries of Goldcrest's operations, had been circulated to shareholders and had even been used outside the company; for example, in the discussions that Chambers, Cruickshank and Lee were then having with the banks from whom they were hoping to secure credit facilities. What was different about the latest draft was that it contained, for the first time, an outline of the management arrangements, board structure and share-option schemes for the new company.

Hitherto, the key policy-making forum within Goldcrest had been the board of Goldcrest Films and Television Ltd, under which umbrella were brought together the interests of Goldcrest Television, Goldcrest Films, GFTP and the myriad of subsidiary companies. The membership of this board had included John Chambers, David Norris, Terry Clegg, Bill Gavin, Mike Wooller and James Lee, as well as David Puttnam, Richard Attenborough, Angus Grossart and other representatives of the principal investors. This was the team which reviewed all the projects, proposals and reports submitted by the television and film arms of Goldcrest. These in turn had their own boards, comprising mostly the same executives but with the addition, on the television side, of Longman's Tim Rix and producer Derek Granger, and, on the film side, of Penguin's Peter Mayer. These operating boards held monthly meetings at which the directors discussed investment proposals in detail.

The old board structure had been complicated only because the over-lapping interests of the partnerships had themselves been so complicated. The point to note is that the managers of the company had sat on the boards that controlled it, and a diagram of Goldcrest's power structure would have resembled a not very high and very flat-topped pyramid. It had been no democracy – Pearson, after all, had held the purse strings throughout – but discussion had been open and, by and large, inclusive rather than exclusive of all the relevant staff.

Naturally, in the reorganization – and especially in the context of Eberts's departure, the importation of Lee, Cruickshank and Lieberson and the establishment of the new company independently of Pearson – all this had to change. But it had not been expected, certainly not by Norris and Chambers, that the new hierarchy would be quite so sharply pointed as was now proposed in the prospectus. A two-tier structure was envisaged, with virtually the entire management team relegated to membership of a subordinate, operating board, while all meaningful power was concentrated in the hands of a higher, holding-company board on which Lee, Cruickshank and Lieberson – the three least-experienced managers of the company – would be the sole executive representatives.

It was not argued that this proposed structure was ideal. In fact, it had come about only as the result of a compromise.

'We got into a very curious situation,' remembers Lee, 'because what I hadn't appreciated was going to happen was that I, for a very short period of time, lost control of the reins. This came as a considerable surprise, because I thought the entire process of transition would happen within my control, but it didn't. Because Pearson was a public company and it was in effect selling some of its assets into a new company, [it] had to be independently advised. They couldn't turn to me because I was an interested party and was going to end up as the chairman of the company. So, quite rightly, Pearson had to have somebody representing their interests in addition to myself.'

The person selected was James Joll and, since Pearson still had a controlling vote throughout the process of reorganization, effective power was, temporarily at least, concentrated in Joll's hands. Lee had hitherto regarded Joll as an ally and was alarmed to find that he was almost immediately engaged in what Joll remembers as being a 'frightful row'.

Lee's two-tier board structure was not in itself controversial – it enabled investment proposals to be scrutinized in detail by the management before they were put to the shareholders' representatives – but his insistence on being chairman of both boards was. Joll was opposed in principle to the idea of chief executives being their own chairmen – in his view, it vested far too much power in the management – and he was particularly against it in this case because the chief executive in question was Lee. ('It wasn't sensible,' he says, 'because James is very headstrong.') He at first argued for the higher board to have a non-executive chairman, which, of course, is what Lee had been in Eberts's day. But Lee adamantly objected to this. Taking the opposite view to Joll, he 'didn't agree with the idea of having a part-time chairman' at all, holding that 'where there was a large board, and the board included other executives who are the subordinates of the chief executive, [then] the chief executive loses a great deal of power if there is in effect a *primus inter pares* between himself and his own executives . . . Essentially, the chairman is able to go over [his] head . . . When everything is OK and there are no crises it doesn't matter. But it was very clear to me that the film business just wasn't like that: it lurches from crisis to crisis, and strong direction is needed.' Joll eventually withdrew – 'in the end he beat us all down and, rather feebly I think, we gave in,' he says – but only on condition that there be a majority of non-executives on the higher, holding-company, board: a majority that could veto, if need be, Lee's or the management's decisions. To this Lee reluctantly agreed.

With Joll, Attenborough, Puttnam, Grossart, Electra's Michael Stoddart and perhaps either Peter Mayer or Tim Rix forming the non-executive majority, the way was open for Lee to nominate four, or perhaps five, executive directors to the higher board. Among them would have to be Lee himself, Cruickshank and Lieberson, which left one, or at the most two, positions still be to filled. But Lee could not fill them. For how could he nominate Norris, say, without Chambers? Or Chambers and Norris without Wooller? He came to the conclusion that matters were best left with just the three most senior executives on the holding-company board.

But this, of course, meant that the rest of the management team, hitherto accustomed to discussing policy on the various boards as among equals, were now, as far as the holding company was concerned, to be subordinates: Norris and Chambers reporting to Cruickshank, who would be the director responsible for finance and administration, Clegg and Wooller reporting to Lieberson, who would be the director responsible for production and marketing, and Gavin, for the time being – since it was thought likely to cause a riot if he had to answer to Lieberson – reporting directly to Lee.

These arrangements were greeted with profound dismay, especially by Norris and Chambers.

'We were there on the [board of the] operating company, but not on the holding company,' explains Norris. 'And it seemed to me that when you saw the plan for decision-making, which was that James could make any investment decision up to £500,000 on his own, the management committee could go up to £3 million collectively – I think subject to review but not approval by the board – and anything above that required the board . . . and knowing that we were not restricting ourselves in terms of the scope of projects . . . I was deeply concerned that . . . there were only going to be three executive directors, Don Cruickshank, Sandy Lieberson and James, none of whom knew much about the business of movies – though Sandy at least knew movies. The rest of the board was going to be Dickie and David [Puttnam], which was fine – [although] probably they knew less of the business, strangely, than I did at the time: I mean, I'm sure that David now knows more than I ever will, but at the time he knew less of the detailed nuts and bolts of the business – and the James Jolls and the Michael Stoddarts and the other shareholders' representatives. They decided that they didn't need the likes of myself, or John or Bill Gavin on the main board.'

To add insult to the injury of being thus disenfranchised, the management team was faced with a share-option scheme which, as they saw it, blatantly discriminated against them. In the past, only Eberts, whose family trust owned 10 per cent of both Goldcrest Films and Goldcrest Television – negotiations for the buy-back of which had, incidentally, become bogged down and not a little acrimonious – and Wooller, who owned 5 per cent of Goldcrest Television, had had any share in the business. But in the draft prospectus, an elaborate option scheme, accounting for 15 per cent of the company's equity, was set out in detail.

'I think between them they [Lee, Lieberson, Attenborough and Puttnam] had 10 per cent – 2.5 per cent each – leaving up to 5 per cent for the rest of the staff,' explains Norris, 'of which about 2 per cent was going to be allocated, say, half a per cent to John, half a per cent to me, half a per cent to Mike Wooller, or whatever it was. And that pissed me off quite considerably – I mean not on a personal level, because I'd never actually valued the share options, so I didn't care if I had none – I just thought it was desperately unfair to the group as a whole, particularly to the rest of the staff.

'I suppose there might have been some justification . . . for the executive directors, James and Sandy, but I could see no justification for giving Dickie and David that level of share options. They had taken substantial fees out of the company for their jobs as producers and directors, and they had done pretty well. Yes, they'd been to board meetings, [and] their input was very valuable . . . but they were not there as businessmen. There was no justification for their taking a very substantially higher proportion than the people who had actually been on the ground making it work: the Terry Cleggs, the Bill Gavins and the Mike Woollers, all of whom had been there longer than I had. *They* were the people who, if you looked at it objectively, had made the operation work. Not David, not Dickie. The only reason for giving it to them that I can see was . . . well, it smacked of a kind of favouritism really.'

What upset Norris most of all – he refers to it as 'sheer impudence' – was the fact that none of this had ever been discussed at the management level: 'The owners of the shop were just saying, "Right, this is it, take it or leave it. You have tuppence ha'penny worth of share options and these guys who actually don't work for the company, but who are on the board, Dickie and David, get 2.5 per cent. And you have no say in running the company." '

The prospectus was to be ratified by the first board meeting of the new company, Goldcrest Films and Television (Holdings) Ltd, the following week. Norris and Chambers were thus forced, in Chambers's words, 'to really crystallize our thoughts. With all the changes we could see happening, we couldn't have something going out with our names on it as part of the management team and then a month later say we're not happy with it.'

Norris made a formal complaint to Lee; Chambers, too, registered his protest. But Lee was not overly sympathetic.

'To be perfectly frank, I never saw either Chambers or Norris as being as central to the success or otherwise of Goldcrest as they did, ever: not in the early days, not latterly and not now,' comments Lee. 'I mean, we hired a head-hunter and he [Chambers] was presented to us as a very good journeyman accountant, a bloody good, competent finance director, which was what we asked for. Quite at what point John changed from being the very skilful accountant into somebody who saw himself as being the be-all and end-all of Goldcrest, I don't know. He was important, everybody was important, but I never saw him in the same light as I saw Jake or David [Puttnam]. It just hadn't occurred to me that he was in the same league. David Norris was something else. He was actually a victim of this blasted non-executive-director thing. Otherwise he would have been involved more closely – but then we would have had the equity problems with John.'

Lee identifies, as the main source of Norris's and Chambers's complaints, their loss of power, and especially the fact that the prospectus 'in every way recognized [Lieberson] as a more important member of the team than them'. His comments are echoed by Bill Gavin, although Gavin names Cruickshank rather than Lieberson as the bugbear.

'Whatever they say, their problem was (a) money and (b) that Cruickshank was above them. They didn't like that at all,' Gavin says, adding that 'Norris felt, even when Jake was there, that he was second-in-command. I don't think Jake ever told him that and I'm not sure that James ever told him that, but David felt that.'

Gavin, who at that time had still not announced his own plans but whose resignation was widely expected, in fact took some care to distance himself from Norris and Chambers. When, on Monday, 20 February, the day before the inaugural holding-board meeting, Norris called him into his office to tell him that he was going to resign, Gavin's only response was to shrug and say, 'No you're not.'

But Norris did resign. He had waited all week for some response to his complaints, and now believes that Lee probably 'acted as a buffer in very much the same way as he had with Jake's own negotiations about salary: he probably never carried anything back – tried to solve it and cope with it on his own'. At all events, no response had been forthcoming.

'I went to see him [Lee] and said, "Look, if nothing's going to happen then I'm going to go," ' remembers Norris. 'He said, "Fine." '

At home that night, Norris wrote out his resignation on his own headed notepaper. He handed it to Lee first thing on Tuesday morning.

'I chose quite deliberately to hand in my notice on the day of the first board meeting,' he explains, 'knowing that he could not ignore that; that he would have to bring it out.'

As Lee received, and accepted, Norris's resignation, a crowd of lawyers, bankers, shareholders, executive and non-executive directors, note-takers and advisers were assembling in the corridor outside the boardroom at Holland Street. Cruickshank, Joll, Attenborough, Lieberson, Angus Grossart and Michael Stoddart were among them. The only notable absentee was David Puttnam, who at that time was working with Roland Joffe on the fine cut of *The Killing Fields*.

John Chambers took the Rothschild representative, Bernie Myers, discreetly to one side and informed him that Norris had resigned and indicated that he, Chambers, might soon follow. 'I said, "I don't know how you're supposed to handle it but I think you ought to know," ' he recalls.

Myers hardly had time to reply before everyone took their seats and James Lee called the meeting to order. The formalities – noting the incorporation of the company and the registration of shareholders, adopting the common seal and logo, and confirming the appointment of auditors, chairman and directors – took only a few minutes. Then the real business of the day, the approval of the main part of the prospectus and discussion of its various appendices, began. This was to be the completion meeting: all preparations were to be concluded, all loose ends tied up and a firm date set for the share offering. It was not expected, at this late stage, that there would be much need for lengthy discussion, still less that there would be controversy.

The proceedings started in suitably businesslike fashion. Banking arrangements, the status of the existing contracts between Goldcrest and various third parties, the procedures for the acquisition by the new company of GFT, GFTP, GFI and Goldcrest Television, the timetable for the reorganization and the fund-raising, an evaluation of taxation liability: all were duly dealt with. Whenever clarification of a legal or procedural point was required one of the outside advisers would be asked to explain, and, once the matter had been dealt with, the meeting briskly moved on to the next item on the long agenda. It was when the meeting was approaching its later stages that, as James Joll remembers it, Lee 'blithely' mentioned, in the context of a review of the share-option scheme, that 'there is one variation: Norris won't be getting any stock options. He's not joining.'

'I said, "Christ – what's this?" ' recalls Joll. 'And he said, "Well, actually, Norris has resigned." '

Lee's casual attitude to the matter struck a wrong note. Indeed, either because he himself did not truly grasp the significance of Norris's decision, or because he believed that everyone present would take their cue from him – that his determination to underplay the resignation would be enough to relegate it to the status of a footnote – he completely misjudged the shareholders' reaction. There was uproar.

'We said, "You can't do this: you can't bloody well have such a senior person leave just like that at this moment in time," ' recalls Joll. 'Everyone was putting their money into this company on the strength of the prospectus, and in the prospectus it said that Norris was the most important man in charge of contracts . . . one of the linchpins of the company. But when it comes to completion we're told he actually isn't joining. We were flabbergasted . . . There was a riot.'

Chambers, who attended the meeting as an adviser, remembers the confused discussion that followed: 'Lee said that he [Norris] was "unhappy with the structure that we have decided upon and he has decided to resign". So Lieberson said, "Oh this is dreadful; perhaps he can have my seat on the board."

'And one of the non-executive directors said, "Well, who's going to take over from David Norris?" And Lee said, "Oh, Don Cruickshank will assume the business affairs and some of the legal stuff." That was the signal for Dickie to really get steamed up. He said, "Well, I think, Mr Chairman, this is absolutely deplorable news" – as only Dickie can, he got really quite wound up – "I've already indicated my dislike of the structure which has been proposed and I foretold that this sort of thing might happen. David Norris has resigned and I'm sure he's not going to be the only one. Jake Eberts culled these individuals at the peak of their careers in the film industry. They were hand-picked and they have stature in the industry. Jake has built them into a team." And he said that if Norris went and if others followed, he would have to reconsider his position as a director of the company.'

Attenborough himself recalls being 'very emotional about it', believing that the exclusion of Norris and Co. from the board was a 'total misjudgement, total folly. The old-style business of "you are the employees and the back-room boys, and we are the board", etc., I don't subscribe to at all. And to allow a position to arise whereby major figures – not front-office figures, but major figures in terms of how you operate in the film industry – to allow them to go, to even contemplate their departure, was, I thought, absolute madness.'

According to the minutes, the non-executive members of the board – Joll, Attenborough, Grossart, Stoddart, Peter Mayer and a newcomer, television producer Philip Whitehead – 'expressed serious concern at these developments and at their potential impact on the fund-raising'. Unlike the earlier part of the meeting, which had been characterized by the steady stream of expert commentary from the outside advisers, this discussion involved only the members of the company. The lawyers, bankers, solicitors and accountants sat on the sidelines, trying, as James Joll remembers, 'to pretend that nothing's happened'. And where the earlier part of the proceedings had been conducted in a cool, technocratic fashion, the present debate was heated from the start. Even so, the most pressing questions – how much or little support did Lee enjoy within the company, what were the real reasons for Norris's resignation and who, if any one, was going to follow him – were left unasked. The debate confined itself instead to the question of the board structure, the reason given by Lee for Norris's resignation. According to the minutes, 'several solutions were discussed, including the adoption of a single operating-company board with strong non-executive representation instead of the proposed two-tier company and board structure'. In the end, it was agreed 'that a fundamental review of the proposals should be undertaken immediately, in consultation with Goldcrest's executive directors and Pearson'. Before the fund-raising could proceed, the minute concludes, 'non-executive directors would require to meet and obtain assurances from each of Goldcrest's senior executive directors that the problems had been satisfactorily resolved and a sound, workable management structure established'.

It would seem from the minutes that the Jolls, Stoddarts and Grossarts, presumably taking their cue from Attenborough, sided with Norris rather than Lee, who thus received a slap in the face from the one camp, the board, upon which he thought he could always rely for support.

The remaining items on the agenda were dealt with in perfunctory fashion and, as soon as the meeting closed, the non-executive directors convened an *ad hoc* meeting, what Joll calls a 'self-elected cabal', of their own. Their discussion revealed not only that Norris's grievances ran deep, but that he was supported by Chambers, who was also likely to resign, and that Gavin and Clegg, for reasons of their own, were probably going to leave the company as well. The non-executive directors asked to see Norris, 'heard his story, and were aghast by the thought of the degree of the revolution which was going on, and the intrigue, none of which had been brought to our attention. There we were setting up a new major company and the chairman and chief executive had lost half his colleagues and was blithely going on without having informed anyone. And we said, "This won't do. Sorry, we can't go on like [this],"' Joll recalls.

The day ended in a flurry of meetings between Lee, Cruickshank, Attenborough, various members of the board, Norris and Chambers. Lord Blakenham himself came over from Millbank to hear, first-hand, what the executives' complaints were.

Whatever the resolution of this crisis, one thing was certain: the share offering was not only going to be delayed once again, but confidence in the company, already weakened following Eberts's departure, would be weakened further. The fund-raising, always in danger of being late, might not even be successful.

Chapter Twenty-seven

Moral Pressure

Ilott: The next day, 22 February, Norris had an early-morning meeting with Malcolm Wilde of Guinness Mahon. Their discussions about setting up 'Goldcrest 2' had reason to be more urgent than before.

Later, Norris joined Lee, Cruickshank and Chambers for a meeting at which all the objections to the management structure and option arrangements were restated, and Lee and Cruickshank, promising, as Chambers recalls, to 'sort something out', went back for talks with Lord Blakenham. Chambers and Norris then went off for a long lunch with Michael Deeley, with whom they again discussed the possibility of moving to Consolidated Productions.

At 3.30 p.m. the meeting with Lee and Cruickshank reconvened.

'They said they had talked to Blakenham and Pearson,' says Chambers, 'and that this was what they were going to propose: that we did away with the two-tier structure, have one board for the holding company, of which we would be members. David and I would report direct to James, [while] Wooller would continue to report to Lieberson. And we had half an hour to decide if we were going to stay or not. And I remember James adding that he "didn't like the way we had handled it". I was dumbfounded and David went berserk, saying, "You don't like the way it's been handled – it's you that have caused all the problems!"

'Here were two guys, terribly upset, in a position they didn't want to be in, very emotional about the whole thing, and to be told that Lee didn't like the way it had been handled was incredibly insensitive, even if it had been true, which it wasn't.

'I mean, what does he expect? He comes into a company, brings two guys in and puts them over the people who work there and have built the whole thing up, and expects them to be happy about it. It showed a complete lack of understanding, of common sense. You don't have to have an MBA to see that.'

It seems that Lee withdrew his demand for an immediate response and the conversation revolved around more general observations and complaints, becoming more amicable in the process. As the working day drew to an end, however, the four of them were joined by Lieberson and Gavin. According to Norris, the discussion then became much more heated and personal. Gavin in particular, he says, became 'very outspoken; more outspoken than I dared be, I think, in terms of personalities'. The focus of Gavin's ire was Lieberson, who recalls, sardonically, that, 'Bill decided that he didn't like me'. His explanation for this antipathy is that Gavin 'really wanted my job', an assertion that Gavin vehemently denies.

Lieberson, Lee and Cruickshank withdrew, leaving Gavin, Norris and Chambers alone in the boardroom. Whatever it was they discussed, it finally persuaded Gavin that he could not stay with the company any longer. The next morning he informed Lee of his decision.

'James said, "Look, Bill, is there anything you want or need to make you change your mind?" I said, "James, no." And, in fact, I remember him ringing me from his office one time and saying, "Seriously, let's talk it out," and I said, "No." I had made up my mind. I wasn't ambivalent about it at all . . . I couldn't see any alternative. I couldn't see anything happening except it all going very wrong. I just couldn't see that structure and that team doing anything else.'

He would leave at the end of the month.

Norris, too, was implacable. Only Chambers, who at that time had not formally given in his notice, was in two minds: 'I remember saying "Well, I don't know." I was completely at sea in that situation.'

For his part, Lee had left the boardroom meeting convinced that matters could still be resolved. Gavin's resignation was a blow, but one which had been long expected (so long, in fact, that sales assistant Guy East had already been groomed to take Gavin's place). And Lee could derive some satisfaction from the fact that the press had not got hold of the story. It seems that no one in the industry was aware of the dramas that were engulfing its flagship company. If Lee could devise an organizational structure that took into account Norris's and Chamber's objections, then all might yet be well. He set to work drafting a letter to the non-executive directors, a letter designed to meet their requirement that they should have 'assurances from each of Goldcrest's senior executives that the problems had been satisfactorily resolved'. On Friday, 24 February, this letter was circulated to the senior executives for their approval. It is worth quoting at length:

Following the events of this Tuesday, I have spent much time with my colleagues at Goldcrest discussing the way we organize ourselves and how we can work together as a team for the future.

We have agreed that neither the board structure that I had proposed for the reorganization, nor the way in which we have been working together for the past two months, has been very satisfactory. We believe that a two-tier board structure would be divisive and would prevent effective communication between the non-executive directors and the senior executives of the company. An opportunity would be lost.

Furthermore, we have recognized that in a company like Goldcrest, with a small team of talented professionals working under intense pressures . . . hier-archical structures are neither realistic nor workable. Accordingly, my proposal to create a hierarchy within the top management was resented and if implemented would have poisoned what has up to now been a collegial atmos-phere. We have reaffirmed our desire and commitment to work as a team.

We have discussed a number of other matters among ourselves, including the allocation of options under the share option scheme. My colleagues feel that we should lay aside a proportion of the share options for a number of other senior managers in both the legal and financial areas, and I agree.

Accordingly we propose that (. . .) should be available for distribution to about (. . .) individuals within the next few months following the reconstruction . . .

Bill Gavin will be leaving us. He really wants to pursue his own interests as an entrepreneur. He will be setting up his own foreign selling agency. He is very confident that Guy East will make an excellent successor and has rec-ommended that Guy take over at the end of the month . . . I am confident that Guy East will do the job very well.

David Norris and John Chambers have agreed to work as part of the top management team, and will report directly to the chairman.

1. We should redesign our organization so that there is a 'unitary board'. This means that the board of Holdings will in fact be the only operating board.

2. The top executive team should be members of the Holding Company board. This means that David Norris, John Chambers and Mike Wooller will join the board . . .

6. The top management team will all report directly to me as chief executive (that is − Sandy Lieberson, David Norris, John Chambers and Donald Cruickshank).

7. Share options will be allocated only to executive directors at the time of the placing, but a second wave should be distributed within three months.

I now believe that we have the basis of a workable organization structure. It is most regrettable that it has taken this trauma to get us to see that the old one would not work. However, every cloud has a silver lining, and I hope that we now have a group of people who will dedicate themselves to working together as a team.

. . . This letter has been considered by David Norris, John Chambers, Donald Cruickshank and Sandy Lieberson, and we are all in agreement. If the non-executive board members are satisfied that the management team can now work together, then I recommend that we proceed with the placing on 6th March as planned.

(East was considered insufficiently experienced to be appointed to the holding-company board immediately. He would instead report to Lieberson, as would Wooller, whose status and role, according to this letter, became even more anomalous than before. The figures for the allocation of share options were left open pending further discussion.)

It was very much against Lee's nature to write a letter such as this, and there is a hint of exasperation in its penitent tone. To this day, while he admits that he had made 'a great mistake' in leaving Norris and Chambers 'out of the play' in the first place, he still takes umbrage at the memory of the 'militant action' by which the duo achieved their ends. But the letter had had to be written – the board meeting had demanded nothing less – and he hoped that the formula he had arrived at would now see the crisis resolved. John Chambers's secretary, Maureen Sheen, thought the same when she saw a copy on Chambers's desk. 'I thought, "Oh good, everything's going to be OK," ' she recalls.

But, of course, the letter, like the draft prospectus, served only to further concentrate Norris's and Chambers's minds.

Norris recalls that the proposals were 'of a cosmetic nature – they were not significant', while Chambers remembers that 'now that we had got the immediate problems sorted out all the underlying things came to the fore'. What concerned them, he says, was 'the way the thing was going to operate and the way the company was going to evolve'.

They had already noted with alarm the ever-growing overheads, which were now running at an annual rate of £2.6 million, a 50 per cent increase on the previous year's £1.7 million, which was itself a significant increase on the figure for 1982. On 1 January eight people had joined the staff, three more had joined in the first week of February and five more were to be added by the end of April, bringing the number of people employed, by the time the revised prospectus was eventually issued, to forty-nine. Seven of these were in sales, eighteen were in the back office and fifteen were in television. The rest reported directly to either Lee or Lieberson.

'If you added up the totality of the James–Sandy group', notes Norris, 'you had nine people . . . three of whom were very, very highly paid . . . effectively taking the place of Jake and Irene [Lyons, who had left Gold-crest to join Eberts at Embassy].'

Norris and Chambers were increasingly worried by what they con-sidered to be the inexperience of the company's two leading adminis-trators, Lee and Cruickshank, and what, in their minds, was the inappro-priate experience of its creative chief, Sandy Lieberson. It was not a question, Norris insists, of having 'doubts about Sandy's ability to choose subjects or to be a production executive: it was really about style . . . I was nervous about the area we were going to get into in terms of development and the costs which I would attribute to Sandy's regime.'

In his own defence, Lieberson says, 'I didn't feel that Goldcrest could be in the area of only making pick-up deals, only sort of buying completed films or waiting until a package was delivered to them. You had to go out and aggressively pursue film-makers, directors, producers and writers and put a package together. And in order to do that you had to spend money on development. I wasn't anxious to finance the development of thousands of screenplays, but to finance a screenplay which is attached to a director or producer or whatever is absolutely necessary to make the kind of films that we wanted to make.'

Eberts: There is a misunderstanding here. What Sandy describes is exactly what I had been doing from the start, except that I had been developing projects with proven film-makers. Goldcrest began life, after all, as a development-financing operation and only later moved into production finance. We didn't do pick-up deals in my day. In fact, it was Sandy and James who were to introduce pick-ups into the company with such investments as *Dance With a Stranger* and *A Room With a View*, neither of which was developed by Goldcrest. The point that is being made here, surely, is that neither Norris nor Chambers had confidence that Sandy would achieve the high level of conversion from development to production that had been achieved when I was at Goldcrest. My conversion rate reflected a certain amount of luck, of course, but it also reflected my background in venture-capital investment, where one is constantly protecting the downside. I was very, very choosy about the projects we backed. Norris's and Chambers's fears about Sandy's likely conversion rate stemmed from Sandy's background in the major studios, where it is all right if only one project in twenty goes into production. Goldcrest could not afford to operate like that.

Ilott: A third area of concern, the seemingly never-to-be-profitable television operation, was one that had been inherited from the old regime. Norris and Chambers argued strongly that television should now be brought under control. Indeed, Chambers especially was in favour of closing it down altogether. Norris recalls that Eberts himself had 'never liked television, wasn't interested in it as an arm of Goldcrest and would have been happy to see it amputated early on'.

The fourth area of Norris's and Chambers's concern was the ancillary activities, in cable, magazine publishing and video, each of which, rather than being a stabilizing or cash-generating venture (as was, say, Bill Gavin's foreign-sales operation) only added to Goldcrest's exposure. Goldcrest's adventure in cable television, the Television Entertainment Group (TEG), caused them particular anxiety. In the fledgling British cable industry, Goldcrest was operating out of its depth in the company of Columbia Pictures, HBO and 20th Century–Fox. The latest development in the cable saga was the formation of Premiere, in which the four partners were joined by Thorn EMI, Warner Bros. and Viacom. Goldcrest's share of the new company was to be 9.8 per cent, compared to its 51 per cent share of TEG, but still the costs were substantial and increasing. An investment limit of £3 million had been imposed by the Goldcrest board, 'until the venture has demonstrated an ability to generate profits', but there was already reason to doubt that any profits would be forthcoming. To Norris and Chambers, cable was an area of high-risk investment in which Goldcrest had no expertise and which was beyond the scope of its modest resources.

Far from serving to placate them, then, Lee's concessions had had the effect of concentrating their minds on what it was they really objected to about the new regime. They refused to endorse his letter. Lee, puzzled and frustrated, retired for the weekend to his country home to try to formulate a solution. An exchange of phone calls followed: Lee to Chambers; Lee to Norris; Norris to Chambers; Chambers to Lee.

'James called me on Sunday evening', recalls Chambers, 'and said, "Look, I've had a long chat with David Norris and he really wants Lieberson's head on the platter. What do you think?" And I said I absolutely agreed. Remember we had all advised against Lieberson, it was a universal thing. And I said to James, "You must look at the guy's record: everything he's been involved with has been a disaster. Even his partnership with Puttnam lost Rothschilds a million quid. You're saying how lucky you are to get him from The Ladd Company, but The Ladd Company is just about to close down and he'd have been out of a job anyway. They've gone through $170 million of Warners' money and Warners have had enough. You can't put all the blame at Lieberson's door but some of it must be his. And Cruickshank – now that you've solved the immediate problem, what does he do? He's not looking after finance and business affairs any more, since David and I are on the board." And James said, "Oh, think how useful he'll be when we go public." Well that's not a reason for keeping on a highly paid executive.'

As Lee saw it, Chambers and Norris seemed to be saying, 'either Lieberson and Cruickshank go, or we go'.

On Monday morning, Chambers called Richard Attenborough and asked for a meeting. It was arranged that, since Norris was going to be spending the morning with Puttnam at the Enigma offices in Kensington, they would rendezvous there. First, however, Chambers had to attend a meeting of the Goldcrest management committee: the first full gathering of executives since the tumultuous events of the previous Tuesday and the first meeting of any kind since the weekend exchange of calls. Lieberson, Cruickshank and Gavin knew most of what they were about to hear, but Terry Clegg, Guy East, Steve Walsh and Mike Wooller, none of whom had been directly involved in the drama so far, listened – 'aghast', according to Chambers – as Lee recounted the events of the past seven days. In Norris's absence, Chambers was put on the defensive.

'I was asked virtually to justify my position,' says Chambers. 'I said "I don't think it's right to say anything without David [Norris] being here", and so the thing was a bit inconclusive. It was left that we would reconvene later in the day, having considered the position.'

Lee and Cruickshank then went for further talks at Millbank Tower, while Chambers made his way down to Kensington. There, he and Norris reported all their grievances and anxieties to Puttnam and Attenborough. Attenborough was sympathetic.

'I would have backed them all the way down the line,' he says. 'I think they are both huge professionals. And I believe in the delegation of authority. You engage people – the best you can get – and you say, "That's yours. I'll know about it presumably if it goes wrong, but while it's going fine you deal with it." Now James wouldn't do that. James wouldn't allow John and David their right of decision in relation to areas in which they were, in my opinion, expert. And it wasn't a matter of judgement, it wasn't a matter of reaching a conclusion about something by debate. It was the fact that John and David, by virtue of their extraordinary track records, just knew the way to go, knew how to deal with things, knew how the industry worked. And it doesn't work in the same way that the City does, or that a publishing house does. It's a unique business, and you can't set down guidelines and rules that have been derived from other forms of activity. We don't have prototypes: we don't make a bicycle and see that it works and then decide to manufacture a quarter of a million of them. It's a once-off operation. And there are certain criteria that have to be applied in arriving at those judgements. David and John are experts. And they just were not listened to. They were not heeded. And I put my backing to them.'

Puttman, however – who, remember, was much closer to Lee than he ever was to Eberts, and who was Lieberson's long-standing friend and colleague – was less encouraging. Indeed, there appears to have been something of a row, in the course of which Puttnam warned Norris and Chambers not only that they would regret leaving Goldcrest but that, if they went through with it, they would never be forgiven.

Meanwhile, in the Pearson boardroom, Lee, Joll and Blakenham were engaged in some straight talking. Lee had earlier been advised to accommodate Norris's demands – 'for Christ's sake, if the management structure is unacceptable to the executives it's the wrong structure' (Joll) – and this, as far as the board structure was concerned, he had agreed to do. But that meant bringing a phalanx of executives on to the holding board, which, since it would otherwise give the executives too powerful a voice, in turn meant, as Joll recalls, telling Lee 'we're sorry, James, we've really got to bring in an outside chairman'.

Lee offered to resign. This was not just a matter of good form. He was by now fed up with the whole thing, regretted the move from Pearson and had already contemplated calling off the reorganization and refinancing. By the spring of 1984, the situation at Goldcrest bore little resemblance to the near-Utopia that he had imagined, and set his heart on, back in the early summer of 1983.

'I would probably have gone,' he now says, 'if I hadn't felt a great deal of responsibility to the company and the situation at that time. I thought, "Jake's gone; if I go there would be no Goldcrest." I had an enormous personal dilemma.'

Lee's resignation offer was withdrawn and he returned to Holland Street to reconvene the adjourned management meeting. But there was no further progress: Lieberson and Cruickshank were not going to be turfed out just to accommodate Norris and Chambers, and Lee believed that he had made every other concession he could to satisfy their demands.

'Lee said, "Well, David and John can't see themselves working with the team,"' recalls Chambers. 'I remember saying, "We may be wrong, but we don't believe that the change in style which is implicit with the structure that we've got now is what Goldcrest is about. We don't think it will work, we don't think it's right. But having said that, it may well work, it may all be terrific – and we hope it is – and it's rather arrogant of us to say anything else. But we're not happy with the position." So it broke up quite amicably. I wrote out my notice and James said he was sorry, etc., etc. And that was it.'

Thus, on the evening of Monday, 27 February, Goldcrest's management structure was in shreds.

The next day there was virtually no work done in Goldcrest at all.

The staff formed a deputation, led by chief accountant Andy Parsons, Chambers's secretary Maureen Sheen and financial controller Ken Simson, which sought meetings first of all with Norris and Chambers.

'We were all very upset,' remembers Sheen, 'and we said, "Can't we do anything? Can't we persuade you?" We said, "Both of you have got commitments, you've got mortgages. And what about us anyway? – we don't want to stay here if you both go." ' (They did not worry about Gavin so much: his resignation, while much regretted, did not affect them so directly and was anyway believed to be final.) They then made similar representations to Lee.

Whether or not the staff action achieved anything more substantial, it probably served to prick the consciences of Norris and Chambers, who were anyway very uncertain about what they had done.

Norris was to be even more affected – 'got at', as he puts it – by a further appeal made at lunch a couple of days later by Rothschild's Bernie Myers, who had been working on the Goldcrest reorganization since the previous August. It was he who had demanded the resolution of doubts surrounding *The Emerald Forest*, and it was his intervention that was now to put an end to the management crisis.

'He said that he understood that I'd resigned and that John had threatened to, and that if we went through with this Rothschilds would have to withdraw from the reorganization,' says Norris. 'I said that I didn't think that either of us was that important . . . He said, "But in our perspective, and no doubt in the perspective of potential investors, you two know more about the business than all the rest put together" – about the *business*, not how to chose a movie, or which one to produce – "you know more about the nuts and bolts of the business. If you are seen to lack confidence in the company and/or the rest of its management, then we have to say we will withdraw, because our recommendation to the investors is based on the confidence of the experts."

'I was shocked and flattered. Flattered to think that anybody actually thought that I meant that much. Shocked that I did mean that much.

'Now I knew that if Rothschilds did not go forward, the reorganization would not go forward. Not because Rothschilds would actually raise the money – most of that would be raised by Noble Grossart – but it was their seal of approval, a blue-chip seal of approval. And it wasn't because I was necessarily a key figure, but because if my resignation stood then that would be an indication to the world at large that a senior executive did not have confidence in this operation.

'When one looks back there was clearly some pressure: you know, "We have made these compromises, what about the fifty people working there who won't have a job in five months' time if Goldcrest doesn't reorganize and raise its money? It will just wither", as it were. In effect, I was being told it was going to be directly my fault.

'So I was got at morally. I had a lot of good friends in the company, people I was very fond of. And I knew there was a lot of potential. So far we had beaten the system – OK maybe with only one or two pictures – but so far we were ahead of the game. And if the reorganization didn't happen then the company would have to be run down to a holding operation just turning over a little bit of capital.'

Norris left the lunch filled with doubts. He called Chambers, who was then attending a meeting at Pinewood Studios.

'David said, "The shit's really hit the fan. They're saying that if we quit they can't go ahead with the placing, Pearson's won't put any more money in and the whole thing will fall apart," ' recalls Chambers. 'So I said to David, "Well, I think in my mind I'm having second thoughts anyway. I'll come straight back and we'll talk about it." '

Their discussion embraced implications even wider than those pertaining to Goldcrest, for Malcolm Wilde of Guinness Mahon, anticipating just such a turn of events, had made it clear to Norris that if Goldcrest's fund-raising failed then the plans for 'Goldcrest 2' would be shelved: it would be pointless, he argued, to hawk a film-finance prospectus around the City at the same time as the industry's flagship was signalling that the effort was not worthwhile. Not only Goldcrest, it seemed, but the future of independent film financing from City sources was at stake. Norris's and Chambers's own careers, as well as those of their friends in the business, could be placed in jeopardy.

These doubts were sufficient for their resignations to be withdrawn.

'They [the board] put right those things which they could put right to my satisfaction,' explains Norris. 'They came back and said, "Right, the option scheme is going to be much wider – it's going to be the whole staff. You're on the board, you don't report to Cruickshank. We're going to see how Sandy goes and back our judgement on that appointment. We're going to see how James goes. Yes, the overheads are getting higher but we're going to have this extra money." So things which affected my day-to-day life were put right, in a way to which I could not object.'

Of particular satisfaction to Norris was the news that Lee was not now going to be chairman.

It was Joll's task to find a replacement. Attenborough was asked, but he declined on the grounds that, having just signed to make A Chorus Line for Embassy, he would be too busy. Joll then approached Michael Stoddart, chief executive of Electra. Stoddart had strongly favoured

Attenborough for the job and was initially reluctant to take it on himself, but in the end agreed. Having made the decision, Stoddart recalls, he then thought that the job would be 'rather fun'.

'I didn't want to get involved on a day-to-day basis . . . You have to believe as a non-executive chairman that you have people working for you who understand the industry and the business that they are in. I felt we had on board somebody who had a first-class reputation, as I understood it, in the television industry: Mike Wooller. We had James Lee, who was obviously the chosen delegate of Pearsons and was perceived at the time to be a first-class chief executive. If one may say one thing about James Lee, he had had a good business career. He may not have been suited to the film industry, but none of us, certainly not I, realized that at the time. We had two experts in the form of Puttnam and Attenborough, who were both, or so I was led to believe, capable of being the gurus of the industry and capable of knowing what was good product and what wasn't good product. And we had a very well-thought-of chap who came in to see to production, very much boosted by Puttnam: Sandy Lieberson.

'Everything', Stoddart concludes, 'augured rather well. Although there [had been] an upset in terms of the management, it was an upset in personality rather than a disagreement over the strategy of the company.'

He now freely admits to having been naive, and considers his acceptance of the chairmanship to have been 'clearly the worst decision I have ever made in my life'. Indeed it is arguable that Stoddart's comparative ignorance of the ways of the film industry (he knew a good deal less than James Joll, for example), and his formidable workload (he had dozens of directorships in all kinds of industries, most of them involving much larger sums of Electra's money than had been invested in Goldcrest; he was, for example, chairman of the Next retailing group), contributed to Goldcrest's later problems. Stoddart was rarely available at short notice, and then never for more than a few minutes. Not being an expert, he could not initiate policy so much as react to mistakes. And, being used to dealing with engineering companies and other highly structured business environments, he always favoured whatever appeared to him to be the most hard-headed approach to a problem – i.e. at board meetings he invariably, and often mistakenly, took Lee's side against Lieberson.

'James could put things to Michael with a plausibility – I don't mean that he did so dishonestly – but a rationale which spoke the professional language that businessmen of that level applied to debate,' explains Attenborough. 'Sandy, or even Jake in some measure, spoke in a totally different language. You could see that Stoddart, bless his heart, didn't know what Sandy was talking about. He certainly didn't understand the values and the arguments. It was a foreign language to him.'

Thus, in the second week of March 1984, the crisis that had at various points involved the proffered resignations of Norris, Chambers and Lee and which coincidentally saw the departure of Gavin – a crisis, in other words, that came close to bringing Goldcrest to a standstill – seemed to have been resolved. In reality, however, although Norris and Chambers were now back in the fold, things were not the same, and they never would be again. 'I wouldn't say that it was an unhappy place,' says Lee, 'but it had changed quite dramatically.'

Not only had the atmosphere been soured by the episode, but Norris's and Chambers's usefulness to the company was much diminished by the distrust that now openly existed between them and the rest of the executive team. They had held a gun to the company's head and it was not an experience that was easily forgotten. It would have taken heroic magnanimity on Lieberson's part, for example, to forgive some of the remarks that had been made about him in the preceding weeks.

And while Lee, according to Chambers, 'took them into his confidence' on almost every important issue for a while, his attempts to forge a comradely style of work 'quickly wore off'. Tension and rivalry – between Norris and Chambers and the rest, between Wooller and the rest, and between Lieberson and Lee – dogged the management team. There was, as Lee himself recalls, 'constant wrangling'.

Nor was the damage limited to the management level. Having fought so hard to secure their right to seats on the board, once there Norris and Chambers felt constrained, both by a sense of loyalty to their fellow executives and by their expectation of the strong disapproval of the non-executive directors, from raising further objections or causing trouble.

'I clearly share the blame, when looked at from the outside,' observes Norris. 'But what I really blame myself for was this: I got the feeling – which may have been paranoia, but John got it too – that at every board meeting after that if we objected to something it was, "Oh, Jesus, those two carping again." No one actually said that, but that was the impression that we got.'

As a result, Norris's and Chambers's opposition to *Revolution*, to Goldcrest's further adventures in cable and other ancillary activities, and to the continuing commitment to television were thereafter never properly voiced at board meetings. The duo, having argued their case at the management level – where they were invariably outvoted – felt obliged by what Norris calls a sense of 'cabinet responsibility' not to go over Lee's head by addressing the board directly. When, about a year later, they could no longer keep their reservations to themselves, they sought assistance outside the formal channels, and what should have been contained within the bounds of normal boardroom debate was to become instead a conspiracy.

Chapter Twenty-eight

Valuations

'Dealing with Rothschilds was a nightmare. We had all these bloody bankers and lawyers and accountants crawling all over us and we had to justify everything. You've no idea what the process is like unless you're in it. Every statement we made had to be justified. Every figure had to be cross-checked. Every part of the background had to be recorded.' – James Lee

Ilott: The revised management arrangements were approved at the second board meeting of Goldcrest Films and Television (Holdings) (GFTH), held in the Holland Street boardroom on Tuesday, 13 March. This meeting, chaired for the first time by Michael Stoddart, was attended not only by the newly appointed directors Norris, Chambers and Wooller, but by Lord Blakenham – presumably he wanted to see for himself that all was now in order – Rothschild's Bernie Myers and representatives of Freshfields and Deloitte.

The new holding-company board had five purely non-executive directors (Stoddart, Joll, Grossart, Mayer and Whitehead), two non-executive but consultant directors (Puttnam and Attenborough) and six executive directors (Lee, Cruickshank, Lieberson, Wooller, Norris and Chambers). It was agreed that a further non-executive director would be appointed. Thus, given that the chairman was now also a non-executive, it would seem that Goldcrest had arrived at the kind of board structure that Joll had wanted in the first place. However, Lee was able to redeem some supra-executive authority by an elaboration of the original two-tier formula that resulted in more power being devolved to Goldcrest Films and Television Ltd, which was to remain as the operating company and which was to have a board of its own. How this was to work is recorded in the minutes of the meeting:

The board of the holding company, being non-executive directors together with leading members of the management team, would be responsible for the overall policy (including finance policy) and strategy of the Group and for all major investment decisions, whereas the GFT board would be responsible for day-to-day management, including the majority of investment decision-making. To this end, Terry Clegg, Goldcrest's production executive, and Guy East and Steve Walsh, marketing executives, would be appointed to the GFT board [i.e., in addition to Lee, Cruickshank, Lieberson, Wooller, Norris and Chambers], which would then establish a committee structure to facilitate the involvement of Sir Richard Attenborough and David Puttnam.

By thus bringing the two expert non-executives, Puttnam and Atten-borough, into a close, consultative relationship with the full management team (and later adding two more non-executive appointments: former newspaper editor and would-be programme-maker Harold Evans, and television producer Derek Granger), Lee guaranteed that the real engine of the company would be GFT, not GFTH. This much was understood and approved by the board. What they certainly would not have approved, had they been able to foresee it, was that, since Lee was to chair the meetings of the GFT board, he would be able to style himself chairman and chief executive of Goldcrest (thus restoring to himself the dual title that he had wanted in the first place). This he did in all his dealings with the industry and the media. That the Goldcrest in question was only the operating company, GFT, and not the holding company, GFTH, was a distinction entirely lost on the world at large. Even within Wardour Street, it was not until the downfall of Lee in 1985 that it became widely known that Stoddart was, and had been all along, the real chairman of the company. Lee's usurpation of his title and public trappings, and especially Lee's habit of signing himself chairman and chief executive on headed notepaper that made no mention of the existence of Goldcrest Holdings, did not please Stoddart, although he makes light of it now.

'My secretary was much more irritated than me,' he says. 'She used to put these things in front of me and say, "Isn't this awful?" and I'd say, "Oh, what does it matter?" '

Nor did the practice impress Lee's colleagues, who could only wonder at the motives for his insistence on the double title. Even David Puttnam, Lee's foremost friend and advocate in the company, was puzzled. 'It was', he says, 'absolutely beyond me.'

The minutes of the 13 March board meeting go on to record that 'the executive directors individually confirmed their satisfaction with the new arrangements', and that 'it was concluded that there was now in place an enthusiastic and united management team'. That this latter assertion was far from being the case is borne out by the fact that Lee had already arranged for a special management conference to take place at his home in Kent later in the week. (A parley, as David Norris remembers it, that was 'intended to clear the air', not only between himself, Chambers and the rest, but between Wooller and the rest, between Lieberson and the rest, and, most notably, between Lieberson and Lee.)

On the advice of the solicitors, Freshfields, it was agreed that some reference to the management upheavals of the past month would have to be made in the prospectus. The company might otherwise be open to the charge of suppressing information of material relevance to a potential investor. The formula arrived at, in a fifty-two-page, 25,000-word document, reads, in full:

The management arrangements proposed to take effect following the reorganization led to a short difficult period during which two executive directors of GFT tendered their resignations and one other threatened to resign. After a period of consultation leading to a revision of the proposed management arrangements, including an increase in the degree of executive representation on the board of Goldcrest Holdings, two of the directors concerned decided to remain with Goldcrest. Bill Gavin has left GFT to become an independent sales agent. The board of Goldcrest Holdings has appointed as chairman Michael Stoddart, who has been involved with Goldcrest since 1977, and James Lee as chief executive. The board has approved these revised arrangements and considers that they provide a sound working basis for the future.

This most cryptic note surely begged an explanation, yet not one of the actual or potential investors in GFTH was to query it.

The re-worked prospectus contained other refinements and reformulations. Deloitte had solved the problem of how best to estimate Goldcrest's true worth by the simple expedient of getting someone else to do it. The firm chosen, Solomon, Finger and Newman, was a New York-based accountancy practice with considerable film and television experience and an impeccable reputation. They in turn had eliminated the problem of putting their name to something unknowable – i.e. what any particular investment might be worth when eventually it went into distribution – by estimating instead the *present value* of the future earnings of the portfolio. It is a fine distinction, but an important one, for it enabled Solomon, Finger and Newman to add a disclaimer to their valuation, to the effect that, 'since the estimated net present value is based on estimates and assumptions which are inherently subject to uncertainty and variation depending upon evolving events, we do not represent it as a result that will be actually achieved'.

Essentially, the method they followed was to have Goldcrest furnish them with all the necessary data – sales forecasts, distribution contracts, budgets and contracted expenses – pertaining to every current film and television investment. Then they measured these against their own experience of the industry. Discrepancies were discussed with the Goldcrest financial team until eventually estimates of future revenues and future direct production and distribution costs were agreed across the whole portfolio. On the assumption that there would be no significant changes, alterations or interruptions to the production and distribution schedule, and that all projects would come in on budget, Solomon, Finger and Newman was able to arrive at a figure – for an investment portfolio with a book value, remember, of just under £16.5 million – of £27.4 million. It was comprised as follows:

	Book value	Present value of estimated net future revenues
Feature films in distribution	£3.68m	£8.34m
Feature films in production	£5.58m	£8.27m
TV programmes in distribution	£2.33m	£3.10m
TV programmes in production	£4.08m	£6.83m
Films in development	£0.31m	£0.34m
TV programmes in development	£0.50m	£0.52m
Total	**£16.48m**	**£27.40m**

Thus, to the question 'how much better was the financial position of the company than that shown in the balance sheet?', the answer now offered was £10.92 million. To the potential investor, Goldcrest's track record might thus appear promising, if not yet impressive. Since 1977, £22.6 million had been invested by the shareholders. Each year since then had shown an operating loss, resulting, at the end of 1983, in an accumulated deficit of about £5.8 million. This had reduced the shareholders' funds to a book value of £16.8 million, of which £300,000 represented the office lease, fixtures and fittings, company cars, cash balances and so on, while £16.5 million represented current film and television investments. The year-on-year trend, however, as more productions went into distribution, was towards profitability, with 1983 almost breaking even and 1984 estimated to show a small profit, most of it to arise from the release of *The Killing Fields*. If Solomon, Finger and Newman's valuation was correct, then, by extrapolation, the future net earnings would give the shareholders an overall profit, before overheads and taxation, of up to £4.8 million on their investment to date. This was not a great deal to show for seventeen feature films, eighty-eight hours of television programming and eight years' exposure in a high-risk business, but given the spectacular rate of growth of the company, its blue-chip shareholders and the calibre both of its directors and of the film-makers with which it was associated, Goldcrest Holdings could be presented, in Don Cruickshank's words, as a 'plausible opportunity' for investment. Certainly, it had the best track record to date of any independently financed film-production company.

Unfortunately, Solomon, Finger and Newman's valuation was not correct. Or rather, it was correct in that it was no more than an estimate of the *present value* of future net revenues. And it is true to say that throughout the prospectus Solomon, Finger and Newman, Rothschild and Deloitte went to great pains to emphasize that an estimate of the present value of future net revenues is not the same thing at all as an estimate of the future net revenues themselves. But it is hard to imagine any potential investor taking note of so fine a distinction. After all, if the valuation was not a guide to the likely future worth of present investments, what was it doing in the prospectus?

On the feature-film side, Solomon, Finger and Newman's valuation was to prove very close to the eventual figures. On the television side, however, it was very far out of line.

Within Goldcrest, and among its advisers, there had long been grave doubts about the viability of the company's television investments. By the end of 1983, nine television productions, in which Goldcrest had invested £3.69 million, had gone into distribution, but they had so far returned only £910,000. Four of these productions had losses written against them and the retained book value of the nine programmes as a whole was only £2.3 million. A further eleven programmes, in which Goldcrest had invested £5.23 million, were still in production. In respect of these, the company had received advances of only £780,000, and provisions had already had to be made against four of them. This was a depressing outlook. Consequently, when it came to putting a figure on the future net revenues of the television portfolio as a whole, all the parties concerned went out of their way to stress the need for a conservative valuation.

In a letter to Gerald Green, of Solomon, Finger and Newman, dated 9 December 1983, for example, Simon Linnet of Rothschild expressed concern that the assumptions on which the television valuation was to be based were not sufficiently pessimistic:

Thank you for explaining so fully the basis of the film valuation last Tuesday. We left the meeting with the impression that, relative to the film valuations (which have been prepared with a certain degree of conservatism), there may be inherent optimism in the valuations of the television projects by reason of the fact that:

a. the television projects, by and large, have only a limited number of potential purchasers in each territory, whereas a film project has a wider market;

b. the television companies tend to set a standard rate per hour of television programme which is only exceeded for 'blockbuster' series such as *Far Pavilions*;

c. certain of the television projects are considered to have only limited appeal . . . which may further reduce the number of potential purchasers;

d. the life of a film project tends to be longer, with greater potential for future exploitation, and this future revenue has been ignored in the valuation;

. . . We appreciate that any film valuation exercise is entirely subjective . . . However, we must believe that the valuations of the film and television interests are prepared with the same degree of inherent conservatism. If you have any difficulty in confirming this, I think we should consider making adjustments to the revenues recoverable on the television projects, to make the valuation approach relatively consistent.

It was as a result of such expressions of concern that the valuation of the future net revenues of the television portfolio, when eventually it was arrived at, was thought by all parties to be distinctly understated. As shown in the table below, the figure in question, £9.93 million, would have suggested a profit of £2.7 million on Goldcrest's television investments to date:

1	2	3 (1–2)	4	5 (4–3)
Cost to date	Revenues to date	Current deficit	Estimated future net revenues	Forecast profit
£8.92m	£1.69m	(£7.23m)	£9.93m	£2.7m

The £2.7 million figure was not, of course, part of Solomon, Finger and Newman's submission. What it represents is an extrapolation from their figures of the profit that would accrue to the investments should everything go exactly according to plan. Things do not, of course, and in reality the twenty television investments concerned were to make a loss of £4.2 million. The 'conservative' valuation, in other words, was not nearly conservative enough. Unfortunately for Goldcrest, each succeeding television investment thereafter, with the exception of a small stake in a production called *Three Sovereigns for Sarah*, was to add to this £4.2 million deficit.

Contributing a significant share of these losses (and threatening to contribute a great deal more in the future) was the *First Love* series produced by David Puttnam's company, Enigma. The *First Love*s were television films that gave new writers, directors and producers a chance to do feature-length work. Their common subject matter, broadly interpreted, was first love, which tended to give the series a wistful and nostalgic flavour. Since the nostalgia in question was for things English, the films had little appeal in the international markets. That was one of the problems. The others were financial. Ideally, the *First Loves* were to have cost about £500,000 each, with Channel 4 putting up between one third and one half of the budgets and the rest being recouped from world television sales, American pay-cable, video and theatrical. As the figures below demonstrate, these hopes diminished as the series progressed:

Titles in order of production	Goldcrest's share of the cost	Goldcrest's net revenue (deficit)
P'Tang Yang Kipperbang	£378,000	£371,000
Experience Preferred But Not Essential	£480,000	£248,000
Secrets	£461,000	£159,000
Forever Young	£420,000	£ 94,000
Arthur's Hallowed Ground	£319,000	(£ 54,000)
Those Glory, Glory Days	£556,000	(£243,000)
Sharma and Beyond	£504,000	(£164,000)
The Big Surprise/Winter Flight	£581,000	(£193,000)

These figures are culled from finance reports dating from October 1987. Even before the end of 1983, however, there was sufficient evidence that the *First Loves* were heading for heavy losses for there to have been calls for the series to be stopped. *P'Tang Yang Kipperbang*, the first of the films, was the only one to achieve net profits, and then only with the help of a tax deal. (Tax deals, in fact, contributed significantly to the revenues of all four films that broke even.) In an interview with *Screen International* at the time, James Lee explained what had gone wrong.

The first three *First Loves*, he said,

were made for very low cost and the Channel Four contribution was very generous: under, but close to half the budget. The subjects were good and proved popular. At the same time, there was strong competition in the US among cable channels looking for something distinctive to buy on a non-exclusive basis. So we had a combination of low-budget films, partly financed by Channel Four, in a fertile market. Now costs have risen, from, say, £400,000 to £600,000, while the Channel Four contribution has not increased in proportion. It's gone up a bit, but where before it might be £200,000 of a £400,000 budget, it's now £250,000 of a £600,000 budget. The gap that we have to fill has been doubled. At the same time, the subjects that Channel Four is attracted by have become less attractive to the international market. And, finally, the competition among the US cable companies has died down. So we face higher costs, a higher share of those costs, for a less attractive product in a less fertile market.

Nevertheless, at the 13 March board meeting Puttnam made a strong case for the investments to continue, on the grounds that among the projects thus developed there would be one or two that could be upgraded to full-scale feature films, and that some of the new writers and directors unearthed by the series would be people that Goldcrest would want to work with in the future. It was, in other words, a low-cost research-and-development operation. The board, acutely conscious of its dependence on Puttnam and the talent that he brought to the company, allowed itself to be persuaded. In all, thirty scripts were to be developed for the *First Love* series, at a cost of £274,000. By the time the holding-company prospectus was issued, in April 1984, ten of these scripts had been abandoned, nine were still in development and eleven had gone into production, of which three, *Cal*, *Mr Love* and *The Frog Prince*, had been upgraded to feature-film status. These upgraded films, too, lost money:

Title	Goldcrest's share of the cost	Goldcrest's net revenue (deficit)
Cal	£396,000	(£118,000)
The Frog Prince	£896,000	(£562,000)
Mr Love	£486,000	(£156,000)

It should be said that Puttnam disputes all the above figures. 'We did an assessment of our own,' he explains. 'And it is really an accounting thing – it's all to do with cash. If you remove the sales-agency fees that Goldcrest took, and the overhead that Goldcrest took, and put them both back into gross receipts, then the *First Love*s made money. That is to say that in cash, in pure cash, Goldcrest came out ahead. Definitely. No question. But if you say, "Well, we are entitled to our distribution fee – why should we cut that? And we are entitled to our overhead – why should we cut that?", then sure, they lost a bit of money. It's purely interpretative.'

John Chambers, however, insists that the figures already discount Goldcrest's share of fees and overheads. It does not matter a great deal either way, for although the board meeting voted to continue with the series, it was soon to be abandoned, along with all the other low-budget television films that Goldcrest had in the pipeline.

That the board did choose to go along with Puttnam's wishes, rather than launch the kind of review which the television division needed, is, of course, largely attributable to the shareholders' desire not to rock the boat in the run-up to the fund-raising. The target figure to be raised was £12 million. Goldcrest's previous outings, in 1980 and 1982, had raised £8.2 million and £9.4 million respectively, in both cases rather less than had been hoped for. On those occasions, the major single source of new money was Pearson. This time Pearson was putting up no new money: in order to keep its holding below 50 per cent the company had decided merely to exchange its shares in GFT, GFI and GFTP for equivalent shares in the new company. Rothschild and Noble Grossart were therefore looking to fill a fairly big hole.

It was by no means certain that they would succeed, for Goldcrest was not the kind of investment opportunity that would set a fund manager's blood racing. For one thing (although this was not made clear in the prospectus), a large part of its good fortune to date was owed to one film, *Gandhi*. By the end of 1983, Goldcrest's completed film and television investments were showing a paper profit (i.e. revenues received plus residual book value) of £1.47 million, made up of a £2.28 million profit on film investments and an £808,000 loss on television. Of the eleven film investments made by the company at that time, three had been development investments only, and one, *Pink Floyd: The Wall*, had been more in the nature of a piece of short-term financial packaging. Of the seven investments remaining, three had recorded losses, and four – *The Howling* (£132,000), *Escape from New York* (£508,000), *Local Hero* (£338,000) and *Gandhi* (£2.67 million) – had recorded profits. Clearly, *Gandhi* was by far the most important of these. Had it been taken out of the equation, the portfolio of completed films would have shown a paper loss to date of £382,000 and the film and television portfolios together would have been running a deficit of £1.19 million. Even by mid-1987, by which time the ruined company had stopped making films altogether, *Gandhi*'s net contribution of £6.3 million was £1 million more than the contribution of all the other profitable film and television productions combined, among them *Chariots of Fire*, *The Dresser*, *Escape from New York*, *The Killing Fields*, *Local Hero* and the first series of *Robin of Sherwood*.

Without *Gandhi*, then, Goldcrest's underlying track record might not have been such as to encourage a new investor to put money in. The point is not that *Gandhi* was exceptional, which it was, but that Goldcrest relied upon such exceptions to make up for the losses that would inevitably accrue to other titles in its portfolio. This was not made clear in the prospectus, which, although scrupulously honest in the detailed presentation of accounts, nevertheless sought to present Goldcrest as a viable trading company operating within a normal business environment. Neither aspect of this proposition was sustainable. Goldcrest, for all that it now employed nearly fifty people, was essentially what it had been from the start: a high-risk venture-capital investment fund. And film finance is far from being a normal business environment.

In the film industry, it is generally accepted that only one film in ten recovers its cost. Goldcrest had a much better track record than most in this respect. Indeed, one outstanding mark in Goldcrest's favour was, or had been until now, its astute choice of projects. However, the company was also much more vulnerable than most, for it did not have other interests, for example in distribution or exhibition, which could generate cash flow and from which the company could recoup its investments even when they failed to achieve net profits.

The problem, the contradiction at the core of Goldcrest, was that everyone – cinema exhibitors, distributors, television stations, video labels, producers, directors, stars, Puttnam, Attenborough, Boorman et al. – was making money, either out of their efforts on behalf of the company or out of their exploitation of its product. But the company itself was making nothing. Goldcrest was trying to operate like a studio without having either a studio's capital or its early access to the box-office dollar via distribution. It was too far down the line of recoupment. For all its energy, verve, nerve and talent, the net profits upon which it relied rarely materialized.

To take the most outstanding example, David Puttnam's entire output for the company – £33 million worth of investments, spread across eight films and nine television features – was to produce, by the end of August 1987, revenues of £25.5 million. The residual book value at that time was put at £6.7 million and the long-term forecast showed a net deficit to Goldcrest of about £420,000. Puttnam made, amongst other titles, *Chariots of Fire*, *The Killing Fields*, *Local Hero* and *The Mission*, all of which he, and Goldcrest, can be proud of. None of his films was shoddily produced, and only three can be counted duds: *The Frog Prince*, *Knights and Emeralds* and *Mr Love*. If Goldcrest found it impossible to make money out of a portfolio such as that produced by Puttnam, then there was surely something wrong with the business.

That no such doubts were expressed in the prospectus is perhaps hardly surprising. *Gandhi*'s impact, however, could have been given greater prominence, as could have the beneficial, but mostly hidden, effects of the fall in the value of the pound, from $2.40 in July 1980, when GFI was founded, to $1.50 in April 1984, when the prospectus was issued.

On the other hand, it is equally surprising that no mention was made of the inherent, but for the most part unquantifiable, sale value of the library that Goldcrest had accumulated. The Solomon, Finger and Newman valuation put a figure on the present value *to Goldcrest* of the future net revenues of all its investments. But to someone else, a media entrepreneur with many means of exploiting product, like Rupert Murdoch, Robert Maxwell or Jerry Weintraub, the inherent value of the library might be, indeed almost certainly would be, a great deal more. Indeed, in recent years there has been something of a scramble to acquire film libraries as satellite, cable, video, deregulated television and new markets in Eastern Europe and the Far East have opened up whole new areas for the exploitation of screen entertainment. Goldcrest, in other words, as well as seeking to make year-on-year profits, was building a library with a long-term sale value. That value, being unquantifiable, would never show up on the balance sheet. Indeed, a figure could be put on it only when, and if, some third party made a bid for the company, as was to happen in 1987.

Chapter Twenty-nine
Production Philosophy

Ilott: On Thursday, 15 March 1984, James Lee played host at his home in Kent to the all-day management conference designed to heal the wounds and clear the air following the recent recriminations and upheavals. As an exercise in democracy it might be counted a small success, but as an attempt by Lee to inspire and fashion his divided executives into a coherent team it was a failure.

The ostensible talking-point at the meeting was Goldcrest's production strategy, for which Lee had prepared a detailed, and typically thorough, discussion paper. Goldcrest, which had put nothing significant into production for months, would soon have a lot of money in the bank. The problem was how best to spend it. Lee's analysis started with what he later formulated in writing as a nine-point interpretation of the production philosophy that had evolved under Eberts. First, follow talent, not themes: try to build relationships with producers and directors rather than worry about genre or subject matter. Second, stay distinctive: Goldcrest could not hope to compete with the Americans at their own game, but it could exploit the apparent weakness of its market position by stressing the uniqueness and excellence of its output. Third, negotiate from strength: offer the studios only those packages owned and controlled by the company and avoid deals that left Goldcrest in the position of junior partner. Fourth, produce both major films and classics (i.e. art movies and low-budget movies with high-brow themes or literary subject matter) in the hope that now and again a classic would break into the mass market, and in the expectation that a regular output of such classics would attract serious film-making talent to the company. Fifth, know the market and its limitations: be sure to identify at an early stage whether a film is for the mass or the classic market, and make all calculations, especially of cost, accordingly. Sixth, retain distribution flexibility: avoid long-term or exclusive relationships with any one US distributor. Seventh, retain foreign rights: avoid worldwide deals with the studios wherever possible, in order to maintain credibility with the independent foreign distributors upon whom the company depended for its risk-covering pre-sales. Eighth, take risks intelligently: for every production weigh up with great care the balance of pre-sales, third-party equity participation and deficit financing required to produce the most attractive risk–reward ratio. And, ninth, keep within capacity: always hold some money in reserve so that the company never has to negotiate from a position of weakness.

Whether or not this could be said to be a fair summary of Eberts's general policy, Lee believed it to be so, and he could see no reason to make any changes. Likewise, he saw no reason to tamper with the three golden rules laid down by the board: spread investments across a wide portfolio, lay off risk by pre-sales and keep a ceiling on Goldcrest's exposure in any one project.

He went on to observe that Goldcrest's deficit financing of television and low-budget features should be minimised, since this was an area that had proved to have little profit potential. In particular, he proposed that television projects should go ahead only if their entire cost were covered by pre-sales in two territories (invariably the US and the UK), leaving sales in the rest of the world to contribute profits. Goldcrest's exposure on big-budget films, on the other hand, should be increased, since this area had proved to be (sometimes) very lucrative.

Lee concluded his presentation by setting out an ideal portfolio, comprising investments in five categories of product: major films, classic films, made-for-television films, mini-series and television documentaries. In each case, he set down rules for investment covering the level of budget, degree of risk and so on.

The discussion that followed was, according to David Norris, 'very useful . . . it did concentrate the mind', while Don Cruickshank agrees that 'some of the theories' that Lee had about the business 'seemed very, very plausible'. But, according to Steve Walsh and others, the debate quickly led into an academic by-way. For Lee's was a strategy in the abstract: it did not address itself to the dozens of actual projects that were then under discussion.

In the few weeks since Lieberson had joined the company, Goldcrest had rejected television dramatizations of Evelyn Waugh's *Scoop* and Dickens's *A Christmas Carol*; a film version of *The Aspern Papers*; a Harold Pinter script, *Turtle Diary*; two projects from Paramount, *Falling in Love*, starring Meryl Streep and Robert De Niro, and *Witness* (at that time with no director or star attached); a Bruce Beresford–Richard Gere film, *King David*; *Mishima*, a Paul Schrader project from Warner Bros.;

and *Fire on the Mountain*, written by Michael Thomas and to be directed by Tony Scott.

Still under consideration were an Alan Parker–Alan Marshall project, *Birdy*; a South African musical, *Dream Song*; an Alan Marshall–Marek Kanievska project, *Horror Movie*; two Richard Attenborough projects, *Tom Paine* and *Biko: Asking for Trouble* (later titled *Cry Freedom*); *Joan of Arc*, a comedy written and to be directed by Bob Kaufman; a series of low-budget comedies to be co-financed with the Samuel Goldwyn Company; a low-budget British drama, *Dance With a Stranger*; and one of Puttnam's upgraded television projects, *The Frog Prince*.

Firm commitments had already been made to *Mandrake*, now with American producer Tom Sternberg attached, a further series of *Robin of Sherwood* and four more *First Loves*. In addition, Goldcrest had a raft of television projects in production or preparation.

While all these proposals could probably have been pigeonholed into Lee's five production categories, and while the categorization itself would seem to be a perfectly valid means of structuring a discussion, it was always likely that within any particular category one project would look more attractive than another, and that there might be, for example, three attractive projects in a category that should provide only one production, or no attractive projects at all in a category that should provide three. The discussion, in other words, could not usefully proceed except in reference to the real projects in question; and this, Walsh insists, did not happen. That it was therefore condemned to be a pointless exercise was proved even before the meeting had ended, as Don Cruickshank recalls.

'It was', he says, 'a classic example of how you could go from one set of thinking to another, in the course of a few minutes . . . James had said, "Look, let's just not spread ourselves all over the place. Let's do these things: let's make these sorts of films and apply our resources in this way between television, this sort of film, that sort of film . . ." And one of the things he said was, "What we're not going to do is make films in . . ." – I can't remember the numbers now: let's say it was the £2.5–6 million range – "that are essentially British films and not international films." And three-quarters of an hour later, after discussion of this, Sandy said, "All very interesting. What do you think about a musical set in Britain in the late 1950s, which might cost about £5 million?" Which was the absolute antithesis of what James had presented: it was the wrong budget, it was a musical, it was a British subject matter, a new director, new producer. Everything James had said we shouldn't do, you could tick off against it. And in an hour at that meeting we'd virtually been convinced by Sandy that, notwithstanding the strategy, we would do this one.'

Thus did Lieberson take a stand for film practice against business theory. Thus, too, did he remind the meeting of his overall authority in the production area. Strategy, product mix, investment guidelines, market analysis: these were certainly all legitimate concerns for the chief executive. But production as such was Lieberson's job. That he felt the need to assert himself, in an area about which it was acknowledged that he knew more than anyone else in the company, is partly explained by the rapid deterioration that had already occurred in his relationship with Lee. So acute was Lieberson's discomfort, in fact, that within weeks of joining the company he had seriously contemplated handing in his resignation. The problem appears to have lain in the sheer force of Lee's energy and personality, for which Lieberson's wry, laid-back, sometimes vague, often indecisive, style was no match. And while it was no doubt proper for Lee to lead the general discussion of production strategy, the fact that the initiative, the ideas and the presentation were all unmistakably his own was bound to diminish Lieberson and, albeit inadvertently, undermine his authority. In this light, it is not fanciful to suggest that Lieberson's intervention in the discussion was an attempt to claim the full power of his office, for fear that, if he did not do so now, he would lose it for ever.

Probably Lee was sensitive to this. Certainly, he had been punctilious in consulting Lieberson before presenting his strategy paper to the meeting. Probably the other executives were sensitive to it too. If so, it would explain why the project in question was accepted in principle, not only against the initial judgement of virtually all those who heard Lieberson's pitch but in flat contradiction of the investment-strategy guidelines just laid down by Lee. The project was called *Absolute Beginners*. It was to have a profound, and disastrous, impact on Goldcrest's fortunes.

In an entirely different way, and for entirely different reasons, the same could be said of another project that Lieberson had introduced a week or so before – *The Mission*. This was the property of Italian producer Fernando Ghia, whose previous credits included *The Red Tent*, *Amarcord*, *Lucky Luciano* and *Lady Caroline Lamb*. In the light of what was later to happen to Ghia, it is as well to establish just how much he had contributed to *The Mission* from the start.

According to Ghia's account he had always been fascinated by the stories he had been told at school of the Jesuit missions in Latin America. In 1973 he had come across a copy of *Time* magazine which had a cover story about the Jesuits. In this story, the missions were given some prominence. Ghia, reminded of the power of those childhood tales, realized that here were the essential ingredients of a movie. He started to do research.

'I read several books and accounts,' he says, 'and when I went to South America to visit the ruins, I found myself going always around one point, which was the Iguazu Falls [on the borders of Argentina and Brazil]. They are ten miles from one mission, twenty miles from another one, one hundred miles from a third. So the geography of the place was dictating a big part of the story: I was thinking of these events taking place on that stage. And that stage, by God, with the river and the jungle, was quite unusual: a world that we in Europe know nothing about.'

Ghia was then very friendly with Robert Bolt, writer of, among other things, *Doctor Zhivago*, *Lawrence of Arabia*, *A Man for All Seasons* and Ghia's own film, *Lady Caroline Lamb*. 'I knew that Robert was the perfect man to handle all this and turn it into something that was dramatic,' he continues. 'But I also knew that there was no way that I would get Robert interested – because history supplies hundreds of such incidents – unless I could give him something specific. Eventually, I went to him and told him a story. I said, "There is a river, a huge river, a mile wide. There are some Jesuits sitting in a canoe, one with a lute, one with a guitar, another guy singing. They are trying to get in touch with the Indians, but they are very frightened, because the Indians want to kill them. To be safe they are rowing in the middle of the river, singing and playing. At a certain moment, on the riverbank a few Indians come out. They look at the canoe and they stand there puzzled. The Jesuit Fathers shake when they see the Indians, but they keep on playing and singing and they don't show any sign of fear. The Indians listen for a while. Then they dip their spears into the sand, which is a sign that they are not thinking of defending themselves. So the Fathers say, 'Let's get closer to them. Keep on playing, don't stop.' And then some of the Indians squat, which is a sign that they are relaxed. And the Jesuits come closer. They have discovered that the music they are playing is an insurance policy. These people are totally taken by the music."

'So I gave Robert this scene, and I told him something of the history of the missions and the discovery and exploitation of the New World and the correspondence between the Pope and the King of Spain and so on. Then I said, "If you decide you want to do this, then, before you do anything else, you have to come and see the place. That is essential." He rang me back some time later and said yes, he did want to do it. So we went to see the Iguazu Falls. And, to make him feel the whole situation, I took him across the jungle on foot, from one river to another. After that, he wanted to do the film very much.'

Bolt's screenplay was paid for by Paramount, who, according to Ghia, professed to love the result. But they did not want to make the film. 'They just said, "No commercial reality," or something like that,' Ghia recalls.

And so began a ten-year search for finance. Ghia took the project from one studio to another, without success. By 1983 he had more or less given up – 'in my heart I was a little defeated' – but then happened to discuss the project with *Chariots of Fire* director Hugh Hudson. Hudson's hands were full with another major production, *Greystoke*, and he was therefore in no position to make a commitment, but Ghia was greatly encouraged by his interest and once again set off on a round of money-raising meetings. By the end of 1983 he was engaged in talks with the new American studio, Tri-Star. It was while in the midst of these negotiations that he met Sandy Lieberson, whom he had known since Lieberson's days as a Rome-based agent in the early 1960s. They swapped notes, Ghia telling Lieberson about his resuscitated South American project and Lieberson telling Ghia about his forthcoming move from The Ladd Company to Goldcrest.

Some weeks later, Ghia received a call from David Puttnam. 'David said, "Where do you stand with *The Mission*? There is a chance to make the picture here with Goldcrest." Of course, I thought we were talking about Hugh Hudson, that this approach was a result of their friendship. He said, "No, no, no, we're talking about a new young director, Roland Joffe." I said, "Who's he?" '

Ghia had known Puttnam for many years and was immediately well disposed towards the idea of being associated with Goldcrest. As he saw it, the company stood in the same awkward gap between Hollywood money and European cinema values as he did. If terms could be arranged, Goldcrest would definitely be 'the best home' for the project. But first he had to find out something about Joffe. He was invited to London to view two hours of *The Killing Fields*, and he was very impressed. 'At the end of the film I saw Roland and I said, "Had I seen this footage by accident I would have phoned you to ask you to do *The Mission*. If you feel the way I feel, then we're home and dry." '

Joffe, who had earlier been introduced to Bolt by Puttnam, had already studied *The Mission* script. 'I didn't like it, but I liked what it was dealing with,' he recalls. 'I thought the script itself was very old-fashioned. It was rather literary. Somehow it wasn't the stuff of a feature film; it read more like a play. But I was very intrigued, for various reasons, with the idea of doing something about Latin America, and particularly doing something that concerned liberation theology, and also that actually looked at the whole complex relationship of Western Europe and Latin American colonization and the relationship of simple peoples with more commercially advanced nations. I thought that that contained some very fascinating things, and that it was a very interesting story.'

Joffe's interpretation of the underlying themes of *The Mission* is almost identical to that given by Ghia in his explanation of what it was that had reawakened his interest in the subject ten years before. Thus, already won over by Joffe's film-making skills, Ghia was further impressed and reassured by the director's sympathetic approach to the story.

As for Bolt, he was a confirmed Joffe enthusiast. The director had written to him, outlining his approach to the story and enumerating the changes that he would like to make to the script. 'He got very excited about this letter,' Joffe recalls, 'and when I went to see him he said, "You've got seventeen points, and, of your seventeen, fourteen are ones that I really want to do." '

Ghia dropped his other negotiations and entered into serious talks with Lieberson. However, there was one obvious and outstanding question that had yet to be answered: what, exactly, was Puttnam's role to be? *The Mission* was Ghia's property, conceived and developed by him, and he, naturally, wanted to produce it. Of this Lieberson was well aware. Why then had Puttnam made the initial call? And why did everyone at Goldcrest talk of it as a Puttnam project?

The answer that eventually emerged was, of course, that Puttnam really wanted to produce the film himself. This was a proposition that Ghia did not wholly reject. He was ready to acknowledge Puttnam's superior skills and, if Puttnam could do what he, Ghia, had failed to do for ten years – i.e. get the film made – then he was more than happy to share the credit. After further discussion, it was agreed that, as a provisional arrangement, Puttnam would be credited as executive producer and Ghia as producer, but that the production team would be Puttnam's – the same team, in fact, that had worked on *The Killing Fields*.

This was not an entirely happy compromise.

'In all honesty it caused me problems,' explains Joffe, 'because Fernando was not suitable to produce the project. It was bigger than anything he'd done before and I think he was frightened of it. And strains began to develop which I thought would be very bad for the project, in that it was clear that David and Fernando were not going to be a good mix. A lot of discussion and heart-searching went on over that.'

The arrangement was amended: the credits would remain as they were, but Puttnam would in fact do the producer's job. As Joffe recalls, Ghia was resigned to the fact that he 'would not take an active part in the production of the film'. Did this not cause resentment?

'I should think it caused some,' says Joffe. 'Fernando is only a human being and nobody likes being told that they're not really up to the job that they feel they're up to, and that they've carried in their mind as something they're going to do for a long time. But the psychology of all that for Fernando, and for everybody else involved, was quite complex. I would have said on Fernando's part there was as much relief as there might have been annoyance.'

By Ghia's own account, it would appear that he took the demotion remarkably well. His resentment is reserved for the subsequent handling of the film itself, which, in his opinion, became overblown and spectacular, emerging as an expensive mid-Atlantic movie rather than a modestly priced and wholly European one. This outcome he traces, with resignation rather than rancour, to Puttnam's influence.

When first presented to the management team in March 1984, *The Mission* was said to be likely to cost about $8 million. This caused Terry Clegg, who had just spent time in Brazil coming to the conclusion that *The Emerald Forest* could not be made for $17 million, to 'express surprise'. He asked to see the script.

Apart from the yet to be resolved commercial and creative considerations, there was one further complication. Puttnam wanted to ensure that *The Mission* – which was not developed by him and of which he was not yet the producer – be regarded as a valid project under the terms of his development deals with both Goldcrest and Warner Bros. Puttnam had a three-year contract with Goldcrest which required the company to pay him an overhead allowance of £135,000 in the first year (increasing by £15,000 each year thereafter) and to advance £30,000 a year against general development costs for which Puttnam's company, Enigma, did not have to give a detailed account. Additional development costs were funded on a project-by-project basis. These advances were recouped from Puttnam's fees and from the budgets of those projects that went into production. In exchange, Goldcrest had first opportunity to finance and distribute Enigma's television films, and second opportunity, after Warner Bros. – with whom Puttnam's deal was similar in structure but considerably more lucrative – to finance and distribute Enigma's feature films. Significantly, Goldcrest ceded to Puttnam 'favourable approval and cutting rights during production' and 'beneficial approval rights in relation to distribution terms'. Puttnam, in other words, retained creative control over his films and had a veto over sales deals.

It should be said that the advances paid by Goldcrest were modest for someone of Puttnam's stature. Other British companies, including Thorn EMI, would have put up double these sums for his services.

Goldcrest was quite happy to include *The Mission* within the terms of this agreement, and the company had no hesitation in funding a reconnaissance in Argentina and Colombia from which a draft budget would be drawn up. Warner Bros., however, took some persuading.

Chapter Thirty
The Goldcrest Myth

Ilott: The constant delays to the fund-raising – it was now five months beyond its original target date – were causing considerable anxiety on the board and were holding up the regular business of the company. No new feature film had been started since *Cal* went before the cameras in September 1983, and the seven-month hiatus since then was bound to have disastrous effects on the company's cash flow in the future. Furthermore, to delay the share offering any longer would be to place it in jeopardy, for the audited accounts and estimates of future earnings contained in the prospectus were already six months old, dating from 30 September 1983. Even the most recent statistics, adding a note to the effect that £1.7 million of the £27.4 million estimated future earnings had already been received, were dated 31 December 1983. If Goldcrest let any more time elapse, the information in the prospectus would be so out of date that it would be invalid. Accordingly, it was agreed to fix a firm date for the publication of the prospectus: Monday, 9 April 1984. This meant that all outstanding matters would have to be concluded by the previous Friday, 6 April.

In order to meet this new deadline, all the remaining preparations were entrusted to a reorganization committee, comprising Lee, Cruickshank, Grossart and the newcomer to the board, Philip Whitehead. Their first task was to draw up a revised proposal for share options. What they devised was a scheme that granted five-year options, of 1.75 per cent to Lee, 1.5 per cent each to Puttnam and Attenborough, 1 per cent each to Chambers, Norris, Lieberson and Cruickshank, 0.67 per cent to Wooller (who also got a carried interest of about 0.1 per cent in respect of his shareholding in Goldcrest Television), and 0.5 per cent each to Terry Clegg, Guy East and Steve Walsh. In addition, 2.5 per cent was set aside to be made available to other staff at a later date. These arrangements met with general approval.

One further problem about share ownership remained, however.

Eberts, whose family trust, Winsome Ltd, owned 10 per cent of both Goldcrest Films and Goldcrest Television, had had the option to sell the trust's shares back to the company at a rate that reflected their value were they to be traded on the open market. It had been hoped that this matter would have been settled long before the new prospectus was issued, but in fact the two sides could not agree on a price. In the end, to avoid adding further delay to the fund-raising, Pearson agreed to indemnify Goldcrest for the costs incurred in the negotiation as well as for the full purchase price of the trust's shares.

Eberts: Needless to say, the price that I thought was fair was far in excess of the price that James Lee and the board of Goldcrest thought was fair, and, after two or three months of tentative and unsatisfactory bilateral negotiations, we agreed to engage the services of an arbitrator.

The choice of arbitrator was Pearson's, not mine, and when I heard that he was an accountant from Touche Ross my heart sank. An accountant would be bound by training and habit to look at the problem from an auditor's point of view. The principal role of an auditor is not to seek opportunity but to ward against disaster, to be as conservative as possible. That's why every audit takes a great deal of time and covers every possible downside risk. An auditor will quickly qualify a report if there is the slightest indication that something is wrong or if there is even a hint of an overstatement of assets. No auditor would dream of taking it upon himself to say that this or that aspect of the company looks great and could really take off. So, to me, an accountant represented the most conservative, the least optimistic kind of valuer. I would have preferred a merchant banker, someone who would have appreciated how the market perceived Goldcrest as an investment opportunity, who took into account the underlying value of the library and who would therefore put a higher price on the trust's shares than would be justified merely by looking at the balance sheet and the profit-and-loss statements.

To present the family trust's case I turned to an old friend, Donald MacPherson of Fielding Newson Smith. Pearson turned to Bernie Myers of Rothschild.

Donald and his team put together a highly professional presentation with charts, stockmarket comparisons and other data showing that the value of the shares should be set at £300,000. Rothschild prepared no documentation at all and relied on Bernie to present Goldcrest's case verbally. At first, the most they were prepared to offer was £150,000, although this was later increased to an absolute top limit of £235,000.

The several meetings that we had were extremely unpleasant. Donald's every claim and observation was met with derision bordering on contempt by the Rothschild people. James Joll, who sat in on the meetings for Pearson, exhibited similar ill-will. This distressed and surprised me because James had always been, and is now, a good friend. But, for some reason, during that interim period, James shared Bernie's attitude and he behaved as if Donald's case deserved no more than to be treated with amusement and disdain.

The arbitrator was very dour and correct. He received the documents and heard the depositions completely impassively, not even remarking on the difference in clarity and preparedness between Donald's case and the case put forward by Bernie Myers. He never gave any indication of which side he favoured, although at the final meeting he did hint that he disapproved of the manner in which Bernie kept interrupting Donald. At the end of that session he informed us that there was no need to meet again, that there was nothing lacking in the submissions and that we should go away and wait for his decision. I left the meeting convinced that he would make a very conservative judgement.

We heard nothing for several days. I took my family on holiday to our farm in Canada and it was while we were there that, early one morning, the telephone rang. It was Irene Lyons, calling to tell me the arbitrator's decision: the trust's shareholding was deemed to be worth £374,000, substantially in excess of even Donald's optimistic claim.

I thought there must have been a mistake, but Irene, thinking the same, had already confirmed the figure herself. I put the phone down in a kind of euphoric trance. My family was at last secure. It was one of the great days of my life.

I expected to find, when I got back to London, a document setting out the reasons for the arbitrator's judgement: a cogently expressed analysis of the value of the company as a whole and of the trust's shareholding in particular. Instead, there was a simple letter, which concluded: 'I hereby determine and certify that the prescribed price of the shares is £374,477.'

I think the Pearson directors were absolutely staggered by it. The Rothschild people were embarrassed to the point of silence. All round there was a general feeling of shock and disbelief, tinged with not a small amount of envy. I decided never to mention the matter to anyone, inside or outside the company, but the first thing that was raised the next time I saw James Lee and John Chambers and James Joll, was: 'Jesus, how did you ever get that price?' They were genuinely upset about it.

Ilott: One enormous obstacle still lay in the path of the fund-raising: the disposal of *The Emerald Forest*. The sale of the film to Embassy had run into unexpected difficulties and, despite daily telephone conferences and the exchange of long telexes, there was a real possibility that the picture would not be off Goldcrest's hands before the 6 April deadline. Goldcrest, which now looked like having to make a choice between stopping the fund-raising and stopping *The Emerald Forest*, instructed John Boorman, who had already started shooting in Brazil, to give the crew two weeks' notice. Boorman ignored the order, believing it to be a ploy on Goldcrest's part to put pressure on Embassy. The crew, getting wind of the crisis, demanded their return tickets to England. The situation was thus not a happy one, least of all for Boorman, whose diary entries of the time give some idea of the conditions in which he was working:

These first two weeks' shooting have been horrendous. It has rained every day, sometimes without respite. We just try to keep shooting, but it is miserable. We are way behind schedule, and we just cannot seem to stem the haemorrhaging budget. All Goldcrest's predictions appear to be coming to pass. Jerry Perenchio is seriously considering abandoning the film . . . He is terrified of runaway costs and I can't blame him . . .

The crew's morale is low. Apart from spending each day wet through, there is a species of mosquito here in Paraty that is excruciating. The body does not seem to be able to deal with it. The bites become hard white lumps sitting on huge welts. Everyone is losing sleep from the unbearable irritation. There is constant anxiety about snakes and biting spiders; tarantulas abound.

The key grip simply walked out this week. He left for London without a word. I suspect others would walk out too if they weren't so attached to their Brazilian girls. The standbys are sluggish and mutinous. I drive the crew on by sheer will-power, cajoling, insulting, threatening. Most of our equipment is still in the customs. I cannot do tracking shots. I have no crab dolly. We are using the Steadicam to get movement and so far it has been a disaster. The electronics are much too delicate to withstand the rain and tropical conditions.

My editor, John Merritt . . . has been sick since he arrived and just cannot take the climate. He is going home.

. . . Powers [Boothe, the actor who played Markham] has done only one scene and is fretting at the hotel. It is the important scene where Markham, after recovering from fever, confronts Wanadi, angrily demanding the return of his son. The scene did not work. It is hopelessly complex, with far too many ideas in it. Markham's powerful emotion, resonating against a spectacular waterfall setting, made the subsidiary ideas simply irritating. Also, the paint on Charley's face gave him a clown-like look. I had to change it and the scene needed to be reshot . . . Charley is working very hard. He is anxious and feels the pressure. Now and then he blows up and screams at me. We have a shouting match and the crew look away . . .

The original deal between Goldcrest and Embassy had been devised by Eberts. The subsequent detailed negotiations, which had dragged on for two months, had been conducted by Ron Beckman and David Norris. But theirs was not a relationship between equals. Eberts had had to persuade Embassy that they needed the film. There was no one else in the company pushing for it. None of the Embassy executives had been involved in setting it up, and none of them would get credit if it was a success. The only reputation riding on it was Eberts's. Beckman, therefore, was under pressure only to get the best possible terms. The longer the negotiations took, the more pressure Goldcrest would be under and the better those terms were likely to be.

Norris, on the other hand, was under orders to close a deal, any deal, just to get the thing off Goldcrest's hands. But even that wasn't easy. For a start, even though the film had commenced shooting on 13 March, there was as yet no signed agreement between Goldcrest and Boorman. The details of his contract had all been agreed verbally, but the final documentation had never been drawn up. One consequence of this was that Goldcrest did not actually own the script, and therefore was not in a position to sell the film and all attendant copyrights to Embassy. Thus, Norris had not only to negotiate terms with Beckman, but had to secure Boorman's agreement to those terms so that he would then sign over the copyright.

Norris flew to LA on 2 April. He drafted yet another outline agreement on the plane and had it typed up at the hotel on his arrival. The next day he presented this draft to Beckman. Beckman, being in no hurry, went through it point by point, listing dozens of minor objections and two potential deal-breakers. First, Beckman would not agree to take over Goldcrest's Brazilian subsidiary, Goldcrest Limitada. This company was the titular producer of the film, the local recipient of currency transactions, the local paymaster and, as a wholly Brazilian company, the point of reference in all dealings with the national and state authorities. Embassy did not want to take responsibility for a company which had already entered into local contracts and which might, at some point down the line, enmesh them in unwanted complications in a distant country. But Goldcrest, for exactly the same reasons, did not want to be left with the responsibility either, least of all as they would henceforth have nothing more to do with Goldcrest Limitada or the making of *The Emerald Forest*.

Second, Beckman would not pay the amount of interest, nor the amount of sales commission, that Norris was demanding for the work already done on the film. Goldcrest had by this time spent £2.9 million ($4.35 million) on development, pre-production and production expenses. In the normal course of things, they would have expected to get that money back, plus interest, plus a fee, making a total of, say, £3.3 million ($4.95 million). Bill Gavin had achieved $3 million of foreign pre-sales (excluding the US deal with Embassy), and again, in the normal course of things, those sales would have earned a commission of 15 per cent (i.e. $450,000). So the cash return that Goldcrest would have looked for, had they sold on the film in ordinary circumstances, would have been not far short of £3.7 million ($5.5 million). In addition, Goldcrest had originally wanted to keep a net profit share of 25 per cent.

Norris had already reduced these expectations considerably. Beckman was to reduce them further.

The contract went through three drafts in as many days. Each time, the terms were less favourable to Goldcrest. In the end, Norris had no choice but to concede to virtually all Beckman's demands. A final agreement was reached on the evening of Wednesday, 4 April. Goldcrest was to recoup its £2.9 million, plus £120,000. Nothing else. And it had to keep the Brazilian subsidiary. It was, says Norris, the best he could do under the circumstances.

Beckman then requested the transfer of copyright, which Norris could provide only with Boorman's agreement. But Boorman, who had had a very favourable deal with Goldcrest, would naturally first want to scrutinize the terms offered him by Embassy. At Norris's request, an outline agreement between Embassy and Boorman was quickly drafted and sent to Boorman's business manager, Ed Gross. This document did not arrive in Gross's office until 5 p.m. on Thursday, 5 April.

Gross read the agreement and found that it was no more than a standard studio contract: good fees upfront and apparently acceptable net-profit participation, but no participation in other revenues and a very conservative – i.e. favourable to Embassy – interpretation of break-even, the point at which net profits begin to be paid. Embassy, for example, insisted on putting into the film's budget a $2 million contribution to overheads, which, according to Boorman, since Embassy had incurred no overhead expenditure on the project to date, was just another way of saying that they wanted the first $2 million net revenues for themselves. The contract also had a performance clause that would reward Boorman if the film came in on time but that would penalize him if it did not. The whole package was, as Norris admits, 'a million miles away' from Boorman's deal with Goldcrest. Inevitably, Gross refused to recommend it to his client.

In London, at 4 o'clock on the following afternoon, Friday, 6 April, the Goldcrest reorganization committee convened for what was supposed to be its final meeting. The committee members present were Michael

Stoddart, Don Cruickshank and a co-opted member, John Chambers. Also in attendance, as an adviser, was Charles ap Simon, of solicitors Freshfields. The agenda of the meeting comprised a long list of formalities: the agreement of transfer of shares from the partnerships to the new company; the authorization for the issuance of new shares; agreement of fees; approval of the final wording of all relevant documents, including the prospectus; approval of the final form of presentation of material contracts; verification of financial data and indemnities, and so on. It would be a long meeting in any event, but it could not close until word came through from Norris that *The Emerald Forest* had finally been sold to Embassy. A call to Norris's hotel established that he had a meeting with Embassy scheduled for 2 p.m. LA time, and that he hoped to have the contract signed by 4 p.m. at the latest (i.e. midnight in London). The reorganization committee settled down for a long wait.

Norris met with Ed Gross at 12.30 and proposed a compromise: that Gross, on Boorman's behalf, should sign an agreement transferring the copyright of the film to Goldcrest, without prejudicing whatever terms would later be agreed between Boorman and Embassy. This could be achieved by placing the transfer agreement in escrow. Goldcrest would then sign a further agreement to release the copyright to Embassy once the terms and conditions of the escrow – i.e. the terms and conditions of Boorman's new contract – had been negotiated and agreed. Embassy, knowing that the copyright was theirs for the taking, would then be in a position to sign the main transfer-of-ownership agreement with Goldcrest. All this could be done within a matter of hours and need have no influence on the protracted negotiation that was likely to ensue between Boorman and Embassy. From Gross's office, Norris called Ron Beckman, who agreed to the arrangement. But Gross himself would not agree. Norris therefore insisted that the matter be referred directly to Boorman.

After three weeks' shooting, Boorman was already two weeks behind schedule. Thus far, the production was a catastrophe. At 6 p.m. on the evening of Friday, 6 April, he returned exhausted and dispirited to his hotel just in time to take the call from Ed Gross, who handed him over to David Norris. Norris and Boorman were old friends. This was not to be a pleasant experience for either of them.

'It was the worst thing I've ever had to do,' Norris recalls. 'My mate was down in Brazil, up to his knees in mud, in very unpleasant conditions, and I had to say, "Unless you tell Ed that he can sign this piece of paper granting copyright to Goldcrest so that Goldcrest can pass it on to Embassy, then I have to tell you, John, with the greatest reluctance, that there will be no cash flow for the production and you will have to close down tonight." '

Two years of preparation and three appalling weeks in the jungle were about to be blown away. If Goldcrest did close down the production, it would never restart. Boorman had no choice but to agree to Norris's demand.

On seeing the transfer-of-copyright document and agreeing the terms of the escrow, Embassy then signed the main purchase agreement. At midnight in London, Stoddart took the call from Norris confirming that *The Emerald Forest* no longer belonged to Goldcrest. He then declared the reorganization-committee meeting closed. All the preparations were now complete and the prospectus would be issued on Monday, 9 April, as planned.

The prospectus first went to all the existing shareholders and four potential new investors. The initial response, however, was not wholly enthusiastic, and the list of potential investors was widened to include first six and then ten new names. By 30 April, the full £12 million had been raised, £6.08 million from existing shareholders and £5.92 million from five new investors, and the offer was declared closed.

The new company, Goldcrest Holdings, which formally opened for business on 4 May 1984, was owned by Pearson (41 per cent), the National Coal Board Pension Fund (10 per cent), Electra Investment Trust (5.5 per cent) and a host of lesser investors, among them the Scottish Investment Trust, London and Manchester Assurance, Noble Grossart, Legal & General Assurance, Coral Leisure Group, various funds operated by the Murray Investment Trust, and the Post Office Superannuation Scheme Venture Capital Fund.

Lee issued a triumphant press release announcing the success of the fund-raising. The release declared that the new money 'effectively doubled Goldcrest's capacity to finance film and television productions', and it went on to trumpet Goldcrest's current achievements and forthcoming attractions. Goldcrest, it said, had six feature films ready for release in 1984, chief among them the eagerly awaited *Killing Fields*. Two Goldcrest films, *Another Country* and *Cal*, had been selected for competition at the Cannes Film Festival, and the company had three major series running simultaneously on US television: *Robin of Sherwood* on Showtime, *Concealed Enemies* on PBS and *The Far Pavilions* on HBO.

'With the new funds in place Goldcrest can now move ahead with an ambitious three-year production programme,' the release continued. 'The company aims to produce five major feature films, ten middle-range features, a series of low-budget comedy films and six mini-series for television as well as a number of made-for-television films.'

There followed a brief survey of projects in development, including Bob Kaufman's *Joan of Arc* and what was described as 'a major project to be produced and directed by Sir Richard Attenborough', neither of which was to see the light of day.

That this press release did not get quite the coverage that it deserved was partly because Goldcrest's fund-raising efforts had been so heavily trailered in the trade press in previous weeks – that Goldcrest had raised the money was noteworthy but everything else about the story was old news – and partly because the release was issued in the week before the Cannes Film Festival. (Goldcrest's failure to command the headlines was the source of some friction between the company and its public relations agency, Dennis Davidson Associates.)

Nevertheless, *Screen International* did manage to devote a whole inside page of its Cannes Festival issue to an interview with Lee.

There is no doubt that the new money did more than give Lee the resources he needed to get back into production: it gave him enormous prestige. The £12 million, plus a £10 million line of credit from the Midland Bank, meant that he had more money to spend than Eberts had ever had. Likewise, the fact that Goldcrest was now an independent company gave Lee a prospective status that Eberts could never have hoped for.

And Lee had been lucky, for not a word of the management crises and internal quarrels of the past months had ever appeared in the press. For all that anyone knew, Goldcrest could still do no wrong. When it wanted more money from the City it had only to snap its fingers and there it was – £12 million. A £10 million line of credit from the bank, access to the US cable channels, co-production deals with American independents, the pick of all the newest and most exciting film and television projects: all were within Goldcrest's confident grasp.

It is little wonder, then, that in the *Screen International* interview, Lee was at his most charming, modest and confident, moving easily between a sober discussion of the problems of low-budget television production and the adverse conditions developing in the US cable market to an upbeat account of Goldcrest's future prospects, stressing especially that it now had enough money to overcome its hitherto absolute reliance on investment partners and pre-sales.

'It's taken us four years to get to the point where we seem credible in the eyes of the investing public,' Lee said. 'We now have enough funds to move ahead on our own resources. In future we will be able to finance projects partly with our own money and partly by simple borrowing from the bank.'

The point he was making was that the greater the proportion of production costs that Goldcrest could finance itself, either directly or by bank borrowing, then the greater the profit share that the company could retain. The example in the back of his, and everybody else's, mind was *Gandhi*, in which, following the failure to secure studio finance and the last-minute falling out of the Patels, Goldcrest had had a much larger share than had originally been intended. That larger share, £5 million, was to yield revenues of £11.5 million, not only giving Goldcrest a huge profit but making an invaluable contribution to the company's cash flow throughout 1983 and 1984.

Similar articles later appeared in trade, business and quality consumer publications. Lee, now with a beard to complement his flamboyant bowties, was establishing a public profile: that of a successful man working in a glamorous business.

In reality, of course, he was faced with enormous problems. The triumphant press release and the upbeat tenor of Lee's interviews glossed over some alarming aspects of Goldcrest's current operations. For example, although it was true that no British company had ever had three television series showing simultaneously in the USA, it was more significant that none of the programmes in question was being broadcast by a major network. As a rule, networks provide 90–100 per cent of the costs of a programme in exchange for the first screening rights in the USA. Everything else – syndication, pay-TV, foreign sales, video, cable and satellite rights – is left to the producer, who thus has a number of markets from which to derive profits. Getting into the networks is tough – it is a phenomenally competitive market – but it is, or was then, one of the few ways to make real money out of independent television production. The problem with cable sales, such as to HBO or Showtime, and sales to the Public Broadcasting Service is that they were simply not lucrative enough to make productions such as *Concealed Enemies* and *The Far Pavilions* profitable to Goldcrest.

Of much greater immediate concern, however, was the fact that having disposed of *The Emerald Forest*, there was now a huge gap in Goldcrest's already attenuated distribution schedule. No major film had been released by Goldcrest since *The Dresser* in December 1983. The next big movie in the schedule was *The Killing Fields*, which now would not open until November in the United States and not until early 1985 elsewhere. After that, nothing. The same was true in the medium-budget category. *Another Country* had opened in September 1983, *Dream One* was to be released in June 1984 and *Cal* was to be released in September. After that there was nothing.

The looming gaps had to be filled, otherwise Goldcrest would find itself using the new money simply to cover its overheads, which were now running at £216,000 a month. Lieberson was therefore under tremendous pressure to get the cash out of the bank and into production as quickly as he could. It was to take him until September to put together a package of films that conformed, however remotely, to the investment criteria laid down by Lee. It was to be certainly the most trumpeted, and arguably the most catastrophic, film-investment programme ever undertaken by a British company.

Chapter Thirty-one

Into the Jungle

'Hitchcock was shooting on location and bad weather had got him behind schedule. "What the hell are you going to do about it?" the studio trouble-shooter demanded. "I shall do whatever is necessary", said Hitchcock in his measured tones, "to complete what, in the course of time, you will come to refer to as 'our film' " ' – story told by John Boorman in the diary he kept during the making of The Emerald Forest; *the diary was later published as a book,* Money Into Light

Eberts: John Boorman never did get a decent contract out of Embassy. Ron Beckman had readily agreed to David Norris's suggestion that the transfer of copyright be held in escrow because he knew that, with filming already underway and with Goldcrest having washed their hands of the project, Boorman would be left in the weakest possible negotiating position. They had him over a barrel, and handled the subsequent negotiations with Ed Gross accordingly. In his deal with Goldcrest, John had agreed to a somewhat smaller than usual upfront fee to help get the financing in place, confident that he would benefit at the back end. For its part, Goldcrest undertook to share all revenues with him, including the proceeds of any tax deal. Embassy did not like this arrangement at all. In particular, they did not like giving John a piece of a tax deal, because tax deals are cash in the pocket. So they put his salary back up to close to his normal level, took away the benefits of the tax deal, and put in a penalty clause to encourage him to come in on or under budget. (They were very concerned, as Goldcrest had been, about an overrun.)

Once the contract had been agreed, Embassy revealed more of their true Hollywood pedigree by the attitude they adopted towards John and towards the film. At Goldcrest, we did not do a deal unless we trusted the film-maker and, once we had agreed on the script, the cast and the budget, we let him or her get on with it. We didn't send people off on location to check up on them. In fact, I never went on location unless I was invited.

By contrast, Embassy had a whole team standing by to interfere. They had a location manager, a production manager, a budget manager, a transport manager. They wanted control: every week, every day, every hour if possible. This did not suit John, who had quite enough problems on his hands without having head office breathing down his neck day and night. Pretty soon fires were raging between him and Embassy. His difficulties with Goldcrest had been as nothing by comparison.

As already noted, the writer of *The Emerald Forest*, Rospo Pallenberg, had been very upset by John's decision to cast his son Charley in the role of the boy. Indeed, Rospo had taken it upon himself (in John's best interest, he said at the time) to warn Embassy that if they went along with that decision they would condemn the film to certain failure. On hearing this, Embassy's already high anxieties about the project got higher still. I knew that John had made every attempt to get somebody else, had failed, and that the only alternative open to him was to use his son Charley. I did not read anything sinister into that. I did not think John had purposely failed to find some other actor. He is an honest, straightforward, practical film-maker. He was not going to concoct a nutty story about screen-testing thirty-two people and then not finding the right one, and falling back at the last minute on his son, who had been doing body-building for six months and just happened to be in good shape for the role. I believed John when he said that Charley was always meant to be a back-up in case no one else could be found.

Embassy didn't believe that. They thought there was great chicanery going on. Of course, that is what you would think if you were based in Hollywood. That's the way Hollywood operates. People there don't trust each other. Trust is a word that sometimes gets mentioned, but only in script conferences, as a motivating factor between strictly fictional characters. It is only among the best people in Hollywood that the films themselves come top of the list of priorities. Among the rest, films come far down the list after a hodge-podge of personal ambitions, rivalries and sectional interests. Films are someone else's problem, someone who can be blamed if they go wrong and someone whose credit can be hi-jacked when they go right.

As if to prove Embassy right and me wrong, however, the first few weeks of production of *The Emerald Forest* were total chaos. Monumental downpours washed props down the river, flooded the stores and left the cast and crew permanently soaked. Equipment was held in customs for long periods. Things that had been promised didn't turn up. Things turned up that hadn't been asked for. Everything which could have gone wrong went wrong. Confusion had arisen over exactly what money had been spent and what further money was available through Citibank's arrangement to buy cruzeiros. Tempers were getting very frayed. Members of the crew were walking off the set. John was under siege. After the first two weeks of shooting, he had accomplished very little: he had practically no usable footage at all. By the end of May, he had been shooting for six weeks and still hadn't made up any of the lost ground.

At Embassy, those executives with ambition (i.e. all of them) were putting a big distance between themselves and this movie, saying, 'I told you this would happen . . . the guy's incompetent . . . we should never have let Jake talk us into this.'

By the last weekend in May, relations between John and Embassy had reached a dangerously low point. It was Memorial weekend in the States and a bank holiday weekend in the UK. I had taken my family down to a rented house in Cornwall. On Saturday night I received a call from Alan Horn, president of Embassy. He was deeply concerned about what was going on in Brazil and said, 'Get your ass down there as quickly as possible and kick Boorman's ass and make sure he gets himself back on track.'

I had not spoken to John for several weeks – he was miles from civilization somewhere in the jungle – and I had no first-hand knowledge of what was going on. I had no alternative but to cut short the weekend, drive back to London, pack a few things and go to Brazil. I took Concorde to Washington; from there I took a plane to Miami, transferred to a flight to Rio and transferred again to a flight to Belém in north-eastern Brazil. At Belém I was met by a private plane which took me to the location deep in the jungle. The whole journey took two days.

I arrived having no idea what to expect: for all I knew the production could have ground to a halt and the crew packed their bags, leaving John sitting in a tent somewhere vowing never to make a film again. In fact, John was nowhere to be seen. He was off shooting in some even more remote part of the jungle. A jeep was procured and I took off into the mist to try to find him.

Everywhere was running with water and, as we crashed and bounced from puddle to puddle, the driver told me more of what had been going on. Entire sets had been washed out, there had been accidents and illnesses, and some of the footage had been accidentally destroyed in the Brazilian labs. Powers Boothe had nearly drowned. At one point the rain had been so heavy that for four days it had been impossible to do anything at all. A dozen of the crew had threatened mutiny and it had taken all John's powers of persuasion to get them to stay. John himself had been arrested at one point: the crew's work permits weren't in good order.

When I got to the place where John was meant to be, he again wasn't there: he had gone even further ahead. The roads beyond were so thick with mud that they were impassable to vehicles and I was told that John had put the camera on his back and set off at a trot to catch a shot before the sun went down. It was the first time sun had broken through the clouds for days. The light was right, the mist was right, the rain was holding off: he just had to get that shot. Here was this man, fifty-one years old, running through the jungle and the mud with a camera on his back. There was no way I could 'kick his ass'. It was out of the question. He was obviously devoting every shred of his energy to the picture.

I returned to the hotel that served as the production headquarters and waited. John got back quite late in the evening. I expected him to be exhausted, but the minute I saw those twinkling eyes and that grin I knew that everything was fine. Indeed, he was in high spirits. He was confronting nature and he was besieged with problems. He was revelling in it. I had a suspicion, too, that he had decided by then that things could only get better.

For all his creative spirit, John is, like most good film-makers (and unlike most desk-bound executives) an eminently practical man: he knows that when a film goes two weeks over schedule there are huge budgetary consequences which cannot be ignored. In round numbers, it was costing about $100,000 a day to pay for the crew and the transport and all the logistics required to maintain the production on location. To be two weeks behind schedule when you're shooting six days a week means that you are $1.2 million over budget. That's the minimum. To replace that time might involve you in other complications – schedules, availability, penalty clauses and so on – that would drive you even further over budget. The only way out is to cut corners and reschedule: i.e. you don't replace the lost time but do without it. You cut some scenes, find easier ways to shoot others, drop others altogether, speed up every process and take advantage of every break that comes your way. John is a genius at that kind of seat-of-the-pants film-making, and I knew that he had already decided in his own mind that by relentless work and ruthless cutting he would find the time within the original schedule to finish the film.

That night I watched some of the footage and it looked wonderful. Thus, even before we had exchanged serious words, John had secured all the moral high ground. In fact he had me eating out of his hand.

At last we sat down alone and, in my least convincing manner, I told him why I was there. I explained that Embassy had asked me to come down, and that it was difficult for me to express what they wanted me to express because I didn't feel the way they did, but they were very unhappy with the progress being made, the lack of communication from John and what they believed to be the lack of control over the production. Was there any way, I asked him, that I could reassure them that the film was going to be fine?

Of course, John got very angry about all this. He had had endless harassment from Embassy, but not one word of encouragement. They had given him a lousy contract, constantly demanded that he supply sane answers to their insane questions, and generally dealt with him as if he were sitting in an air-conditioned office surrounded by a dozen secretaries and the latest communications technology, ready instantaneously to respond to their every request. Now they had sent his friend down to 'kick his ass'. The whole thing stank as far as he was concerned. However, having got all that off his chest, he calmed down and gave me the assurances – details of script cuts and so on – that I needed.

The whole episode was distasteful to me too, because I was acting on someone else's instructions, bringing a message I did not believe in to a man who was doing everything within his power to get the picture made. This kind of thing had not happened to me before. At Goldcrest I had been the boss and everything I did, I did with conviction. At Embassy I was an employee, under orders.

I flew back to Belém and spent a lot of time over the next couple of days in the production office going over the figures and telephoning Alan Horn in LA to reassure him that things were not as bad as he had thought and that it was going to be OK. But Alan was not easily convinced. This was the first feature film undertaken by his administration. Like him, all the senior people at Embassy came from television. Their idea of production was shooting a television series in a studio, where the costs are very controllable, and where you shoot very quickly, and where you have rehearsed a great deal before production starts. To go from that into the feature-film business, especially on a film which was being shot in the jungles of Brazil, was more than they could cope with. They were extremely frustrated by what they felt was the lack of co-operation from John, and were beside themselves with anxiety because there was no way they could supervise the production directly. It was probably an unfortunate first project for them to have been involved in.

In the end, and to everyone's amazement, John brought the film in on schedule and under budget. This gave me particular pleasure, not only because it got the critics at Embassy off my back and got John his well-deserved bonus, but because it proved to the sceptics within Goldcrest that they had been wrong all along. Had Goldcrest kept the picture, they would have filled one of the gaps in their distribution schedule, boosted their cash flow and made substantial profits. Even the much disputed casting of Charley as the boy was vindicated. His performance was one of the strengths of the film.

I returned from Brazil to London and went back to work at my office in Audley Square. By title, I was president of Embassy Communications International, but, in fact, there was no such company. It was just a name dreamed up so that there was something to put on my calling card. I had no corporate role at Embassy at all. I was not part of the hierarchy, had no managerial responsibilities and, other than my personal assistant and my secretary, had no staff reporting to me. My job was to raise money for Embassy Film Associates (EFA) and, when that was done, to bring projects and film-makers to the company.

EFA was to be a limited pool of capital to be used for a fixed term to finance the production of a limited number of feature films. These would be distributed by Embassy in the US domestic market and sold to independent distributors in the foreign markets. The investors would receive a very favourable deal compared to other available film investments, because Embassy was going to charge only one third of its normal distribution fees. In other words, it was going to share profits on a much more equitable basis than would normally be the case. To make it even more attractive, Norman Lear and Jerry Perenchio were going to invest a very substantial amount of their own money. Given these attractions, we thought we would have no trouble raising the $100 million that was our target figure. In fact, we were to encounter almost insurmountable problems and I was to spend the best part of a year in a frustrating search for investors. I spent very little time in London and saw very little of my family.

Chapter Thirty-two

Dark Days

'As far as Jake was concerned, Goldcrest was his. And he was very proud of it. And it really upset him and distressed him that it was going wrong.' – Richard Attenborough

Eberts: The first step in raising money for EFA was to find an investment bank that would play the same role for Embassy as E. F. Hutton had for IFI. I spent weeks with Jerry in the States lining up meetings on Wall Street. Perhaps our most promising relationship was with Bear Stearns. The first meeting with them was a very formal and very businesslike luncheon. The assembled executives asked all sorts of questions, which Jerry and I answered fairly adroitly. Further discussions took place over the following days and the matter moved forward, as these things always do in the banking world, step by step. This was not a fast enough pace for Jerry. As weeks went by, and meeting followed meeting, I could see that he was getting impatient. However, we eventually got down to the finer details of how the two sides were going to work together and, after one particular meeting in New York, we were within an ace of concluding the negotiation. Jerry had to fly back to LA that evening to host a charity dinner in honour of his friend Pierre Cossette, and so it was agreed that we would finish our discussion with the bank in a coast-to-coast conference call first thing the following morning.

Jerry invited me to the dinner and we flew back together to the West Coast in his private plane. We cleaned ourselves up at his Century City apartment and went straight off to the Beverly Hilton. Norman Lear was there, and Andy Williams, and a lot of other stars and friends whom Jerry had invited. Jerry Lee Lewis performed on stage and Bob Newhart gave a very funny speech. It was a pleasant evening with a lot of drinking and laughing.

As the formal part of the proceedings wound down we repaired to Trader Vic's bar and had more drinks. Angie Dickinson, British producer

Barry Spikings and a number of other people, mostly friends of Jerry, joined the party, which went on until about 4 a.m., when finally we got into our respective limousines to go home.

At 6 a.m. (9 a.m. in New York) Jerry and I were scheduled to have the conference call with Bear Stearns, immediately after which we were going to fly to Chicago to meet with an important potential investor. There was only time for a shower and a quick nap before being ready for the call.

By 6 a.m. I had pretty well sobered up. The telephone rang and the operator came on the line and said, 'Hello, is that Los Angeles on the phone? Mr Eberts and Mr Perenchio?'

'Yes, we're both here.'

'Hold on one minute. I'll get the Bear Stearns New York office on the phone.' So the Bear Stearns New York office came on.

'Hello, hello, is that Bear Stearns New York?'

'Yes.'

'Hold on one minute.' And the operator then got Bear Stearns Chicago and Bear Stearns some other place. We could hear all this going on and had to wait, telephones to our ears, while all the necessary connections were made.

To pass the time, Jerry, still in a very good mood, began singing 'Blue Moon', one of Andy Williams's biggest hits. Jerry, who has a very good voice, is a great friend of Andy's and Andy had been singing the song three hours earlier at Trader Vic's. So, 'Blue Moon, you saw me standing alone . . .'

I wasn't sure that this was the right approach. I could just see all these serious, blue-suit types back in New York listening to Jerry singing and not being amused. Whether or not he intended it, Jerry's message was pretty clear: 'Come on, fellas, let's get cracking.'

He was still singing when all the connections were in place and we were ready to go. A very serious, disapproving voice cut his crooning short: 'Mr Perenchio, I don't think you're taking this conference call too seriously.'

Jerry replied abruptly, 'Oh yes I am. What can we do for you gentlemen?' As always he was polite, but there was an unmistakable edge to his voice.

Whether it was just to get the ball rolling or whether it was seriously put I don't know, but one of the Bear Stearns executives kicked off with a really basic question which had been asked and answered many times before. Jerry exploded. 'If, after all this time,' he said, 'you guys are still jerking us around and asking that kind of question there is simply no interest on our part in ever dealing with you again.' And he hung up.

I was aghast. After weeks of negotiation, with one of Wall Street's most important banks about to commit to help us raise the $100 million, there was Jerry singing 'Blue Moon' on the phone and telling them to get lost. The whole deal had disappeared in a second.

Jerry turned to me and said, 'Let's get dressed and go to Chicago.' I was in no position to argue.

After that we never had a conversation with Bear Stearns again. In fact, although one or two other investment banks showed an interest, we never did secure the assistance of a bank. I think Jerry took the attitude that we would show them and do it all on our own. This was not a good move. In 99 per cent of cases where you are trying to raise money, you have an investment bank acting for you. They take a fee, in some cases a very substantial fee, but they earn it: they can open doors for you; they put a stamp of approval on the project; they help you structure the deal. It is very unusual not to have an investment bank's name on a prospectus and, looking back on it, I think that it was a big mistake – $100 million in equity is a lot of money to try to raise on your own.

Anyway, we got dressed and were whisked out to Jerry's private plane. It was 7 a.m. LA time, and 9 a.m. in Chicago. Our meeting was scheduled for midday in Chicago, so we were already tight for time.

It was a gorgeous, blue-sky day. Jerry, sitting in the back of the plane, promptly fell fast asleep. He was still recovering from the exertions of the previous night. The little Lear Jet winged its way northward. Suddenly I heard one engine falter. There are only two engines on the plane, and one went '*nnnnn – nnnn – nnn – nn – n . . .*' – and then just shut right down. It was unmistakable. I could see the two pilots sitting up at the front talking excitedly to each other and playing with the controls. Then one of them got out the instruction book.

I was absolutely petrified. I said to myself, 'Jesus, if these guys have to look in the instruction book to figure out what to do, we're in deep trouble.' The pilot was flipping through the pages, trying to find the section headed 'What to Do When the Engine Fails'. Jerry was asleep, oblivious to what was going on. I stared out of the window into the vast space between us and the desert below. I was seized by a deep panic, sweating cold sweat and grasping the edge of my seat. I breathed hard and long and eventually managed to get sufficient grip on myself to leave my seat and go up to the cockpit.

I said, 'H-H-H-H-Hi fellas [my stutter had made a spectacular return],

I noticed that one engine's just gone down. What are you going to do about it?'

The pilot said, 'Well, we're going to do something in just a few minutes,' and he went on flipping through the book trying to discover what to do.

And I said, 'Well, shouldn't we just try to land? We've only got one engine left. If we lose that one, then we're really in trouble. The plane will drop like a rock.'

He said, 'Don't worry about it. Even if the second engine goes, we can glide sixty miles.'

I said, 'Well, are we sixty miles from the nearest airport?' We happened to be at that time flying over the Arizona–California border. I could see that down below was a town.

'Why don't we just land at the nearest possible strip?' I suggested. 'Why don't we just go down there? There must be an airport of some sort. Let's not take a chance on losing the second engine. Who knows . . .'

According to the manual, Lear Jet had its principal repair facility in Phoenix, Arizona, and the pilot decided that the logical thing was to get ourselves to Phoenix. Well, Phoenix was 120 miles away, south-east – in the opposite direction from Chicago – and Flagstaff, Arizona, was right below us.

So there I was pleading with the pilots to land the thing at Flagstaff and not to worry about getting into Phoenix. 'We'll deal with Phoenix later, but let's get down on the ground first,' I said.

And they said, 'No, no, we'll get to Phoenix.'

I said, 'How long will it take?'

'It'll take twenty-five minutes.'

I said, 'Jesus – what if the second one goes? – we're really in trouble.'

'Don't worry, it's not going to go.'

So we headed south-east for Phoenix. Jerry was still sound asleep, snoring loudly. I didn't want to wake him. I felt there was no point: if we were going to go down, he might as well go down sleeping as awake.

We lasted the twenty-five minutes. The pilot had radioed ahead and the airport people had fire engines out. We circled a couple of times to make sure that everything was ready, then we came in on a very long, slow, gliding path: with only one engine we did not have much manoeuvrability. The landing was fine. I stumbled gratefully out of the plane, glanced up and saw the airport sign: 'Tucson'. The pilot looked puzzled.

Jerry woke up after we landed and treated the episode with disdain. He had been a pilot in the Air Force. In fact, he had been in a bad crash and had a back injury which still gives him problems. But he just loves planes and was completely relaxed about the whole thing. Within ten or fifteen minutes we were on board a second plane, which Lear had put at our disposal. We landed in Chicago and got to our meeting only a few minutes late.

Unfortunately, the Chicago investor decided not to invest in EFA. He was not alone.

The one criterion that Jerry had set was that the minimum investment should be $1 million. His theory was that he could get $100 million from a small number of friends of his, or people who knew of his activities. He had, after all, been a very successful entrepreneur. He and Norman knew a lot of very well-heeled people and they believed that these friends could be persuaded to put up the $100 million with little problem. They were so confident of this, in fact, that they had no plans to seek institutional investors.

Their confidence was misplaced. We got very little money from individuals. In fact we got very little money at all.

Jerry and Norman had a wonderful track record in television – I think at that time they had six or seven series running on the networks and three or four series running in syndication – but they had no track record in feature films. Everyone we approached would immediately check us out with a contact in Hollywood. In Hollywood, of course, no one will ever enthusiastically support another person's deal: they will always find some reason to recommend against it. So if Joe Bloggs in Chicago, who had made his money in the chemicals business, wanted to take a flyer on Embassy's film fund, he would first ring up his friend in California and say, 'What do you think of these guys from Embassy?' His friend would say, 'Well, Jerry's a great entrepreneur and Norman's a terrific television producer, but they know nothing about the feature-film business. There are better places to put your money.'

So instead of spending a few weeks, as had been expected, I spent very nearly a year on the road, knocking on doors. I contacted probably fifty potential investors in Japan, France, Italy, Germany, Switzerland and the UK, and over 260 carefully chosen and researched individuals and institutions in the States. I moved down the list from Jerry's and Norman's friends, to associates, to wealthy industry professionals, media entrepreneurs, wealthy investors in other venture-capital areas, to millionaires with no relation to the business or venture capital at all. And I came up with nothing. I moved on to the institutions: pension funds, insurance companies, private investment companies, trusts, merchant banks and venture-capital funds. I called, I visited, I fixed meetings. Nothing. And I wasn't the only one working on it. We had a team of four or five doing this, spread out across the country. They came up with nothing either.

I would go to the States for two or three weeks, come back to London for four or five days, see my wife and kids, spend a couple of days taking care of whatever business was on my desk, make a few calls and appointments, then fly off again. It was a very difficult time for me and my family.

And it became deeply frustrating for Jerry. Jerry is a very impatient man. He just could not understand why I was not raking in the cash. Our personal relationship began to sour. He had been criticized by his colleagues for agreeing to pay me so much money – my salary was considerably out of line with the rest of the Embassy employees – and he had justified it by saying that I was a great fund-raiser and would bring in tons of money for EFA. When I didn't, I think he probably felt cheated, perhaps betrayed.

And the more difficulty I had in raising the money, the less Jerry wanted me to get involved in other things. He didn't want me to deal with film-makers, he didn't want me to deal with projects. Partly, no doubt, this was the result of pressure he was under from other people in the company, for I was not a popular man. My lack of corporate responsibility was resented almost as much as my salary. Of course, precisely because I had no responsibilities and no staff answering to me, I had no power base, and it was therefore easy for the Embassy management to marginalize me. Sometimes I would show up in LA and sit in on a production meeting. But the discomfort was palpable on both sides. In fact, Jerry's efforts to keep me out of the production area were hardly needed: I didn't want to encourage film-makers to bring me their projects, knowing that there was a strong likelihood that Embassy would turn them down simply because they had my name attached.

Likewise, although I had initially been encouraged to bring investment ideas to Jerry's attention, he wanted that to stop too. I knew a lot of people on Wall Street, old friends from Harvard, Laird and Oppenheimer, and I kept hearing about deals. For example, I had lunch one day with some friends on Wall street and we got on to the subject of Storer Broadcasting. Storer had been talked about as a potential leveraged buy-out, and it was at that time coming into play, meaning that if you had the right kind of approach and the right kind of money you could probably acquire enough stock to get control of the company. I decided to call Jerry to tell him about it. I couldn't get him on the phone so I sent him a telex, simply outlining why, at about $40 a share, Storer was a pretty good buy.

I got a brief telex back: 'Don't waste your time on Storer Broadcasting. Get the money. Get the money. Get the money.' That was all. (Storer Broadcasting stock quickly went up to about $88 a share, the company was the subject of a leveraged takeover and a lot of people made a lot of money out of it.)

Jerry does not hide his feelings. His frustration was obvious and we had a very strained relationship from about April 1984 onwards. He stopped being friendly. He stopped inviting me to his house. He restricted our conversations to business. It was very distressing for me and, to some extent, I could not help but feel that Jerry's earlier personal warmth had been merely a ploy, part of his seduction technique to get me to join the company. It seemed that once I had joined I ceased to be a friend and became an employee, simple as that.

I spent most of that year working out of Norman Lear's office in New York. As luck would have it, Embassy's next major picture, *A Chorus Line*, was just starting production in the Mark Hellinger Theater on Broadway. The director was Dickie Attenborough.

Dickie had been anxious to do another musical ever since the success of *Oh What a Lovely War!* I think he felt, too, that *A Chorus Line* was an opportunity for him to prove that he had the talent to make a popular film in a popular idiom. The only problem he had was with the script. He laboured long and hard over it, as many had before him, but I don't think he was ever very happy with the result.

It was during that period of trying to get the script right that I spent a lot of time with him. It was a relief for me, after spending a day trying to raise money, making cold calls and getting only rejections, to wander over to the set and spend some time with Dickie and his leading man, Michael Douglas.

The summer of 1984 was a very unhappy one for me, worse even than the dark days at Oppenheimer, probably the worst I have ever had. I was seeing nothing of my children. Jerry had turned from being a friend into being a distant and demanding boss. My self-esteem was taking a beating as I failed to raise money for Embassy. The prospect of graduating to the next stage, of bringing in projects and film-makers, receded into the far distance. By June or July there was no escaping the conclusion that going to Embassy had been a terrible mistake. Apart from the money, the company had nothing to offer me at all. Worse, I had nothing to offer it. No one at the company was interested in what I was doing or what I was saying.

But although I realized that going to Embassy had been a mistake, I did not regret having left Goldcrest. In fact, I did not really miss Goldcrest at all. I missed it even less when I heard from Dickie, and from the Goldcrest people I met at festivals and markets, that things were far from happy under James Lee's leadership. I had heard about the threatened resignations of John Chambers and David Norris. I knew, of course, about Bill Gavin's departure, and I was aware of the low morale that was said to be engulfing the company. But, by and large, I made it my business not to pry. I wished them well, but it was nothing to do with me.

Ilott: On the contrary, according to Attenborough, in their discussions on the set of *A Chorus Line*, Eberts constantly asked about Goldcrest. In those conversations, too, Attenborough made no secret of the fact that, in his opinion, Eberts, who was so clearly unhappy at Embassy, should come back to Holland Street.

'I believed that Goldcrest was going down the drain without him,' Attenborough says. 'I believed that the situation that was materializing – of James taking more and more control in areas where he was ill equipped – was disastrous. And I never stopped saying to Jake, "Look, you'll have to come back sometime if Goldcrest is to survive." And I am sure he had a belief that one day he would come back.'

As long as Attenborough could discern, or sustain, Eberts's warmth for Goldcrest, then so long would Eberts remain the King Across the Water: a potent figure, of whom Lee, for one, was very much aware.

There was no plan that Eberts should return, still less a plot. It was just an idea. Whether anything more would come of it would depend on developments within Embassy as well as within Goldcrest. As far as the latter was concerned, the main event was Sandy Lieberson's production programme.

Chapter Thirty-three
Plugging the Gaps

Ilott: Lieberson's attempts to put together a production programme were hampered by the continuing deterioration in his relationship with Lee. We know that Lee had all along been eager to be involved in production decisions, but there was, in theory at least, a clear-cut division of labour between the two men. Lieberson's job was to attach scripts, casts, crews and budgets to those projects that he felt were worth putting forward as opportunities for investment. Lee's job was to marshall all the relevant information from his sales, legal and financial departments in order to arrive at an informed decision about whether or not such investments should be approved. The criteria by which Lieberson made his decisions were mainly creative: was it the right subject, the right cast, the right director, the right script? The criteria by which Lee made his decisions were mainly to do with business, embracing such considerations as cash flow, management of risk, sales forecasts, overall balance of the production programme and the needs of the distribution schedule.

In the film business, of course, it is not possible to have things as simple as that. Lieberson's creative choices were heavily dependent on his commercial judgement. By the same token, Lee, for all that he would have preferred movies to conform to predetermined and rigorous investment criteria, knew that he was operating in a hit-and-miss business; one that required him, at some point, to set his plans and projections to one side, stick his neck out and take risks on the basis of nothing more than a strong feeling for the projects in question.

Thus, even in the best of circumstances, Lieberson's and Lee's judgements were bound to overlap. Given the growing unease between the two men, and given Lee's tendency to trespass too readily on Lieberson's areas of responsibility, this could only cause unhappiness.

The scale of Lee's ambition and, hence, of Lieberson's task, can be gauged by a minute from the board meeting of 18 June 1984, in which it was noted that, on the basis of a capital turnover cycle of eighteen months, and with up to £50 million available for investment, made up of £33 million share capital and £15 million loan finance (Lee was already planning to supplement the Midland Bank's £10 million credit facility), 'the group might produce turnover of £35 million per annum by 1986, and, assuming a reasonable increase in the overall gross margin, pre-tax profits of £10 million in that year'. For comparison, turnover in 1983 amounted to £12 million and projected turnover in 1984 was £16 million. Lieberson, in other words, was being asked to produce a programme that would more than triple Goldcrest's current level of operations.

Although Lieberson and Lee were committed to investing only in projects that had been developed in-house, the gaps in the distribution schedule were so alarming that it was decided, as an interim measure, to pick up projects from other sources that were already in, or about to go into, production. *Dance With a Stranger*, a low-budget, period drama, was acquired for this reason.

As a creative package, *Dance With a Stranger* had had nothing to do with Lieberson or Goldcrest at all. The work had all been done by producer Roger Randall-Cutler, writer Shelagh Delaney and director Mike Newell. In fact, Goldcrest did not even invest its money – £253,000 in exchange for worldwide distribution rights and a 12 per cent equity interest – until the film had started shooting, and Randall-Cutler has bitter memories of the toing-and-froing that attended Goldcrest's decision to invest. (The picture had at first been rejected, and there was considerable opposition amongst the Goldcrest management even to the relatively modest commitment that was eventually made.) Randall-Cutler's frustrations were as nothing, however, by comparison with the difficulties that were encountered in bringing most of the other projects to fruition.

Lieberson was burdened by the weight of high expectations: Eberts, after all, had left an Oscar-laden legacy. He was also under intense pressure of time. Goldcrest, having turned down *The Mosquito Coast* and ditched *The Emerald Forest*, and having then been bogged down in the reorganization and fund-raising, had not properly functioned as a film company for seven months.

'There was nothing in the pipeline,' Lieberson recalls. 'There were forty or fifty employees. There were huge overheads. There was tremendous pressure from the board: "When is our next film project? When is our next film project?" So I had to get things started quickly. There was very little time to consider things carefully.'

In a helter-skelter seven months, from March to September, he read, rejected, sought out, was offered, pleaded for, grabbed, failed to grab, commissioned and decommissioned dozens of ideas, treatments, scripts and packages. He assembled a creative team and between them they managed to put some order into the otherwise unmanageable mass of paper that was piling up on his desk. The vast majority of ideas were quickly rejected as being uncommercial, unfilmable or simply uninteresting. It was among the rest that the real struggle took place.

By the end of March, *The Mission*, the South African musical *Dream Song*, the Alan Marshall/Marek Kanievska project *Horror Movie*, the series of low-budget comedies to be produced with the Samuel Goldwyn Company, *Absolute Beginners* and *Mandrake* were on the probables list; *Dance With a Stranger* and Richard Gere's *King David* had been turned down; the Paul Schrader project, *Mishima*, and the Tony Scott project, *Fire on the Mountain*, were under consideration. By the end of April, the decision on *Dance With a Stranger* had been reversed and a $6 million spoof, *Joan of Arc*, had joined the probables; Attenborough's long-cherished *Tom Paine* project was in limbo; *Falling in Love* and *Witness* had both been offered by Paramount and were under consideration. In May, Attenborough's new South African project *Biko: Asking for Trouble (Cry Freedom)*, and an idea introduced by Lieberson himself, *Rita, Sue and Bob Too*, as well as the proposed film version of J. P. Donleavy's *The Ginger Man*, joined the probables; three low-budget films from David Puttnam, *The Frog Prince*, *Knights and Emeralds* and *Mr Love*, were turned down, as were *Falling in Love* and *Witness*; Ridley Scott's *Legend*, Peter Yates's *Eleni* and Franco Zeffirelli's *Toscanini* were under consideration. In June, the decision to reject the three Puttnam films was reversed; it looked as if script and financial problems would force *Tom Paine* and *Absolute Beginners* out of contention; *Eleni* and yet another Puttnam project, *Defence of the Realm*, were rejected; a possible Al Pacino vehicle, *Crystal Clear*, was under consideration. In July, *The Mission*, *Horror Movie* and *Mandrake* were given top priority; new projects – *The Lightship*, *Toys*, *Trojans* and *Doctor Slaughter* – were under consideration; *Toscanini* and *Crystal Clear* were withdrawn. In September, a new Hugh Hudson–Irwin Winkler project, *Revolution*, was added to the list of probables, and an investment in Martin Rosen's *Fifteen (Smooth Talk)*, supported by James Lee, was approved.

Each new selection of probables was subjected to the scrutiny of John Chambers and Guy East: the former to calculate the impact on cash flow and borrowing requirements, the latter to attach to each project a forecast of likely sales revenue.

Even when he had selected the projects that he liked, Lieberson was hostage to the simple unpredictability of the development process itself: *Mandrake*, *Horror Movie*, *Joan of Arc* and *Tom Paine* were among those feature-film projects the creative problems of which were never to be resolved, either because they were intractable or because Goldcrest ran out of time; while *Revolution, The Mission* and *Absolute Beginners* all changed dramatically in the period between Goldcrest's first commitment and the start of shooting.

'Don't forget, too, they wanted to make British films,' continues Lieberson. 'It wasn't as if I could dash out and get American movies as such. This was a British company, and it was very clear – this was a directive from the board – that we were there to make British movies. There was nothing to say we couldn't have an American director, or an Italian, or something like that, but essentially they [the films] had to be British. I had a number of approaches from American directors, producers, writers and agents, all anxious to work with us, but in most cases I told them, "Look, we are trying to get a programme of British-based films going. The future will be the future." '

A further constraint was that Lieberson was bound to accommodate the family of producers and directors that Eberts had gathered under the wing of the company. Between these film-makers and Goldcrest there had once existed a genuine sense of partnership: if Bill Gavin is to be believed, Alan Marshall, David Puttnam, Peter Yates et al. 'would have died rather than go over budget and let Goldcrest down'. But the fine feelings had quickly begun to wane after Eberts's departure. John Boorman, for example, was unlikely to want to work with the company again. Alan Marshall had *Horror Movie* in development, but his other project, *Birdy*, to be made with Alan Parker, was never approved. (It was later made with Tri-Star.) Peter Yates found *Eleni* rejected. (He eventually found backing at CBS Theatrical Films.)

Then there was Attenborough, not only the most senior film-maker associated with the company, but, in money terms, by far and away the most successful. Attenborough was, and is, very close to Eberts; Lieberson, on the other hand, he hardly knew. As for Lee, he did not get on with him at all: there was, he says, 'no rapport' between them. Neither *Tom Paine* nor *Cry Freedom* was to reach fruition at Goldcrest. Indeed, Attenborough, although he served Goldcrest loyally through all its subsequent crises, was never to make another film for the company.

Even Lee's mentor, David Puttnam, in whom Lieberson professes to have had 'sublime confidence', was soon to find it necessary to take his rejected projects elsewhere. Puttnam knew that he could rely on Goldcrest's backing for *The Mission*, even if formal commitment depended on the participation of Warner Bros., or, if Warners turned it down, on the participation of another major studio. (Tri-Star, introduced to the project by Ghia, was still keen.) The same, however, could not be said for the two upgraded *First Love* films, *The Frog Prince* and *Mr Love*, and a third low-budget picture, *Knights and Emeralds*, about which Lieberson and Lee were at best lukewarm and to which the rest of the management was definitely opposed.

The three low-budget films had first been proposed as a package for investment in May. By that time, John Chambers had completed a profitability study of Goldcrest's low-budget investments, in the light of which it appeared that these three projects had no hope of recouping their costs. They were not accepted. But they were not rejected either. As David Norris recalls, Goldcrest 'prevaricated'.

'David [Puttnam] was so upset that he said, "Look, EMI always want to do films with me – I'll take them off there," ' Norris recalls. 'So we said, "Fine, let's see if we can do it together with EMI." So Gary Dartnall [head of Thorn EMI's Screen Entertainment division, TESE], who wanted to work with Puttnam, and would have moved heaven and earth to have done these films, got his boys to do their numbers. And John Reiss [TESE's finance director] came to see me and said, "Look, these numbers don't add up." I said, "I didn't expect them to add up for you, because they didn't add up for us." He sat there trying to make them work, even to the extent that Thorn EMI were prepared to do, as it were, an internal tax deal – i.e. factor into the arrangement the capital allowance benefit that they, inside the Thorn EMI group, could take. But even allowing for that, which actually made quite a generous contribution to the cost, about 20 per cent, it still didn't make sense on their sales predictions, which were totally in line with Guy East's.'

In fact, only two of the films, *Mr Love* and *Knights and Emeralds*, were considered by EMI. When these were rejected, in June, Lee put to the management meeting the options that remained: Goldcrest could (a) abandon them; (b) leave them on the shelf until new sources of finance were available; (c) have them revert to the status of television films in the hope that they could be financed that way; or (d) 'breach all Goldcrest standard production finance criteria' and put them into production 'in the knowledge that a loss was likely'. The meeting voted for the third option: to re-format the pictures as television films.

The third film, *The Frog Prince*, was deemed, at that same meeting, to have 'no greater appeal' than the others. But *The Frog Prince* was already under consideration by Warner Bros., and it seems that Puttnam later managed to elicit Goldcrest's agreement that a commitment might be made to finance all three films if Warner Bros. (who, after all, had the right of first look at Puttnam's feature projects) were to come in as a partner. According to Norris, the Goldcrest management went along with this only because 'there was strong optimism that Warners would turn it down'.

Puttnam then primed Warners, presenting the three-film package as the start of a cut-price research-and-development operation, much as he had sold the original *First Loves* idea to Goldcrest and Channel 4: if the comparatively low cost of the films were to be shared between Warners and Goldcrest, and if the writers and directors involved agreed to option their future services to Enigma, Warners and Goldcrest, then, at minimal risk, the partners would have access to a host of new talent, amongst which there might be, somewhere down the line, one or two money-making film-makers. 'I liked the concept a lot,' recalls Warners chief, Terry Semel. 'We felt that if we did four or five of them, then, if we had one winner out of that four or five, we would cover the total investment and maybe we would inherit two or three good writers and two or three good film-makers.'

Semel and his team still had their doubts about the scripts in question, however, and it would appear that they came to much the same conclusion as Goldcrest had: only if their transatlantic partner were prepared to put up a substantial share of the cost would they go ahead. Thus, when Lieberson flew out to talk to Semel in June, and said, in effect, 'We'll do them if you'll do them', both sides found themselves, somewhat to their surprise, committed. According to Norris, nobody at Goldcrest had the slightest enthusiasm for the three films, and the fact that the commitment was made in this way was, in his view, more than an error of judgement: it was a dereliction of fiduciary duty.

'It was a deal agreed out of corporate cowardice,' he says. 'A real disgrace to us all collectively . . . a bigger shame, from the point of view of corporate and individual behaviour, then *Revolution*, which at least people did feel strongly and passionately about, for or against, and which was a genuine error rather than a political error . . . The management committee took a vote around the room, and John [Chambers] and I said no, and everyone else said, "Well, if I'm forced to make a decision I'll go along with everyone else", or whatever. But John and I said no because we'd done the numbers and they didn't stack up . . . both Warners and Goldcrest corporately shirked saying no to David.'

Mr Love, in which Goldcrest invested £486,000, went into production in July. *The Frog Prince*, in which Goldcrest invested £896,000, started shooting in September. *Knights and Emeralds*, in which Goldcrest invested £1.1 million, started in May 1985. Apart from the general lack of enthusiasm for the scripts and the doubts about their commercial viability (Lieberson and Lee hoped that at least one of them would be a hit, but they do not seem to have had any clear idea of which one it was likely to be), there was a further factor that, had they known it, would have warned Goldcrest off the pictures: throughout the period in question – July 1984 when *Mr Love* started, to July 1985 when *Knights and Emeralds* wrapped – David Puttnam was preoccupied with the release of *The Killing Fields* and the production of *The Mission*. He did not have time personally to oversee the three small films as well. As Terry Semel now realizes, this was a major defect in what might otherwise have been a viable scheme.

'What a film needs more than anything else, in addition to financing, is an experienced person to really be there all the time, to really help them [the young film-makers] with their projects and to make sure that what they are doing has a hope of being commercial,' he says. '[But] it turned out to be one of the younger people in [David's] company who was spending time with those film-makers. Now what you can't do is take a bright young person who works in your company and put them in charge of all these other bright young people, because, to some degree, it's the blind leading the blind.

'We didn't think we could lose very much,' Semel concludes. 'But we were wrong. I don't think any of them turned out to be commercial in the UK [in fact, the three films lost Goldcrest £1.4 million], and they certainly didn't in America.'

Warner Bros.' role in the decision to invest in these three films serves to illustrate a further constraint on Lieberson's freedom of choice in devising a production programme: for all that there was now a large sum of money in the bank, Goldcrest still relied on partners, either co-financiers who shared the equity or distributors who put up advances prior to production. The rule was simple: no partner, no picture. But once Goldcrest did secure such a partner all major decisions concerning budget, casting and script had to be made jointly, an exercise that was fraught with conflict and compromise. Given the historically close relationship between Warner Bros. and Goldcrest, and, even more, the first-look contractual bond between Warners and Puttnam, it was inevitable that Warners would be Goldcrest's principal partner and that Warners' choices would have a considerable influence on the eventual shape of Goldcrest's production programme. It is in this light that the personal relationships between Semel and Lieberson and, much more importantly, between Semel and Lee, were to prove of crucial significance.

In the second week of June 1984, Lee's deputy, Don Cruickshank, resigned. He had had two areas of responsibility at Goldcrest: cable television and the preparations for the fund-raising. The cable venture, the Television Entertainment Group (TEG), formed in May 1983 in partnership with CBS, Columbia, HBO and 20th Century–Fox, had been launched in the expectation that television in Britain would be transformed by cable the way it had in America. The British government, thinking the same, had awarded franchises to cable operators in a number of key urban areas. TEG was to supply these with a subscription-based movie channel. It had quickly become apparent, however, that introducing cable to Britain was not going to be an easy matter. In the first place, the high cost of laying the cables meant that the plans of many franchise-holders never got further than the drawing board. In the second place, the British public showed no great interest in cable services: they were, by and large, happy with what was available on the existing television channels. The one area in which there were calls for greater choice was movies, but home video, which in the UK reached a greater proportion of television homes than anywhere else in the world, was already well ahead of cable in meeting this demand.

With cost projections rising and sales forecasts falling, the TEG partners had, in March 1984, joined forces with their erstwhile rivals, Thorn EMI, Viacom and Warner Bros., to form Premiere. Where Goldcrest had been a major player in TEG, and Cruickshank's had been a leading voice, the company was a distinctly junior partner in the new consortium. Cruickshank's role was correspondingly diminished. By the summer of 1984 it was clear not only that there was no work to occupy him at Premiere but that Premiere itself was doomed to failure.

As for the fund-raising, Cruickshank's efforts came to an end with the publication of the prospectus in April. Thus, by May 1984, he was left with no real role to play – proving, if proof were needed, that, despite Lee's high hopes, there had never been a long-term role for him at Goldcrest at all. Indeed, his importation into the hierarchy had served only to cause enormous upset, confusion and expense.

Richard Branson, head of the music, video and film group, Virgin, was at that time looking for a managing director who would prepare his company for public flotation. Branson approached Puttnam, who, after consultation with Norris and Chambers, recommended Cruickshank. It was too good an opportunity for Cruickshank to refuse.

Cruickshank's loss was a considerable blow to Lee, not only because he was a friend and a like-minded colleague but because the Goldcrest that Lee had dreamed about was a Goldcrest with Cruickshank in it. Eberts had gone, Gavin had gone, now Cruickshank had gone and Clegg was going. Norris and Chambers had questioned Lee's leadership and Lieberson wasn't talking to him. This was not at all the picture that he had had in mind when he had made the bold decision to leave Pearson ten months before.

Chapter Thirty-four

Relations with Warners

'These guys, most of them have learned to keep all their teeth in their mouths; you know, they are pretty good business people. And they have an arrogance of power that is very difficult and very seductive to outsiders. Outsiders think they are getting inside, only to find that they never get inside.' – Sam Goldwyn Jnr., on the heads of studios

Ilott: In the geography of the California film industry, Burbank, Culver City, Universal City, Century City and Hollywood are satellite work stations around the central residential and recreational hub of Beverly Hills. At the heart of each of these work stations is a studio: Fox, Universal, Paramount, what used to be MGM, Disney, Columbia and Warner Bros. Surrounding them, often at a considerable distance, are further, peripheral offices, housing the studios' ancillary divisions.

At the heart of Burbank are the Burbank Studios, until recently home to both Warner Bros. and Columbia Pictures. While Columbia was housed at the back of the lot in sleek modern offices of glass and steel, Warner Bros. had its headquarters in a low, old-fashioned, tile-roofed building by the gatehouse. In the mid-1980s, the interior of this building was furnished and decorated in the authentic style of the movies: 1930s art deco. Upstairs, through double doors, beyond both outer and inner reception areas, were two, interconnecting, offices: straight ahead, that of the chairman and chief executive of the studio, Bob Daly; on the left that of the president and chief operating officer, Terry Semel.

Semel's office is large, cool and sophisticated, with marble surfaces, chrome-and-glass furniture, pastel shades and recessed lights. It is a workroom: clean, formal and efficient, but at the same time comfortable enough for his supplicants, the writers, directors and producers hoping for a green light, to feel at ease. Like most modern executives, and like everybody in the film industry, Semel works mainly on the telephone. Incoming calls are intercepted and noted by his secretary, and his last task each day is to go through the log, indicating which calls are to be answered and in what order; which are to be put through should they call again; which are to be delegated to one of his lieutenants; and which are to be left on the list to see whether they will rise up in the order of priorities or sink down to the category of those which are of insufficient importance to warrant personal attention. Semel's incoming telephone log normally covers two or three weeks and details some hundreds of calls, several dozen of which are in the high-priority categories. Among them, in the mid-1980s, were all the calls from Goldcrest.

The relationship with Goldcrest was for a number of years the most important independent production relationship that Warner Bros. had. Likewise, Warner Bros. was, by 1984, the most important of all Goldcrest's partners in Hollywood, taking the place once occupied by Columbia.

Warners and Goldcrest first met via David Puttnam, whose *Chariots of Fire* was acquired for North America by The Ladd Company, which at that time distributed all its films through Warner Bros. So impressed were they by this film that Warners quickly signed development deals with both Puttnam and the director Hugh Hudson. The studio subsequently either co-financed or acquired the rights to three Puttnam projects, *Local Hero*, *The Killing Fields* and *Cal*, as well as to Hudson's Tarzan epic, *Greystoke*.

Through Puttnam and Eberts, with whom Semel quickly developed a good rapport, Warner Bros. was able to keep abreast of developments in the British industry. The favourable exchange rate, the tax breaks and a long-established levy system that put money from the box office directly into the pockets of producers of British-made films, as well as the emergence of successive crops of new talent from television and commercials, made Britain an attractive production base throughout the late 1970s and early 1980s. Goldcrest itself, of course, had played a large part in this.

'In effect, David Puttnam as a producer became our eyes and ears in Europe,' explains Semel. 'And in looking upon Goldcrest as an entity and David as an individual – and I think one would assume, as later became the case, that they would also relate to each other in various ways – then for us it was an opportunity to get involved in two, three or four movies a year that really had their origins in Europe. And for us to be exposed to the up-and-coming film-makers, many of whom we had never heard of at that point in time: whether it turned out to be Roland Joffe on *The Killing Fields*, or Hugh Hudson on *Chariots of Fire*, or Bill Forsyth on *Local Hero*. And the combination of that with what Goldcrest's goals were – to develop these projects and help bring them to script stage and then look outside for either partnership financing and/or partnership distribution – was perfect for us. We were able to allow them to exercise their expertise as to what they felt would work in Europe, and we would look at it to see if it had any chance of working in America, and/or go forward with them in an even bigger partnership that included most of the world.'

According to Semel, the original idea had been to deal with 'less costly films', there being at that time a growing market in America for low-budget, art-house and specialist movies.

'But, hand in hand with that,' he continues, 'we had agreed from the beginning that, since we had a big appetite, then when they were excited with something that would be more costly they should not shy away. We could work out a partnership arrangement where we would pick up a portion, or, depending on the circumstances, a lot of the [additional] negative financing.'

None of this was enshrined in a formal contract between the companies, nor, as Semel explains, was any such contract thought to be necessary: 'We had a handshake to say that whenever we needed help with financing or were looking to perhaps sell off European pieces, we would look to them, and, in turn, if they needed help they would look to us.'

This arrangement worked partly because there was a clear identity of interest between Goldcrest and Warner Bros., but mainly because the individuals involved, especially Semel and Eberts, enjoyed exceptionally good personal relationships.

'Jake was very easy and very accessible to talk with,' notes Semel. 'It was like one-stop shopping between Jake and myself. One of us was able to pick up the phone and say, "I have a script that I really think you should read", and the other one would read it and by the next Monday or so call back and say, "I have a real interest." And you'd say, "Let's try a budget", or "I have a budget – it's going to cost that; how much would you like to spend?" And then we would, within the course of that conversation, shape a deal that would accommodate how much either they felt like spending or we felt like spending, in terms of who kept which rights.

'And we helped each other. Jake helped us with some production problems in Europe and also European financing and . . . when they needed introductions to American television and access to other people in America, when we weren't involved, then we in turn helped them. So it was a wonderful working relationship, and we were very excited about it.'

Eberts's departure from Goldcrest in 1983 had caused Semel no surprise: 'I always knew that Jake was earning at best 25 per cent of what a comparable executive in our company would expect, [so] there was no question that he would probably not be long-term at that company.'

Nor had it caused him anxiety. He looked forward to establishing a good relationship with Lieberson – 'Sandy we had known for many years and liked' – and, more especially, since 'at the end of the day, James was calling the shots', with Lee.

'I thought that James Lee, who I had met a number of times before, was a very intelligent man, and seemed to be a very thoughtful and very smart person,' says Semel. 'And I thought that, although he had a lot to learn, that by surrounding himself with the appropriate people and being a good executive, it would probably work out almost as well, or as well, as it had with Jake.'

Unfortunately, and notwithstanding the genuine desire on both sides to make the new partnership work, it didn't. This failure is entirely attributable to the inability of Lee and Semel to establish a rapport.

'You very rarely think, and I never do with big companies, that one person could make the difference,' comments Semel. '[But] in Goldcrest's case, to us it made a dramatic difference: it was night and day, just night and day. I think that James had the ability to learn but chose not to take the time to learn. Rather he plunged straight in and decided what it was he was going to change. It was very obvious that we could not deal the way we used to deal. The one-on-one relations, the ease of picking up the phone and saying, "Please read this", had clearly changed.'

Not only was their personal relationship lacking, but there was a gulf of experience and knowledge, of both the business and creative aspects of film-making, between Semel and Lee that could not easily be bridged. Semel had spent his adult life working his way up the industry; Lee had come in straight at the top.

On the creative side, says Semel, 'it was difficult because somebody who doesn't spend at least a few years working on screenplays and working with talent should probably come into it a bit more gradually and bring a few executives with him. It was quite obvious from the outset that James was attending script meetings one on one with the directors and the writers and was being very adamant about his point of view. In my own case, I probably stayed as an active participant, or observer, for three, four or five years before I let my presence be deeply felt in those meetings; until I really felt that I knew what I was talking about. But he [Lee] almost eliminated the training period and went immediately to the decisions.'

On the business side, Semel says, 'the ease with which Jake and I would turn to each other and say, "Fine, if you would like another dollar, great, can I have another country?", was almost totally out of the question when dealing with James. I really thought a lot of it was James's uncertainty about his own knowledge of exactly what was going on. And rather than saying, "Let me go back and discuss that with some of my people", which, frankly, even after twelve years helping to run Warner Bros., I still do. I'll often say, "Excuse me, that's not my expertise. I'll come back to you with an opinion." James made decisions right there on the spot. And I'm not sure that they were often the right decisions. You can be wrong even with a lot of experience, as we all know, but sometimes experience is a good teacher.

'So he had a lot to grasp all at once in terms of "This is how we deal with the business side of it, and this is how we deal with the creative side". He kind of tackled them all at the same time.'

Semel recalls that their first meetings, in the early summer of 1984, were 'very rocky meetings, very difficult meetings. I'm sure they were difficult from both sides.' So fraught were they, in fact, that, according to Semel, Warners 'came very close to not making any deals' at all with the new regime at Goldcrest. Matters were not helped by the fact that Semel was well aware that Lieberson and Lee, 'although they were still coming here first', were 'busy kind of shopping the whole marketplace, entertaining other companies here in America that they could deal with at the same time'.

In all, seven films were offered to Warner Bros. by Goldcrest in 1984. The first three comprised the Puttnam package of low-budget films, to which Warners made a commitment in June. The fourth was *The Mission*.

The Mission tells the story of Gabriel, an eighteenth-century Jesuit missionary who establishes an Indian Christian community in the South American jungle. Gabriel is joined by a former slave-trader, Mendoza, who is full of remorse, and is hence reformed, after killing his own brother in a duel. The two unlikely companions defend their commune, and their Indian converts, from attack by marauding Spaniards and Portuguese, for whom the mission is no more than an obstacle in the path of their quest for plunder and a source of human bodies for the slave trade.

'We were knee deep in *The Mission*, but we were at real loggerheads on how to do it and how to make it fly,' Semel recalls. 'We read it with the original intent that we, Warner Bros., probably could have financed the whole world, or a lot of it. But we were worried and concerned that it had a bleak ending. It's very rare that movies become commercial movies when the stars in the movies are all killed. And we were concerned that not only were the stars all killed, or dying, but we weren't really sure exactly what they had accomplished by the time they died. You know, "What new hope have you brought to the world, and how have you changed the world, as a result of bringing us on this two-hour journey?" We wished it had an ending more like *The Killing Fields*, where the two guys hugged and embraced. Now that ending was not in the original screenplay of *The Killing Fields*. That came about because, with Roland [Joffe] and David [Puttnam] and Jake, we talked and talked and talked and went for a more upbeat ending, to make it more emotional and more exciting.

'Roland and David, probably correctly, both felt that they could not do that with the ending of *The Mission*, that they wanted to be true to the screenplay and to the story. We were not convinced. We felt that it wasn't exactly a story that everybody knew the ending of, it wasn't a famous book, so who's going to know? But they had good reasons as to why they weren't going to change it. They would consider giving it a more moral touch . . . It didn't basically change the story, but we hoped that it would be a more moral ending: you know, when the bishop comes back on the screen and talks. That was not in the original screenplay.'

The fifth project to be offered was *Absolute Beginners*, the British musical that Lieberson had introduced at the special management conference in March. The film has two main characters but no strong storyline. Instead it attempts to re-create, in a series of dramatic scenes and musical sequences, the atmosphere of London in the 1950s.

'At the time it had a fairly high budget and we thought, for the cost, that it was very different, very unusual and probably not very commercial for America,' says Semel. 'By and large musicals *per se* are a bit difficult. Not that it hasn't been tried in recent years, but whether it was *Flashdance* or *Footloose* or any of the young people's musicals, they were basically made at very low cost. This was much more expensive and we felt it was much more of a British musical than a worldwide musical . . . The movies that Goldcrest had put their money into, with the exception of the small movies that David Puttnam helped bring about, had been significant, worldwide films. Whether it was *Gandhi*, or *Chariots*, they were very emotional, very dramatic and very international subject matters. This was a much riskier try.'

Warner Bros. turned it down.

The sixth project was Alan Marshall's and Marek Kanievska's *Horror Movie*. The script, by Stephen Volk, attempts to involve the real cinema audience in a horrific story about a cinema audience watching a horror movie that envelops them in horror.

'They were very excited about it, thought it was fantastic,' Semel recalls. 'We thought it was an awful idea for a movie and didn't want any part of it. None of us saw it as a commercial selection.

'When you make a horror movie you only make it for one reason and that is to see how commercial it can be. They don't win awards, they don't have to be greatly executed, they just have to be scary and exciting. This was neither.'

The seventh project was *Revolution*.

Chapter Thirty-five

Revolution

Ilott: The idea of a father–son love story set in the American War of Independence came to producer Irwin Winkler while working on his ill-fated epic of American heroism, *The Right Stuff*. Winkler is one of the most successful, and certainly one of the most wealthy, producers in Hollywood, with more than thirty films, from *Raging Bull* to *Rocky*, to his credit. Most of these were made with his former partner Bob Chartoff. Although that partnership is now dissolved, the two men still share a nondescript, two-storey office building in Culver City, opposite what used to be the MGM studios. Above the entrance a large sign bears the legend 'Chartoff–Winkler Productions'. Inside, the offices are comfortable rather than grand, and the atmosphere is efficient rather than hectic. Framed posters, of *Rocky, Raging Bull, Round Midnight* and other Winkler films, fill the walls. Winkler's personal office is light, spacious, white-walled and pine-floored. There is no macho leather or mahogany, and there are no executive toys. Winkler himself is neat, almost dapper, and quietly spoken. In Hollywood, he is, by all accounts, a well-liked, sociable figure and he is said to be especially popular with writers and directors. He is also known for his expensive tastes: always flying Concorde across the Atlantic; insisting that a personal chef be provided on location; staying only in the most luxurious hotels. He has a garage full of expensive cars and the walls of his home are hung with expensive paintings.

His large desk is not cluttered, his large desk-diary is not full. He has no need for a telephone log. He sets his own agenda and appears to conduct his business life at a measured pace. In this manner he has made, on average, three films every two years for the last two decades.

Although always credited as producer or co-producer, Winkler's real strengths are in developing and packaging: he invariably has three or four scripts in hand, he is good with ideas and he knows how to treat talent. He is not noted, however, for his hands-on production skills. As Terry Semel observes, Winkler is not 'the kind of person you normally look to to be on top of your budget'. Where he has worked with 'responsible' directors, like Martin Scorsese, his practical, on-the-set shortcomings have been of no consequence. Where he has worked with 'wayward' directors, like Phil Kaufman on *The Right Stuff*, the results have been disastrous.

Two observations relevant to the Goldcrest story can be drawn from this description of Winkler. The first is a general one: a rich, relaxed, hugely successful Hollywood producer who has expensive tastes and a very laid-back attitude to the details of production, was not the kind of person likely to command respect among the generally puritanical, workaholic executives of Goldcrest. Winkler was, in Chambers's dismissive description, 'a typical Hollywood front-man producer'. The second observation is more specific: Winkler's chosen director for *Revolution*, Hugh Hudson, although very talented, can be as wayward as they come and, given the scale of the movie in question, their proposed collaboration was a cause for concern.

Winkler originally conceived his story as being about a common man. After *The Right Stuff*, he says, 'I'd had enough of famous historical figures in my life for a while'. He chose the setting of the American Revolution because 'there had never really been a film about the American Revolution since D. W. Griffith's time. It seemed a good subject to go after.'

He took the idea to Warner Bros., with whom he had a development deal, and they agreed to finance a script. However, the screenplay handed in by writer Robert Dillon did not impress Terry Semel enough for him to want to finance it, and the project was put into turnaround. Winkler, having higher hopes, bought back the property himself. The screenplay, meanwhile, had landed on Hugh Hudson's desk in England.

Hudson, who was looking for a project to follow *Greystoke*, was attracted by the subject matter, an anti-colonial war that for him held obvious parallels with Vietnam, and by the writer's ground-level, grassroots approach. He called Winkler and, shortly after the Cannes Film Festival in 1984, they met and agreed to collaborate. Throughout the summer, Winkler went from studio to studio looking for finance, but without success. Hudson suggested that he call Sandy Lieberson at Goldcrest.

'I have known Sandy for twenty-five years, so I thought, "Well, why not?" ' Winkler recalls. 'We also thought that the way we could make the picture cheaper was to make it in England. [The exchange rate by this time was down to £1:$1.30. Americans got huge value for their dollars in the UK.] So it all kind of fitted in: Goldcrest seemed to be the right place for it.'

Hudson sent a copy of the script to Lieberson at the end of July. Lieberson was bowled over.

'I thought it was wonderfully written,' he says. 'It had a real sort of scale to it. It was romantic. It had a strong narrative. It had a central hero. It was about the American Revolution. It didn't have to be expensive. It could be done in England. We had all the locations here. It was a perfect opportunity, as I saw it, to make a British film in England with international potential.'

Revolution was attractive for another reason. In Lieberson's battle to put together a production programme, there were already worries about the number of low-budget films that were pushing their way to the top of the list. *Dance With a Stranger, Dream Song*, the Goldwyn comedies, the three upgraded Puttnam films, Lieberson's own project, *Rita Sue and Bob Too, Smooth Talk*, a new project from the *Cal* creative team, *Lamb*, and a new drama project, *The Lightship*, were all strong contenders. The problem with them was that, although their costs might be modest, so was their audience appeal. It was not enough to make £108,000 profit on an investment of £253,000, as Goldcrest was to do with *Dance With a Stranger*; it would take twenty-five such films, and for every one of them to be as successful, just to cover Goldcrest's £2.7 million annual overhead. What was needed was a couple of films of the stature of *Gandhi* or *The Killing Fields. Revolution* was of that scale.

Amanda Schiff, a member of the development team working with Lieberson, was one of the first to read the 108-page screenplay. It told the story of Ned Dobb and his father, Tom, who become embroiled, more or less accidentally, in the fight against the British in 1776. Tom meets and makes love to Daisy, a committed revolutionary. They fall out. Ned is taken away by British troops and Tom sets out to rescue him. Various battles and adventures follow, including a sojourn with Indians who nurse Ned's wounds. Tom rescues Ned and meets Daisy again, but they are no sooner reconciled than Daisy, in the thick of the fighting, is shot. In the confusion it is impossible for Tom to know whether she is alive or dead. Five or six years later, after the war is over, Tom meets her again by chance.

Schiff filed the following report.

From: Amanda Schiff

To: Sandy Lieberson

Re: REVOLUTION by Robert Dillon
submitted by Hugh Hudson   Date: 7 August 1984

The writer has got very hung up on the sound of the words, and it makes most of it read like prose – sometimes it's very poetic, others it becomes sentimental, hyperbolic and pretentious. There is a strong documentary feel about the script – there's very little *real* drama, it's mainly background. It seems like a cross section through a moment in history – there is no sense of what comes before or after, either in the characters' lives or the history.

I couldn't grasp what exactly was propelling the central characters through the narrative. It resembles an eighteenth century picaresque novel by Smollett or Defoe – but without the satire or irony.

What I found most disturbing of all was the lack of resonance. It's halfway between the epic and the intimate, but doesn't relate one to the other. There is no use of counterpoint or metaphor. NED and TOM are caught up in the moment, and it would be nice to see some significance about their actions or destinies.

The screenplay is written at a distance – there is no involvement with the characters. TOM and NED don't really change – other than (unsurprisingly) they become stronger, fitter, leaner, and more proficient soldiers. I found all the accidental meetings between father and son, and the lovers of each, too hard to swallow.

I liked the sequence of TOM rescuing NED and MERLE, and TONTI and the Hurons taking care of them in the Hogan – it had a lyrical, Thoreauesque feel to it which is so American.

The fighting scenes are always doing the same thing each time they occur – providing blood, thunder and excitement in lieu of real drama, and again the documentary interest in how war was fought in Olden Times. There is too much room for visual excess in this screenplay – fogs rolling across rivers, antique houses, the epic squalor of New York (the glamour of the underworld!) and although it would all be undoubtedly stunning and lovely to admire, it diverts attention from the basic lack of narrative drive (as they say) in the story. This will be an expensive film and apart from appealing to American jingoism (no doubt a commercial element at the moment) it needs more steel in its structure to justify the expense. Apart from telling us the English were bastards and the Americans heroes, it doesn't answer a lot of questions I'd like to have known.

The following day, Goldcrest script reader Honor Borwick delivered a standard reader's report, establishing the period and dramatic category and summarizing the plot. She added the following comment:

This has the feeling to me of one of those children's pictorial history books. It's sort of a cross between a Walt Disney and World War 2 propaganda film. It left me really cold, and, however epically it was filmed, I just don't think it's gripping or exciting enough to draw the audiences. I *would* like us to do something with Hugh Hudson, but I don't think this is it.

Lieberson accepted that the script needed work, especially on the relationship between Daisy and Tom, but he felt that this was a matter that could easily be remedied. On Friday, 31 August, when Lee and other senior executives were back from their summer vacations, he circulated copies of the script. Reactions were mixed, at best.

'Some people had reservations about it,' admits Lieberson. 'Everybody read the script and had their opinion. Some people liked it. Some people thought this was wrong with it and some people thought that was wrong with it. So I mean everybody didn't kind of leap on their desks and say, "This is it." Certainly James Lee was very enthusiastic about it, [and] the sales people were. Hugh Hudson had just done *Chariots of Fire* and *Greystoke*. Irwin Winkler is a man with experience who has made some of the biggest grossing movies of all time. Anyway, they [Goldcrest] weren't dragged kicking and screaming into *Revolution*. Everybody was very excited about it.'

Lieberson does admit that he 'can't speak for John Chambers and David Norris. They may not have wanted to do it – I don't remember.' In fact, Norris was so much against it that he put his objections down in writing.

'Friday evening the script came round, which is something Sandy never did before or after, with a two-line memo saying, "This is the best script I have ever read. Would you please try and read it before Monday's meeting," ' Norris recalls. 'And I read the script and my memo said: "It is not the greatest script I have ever read, it is banal. I think the coincidental meetings of these two people are stretching the imagination beyond belief. Quite frankly I can't believe in their relationship, and the only thing that works for me is the father and son. As far as I am concerned it is something we shouldn't make." Period. Funnily enough I expressed that view quite strongly to James. I went into his room and said, "Look, James, I really think this is garbage, junk," and he actually agreed with me – privately.'

Chambers remembers reading the script and thinking, ' "Oh dear, I don't like this at all." And the first person I talked to was Guy East and I said, "God, I don't like this script," and he said, "Read it again." So I read it again, but I still didn't like it. There was no bloody story.'

Terry Clegg, who was coming to the end of his time at Goldcrest, only recalls a general 'lack of enthusiasm' for the project. 'The proposal for *Revolution* had come to management I think a few weeks before I left,' he says. 'And I remember when it was first mentioned at management level there was very non-committal feeling around the table. Nobody was particularly for it. It was just a proposal that had been put forward and it seemed quite interesting, no more than that.'

At the management meeting, it was stated that the project had a budget of £7.5 million ($10 million at the then exchange rate) below the line – i.e. not including the cost of the director, producer and leading actors – and that it was intended to star Sam Shepard. A quick decision was urged in view of the fact that the project already had a February 1985 start-date. (Given Goldcrest's urgent need for major movies, this was a significant attraction.) It was agreed that, while Goldcrest was well disposed towards the project, the final decision would await the outcome of further talks with Winkler and Hudson and an analysis of the sales estimates and cash-flow forecasts. The most important pre-condition, however, was that Goldcrest had to have a US partner. Warner Bros. was the first studio to be approached.

That they were not now being required to finance the entire picture certainly made *Revolution* much more attractive to Warners. But it was still not an easy sell. For one thing, Terry Semel had recently worked with Hudson on *Greystoke* and with Winkler on *The Right Stuff*, and neither experience was one that he would care to repeat.

'We realized that, while Hugh is a talented director and an intelligent man, we had had a hard time with the budget process on *Greystoke*, and had every reason to believe that, if nothing else, he was a perfectionist,' Semel explains. 'He was a guy who was not going to cut any corners, and not cut any corners particularly if he thought that it would in any way be a sacrifice on the part of the movie. I don't mean that other film-makers sacrifice their movies, but they will be more conscious of their budgetary obligations and will make compromises to stick to the budget. Hugh certainly didn't do that on *Greystoke* and we weren't quite sure he ever would do it again.

'Would we do a movie with Hugh Hudson, or would we have liked to be involved in a movie that Hugh was directing? Definitely. Would it be the right time in his career to believe he was going to bring the movie in on budget? There was no reason to expect that. We certainly wouldn't want to be the people responsible for where the budget would go in Hugh's hands. That was no secret from anyone anywhere in the world, certainly no one in England, because they had seen Terry Semel there once a week, or once a month, on *Greystoke*.'

Semel had no such qualms about Winkler. 'I like Irwin a lot; he is a good friend. We have worked together for a long time. He is a good mediator. He is a different kind of man certainly than a David Puttnam. In David's eyes he's maybe a lot worse, I don't know. In my eyes they are just totally different kinds of people. David is very straight and narrow, and that's great, because whether he's doing a movie or taking your baby to the supermarket he will do it meticulously and you can sleep well at night. David would be upset that Irwin would take a first-class hotel room, while he is pinching pennies to save money for a movie. David would make sure everything was tight, and to get a movie made he would cut his own salary, and that is all very admirable. Irwin won't do any of those things, but that doesn't mean Irwin can't also deliver hit movies. He has and he will again.'

But one thing of which Semel was very much aware was that 'you wouldn't normally look to Irwin Winkler to be the line producer on a very expensive movie, because it is not his forte to be on top of production full time.'

Revolution, then, had a producer and a director neither of whom could be relied upon to keep the production on the rails. With this in mind, Goldcrest and Warners discussed the need for especially strict budgetary control, agreeing that an experienced line producer would have to be brought in from the start.

What is crucial to grasp at this point, however, is that the budget was Goldcrest's problem, not Warners'. Warners would put up a fixed sum in exchange for US distribution rights. It made no difference to them how much the film eventually cost.

What would make a difference to them was the quality of the product, and that, in Semel's view, depended on sorting out the problems in the script. For Warners had much the same view of Dillon's work as had Norris, Chambers, Borwick and Schiff.

'We wanted to be involved, and I wanted to be involved,' says Semel. 'But I really wanted us to continue working on the screenplay before we went too far down the line.'

From the outset, according to Semel, Warners had been interested in the American Revolution only 'as the backdrop, and in the foreground have an emotional, dramatic film about two relationships'. They did not want to 'get into a gory war, where people saw off their legs and shoot off their heads. We've seen it fifty times before and it doesn't make good entertainment. Put the war in the background, put the two relationships in the foreground. And when the father and son hug and go for it together, you cheer for them. And when the father and the woman fall in love, well, you feel romantic, you feel wonderful. And at the end have a real feeling of hope.'

The problem with Robert Dillon's original script, he says, was that at the end 'they returned to New York or wherever it was, and it was all blown up, it was devastated, it looked like the jungle and felt like shit. And the father was going to be on his own, and the war was over, and it was renegade time. And you said to yourself, "My God, why did I make this journey?" '

It was the perceived weaknesses in the script, and the likely cost – Winkler's first budget estimate, without a star, was $13 million (the figure was only later revised down to $10 million when it was proposed to shoot in England) – that had caused Warners to put the project into turnaround in the first place.

Hudson mailed off a revised version of the script, to both Goldcrest and Warners, in September. A meeting of all the parties was arranged, in Los Angeles, for the following week.

What happened next was, according to Semel, 'quite symbolic. It wasn't symbolic of someone not being nice or not being intelligent; it was symbolic of someone with a lack of experience, a lack of maturity.

'We had worked feverishly after reading the [revised] script. We were quite concerned about a lot of things in it and we had put together what I thought would be a really comprehensive list of storyboards and notes and things that absolutely desperately needed changing. Rather than Goldcrest doing [the same] and then coming to the meeting with us all – and I remember this quite clearly – they called Hugh Hudson and Irwin Winkler and congratulated them on the screenplay and told them that they thought it was excellent and that they were ready to go ahead.

'I was furious. I called James up and said, "Please – to begin with you are our partner. Why would you not talk to your partner first before you would talk to the film-makers? Second, you are absolutely wrong. The screenplay is nowhere near ready to start principal photography. It needs lots of work, a full rewrite. You can't even budget this screenplay because it's so poorly written in parts. At least give us the courtesy and advantage of understanding what our concerns are before you start to congratulate people." '

As far as Semel was concerned, the revised script 'was clearly not the movie we were going to make, not even the movie we were going to part-finance. James and I had one or two very right-on-the-nose conversations and I told him that if this is the screenplay he's financing, and this is the screenplay Goldcrest goes for, then we are out. And if we don't have the authority to sit in a meeting and tell Hugh Hudson to make the following changes, we are also out.'

Goldcrest was under no obligation to listen to Warners: the studio had been offered the picture, but as yet it had made no commitment. As Semel confirms, 'Goldcrest could have said, "Thank you very much, we like what we have, goodbye." ' But in the event, Lee 'apologized and said, "You're right, we shouldn't have done it that way." '

In fact, the opinion of the Warners team was that Hudson's revision was, in many respects, worse than the Dillon original.

'It was a mish-mash,' explains Semel. 'Certain areas had improved, certain areas had gone backward. It was actually a much bleaker look, a more severe look, at the American Revolution. Not that maybe it wasn't factually done – I'm not stating a case for that – but it certainly seemed a lot less entertaining. And there were aspects of the relationships in the revised screenplay that we read that were very disturbing. [In the original version] the girl ultimately ended up with the father at the end of the movie. [In the new version] she died about three-quarters of the way through and was out of the script. And the son left the father to go off with his wife. And the father really was meandering at the end of the movie, with almost no purpose; all the people who were close to him were gone. It just didn't have any focus, you really didn't know what the story was. Once you got through the documentary about the American Revolution you said, "Well, now what? What have we just done?" '

The Warners executives were also alarmed to find that the film had become 'non-emotional'. 'There was almost a blank wall between the father and the girl and the father and his son. They were almost stand-offish,' recalls Semel. 'You would see these two people running through a field together and it would look great. But the couples never touched, they never hugged, they never made love, they never opened up. Some of it was the direction that Hugh wanted to take the movie in; to make it father–son, and therefore we don't care what happens to the girl at the end, and therefore we shouldn't have any emotional scenes with the girl and so on.

'It was absolutely *déjà vu* for us because we had the exact same conversations on *Greystoke*. *Greystoke* was one of the greatest screen-plays ever written. By Bob Towne. Wonderful. The end of the script was written in a very romantic way: Jane would go back into the jungle and they would live happily ever after. Hugh cut that. He felt it was better for them not to have a romance. It got rewritten to the point that it was no longer about Tarzan and Jane, but about Tarzan and the ape tribe. It was all about men. He didn't even want to call her Jane. In fact, he almost wrote her out of the script. Those scenes when they were back in England, and she was teaching him, and they would dance, and he would comb her hair: those were the scenes we fought for and made him put back in the movie.

'When we came to *Revolution* we were facing exactly the same situation. I mean I stood up and said, "You are serious, aren't you? You don't want the emotion. You don't want the boy and girl to end up together at the end. You want the boy to end up alone. You want her to be gone. You basically want to take away the emotional aspect and the love aspect and make it more brutal." I mean the screenplay of *Revolution* was *brutal*. The sergeant was buggering the young boys when he captured them – and that was *after* he had beaten them.'

Warners, Semel says, 'clearly would have none of it. We didn't want a rosy-type ending where they all lived happily ever after, but what we did want was a feeling of hope, of a future, of the war providing them with a launching-pad to a better life.'

The script meetings, held in the Warners offices, in Winkler's house and, later, in Semel's house, were, as Semel remembers them, 'very comprehensive and very long; we really tore apart many points of the screenplay'. In the course of these discussions, he says, two things became clear. The first was that 'the script needed another rewrite'. The second was that 'James was taking positions on everything'.

'Gone was the bow-tie and on came the beard, if I recall correctly,' says Semel. 'James had gone Hollywood. From the man who used to sit and talk about numbers, here was this whole new person in the room. And he immediately jumped right into the screenplay: "I think this is a good idea", or "I think that is not a good idea". And we looked at each other and thought, since it was probably the first story meeting he had ever attended, that it would have been more intelligent to just sit there and let someone like Sandy Lieberson do all the Goldcrest remarks. As I think back, I am not even sure that Sandy attended those meetings. I think, in retrospect, that James told Sandy that he would handle those meetings himself. Which put me back a little. I remember phoning Sandy and saying, "Please, your input into this should certainly be to the extent of what is right and what is wrong with the script. Let James go to the meetings about the business part of it. But what you are doing is the reverse: James is coming to *this* meeting." It was apparent that, assuming Sandy had the ability to do these things – I have never worked that closely with Sandy but I assume that he can because he has been at it for a number of years – that James was not allowing him to do them. It was apparent that James saw himself as the person to do that for Goldcrest. And he did a very poor job.

'Frankly, James is a very nice man and I am sure a very intelligent man, but he was really miscast. He didn't belong in those meetings. He was out of place. He was not welcome there. He should at least have said to himself, "When I come to a business meeting I will bring my business person with me, and when I come to a story meeting I'll bring all the creative executives with me", and not sit – a man who has no experience of any of these fields – in all of those meetings on his own. It was very destructive, it made him difficult and it was embarrassing for

Goldcrest. Most of the people who were in those meetings are very professional, whether they were Irwin Winkler, who's done dozens of movies, or myself, or the writers. And the feeling afterwards was, "Oh boy, do we have a problem on our hands." We all knew we had a problem.'

On the occasions that Semel did deal with Lieberson he was never quite sure how much authority he had. He didn't know, he says, 'who was in the driving seat . . . Sandy could have probably been more helpful to James had they worked better as a team between themselves. You always got the feeling that James was listening to Sandy about as little as he was listening to each of us. So you never quite knew, when you were sitting in a meeting, who was able to call the shots. In fact, I would even call James from time to time just to be sure it was him who was making the decisions rather than the [Goldcrest] board, because some of the decisions just didn't seem to be well thought out.'

Semel draws a comparison between the decision-making process on *Revolution*, which concerned Hudson, Winkler, Lieberson and Lee, and the equivalent process on *The Mission*, which involved only Puttnam and Joffe.

'We all respond to projects in what we like to call a creative way,' he explains. 'It's creative, it's business at the same time, and it's instinctive at the same time. And a lot of it has to do with presentation. When you're on the fence, or you have certain doubts, a lot of it has to do with how convinced the other guy seems to be and how much you trust his judgement. So that when Roland Joffe and David Puttnam were talking about *The Mission* and they were much more enthusiastic about it than perhaps I was, I had to put some of that enthusiasm into my own formula. When you sit in a room and David says, "Trust me. *The Mission* is great: it will win awards and make money," you have to remember all the old conversations about why he thought *Chariots* was great and why he thought *The Killing Fields* was great. In Jake [Eberts] and David Puttnam you have people with lots of experience and lots of reliability and you do value their opinions.

'With James and Sandy it was different. In fact, they had a credibility problem. You would sit there and think to yourself, "To what extent do I care that these two people are very excited about this project? I am not sure that their opinion is very worthwhile." You find yourself in a meeting with people who are telling you why *Absolute Beginners* is going to be a huge hit, and why *Horror Movie* is going to be a huge hit, and then, after you go past those two, why they are going to fix the script on

Revolution, which you just put into turnaround. You start off with a credibility gap.'

It has to be said in Lieberson's and Lee's defence that the fact that they were not much involved in *The Mission*, but found themselves endlessly embroiled in *Revolution*'s problems, says as much about Winkler, Hudson and the *Revolution* script as it does about their own credibility. Puttnam, remember, was Lee's model of what a producer should be. Had they all been like him, Lee might never have got involved in script meetings at all.

For a long time Warners were undecided about *Revolution*. After the first script meetings, and especially after hearing Hudson's interpretation of the story, they were, says Semel, 'ready to leave . . . But the screenplay got considerably better, and she didn't die and the ending wasn't so dismal. It wasn't very good, but we felt that, for the kind of money we were in for, it would be a decent try, and Hugh, being a good director, might pull off some good reviews when it was all over. If the critics jumped on it even in a nice way, for our investment we could earn a profit.'

All that remained was to agree the terms. This, too, proved to be a far from easy process.

'It was unlike dealing with Jake. Jake and I could agree to the concept of which countries, and how much money, and who keeps which piece of the gross, in a half-hour phone conversation. With James it went on endlessly,' recalls Semel. 'I think a lot of it was his inability to comprehend what was going on. I was always asking him, "James, please don't do this yourself. Please put David [Norris] on the phone with you, or better yet let Jim Miller [Warners' head of business affairs] and David do it. Because either you don't have the ability to say yes or no to things, and therefore you are taking what I'm saying someplace else, or maybe some of the things I am saying are confusing. Or maybe I don't understand you. But one or the other is happening here, James, and it's not fair. It is not appropriate to keep me here on the phone talking. You are not making any decisions on any of this stuff." He said, no, he wouldn't hear of it: he was going to be the deal-making person. Which was absurd. I could not do that for Warner Bros. – you know, sit on the phone with the president of Paramount and start negotiating a deal. I would be smart enough to have my lawyer on the phone with me at least. But he wouldn't do it. He attended story meetings on his own, he attended negotiations on his own.

'Then, in the course of everything, he called me and he was a little embarrassed: we were negotiating for several territories and he had just discovered that one of his salesmen had already sold those countries! I mean, how could you do that? "We are negotiating and you are telling me that he just sold all Latin and South America?" "Yeah, I'm really sorry." That was on *The Mission*. It was totally unco-ordinated. There was no leader, no leader on the deal-making side.'

In his own defence, Lee says that he found himself 'in an extraordinarily difficult position . . . Almost every single decision had some sort of opposition from one or other of Guy East, John Chambers or David Norris. There was constant wrangling going on behind the scenes about "should we be making these films?" And my view was that, as chairman and chief executive of the operating company, that was what being leader of the organization was all about: I had to stand by my judgement. But it was terribly difficult. I had long discussions later with people at Orion about how every film company has this problem: that you have either got to be a Sam Goldwyn Snr., a total autocrat – "I'm running this show and this is what I say" – or you have got to accept total democracy and live by it.

'Furthermore, there was some confusion about precisely whose role it was to do certain things. David Norris wanted to evolve very much as the head of business affairs in the way that the head of business affairs exists in a Hollywood major: not only the chief legal officer but the negotiator of most things. Sandy felt that, as head of production, organizing the producers' deals, deciding how many points Irwin Winkler had and so on, was what the head of production did, and then he passed it over to the head of business affairs for the administrative task of translating the agreement into reality. And, as a result of this, I found myself increasingly sucked into matters which I really didn't want to have anything to do with. I found myself sitting eating breakfast in the Polo Lounge in Beverly Hills with Irwin Winkler discussing his contract, which was quite wrong. Why was I doing that? Really because some unfortunate difference of opinion had occurred between business affairs and production.'

All that can be said in favour of Lee's interpretation of affairs is that had a strong personality, like Puttnam, or Alan Parker, or Alan Marshall, been head of production, then Lee would probably have confined himself to his business plans and staff charts. Any one of them would have rebuffed him had he tried to interfere in their area of responsibility. Lieberson, however, was made of less stern stuff.

'Nine times out of ten there was quite an unpleasant atmosphere between Sandy and James,' recalls Norris, 'and he [Sandy] just gave in in many respects. He withdrew and withdrew. He had a very strong contract whereby he would be the boss of everything . . . but then, having ensured that he had that responsibility, he didn't take it . . . from quite an early stage.'

Pearson's James Joll, always a significant figure behind the scenes, also quickly grasped that Lieberson was not exercising the power that was vested in him. But neither, in his opinion, was anyone else. Norris, Chambers, Wooller, East: all, he says, were 'overawed' by Lee.

'The trouble with James,' says salesman Steve Walsh, 'was that he wanted to do everything himself. As a result, there was a general feeling that the company didn't know where it was going. It was no longer a team. You'd see them all sitting there, and, with few exceptions, they were not on the same side any longer. Jake always listened to people and he always made it his business to try and find out what he didn't know. He tried to combine his qualities and skills with those of the people he worked with, so that we all had the feeling that we were working together on the same thing. That went out the window when James took over. Nothing we discussed ever came to agreement. We'd sit around the table and agree that we didn't want to be involved in *Dance With a Stranger* and next day we'd find that we were involved all the same. It seemed it no longer mattered what we had to say.'

Whether Lee had, as Walsh suggests, crudely seized power, or whether, as Lee himself maintains, he was merely picking up the pieces dropped by his demoralized and fractious colleagues, is not a point that can be determined here. The fact that concerns us is that, when Lee sat down with Semel in Hollywood, he was acting very largely on his own. That was the problem that Semel was having to deal with.

It had been agreed by both Warners and Goldcrest that the distribution deals on *The Mission* and *Revolution* would follow the *Killing Fields* model. In summary, this meant that, for each film: (a) Goldcrest would finance – i.e. wholly own – the production; (b) Warners would put up an advance, equivalent to roughly one third of the cost of the picture, for all North American rights in perpetuity, and might put up further advances for other rights in other territories; (c) the budget, director and leading actors would be subject to approval by both Goldcrest and Warner Bros.; (d) from the North American theatrical release, Goldcrest would receive 30 per cent of either the first $20 million of the distributor's gross (i.e. after the cinema exhibitors had taken their cut), or two and a half times Warners' distribution expenses, whichever figure was the lower; (e) Goldcrest would receive 40 per cent of the next $5 million distributor's gross, 50 per cent of the $5 million after that, 60 per cent of the $5 million after that, and 65 per cent of all gross theatrical revenues thereafter; and (f) Goldcrest would receive 75 per cent of the gross in video, 70 per cent of the gross in syndicated television, 77.5 per cent of the first $6 million gross revenues from cable television and 77.5 per cent of the first $4 million gross revenues from network television. (As an incentive, Warners would take a bigger commission should more money be earned in cable and network television.)

According to David Norris, this deal structure was exactly the same as that which applied to the much-admired *Killing Fields* deal negotiated with Warner Bros. by Eberts. The actual figures did not differ much, either. Where Warners had put up $4.75 million as an advance for North American rights to *The Killing Fields*, they initially put up $4.25 million for *Revolution* and $5 million for *The Mission*. (Both figures were later increased, to $5.6 million and $5.5 million respectively, when Warners agreed to contribute to the costs of Al Pacino and Robert De Niro). And where Warners had paid $4 million for a whole clutch of foreign territories for *The Killing Fields*, subsequent negotiations on *Revolution* added the UK, South Africa, France, Belgium and Switzerland, for all of which they paid an advance of $1.25 million, and Spain, for which they paid an advance of $300,000. For *The Mission*, Warners took the UK and South Africa, for which they paid $350,000, Spain, for which they paid $300,000, and video rights only in Italy ($100,000) and France, Belgium and Switzerland ($115,000).

However, while the structure and the level of advances were much the same, there were, nevertheless, significant differences between the *Killing Fields* deal and the deals for *The Mission* and *Revolution*. In the first place, of course, the first film cost about half as much as each of the later two. To be paid an advance of $5 million on a film that costs £10 million is a very different thing to being paid the same sum for a film that costs £18 million. (Lee cannot be blamed entirely for this, for at the time the deals were first discussed it was thought that *The Mission* and *Revolution* would cost the same as *The Killing Fields*.) In the second place, IFI had put up $2 million of the cost of *The Killing Fields*, whereas there was as yet no equity partner in either *The Mission* or *Revolution*. And third, in the case of *Revolution*, Warners insisted on the right in their territories to make their own final cut. This demand was inspired largely by their doubts about the screenplay and the experience they had had with Hudson on *Greystoke*. Although an undertaking had already been made by Hudson and Winkler to the effect that the film would be, as Semel recalls, 'much more gentle, and he [Hugh] wouldn't shoot the guy sawing off the leg and all that', Warners wanted to be certain that the end result would be a film acceptable to the mainstream American audience.

A subsequent revision of the deals – the outlines were first agreed in an exchange of telexes in September, but negotiations dragged on into the new year, by which time, crucially, Warners had released *The Killing Fields* – introduced a further difference. It was small, but it proved to be significant. In the case of *The Killing Fields* there was no cross-collateralization between the theatrical and the ancillary revenues: i.e. Warners were obliged to recoup their entire advance from the theatrical release only. In the event that this proved impossible – in the event that the film was a flop – then the commission that Warners earned on video and television sales could be increased, from 30 per cent to 50 per cent, but no more than that. Goldcrest, in other words, was guaranteed its theatrical advance and not less than 50 per cent of the video and television earnings even if the film did not take a single dollar at the box office. When it came to *Revolution* and *The Mission*, Warners insisted that they be allowed to make good their entire theatrical advances, should they need to, from the video and television revenues. Only when Warners had been thus 'made whole' would Goldcrest receive revenues in the manner outlined above. Warners' head of business affairs, Jim Miller, explains how, and why, this came about.

'After we make a deal, we see the picture go out, and we examine it and see how it worked. We found an exposure that we hadn't anticipated on *The Killing Fields*. We made a gross deal on an expectation of what our cost of distribution would be. We found that when we got it, because of the nature of the film, we spent a lot more than we thought. And so we got squeezed. I guess it pretty much met our expectations in terms of gross, but we got squeezed on our profitability, and we found ourselves living off the television fee and the video-cassette income. So we thought it more equitable in *The Mission* and *Revolution* to make that slight change.'

The 'slight change' would have been of no consequence had either *Revolution* or *The Mission* been a success: Warners would have recouped their advances from the theatrical releases as planned and Goldcrest would have received its full share of the revenues as planned. Winkler, Hudson and Puttnam are right to point out (as they have done, vehemently and at great length; this despite the fact that they were apprised of the deals and approved them) that the deals negotiated by Lee were worse than those negotiated by Eberts. But they cannot be allowed, by drawing attention to that fact, to gloss over the real cause of the damage done by the films to Goldcrest's finances: first, *after the distribution deals were all in place*, the budgets for both films were revised upwards (*The Mission* was first approved at £11.5 million but had a final budget of £17.6 million; *Revolution* was first approved at £9 million and had a final budget of £16 million); second, in the case of *Revolution*, even the revised budget fell well short of the final cost (£19 million); and, third, neither film performed at the box office. Set against these factors, Lee's supposed shortcomings as a deal-maker are hardly significant.

In fact, according to Norris, no great friend of Lee's by this time, he was not so bad at deal-making anyway. While it is true that the advances were relatively low and that the amended terms protected Warners' downside by allowing them to invade Goldcrest's share of ancillary revenues, it was still the case that on the upside – i.e. in the event that the films were successful – Goldcrest had exceptionally good terms: according to Norris, 'the most that Warners could ever make was 24 or 25 per cent of the gross'.

'I was with him [Lee] on the occasion when those things were negotiated,' Norris says, 'and there is no doubt that they were the best terms we could get. I do not think that Terry Semel was bluffing when he said they were the best terms they would offer. Because by this time I had had discussions with Fox and Paramount. I said to them, "We'll do the same deal as we do for Warners." And I laid the deal out for them. They analysed it and came back and said, "Forget it. We can get 25 per cent maximum out of this and we need 32 per cent. And that's the bottom – we talk up from 32 per cent." They were both adamant that they wouldn't take any kind of deal that gave them less than 32 or 33 per cent of the gross. So I had no doubt at that point that when he [Semel] said he wouldn't do more, he wouldn't do it. He really would have pulled out. James didn't give in really until both arms were twisted right up his back.'

It is in the light of all this that one has to interpret Semel's answer to the question: did Warners pay too little?

'I think in the final analysis we certainly did,' he says. 'Don't forget that we made a deal predicated on the budget of the movies, which is the way everybody pre-sells movies, not just Goldcrest. So it behooves you to keep your movie real close to the budget anytime you are pre-selling the pieces. So if you think you have a $10 million movie, and your pre-sold pieces add up to $7 or $8 million and you're going to keep a little risk, and you then make the film for $17 million, you are in big trouble. The risk is enormous. Warners were in for a fixed amount of dollars. We felt that if the movie [*Revolution*] was OK, we would do fine financially. If it was good, we would do very well out of it. We had very little downside. We were not on the line for completion: if it cost five times that amount it was not our concern. We were not the producing company, so we weren't on the line.'

On this basis, on 18 September 1984, Warners telexed their commitment. *Revolution*, if the Goldcrest board approved, was a 'go project'.

Chapter Thirty-six

Absolute Beginners

Ilott: By the summer of 1984 Lieberson had *The Mission* and *Revolution* virtually committed; he had *Dance With a Stranger* to fill the immediate gap in the distribution schedule; he had the three low-budget films from David Puttnam, one of which, *Mr Love*, was to go into production immediately; he had two projects developed in-house and for which everyone had high hopes, *Mandrake* and *Horror Movie*; he had a musical set in Africa, *Dream Song*; he had Lee's choice, *Fifteen* (*Smooth Talk*); and he was making progress on the comedy series to be co-financed with the Samuel Goldwyn Company. His production programme, in other words, was beginning to fall into place. All his efforts were now directed towards imposing some sort of order on the project that was probably closest to his heart, *Absolute Beginners*.

Absolute Beginners started life as a novel written by Colin MacInnes, a high-born but low-living British writer of the 1950s and 1960s. When MacInnes's reputation was set for a revival, in the early 1980s, one of the first of the new generation to read his work was Don MacPherson, at that time editor of the films section of the London listings magazine *Time Out*. MacPherson was a close friend of director Julien Temple, with whom he had worked on a number of pop promos. Temple in turn was a partner with Michael Hamlyn in a company called Midnight Films. It is not clear exactly how the subject arose, but, sometime in 1983, MacPherson, Temple and Hamlyn agreed to turn *Absolute Beginners* into a film musical.

MacPherson wrote a script, but it seems that no one liked it. Richard Burridge, an old friend of Temple's from film-school days, then wrote another script, paid for by the National Film Development Fund; the NFDF person supervising the work was Amanda Schiff, soon to be working in the script department at Goldcrest; Schiff, in turn, answered to a board that included Sandy Lieberson, soon to be head of production at Goldcrest. Burridge's script was long, but it was generally liked. MGM was approached to provide production finance; the studio expressed interest, but nothing was ever finalized. The project was submitted to Jake Eberts, who was then still at Goldcrest, and he turned it down. He was approached again at Embassy, and again he turned it down. MacPherson, Temple and Hamlyn then approached independent film producer Steve Woolley. Woolley's version of what happened next is, for our purposes, as good as any.

'Don MacPherson came down to Shepperton, where we were working on *Company of Wolves*, and said, "Why don't you get involved?"' Woolley recalls. 'I read the script [Richard Burridge's] and I liked it. Then I spoke to Julien about his plans for it.

'I've known Julien for a long time. Not as a friend, but I've known him. Our paths always crossed. If I went to the Electric to see a Sam Fuller film there'd be two other people there and one of them would be Julien. If I went to the NFT to see a Nick Ray film there'd be seven people there and one of them would be Julien. So we ran into each other all the time, and it was that kind of area of cinema – Nick Ray, Sam Fuller, Douglas Sirk, Vincente Minnelli, Frank Tashlin, the 1950s period – that Julien was obsessed with. So I knew we had a lot of kinship. We thought similarly about cinema.

'So I said that, yes, I could become involved. And they said, "Great, let's work out a deal." We did a deal at Kettners, on one of those paper tablecloths, that Michael [Hamlyn] and I would co-produce it. I took it to Sandy Lieberson at Goldcrest with Michael. And Sandy said, "Oh great, guys, it sounds terrific. Let's see if we can pursue it. If there are problems with the script, talk to Amanda [Schiff]." So I started work on it: on the script and on raising money.'

Woolley had not progressed far with the project before Hamlyn and Temple asked him to step down, for they had secured the promise of production finance from Richard Branson's Virgin Group. At that time there was bad blood between Virgin and Woolley's company, Palace, and it was thought by Temple and Hamlyn that Woolley's involvement would not be welcome to Branson. The news was broken to Woolley at a very drunken dinner in Soho. 'There was me, Michael and Julien,' Woolley continues. 'Basically they were saying, "Virgin are doing it and there is no role for you." So I said, "Fine, OK". My hands were full anyway [with] *Company of Wolves* . . . So at the time I didn't really think anything of it. The other thing was that Julien insisted on it being shot that summer [1984]. Virgin said it would be that summer.

'Then at the wrap party for *Company of Wolves* Julien turned up. I'd not spoken to him for three weeks, assuming they were off getting the film made. And he expressed grave doubts about Michael Hamlyn's ability to produce the film, because he thought that they'd been sold a dummy by Virgin. What had happened was that when they got to sign the contract, suddenly it wasn't *that* year, suddenly it would be *the next* year. Virgin said, "We're not going to make it this year because you're not ready."

'Julien is a *very* emotional man. And he came to me in a real two-and-eight, a real state. "The world is ending. Everybody has lied to me. Michael has cheated. He's put a knife in my back. He's conniving with Robert Devereux [head of Virgin's film and video division]": statements that he would later probably want to retract. He was totally upset. And he asked would I get involved again. So I said, "All right, give me a week." And I spent the week after *Company of Wolves* with Sandy Lieberson at Goldcrest. On the phone to Fox. On the phone to MGM. Just to see if it was possible to put the deal together without Virgin.

'In that week I bought all the rights from Julien, because he hadn't actually signed the deal with Virgin. So I went and did the entire deal myself as Palace, and just took everything that there was on the film.

'Virgin went absolutely ape-shit. They went *completely* up the wall because we'd done this. So myself and Nik Powell [managing director of Palace] had meetings with Virgin and said, "Look, it's very simple. Why don't we get the finance 50 per cent from you and 50 per cent from Goldcrest, if they're still interested. Because the budget isn't going to be £3 million" – which I think was the figure we were talking about – "it's going to be more than that. And if it is going to be more than that then we are going to have to share it. And we'll have to get another financier."

'They hummed and haa'd, because they had just done a deal with MGM, on a film called *Electric Dreams*, which was a very advantageous deal to them financially. So they were riding high with MGM, and they had done a deal on *Secret Places* with Rank, and I think they were kind of buoyant at the time. And they were very upset that, as they saw it, we had muscled in and stolen the project.

'So what I did was to try and put all the parties together – MGM, who had an interest, Virgin and Goldcrest – and do a deal between all of us. Goldcrest were at the time very enthusiastic about the project. Extremely enthusiastic. Sandy was very keen, I think, to work with me and I was keen to work with him, because I really liked him a lot. Thought he was great.

'Again, Goldcrest, like Virgin, were very, very buoyant. They wanted in on new films. They wanted to take their reputation and say, "Look we've got the new Hugh Hudson film, *Revolution*, and we've got the new David Puttnam–Roland Joffe film, *The Mission*, and we've got this even more exciting thing, this *big* musical, *Absolute Beginners*." It seemed a great thing. James Lee and Sandy were very keen.

'We were soon hurtling into pre-production. It's the only way: if you want to get a film together you have to start, because if you don't start nobody else will. So we'd started, basically.

'But Robert Devereux at Virgin was still smarting from our move, and he got together with James Lee and said to him, "I don't think they are sufficiently prepared for this year." By this time, too, MGM wanted out. There was no American money. The film had to stop.

'We'd already gone into pre-production to the tune of £300,000, all of which was Palace's. No one else's. They had promised to do a deal, to sign contracts. But you can't take the promise of a signed contract to a rigger and ask him to build a piece of wall. He wants money. So the money was us, on the assumption that we were going to get paid back, on the assumption that we trusted our partners, Goldcrest and Virgin. We were way out there on a limb.

'Julien was completely upset that the film had gone again. And everything that he feared would have happened at Virgin, had actually happened with Virgin and Goldcrest. But to be honest, if one analyses the situation, Goldcrest had no choice. On the other two projects they had, *Revolution* and *The Mission*, Warner Bros. were in on both. On our film they'd lost the American coverage. By now the budget had gone from £3 million to £5 million. So they had a £5 million film without coverage. They had unknown producers, myself and Chris Brown [Woolley's co-producer on both *Company of Wolves* and *Absolute Beginners*]. They had an unknown talent in terms of cinema. Sure, Julien had done videos and *The Rock and Roll Swindle*, but he was not a known quantity in feature films. And we had no stars, except for music stars – and they don't sell a movie. So what could Goldcrest do?

'They said, "Look guys, we're not going to make the film, so stop spending money." We'd put everybody on to the film: the art director, the set designer; Gil Evans was over here doing the musical arrangements; Sade, David Bowie, Ray Davies had all been commissioned to write songs. It was all happening. Stages were booked.

'We then had to go and do a deal with Goldcrest and Virgin to get our money back. We got some back, but we [Palace] were out by £100,000 by the end of this awful summer.'

By June 1984, it looked as though *Absolute Beginners* would never happen. But part of the deal between Goldcrest, Virgin and Palace stipulated that if Palace could raise 40 per cent of the budget from an American distributor then Virgin and Goldcrest were bound to furnish the remaining 60 per cent. Woolley went looking for the money.

'Julien and I went to America,' he recalls. 'We got a very good feeling from Tri-Star. Lynda Obst at Geffen also liked the film a lot. So those two were our main hits. But it was, "Well, if you just make *these* changes, and if you just make *those* changes . . ." By this stage, Don MacPherson had been doing rewrites for us. I'd gone as far as I could with Richard Burridge, who wouldn't do anything I'd asked him to do. The relationship between Richard and Julien, because they'd gone to film-school together, was that this was a *pure* work, and Richard had gone as far as he would go. So I'd brought Don in to work with Julien on making some of the changes that were necessary for the budget and for the Americans.

'Then I went in to see a company called Orion. I showed it to Mike Medavoy, who was in charge of Orion's production.

'Meanwhile, Julien had met Bob Dylan's manager, because Bob Dylan wanted Julien to direct *Maggie's Farm*, which he was re-doing. So I went to see Mike Medavoy on my own. And I think Bob Dylan's manager had rung him up and said, "Mike, you should get involved in this." Anyway, Mike liked the project a lot. Orion at that time were far more adventurous in production than they have subsequently become. They were riding on the wave of *Desperately Seeking Susan*. They had *Terminator*, which was a big hit. They were very hot and they wanted youthful, exciting things. So Mike said he'd do the deal. We got exactly 40 per cent of the money.

'The budget by this stage was £6 million. We had incurred costs in cancelling the production, and we had added some costs in the rewrites, because there were things the Americans loved, like David Bowie dancing on top of the world. So we'd really upped the budget by changing the script for them: for Goldcrest, for the Americans and for Virgin.

'And that was it. We came back with the 40 per cent Orion deal – this was September 1984 – and, with Virgin and Goldcrest committed, we restarted pre-production on the film.'

Attenborough and Chambers hated the project. Guy East was doubtful about its sales prospects. Lieberson and Lee, however, were keen and even Norris gave it his blessing.

Chapter Thirty-seven
Folie de Grandeur

'You've always got to presume that, however well you research, there are chances that new ventures can go wrong. In which case, you must never over-bet the company, must you?' – James Joll, talking about the Goldcrest production programme

Ilott: On 25 September 1984 Lee presented to the holdings board a strategy document that outlined the now complete production programme for the coming year. After a restatement of the nine-point production philosophy – that Goldcrest should follow talent, not themes; stay distinctive; negotiate from strength; produce films for both mass and specialized audiences; know the market; retain distribution flexibility; retain foreign rights; take risks intelligently; and keep within capacity – Lieberson and Lee (the document was signed by them both) set out their choices: five major films, *The Mission, Revolution, Horror Movie, Absolute Beginners* and *Mandrake*; and five low-budget classics, *Mr Love, The Frog Prince, Knights and Emeralds, Dream Song* and *Fifteen* (*Smooth Talk*). The document outlined the plot, and gave details of cast, director, producer, etc., for each of these, before going on to give Lieberson's and Lee's reasons for putting them forward for approval:

THE MISSION – The film has strong worldwide potential . . . our aim is to cover the budget of approximately $17 million from $5 million advance from Warner for the US and Canada and $5 million of pre-sales in foreign territories. The aim is to limit our cash risk to no more than $5 million, or one-third of the cash budget. The final screenplay will be available at the beginning of October . . . however the board should be aware that we are already proceeding on the assumption that this film will go ahead . . . By mid-October we will have invested some £400,000 . . . Our enthusiasm is based on (1) the Joffe/Puttnam axis (2) the Bolt screenplay (3) the scale and impressiveness of the locations, and (4) the opportunity for a prominent, highly promotable central heroic role.

REVOLUTION – We believe that the film has very strong worldwide potential and that the opportunity for significant foreign pre-sales is very good . . . We are looking for an advance from the US and Canada for approximately one-third of the budget of $15 million. We expect, therefore, to get $9 million in risk cover: $5 million from Warner, $4 million from foreign pre-sales . . . We hope to restrict our own cash risk exposure to no more than $4 million. Our interest is based on (1) Hugh Hudson's reputation . . . (2) the strong visual element and the opportunity for action and adventure in the screenplay, and (3) to a lesser extent the very strong interest in patriotic themes in the US at this time under the influence of President Reagan.

HORROR MOVIE – We are looking for an advance from the US and Canada of half the budget of $9 million. We hope to succeed in securing between $3 million and $4 million on foreign pre-sales, and, if successful, our cash investment should be almost fully covered. In return for a 50 per cent advance from the US and Canada, we are expecting slightly less favourable distribution terms than those achieved from Warners for the other two films . . . We aim to commit to production as soon as we have a satisfactory screenplay and a US distributor is unconditionally committed . . . Our interest is based on (1) the strength of the story itself (2) the almost instantaneously positive response received from all those who have been in contact with the project, and (3) the qualities of the Alan Marshall/Marek Kanievska team.

ABSOLUTE BEGINNERS – We believe that it has strong potential outside the United States, but requires careful marketing to be successful in the United States. We therefore believe this to be a high-risk project. Goldcrest and Virgin together will sell foreign rights, but we will be looking for half of the budget of £5 million ($7 million) cover out of the US and Canada . . . A new screenplay will be written before the end of this year . . . The foreign pre-sales potential is below average, and a pre-sale of $1–2 million is all that can be expected. We aim to limit our own cash investment to no more than $1 million . . . Our interest is based on (1) Virgin's ability to set musical trends and to promote music (2) the proven success of the story among teenagers (3) the strong soundtrack and exciting choreography, and (4) the young director, Julien Temple.

MANDRAKE – Our final decision about the financing and distribution strategy must await the final screenplay, but at the moment we assume that the budget could be as high as $20 million. We would hope to secure one-third of the budget from the US and Canada as an advance against a gross deal, and in excess of one-third of the budget from foreign pre-sales.

The low-budget films were dealt with in like fashion, and a note was added to the effect that, in addition to the films listed, the company was committed to the Goldwyn comedy series. The document then went on to explain the financial arrangements:

We have produced a cash flow for the period to December 1985 based on our best assumptions about inflows and outflows from existing projects, and our existing overheads. This analysis shows that we have £13 million ($17 million) of equity and £10 million ($13 million) of debt capacity available.

The financial implications of the ten priority projects described are shown below.

	Approx. budget	Approx. cash cost	US advance	Foreign pre-sales target	Goldcrest risk
The Mission	17	15	5	5	5
Revolution	15	13	4.5	4.5	4
Horror Movie	9	8	4.5	3.5	–
Absolute Beg'rs	8	7	4	1	1*
Mandrake	20	18	6	7†	5
Mr Love					
Frog Prince	6	5.5	2.7	0.3	2.4
Knights & Em'lds					
Dream Song	2	2	–	–	0.3*
Fifteen	1	0.9	0.5	–	0.4
Total $ million	**78‡**	**69.4‡**	**27.2**	**21.3**	**18.1**
£ @ $1.30	**60**	**53.4**	**21**	**16.4**	**13.9**

This table clearly shows that we do not have the resources to complete the entire programme, particularly taking into account the fact that we also intend to produce at least three significant TV productions during the same period. It is clear therefore that one of the five major films will have either to be aborted, postponed or financed in a different way.

In considering this programme, one must distinguish between what might have been apparent at the time and what only became apparent with hindsight. At the time, alert members of the board would have noted that all the major productions were said to have script problems. It might further have been observed that some of the reasons given for recommending the projects amounted to little more than wishful thinking: 'very strong interest in patriotic themes in the US' in the case of *Revolution*, for example, and the 'instantaneously positive reaction' to *Horror Movie* (a project which Terry Semel thought was 'an awful idea' and for which not one US distributor could be found to put up an advance). Other reasons given for recommending the projects were either wrong – 'Virgin's ability to set music trends' and 'the proven success' among teenagers of *Absolute Beginners* (a book that was only ever read by graduates) – or, as in 'the scale and impressiveness' of *The Mission* locations and 'the strong visual element' in *Revolution*, of marginal significance.

It is unlikely, however, that any of these things was noted; certainly

* The exposure on *Absolute Beginners* and *Dream Song* was to be shared with co-investors. Hence the low figures in the right-hand column.

† *Mandrake* had been in development at Goldcrest for more than two years. It had been plagued with script and personnel problems. However, there was tremendous interest in the project in the foreign markets and this explains the $7 million pre-sale target.

‡ The difference between budget and cash cost (the left-hand columns) arose from the fact that the budget included items, for example overhead fees, that were payable to Goldcrest itself and that did not, therefore, require cash advances.

they are not referred to in the minutes. Nor were the projects themselves subjected to any great scrutiny. The board comprised executive directors (i.e. the Goldcrest management) who had already agreed to the programme, and non-executive directors who, with two exceptions, were businessmen not film-makers; they did not see it as their job, nor would they have been expected to make it their job, to question the wisdom of Lieberson's and Lee's creative choices. The two film-making non-executive directors, Attenborough and Puttnam, were absent from the meeting. Puttnam later congratulated Lieberson on his choices; Attenborough said nothing.

Rather than concentrating on the films, then, the board's discussion focused on the matters raised by the cash-flow forecasts, borrowing requirement and profitability studies prepared by John Chambers. He produced detailed figures for the only films which at that time had a US distributor in place, *The Mission* and *Revolution*. The following tables are a summary of his findings.

Goldcrest Profitability – *The Mission*

	Best likely	Probable	Worst likely
A: Goldcrest investment ($000)	**(16,917)**	**(16,917)**	**(16,917)**
sales income (advances)	16,917	16,917	10,271
interest	1,000	1,200	0
completion/production fees	1,917	1,917	1,917
distribution fees,			
UK	130	100	35
rest of the world	2,234	1,397	672
overages	10,742	775	0
B: total income	**32,940**	**22,306**	**12,895**
B−A: contribution (loss)	**16,023**	**5,389**	**(4,022)**
percentage return (loss)	94.72%	31.86%	(23.77%)

Goldcrest Profitability – *Revolution*

	Best Likely	Probable	Worst likely
A: Goldcrest investment ($000)	**(13,581)**	**(13,581)**	**(13,581)**
sales income (advances)	13,581	13,581	10,488
interest	800	1,000	0
completion fee	711	711	711
deferred fees	817	817	0
distribution fees & expenses	1,961	1,436	0
less distribution expenses	−600	−500	−400
overages	9,825	1,113	0
B: total income	**27,095**	**18,158**	**10,799**
B−A: contribution (loss)	**13,514**	**4,577**	**(2,782)**
percentage return (loss)	99.51%	33.70%	(20.48%)

(Sales income is the money put up in advance by distributors for the right to distribute the film in their territories. Interest is recouped by Goldcrest in respect of its expenditure on the film – on script, location-finding and so on – prior to and during production. If the film performs well, this money is recouped quickly and the interest payable is correspondingly less than when the film performs only modestly, in which case recoupment takes longer and the interest payable is greater. If the film performs so badly as to not recoup its costs at all, then no interest will be paid. The completion fee, which we will come back to later, is money earned, and taken out of the budget, by Goldcrest for itself acting as guarantor. Deferred fees, in the case of *Revolution*, are overhead fees – i.e. that part of the cost of the film accounted for by Goldcrest's office services, contract work, bookkeeping and so on – the recoupment of which Goldcrest agreed to defer until the film went into profit. The company did this, as did Irwin Winkler and Hugh Hudson in respect of their fees, in order to keep the budget down. If, in the worst case, the film didn't move into profit, then the deferred fees would not be paid. Distribution fees are earned by Goldcrest for selling the films around the world and are paid out of gross receipts. Overages are revenues remaining after the distributors have recouped their advances and fees. Only successful films return overages to the producer. The contribution is the money remaining, if any, when all the receipts have come in and the original investment has been recouped. It is called the contribution because it is the money that contributes to the company's general overheads.)

The huge disparity between Chambers's best-case and worst-case figures does not mean that these numbers were plucked out of the air. They were arrived at after careful appraisal of the distribution deals that were likely to be concluded between Goldcrest and Warners in the US, and between Goldcrest and independent distributors in the foreign territories. The disparity arises from the simple practice of taking those distribution deals, looking especially at the back-end terms, and applying to them the questions: what if the film is a hit? what if it does OK? what if it is a flop? (To the questions: *will* it be a hit? *will* it be OK? *will* it be a flop? there are no answers, only guesses.)

If you were asked to invest £10 million in a film (*Revolution*) which might double your stake or might make a loss of £2 million; or if you were asked to invest £12.5 million in a film (*The Mission*) which also might double your stake or might make a loss of £3 million; and if you knew that in each case you had only one throw of the dice and that in neither case could you, or anyone else, predict whether the higher or the lower figures were likely to be nearer the mark, what would you do? If you were sensible, you would ignore the higher figures and concentrate on the low ones. Yes, the films might make money, but that is not something that you, the investor, can influence. The only thing you can influence is the risk that you enter into when making the investment: you ensure that, even if the films turn out to be disastrous failures, you don't lose your shirt.

And that is exactly how the Goldcrest board approached the discussion.

Chambers was questioned about the calculation of the worst-case figures and Lee was asked to explain his policy of risk management, which was essentially to cover 50 per cent of Goldcrest's investment by pre-sales and to find as many third-party investors as possible to share the remaining 50 per cent. What emerged from the discussion was the classic gambler's dilemma: if risk were eliminated altogether there would be no danger of losing money even if the films did badly, but, by the same token, there would be little chance of taking a significant share of the profits if the films did well. The example that yet again sprang to mind was *Gandhi*, for which Pearson and GFI had been on the line for more than £5 million at one point, without any distribution deals being in place – in other words, the entire sum was at risk. In the event, *Gandhi* did exceptionally well, taking $25 million rentals in the US and $30 million rentals from the international markets. With the addition of television, *Gandhi* has grossed over $80 million to date, of which $32 million has been available to Goldcrest, its co-financiers (IFI, Pearson and the Indian government) and profit participants (including Attenborough). After paying nearly £5 million in interest, the film has earned £12 million in net profits. Even after buying back the Pearson stake (giving Pearson a profit of £1.1 million), the contribution to Goldcrest to date has been £6.3 million – a 128 per cent return. Had Eberts been successful in his efforts to lay off a larger part of the *Gandhi* risk, the returns to Goldcrest would have been commensurately reduced.

Clearly, the lesson of *Gandhi* was that Goldcrest, if it wanted bonanza profits, had to keep some risk. The right-hand column of the first table set out above shows the amounts that Lee was prepared to gamble: a $5 million exposure on *The Mission* and *Mandrake*, a $4 million exposure on *Revolution*, a $1 million exposure on the 'high-risk' *Absolute Beginners* and no exposure at all on *Horror Movie*. As long as the distribution deals matched Guy East's expectations, *and as long as the costs were kept down to the levels quoted*, then Lee's judgement would seem to have been entirely reasonable.

From the evidence of the minutes of the meeting, it seems that three further points had to be dealt with before the board would give the programme its approval. The first was the observation that, notwithstanding the golden rule of making investments across a wide portfolio, the company was now putting itself in a position where the entire results for 1986 would depend on returns from just four films – *Revolution, The Mission, Absolute Beginners* and either *Mandrake* or *Horror Movie* – which between them would probably account for $15 million of the proposed $18 million risk investment. The justification given for this was that, it having been proved that low-budget films generated considerable back-office costs without making any significant contribution to over-heads, Goldcrest, which was now costing nearly £3 million a year to run, *had* to invest in big films. Four films was the most they could afford to do at one time. There was logic in this position, but it did not answer the question.

The second problem was that, even allowing Lee's point that one of the major films (either *Mandrake* or *Horror Movie*) would have to be deferred, there was still the prospect of a cash shortfall – the company would have spent all its money and used up its entire overdraft facility – once the bulk of the production programme was under way. Would it not be more sensible, Lieberson and Lee were asked, to stagger the production schedule by delaying a couple of projects, at least until the results from the release of *The Killing Fields* were known? Again, the company was faced with a dilemma: it had been so long out of production that deliberately to postpone a film now, when past experience had shown that productions, even after they have been approved, are them-selves subject to all manner of unforeseen delays, could leave the com-pany with still further gaps in its distribution schedule a year or two hence. There was money in the bank, after all, and it was there to be spent. The board accepted the logic of this position too, and turned its attention to a discussion of how the cash shortfall might be covered. No conclusion was reached. Again, the question was left unanswered.

The third problem concerned logistics: did Goldcrest have the capacity to cope with this burden of work? Goldcrest had made one big film, *Gandhi*, in 1980–1; it had made another, *The Killing Fields*, in 1983–4. In between it had made two medium-budget films, *Local Hero* and *The Dresser*. Its entire turnover in 1983 was just £12 million. The £60 million ($78 million) production programme now put before the board thus represented a huge leap in ambition. Lieberson conceded, or argued, that the production and sales departments would have to be further strengthened – i.e. more people would have to be brought on board. And Lee spoke of the possibility, somewhere down the line, of taking investment positions in American-produced films as a way of easing the production burden in the home office. On the evidence of the minutes, the board seems, in a general kind of way, to have been satisfied with this discussion, even though, again, no particular conclusion was reached.

The entire programme was duly approved. It was agreed that a press conference would be held once final details had been agreed with Warner Bros. on *Revolution*, and the Ghia–Puttnam problem had been resolved on *The Mission*. The press conference would be used to announce to the world that Goldcrest was not just back in business, but back in business with bigger and better films than ever.

Before going any further with this story, it is important to emphasize two things. First, the seeds of the crisis that later engulfed the company were sown at the 25 September board meeting not just because fateful investments were approved but because the board allowed its three vital questions to go unanswered. Goldcrest *was* putting too much money into too few projects. In fact, the welfare of the company was not to depend on four major films but on three, since neither *Mandrake* nor *Horror Movie* ever went into production. Likewise, there *was* to be a cash-flow crisis, one that nearly broke the company even as the films were still in production. And third, Goldcrest, for all its enormous overhead, *did not* have the resources in the right places to cope with the workload. In particular, there was never adequate supervision of the two productions based in England, one of which, *Absolute Beginners*, was in the hands of an inexperienced production team, and the other, *Revolution*, had a producer and a director who were known *from the outset* to be weak on budgetary control.

None of these problems need have been of such enormous conse-quence were it not for the fact that *no sooner had approval for the programme been given* than the budgets of all the major films were revised upwards. Lee's entire strategy of risk management depended on costs being kept down. But Goldcrest, instead of facing a maximum exposure of £14 million spread across five major films and five classics, ended up with an exposure of £17 million spread across just three major films and four classics (*Dream Song*, like *Mandrake* and *Horror Movie*, never went into production). Even if this programme had achieved an average rate of success it would not have been enough: by the most optimistic calculation, two, at least, of the major films would have had to have been as successful as *Gandhi* for there to have been a chance of recouping £17 million from the back end. That was *before* the films went into production: the subsequent overcosts on *Revolution* and *Absolute*

Beginners merely ensured that an already precarious position was made untenable.

A final point to note while on the subject of the fateful 25 September board meeting is that, although neither Puttnam nor Attenborough was in attendance, both men received copies of the production programme, financial projections and the minutes as soon as these were available. Whether they read these documents or not – and Attenborough, who was directing *A Chorus Line* at the time, thinks probably he didn't – they were duty bound to do so. Stoddart, Chambers, Grossart, Joll, Lee, Lieberson, Peter Mayer, David Norris, Philip Whitehead and Mike Wooller, all of whom *were* present, knew exactly the sums that were being committed and the initial risks that were being undertaken. Lee, who was later made the scapegoat for every disaster that befell the company, can be blamed neither for the choice of films nor for the decision to make them. He may or may not have overawed his executive colleagues, but no one has ever claimed that he overawed the board: Stoddart was his senior in age and experience, Joll at least his equal in force of personality, Mayer his match in energy and judgement. Their voices were heard as well as his.

Whatever they may later have claimed – and in 1986 there was to be a lot of buck-passing and rewriting of history – responsibility for the decision to make these investments must rest with the board as a whole.

At lunchtime on 8 October 1984, television crews, radio journalists, trade and national press gathered at Maxim's restaurant in London's Leicester Square for the Goldcrest press conference. Sandy Lieberson was given the honour of introducing what the accompanying press release described as 'one of the most ambitious programmes of film production ever to be wholly financed and based in Britain'. Referring to the directors and producers who had been assembled for the occasion – among them Robert Bolt, Roland Joffe, Fernando Ghia, Hugh Hudson, *Horror Movie* writer Stephen Volk, Julien Temple, *Absolute Beginners* co-producer Chris Brown, and the co-producers of *Dream Song*, Michael Raeburn and Gavrik Losey – Lieberson emphasized the 'sheer quality' of the line-up. He then described each film in outline and answered questions on budgets and casting. *Revolution* and *Horror Movie*, he said, would start production in February 1985, *Absolute Beginners* and *The Mission* would start later in the summer and *Mandrake* would start in the autumn.

Lee then took the floor. There was no change, he said, in the company's film policy, 'except that if anything Goldcrest has gone for more large-scale productions and fewer smaller-budget films'.

'For the first time for more than a decade,' he declared, 'there is a British film company with both the will and the resources to give our creative talents the support they so richly deserve.'

The tenor of the press conference was upbeat to the point of being triumphant. Not everyone, however, was impressed. Chambers and Norris hated the production programme and were embarrassed by the ballyhoo that accompanied its announcement. Michael Stoddart, who professes to have had no opinion about the films themselves, was nevertheless alarmed by the scale of the investments. He was also worried, and said so at the time, that the press conference was a manifestation of *folie de grandeur*. Richard Attenborough, working on the set of *A Chorus Line* in New York, was shattered to hear of the inclusion in the list of *Revolution*, since it would mean the end of his own long-treasured project, *Tom Paine*, which was to have dealt with the exactly same period of history. When he later had time to study the whole production programme in detail, his reaction, he recalls, was one of horror: 'Because the production programme exceeded any sensible financial base. What I mean is that our capability of calling upon assets, of funding – not cash flow directly, not until further down the line – but our commitment to these scales of investment, all without any knowledge of what was coming in, without yet knowing what the results of *The Killing Fields* were going to be, without reference to any fiscal concern whatsoever, was madness, unutterable madness. You would need to be a major studio to be backing that sort of production programme. It was lunatic.'

Chapter Thirty-eight
The Great Television Debate

'The primary interest of companies in the UK is creativity: we like to make programmes, which is a very different philosophy from that in America, where they want to make money.' – Mike Wooller, managing director of Goldcrest Television, interviewed in August 1984

Ilott: The financing of Lieberson's film-production programme for 1985 could not be considered except in conjunction with the company's television commitments over the same period; television, after all, had accounted for about 40 per cent of Goldcrest's investments to date. But television itself was the subject of a major review that had been launched in July and that was to be the main item for discussion, at both management and board levels, now that the film programme had been agreed. For television, always a point of contention first with Eberts and Gavin and then with Norris and Chambers, had now become the focus of considerable misgivings on the part of virtually every executive in the company other than Wooller.

Wooller had undertaken a massive production programme when Goldcrest Television was first launched in 1981. In all, he had committed finance to more than twenty projects, totalling eighty-eight hours of screen time, at a projected cost of more than £18 million. The first of these projects, *The Body Machine*, *The Far Pavilions* and *Red Monarch*, went before the cameras in the spring of 1982. They were quickly followed by *Runners*, *The Ploughman's Lunch*, *The Wine Programme*, *The World: a Television History* and a trio of *First Loves*. By the summer of 1983, Goldcrest had invested about £9 million in television, of which £3.7 million represented completed productions that had already gone into distribution. But the revenues received by this time totalled only £1.7 million. Not only were Wooller's programmes much more costly and taking much longer to produce than had been planned, but in style and content they were unsuitable for the international markets from which so much of their cost was to have been recouped.

Some programmes, such as *Arthur's Hallowed Ground*, which told the story of a groundsman's love of his cricket pitch, were parochial in subject matter. Others, such as *The Wine Programme*, were made in such a way – the presenter speaking English to the camera, the prices of wines in British supermarkets being quoted – as to render them unsaleable outside the UK.

Head of sales, Bill Gavin, had felt that the demands being made of him to recover the cost of these programmes were unrealistic. Shouting matches between Gavin and Wooller; threats by Wooller to resign; and accompanying exhortations by Chambers that the resignations be accepted, had been a regular feature of the hectic life at Holland Park Avenue.

Eberts could have put a stop to it while he was still at Goldcrest, but he admits that he had 'preferred to muddle through'. When he left, he advised Lee to close the television department altogether and to put Wooller on an independent producer's contract. But Lee was no more keen to grasp the nettle than Eberts had been.

The appointment of Lieberson as head of production, with responsibility for television as well as films, made the already difficult task of bringing the high-spending but loss-making television division under control, virtually unmanageable. Lieberson had never worked in television, knew nothing about it and appeared to care about it less.

By the summer of 1984, it had become clear that Solomon, Finger and Newman's valuation of the television portfolio in which they had predicted future net revenues of £9.93 million on the existing investments, giving Goldcrest a return of £2.7 million overall, had been over-optimistic. Chambers produced figures to show that not only was the *First Love* series bound for heavy losses, but that virtually every television production on the list was going to lose money. The only significant exception was the *Robin of Sherwood* series.

In July 1984, by which time £15 million had been spent on television, Lee instituted some major policy changes. All forms of programming other than drama were to be dropped. Within drama, the emphasis was to be on mini-series. And he insisted that no television programme was to go ahead unless its entire cost had been covered in advance by sales in two territories, leaving the rest of the world from which to derive profits.

Even this did not placate Wooller's critics. But while Chambers, Norris, Lieberson and television salesman Steve Walsh agreed that television had lost money, was losing money and would continue to lose money, they were divided on what to do about it. The review was Lee's attempt to arrive at a solution by consensus.

Papers were commissioned: John Gau on factual programming, Derek Granger on drama and films, and Steve Walsh on co-productions and US representation. Wooller himself was to write a paper on overall strategy.

While these preparations were under way, Wooller presented a rough draft of his proposed production slate for 1985. It included five made-for-television films: *The Crack*, which was planned to go into production in March 1985; *The Blunderer* and *The Twelve Vice-Consuls*, to start in June; *Girl on a Bicycle*, to start in July; and *Redcoat*, which would not start until April 1986. It also included three mini-series: *The Monte Carlo Casino Story*, to start in July; *Thirteen Days*, to start in September; and *Triads*, which would not start until September 1986.

This programme was already much more modest in scope and more international in appeal than Wooller's first. But still it was judged by the management team to contain too many television films, expensive one-offs that had little appeal outside the UK, and not enough mini-series, which were then flavour-of-the-month in the world's television markets. Wooller and Lee discussed the matter, and a revised programme, containing only three made-for-television movies, *The Blunderer*, *The Twelve Vice-Consuls* and *Girl on a Bicycle*, and adding a further mini-series, *The Matterhorn Flyers*, began to take shape by September.

A question mark, however, was hanging over the company's most successful, and most promising, television production to date, *Robin of Sherwood*. Thirteen episodes of this adventure series had been sold to Showtime in the United States. Chambers's projections suggested that the £2.6 million that Goldcrest had invested in these programmes would result in a net contribution to the company of between £800,000 and £1 million. As *Gandhi* was to film, so the first thirteen episodes of *Robin of Sherwood* were to television: in terms of profitability, nothing else came close.

Unfortunately, there were problems getting a further series of thirteen programmes off the ground. The star, Michael Praed, who had a considerable personal following among *Robin*'s audience, became unavailable, and without him the co-producer, HTV, was reluctant to make a commitment. Showtime, too, was lukewarm: the ratings in the States were not outstanding. Furthermore, Goldcrest was having great difficulty in the international markets. *Robin of Sherwood* was made under standard British television contracts that stipulate that all artists should be paid a fee, known as a residual fee, in respect of every single foreign and ancillary sale. This not only entails a daunting amount of administration, but seriously undermines the value that foreign sales might have to the producer. According to Goldcrest's in-house solicitor Peter Coles, the residuals bill for the sale of *Robin* in the Soviet Union, for example, was about the same as the deal with Soviet Television was worth.

The solution to this problem is to buy out all the artists from the beginning. To want to undertake that expense, however, the production company must have a strong incentive: at the very least the programme must have good foreign-sales potential (which the vast majority of programmes do not) on which the company is relying, to some degree, for its profits. This was certainly Goldcrest's position, but it wasn't HTV's. HTV, an independent television station in the west of England, was the end-user, after all, and it had acquired a very attractive series, at a reasonable price, which it could network in the UK and on the back of which it would make handsome advertising sales. The artists' residuals were not bought out, and Goldcrest, which sold the series to more than twenty countries, was to pay the price: £810,000 in residual payments on the first thirteen episodes and £1.2 million on the second. From being a major profit-earner, *Robin of Sherwood* was to end up losing about £1.2 million overall.

With the discussion papers and Wooller's much-revised production slate as the main texts, the television debate was launched in September 1984. Steve Walsh's description of the various meetings, which he recalls as having been 'futile exercises in democracy', strongly resembles Don Cruickshank's account of the management conference at which *Absolute Beginners* had first been introduced back in March.

'We spent a whole day discussing television strategy,' Walsh says. 'And we decided that we were going to do X number of television movies, Y number of mini-series, and so on. But all the discussions were about theory not about practice. We were not talking about *this* project or about *that* project; we were trying to work out whether we would be capable of producing four television movies a year, *without knowing what those movies were*. This was obviously the wrong way to do it. What they should have been saying was, "Look, there are all these projects, let's throw them all out the window because none of them are starters, and let's see if we can't find two really good projects, sell them to a network and get on and make them."'

If Goldcrest was to stay in television, says Walsh, it had to 'go out and out commercial, really go downmarket'. Wooller, he says, was 'totally opposed' to this approach: mini-series, maybe, but downmarket, never. Among the satellite producers, continues Walsh, 'the only one who was commercially minded enough to make the kind of television that large numbers of people will watch willingly was Paul Knight. None of the others were really interested in that.' As for Lee, he remained, in Walsh's view, unrealistically optimistic. As a result, says Walsh, the discussion, certainly among the television people themselves, became mere 'pie in the sky'.

As between the television people and the rest, it quickly became acrimonious. Wooller, who had 'no doubt at all' that Lee was the only member of the management team on his side, was on trial and he knew it. 'I felt at the time', he says, 'that I was becoming the fall-guy. There was a feeling that television was of little consequence and that it was never going to make any money. They were a feature-film operation and they despised the television operation, thought it was peanuts and not worth worrying about.'

Many people have testified that there was, indeed, a real feeling of 'us and them' between the two sides of Goldcrest. Of the fifty-two people then employed by the company, eight could be identified as working solely in feature films and eleven as working solely in television. But of the rest, in sales, legal affairs, finance and administration, the majority seem to have had a much greater respect for Goldcrest's film producers than they had for what accountant Andy Parsons calls the 'fly boys' of television.

'The TV boys', Parsons says, 'had been cosseted by the big companies all their lives, and when they had to come out on their own they were like babes. They still had these creative ideas, but they couldn't relate them to proper business sense.' As a result, he says, 'a lot of money was poured away'.

Such views were widespread within the company, and one does not have to paint a lurid picture of some kind of *cinéastes'* conspiracy to appreciate why it was that Goldcrest's feature films were generally more highly regarded by the staff than was its television output. Britain's television culture is very sophisticated and there is available a deep pool of writers, technicians, producers, directors and actors whose mastery of the medium is probably unmatched anywhere in the world. Making good-quality programmes is thus, comparatively speaking, not so difficult. Being not so difficult, it is not so impressive. Britain's film culture, on the other hand, is under-developed even in European terms, and it is dwarfed not only by Hollywood but by the very television culture that surrounds it. There is a tiny pool of film talent on which to draw and, unlike television, which has well-established structures for training and advancement, film requires each generation of newcomers to make the same mistakes over again. Making films in Britain, and especially making films of the calibre of *Gandhi* or *The Killing Fields*, is a process akin to re-inventing the industry. It is, in its way, a heroic undertaking, and it attracts people who in themselves combine extraordinary abilities. Jeremy Thomas, David Puttnam, Richard Attenborough, Alan Parker, Alan Marshall, Richard Lester, John Boorman and Derek Jarman, to take a representative sample, are variously entrepreneurs, impresarios and/or artists, who, among the many things they have in common, are tireless and highly skilled. On these grounds alone, their achievements are worthy of admiration. They are, in addition, bound by commercial considerations in a way that television people have never been; they understand the minutiae of budgets and the broad outlines of distribution deals; they appreciate the financial implications of their creative choices; and they stand to lose or gain not just by the critical success but by the profitability of their work. All this only adds to their status in the eyes of the Andy Parsonses and John Chamberses of the world.

Furthermore, film is, of course, more glamorous than television, just as the Oscars are more glamorous than the Emmys, and Richard Attenborough is more glamorous than Mike Wooller. In a company that had already received twenty-three Oscar nominations and won twelve, and that had another Oscar contender, *The Killing Fields*, about to be released, it would have taken a small-screen fixation for the Goldcrest employees to find the television side of the company as interesting as the film side.

Having said all that, it would still be wrong to portray Wooller as a victim of the feature-film bias at Goldcrest: his real problems were not with the film community, after all, and certainly not with the film people in his own company, but with the sharp end of his beloved world of television. To this day, Paul Knight believes that Channel 4, HTV, Showtime, HBO and the US networks 'took Goldcrest for a ride', and he observes that when the company finally collapsed, 'the television establishment were laughing up their sleeves'. It was this sharp end of television that Wooller had never had to deal with before, and he was never to come to terms with it, certainly not while he was at Goldcrest.

Nor was Wooller's own voice always moderate or conciliatory in tone. His general view of film people is that 'they are shits, they really are'. He talks of 'the vast salaries and vast amounts of money' that swill around in the film world and contrasts that with television, where people 'tend to be much straighter and much more with their feet on the ground'. He 'didn't have a great deal of respect' for John Chambers, and thought that David Norris 'really didn't spend the time he should have done on television, because there was always some massive film deal he had to do and television always seemed to go to the bottom of the pile'. Most of all, he loudly resented the lack of effort that went into selling the product that he had created, even though this was an area for which he, as much as anyone, was responsible: he was managing director of Goldcrest Television, after all, not merely its head of production. According to the testimony of Knight, Gavin and Walsh, Wooller was as little interested in television sales as, say, Eberts had been in television production.

'His attitude was extraordinary,' comments Knight. 'They spent vastly too much money going to places like MIP-TV [the major television market] . . . but Mike never took much interest in what had been sold. I would be on to our distribution guys every day: "How's it going? What are you doing? What have you sold?" But Mike didn't seem to care.'

None of which is to say that Wooller wasn't a good-natured colleague whose skills as a producer were held in high regard even by his sternest critics. It is merely to point out that in the debate between film and television, which is what it came down to, feelings ran high on both sides and Wooller was more than capable of fighting his corner. He also had a trump card: the support of James Lee.

The debate, not surprisingly, failed to arrive at the hoped-for consensus. Chambers argued, as he had done for more than a year, that the television operation should be closed down altogether. Norris agreed. Wooller, naturally, argued that television should carry on. Like Puttnam, he believed in taking the long view: at the end of the day, television, which in his opinion (an opinion shared, it should be said, by almost nobody else in the business) has a longer shelf-life than feature films, would prove profitable. Steve Walsh, the second most senior television executive in the company, also argued that television should carry on – only Walsh wanted to write off everything that had been produced to date and start again, with internationally acceptable (i.e. commercial) programming and without Wooller. Lieberson, nominally in charge but in reality increasingly remote from the debate, also argued in favour of starting again, but he wanted to ditch Walsh as well as Wooller. Lee, who was aware of all these points of view – they were not so openly expressed in the debates – but who had, in addition, pressure from the shareholders to contend with, favoured a compromise: a slimmed-down department, with Wooller still at its head, producing the kind of commercial programming that Walsh argued for.

Lee's was the one view that satisfied nobody. It was, however, the only formula that was going to bring the unsatisfactory discussion to an end. The final decision would anyway be up to the holdings board, to whom Lee and Wooller presented the broad conclusions of the debate on 16 October.

According to the minutes of this meeting, Wooller, who introduced the debate, drew the board's attention to 'several factors' which had influenced what he surprisingly referred to as Goldcrest Television's 'success in the international marketplace'. He assured the board that the strategy that was now proposed 'involved the continuation of a trend established over the last year rather than a major departure from the existing mode of operation'. He pointed out that while Goldcrest had achieved 'notable successes in the crucial American market with the *Robin Hood* series and its two mini-series [*Concealed Enemies* and *The Far Pavilions*], and prospects for the two major documentary series [*The Living Body* and *The World: a Television History*] had greatly improved, losses had been incurred on short documentary series and on almost every individual television film produced for Channel 4'. Management, he said, 'had now concluded that these last two categories should generally be avoided, and efforts concentrated on drama series and major documentary series, particularly those large-scale and complex productions which UK and European broadcasters might find difficult to produce alone.' It was felt, he added, that Goldcrest also had 'a valuable role to play' in arranging co-productions between UK broadcasters and the US, something towards which 'both the BBC and ITV companies were becoming more favourably disposed'.

It would appear that the non-executive directors – Angus Grossart, James Joll, Peter Mayer, David Puttnam and Philip Whitehead were at the meeting – reacted strongly to Wooller's preamble. Perhaps not fully aware of the bitterly divided opinions within the management, unable to challenge the assertion that prospects for the two documentary series 'had greatly improved' (they were, in fact, to lose over £2 million between them) and knowing only that there was a lot of money sitting in the bank that ought to be invested, they 'voiced strong concern that Goldcrest should not abandon altogether its previous television philosophy and strategy in favour of production aimed exclusively at the American market'.

Lee, who was chairing the meeting in Stoddart's absence, was taken aback by the non-executive directors' reaction, which threatened to take the wind out of the sails of his proposed reforms. The minutes record that he sought to 'clarify the intentions behind the proposals', which, he said, 'had been misunderstood'. Goldcrest, he assured the company, 'remained committed to British production of distinctive television programming. It should not attempt to compete directly with US network suppliers, nor with BBC and ITV production departments, but rather exploit openings in the market, such as those for large-scale drama series.'

The board's attention was then drawn to Lee's rules on deficit-financing (that no television production could go ahead unless its entire cost was covered in advance by pre-sales in two territories), the prospects for co-productions and the difficulty of coming up with projects that had real international – and, the non-executive directors' blandishments notwith-standing, that meant American – potential. On this latter point, it was suggested that Goldcrest would be better placed if it opened a US office, appointed a US agent, aligned itself with a US television company and/or increased the amount of personal contact between Goldcrest executives and the US networks. (There seems to have been no clear view of which of these approaches would be for the best, although Lee was soon to propose a co-venture with Warner Television, an initiative that was to be drowned in the flood of crises that later engulfed the company.)

The discussion moved on to consider the ineffectiveness of the satellite-producer relationships, only one of which, that with Paul Knight, was thought to have proved satisfactory to both sides.

The debate eventually came to an end and Lee summarized its conclusions as follows:

1. Although the board supported the close re-examination of television strategy, it was concerned that management should not overreact to poor financial returns in specific programming areas.
2. There was general support for narrowing the range of programming interests, and concentrating on fewer, larger-scale productions.
3. The satellite producer concept was not working and would be abandoned. Relationships with talent should be secured through the provision of development finance for specific projects.
4. Management should prepare more detailed proposals regarding US representation.
5. Goldcrest's team needed to be more aggressive in marketing and sales.
6. The new rules on deficit financing had already been implemented and would be adhered to in all but special cases.

These guidelines were taken back to the management for further consideration. Walsh, Chambers and Norris could see nothing in them but still more prevarication. In their opinion there were two decisions that had to be taken before any good could come of 'preparing detailed proposals regarding US representation' or exhorting the Goldcrest team to be 'more aggressive in marketing and sales'. First, Wooller had to go. Second, all television projects currently in development and production had to be reassessed according to commercial criteria. If that meant that the majority, or even all of them, should be closed down, then so be it.

Chambers and Norris made further representations to Lee on the matter of ditching Wooller, as did Lieberson, who apparently gave Lee a choice along the lines, 'either I run this department, in which case Wooller goes, or Wooller stays and I give up television to concentrate on films'. Lee was sufficiently persuaded by these approaches to raise with Michael Stoddart the possibility of sacking Wooller. But Stoddart vetoed the idea, on the grounds that there had been enough upheavals at Goldcrest for one year; that to sack Wooller now would upset the shareholders; and that the important thing was to stop the seemingly endless internal squabbles and get back into production. Lee reported this back to Lieberson, who asked to be relieved of all further responsibility for the television division.

Walsh, who had concluded that it was 'quite clear that we were not going to go anywhere on the television front and that there was no role for somebody like me in the company', decided it was time to quit. He had been considering a number of approaches from American companies during the summer and was now offered a job at Consolidated Productions, the same company that had wooed Norris and Chambers back in March. He left Goldcrest at the end of the year. It would not be unfair to say that Walsh's departure was greeted with relief by Wooller, who surmised, rightly, that Walsh had all along been after his job.

The manner of Walsh's departure caused Paul Knight, who was clearly not overly impressed by Walsh's achievements, to raise a quizzical eyebrow. 'He was allowed to leave and go to Consolidated quite quickly and he wasn't even particularly debriefed,' Knight says. 'I don't think they ever knew what he'd been up to for a year and a half. They didn't sit down and say, "Well, what have you actually done? Where are all these contracts? Where are we in all these negotiations?" '

Knight's remarks form part of his general observation that the television division was never in the hands of a competent administrator, let alone a competent entrepreneur. Regardless of the other failures in policy, he says, television was simply mismanaged. 'They didn't channel their energies and wasted an enormous amount of money,' he says. 'I had a list of what they'd developed, projects which never got past the post, which made hair-raising reading: £1,000 here, £25,000 there. I think they spent over £1 million on development. Most of the satellite producers didn't actually make anything. Money was drained into the *First Loves*. People were allowed to drift in and out, take a lot of money out of the company and never be accountable.

'Let's face it,' he concludes, 'Goldcrest Television was a very easy ride for a lot of people.'

After further discussion of television strategy with the management team, Lee reported back to the board for what was expected to be the last time on this subject. He proposed two organizational changes. First, Lieberson, at his own request, would relinquish control of television, which was to be run by Wooller reporting directly to Lee himself. This was agreed. One consequence of this decision was that there would henceforth be two weekly management meetings: one for film, one for television. The rift between the two sides of the company, far from being healed, was thus actually made formal. Second, to replace the now abandoned satellite-producer relationships, Paul Knight was to be appointed executive producer of drama and drama series. He would report to Wooller, but was to be given direct charge of all the mini-series and television movies that were then in development. This too was agreed.

The television debate was thus brought, temporarily, to an end. Its main achievement seems to have been to dress up in strategic and theoretical terms what had already become the case in practice. The emphasis on drama, and especially mini-series, had been accepted by Wooller back in July, since which time too Lee's new investment rules had been in place. The abandonment of the satellite-producer relationships only confirmed the general management view, shared by Lee, that none of the contracts in question should be renewed. Lieberson's handing over of responsibility for television amounted to little more than a belated recognition that he had never exercised authority in the area anyway.

Wooller, his empire in tatters, was thoroughly demoralized. Norris and Chambers were still dissatisfied: nothing had been done about the loss-making projects that were currently in production and, apart from ending the satellite-producer relationships, no move had been made to slim down the costly television department. As for Lee, he was having to preside over what was unmistakably the demise of an initiative begun by himself and David Puttnam back in the early months of 1981.

Chapter Thirty-nine

Nominal Profits, Rising Costs

Ilott: At the end of October 1984, *The Killing Fields* opened in the United States to reviews that were both excellent and alarming. Excellent because the critics recognized the film's quality, and immediately tipped it as an Oscar contender. Alarming because nearly all of them strongly emphasized the film's realistic handling of what was a very gruesome true-life story. 'Gripping, frightening, drags you right into what was happening', 'gut-wrenching', 'compelling and harrowing', 'makes audiences bleed and sweat', were typical of the comments in the American media.

The problem with films that are gut-wrenching and harrowing is that most people, for whom cinema is, after all, a form of entertainment, don't want to go and see them. As if to warn them off, one American critic, who announced that the film was 'the most compelling experience I have had in years', observed that 'many things on the screen are hard to bear: shattered bodies, human cruelty, pervasive fear'. Another, overwhelmed by the importance of the film's subject matter rather than its entertainment value, said, 'Try to find someone who wants to see *The Killing Fields* a second time. You won't. It's too real and too powerful.'

By the time the film opened, Goldcrest had covered its entire investment of £8.4 million ($11 million). Eberts had secured an excellent deal with Warner Bros., and the initial forecast, of $17 million rentals in the United States, would see Goldcrest not only recoup but take a net contribution from the film of about £2 million ($2.6 million at the then exchange rate of $1.30). The reviews that stressed the bleak and, in terms of entertainment value, negative side of the film were unlikely to jeopardize this prospect. What they might do, however, was inhibit the film's chances of really opening out, of taking not $17 million, but, say, $27 million, from which Goldcrest would net not £2 million, but, with network, cable, video and television syndication prices all tied to theatrical performance, as much as £5 million. Not only would such a return make a handsome impact on profits in 1984 and 1985, but the concomitant cash inflow of £6 or £7 million would do much to relieve the company's borrowing requirements when the new films went before the cameras in the summer of 1985. It was just such a bonanza that everyone at Goldcrest was hoping for.

When the first box-office figures came in, it looked as if their hopes might be realized. Indeed, Warner Bros. were soon predicting that *The Killing Fields* would do better even than *Chariots of Fire*, which had taken $31 million rentals in 1981. In that expectation, they increased their spending on prints and ads. and started to open in more theatres. But then the box office softened: the film, it seems, *was* too gruelling, too serious, and perhaps too masculine, for the wider cinema audience. At the end of the day, it was to be a modest success, taking $15 million rentals. But to achieve that figure Warners had had to spend about $13 million on prints and ads. (Of Warners' $4.75 million advance to Goldcrest, $130,000 was still unrecouped at the end of 1988. It was this prospect that had prompted their concern that in the cases of *The Mission* and *Revolution* they should be able to recoup their advances, if need be, from television, cable and video sales.)

The Killing Fields went on to do as well or better than predicted in most foreign markets, and its eventual contribution to Goldcrest, £2.2 million, was almost exactly as originally forecast.

Once the film's early returns were in, it was possible to draw up the company accounts for 1984, the first full year of Lee's regime.

He could look back only with mixed feelings. He had endured twelve months of gruelling work, but most of the effort for most of the time had been inwardly directed: raising new money, simplifying the labyrinth of partnerships and cross-holdings, establishing a new command structure and management organization, settling strategic policy questions, and addressing, if not solving, the problem of the loss-making television operation. Other than *The Killing Fields*, only two films had been released: *Cal*, which lost about £100,000, and *Dream One*, for which Columbia was still refusing to pay its $2.8 million distribution advance and which was eventually to lose Goldcrest about £600,000. A lot of television product had gone into distribution during the year but, with the exception of the first series of *Robin of Sherwood*, none of it had made money.

Having rejected *The Mosquito Coast* and ditched *The Emerald Forest* Goldcrest had put no major feature film before the cameras during the course of the year. In fact, the only film production starts were Roger Randall-Cutler's *Dance With a Stranger*, which can hardly be counted a Goldcrest production; two of David Puttnam's upgraded *First Loves*, *The Frog Prince* and *Mr Love*; and Martin Rosen's *Smooth Talk*. Goldcrest's share of these investments added up to less than £2 million. New television starts, too, had come to a faltering halt.

The money that had been raised in May was thus still in the bank, earning interest. To this interest was added the continued inflow of cash from earlier Goldcrest releases, especially *Gandhi*, which provided a further £5 million (the film having long since broken even, all this money was available to contribute to overheads), and to a lesser extent *Local Hero* and *Another Country*. Further cash inflows were received from the sale of *The Emerald Forest* and from the completed television productions, the delivery of which triggered substantial payments from such end-users as Channel 4, HBO and Showtime. Thus, with so little going out and so much coming in, it was no great surprise that, at the end of 1984, Goldcrest could report profits for the first time: £1.6 million on a turnover of £14 million and average capital employed of £23 million.

In other circumstances, the posting of first profits after eight years of sustained investment would be the occasion for self-congratulation. Goldcrest, however, announced the 1984 results without fanfare (its press release was blandly headed 'Goldcrest Publishes Results for the First Time') and chairman Michael Stoddart, in his introduction to the company's annual report – not published until June 1985 – was unusually frank in admitting that the figures were 'well below target'. In fact, as the profit-and-loss account for 1984 shows, the £1.6 million surplus was more in the nature of a windfall arising from the reorganization of the company than a true operating profit.

Profit-and-loss account	1983 £000	1984 £000	Change %
Turnover	12,402	13,990	+13%
Direct costs and amortization	(9,338)	(10,350)	+11%
Gross profit	3,064	3,640	+19%
Operating expenses	(1,741)	(2,501)	+44%
Operating profit	1,323	1,139	−16%
Associated companies, non-film write-offs, surplus on currency exchanges, etc.	(198)	(127)	−
Profit before interest	1,125	1,012	−10%
Interest receivable	148	699	+472%
Interest payable	(1,444)	(97)	−1,500%
Pre-tax profit (loss)	(171)	1,614	−
Taxation	(864)	(30)	−3,000%
Profit (loss) after tax	(1,035)	1,584	−

Clearly, the turnaround from a net loss in 1983 of £1.03 million to a net profit in 1984 of £1.58 million was entirely due to two non-operating factors: interest receivable and taxation. The much-reduced tax bill was a technical adjustment, reflecting the utilization of previous partnership losses and the release of deferred tax provisions that had already been accounted for. As to interest, the £1.4 million payable in the previous year had been in respect of borrowings (£384,000) and loan stock (£1.06 million). Following the recapitalization, Goldcrest, with £10 million in the bank, was no longer in need of major borrowing. And with the reorganization, the loan stocks that had constituted the GFI and GFTP partnerships had been converted into simple equity. Thus Goldcrest found itself free of an interest burden of nearly £1.5 million, and in receipt of interest payments totalling nearly £700,000.

If one sets aside interest receivable and tax, then the 44 per cent increase in overheads meant that, in operating terms, the company's performance was actually worse in 1984 than in 1983. The average number of staff employed had increased by 40 per cent, from thirty-five to forty-nine (the year ended with a complement of fifty-two), and, with so many of the new additions coming in at the top end of the hierarchy, direct staff costs had risen by a massive 85 per cent, from £670,000 to £1.2 million a year.

The balance sheet, too, gave cause for concern. As shown below, it clearly indicated the dramatic fall in the value of new investments: only £3.8 million in 1984 compared with £10 million in 1983. It would have been reasonable to expect the eventual cash inflow from these film and television productions to be correspondingly modest, the more so as they included *The Frog Prince, Mr Love, Smooth Talk*, the two television documentary series, *The Body Machine* and *The World: a Television History*, and a general-interest series, *Assignment Adventure*, from none of which large cash receipts were expected. Lee in fact estimated that cash inflows from current investments would total only £9 million over the eighteen-month period beginning 1 January 1985, and that of that £9 million, £3.5 million would be absorbed by overheads while a further £2.3 million was already earmarked to be charged to Pearson as repayment of a guarantee. Thus, only £3.2 million in cash receipts would be available, to be added to the £10 million sitting in the bank, for investment purposes. Given the enormous production costs to which Goldcrest was soon to be committed, this dearth of cash inflow from current investments was bound to put the company under severe financial strain.

But James Lee still had everything to play for. On the one hand, he was presiding over the activities of a newly profitable company which

Balance sheet	1983	1984
	£000	£000
Assets:		
office equipment, motors cars, etc.	138	192
associated companies (mainly cable TV)	383	227
films/TV in distribution	5,388	14,508
films/TV in production	10,477	3,760
films/TV in development	724	862
fixed assets	17,110	19,549
current assets (bank balances, etc.)	673	10,472
	17,783	30,021
Liabilities		
creditors	(307)	(545)
deferred taxation	(616)	(273)
Net assets	16,860	29,203
made up of, share capital and reserves	22,407	33,119
accumulated losses	(5,547)	(3,916)
	16,860	29,203

had no significant debts, a large cash reserve and plans for an unprecedentedly ambitious production programme. On the other hand, the cupboard of current productions was almost bare, the company was sustaining a very high level of overheads, the television-production programme was losing money, and there was more than £1 million invested in a cable venture, Premiere, the success of which looked ever more remote. Nevertheless, at this point, December 1984, there was no more reason to think that the company would be a failure than to think that it would continue to be a success.

Certainly, as far as the majority on the board was concerned, everything augured well. The upset over the management arrangements and share options earlier in the year had been resolved. The subsequent fund-raising had been a success. Bill Gavin had been very satisfactorily replaced by Guy East. Lieberson had come up with a production programme that had received widespread praise. The television problem was thought to have been faced squarely.

In fact, there were only two causes for anxiety. The first was the problem of how best to improve profitability: a £1.6 million surplus, even if it had not been the result of bookkeeping adjustments, represented a very small return on capital employed. The second was the still unanswered question of how to manage the cash-flow requirements of the forthcoming production programme. These two points were addressed at the last board meetings of the year.

On 19 November chairman Michael Stoddart suggested a pre-tax profit target of £7.5 million – a rate of return of about 25 per cent. 'It was considered', record the minutes, 'that this objective would be extremely difficult to achieve.' Lee, having explained that the new production programme would take time to show results, set his own profit target of £6 million – a 20 per cent return on capital – by 1987.

It is debatable whether annual rates of return are relevant measures of performance for a venture-capital investment like film financing. The point, surely, is not to aim for consistency but to stay in the game until you throw a double six like *Gandhi*. Furthermore, return on capital employed gives no indication of the true value of the company's greatest asset, its library of films. Probably better measures of the success of a company like Goldcrest are (a) that its losses are sustainable; (b) that it continues to attract the best talent and ideas; (c) that it has the calibre of management to select wise investments; and (d) that the sale of its library would at any point produce a surplus on the total capital invested.

Such, however, was not the view taken by the Goldcrest board. And one can see why. Goldcrest, with more than fifty employees, was looking less and less like the investment vehicle that Eberts had first designed and ever more like a regular company. And although the nature of Goldcrest's business had not changed, the expectations that it engendered had. Instead of sitting round a table discussing the merits of this or that proposed investment, which had been the sole business of the very first GFI board meeting at which the commitments to *Gandhi*, *The Killing Fields*, *The Howling* and *Escape from New York* had been approved, the board found itself increasingly bogged down in questions of overheads, rates of return, staff contracts, share options – all the paraphernalia, in other words, of a regular business.

Stoddart was merely responding to these developments: since we now look like a regular enterprise, he seemed to be saying, we'd better show regular profits. It is a shame that he did so, for what had long been needed was for someone on the board to rummage through all the accumulated management bric-à-brac and recover the nuggets of what was still essentially a venture-capital project. A discussion of optimum rates of return on capital employed had nothing at all to contribute to this. Like the discussion of an optimum film slate in March, and the similar discussion of an optimum television slate in September, it was abstract and wide open to wishful thinking. No doubt it had its uses, but it also had the terrible effect of diverting attention away from the real points at issue. These had never changed and can be easily summarized: what investments are being made and why. All the rest was noise.

The noise proceeded along the lines laid down by Stoddart and Lee. The minutes of the meeting record that three main constraints on profitability were identified: (a) overheads, which at the end of the year were running at about 9 per cent of capital employed; (b) the limitations imposed by the currently low levels of cash inflow; and (c) the long wait between production investment and recoupment from distribution. Goldcrest, it seems, was not turning over enough money quickly enough. The obvious solution was to employ more money, thereby reducing the proportion absorbed by overheads, improving the cash-flow position and, since investments would be spread across a wider portfolio, diminishing the significance of the lead-lag time during which capital was tied up in current productions.

But Goldcrest, of course, couldn't go back to the market and raise new capital just like that. Most of the £12 million it had raised in May was still in the bank, after all. Nor were the shareholders disposed to put more money in. They wanted to see results first. The only viable options were: arrange additional borrowing facilities in the short term; bring forward to the earliest possible date the flotation of Goldcrest as a public company; and in the interim take minority positions in other people's films that were already in advanced states of preparation, or even production, in order to speed up the capital turnover.

The discussion was continued at the next meeting, held on 18 December, at which Chambers presented a draft budget for 1985. In doing so, he noted that Goldcrest would revert to being a substantial interest-payer in the coming year, since the production programme would require considerable borrowings. His figures assumed that *Revolution, Horror Movie* and six programmes in the *Robin of Sherwood* series would be released in 1985, thereby recovering their costs and making some contribution within the financial year. On that basis, he predicted a pre-tax profit of £1.5 million. Should *Horror Movie* be delayed, as seemed likely following the hiring of yet another new writer to work on the script, then the profit forecast would be reduced to £700,000.

These low figures, which were obviously vulnerable to exchange-rate fluctuations, overcosts in production and even fairly minor shortfalls in sales performance, alarmed the board. A public flotation depended on increasing profits over a period of three or four consecutive years. To flicker into profit in 1984 and then flicker out again in 1985 was no way to impress the investment community. The board urged that the management should push harder on sales. It reiterated that some of Goldcrest's capital should be invested in other companies' productions that would be ready for release in 1985 (and hence contribute to the year's profits), while greater third-party participation should be sought for those Goldcrest projects that would not be ready until 1986. And it urged a clampdown on development expenditure.

As for cash flow, apart from the general anxiety about covering the costs of the new production programme, there were two specific causes for concern. The first was Columbia's steadfast refusal to pay its $2.8 million advance for *Dream One*. Goldcrest had given up hope of making any profit on the picture, but it desperately needed the cash in the first half of 1985, when the new films would get underway. Columbia had drawn up a list of contract violations relating to the technical quality of the film and the appearance in it of one character who, for copyright reasons, was supposed to have been omitted, and while Norris was confident that these points could be dealt with, Goldcrest now faced the prospect of long, and costly, litigation. The second cause for concern, by comparison with which the *Dream One* problem was soon to pale into insignificance, was the startling jump in the anticipated cost of *The Mission*.

The Mission had been approved by the board on 25 September, at which time the estimated cash budget was £11.5 million ($15 million). The board's approval was conditional on the project's being resubmitted should the budget go any higher. On 6 November, only six weeks later, Puttnam informed Lieberson and Lee that the budget had indeed gone higher. Lee summarized the position in a memo that he circulated to Goldcrest's senior executives the next day:

Sandy and I met with David Puttnam last night to discuss the *Mission* budget. At this stage we have the following:

Below-the-line	£12.38 million
Above-the-line	£ 1.07 million
Turnaround payments	£ 0.25 million
Principal cast	£ 0.75 million
Total	**£14.45 million**
Completion fee	£ 0.87 million
	£15.32 million

Thus, before accounting for Goldcrest overhead, we have a $20 million film on our hands.

David has identified budget savings of a total £1.05 million, but these depend on reducing the period of principal photography by one week, from 14 to 13 weeks, and involve certain other reductions, particularly in sets and props. These savings are by no means secured. We know that Garth Thomas remains concerned about the ability of the team to shoot in 13 weeks.

In the light of these facts I propose that we take the following action.

1. I begin negotiations with Warners to remove the limit of $5 million on their advance. I propose to ask for one-third of the total budget.

2. Guy is briefed on the budget change and asked to ensure that his advances are consistent with those justified by a $20 million picture.

3. Sandy and Garth prepare a full analysis of the budget, including a firm top sheet (we do not have one yet).

4. Garth analyse the budget in detail with Iain Smith to recommend

    (a) possible areas of saving, if any; and,

    (b) completion risk associated with the finally agreed budget.

5. David Norris will investigate the possibility of getting up to $6 million as equity finance from Mitsubishi (believed to have blocked funds in South America).

6. John Chambers will prepare a breakeven analysis to find out what levels of gross worldwide would be required to breakeven on a $20 million budget.

I think it should be made clear that at this stage Goldcrest are not committed to production on a $20 million budget. I remain convinced that this subject warrants a $15 million investment, not $20 million. However, I am equally determined that Goldcrest should not lose this opportunity and we will make every effort working on two fronts – firstly, to reduce the cost of the film, and, secondly, to introduce additional equity financing to share the downside risk.

The central question is whether or not we think we have a film with true mass market potential. If we have, then the $20 million budget should not deter us. If, on the other hand, *The Mission* is a film that we believe to have limited appeal (i.e. a film that performs well but gets only $20 million in rentals) then a $20 million budget is problematic to say the least.

In discussions with Robert Bolt, I at least have the assurance of the author that he has written a screenplay intended for a general audience.

This film has become our top priority because the clock is running. I hope that we can all complete our tasks as soon as possible and at least before the Holdings Board meeting on Monday, 19th November. Before that date I will have to decide whether or not to recommend going ahead at a higher budget level than $15 million, since that is the limit of our authority from the Holdings Board at this stage.

(The turnaround payments noted in Lee's budget summary refer to monies owed to United Artists and Paramount, both of which had been involved in developing the script with Ghia and Bolt ten years before. Below-the-line costs are the direct costs of physical production, including sets, costumes, accommodation, travel and wages. Above-the-line costs are the fees paid to the producer, director and leading actors, and the costs of the script. It had been agreed that Goldcrest's overhead – that part of the film's costs accounted for by Goldcrest's office services, contract work, administration and so on – was to be recovered from revenues after the film was released rather than, as is normally the case, from the budget. Goldcrest, in other words, was throwing in its overhead fee as part of its investment. Had the overhead been included it would have added about £900,000 to the budget. Garth Thomas was the newly appointed production supervisor, replacing Terry Clegg, who was now working with Sydney Pollack on *Out of Africa*. Iain Smith was *The Mission*'s associate producer. He was the person most responsible for the detailed and day-to-day management of the production. He had done the same job, very successfully, on *The Killing Fields*. A standard production budget runs to about thirty pages and includes details of every single expense in every department, from wardrobe to laboratory charges, for the duration of the production. The top sheet is the summary that provides the rounded-up totals of above-the-line, below-the-line and indirect costs, such as interest, overheads and legal fees, department by department. Added together these provide the total budget figure. Blocked funds, monies that cannot be repatriated from the country in which they are earned, were at that time thought, by Norris in particular, to be a likely source of third-party equity participation, since they could be used to cover location costs in the local currency. The availability of such blocked funds could even decide in which Latin American country, or countries, the film was to be made.)

That evening, in accordance with the first point in his plan of action, Lee telexed Terry Semel:

Dear Terry

I was delighted to receive Warner's telex today confirming approval of *The Mission* screenplay. Our original proposal was, as you know, based on the assumption that we would be able to contain the budget to a figure of $15 million (excluding Goldcrest overhead but including completion guarantee fee). When we met in New York I mentioned that we were having 'certain budget difficulties'. Sandy and I met David Puttnam last night to review the budget and at this stage we have a budget of $19.8 million including completion fee but excluding our overheads. We have discussed budget savings amounting to $1.3 million, but these are by no means secured as yet. Thus, for the meantime, Goldcrest and Warner should be thinking in terms of a picture costing $20 million, not $15 million. We agreed that Warner would pay one-third of the budget as an advance against US and Canadian rights, subject to an upper limit of $5 million (one-third of $15 million). In the light of the new budget we must ask you to remove that limit of $5 million.

Kind regards,

James Lee.

Semel did not respond to Lee's request immediately, but it is probable that he knew already what his answer was likely to be. He was confident that *The Mission* would be a well-produced and well-realized production, just as *The Killing Fields* had been, and on those grounds had originally been prepared to offer Goldcrest a worldwide distribution deal. But even his best-case estimates told him that the film, by virtue of its subject matter, was not for the mass audience. It was therefore, in his words, 'a film to be made at a price'. And that price was $15 million, of which Warners would put up one third. The only increments that Semel was prepared to discuss were for the principal cast (if it was thought that the addition of a star-name would add box-office appeal) and for prints and ads. (if, when the film was delivered, it was thought to warrant a wider release). In this respect, *The Mission* was perceived quite differently than was *Revolution*, for which Warners initially wanted distribution rights only in North America and France. For, while Semel and his team had doubts about the script, and even bigger doubts about Hudson's ability to bring the film in on time, they recognized that an action–adventure picture about the American Revolution was inherently attractive, as a subject, to the mass audience. Whether it reached that audience would depend on how it was made. In the case of *Revolution*, therefore, Warners had agreed to put up one third of the budget, as they had with *The Mission*, but without a ceiling, additions to the initial estimate of $15 million being a matter for further discussion.

Semel was not of a mind to revise his view of *The Mission*, but, ever cautious, he opted to discuss Lee's request with his lieutenants before making a reply.

Iain Smith and Garth Thomas, meanwhile, were working on possible budget savings. On 8 November, Smith worked out a thirteen-week schedule that would cut £900,000 from the budget, bringing the below-the-line costs down to about £11.4 million ($15 million). As this figure did not include fees for the producer, director, scriptwriter and principal actors, it was still, as far as Lee was concerned, too high. On 9 November he wrote to Sandy Lieberson:

The Mission Budget

Unless we take a very determined stand, I think there is every possibility that we will be sucked into a financial commitment on *The Mission* well beyond that which you and I agree is sensible.

I therefore think that you and I must agree now a maximum figure that we are prepared to tolerate, and then we must stick with it through thick and thin. I have already accepted in my own mind that $15 million is unrealistic. I think you have known that for some time!

Garth Thomas seems to feel that savings of £1 million are achievable, and that an additional £500,000 could be squeezed from the budget without requiring radical changes to the script or the scale or quality of the film itself. This suggests therefore that, in theory, the below-the-line cost could be reduced to just below £11 million, but not much more.

We know the above-the-line costs for scripts, director and the three producers amount to £1.07 million, and there are other costs associated with the screenplay of £300,000.

The provision for the three principal parts, Mendoza, Gabriel and Altamirano, has not been established. We know that there are pressures for major cast, and Clint Eastwood has been mentioned. I have devoted a lot of time to thinking about the pros and cons of a major star for this film, and the implications for the budget. Despite the fact that Roland Joffe is becoming increasingly enthusiastic about a major star (and we should listen carefully to him), I am not convinced.

I would have thought that we should make a provision of only $1 million in the budget for the three stars therefore, although I would like your advice on this. Whatever we decide, I think we should decide now, and make it clear to David and Roland that this is not the next round in the rather woolly negotiations that we seem to be having.

On these assumptions, the situation would seem to be as follows:

	£ million
Minimum below the line	11.0
Above-the-line	1.1
Additional script payments	0.3
Cast	0.8
	13.2
Additional provision	0.3
Proposed budget limit	13.5

£13.5 million at today's exchange rate is $17.5 million.

Lee's figure, a compromise between the originally approved budget and the Puttnam team's latest estimate, did not include overhead or completion fees – which together would have added another £1.5 million – since these were not direct cash costs and could be recovered by Goldcrest out of first receipts. (He later seems to have changed his mind and found space for the completion fee within the £13.5 million.) But he did intend that it should include a contingency – the sum, usually 10 per cent of the below-the-line budget, set aside for unforeseen overages, and without which it is impossible to calculate the completion fee. There was later to be great confusion over the *Mission* budget, so much so that the company, at Puttnam's behest, at one point issued a press release on the subject. Most of that confusion had its origins in the different opinions about whether, and to what degree, and on what basis of calculation, a contingency figure and completion fee were included in the budget.

Lee decided that he would recommend the board's approval of a £13.5 million ($17.5 million) cash budget, subject to two conditions: first, that

Warners put up $6.5 million, rather than $5 million, for the American rights; and, second, that Norris was confident of securing an equity deal using blocked currency. In making this recommendation, Lee was very aware of the fact that Puttnam and his team had already spent more than £500,000 of Goldcrest's money. If the board decided to pull out, this money would be lost.

On 15 November, four days before the board meeting at which this matter was to be discussed, Lee wrote to Puttnam:

Dear David,

This is a formal letter to clarify Goldcrest's position on *The Mission*.

We have so far spent more than $750,000 on development and pre-production, but at this stage no firm decision has been taken to proceed with production. Subject to our Holdings Board meeting on Monday morning, Goldcrest will be in a position to provide you with sufficient production finance to cover the following:

1. No more than £11 million of below-the-line cost (including completion fee, but excluding Goldcrest's standard overheads).

2. All agreed payments for producer and director, including Fernando Ghia's additional settlement payments.

3. The option and turnaround payments.

4. No more than £750,000 of above-the-line cast costs to cover the three parts, Mendoza, Gabriel and Altamirano.

The existing budget for below-the-line costs, excluding completion guarantee, is £11.4 million. Thus, further significant savings will need to be made.

To help you consider these savings I have included our own computer analysis of *The Mission* budget compared with *The Killing Fields*. While we recognize that there are great differences between *The Killing Fields* and *The Mission*, nevertheless, there are certain obvious questions raised by the comparisons. For example, have a look at production management, assistant directors, production accountancy, art department, camera equipment rental, film and lab charges. Increases in these categories range between 33 per cent in the case of production management, and 96 per cent in the case of film and lab charges.

I hope that you find the analysis useful as a basis for agreeing with Iain Smith and Roland Joffe how best to make the savings that remain to be achieved.

Kind regards,

James G. Lee

The computer analysis that Lee attached to his letter listed *The Mission*'s forty-two below-the-line budget items and compared them with the same items on *The Killing Fields*, expressing the differences as percentages. *The Mission*'s total, £11.4 million, was 54 per cent more than *The Killing Fields*' £7.9 million.

Puttnam replied immediately:

Dear James,

. . . We are faced with an overall budget figure which is onerous, and substantially greater than that which I had originally conceived as being appropriate for the film. There are three issues worth citing in mitigation:

1. The new screenplay is far more of an action–adventure story than was the original, slightly polemical piece. It's no small miracle that this has been achieved without any diminution of the original project.

2. *The Killing Fields* was the first picture by Roland Joffe, which was the risk we all decided to take, and it is fair to say that in return Roland took risks, in agreeing to the original schedule and budget, which would be crazy for him to contemplate in his present situation. By this I do not for one moment mean that he will work less hard, and we will in fact have the benefit of the experiences he went through in Thailand. It is merely that he will be a lot less ready to compromise, and I would be doing no one any favours by pretending that this is not a budgetary factor.

3. The current buoyant state of the film production sector of the industry has had its effects on the salaries demanded by top technicians. Furthermore, I would never contemplate undertaking a film of this complexity without being surrounded by the very best people money can buy. I am only sorry it's costing so much to buy them!

. . . I fully understand the points you make, but it would be wrong to mislead you or the board into believing that this film can be made for the £11 million figure referred to. I was very grateful for the copy of the computer analysis that you sent me, which compared the budget of *The Killing Fields* with the proposed budget for *The Mission*. I feel that I have at last got an opportunity to correct some of the mis-assumptions which are in the air.

a. Salaries. If you look at the social security section of *The Mission* budget you will find a zero figure. This doesn't mean that we will be making no social security payments, it rather means that the computer available to us has, for the first time, enabled us to calculate those social security payments into the individual line items for each department. In this way we have absorbed what in the case of *The Killing Fields* was shown as approximately £222,000 worth of social security payments into the body of other parts of the budget.

b. Film stock and lab charges. It was an error to make a comparison with the budget for *The Killing Fields* and not with the final stock statement. Much of the budget exercise on *The Mission* has been helped enormously by the practical expertise gained by Brian Harris [production accountant] and Iain Smith in working two years ago with Roland Joffe. One of the things we discovered is that Roland, whilst able to accommodate savings in other areas, uses a great deal more stock than most directors. In this particular area, we incurred an overage on *The Killing Fields* of £190,000, in using some 650,000 feet of film stock. Some of this, without doubt, was due to inexperience, and we have on this occasion budgeted at 500,000 feet, albeit at the slightly increased figure per foot which Kodak indicated will comprise next year's price list. In this way, it can be readily seen that we are estimating to incur almost £40,000 *less* on this particular item, not, as would appear from your figures, £154,000 more.

c. Production accountancy. A quick check around the business has thrown up the fact that, at £1,350 per seven day week, Brian Harris represents a 10 per cent saving on the current industry norm. Furthermore, he has agreed to head a department of three rather than the four people who would tend to be standard for this level of production. The substantial increase over his salary for *The Killing Fields* is entirely explained by the fact that we took advantage of the weak negotiating position he found hmself in two years ago, the details of which I can more easily explain to you in person.

I have enclosed, unedited, the telex I got from Iain Smith last night. This followed a fairly acrimonious conversation, during which I attempted to corner him into a re-think. What he has to say is in all respects entirely correct, and his conclusion should also be yours, namely that Goldcrest make the final decision knowing that the production team will conscientiously spend not one penny more than is needed to make a motion picture which conforms to the expectations that have been raised by the production of *The Killing Fields*. It is on the basis of *The Killing Fields* that this picture is being funded, and it is on the basis of *The Killing Fields* that it will be judged.

I hope this is all of some help.

Kindest regards,

Yours as ever,

David Puttnam

The enclosed telex from Iain Smith, who was at that time in Colombia – the favoured location – dealing with such matters as labour laws, insurance, hotel rooms and transport arrangements, for the most part reinforces the points made in Puttnam's letter to Lee. It then goes on to say:

Everyone keeps telling me I've been protected on previous films. I never want to be unreasonably protected. I know my productions inside out. Lee Katz [completion guarantor] scrutinized *The Killing Fields* and I enjoyed that because he climbed on a plane and sweated along with us for two weeks. I am always open to scrutiny, as long as it is professional and informed, hard working and exhaustive. You know the outcome of his visit and how we were vindicated in the final analysis. If Garth or Sandy or Jimmy Swann [completion guarantor] or Lee Katz get on a plane, I promise you I will take them round every location and facility and as guarantors they will not wish to reduce our budget. In the case of Lee it would be quite the opposite. What is difficult for me to respect are the armchair opinions which are accepted as some kind of received truth. Believe me we are trying everything in our power to make this film as inexpensively as we can whilst keeping quality commensurate with your name and Roland's high standards. For your information we are spending around £25,000 per week just now, which will increase to around £31,000 in December. Approximately half of these [expenditures] are inescapable [basic salaries], payable in any event. The rest are manifestations of work done. We are now pressing so tightly against the preparation time needed for an April start that my concern is for a Yes: go, or, No: stop, decision as soon as possible.

Yours loyally,

Iain

Faced with such a carefully calculated display of expertise and indignation – the enclosure of Iain Smith's telex was a Puttnam master-stroke – what was Lee, who knew nothing about the making of films, to do? Inevitably, he gave in: £11.4 million became the accepted below-the-line figure.

Guy East, Garth Thomas and John Chambers had meanwhile done the work requested of them, and Lee entered the November board meeting armed with revised sales, break-even and profitability projections. He analysed the new budget and compared it with the budget submitted in September:

The Mission – budget £000	24.9.84	19.11.84
Above-the-line (stars, director, producer and script)	⎱	2,236
	⎰ 11,538	
Below-the-line		11,471
Operating contingency	–	–
Agreed operating budget	11,538 ($15m)	13,707 ($17.5m)
Additional contingency	–	685
Completion guarantee fee	692	822
Budget for completion fee purposes	12,230 ($15.9m)	15,214 ($20m)
Goldcrest overhead (deferred)	783	962
Total including deferments	13,013	16,176 ($21m)
Actual expenditure to date	231	531

(The £685,000 additional contingency in the November budget was a notional figure arrived at solely for the purpose of calculating the completion-guarantee fee and rebate.)

Lee pointed out to the board that the increases in the second budget 'would have a significant impact on Goldcrest's likely return'. Warners, he reported, were 'unlikely to raise their $5 million advance', but East's sales forecasts suggested that Goldcrest's exposure could still be limited to 'around $5 million, as originally anticipated'. He noted that only $1 million was allowed for the casting of the three principal roles, but said that Warners would be 'pressed to bear the excess' of cast costs above this figure. He concluded by recommending that the company proceed with the project while seeking further cost reductions and actively pursuing third-party equity investors to share Goldcrest's risk. The board agreed.

Lee telexed Semel, informing him of this decision and adding:

. . . We would be prepared to accept the Warner offer of $5 million for the US and Canada on the agreed terms, provided that:

1. Warners will agree to cover 100 per cent of any principal cast costs in excess of the $1 million in the Goldcrest budget, and,

2. We can reach agreement on an appropriate mimimum guaranteed level of investment by Warners in prints and ads.

We should aim to finalize a deal this week . . .

Kind regards, James

Puttnam missed the November board meeting because he was attending to arrangements for the London opening of *The Killing Fields*. It is reasonable to suppose, however, that even if he had not had pressing engagements elsewhere he would have given the meeting a wide berth. He was firmly wearing his producer's hat by this time and, since he knew that the board's main business would be the approval or rejection of his own film, he probably thought it better to let them decide the matter without having to deal with his intimidating presence. The vote went in his favour and Lee wrote to him after the event, saying that he was 'absolutely delighted that we are at long last moving ahead with this production. The only remaining questions concern the start and finish dates. I had hoped that it might have been possible to get some limited release before 31 December 1985, but I understand that this is impossible. We must ensure that Warners are prepared to distribute the film in the spring of 1986. We would not want to wait until Christmas 1986 to release this film on an eager world.'

Whether or not the world was eager, it was going to have to wait: *The Mission* did not open until October 1986. But even before the film had started shooting there were to be many occasions on which Lee would have cause to be something less than 'absolutely delighted' with the project.

The first came in the second week of December, less than a month after the board had approved the new budget. Robert De Niro was persuaded by Roland Joffe to play the part of Mendoza. His fee, which was the subject of much hard negotiating between De Niro's agent and David Norris, was to be $1.5 million, plus expenses, plus 13 per cent of net profits. Warner Bros. approved the choice, but would put up only their 'share', $500,000, of De Niro's cash fee. Goldcrest's $1 million above-the-line cast provision was thus used up on one actor.

The Mission's ever-growing budget not only jeopardized Goldcrest's cash-flow and profitability projections, but put further pressure on *Revolution*, which *had* to go into distribution in 1985 if the company was to avoid reporting substantial losses in the year. Although the project had first been approved, subject to budget, at the 25 September board meeting, the wrangling over the script continued for many weeks thereafter. Richard Gere had replaced Sam Shepard as the preferred lead, but no terms had been agreed. None of the other parts could be offered to actors or actresses until both the script and the leading role had been settled. Nor could the budget be fixed.

To make a film in a year – from approval of the screenplay to the release of finished prints – is not uncommon, but it requires very thorough preparation. The more complex the film, the more thorough that preparation has to be. *Revolution* was a period epic to be filmed exclusively on location. To attempt to make it in less than a year, when the script was known to be unsatisfactory, when the director was as meticulous as Hugh Hudson, and when the producer was concurrently making another film in another country (Winkler's contract allowed him to work for part of the time in Paris, helping Bertrand Tavernier with *Round Midnight*), was thought, by at least two of the key people involved, Terry Semel and Hudson himself, to be unwise.

'We found ourselves heading quickly down the track of making the movie when we had a screenplay that basically didn't work,' Semel recalls. 'A lot of changes were made, a lot of changes were promised. The writers were flying wherever the heck they all went, working feverishly to change the screenplay. But it was a very haphazard way of going about it. If that had been our movie at that point in time we would have put the brakes on. We would have slowed down the process. We simply would have said, "This script is not ready to go." '

Hudson remembers that both he and Winkler 'cautioned Goldcrest and said, "Look, we're going too fast – we need two or three more months' preparation." And they said, "No, no, we've got to have the film by next Christmas. We've got to have it, got to have it, got to have it." So we had to accelerate. And that was a terrible error. I should not have let it happen.'

By early December, the *Revolution* budget was put at £11.3 million ($14.7 million) above and below the line, including a 6 per cent completion fee and $1.5 million above-the-line cast allowance. Lieberson warned that $1.5 million would not be enough for the calibre of cast that Hudson had in mind. More importantly, Hudson regarded the budget as a whole as no more than 'a thumbnail budget, to see where we were'.

'It was done before we had even a cast or finalized locations,' he says. 'We didn't know when we were going to shoot, how we were going to shoot, where we were going to shoot. We said, "Maybe it's possible, it depends on where we go." But unfortunately they had got that budget, that figure, into their heads and they wanted to stick with it whatever we did.'

One place that Hudson at first adamantly refused to go was Norway.

David Norris had secured $4 million of equity investment from a Norwegian tax-shelter fund, Viking Film, but it was conditional on some part of the production taking place in that country, thereby making the $4 million eligible for the Norwegian tax breaks that were the real reason for the investors' interest. Only after much argument did Hudson give way.

Chapter Forty

Forecasts and Guarantees

Ilott: In the first week of January 1985, James Lee, John Chambers and management accountant Tony Kelly reworked their cash-flow projections. On the assumptions that *Horror Movie* and *Revolution* would be made and released before Christmas 1985 and that substantial third-party investors would be found for *Revolution* and *The Mission*, they came up with a rough projection that covered the eighteen-month period to June 1986.

Cash required for film investment	**£13.0 million ($17m)**
Cash in the bank	£10.8 million
Cash inflows from current investments	£ 9.0 million
Repayment of Pearson guarantee	(£ 2.3 million)
Overheads	(£ 3.5 million)
Cash available	**£14.0 million ($18.2m)**

While it was thus true that, as Lee noted at the time, 'it looks like our requirement for film investment will be . . . just within the available finance', there remained little room for error (and, incidentally, no room at all for television). The actual flow of cash, in and out, was, of course, bound to be uneven and would necessitate the bridging finance that was available from the Midland's £10 million line of credit. Chambers estimated that the peak borrowing requirement would be about £5.7 million and that this would be reached in November. However, the terms of the arrangement with the Midland required Goldcrest to furnish proof of confirmed distribution contracts to the value of £1 for every 75 pence borrowed. Thus, although the credit ceiling of £10 million was a substantial cash mattress on which to fall back, Goldcrest could fully make use of it only if it had £13.3 million of sales contracts to match.

Warners' advances for *The Mission* and *Revolution* (which were to be paid during the course of production) had already been discounted in Lee's and Chambers's calculations; it was therefore from the rest of the production slate, and from the foreign markets, that the required sales contracts had to come. In February, Tony Kelly, in consultation with

Guy East, produced an analysis that showed that £3.9 million worth of sales had then been contracted, and that a further £2.4 million were in negotiation. Even in the unlikely event that these deals were closed one after another just as Goldcrest needed them, they would still fall £1.2 million short of the £7.5 million worth of contracts needed to cover the £5.7 million peak borrowing requirement. Furthermore, one of the contracts in question was the advance for *Dream One* that Columbia was refusing to pay.

Goldcrest was thus entering into a production programme with only the most slender margin of spare financial capacity and still without any means of fully financing its cash-flow requirement. One of the nine golden rules for investment that Lee had laid down at the September 1984 board meeting at which the production programme had been first approved, was 'Keep Within Capacity'. In the strategy document circulated at that time, he said: 'a film company that lives beyond its means inevitably gets into trouble. Negotiating from a position of weakness in a brutal marketplace is not fun. Consequently, our policy is to tend to operate somewhat below a reasonable projected capacity, leaving room for manoeuvre.' With these principles in mind, Lee now proposed (a) that Goldcrest seek additional borrowing facilities; (b) that either, or both, *Absolute Beginners* and *Mandrake* be rescheduled; and (c) that a production partner be found for either, or both, *The Mission* and *Revolution*.

'In the meantime,' he wrote in a memo to Sandy Lieberson, 'we should assume that we have no financial capacity to commit to further productions beyond those already announced.'

The cash-flow problem was put before the full management committee at its regular Monday morning meeting on 7 January. The next day, Lee circulated the following memo:

I am conscious of the fact that at yesterday's management meeting I may have raised undue alarm about our cash flow situation. My purpose was to make it clear to everybody that our production programme for 1985 was going to stretch our financial capacity to the limits, particularly if the Columbia/*Dream One* situation cannot be resolved.

John Chambers and I have decided to make the following assumptions when thinking about our cash flow next year.

1. We will succeed in securing third-party equity investment in both *Revolution* and *The Mission*. (This means that the Norwegian arrangement will be sorted out, and Cinema Group or another investor will be secured for *The Mission*).

2. The pre-sales programme forecast by Guy is implemented 100 per cent and on the projected dates. This is very important, and I am relying on Sandy to work with Guy to make sure that this is given all the help that it needs.

3. We start *Horror Movie* in April, and that it is available for delivery seven months later in November.

4. We succeed in securing a third-party investor for *Horror Movie* as well.

5. We reach a settlement with Columbia that will give us at least 50 per cent of the $2.85 million owed by the end of March.

6. We remain flexible about the start date of *Mandrake*.

7. The only major television expenditure is the next 13 parts of *Robin of Sherwood*.

On the basis of the above assumptions, I am confident that we should have no difficulty with the 1985 cash flow. However, it should be clear that some of these things require a lot of effort, and will be very difficult to achieve.

(Cinema Group is a US film company, whose president, Harry Gould, had already had a number of conversations with Lee about investing in *The Mission*. That Sandy Lieberson was asked to work with Guy East on the pre-sales programme reflected not only on East's comparative lack of experience, but on Lieberson's extensive knowledge of the international marketplace. His range of contacts and his abilities as a salesman were to be remarked upon even by Chambers, who otherwise had little respect for him. At the January board meeting it was agreed that Norris and Lee would negotiate some kind of compromise with Columbia on the question of *Dream One*. They eventually secured a reduced payment, $2.2 million, payable in two instalments in 1985 and 1987. Lee's reference to *Robin of Sherwood* as the only major television expenditure to be allowed for the foreseeable future drove a further nail into the coffin of Wooller's empire. At this time, the scale of the problem of artists' residuals had not become fully apparent, and there was no reason, as Lee saw it, why *Robin* shouldn't become a long-running profit-earner. Accordingly, he had exerted considerable pressure on HTV, who had at last agreed to co-finance a further thirteen episodes. There was as yet no firm American deal in place, but Lee was confident that Showtime, although it had not reported good ratings for the first series, would exercise its option for the second. Thus, with Jason Connery signed for the lead in the place of Michael Praed, the second series was given the go-ahead to start in February.)

Not only were many of the assumptions set out in Lee's memo not achieved, but, with escalating budgets and overcosts, the cash requirement itself was to be constantly revised upwards.

On Friday, 11 January, the first bombshell landed: Iain Smith, who had just returned from Colombia, met with Lieberson and informed him that pre-production expenditure on *The Mission* was already substantially over budget. In a later memo, he itemized the overages as follows:

Wardrobe staff	£150,000
Wardrobe materials	£100,000
Props	£175,000
Additional dubbing requirement	£ 55,000
Insurance	£ 13,750
Unit overtime	£ 45,000
Film stock and lab charges	£ 15,000
Camera and lighting	£ 10,000
Special effects	£ 10,000
Legal costs	£ 15,000
Music	£ 10,000
Transport	£ 20,000
Other items	£ 31,250
Total	**£650,000 ($850,000)**

Some of these overcosts, for example insurance and overtime, were knock-on expenses arising from increases in other areas. Others, such as those in wardrobe, props and dubbing, reflected unforeseen increases in either the amount of work needed to be done – arising, for example, from script changes – or in such sub-contracted costs as shipping and transport. Others again, such as special effects, music, legal and camera, were additions in areas that were thought to have been under-budgeted in the first place. Smith concluded his memo by warning that there might be a further £250,000 overcost should the picture go over schedule in Argentina, as seemed likely.

Lee and his team thus found themselves facing a production the costs of which kept going up. The operating budget (i.e. leaving aside provisions for contingency, completion fees and Goldcrest's overhead) had originally been approved, at the September board meeting, at £11.5 million ($15 million). At the November board meeting this had been revised to £13.8 million ($18 million). In December, an agreed above-the-line increment of £695,000 ($900,000) had been added following the signing of De Niro. Now Iain Smith was reporting overages of £425,000 already spent in wardrobe and props, a further £225,000 to be spent in the other categories listed above, and the likelihood of a £250,000 overrun in Argentina. With the concomitant increases in indirect costs such as overhead fees, Goldcrest was, as Lee noted at the time, looking at an additional overcost of £1 million. Given the margins within which the company was trying to operate, this was just not allowable.

At the management meeting of 21 January, at which *The Mission*'s unauthorized overspend was said to indicate 'alarmingly poor production management and control', Lee emphasized that an increase in the recently approved budget, such as the production team 'seemed to be seeking', was 'out of the question'. Garth Thomas was to demand detailed accounts for the various overages and an explanation of why they had not been identified before the budget had been approved in November. It was further agreed that weekly cost statements, such as are usually provided only when a film is actually shooting, would have to be furnished from now on; that all overages would require Goldcrest's prior approval; that the production team would be reminded of Goldcrest's responsibilities, and powers, as completion guarantor; that Thomas would visit the locations in Colombia and Argentina in his capacity as the completion guarantor's representative, and, on the basis of his inspection, would decide whether a permanent representative, empowered to overrule Puttnam and Joffe on any matter that might incur additional costs, was required; that Lieberson and Thomas would meet with Puttnam, who was at that time still in Colombia, to discuss the situation; and that Puttnam's and Joffe's contracts would be revised to include the specific requirement that the film be no more than two hours in length (Joffe's tendency to overshoot being considered the most likely cause of further unauthorized costs).

In a memorandum circulated to the Goldcrest management team that afternoon, Lee sought to clarify the position, so that 'all of us are clear how the company stands and who is responsible for what'. He traced the history of the project to date, pointing out that Goldcrest had all along insisted that the film be made within given cash limits. These had already been substantially revised. The company could not allow them to be revised again: the budget would remain at the amount approved at the November board meeting plus the agreed above-the-line cast overage. Since additional monies had already been spent in wardrobe and props, this meant looking for savings elsewhere. Lee added that, 'as far as the psychology of the production team is concerned, there should be a full and frank exchange of points of view between Goldcrest and the team to clear the air before it is too late to prevent serious problems'.

On the same day, Lieberson wrote to Smith:

Your memo of January 16th has caused us tremendous concern. It is particularly worrying since we haven't yet begun the intensive construction, and there is the possibility of something going wrong during principal photography which would extend our shooting schedule.

As you know, we are acting as completion guarantor on *The Mission* entirely due to the fact that it is controlled by David and yourself. We are relying on both of you to a much larger extent that we would normally do on any other producer.

My first concern is to ensure the quality of the film, but we also have to exercise the responsibility we have as completion guarantors and financiers. We obviously can't accept the situation as you've outlined it in the memorandum.

Where you have already spent the money there is nothing to do. Where it is not yet committed or spent you will have to examine each area of possible overage and then agree them with Garth.

We desperately need your and David's co-operation and commitment to try and make this for the budget we previously agreed.

Look forward to hearing from you as urgently as possible.

Sandy

Smith replied:

I am well aware of the tremendous concern being expressed within Goldcrest with regard to the projected overage of £650,000, and as I explained at our meeting, I fully appreciate Goldcrest's position both as financier and as completion guarantor.

Please be assured that you have both David's and my co-operation and commitment both in ensuring the quality of the film and in maintaining budgets, and I wish to make it quite clear that I will make full use of your support in the memo in order to effect whatever cost savings are required.

I will keep Garth informed on a regular basis.

Iain

All of this was reported to the January board meeting. Lee made no recommendations and there was no vote to be taken. All that Stoddart, Joll and Co. could do was to express concern and await further developments. Certainly there was no question of pulling out: by this time, Goldcrest had spent £1.6 million on the picture.

Garth Thomas, whose 'authority to exert control on a line-by-line basis' had been confirmed by Lee, and whose mandate it was to bring the production to heel, went through the overages with Smith. But in a memo dated 28 January his tone was already forgiving. He thanked Smith for 'bringing the details to our attention so quickly', then confirmed that many of the overcosts did indeed seem to be justified. Those that he queried could best be dealt with, he said, when he visited the production in February. Smith replied in equally conciliatory tones, pointing out that the projected overages were 'worst-case' figures, which, with luck, could still be avoided. 'You can be assured', he told Thomas, 'that this associate producer and his team will be effecting every possible cost-cutting exercise.'

Smith nevertheless went to some lengths to elaborate on the many difficulties encountered when filming in Colombia. With reference to those areas of the budget in which overcosts had already been incurred, he said that the country 'affords us very few suitable materials for anything other than the simplest costumes', and, there being a 'significant lack of movement between Colombia and the UK, in both shipping and air freight', they found themselves 'victims of lengthy shipping times', which in turn meant longer hire-periods for props and equipment. In effect, there being no significant film industry in Colombia, it was necessary for Smith and his team to import everything.

Lee, meanwhile, was giving top priority to the task of finding investors to share Goldcrest's risk in the picture. By 30 January he was confident that agreement would soon be reached with Harry Gould's Cinema Group. In essence, the deal that he proposed can be summarized as follows:

1. The budget would be regarded as being in sterling for investment and recoupment purposes. Cinema Group's investment would be in sterling.
2. Goldcrest would act as completion guarantor, for which purpose a 10 per cent contingency would be added below the line. The company would reinsure its completion risk either through Lloyd's or with a completion guarantor such as Film Finances.
3. Finance for the production would then be provided (a) by Warners' advance of $5.4 million (including a contribution to the cost of De Niro); (b) by a £4 million loan provided by Goldcrest; and (c) by equity investment, split fifty–fifty between Cinema Group and Goldcrest.
4. Overheads would not be included in the budget but would be recouped from revenues, the first £250,000 going to Goldcrest and the rest being split between Goldcrest and Cinema Group equally.
5. The proceeds of any tax or currency deals would go into the pot and be treated as revenue.
6. Recoupment would then to be in the following order: first, recovery of Goldcrest's £4 million loan, with interest; second, recovery of Goldcrest's and Cinema Group's equity, with interest; third, payment of Goldcrest's sales commission (15 per cent on all but the Warner territories), of which Cinema Group would take a small share; fourth, payment of deferments, including overheads; and fifth, distribution of net profits, 50 per cent to Goldcrest and Cinema Group as financiers, and 50 per cent to Puttnam, Chia, De Niro, Bolt, Joffe and all the other participants.

(It is an interesting footnote to this story that there were so many profit participants in the film that Puttnam ended up with a personal stake of less than 5 per cent. Furthermore, his production fee, £250,000, was certainly less than half his market value at the time. While a certain amount of this has to be discounted against the development deals that he had with both Goldcrest and Warner Bros., it is still true that he was giving both companies, and Goldcrest in particular, good value.)

Lee drew up a rough budget summary for the purposes of his discussions with Cinema Group:

Above-the-line	£ 3.67 million
Below-the-line	£11.47
	£15.14
Completion fee	£ .90
Legal costs	£ .10
Contingency	£ 1.15
	£17.29
Overhead	£ 1.08
Total	**£18.38 ($24 million)**

On this basis, Cinema Group would be asked to put up about £4.5 million ($5.8 million). Goldcrest would put up the same, plus the £4 million loan.

Lee was confident that the Cinema Group's investment would be confirmed by about the middle of February.

On 24 January a revised business plan for the year was put before the board. Pre-tax profits of £1.7 million were predicted, a marginal improvement on the previous forecast but still a miserable rate of return (less than 6 per cent on capital employed) for the shareholders. Lee, typically, sought to put the best possible gloss on the forecast, pointing out that, while 1985 would be a lean year in terms of profits, the benefits of the high levels of current investment would be felt in 1986 and thereafter. He was also able to point to the new rules governing television investment, which in future would be undertaken only on a no-risk basis. And he promised that the level of write-offs (scripts that had been developed but which had failed to go into production), which had accounted for the equivalent of 10 per cent of net revenues in 1984, would be reduced 'through a determined and vigorous control of development'.

Chambers, equally typically, emphasized the more problematic assumptions underlying his calculations. First, it had had to be assumed that *Revolution* would be delivered before the end of the year. This allowed no time for production hold-ups, yet there were already major construction delays in the Norfolk town of King's Lynn, large parts of which were being dressed to serve as late eighteenth-century New York. Second, it had had to be assumed that *Horror Movie*, too, would be released before the end of the year. But, this, as the minutes record, was 'even more problematic', as the script was being written afresh. (In fact, it was to be agreed before the end of the meeting that *Horror Movie*, on which Goldcrest had now spent more than $300,000, should be taken out of the 1985 revenue projections altogether.) Third, it had

had to be assumed that some part of the second series of *Robin of Sherwood* would be delivered and transmitted during the year. Showtime, however, from whom Goldcrest expected to receive the biggest single contribution to the cost, had not yet made up its mind whether to exercise its option.

As the minutes record, 'in these assumptions, and in Goldcrest's position as completion guarantor on *The Mission* and *Revolution*, lay the major downside risks to the plan'.

The question of completion guarantees had always been a divisive one at Goldcrest, even in Eberts's day. In the case of *The Killing Fields*, David Puttnam had persuaded Goldcrest not to have a completion guarantee. Or rather, he had persuaded them to take out war insurance only and keep the completion risk themselves (giving Goldcrest first call on an amount of money equal to a completion fee for having taken the risk). After a detailed study of the budget and the locations by an independent completion guarantor, Eberts had readily agreed to this proposal. It suited his policy of trust between film-maker and financier.

The Killing Fields had come in on time and Goldcrest had earned its fee. There was general enthusiasm, therefore, for the proposal that the procedure be repeated on *The Mission*, which was in most respects a very similar kind of production to *The Killing Fields* and was even to be made by the same team. One complication was that, since Goldcrest wanted to involve third-party equity investors who probably would not wish to participate in the completion risk, it had to set out formally just how, and at what point, it would recoup its fee, since the money in question would have to be recovered before the partners started sharing the remaining revenues – hence the reworking of the budget for the purposes of Lee's discussions with Cinema Group. A further complication was that it was felt prudent, since Goldcrest was entering into a much greater risk across its entire production programme than it had ever done in the past, to reinsure part of the completion risk with an outside finance company – hence the reference, in Lee's proposed Cinema Group deal, to reinsuring the completion risk 'either through Lloyd's or with a completion guarantor'.

Lieberson did not like to use completion guarantors any more than Puttnam did, and he was generally in favour of the arrangements proposed for *The Mission*. But when the question arose in the cases of *Revolution* and *Absolute Beginners* he was much more cautious and advised against Goldcrest's taking the completion risk itself.

With *Absolute Beginners*, the main cause of Lieberson's anxiety was that, although it was a very ambitious project, its production team was not very experienced. In this view he had the support of the management team. It was proposed, therefore, that Goldcrest should share completion risk on *Absolute Beginners* with the completion-bond company Film Finances. Should the film get into difficulties, a 15 per cent contingency on the below-the-line element of the £6 million ($8 million) budget, would be financed by Goldcrest. The first costs above that contingency, to an amount equivalent to 10 per cent of the budget, would also be financed by Goldcrest. Beyond that, everything would be the responsibility of Film Finances. Goldcrest would recover its contingency, partly from first receipts and partly from an enhanced profit position. The completion fee, to be shared between Goldcrest and Film Finances, would be 6 per cent, half of which would be rebated should the film come in on, or under, budget.

The attraction of these arrangements from Goldcrest's point of view was that, should the film come in on schedule, the company stood first in line to recover its fees, with interest, as well as an enhanced profit share. In addition, while as a proportion of the budgeted costs these additional revenues were not of any great magnitude, as a proportion of Goldcrest's share of those costs, about £2 million, much of which was to be covered by pre-sales (from which Goldcrest was taking a sales commission off the top), they were very considerable indeed. Taking the completion risk, in other words, could result in a considerably enhanced rate of return on the investment. The main shortcoming of these arrangements was that Goldcrest was proposing to take the first element of risk itself: Film Finances would be required to put up the end money only if the film went massively – 20 per cent or more – over budget.

Even if the film did go over budget, however, and Goldcrest found itself financing as much as £1.1 million (the contingency plus the first 10 per cent) of extra costs, that money would still be recoverable from revenues. Problems would only arise (a) if Goldcrest did not have the cash to pay the additional costs; and (b) if the film subsequently failed to perform in the marketplace, in which case there would be no revenues from which to recoup.

In the case of *Revolution*, Lieberson's problem was Hudson and Winkler, both of whom had recently had bad experiences with films, *Greystoke* and *The Right Stuff* respectively, that had experienced budgetary difficulties. In support of Lieberson, Garth Thomas made it known that he had no confidence that the production would be tightly controlled. This was despite the fact that an associate producer, Chris Burt, had been assigned to work with Winkler.

Thomas and Lieberson both argued that the entire completion risk on

Revolution should be handed over to Film Finances. This proposal provoked a lively debate at board level, and it is not clear, from the evidence of their own later testimony, that Stoddart and Joll, who, along with Angus Grossart, were the most sophisticated and experienced financiers on the board, ever fully understood the implications of the choices before them.

Lee argued against Lieberson and Thomas. He wanted Goldcrest to keep some of the completion risk. As in the case of *Absolute Beginners*, the attraction to Goldcrest of taking part of the risk itself lay in the high level of recoupment compared to the company's actual level of exposure: once the Warner deals, the pre-sales and the $4 million of Norwegian money had been discounted, it was estimated that Goldcrest would have no more than $5 million at risk on *Revolution*. (This estimate was soon to come down to less than $2 million following the promised involvement of another third-party investor.) Lee therefore proposed that Goldcrest should bear a 10 per cent contingency and all overcosts up to a further 10 per cent of budget, after which completion monies would be provided by Film Finances. Goldcrest and Film Finances would share the 6 per cent fee equally.

Lee's view carried the day. As the arrangements he put forward involved essentially the same risk and fee structure proposed for *Absolute Beginners*, and as Goldcrest was anyway looking to reinsure part of the completion risk on *The Mission*, it seemed sensible for all three films to be packaged together in an overall completion deal. As the minutes of the 4 March management meeting recall, 'this would be a private arrangement between Goldcrest and Film Finances: details need not be disclosed to production teams and, in its dealings with them, Goldcrest would act to control costs to the approved budget excluding any contingency'. Goldcrest, in other words, would not be above exerting moral pressure on the film-makers by letting them believe that it was on the line for every penny that their productions went over.

However, having agreed to take part of the completion risk, Goldcrest now had to ensure that the budgets of the three films were watertight – that there should be no possibility of the productions having to have recourse to their contingency allowances, let alone to completion funds.

There was already considerable concern on this score, for all three films seemed to be getting more and more expensive. At the January board meeting, the non-executive directors were surprised to be informed by Lee of the £650,000 overages already added to *The Mission*. They had, after all, given their approval to a substantially revised budget only six weeks before, and in the interim had allowed a further increase in the above-the-line costs to accommodate Robert De Niro. The film was still many weeks away from the start of production: how many more budget increments were there to be?

They were rocked back in their seats when Lieberson then reported that Al Pacino was now favoured by Hudson and Winkler for the leading role in *Revolution*. The above-the-line cast allowance on this picture was $1.5 million − a figure, admittedly, that Lieberson had already warned would probably not be enough. But even he had not had a star of the magnitude of Pacino in mind. Pacino wanted $3 million, plus expenses, plus 10 per cent of the gross.

Pacino's $3 million fee was then worth about £2.5 million, which, with the addition of expenses and profit points, brought the cost of hiring him to something close to £3 million. As this was the limit beyond which all commitments had to be referred to the board, and as £3 million anyway constituted a substantial material addition to a budget that had already been approved, the casting of Pacino had to be put before the directors. Thus, Michael Stoddart, Angus Grossart, James Joll, Peter Mayer and Philip Whitehead found themselves voting on Hudson's choice of actor, albeit in the guise of voting for or against an increase in the budget. They were perfectly right, indeed obliged, to do so, but it was still a curious position for a group of financiers, a publisher and a television producer to find themselves in.

'I remember distinctly saying something, in a rather naive way, [about the wisdom of it] at that stage,' recalls Michael Stoddart, 'and they said, "If you have a man like Al Pacino you get $3 million straight back at the box office." There is no doubt that I voted in favour, because the experts sitting around the table all said that this was the right thing. Mr Hudson was the man who was recommending it and it would have been a very foolish chairman, who wasn't experienced in the industry, who would stand up and say, "We don't have Pacino." The consequence of that would be that the director would be absolutely horrified. The producer would say, "What are these people doing? Here's our recommendation. We're putting our artistic talent, reputations and so on, at stake." So, I'm jolly sure I voted for it. But the vote wasn't on whether he would make a suitable actor or not, because that was a foregone conclusion − the experts had told us that he was − the question was, could we get the extra money back? We were informed that we could.'

In Chambers's recollection, the experts' opinion was far from unanimous.

'David [Norris] and I were particularly against Pacino,' he says. 'We didn't think he was the right man and he was very expensive. We didn't see what he was really going to add to the film. We were doubly worried, since the combination of a Hollywood star, a front-man producer and Hudson was capable of producing terrible problems in itself. Our view was shared by Film Finances. We had an open discussion at the main board meeting and we were asked individually whether we thought Pacino should be hired. David and I said no. Lieberson wouldn't say yes or no: it was almost like he wasn't part of the company at all; he was like some sort of outside consultant, saying, "Well, if you want to do it, do it, if you don't, don't." '

The vote nevertheless went in Hudson's favour, partly, no doubt, because it had been suggested that he would withdraw from the picture if Pacino were not hired. The board's approval, however, was subject to the negotiation of satisfactory terms, since Goldcrest could simply not afford to give Pacino part of its share of the gross.

Meanwhile, out at Shepperton Studios, the first week's shooting of *Absolute Beginners* had just started. Orion, now confirmed as the US partner, had insisted that the film go into production before the end of January. It didn't matter if it was only for one day. Nor did it matter if the camera focused on a tea-cup. As long as principal photography could be said to have started before 31 January 1985, then *Absolute Beginners* could be included as the last film in a ten-picture pay-TV package that Orion had signed with HBO. This had been agreed and the one-week shoot had been arranged.

The fact that the film was under way was noted with approval by the non-executive directors at the board meeting. What they did not know was just how elaborate a street-set for the film was being built on the backlot. An equally elaborate construction was going up on H-stage. Terry Clegg, who was of course very familiar with the project and with the production team ('nice lads and well-intentioned, but they really didn't have their act together'), had just returned to his office at Shepperton after working on location on *Out of Africa*. The *Absolute Beginners* sets were creating a lot of excitement at the studio and he wandered over to have a look.

'I looked at H-stage and I looked at the set that was on the lot,' he recalls, 'and I thought, "I don't know what they're doing here, but this is a very expensive construction. This is a big-budget movie." It was way above what I had understood they were making. And I spoke with David Norris – he came down to lunch one day – and I asked him what sort of money they were making the movie for and he told me, and I said,

"Well, somebody's fooling somebody, because I can tell you there is no way that picture can be made for that price." '

Absolute Beginners was, as Clegg had guessed, already overspending heavily.

The film's budget, in fact, was still the subject of much contention, for it stubbornly refused to come down from the £6 million estimated by producer Steve Woolley to the £5.5 million ceiling that was being insisted upon by Goldcrest and Virgin. Moreover, Woolley's figure did not include contingency or completion fees, whereas Goldcrest's did. One upshot, should the higher figure be conceded, was that Orion's advance would account for 33 rather than 40 per cent of the budget. Another was that every addition to the cost would eat into the contingency funded by Goldcrest.

Goldcrest was at that time also having difficulty with David Puttnam's package of low-budget films. The first two, *The Frog Prince* and *Mr Love*, had already gone into production, but there was no great enthusiasm for the third, *Knights and Emeralds*, which Goldcrest now wanted to shelve. However, it appeared that Warners were obliged to take the films only if all three were produced, and, furthermore, that Goldcrest was committed by the terms of its agreement with Enigma to make all the films as long as the aggregate cost did not exceed £4.4 million ($6 million). The first two at that time had an estimated final aggregate cost of £2.9 million ($3.8 million) and the budget for the third was put at £1.5 million ($2 million), so Goldcrest was still bound by the deal. However, Warners agreed that it might be better to postpone the third film for six months, by which time the results of at least one of the first two would be known. Should either of them do well, then any surplus revenues earned could be used to enhance the budget of the third, in order to improve its quality. Also, if the third picture were delayed for six months, Puttnam might by then be sufficiently free of his production chores on *The Mission* to take it over himself.

Puttnam was not happy with this. As he saw it, there was already money enough to make the third to the standard required. His view prevailed and the film duly started production, as originally scheduled, in April 1985. (It was to cost £2.2 million. Goldcrest's share of the cost of the three films taken together was about £2.5 million, on which it made a loss of about £1.5 million.)

As for the other films on Lieberson's list, *Horror Movie* was stuck in rewrites; *Mandrake*, on which Goldcrest had spent $482,000, had gone back to the drawing board; and *Dream Song* was stalled for want of promised third-party funds.

Chapter Forty-one

High Anxiety

Ilott: After more than a year of inaction, Goldcrest was at last throwing itself back into production, and this should have been the occasion for rejoicing. But the mood inside the company was, in Attenborough's words, 'filled with dread'. For everyone was aware that Goldcrest's resources were finite and, in the scale of things, modest; and that the production programme, which invested virtually the company's entire capital in *Revolution*, *The Mission* and *Absolute Beginners*, was a three-way bet that Goldcrest could not afford to lose. None of the films enjoyed the wholehearted support of the Goldcrest staff, or even of the management team. *The Mission*, which was the least contentious from a creative point of view, was thought to have the smallest chance of commercial success. It was simply too expensive for the kind of audience it was likely to attract. *Revolution*, which was the most contentious from a creative point of view, was acknowledged to be the one film on the list that could make serious money. *Absolute Beginners* inspired loathing (Chambers, Attenborough) and bemusement (Norris, Thomas) in more or less equal measure. Only Lieberson and Lee were unreservedly in the film's favour, although it is true that East, on finding a much more positive response than expected from international distributors, managed to work up some enthusiasm for it (even to the point of increasing his pre-sales forecasts from $3.3 million to $4.5 million).

None was more aware of how close the company was to being placed in jeopardy than were Norris and Chambers, whose alliance had become, by February 1985, as significant a factor in the management of the company as had the cold war between Lieberson and Lee. After what had been a relatively long period of silent but resentful acquiescence in Lee's conduct of the company's affairs, Norris and Chambers now decided that the time had come to break ranks and protest.

Chambers, a man of considerable ambition, was at that time eager to advance from his role as principal manager of the back office. The only place to which he could advance was the front office, then occupied by Lee in the chief-executive's chair, Lieberson in production, Mike Wooller in television and Guy East in sales. Chambers had long held Lee, Lieberson and Wooller in low regard; East, his junior in age and experience, he merely tolerated.

Chambers had built up a staff, in finance, administration and personnel, of some eighteen people – by far the largest single group within Goldcrest. They were very loyal to him and they shared, to some degree, his antipathy towards all other departments in the company other than that led by Norris. In part, this no doubt reflected the traditional, possibly inevitable, rivalry that exists in most companies between the back office, which tends to regard itself as responsible and hard working, and the front office, which it regards as irresponsible and lazy.

Norris, too, is a man of considerable ambition. And, as with Chambers, that ambition, in the early months of 1985, had yet to find full expression. Norris had seven people working under him in legal and business affairs, and he not only enjoyed their support but, because of his alliance with Chambers, he enjoyed considerable support from the finance and administrative staff as well.

It would be broadly true to say that the entire back-office staff looked upon Norris and Chambers as the true leadership of Goldcrest and upon Lieberson and Lee as interlopers who were wrecking the company.

It should be said, of course, that Lieberson's nine production staff, the six working for Wooller in television and the twelve working for East in sales, all had loyalties and alliances of their own. Among some of them, Chambers, for example, was not a popular man.

That Goldcrest was thus composed of departmental fiefdoms that were virtually condemned to exist in a state of constant rivalry was arguably Lee's fault. He had designed the company that way. It was part of his grand vision. From the day that he took over from Eberts there had issued from his office a steady stream of staff and organizational charts enshrining the departmental principle. At the beginning of 1985 there were fifty-five people at Goldcrest and Lee might have been expected to know them all. Instead, he required his departmental heads to supply written, confidential staff reports. It was a style of management derived, presumably, from his training at McKinsey. It was appropriate for a big corporation. It was surely inappropriate for Goldcrest.

To this day, Norris and Chambers find it difficult to agree on just how calculated was their decision to break the spell which seemed to have been cast over the company. Norris tends to play down the element of conscious politicking. Chambers tends to play it up, presenting their manoeuvres as a planned conspiracy. What is certain is that, from February onwards, they acted increasingly not only as an opposition but as an alternative leadership. In the four months to June 1985, they were often to be found in one or the other's office, long after hours, deep in discussion. Lee, Lieberson and Wooller, they concluded, had to go. Television had to be closed down. All the peripheral activities had to be curtailed. Development costs had to be cut back. Overheads had to be reduced. *Revolution* had to be either put under the supervision of a super-tough producer like Alan Marshall or stopped altogether. It was too late to stop *Absolute Beginners*, but that too had to be brought to heel.

To achieve all this, the support of the back-office staff was not enough. Norris and Chambers needed the support of the board. But the board, they knew, while it might give them a hearing, would not give them the reins of the company. A new leader had to be found. There was only one possible candidate.

Eberts: The fund-raising exercise for Embassy Film Associates was more or less wrapped up by the end of 1984. It was judged within the company to have been a failure, although this wasn't something we cared to admit in public. Some money was raised, and the deal was eventually closed, but it was not the amount that we had hoped for – we managed just $55 million of the $100 million target – and none of it came from the kind of people we were expecting it to come from: apart from one lucky telephone call by me that resulted in $10 million from a pension fund in Oregon, everything came from in-house sources and from a trade-out with Technicolor. Almost half the money came from Norman Lear and Jerry Perenchio themselves.

Jerry was very upset about it all. Whether he blamed me I don't know, but clearly the large salary I was being paid had not been justified in his eyes, or in the eyes of anyone else in the company. I rarely saw him, and only occasionally spoke to him on the telephone. Our conversations were brief and businesslike and his general tone left me in no doubt about his displeasure.

I was hurt by this attitude. After all, no one felt the lack of success more than I did. Nor could I accept that the failure was my responsibility entirely: we had no investment bank to assist us – thanks largely to Jerry's 'Blue Moon' outburst – and Jerry and Norman, who as joint owners had complete control over the company, had no track record in feature films in which investors could have confidence. Proof of that, if needed, is that not one of their film-industry friends or associates, who, after all, were supposed to be our prime targets, put money into the fund.

I was upset, too, because Jerry's attitude undermined everything that had gone before. I didn't blame him – his job was to build the company, not make friends – but I regretted having been taken in by his earlier displays of warmth and companionship. Business is not the most important thing in life, and opportunities for real friendship, such as Jerry seemed to offer, are not so plentiful that one can treat them lightly. In fact, my way of conducting business – perhaps the one lesson I had learned by then after sixteen years as an entrepreneur – was not to exploit, but to build on friendship.

I wasn't the only one having difficulties at Embassy. Alan Horn was going through a very tough time. He knew that Jerry and Norman were looking for someone else to run the company, someone with feature-film experience at a very high level. (Like Jerry and Norman, Alan came out of television.)

I don't doubt that Alan resented the fact that I was getting paid an awful lot of money, but he didn't let that become a personal thing. Indeed, he was always correct and courteous in his dealings with me. Professionally, however, it was clear from the first day that he had no use for me at all. The ideas I had for films were all of the classy, prestigious, Goldcrest type, and that was not what interested him. He wanted mainstream, audience-pleasing entertainment. I didn't object to that. The real difference between us was that the audience I wanted to please was a little older than the cinema mainstream. The film-makers I was talking to at the time were mostly Europeans: commercially minded for sure, but in a very different way from most film-makers in Hollywood. Even the American film-makers with whom I was associated – Jerome Hellman, for instance – tended to steer clear of the high-concept, formula movies designed for sixteen–twenty-two-year-olds that were Alan Horn's principal interest.

So, having failed on the fund-raising front, I now found myself without a role in Embassy. And I had no authority at all. Forget committing money to projects and film-makers: I couldn't commit a taxi fare without getting approval from LA. I couldn't even help those film-makers who were already working for the company, for I had no access to Jerry and no influence with Alan. John Boorman had known, when I was sent to 'kick his ass' in Brazil, that I had no power, that I was just a hired hand.

Dickie's experience was not quite as bad as John's, but it was similar. I spent a lot of my time with Dickie saying, 'Don't worry about Embassy. Just relax. They're good guys.' This was in spite of the fact that he was continuously harassed by them about every aspect of *A Chorus Line*, and most importantly the casting. They used to drive him mad.

Just before Christmas 1984, I had put to Jerry and Alan the outline of a proposal which would enable me to do what I wanted – develop relationships with film-makers – while still being of use to them. My idea was to set up a development fund with capital raised from outside the company. I would run it myself from London. All my projects would be offered first to Embassy, and if they went ahead with one then my packaging fee would be taken out of my salary. If they did not want a project, I would be free to take it elsewhere. Any fees that I then earned from a third party would likewise be set against my salary. In other words, my salary, to which Embassy was contractually committed for a further two years, would become an advance against fees, whether earned from Embassy or from another company.

A provision already existed in my contract for an arrangement along these lines, but it stipulated not only that Embassy would themselves put up the necessary development funds, but that if they passed on a project I was not allowed to take it elsewhere. Given the gulf that existed between my ideas and those of Alan Horn and his colleagues, it seemed unlikely that I would ever come up with something that they would want to develop.

I did not want to endanger my contract but neither did I want to sit on it, taking the money but doing nothing in return. Most of all, I wanted to restore my now faltering relationships with the film-makers of my acquaintance.

Jerry made no direct response to my proposal. Instead I had a call from Alan Horn saying that it had been considered very briefly by himself and Jerry (and I presume Norman), and that they really weren't interested in it. I said that I would like to leave it on the table for further discussion. As I was due to be in LA sometime in January 1985 we could talk about it then. This was agreed.

I did not get to LA until February. After several fruitless attempts to fix a meeting with Jerry directly, I received a cryptic telex from Alan Horn saying, 'Jerry will see you at 11 o'clock on Tuesday morning at his house in Malibu.' It would be the first time I had been there in almost a year.

I got to town on the night of Monday, 18 February, and checked into the Beverly Hills Hotel. In the morning, I had an early breakfast, then drove out on Sunset Boulevard to the Pacific Coast Highway and up to Malibu. On the way, I rehearsed the arguments in favour of my scheme. To be honest, I didn't think I had much chance of getting it approved.

On the other hand, it wasn't going to cost them anything and it would at least enable me to be of some use to them, if only for the duration of my contract. It was worth a try.

When I got there, I found Alan Horn standing outside the entrance to Jerry's house. I hadn't expected to see him: what I had to say wasn't so important or so complicated that it required the attention of Jerry and Alan together. It was odd, too, to find him waiting outside – as if he had been assigned to be my escort.

Alan is not an easy-going man, but he makes an effort to be friendly and he overcomes his natural inhibitions when greeting someone by patting them on the back or giving them a Hollywood hug. But there was none of that on this occasion. He was very sombre.

He said nervously, 'Jerry's inside waiting for you.'

The big house was being redecorated and Jerry was temporarily camping in one of the guest houses. Alan ushered me inside. Jerry, who was sitting down to an unusually late breakfast, was having trouble with his back and was not able to stand up to greet me. I had the feeling, nevertheless, that he was happy to stay sitting down: it created an 'I'm-the-boss' impression. Certainly there was nothing of the warm, outgoing, super-host reception which I had always associated with him. I had not seen him for several months and had not been able to establish any kind of rapport with him following the collapse of what I had once regarded as our friendship.

After the rather stiff 'hellos' there were no pleasantries and no attempt on Jerry's or Alan's part to make small talk. I took my cue from the silence and started to outline my plan. I had not spoken for more than a few seconds before Jerry waved his hand and said, 'Wait, wait, wait, wait.' He glanced at Alan, then turned to me and said, in a matter-of-fact tone of voice: 'Jake, I think that our relationship has to come to an end.'

I was stunned. For matters to have gone this far they must have been talking about it for weeks. I had no idea.

I said, 'Well, if you've made that decision and it's unequivocal then there would seem to be no point in going on with my proposal.'

Jerry said, 'That's right.'

It was as simple as that. We were no longer colleagues.

Jerry went on, 'I think you should get together with Alan and work out some sort of severance terms.' Then he added, 'Would you like a cup of coffee?'

I was struggling to find appropriate words, and managed only to say something along the lines of, 'Well, I'm sorry that it didn't work out. I guess these things happen in life.'

There was tension in the air: the weight of all the things that were left unsaid. But there was no unpleasantness. Nobody was rude. There was no shouting. We just cut the cord and had a cup of coffee. After a couple of feeble attempts at light conversation, I said, 'Well, I see no point in prolonging the agony. I guess I might as well get on my horse.'

Jerry struggled to his feet, we embraced, and I walked out. The meeting had taken no more than five minutes.

Alan Horn accompanied me out into the bright sunshine and said with a pained smile, 'We should work out some sort of deal.'

Equally uncomfortably, I replied, 'I'd better speak to my lawyer first. I'll get back to you. Don't worry, I want to settle the thing quickly, get it done and move on.'

We shook hands and he went back into the house. I walked across the street to where Jerry Hellman lives. I often used to go to his house for dinner or drinks, and he was now a friend at hand, someone I could turn to. I was in a bit of a daze.

We sat in his living room, right on the edge of the beach, looking out across the deck to the sea. I told him what had happened and we talked about what I should do next. I called my lawyer, Tom Lewyn, and I called my friend, CAA agent Marty Baum. Marty and Tom had negotiated my contract with Embassy and I wanted to put them in the picture and get their advice.

I am sure Embassy felt much as I did – that it would be best to get the severance dealt with as quickly as possible – but it still took a couple of weeks. I was on a pay-or-play contract, which meant that I had to be paid for the term of our agreement whether I was working or not. I didn't want to stick Jerry with the full amount, because I didn't think that was fair. He hadn't really got what he had been hoping for, after all. On the other hand, I had given up my job at Goldcrest and had been seduced into going to Embassy on the understanding that certain conditions would be fulfilled. As far as I was concerned those conditions had not been fulfilled at all. So I wasn't going to roll over meekly and say, 'All right, it hasn't worked, I'll just go away.'

Pay-or-play contracts usually have what is known as a mitigation-of-damages clause. This means that if the company is obliged to pay you your full salary during the unexpired period of your contract and you then go out and earn money from a third party, you have to reduce the amount which is owed to you by the amount of your new earnings. So my first option was to say, 'All right, I will repay you the amount I earn elsewhere during the unexpired period of my contract.' The second option was to say, 'Rather than go through all the accounting mess and documentation and arguing, let's just settle on a figure now. It will be less than the full amount that you owe me, but if I accept it I do not then have to reimburse you for any other money I may earn.'

A third alternative was put to me by Tom Lewyn, who said, 'If you want to, you can go and sit on a beach for two years. You can do nothing and continue to collect your salary. But if you do that you're going to lose touch with the business; you're going to lose touch with your friends; you're going to lose touch with what's going on; and, when you try to come back in two years' time you'll have a terrible struggle getting yourself re-established.'

I am anyway not the kind of person who can do that. I couldn't sit on a beach for more than twenty-four hours without getting fussed. I could possibly go on a two-week skiing trip somewhere, or I might last six weeks exploring the Antarctic or fishing in Australia, but I couldn't take two years off. I would go mad. So that was not a practical alternative. Nor was the idea of accounting for other earnings: I did not want Embassy scrutinizing my personal finances. So, over the next couple of weeks, Tom was to work out with Embassy's legal department a settlement by which they made a final payment, acceptable to us both. Once that had been done, we were to sever all further connections.

Having discussed these various options with Tom and Marty on the telephone from Jerry's living room, I began to relax. In fact I felt nothing but relief. I had money in the bank, I had my development-fund idea and I was rid of a job which had only caused me unhappiness. My time at Embassy had been as bad as the Oppenheimer days, when all my ventures – the Marbella Hilton tennis club, the Frankfurt office development and the insurance company – had failed. What you enjoy in your working life is not necessarily what other people think that you've done, but what you think you've done. At Embassy I knew that I had done nothing.

All I had to do now was decide what to do next.

Chapter Forty-two

Over-exposed

Ilott: David Norris spent several hectic days at the beginning of March hammering out a deal with Al Pacino's agent. Warner Bros. had already indicated that, while they approved of the choice of Pacino and were prepared to put an additional $750,000 into the above-the-line cast allowance to help pay for him, they would not bear any share of his proposed gross participation. This left Goldcrest in a difficult position, for there was no way that the company could surrender the equivalent of 10 per cent of the gross from its share. Either Pacino would have to settle for a piece of the net profits or another actor would have to be found. The latter outcome raised the spectre of Hudson and Winkler withdrawing from the picture altogether.

Norris eventually secured terms whereby Pacino would get his $3 million, payable in weekly instalments during the course of the production, plus expenses ($2,500 a week in London, $1,500 a week on location), plus a secretary, a cook and a chauffeur-driven car, as well as 20 per cent of the net profits. The non-financial clauses in his contract gave him rights to rehearsal time and approval of script changes.

These terms having been agreed, Goldcrest's main worry was the impact that Pacino would have on the style and scope of the production. 'Not that Pacino was anything other than a 100 per cent professional,' notes Norris. 'But Sandy warned that when you cast a Hollywood star you really ought to add two weeks to the schedule. Not because of temperament but because of the influence they will have. That level of casting creates a mind-set and everybody then starts getting grander and time gets added. So the budget was on the way up by more than just the amount of the fee.'

Garth Thomas's avowed lack of confidence in the Hudson–Winkler team meant that a considerable burden of responsibility was placed on the shoulders of *Revolution*'s associate producer, Chris Burt, whose 'effectiveness', the minutes of one management meeting tell us, 'would be particularly important'. Associate producer is the official title of the person usually known as the line producer. It is his, or her, job to make sure that everything goes according to schedule.

Burt was then forty-three and had spent most of his professional life in British television, working as a director, associate producer and editor on such popular detective series as *The Sweeney*, *The Professionals* and *Van Der Valk*. He had most recently produced the high-gloss mini-series *Reilly, Ace of Spies*. His feature-film experience, however, was limited to *The French Lieutenant's Woman*, of which he had been production manager. It is not apparent from his background that he was ideally suited to take charge of a big-budget picture with a difficult director and a star of the calibre of Al Pacino.

Burt spent most of January and February supervising *Revolution*'s preproduction. 'To get a film of that size ready by the middle of March, not having started really until the New Year, with all the complications of troops, costumes, movement, catering and all the rest of it, was a huge operation,' he says. 'You are not talking about taking over a small area; you are talking about taking over the streets of King's Lynn, and going round to every single house and getting permission to take down aerials and all the rest of it. Then we wanted to shoot on Dartmoor, because we were looking for undomesticated land, huge tracts without hedges, like America at the time of the Revolution. But we had problems with the Duchy of Cornwall, who had had film crews on Dartmoor before and didn't want it spoiled. It was all done under great pressure of time. But we were ready to shoot. Hugh had everything he wanted. There were never any hold-ups because of fuck-ups.'

While this was going on, Hudson himself was in New York. 'Given the time limits, I couldn't be everywhere,' he says, 'and I had to be with Al Pacino, the main character. In this kind of film you have to work on the major character, rehearsing, going through the script, trying to help his character. I went over to New York for three weeks, while the rest of the casting was going on [in London]. Everything was happening one on top of the other.'

The importance that Hudson attached to the casting of Pacino, and the trouble that he took to prepare him for his role, contrasts with the hurried and, by his own account, none-too-careful casting of Nastassia Kinski in the role of Daisy McConnahay and of Donald Sutherland in the role of Sergeant Peasy. Hudson had not even met Kinski, and was not to do so until the first day of shooting.

'We didn't have anybody and she was free,' he explains. 'I've always liked her work, so we cast her.'

He now believes that she was a bad choice. 'The way you see it – Pacino, Kinski and Sutherland – you expect Pacino and Kinski to be a love story set against history,' he says. 'And of course it wasn't, and people were disappointed. It would have been better to cast an unknown English actress. Then, I think, the audience would have accepted the way the character was written.'

Kinski was not just, in Hudson's view, wrong for the part (when the film was released the critics objected far more strongly to the anachronistically Brooklyn-accented Pacino and the bizarrely Glaswegian-accented Sutherland), but she was ill through much of the shooting, disappeared for several crucial days, and developed something of a loathing for her director. Nor was she cheap: like Sutherland, she was to receive $500,000 (part deferred), plus expenses, chauffeur-driven car and cook.

Pacino could not start the film until he had had time to rehearse with her, as many of their more difficult scenes together were scheduled for the beginning of the shoot. And there were still arguments over the script, the ending of which did not satisfy Hudson. He wanted to bring in a writer, Colin Welland, before the film started shooting, but Lieberson refused, ostensibly on grounds of time and cost, but more likely for the reason that he simply did not want further changes. At one point he had to telex Hudson to the effect that as far as Goldcrest and Warner Bros. were concerned the investment was 'conditional upon production of the agreed ending only. An alternative ending should not be provided.' Undaunted, Hudson later took advantage of the stand-off between Lieberson and Lee to secure Lee's approval for the changes he required.

The need for rehearsal, continued script arguments and further construction problems pushed the start-date back from 7 February to 18 March, adding significantly to the costs. Indeed, overages had already been incurred in pre-production and it was predicted that there would be further overages in post-production, especially in overtime and editing costs, if the film was to meet its December deadline. Lieberson reported to the March board meeting that there was now room in the schedule for only one preview and re-cut, whereas Hudson's contract allowed him three. Such privileges are usually jealously guarded by film-makers, but Hudson, Lieberson said, was personally committed to the delivery date and was prepared to forgo his rights in the matter. It was but one of many decisions that Hudson was later to regret.

In the second week of February, Chambers produced a revised cash-flow forecast. It showed, to no one's surprise, that Goldcrest's maximum borrowing requirement would not be £5.7 million, as predicted only a few weeks before, but the whole of the Midland Bank facility of £10 million. As there were insufficient sales contracts to cover this, Lee and Chambers started looking for sources of additional credit. Their first calls were to the European American Bank and the First National Bank of Boston. At the same time, they intensified the search for third-party investors for *Revolution* and *The Mission*. (The financing of *Absolute Beginners* was, in theory anyway, never a problem: Orion had guaranteed a US advance of $2.5 million and Virgin and Goldcrest were to split the remaining cash costs.)

According to Norris they needed to raise £7 or £8 million ($10 million), shared more or less equally between the two films. Norris had already done the deal with the Norwegian Viking Film, which was to put $4 million into *Revolution*, and Chambers had found an American investment fund, managed by an acquaintance, Howard Schuster, which might put a further $4.5 million into the film. Lee was still negotiating terms with Cinema Group, whose boss, Harry Gould, had originally wanted to put money into both films, but, since *Revolution* seemed to be already covered, Lee now steered him towards putting the whole of his $5 million into *The Mission*. Puttnam's and Joffe's film might also benefit from the proceeds of an Australian tax-shelter scheme, managed by Westpac, which looked likely to produce a further $5.75 million.

In a memo to the board, dated 27 February 1985, Lee included these potential third-party investors in a summary of the anticipated funding arrangements for the two films. Including contingency, deferments and overheads, *Revolution* was to cost £16 million ($19.3 million) and *The Mission* was to cost £17 million ($20.2 million). These costs were to be met as in the table below.

Revolution	$ million
Deferred Goldcrest overhead	1.0
Other deferments	1.2
Goldcrest completion fee	0.4
Warner advance	6.4
Norwegian investment (Viking)	4.0
US investment (Howard Schuster)	4.5
Goldcrest cash investment	1.8
Total cost	19.3 (£16 million)

The Mission	$ million
Deferred Goldcrest overhead	1.0
Other deferments	0.7
Goldcrest completion fees	0.5
Warner advances	5.5
Cinema Group investment	5.0
Goldcrest cash investment	7.5
Total cost	20.2 (£17 million)

Goldcrest's overheads – that part of the cost of the films accounted for by the company's legal, office and administrative services – were to be deferred, i.e. not paid out of the budget but recovered from receipts. Half of Hudson's fee, all of Winkler's and a proportion of both Puttnam's and Ghia's were likewise to be deferred and are included here under the heading 'other deferments'. The completion fees were the monies that the Goldcrest would receive should the films come in on, or under, budget; again, these were items that Goldcrest was happy to recover from receipts. Taken together, all these deferments reduced *Revolution*'s funding requirements by $2.6 million and *The Mission*'s by $2.2 million. The bulk of the rest of the money – the actual cash to be advanced to the productions – was to be provided by Warner Bros., Viking, Schuster and Cinema Group, leaving Goldcrest with a $1.8 million cash investment in *Revolution* and a $7.5 million cash investment in *The Mission*. Of the latter sum, $5.75 million was expected to be covered by the Australian tax-shelter deal (Westpac), leaving Goldcrest with a true exposure of only $1.75 million.

Further cover was provided by the foreign pre-sales (other than for the territories taken by Warner Bros.) which had reached $5.4 million for *The Mission* and $1.8 million for *Revolution*. The latter, relatively low, figure reflected the fact that Guy East could not sell *Revolution* in two major territories: Japan, where there was said to be no interest in the subject, and Germany, where no distributor liked the script.

On the face of it, these arrangements would seem, from Goldcrest's point of view, to have been very satisfactory. As Lee emphasized in his memorandum to the board, the company looked like being able to finance the production of two very big films at very little risk to itself, despite the fact that the budgets had increased significantly in both cases. Of course, by having so many partners, the company's share of the profits was bound to be diminished, but even so Lee was able to estimate that, at the expected level of gross receipts, Goldcrest would receive net contributions of about $3.3 million from *Revolution* and $6 million on *The Mission*. This was a very acceptable level of return given the small amounts of money at risk.

Two observations about Lee's presentation have to be made, however. The first, of course, is that everything depended on the deals with third parties. Of these, only Viking's $4 million investment in *Revolution* was confirmed. Cinema Group, the Australian tax deal and Schuster were still in negotiation. The Schuster money depended on a private fund-raising, the outcome of which was beyond Goldcrest's, or even Schuster's, control and would not be known for some months. Cinema Group had already objected to the degree of Westpac's proposed profit participation, and Westpac, in turn, was having trouble getting its fund approved by the Australian tax authorities. Should any of these third-party deals fall through, Lee told the board at its next meeting, Goldcrest 'would require additional financial resources beyond its existing capacity'. As a 'last resort', shareholders would be offered 'direct participation as had been done in the financing of *Gandhi*'. (Lee was here referring to the $4 million put up by Pearson to replace the suddenly withdrawn Patel money.)

Whether the shareholders would want to participate directly in this way would depend on the scale of the finance required, which in turn depended on the other major assumptions in Lee's presentation: that the budgets remained at the newly agreed levels, that the films did not go over and that there were no significant shifts in the exchange rates.

Which brings us to the second observation: that in all these calculations Lee took a very optimistic view of the downside – i.e. Goldcrest's risk.

John Chambers had produced detailed figures that looked at the revenue expectations, rather than the funding arrangements, for the two films, and it is from these figures that we can arrive at a 'worst-case' assessment of Goldcrest's risk.

The Mission – Revenue and Profitability

	Best likely	Probable	Worst likely
Goldcrest Investment (cost of the film less Cinema Group's $5 million) ($000)	(14,595)	(14,595)	(14,595)
Receipts:			
North America	26,500	16,900	6,750
UK	1,952	1,252	525
Rest of world	11,243	8,728	5,458
Westpac leasing deal	5,750	5,750	5,750
Total receipts	45,445	32,630	18,483
Less distribution expenses	(600)	(500)	(400)
Less third-party shares:			
Cinema Group	(8,895)	(7,881)	(4,227)
Westpac	(4,806)	(2,263)	0
Puttnam, Ghia, De Niro, etc.	(5,600)	(260)	0
Goldcrest share of receipts	25,544	21,725	13,856
Less investment	(14,595)	(14,595)	(14,595)
Contribution	10,949	7,130	(740)
Rate of return	75%	49%	(5%)

These revenue figures depended on the participation of Cinema Group and the tax-shelter deal with Westpac. Were they both to drop out, then the effect would be to increase the upside (profit) potential, since revenues wouldn't have to be shared, but only at the cost of an even more dramatically increased downside risk, as the following extrapolation from Chambers's table shows:

Contribution forecast without Cinema Group and Westpac ($000)	Best likely	Probable	Worst likely
	13,495	6,120	(7,667)

But even in his computation of the 'worst-likely' outcome, Chambers presupposed that *The Mission* would stay on budget – i.e. he included the completion fee, now put at £900,000, in Goldcrest's share of receipts, but he did not make a 'worst-likely' computation that called upon any of the £2.5 million completion risk (the contingency plus the 10 per cent override for which Goldcrest was responsible according to the terms of its as yet unsigned deal with Film Finances). If we do so now, moving, so to speak, from 'worst likely' to 'worst possible', and include as well Goldcrest's overhead fee (£1 million), which, being deferred, was also at risk, we arrive at a maximum downside of just over £10 million ($12 million).

Revolution's revenue forecast told much the same story:

Revolution – Revenue and Profitability

	Best likely	Probable	Worst likely
Goldcrest Investment (cost of the film less Viking and Schuster investments) ($000)	(8,922)	(8,922)	(8,922)
Receipts:			
North America	27,000	17,150	6,563
Other Warner territories	2,035	1,600	1,495
Goldcrest territories	8,677	6,022	2,597
Total receipts	37,712	24,772	10,655
Less distribution expenses	(400)	(400)	(400)
Less third-party shares:			
Viking	(5,578)	(4,753)	(2,167)
Schuster	(7,604)	(6,343)	(1,580)
Hudson, Winkler, Pacino, etc.	(8,048)	(1,275)	0
Goldcrest share of receipts	16,082	12,001	6,507
Less investment	(8,922)	(8,922)	(8,922)
Contribution	**7,160**	**3,080**	**(2,415)**
Rate of return	80.3%	34.5%	(27%)

Were Schuster to drop out, then, as in the case of *The Mission*, the upside would be improved, since Schuster's share of receipts would be divided between Viking, Goldcrest and the talent, but, again, only at the cost of a very much greater downside risk:

Contribution forecast	**Best likely**	**Probable**	**Worst likely**
without Schuster ($000)	11,264	5,923	(7,495)

Adding Goldcrest's completion risk (£3 million) and overhead fee (£1 million) we arrive at a 'worst possible' downside risk of about £9.2 million.

Thus, in the worst possible case – i.e. both films failed to secure expected third-party participations, ran crazily over budget, and neither attracted further sales nor performed well enough at the box office to produce overages – Goldcrest would face losses of nearly £20 million.

This is a far cry from the levels of risk suggested by Lee's memorandum, in which he predicted a maximum downside of a $1.4 million in the case of *Revolution* and $1.5 million in the case of *The Mission*.

Lee's optimistic forecasts were soon to be revised, for, within a week of circulating that memo, he met with Puttnam for yet another review of the financial arrangements for *The Mission*. The main outcome of their discussion was an agreement to add a further £750,000 to the budget. This sum, referred to as the 'operating contingency' – the real margin into which the production could trespass without incurring completion problems – was included within the notional 10 per cent above-and-below-the-line contingency that had already been added for purposes of calculating the completion fee and rebate. It thus added to the cash cost without affecting Lee's projections of risk and profitability. The latest *Mission* budget (including, also, the additional cast allowance for De Niro) compared with the previous versions, as in the table below.

The Mission – Budget £000	24.9.84	19.11.84	6.3.85
Above-the-line	} 11,538	2,236	3,162
Below-the-line		11,471	11,471
Operating contingency	–	–	750
Agreed operating budget	**11,538**	**13,707**	**15,383 ($18.5m)**
Balance of 10% contingency for completion calculation	–	685	713
Completion guarantee fee	692	822	878
Budget for completion purposes	12,230	15,214	16,974 ($20m)
Goldcrest overhead (deferred)	783	962	1,067
Total including deferments	**13,013**	**16,176**	**18,041 ($22m)**
Actual expenditure to date	231	531	approx 3,000

At the board meeting of 21 March, concern was again expressed at the constantly rising cost of the picture: the operating budget was now 33 per cent greater than it had been when first approved in September.

Puttnam pointed out, with some justice, that the below-the-line cost (the day-to-day expense of making the film) had not changed. The increments were in approved above-the-line cast overage and contingency. He acknowledged that these items did, all the same, jeopardize the profitability of the venture for Goldcrest. Indeed, he went further and questioned some of the more optimistic assumptions in Chambers's profit forecast, which, as we have seen, predicted a 'worst-likely' net loss to Goldcrest of £616,000 ($740,000), a 'best-likely' net contribution of £9.1 million ($11 million) and a 'probable' net contribution of £5.9 million ($7 million). Amongst Chambers's assumptions in arriving at these figures were North American gross receipts (i.e. what remained of the box-office rentals and ancillary sales after Warner Bros. had taken its share) of, at worst, $6.8 million, at best $26.5 million, and, most likely, $16.9 million. This latter figure assumed US theatrical rentals of $25 million. *Chariots of Fire*, remember, had achieved rentals of $31 million, and at one stage Warners were talking of *The Killing Fields* doing the same. But by now it was clear that *The Killing Fields*, in its seventeenth week on release, was not going to get anywhere near that figure. Puttnam, who had always placed the three films in the same audience bracket, concluded that this sector of the market was softening and that *The Mission* should not be expected to do better than *The Killing Fields*, still less that it should do as well as *Chariots*. According to the minutes, he 'queried the definition of "best likely" and "probable" used in the analyses and suggested that several figures, particularly the $25 million shown for domestic rentals, were over-stated'.

Puttnam's was not a view to be ignored. His blunt advice to the board, that the picture was unlikely to perform as well as they were hoping it would, was followed by the suggestion that Goldcrest might want to withdraw from *The Mission* altogether. He had made this suggestion before. Indeed, as far back as May 1984, when the project had first been introduced, Puttnam had constantly fought against what he saw as Goldcrest's unreasonable expectations as regards costs. At that time, Lieberson had made a rough budget forecast of $10 million. This, of course, had soon been revised. But the next level of forecast cost, $15 million, became a kind of benchmark. This was the figure beyond which, as Warners' Terry Semel had all along insisted, such a film should not go, and every increment thereafter was approved only grudgingly by Goldcrest.

'They were putting pressure on me to make the film for less,' Puttnam recalls. 'I said, "I can't make the film for less. If you want to make it for less, don't make the picture, make a different picture. Maybe it is too much, but that's what it's going to cost." '

The problem, of course, was that each time Puttnam proposed that Goldcrest might like to withdraw – i.e. each time there was a significant budget increase – there was a price to be paid. In September 1984, when the budget was approved at £11.5 million ($15 million), the cost of pulling out would have been not less than £250,000. In November 1984, when the budget was approved at £13.8 million ($17 million), the cost of pulling out would have been not less than £600,000. In January 1985, when, with the casting of De Niro, the budget had been approved at £15.4 million ($18.5 million), the cost of pulling out would have been not less than £1.8 million. Now, in March, with less than four weeks to go before the start of shooting, the cost of pulling out would be not less than £3.4 million. That does not include whatever compensation would have to be paid to the cast, crew and suppliers of equipment and services with whom contracts had already been signed. At this point, it simply was not worth pulling out: the film would have had to have been one of the great flops of all time to lose more than £3.4 million.

The board was anyway in no mood to withdraw. Its prospective third-party deals would, so it was thought, reduce its risk to the acceptable levels outlined by Lee and, notwithstanding Puttnam's counsel, the management team had great confidence in the film's potential. The minutes report that 'whilst it was accepted that the film was of a type typically generating domestic rentals of $15–18 million, executive directors expressed confidence that $25 million rentals would be achieved in this case'.

Their confidence had doubtless been boosted by the rapturous reception given to the film by international distributors at the American Film Market, which had taken place only the week before.

The fifth annual American Film Market (AFM) was held in the Hyatt Hotel on Sunset Boulevard. Eighty-five independent film companies, Americans mostly but with a sprinkling of Europeans, took over the entire building, setting up offices in the rooms and suites and attaching posters and screening schedules to the walls. Groups of salesmen standing in the doorways transformed the narrow hotel corridors into the alleys of some misplaced bazaar. Eighteen non-film companies – laboratories, trade publications, studios and facilities houses – brought the number of stallholders to a record 103.

The hotel is a simple oblong, with six floors. On each floor a single corridor runs the length of the building, with rooms leading off to right and left. In the middle of each corridor is a central elevator and stairwell. The offices on either side of the elevator section were sought after, since they were in the thick of the traffic. But the suites at the end of each corridor were even more highly prized, since, by taking the rooms on both sides, a company could have an end-zone all to itself. These were booked by the big independents: Cannon, PSO, EMI, New World, Orion and Goldcrest.

When the doors opened on 7 March, the market was flooded with 3,000 buyers: independent distributors from every country of the world.

Most of the films that you see in the cinema are produced and distributed by the major studios. They do not participate in markets such as this. The AFM is strictly for the independent producers and distributors, much of whose stock in trade – low-budget horror, action–adventure, sex romps and teen comedies – is destined to go straight to the video market. Some independent producers, however, have higher aspirations. In 1985 none was more ambitious than Goldcrest. Its suite was dominated by life-size posters of Robert De Niro and Al Pacino. They created a sensation. From the first day, Guy East and his sales team were under siege.

'People will say, why on earth did Goldcrest get involved [in these big-budget pictures]? But look what we had,' East says. 'We had *The Mission*. A script written by Robert Bolt, an Oscar winner with *Lawrence of Arabia, Doctor Zhivago, A Man for all Seasons*. A wonderful scriptwriter. We had a cameraman, Chris Menges, Oscar nominee for *The Killing Fields*. We had De Niro and Jeremy Irons. We had an editor, Jim Clark, also an Oscar nominee for *The Killing Fields*. Roland Joffe, an acclaimed new director. David Puttnam, producer of *Chariots, Midnight Express, Local Hero, The Killing Fields*. And Fernando Ghia, who, while not, if you like, in the Oscar category, was a very well-known producer. Every major member of that crew was an Oscar winner. That was a fantastic item to go to the market with.

'We had *Revolution*: the producer of *Rocky*, the director of *Chariots of Fire* and three major stars, Pacino, Sutherland and Kinski. A film that told the story of an ordinary man who risked his life to save his son, set against the huge backdrop of the American Revolution – lots of colour and glamour – and in the middle a love story. It was snapped up in the foreign markets straight away.

'We had *Horror Movie*, which was a wonderful, wonderful horror script and, coming from Goldcrest, would have been a very, very classy horror movie. It excited everybody. We had *Dance With a Stranger*, which had opened in England about two weeks before the AFM. We had spent a lot of money promoting it so that we could go into the market with *Dance With a Stranger* way up. I think it was number one in England that week. So that was a small-budget film to put into that group.

'And we had *Absolute Beginners*. At that time it was a medium-budget musical with an interesting mix of talents. Palace were producing it, which was interesting. Virgin were doing the music, which was interesting. It was a good punt, if you like, to put into that group.

'So you had a package of five films, which was a very exciting bet: two huge films, a horror movie, a musical and a low-budget film. If you were a buyer looking for a spread of films, that was a great spread, an amazing spread of films. Congratulations to Sandy for getting it together.

'I knew that there was nobody to compete with us and that the buyers would be pouring into our office. When you walked in the door, bang! You were hit by these two famous, famous stars, Pacino and De Niro, who are not normally available in the independent marketplace.

'And you put that in the context of Goldcrest having just won Oscars with *Gandhi*, and seven nominations for *The Killing Fields*, and with all those marvellous films: *The Dresser, Local Hero* and *Another Country*. I mean, for the buyers, that was a hell of a line-up, a fantastic line-up. They were fighting to get in. Myself, Greg Phillips [the newly appointed sales director], Anne Barson [sales executive] and Diana Hawkins [head of marketing and publicity], we worked twenty-four hours a day. Hardly slept.

'We sold *Absolute Beginners* fantastically well. We sold *The Mission* fantastically well. We sold *Horror Movie* very well. We sold *Dance With a Stranger* very well, which was astonishing for a low-budget British film. On *Revolution*, the only countries we didn't pre-sell were Germany and Japan.'

East's report to the management meeting of 18 March included a schedule of agreed sales and offers 'that in every case except *Dance With a Stranger* totalled more than the previous estimate of possible sales'. This confirmed, East told the meeting, 'the wisdom of casting major stars' in *Revolution* and *The Mission*. He drew special attention to the 'exceptional' reception given to *Absolute Beginners*, 50 per cent of the budget of which was now covered by pre-sales.

It was this bumper harvest that had encouraged the Goldcrest management to make the optimistic forecast of *The Mission* rentals. It even gave Lee the confidence to stretch Goldcrest's financial commitments a little further. The board had been pressing him to take investment positions in other people's films that were already in an advanced state of preparation and the revenues from which could be added to Goldcrest's 1985 profit-and-loss account. One such opportunity now arose, which, while it did not inspire any great enthusiasm among the management team, did look a very safe bet. It was *A Room With a View*, a £2.6 million project to be produced and directed by the long-standing partnership of Ismail Merchant and James Ivory. It was to prove a far more significant investment than anyone expected at the time.

Chapter Forty-three

The Whiff of Catastrophe

Ilott: On 4 February 1985, the British Academy of Film and Television Arts (BAFTA) had published the list of nominees for its 1985 awards. The BAFTA Awards are not limited to British-made or British-financed productions: like the Oscars, they seek to honour outstanding work from wherever it comes. They embrace television and film more or less equally and they cover all aspects of production, from make-up to music. Like the Oscars, too, they are voted on by a membership that includes the industry's most senior personnel, for whom the nominations count nearly as much as the awards themselves. That year, Goldcrest productions received twenty-five nominations. *The Killing Fields* alone was named in thirteen categories, including Best Film, Director, Actor, Score, Cinematography and Editing. *The Dresser* was named in six: Best Film, Director, Screenplay, Actor (two nominations: Albert Finney and Tom Courtenay), Make-up and Supporting Actress. *Another Country* received three nominations, including Best Screenplay, and *Cal* received two, for Best Actress and Outstanding Newcomer. On the television side, there were five nominations for *The Far Pavilions* and one for *Robin of Sherwood*. It was an unprecedented achievement.

Two days later, the American Academy published the list of Oscar nominees. *The Killing Fields* was named in seven categories, including Best Film, Best Director, Best Actor and Best Supporting Actor.

One would have expected David Puttnam's morale to have been boosted by these accolades. Not only was his film highly favoured, and his company honoured, but the British film industry itself, to which he has always been fiercely committed, was again the dominant presence on the Oscar lists: alongside *The Killing Fields* were David Lean's *A Passage to India* (eleven nominations); Albert Finney (Best Actor, *Under the Volcano*); Ralph Richardson (Best Supporting Actor, *Greystoke*); and Vanessa Redgrave (Best Supporting Actress, *The Bostonians*). This was to be the fourth consecutive year in which, as one observer put it, 'the Oscar nominations look like a benefit night for the British film industry'.

But Puttnam was far from happy. In the first place, the British government had decided to withdraw the limited but very important forms of support hitherto provided for British films. In the second place, an initiative to which Puttnam and Richard Attenborough had lent their considerable energies, British Film Year, was in danger of folding under the weight of Wardour Street's indifference. British Film Year was aimed at reviving the cinema-going habit in the television-addicted British public – an ambition in which it proved to be successful beyond all reasonable expectation: the downward trend of cinema admissions was reversed for the first time in more than thirty years. Yet the very people who stood to gain most from the campaign were refusing to support it.

Puttnam was not alone in finding this attempted suicide by sloth almost unendurable. For the first time in sixteen years, he said, he 'despaired that we would ever pull together as a business'. He characterized the British industry as being dominated by a 'terrible apathy and scepticism' and described the attitude towards British Film Year as 'niggardly, fragmented and incohesive'. Not only were the 'old grey men of Wardour Street', as he called them, disdainful of a campaign that sought to put right many of wrongs which they themselves had perpetrated over the years, but they had insinuated – in private meetings, not in public – that Puttnam and Attenborough were using British Film Year for purposes of self-aggrandizement.

'What makes you bitter', Puttnam complained at the time, 'is that the people who criticize your efforts don't have one third of your workload.'

A further source of disenchantment was his own company, Enigma, which, like Goldcrest, had grown far bigger than had ever been planned. Enigma was not only becoming something of an administrative albatross around Puttnam's neck but was also in financial difficulties. Its main business now was to see *Mr Love*, *Knights and Emeralds* and *The Frog Prince* through to completion. Once they were out of the way, Puttnam decided, the company would do no more than administer his own affairs. The staff were given notice. Most were to have left by the end of the summer.

Puttnam was also carrying a considerable burden of personal debt at the time, and the terms of his deal with Goldcrest meant that his earnings from *The Mission*, which was to occupy him for the next year and a half, were unlikely to reduce it.

All these things combined to give him the feeling that he was, as he said at the time, 'on a treadmill'. On top of it all, he was subjected to a scathing public rebuke from film-maker Derek Jarman, who not only criticized the cosily reassuring themes of Puttnam's films, but came close to questioning Puttnam's motives. On neither count were the criticisms entirely unfounded, a point that Puttnam himself acknowledged when he said of the attack merely that he 'didn't agree with all of it'. But he was stung by it, nevertheless, for Jarman had touched upon matters about which Puttnam was particularly sensitive.

In an interview conducted at the end of January 1985, Puttnam, then forty-four, confessed that he wanted to get out of films, at least for a while. He had been offered a board-level position at advertising agency Saatchi & Saatchi, which would give him a lot of money and a break – 'a chance', as he said, 'to do something completely different for three years'. But he knew already that he would turn it down. More attractive was the prospect of an exchange deal with Harvard University: Puttnam would teach film-making for part of the time, and for the rest would study 'politics, moral philosophy, ethics, law: the interface within which films exist'. Although the Harvard post was unlikely to be lucrative, the fact that it would take Puttnam out of the UK for a year would help his personal tax position considerably.

'Making films can be very punishing and unrewarding,' Puttnam explained. 'I've made twenty films in sixteen years and I am very tired. I'd like to think that in the second half of my career I'll make as good films as I have made in the first half, but to do that I need a break. I've got to be able, at the very minimum, to ask the right questions. As presently equipped as a film producer, I can't do better than *The Killing Fields*. I'm very proud of it. But how sure am I that *The Killing Fields* is a fair depiction of events?'

Many would be happy to think that they could do even as well as *The Killing Fields*, but Puttnam, always conscious of his lack of formal education – he left school at sixteen and did not go to college – wanted more. He wanted to be sure of the significance of what he was doing.

'If you're going to spend two or three years on something, it's got to be worthwhile,' he said. 'I may come out [of Harvard] disappointed with what's learnable, but I don't want to look back at sixty-five and see my apotheosis at forty-three.'

He never did go to Harvard, but his desire to do so, which appeared to be genuine at the time – he planned to make the move in the late spring of 1986, when *The Mission* and the three low-budget films would be finished – tells us something about his degree of commitment to Goldcrest at the very moment at which it was about to plunge into crisis. It has often been said about Puttnam that he is the first to walk away from trouble. (This need not be a wholly cynical observation: it may be that the first rule of being a successful film producer is knowing which crosses not to bear.) It would certainly be consistent with what we know of his character for him to have put a distance between himself and the company as soon as he detected the whiff of catastrophe. The announcement of his decision to go to Harvard was the beginning of this process.

Puttnam was not the only one making other plans.

In the first week of February, Sandy Lieberson had accompanied Guy East on a sales trip to Australia and the Far East. It had been, by all accounts, a great success. The new slate of films had been well received everywhere, and Lieberson, according to East, had proved an invaluable guide. Upon their return, however, Lieberson confided to Attenborough that he was going to take the option in his contract that allowed him to relinquish his executive responsibilities: at the end of the year he would cease to be head of production and would become instead an independent producer for the company.

'I knew from the third or fourth month that I was there that it was an intolerable situation,' Lieberson now explains. 'It was not something that I could work under. It was a wonderful opportunity to get some films made, but at the same time it was an unhappy experience. We were all very different personalities with different concepts of what Goldcrest was. It was very unpleasant.'

Attenborough recalls that his first meeting with Lieberson on this subject took place in the Goldcrest offices, and that the two men subsequently talked at greater length over lunch. 'Sandy thought that James didn't know his arse from his elbow, and didn't grant him, Sandy, the autonomy that he should have had,' Attenborough recalls. 'And in a way Sandy ultimately became impotent. He said, "Either I have the control or I don't, but I can't be answerable to somebody who simply doesn't know our language, who doesn't know the criteria by which we apply our judgements." He told me that the situation was absolutely intolerable, that his authority was being totally eroded and that what he believed was to have been his position – the grounds on which David [Puttnam] had persuaded him to join the company – just hadn't worked out, and that he was not going to remain.'

The most noteworthy thing about Lieberson's decision to quit was the timing: he had just committed the company to a hugely ambitious production slate which he would not now see through to completion. When his decision was eventually made public, it robbed him also of what was left of his authority. This was to have disastrous consequences, especially for *Revolution*.

Lieberson's decision to remove himself from the corporate battlefield coincided with Norris's and Chambers's decision to try to rescue the company from what they saw as the jeopardy in which it had been placed by Lee. In this task they needed the support of the non-executive directors. They would of course have to approach them outside the board's regular meetings and without Lee's knowledge. This was something, Norris now maintains, that they should have done 'months before'.

The first person they approached was Attenborough.

As Norris tells it, the meeting, held in Attenborough's central London office, was 'absolutely not' the beginning of a conspiracy. But it is noteworthy that he made sure that there was no written record of the appointment. 'I had the feeling that it was better not put in my diary,' he admits.

For his part, Chambers is quite clear that it was the first step in a campaign to drive a wedge between Lee and the board. And while Norris insists that they chose Attenborough because he was the only non-executive director who knew about films and was available – Puttnam's hands being full with *The Mission* – he can hardly have been unaware that they were likely to get a much more favourable hearing from the man who had sided with them throughout the management crisis of the previous February, than from Puttnam, who was Lee's closest, if now somewhat lukewarm, ally.

What they put to Attenborough, remembers Norris, was that 'certain of the five or six key areas' about which they had made their strong protest the year before 'weren't showing any improvement'.

'Overheads were still rising. Development had got out of hand: at that time, on a capital base of, say, £29 million, we had tied up between £1 million and £1.4 million in development. We were still in the cable-television consortium, which was just a drain, a comparatively small one, but a drain nevertheless,' he explains. 'And we had embarked by then upon a programme of films which John and I knew, and James knew, we didn't have the resources for.'

Prominent on their list of grievances was *Revolution*, which had that very day started principal photography in King's Lynn. This was a subject about which Attenborough, who had by now read what he describes as the 'ill-structured' screenplay and found that there was 'no story' in it, could be relied on to be an attentive listener, even if his remarks were tempered by his rule of not commenting on the intrinsic merits of other Goldcrest projects than his own.

When Norris and Chambers had exhausted their litany of complaints, Attenborough told them his own piece of news: that Lieberson had decided to opt out. This came not so much as a revelation as confirmation of what had long been expected. It was welcome none the less. As Chambers puts it, 'it was something to be encouraged'.

'Before we made any move,' Chambers explains, 'it was obvious that we needed to allow Lieberson to continue in his intention of leaving and to actually take up his option. Because in our view, if you got rid of Lee and then Lieberson said, "Oh, great, Lee's gone, now I'll stay," it would be just as bad.'

At the end of the meeting, Attenborough asked Norris and Chambers to put everything they had just told him down on paper, as he wanted to discuss the matter privately with 'one or two members of the board' before taking it further. To this suggestion, Norris and Chambers readily agreed. But whether because they were too busy or because they were not sure that it was the right thing to do, they didn't get round to writing their report for more than six weeks. Had they acted earlier, Norris now believes, the disaster that was soon to befall the company might have been averted.

On the same day, over lunch at the Grill Room of The Dorchester, Jake Eberts was talking to a journalist from one of the film trades. No word of Eberts's departure from Embassy had yet been mentioned in the press, and, having now settled his severance terms with Perenchio, he chose this occasion to break the news.

'I have to say that my parting with Embassy is entirely friendly and I have nothing but affection for the people I have worked with in the company,' he declared in time-honoured, best-leave-the-door-open fashion.

He then outlined his plans for the future.

Eberts: I had decided to retrace the steps of my career and start again, setting up a film-development fund just as I had done when I launched Goldcrest back in 1976. I had discussed the idea that day in Jerry Hellman's house and everyone had seemed very much in favour. As Tom Lewyn said, if I didn't want to work for another studio, which I didn't, then I really had no choice but to strike out on my own.

I was by this time convinced that the film world was not as friendly a place for an independent as it had been nine years before: the independent sector was overcrowded and smaller companies too often found themselves producing films that got no more than a token theatrical release. The pendulum had swung back in favour of the major studios, who, after the dramatic decline in their fortunes in 1982, were now taking an ever greater share of every market. When I had first set up Goldcrest,

I had done it with independent sources of finance and without any ongoing development or distribution arrangements in Hollywood. Our early deals had been with independents like Embassy. Later on, we had traded on a film-by-film basis with Columbia, Warner Bros., Orion, 20th Century–Fox and the Samuel Goldwyn Company. In my view, this was no longer the right way to go about things: if I wanted to get anywhere, I had to have a relationship with a studio from the outset.

At that time there were maybe sixty or seventy independent producers or packagers who had development deals with the studios. David Puttnam was one of them, indeed the only one in the UK. I wanted to be another. The proposal that I had tried to put to Jerry Perenchio needed only a few adjustments to be suitable for this purpose. In outline, it envisaged the launch of a new company, financed, as Goldcrest had been, from independent sources, and whose sole business would be to develop feature-film projects. Unlike Goldcrest, but like David Puttnam's Enigma, the new company would be tied by a development deal to a major studio.

My first call, made from Jerry Hellman's house, had been to Terry Semel at Warner Bros. I said, 'Terry, my relationship with Embassy has come to an abrupt end and I'd like to come and talk to you about an idea I have to set up a development fund.'

'Love to talk to you about it,' he said. 'Come on over.'

Thus, within hours of parting company with Jerry Perenchio, I found myself driving back along the Pacific Coast Highway and over the Hollywood Hills to the Warner building in Burbank.

I have always found Terry Semel an exceptionally businesslike, pleasant and clear-thinking man. He is very slow to come to a decision, but once that decision is made he will stick to it. In our previous dealings, when I was at Goldcrest, he always knew exactly what he was looking for. That made it easy for me to keep a hold on what I was looking for, and if we disagreed it was a clear-cut disagreement: there was never any misunderstanding over who said what to whom, or what had been intended.

Terry was very interested in my proposal and was prepared to agree to it there and then. However, I wanted to talk to the other studios first, just in case one of them came up with a better idea or better terms. Terry encouraged me to do this and was happy to let me take my time.

I went to see Frank Mancuso, who was by then head of Paramount. We spent a very pleasant hour together, but it was clear within five minutes that what I wanted to do, in terms of the film-makers I wanted to work with and the kind of films they would want to make, was quite different to what he wanted to do. Like Alan Horn, Frank was really only interested in the cinema mainstream: Eddie Murphy, *Fatal Attraction* and *Top Gun*. There wasn't the remotest chance that I would come up with that kind of material from London. Maybe once every three or four years I might put together a package that would interest Paramount, but that was not a sufficient basis for a contractual relationship. Accordingly, although Frank was willing to do a deal, the terms were not very favourable and I didn't get the feeling of real commitment.

I went to see Jeff Katzenberg at Disney. He liked the idea in a vague kind of way, but not enough to put up serious money for it. The same was true at Columbia.

So within a couple of weeks I was back in Terry Semel's office. Warner Bros. was to be my home. Without wanting to draw any comparisons between myself and David Puttnam, it may be that Terry, mindful of David's stated intention of dropping out of films for a while, wanted to keep his contacts in Europe. Between Puttnam and Goldcrest, after all, Warner Bros. had acquired interests in *Chariots of Fire*, *The Killing Fields*, *Local Hero*, *The Mission*, *Revolution*, *Mr Love*, *Knights and Emeralds* and *The Frog Prince*. That was an exceptionally good haul for a relationship that was less than five years old. The people I now wanted to work with were the same group as before: Alan Marshall, Hugh Hudson, Alan Parker, Peter Yates, Dickie Attenborough and John Boorman, with the addition of a handful of Americans, among them Alan Pakula and Jerry Hellman. In terms of track record, this was a pretty bankable list. Warners were not exactly about to launch into the unknown.

Tom Lewyn handled the negotiations on my behalf. Warner Bros. would pay an annual advance plus a contribution to my overheads guaranteed for three years, in return for which they would have first look at all the projects that I developed or packaged. If they didn't like a project, I would be free to take it elsewhere, although I had to re-submit it to Terry if the terms I negotiated with another studio were better than those I had offered to Warner Bros. in the first place. Every time a project of mine went into production, whether with Warners or another studio, then part of the fees would go to my company. The remainder of the fees would go back to Warners until they had recouped their advance. Terry was thus gambling on my ability to put enough packages into production to cover his investment in me. If I didn't, the relationship would not be extended beyond the third year. His upside potential, of course, was that one of my projects might be a *Chariots* or a *Gandhi*. If

I came up with just one of those in three years he would be more than satisfied.

Having agreed all that, I then set about forming the new company. It was to be called Allied Filmmakers. It was not a very original name, perhaps, but it perfectly expressed the nature of the project.

There was much talk at the time that I was setting up Goldcrest Mark 2. This was never true. In the first place, I didn't want to get involved in foreign sales, nor did I want to get into production finance or television. In the second place, unlike Goldcrest, I now had an ongoing relationship with Warner Bros. In other respects, of course, there were obvious similarities, especially with the pre-1981 Goldcrest.

My hope was that at Allied I would at last get the balance right: that I would have neither the burden of responsibility that I had had at Goldcrest, nor the frustration that I had experienced at Embassy. I wanted to be the boss, but I wanted to be the boss of a company with no employees other than myself and my secretary. I would then be free to do what I was best at: making deals.

I had in mind a $5 million fund, which, with the Warner advances, would be enough for me to package three, four or five films a year. That would be as much work as I could handle. To raise $5 million, I needed only a half-dozen or so investors. Their money would be spent on scripts, research, the acquisition of rights and, in some cases, a contribution to the overheads of various film-makers. These costs, like the Warner advances, would be recovered, with interest, when a project went into production. In addition, Allied would earn packaging fees and it would take a net-profit position – in some cases as much as 15 per cent – in every film. It was from these profit participations that Allied stood to make real money. Furthermore, since the Warner advances paid Allied's operating costs, Allied was to be an overhead-free fund.

With all this documented in the form of a prospectus – I was by now an expert at drafting these things – and with Warners' commitment already in my pocket, I went in search of investors. My first call was to Michael Stoddart at Electra. He was keen, but he felt that he had to seek the approval of the Goldcrest board before making an investment, in case it was thought that there was a conflict of interest between Goldcrest and Allied. In anticipation of this, I had gone to great lengths to emphasize that Allied would not be in competition but would be compatible, even complementary, with Goldcrest – in the way, say, that Enigma was. The matter was duly put to Goldcrest directors at their March board meeting and no objection was raised.

With Warners and Electra now committed I was able to approach investors in France, Norway and the UK. In total, seven institutions were to be involved, most of them people I knew well in the film or investment-banking communities. It was nice to be back at Warners with Terry Semel and all my old friends. I felt even more at home when Terry invited me to a pre-Oscar dinner for the nominees from *The Killing Fields*. I was back in business.

Ilott: On 25 March 1985, *The Killing Fields* was awarded three Oscars. Pictures developed or financed by Goldcrest had now picked up thirty Oscar nominations and fifteen awards in four years.

Chapter Forty-four

Disaster

'This epic period of American history has not been featured on such a scale since D. W. Griffith's classic 1924 production, America.' – Irwin Winkler, March 1985

'The people of King's Lynn had never been better off, with everybody being paid as extras in the town. Dom Perignon in buckets by the sound of it.' – James Joll, August 1987

Ilott: *Revolution*, which started shooting on 18 March, was by far the biggest investment that Goldcrest had ever undertaken. Its budget, finally settled at just over £16 million ($19.3 million), was, in sterling terms, as much as the combined costs of *Another Country*, *Gandhi*, *The Dresser*, *Local Hero* and *Cal*, and considerably more than the company's entire turnover in 1984. A proportion of this budget was, of course, covered by pre-sales, by the distribution deal with Warner Bros. and by the $4 million equity investment by Viking Film of Norway, and there were still high hopes that Howard Schuster's fund would come up with $3–5 million. Even so, and notwithstanding James Lee's earlier best-case estimate of a maximum cash exposure of $1.8 million, at the start of production, in March 1985, Goldcrest had as much at stake in the picture as it had had in *Gandhi* in 1980. From the point of view of Goldcrest's financial interest, the most significant of the many differences between the two projects was the outcome: *Gandhi* worked, *Revolution* didn't.

There are doubtless many reasons why *Revolution* went wrong. The script was never satisfactory, there was an element of miscasting, the production was ill prepared, bedevilled by illness and plagued by bad weather, and the post-production was rushed. That much is agreed by everyone, including director Hugh Hudson. There were also accusations from the Goldcrest head office of profligacy, perfectionism and incompetence on the set, and counter-accusations from the production team of head-office carping and interference.

But it is as well to remember that, had *Revolution* been the box-office success that everyone thought it was going to be, then all these things would have been forgiven and forgotten. There are many examples of successful films that have gone over budget where this fact is neither well known nor held to be of any significance. The films were successful, and that's all that counts.

One thing that can be said about *Revolution* is that the film that Goldcrest had agreed to fund was quite different from the film that Hudson set out to make. The former was the one that Winkler had originally conceived, that Robert Dillon had written and that Lieberson, Lee and Hudson had had in mind when they first discussed the project. It was to have been an intimate drama concerning ordinary people caught up in extraordinary events. It was to have been filmed close to the action, so that the sights and sounds of battle were to be viewed from the perspective of the ordinary soldier rather than from the high ground occupied by the general staff. The sweep and scheme of history were likewise to have been suggested only remotely, somewhere in the distance, out of focus. As Lieberson recalls, the model for this version was a celebrated British television production, *Culloden*, which told the story of the suppression of the Scots by the English in the mid-eighteenth century and used hand-held cameras to involve the audience in the awful bloodiness of battles fought with axe and sword. (A useful comparison could be made between *Culloden* and a more recent and better-known film, *Platoon*, which had a lot in common with *Revolution* and is spoken of in terms of the highest praise by Hudson.)

In keeping with this general approach, the first version was to have been fairly modest in cost, without major stars or extravagant production values.

The second film, which emerged from the mind of Hugh Hudson as the project developed, was to be an epic re-creation of the entire period of the American War of Independence. Hudson wanted to keep what he calls a 'ground-level, working man's view of war' while at the same time conveying the texture of those days, in terms of the physical conditions of life, the social fabric and the conflict of ideas. Hudson has an interest in history, and the many political parallels between that first anti-colonial war and the wars of liberation of our own time both intrigued and inspired him.

From Goldcrest's point of view, the difference between these two versions was essentially one of scale: what Hudson had in mind was a good deal more ambitious, and therefore more costly, than anything that had been agreed with Lieberson and Lee. Where the first film called for only a sketchy treatment of the period background, the second required extensive and minutely detailed sets and props. Where the first called for the personal drama to be in close-up and the historical events to be crowding in, so to speak, from the edges, the second placed the personal drama squarely in the midst of the historical action, sometimes, indeed, overwhelmed by it, so that the leading actors found themselves at a distance from the camera and almost out of range of the microphone. Filling up the spaces in between were to be extras: hundreds of them, all perfectly attired in expertly re-created costumes of the period.

Goldcrest was not at first aware of Hudson's grand plan, and was persuaded to accept his changes in piecemeal fashion. As Lieberson remarks: 'Little by little you get drawn into these situations, and little by little it began to change the course of the kind of film it was intended to be.'

But the watershed, at which point, or shortly thereafter, it became clear that there were two quite distinct versions of the film on offer, was the casting of Pacino. Had Goldcrest voted down Pacino, the original concept of the film might have been saved. Once he had been accepted, however, the original concept was lost; not necessarily, or not only, because Pacino was wrong for the part, but because the vote emphatically handed over the film to the director.

As to Hudson's concept, however, Goldcrest had neither the will nor the money to see it to fruition. The budget increments to pay for Pacino, Sutherland and Kinski were as far as the company was prepared to go in terms of enhancing the production values, and therefore the cost, of the picture. But Hudson needed to go further. His first detailed budget, drawn up less than a month before the film started shooting, came to about £18 million: £4.8 million above the line, £10.7 million below the line and £2.5 million in indirect costs, including a notional contingency and completion fees. This budget was rejected by Goldcrest. Since the above-the-line figure – the cost of script, stars, producer and director – was fixed, and since the indirect costs were contingent on the above-and-below-the-line total, it was on the below-the-line budget – the direct, day-to-day costs of making the film – that the dispute was focused. Hudson would have to rein in his ambition, even cut scenes if that was necessary, but at all costs the below-the-line figure was not to go above £8.9 million. Hudson and Winkler signed the final budget document, so one must assume that they agreed to this. That they did so with reluctance, however, was no secret at the time and is not denied by Hudson now. In fact, the two sides immediately became engaged in a war that did not end even when the film was finished. Lieberson, initially the project's most enthusiastic supporter within Goldcrest, and until then a longtime friend of both Hudson and Winkler, became first alarmed, then angry and finally so disillusioned that he wanted to wash his hands of the enterprise altogether.

The first battle was over construction costs. 'Everything began to be on a larger scale,' Lieberson recalls. 'The sets became higher, longer, wider, which means you photograph more, more time is needed. In other words, it began to grow. Whereas before it was going to be tight and intimate and dramatic, all of a sudden it's on a magnificent scale. That was never agreed to, never discussed, never even contemplated by us.'

The second battle was over costumes, props and extras. Accountant Andy Parsons, across whose desk all the expenses of the production had to pass for approval, remembers that *Revolution* was 'well over budget before the cameras started rolling . . . The commitment to extra artistes over and above those allowed for in the budget, the costumes – if you say in a budget that you want a crowd of 200 on this day and in fact you've got a crowd of 800, then you've got four times as many uniforms to provide, four times as many meals and so on – all added to the cost. *Revolution* was becoming a big, big problem.'

The third battle was over the supporting cast. Hudson believed that it was essential that the secondary actors should be of sufficient calibre to stand up to Pacino on the screen. 'I was accused of spending too much money on actors,' he says. 'Irwin's and my defence was quite simple: "Yes, we have done it. We shouldn't have done it, but we have. If you look in the budget you will see that all these small parts which we have decided should be played by actors were budgeted for extras. Now if you have actors like Al Pacino and Nastassia Kinski you do not give them extras to play against. You just don't do it. If you do, they won't play. They'll walk away. You've got to give them decent actors to play against. Otherwise, first of all it will stand out as being obvious to the audience, and secondly it's incredibly short-sighted, because you won't get any good work from the stars." That was our argument. But Goldcrest wouldn't hear of it. They buried their heads in the sand and said no.'

By his own admission, Hudson then went ahead and hired the actors he wanted anyway, spending, he says, 'about $750,000' more than was provided for in the below-the-line cast allowance.

The fourth, and hardest-fought, battle was over the script. There had already been a long process of revision and rewriting, in which both Goldcrest and Warner Bros. had played a part, and there were still many reservations about the final draft. But once it had been approved, Lieberson insisted that there be no further changes.

'We were very happy with the screenplay,' Lieberson says. 'We always assumed that the writer, Robert Dillon, who is an experienced screenwriter, would be able to do the fine-tuning, and that that was going to be done for the actors. As a matter of fact, Dillon did do the changes that were required by the casting of Pacino. We had talked about the possibility of bringing another writer in to polish some dialogue – Hugh had all kinds of ideas about that – but essentially I was insistent that we had agreed to make one screenplay and I wasn't interested in bringing in a lot of other writers. I was happy with the script we had.'

In February, Hudson pleaded to be allowed a writer 'to help me on the relationship between the man and the woman'. Lieberson, making what Hudson calls 'the stupidest decision', refused. A script editor, Shawn Slovo, who had been hired to record the actors' dialogue changes and provide notes on characterization and relationships, was all that was to be allowed.

Hudson would not accept this. He took the opportunity of a visit to the set by James Lee, soon after the film had started shooting, to press his case afresh.

'Hudson decided, and I believed in this case correctly, that some of the script really just didn't hold together,' Lee recalls, 'and that it was necessary to do some rewriting. He got hold of me while I was down there and said, "You know, we always assumed that the script needed a lot of polishing up." [He said] Colin Welland could do it – because Robert Dillon wasn't available – and that this could be done at no cost. Thinking that in the general run of things this was a fairly minor request, because he was being asked to rewrite six pages, or parts of six pages – it wasn't as though we were tearing up the script – I got an assurance out of Hudson that the rewrites that Colin Welland would be associated with (i) would be approved by Sandy, as head of production, and (ii) would have no cost implications – i.e. they would not change the scale or the nature of the film.

'Well, needless to say, no mention was made of the fact that Sandy had already been consulted about this and had said no. So when I got back Sandy was absolutely incensed: "What the hell have you done?" And I said, "Well, come on, we all knew the script was going to have to be developed during the course of production. We've got nothing against Welland and it's not going to add any cost . . ." And he said, "But no, that's not the point. Hudson had already asked us and we had said no. We really have got a problem now." And I thought, Christ, I have really been screwed here. Because, of course, there was much more to this than just a matter of polishing up the dialogue with no implications of cost.'

Hudson now admits that far from requiring work on only half a dozen pages, the script 'needed to be rewritten, re-thought'. But it was far too late for that. And no sooner had Welland started work than his revisions fell foul of Pacino, who liked the original script and had insisted that there be no changes. In Lieberson's recollection, Hudson and Pacino immediately became involved in 'tremendous fights' over Welland's revisions. Line producer Chris Burt, however, recalls that Welland only 'came in for a little while and wrote some of the scenes for Daisy and Daisy's father and mother'. He admits, however, that even these changes led to 'difficulties' between director and star. Welland, he says, 'on the whole left Al's lines well alone, because I think that would have caused major problems . . . Hugh's relationship with Al was on and off really. I think Hugh was more comfortable with English actors, who come along and discuss the part as a sort of intellectual process rather than an emotional process . . . he is obviously good with someone like Donald Sutherland . . . What Hugh found difficult was the fact that people like Al and Kinksi demand your whole being, really. Al's whole life is acting . . . Hugh doesn't arrive at the same way of getting a performance as Al . . . And there were difficulties between the two of them. But nothing that ever caused Al not to come out of his caravan.'

The really difficult relationship, according to Burt, was between Hudson and Kinski, who, he says, 'is wonderful on the screen, but was like a child off it. She was going through problems with her marriage and God knows what else: all sorts of emotional and psychological problems. And she and Hugh just didn't get on, not at all.'

The fifth battle, then, was between the various personalities involved. In this, Lieberson probably suffered the heaviest losses: Hudson and Winkler, who started the film as his friends of twenty years' standing, ended it his sworn enemies.

The film started shooting in very wet and very cold weather in King's Lynn. Pacino promptly fell ill. From then on, one disaster followed another: there was a fire; a £250,000 crane fell over a cliff; it rained when they needed it to be fine, and it was fine when they needed it to keep raining. And then Kinski, too, fell ill.

'Al and Nastassia seemed to fall ill out of sync. with each other at every available opportunity,' remembers Burt. 'So you had got Al by himself but you were in a set where they were meant to be together. I think Nastassia had some internal medical problem: a big problem, she was crying and weeping and coming out in spots, internal bleeding. Al had the flu, which never really went away because it was so bitterly cold up there in King's Lynn. And then we had such an awful summer – it was always raining. It ended up that we had to shoot a lot of stuff in the rain, even when it wasn't raining, just for continuity. So the poor bugger is running round being drenched even on the dry days. He fell ill frequently and it put enormous pressure on the schedule. We had to keep changing the schedule the whole time.'

Winkler recalls that, 'What would happen was that we would shoot a scene and have no location to go to the next day. There were guys out there looking for stuff, and things weren't ready. If you get into that situation then you get real problems, especially when so many of the scenes needed such big crowds.'

By the end of the second week, says Lieberson, 'We could see that the material just wasn't being shot. We could see we were already days behind. The rushes looked great from a visual point of view, but Hugh kept on rescheduling the film, so that there were no dramatic scenes for at least the first four or five weeks of the movie. And that was another area of contention: although we had these incredibly highly paid actors, they were turning in a snippet here, a snippet there, running here, a battle charge there, but the dramatic scenes were pushed further and further back into the schedule.'

This rescheduling was mainly caused, as Burt has noted, by illness and weather conditions. But by the second or third week, Burt, too, had doubts about the way that the film was being shot. 'This is very difficult to say, because you never know when you are shooting a film whether you are right or whether you are wrong. I spoke to Irwin about it in some detail and Irwin said, "Look, I've seen a lot of pictures that I didn't like and they have turned out to be absolutely terrific." And he is quite right. It is very difficult. My feeling was that having got Al in there for $3 million, the only way the picture could work was to do what John Ford would have done. He would have taken that central character; within three minutes he would have established the relationship between the father and the son – the audience would have gone with that relationship; and then, using that actor, he would have taken the audience through the picture. What happened on *Revolution* was that Al was treated almost like an extra in lots of scenes. It was a Ford script which Hugh shot as a Pontecorvo movie, and the two didn't meet.'

(As part of his preparation for *Revolution*, Hudson had screened a number of films, the most prominent amongst them being, according to

Burt, a clutch of westerns by John Ford, *Gone With the Wind*, Andrzej Wajda's *Danton* and Pontecorvo's *Battle of Algiers*.)

Burt was also worried by Hudson's perfectionism: 'He would do a shot ten or eleven times, of Al walking through a crowd. Well, that's just ridiculous. And Al thought it was ridiculous.'

Pressed on this point, Hudson says, 'Maybe I am [a perfectionist] and maybe it's a fault. But I think it's better to be a perfectionist than to be sloppy. If anything, I wasn't particular enough. I should have insisted on having a scriptwriter when I wanted him. If I'd done that – if they had allowed me to do that – I would have saved a lot of money for them. I wasn't particular enough.'

As for the charge of extravagance, levelled at him by Lieberson and the Goldcrest team in London, and even by Puttnam, who was soon in receipt of regular reports from the *Revolution* set while he was out in Colombia, Hudson protests: 'What can I say? We had two or three hundred extras each day, sometimes a thousand, and they each have to be dressed properly. And we had good people doing it. John Mollo [*Revolution*'s costume designer] is not an extravagant man. We were trying to re-create a period, which is a very difficult thing to do. I wanted to make my battle scenes really good, and I think they are good in the film, as good as any period battle scenes that have ever been shot. I did everything with an open heart and I was hoping for a big success. I didn't do it just to get my rocks off.'

Hudson was under enormous pressure not only to make a great film but to deliver it by December, in time, as everyone was aware, to be eligible for the 1986 Academy Awards. (There was a strong feeling that *Revolution* and *The Mission* should not compete for honours and that therefore they should be released in separate years.) It led, as Hudson himself describes, to a kind of delirium. 'We were going so fast, too fast even to keep control of it in a way,' he says. 'Everybody was in a rush of euphoria in production, and we left the accounts department behind. You shouldn't be going too fast, of course, and eventually there has to be a day of reckoning. But it's very difficult, when you have embarked on something like that, to stop it.'

The production accountant finally caught up with all the invoices and receipts in the third week of shooting. He found that the film was already £1.2 million over budget. Goldcrest's days were numbered.

On Monday, 15 April 1985, Garth Thomas, accompanied by freelance production accountant Bobby Blues, hurried to the *Revolution* set, which had now moved from King's Lynn to Devon, to investigate. Blues set to work on the books, while Thomas conferred with Hudson, Winkler and Burt. At the management meeting in London that day, it was reported that while Thomas was 'reviewing all aspects of the budget and schedules with a view to holding the overage to £1.2 million . . . further overages were likely during post-production to ensure delivery in time for a pre-Christmas release'.

In fact, the situation soon proved to be a great deal worse than had been thought. On Thursday, 18 April, the Goldcrest directors, assembled for their monthly board meeting, were informed that 'after four weeks of principal photography, a £3 million overage at completion was being estimated'. According to the minutes of that meeting, this overage was attributed to three main factors:

1. delay in the commencement of principal photography,
2. an insured loss, giving rise to a claim for up to £0.5 million, and,
3. an apparent lack of serious intention on the part of the producer, Irwin Winkler, and the director, Hugh Hudson, to shoot the film in the manner envisaged by Goldcrest, despite assurances given by them in pre-production discussions.

The minutes continue:

The problem had been exacerbated by the failure of the production team to appreciate the true level of total expenditure. The following actions were being taken to alleviate the situation:
1. certain expensive scenes were being curtailed or deleted altogether,
2. Goldcrest's prior written consent would be required for any additional expenditure in budget areas where overage had already been incurred,
3. the appointment of a full-time permanent Goldcrest representative was being considered.

Garth Thomas, Goldcrest's production executive, who had worked with Hudson on previous films, was currently on location investigating the position and implementing appropriate measures.

Although Chris Burt is a competent associate producer, he appears to have been deceived by others involved in the picture. Mr Norris explained the contractual position as to penalizing the producer and the director: on this project, however, Winkler had deferred all his fees, and Hudson half of his. Although both were responding positively in the crisis, the new controls and screenplay cuts would reduce Goldcrest's dependence on their financial performance. The executive directors advised that to go further at this stage, by exercising the right to take over the production and fire Hudson, would be counter-productive.

(The insurance claim for 'up to £0.5 million' was in respect of the loss of the camera crane that fell off a Devon cliff. The production team's 'failure to appreciate the true level of total expenditure' is a euphemism for not keeping proper accounting records. The 'others involved in the picture' who had 'deceived' Chris Burt were, of course, Hudson and Winkler.)

There is no record of the board's response to all this. There is no doubt that the overcost was calamitous, and would have been seen to have been such. An overage of £3 million not only destroyed the potential profitability of the film as far as Goldcrest was concerned, since the company, as completion guarantor, would have to put up the additional money itself, but it jeopardized the participation of the still unconfirmed third-party investors, and, most pressing in the short term, it added a further £3 million to the already unmanageable cash outflow.

Thomas was instructed to issue a memorandum to Chris Burt 'exercising Goldcrest's right, as completion guarantor, to demand certain actions and control procedures to contain overcost', and threatening the appointment of a 'full-time managing supervisor to take over control of the production'. This he did on Friday, 19 April. At the weekend he was joined in Devon by Lieberson. The two of them went through the budget and such schedules as existed, marking the cuts and economies that would have to be made to ensure that there were no further overages. These cuts were agreed with Burt, Hudson and Winkler, and Lieberson and Thomas returned to London in time to attend the management meeting on Monday, 22 April. The minutes of that meeting provide a somewhat more detailed explanation for the overcost than that offered to the board:

1. the director had determined to produce on a much larger scale than agreed with Goldcrest and budgeted for,
2. sets, props and the numbers of actors and extras all increased substantially,
3. production accountants and administrative staff were unaware of the extra commitments and expenditure,
4. no detailed schedule had ever been prepared, and,
5. the dialogue in individual scenes required to be changed.

Substantial cuts were necessary to reduce final costs, and Garth Thomas had ordered a re-scheduling, re-budgeting, and re-timing of the film, which must take into account the instructions in his memorandum and other savings still achievable. The re-budget would also provide Goldcrest with an accurate, up-to-date cost statement.

From this minute it would seem that no proper schedule or cost statements had been available hitherto, either to the production or to Goldcrest. If that was indeed the case, it would bear out Lieberson's contention, vehemently denied by Hudson, Winkler and Burt, that the production was 'out of control'. The management meeting further agreed that:

1. the production team be advised immediately that a full schedule, rather than a 'one-liner', must be prepared,
2. Bobby Blues be asked to return to Devon as soon as possible to help with

production accounting and the re-budgeting – this would emphasize Goldcrest's resolve, and,

3. a new cash flow would be prepared.

The re-budget was to be ready on Friday (April 26), and thereafter refined and agreed: a projected overcost of £4 million or more would be considered unacceptable . . . The appointment of a full-time manager was considered. There were psychological disadvantages and, unless Garth Thomas were appointed, a time lapse while the appointee acquainted himself with all aspects of the production. Garth Thomas believed that Chris Burt still commanded the respect of his team, and both Winkler and Hudson were understood to be amenable to the actions proposed by Goldcrest. However, if Goldcrest's legitimate demands as completion guarantor were not met, the resignations of Burt and Winkler would be sought. If Burt resigned in that event, or otherwise, Garth Thomas would assume production management and control responsibility.

Accordingly, it was agreed to postpone the appointment of a full-time production manager pending the outcome of the actions and initiatives already undertaken. David Norris would accompany Garth Thomas on his return to Devon to review the general situation and the compliance with each of Goldcrest's demands. He would emphasize that Goldcrest's rights as completion guarantor were now exercisable, in particular as to the take-over of the film.

Viking, the Norwegian investors, were aware of the production problems . . . Schuster would be advised . . . once the situation was clearer. The effect on the Schuster investment could be significant because of the impact of the overcost on net profits . . . Film Finances were well aware of the situation. Because the agreement with Film Finances was not yet in place, there was concern that they would insist upon substantial additions to the budget, apart from the 20 per cent margin of contingency and Goldcrest overcost, before they would bear any liability.

(Only in the film business, one feels, would it be possible to enter into a £16 million high-risk investment with the completion insurance 'not yet in place'. Indeed, when *Revolution* started shooting, the property didn't even belong to Goldcrest, nor even to Winkler, from whom Goldcrest was supposed to have purchased it, for he had not signed the release documents with the original owners, Warner Bros. Nor had Winkler signed any contract with Goldcrest, and since he was receiving no fee – it having been deferred – he was, strictly speaking, free to walk off the picture at any time.)

Eberts: In the midst of all this – I knew nothing about it, of course – I arranged to have a meeting with James. I was back in London, working hard on getting Allied's first projects off the ground. I had pledges of capital, I had the relationship with Warner Bros. and I had the beginnings of a pool of film-makers to draw on. What I needed was a foreign-sales connection. It is much easier to finance a film if the studio you're dealing with has the option of either taking the whole world or just taking the

US, sharing the risk with foreign distributors. An example of this was one of the first Allied projects, *The Name of the Rose*, produced by Bernd Eichinger. It had a budget of $14 million, was to star Sean Connery and F. Murray Abraham and was to be directed by Jean-Jacques Annaud. It was a very European-flavoured film – the book on which it was based had been a publishing phenomenon in Europe – and Warner Bros. said they would be interested in doing it, but only if their investment could be limited to $5 or $6 million, for which they would take US rights only. To make up the gap, I had to find a very substantial advance from the foreign markets. I could get $3 or $4 million from Germany and Italy, the territories in which the book had had its greatest success, but I still needed $4–6 million from elsewhere. Obviously, the thing for me to do was to have a relationship with a foreign-sales company. At that time, the best foreign-sales company in the business was Goldcrest.

I called on James one afternoon in April. Although I didn't feel as comfortable with him as I had before – he was now very much the boss – the meeting was entirely cordial. Throughout it, he kept looking at his watch: he could spare me only half an hour and he was clearly under a lot of pressure. But he was in high spirits and the tone of his conversation was very upbeat. Goldcrest had just got back into production after having been effectively out of action since my departure at the end of 1983, and I think he was very pleased to be able to enthuse about Al Pacino and Robert De Niro, the fabulous sets for *Absolute Beginners* and all the television activity.

In fact, his enthusiasm was such that it made it a little awkward for me to present my proposal, for I did not want to appear to be critical of the way things were going in the company.

Goldcrest, I said to him, had its own development and production arm of nine or ten people. They were the ones who created product, invested money in scripts, acquired rights and prepared packages for James to go and sell to the Hollywood studios. I knew that Sandy, who was in charge of all this, was unhappy and was unlikely to stay beyond the end of the year – there was no mystery about that: everyone in Wardour Street knew it. In my opinion, the development strategy followed by Sandy and his team was wrong-headed: they were spending far too much time and money and manpower looking at hundreds of ideas which didn't have the remotest chance of getting made because they didn't have major film-makers attached to them. For a company in Goldcrest's position, with limited investment funds available and a consequent need for a very high conversion rate of development deals, it was a waste of time dealing with untried talent. That may sound a little hard on all the newcomers who might be the Alan Parkers and Roland Joffes of tomorrow, but the plain fact is that it was no part of Goldcrest's brief to use its resources to nurture up-and-coming film-makers – a job that was best left to people like David Puttnam, non-commercial sponsors such as British Screen Finance, or, in the US, the major studios.

I had also heard, I told James, that Goldcrest's overheads were going through the roof. Everyone in town was talking about the ever-growing staff. Sandy's development operation was clearly contributing to that.

What I proposed was that Allied should become in effect the development arm of Goldcrest. This would solve the problem of replacing Sandy, save the company substantial risk capital in the development business, reduce the workload, cut the overhead and, at the same time, expand the sources of product. Goldcrest would pay Allied an advance, recoverable from the budgets of those projects that went into production, in exchange for which they would have second look, after Warner Bros., at all Allied projects. This was not as bad a deal as it seems, because in fact – and I knew this better than anyone – Goldcrest and Warner Bros. had been acting as partners for some years and the arrangement had been very beneficial to them both. 'Second look' in this context was tantamount to formalizing that relationship, making Goldcrest and Warners true partners in all Allied projects.

Of course, I realized that what I was saying might not be altogether palatable to James. I didn't want to imply any criticism of his set-up there, nor did I want him to think that I was trying to get back into Goldcrest. I therefore deliberately went out of my way to couch my proposal in respectful terms.

'James,' I said, 'I hope you don't feel that this is in any way an attempt to encroach upon what you are doing. Believe me, nothing could be further from the truth. The fact is that you're too busy running the company to spend time attracting talent and negotiating deals, and this is a possible solution for you.'

He waved aside any suggestion that my approach was unwelcome. He listened attentively to the proposal, and I had the impression that he would take it away and give it serious consideration.

Shortly after that meeting – it may even have been in the same week – David Norris and John Chambers came round to see me at my apartment in Kensington. I think they really wanted to talk about the problems within Goldcrest, although, if that was the case, by the time they arrived they had clearly thought better of it. Instead, we had a social drink and I took the opportunity to explain to them the proposal that I had put to

James. They seemed very keen, and even undertook to speak up for it, when, and if, it was put before a management meeting.

Ilott: Norris admits that the purpose of going to see Eberts was 'quite frankly, to see if he was prepared to come back, whether [coming back] was something that would interest him'. But the tenor of the meeting, he says, was 'completely non-cabal like . . . There was no "Let's plot and plan and overthrow." What we were trying to do was to see what Jake's state of mind was. It was a bit naive, because I guess what was much in my mind, probably not in John's, was to turn the clock back two years. Two years before it was smaller and tighter, less grandiose in its aspirations.'

It is not clear from Norris's account, nor from Chambers's, whether Eberts's return to Goldcrest was actually raised at that meeting, or whether, as Eberts maintains above, it had been set aside even before the meeting began. Both Norris and Chambers do remember, however, the discussion of his Allied proposal, and both were indeed very much in favour of it. It was to be the cause, at a subsequent Goldcrest management meeting, of what Lee describes as 'internal friction'.

'At the time, we were busy trying to work out which assassin to use to kill Hugh Hudson – which hit-man would do the cleanest job,' Lee says, 'and I was being put under this terrible pressure to sign up that deal with Jake. Sandy appeared in some way to sit on the wall on the issue . . . [but] John Chambers, David Norris and two of the non-executive directors were determined that we should go for it . . . And I said that we did not need to support Jake's overheads to get access to his product, because the one thing that was absolutely clear was that, if Warners turned it down on the first look, the next place he would go would be Goldcrest. We didn't need to pay him to do it.'

Eberts called Lee a few days later and was told that Goldcrest was not interested. Then Norris and Chambers called Eberts to arrange another meeting. This time the idea of him coming back into the company was discussed, and at length.

The three men met for dinner in a restaurant not far from the Goldcrest offices on the evening of 22 April. This was the very day of the management meeting that had been held to consider ways of dealing with Hudson and Winkler. Indeed, *Revolution*'s overcost became one of the many subjects of the evening's conversation, for Norris and Chambers used the occasion to explain to Eberts the state of affairs, as they saw it, within the company: the looming cash-flow crisis, the ever-growing overheads, the television losses, the *Revolution* débâcle and the undeclared state of war between Lieberson and Lee. Something, they said, had to be done. What they proposed was not that Eberts should take up the reins of running the company, but that he should bring Allied into Goldcrest and become its creative head and chief deal-maker. While he would of course have to be the titular boss, it would fall to Norris and Chambers actually to attend to the day-to-day affairs of the company as joint managing directors. Their plan sounds very much like a combination of Eberts's own proposal and an idealized version of the situation that had prevailed in the summer of 1983, before Eberts had left for Embassy.

'He liked the idea,' says Chambers, 'but he said, "What about Lee? You can't get rid of Lee." And I said, "Well, if it can't operate with him then he will have to go." '

Chambers insists that the whole discussion, and especially that part concerning Lee, was conducted in an ethical manner. 'Of course we couldn't do anything formal with Jake. There couldn't be any note of conspiracy. Jake behaved very correctly and kept right away from it. In other words, he was ready to come back if the way was clear, but he didn't want to be approached formally until something had happened. Which was a perfectly right and proper way to operate.'

In these affairs, there is clearly a very fine line to be drawn between acting responsibly in the best interests of the company and its share-holders, which is what Norris and Chambers undoubtedly believed they were doing, and acting conspiratorially in one's own interest, which was equally undoubtedly a significant component, conscious or otherwise, in their thinking. They had not forgiven Lee for his attempt to disenfranchise them at the outset of his regime and they continually bridled at what they believed to be his high-handedness.

Eberts: In my recollection, Norris's and Chambers's main concern at that meeting wasn't James, with whom they clearly were not very happy, but Sandy. Sandy, they said, constantly ducked responsibility for production decisions, always looking to defer to a third party – either James, or the board or his management colleagues. They were very anxious that Sandy should announce his intention to leave at the end of the year – so far he had told only Dickie; none of the board members knew of his plan – and that, as soon as he did so, his department should be slimmed down, or abolished altogether, and that Allied should come in to fill the gap.

We talked in general about overheads, the cost of the films and the uncommercial nature of some of the projects. I had the impression throughout our conversation that John and David had no doubt that they should be running the company.

My own position was that, although I was very willing to have some role to play in Goldcrest – I had proposed as much to James already – I was not anxious, after what I had been through at Embassy, to get involved again in corporate politics. I was very happy with the deal I had done with Warner Bros. and I was pleased with the progress I was making with Allied. There was nothing I had to prove that would require me to roll up my sleeves and get stuck into Goldcrest. So while my response may have given John and David encouragement, it actually amounted to very little more than saying, yes, I would like Allied to work with Goldcrest, and, no, I didn't want anything to do with running the company.

As for the issue of James's future, it had nothing to do with me at all. I had my own views about what James was doing at Goldcrest, but, out of prudence as well as principle, I kept them to myself.

Ilott: It is unlikely that a meeting between Eberts, Norris and Chambers could have been held in a public place in London without being noticed. Michael Deeley, head of Consolidated Productions, heard about it and mentioned it to Steve Walsh. After that, rumours that Eberts was being lined up to return to Goldcrest gradually filtered into the Wardour Street mill.

On Tuesday morning, 23 April, Lee received a call from Bobby Blues, who had returned to Devon to oversee the *Revolution* accounts. Garth Thomas's instructions, he said, were being ignored and the situation, instead of getting better, had in fact got worse. Notwithstanding the previous day's decision to await 'the outcome of the actions and initiatives already undertaken', Lee decided there and then to get rid of Irwin Winkler. He called a meeting with Norris and Chambers, and consulted Lieberson, who was now in San Francisco working on the script of *Horror Movie* with writer David Peoples, by telephone. All were agreed that Winkler had to be banned from the set – since he was not technically under contract he could not be fired – and that Hudson was to be warned that, should there be any further failure to follow instructions, he, too, would be taken off the picture.

On Wednesday afternoon, Norris, accompanied by Garth Thomas, took a private plane to Plymouth. 'I'd arranged to meet Irwin at 11 o'clock on Thursday morning, in a disused warehouse that they were using as an office-cum-prop-store in Plymouth,' he recalls. 'I was told by Garth on the way there that, although the office had been there for three weeks, Irwin had never been in it. We got there, I suppose, at 10.30. And within five minutes of him [Irwin] due to arrive, I had this phone call from

Sandy in San Francisco. It was 3 o'clock in the morning his time. He said, "Have you met with Irwin yet?" I said, "No, he's on his way." "Oh, I've just had him on the phone for an hour. Whatever you do, Dave, mollify him, pacify him, don't do a thing to upset him. And, whatever you do, don't fire him." I said, "Why not?" "Well," he said, "the entire cast and Hudson are on his side. If he walks, or is forced to walk, they'll all walk." I said, "Sandy, really, they won't. They're a professional crew, their careers are too important to them." "Well, he has assured me that they will and I believe him. So whatever you do you have got to keep him sweet. Check with James."

'So I then call James, and at that moment in walks Winkler. "James, what do you want me to do?" I asked. "Yes, yes, I have talked to Sandy," he said. "You must not fire Winkler." So there I am in the office of the guy I'm supposed to sack, who is standing right next to me, and someone had just cut my balls off.'

Winkler, it seems, realizing the nature of Norris's mission, had called Lieberson and threatened, in effect, to stop the picture. (According to Lieberson this was a manoeuvre that the producer used on more than one occasion.) Knowing that no completion-guarantee contract had been signed and faced, therefore, with the prospect of saying goodbye to the £4 million or more that had already been spent, Lieberson had immediately called Lee, who, presumably reluctantly, had agreed that Norris's mission should be aborted. One supposes that while Norris had been trying to contact Lee, Lee had been just as feverishly trying to contact Norris.

Norris continues the story: 'So now what was I supposed to be there for? Before I had even opened my mouth, Winkler, who had deferred all his fee in the expectation that the film would take $100 million – it didn't hurt him; he lived like a lord and his expenses were horrendous – actually said, "Now I've got to tell you something. I agreed to defer my fee on this picture, but that's costing me money because of the way I structured my deal with Warners, and unless you promise to pay $250,000 of my fee now, in cash, then I think I'm going to have to stop working on this picture, and you know that will mean that Hudson will stop working and Pacino will stop working." And this is the guy that was to be sacked for incompetence! And I've got ringing in my ears: "Whatever you do, don't fire him, don't upset him."

'I didn't fire him. I didn't even threaten to fire him. I just told him that there was no way that he was going to get $250,000. I said that the best I would ever agree to was to see that, if from that point on things improved, that they picked up some of their lost costs, then we would put his request to the board for their consideration. By the time we parted, he was happy to carry on and for his $600,000 fee to be deferred, knowing that I was a fair man who would treat his case reasonably in relation to the $250,000 in due course. That was bullshit on his part, and bullshit on mine. And the rest of the day I became a spare prick at a wedding, just wandering about the set. The chance of bringing the film under control was dead, gone, wallop. Not that everything was Irwin's fault, necessarily. But he was the most expendable, making the least contribution. It needed a shock to stop the rot.'

But the matter, of course, could not be left there. All that Norris's mission had achieved was the throwing up of a $250,000 smokescreen that would only add to the acrimony between the production team and head office. The problem of forcing Hudson to work within the limits set by Garth Thomas remained. Lieberson and Lee sought the advice of Terry Semel, who had experienced similar problems with both Winkler and Hudson in the past.

'Irwin could not control Hugh any more than I can', Semel recalls, 'in terms of the budget of the movie. Hugh just saw things bigger. He saw a hundred extras, and he needed someone to say, "Well, you're not going to get a hundred – you get ten". But although Irwin couldn't control Hugh, what he could do was compromise him.

'I talked to James. I said, "If you don't have Irwin there now it's not better, it's worse. Because at least Irwin and Hugh talk to each other all day long." And they did, they were together. "What you have with Irwin is someone that Hugh at least respects, and doesn't feel is out to get him. And therefore he can accomplish a lot of the things you want to accomplish. I don't think you'll solve the dilemma by giving Hugh someone he doesn't know right now. He won't hear of it. He won't deal with it. He'll just totally withdraw into his shell. Every day that he starts having a headache it's going to cost you a few hundred thousand dollars. And he will really make it a game. Because of his insecurities and his paranoia, you are probably better off keeping someone he does know, and at least he trusts, and what you've got to do is really work on that person. You've got to be on Irwin Winkler's back day in and day out, every single day. You've got to get Irwin to feel inclined to think that you are right about this. And then Irwin can accomplish half or three quarters of the things you think you want." This was difficult because they were all so alienated from each other, they all disliked each other. James, Sandy, Irwin – I don't think any of them were basically talking to each other.'

Semel's views carried considerable weight, of course, and, for the present all thoughts of firing Winkler were set aside. At the management meeting of 7 May it was noted that 'it was essential to maintain pressure on the production team through frequent visits by Goldcrest's senior management', a task that fell increasingly to Lee, with whom Hudson and Winkler maintained more or less cordial relations.

Lieberson turned his attention to *The Mission*.

Chapter Forty-five

Staunching the Flow of Cash

'In Colombia you are constantly aware of death. Three men on the film died when we were there. One was shot by a policeman at home in front of his mother, one was murdered at a party and another died in an accident. One day a man walked into my office with a machete, wanting to be paid. This was the atmosphere we were in. It was not like the cosy boardroom in London, and it was not like King's Lynn.'
– Iain Smith, associate producer of The Mission

Ilott: At the beginning of 1985, Chambers had predicted a maximum borrowing requirement of £5.7 million, peaking in November. This had been deemed manageable within the terms of the Midland Bank credit facility. In February, he had increased the forecast requirement to £10 million, and indicated that it would peak much earlier in the year. Again, this did not cause any great alarm. Although it was clear that the funds available within the terms of the Midland facility would not meet Goldcrest's needs, arrangements were already in hand to secure bigger and more flexible credit arrangements with a bank that had specialist expertise in film finance. David Berman, of the European American Bank, was invited to the offices at the end of March, and on 17 April Frans Afman of Credit Lyonnais had lunch with Norris, Chambers, East and accountant Andy Parsons. At the April board meeting, by which time *Revolution*'s overcost had to be included in the calculations, the worsening cash-flow position was set out in some detail, but, once again, the discussion appears to have been conducted with no great urgency. Now, on Monday, 29 April, two weeks after that board meeting, Chambers produced another revised forecast. This showed a peak borrowing requirement of £12.4 million, occurring in June. In other words, Goldcrest would run out of cash and credit within six weeks.

The urgency of the situation could no longer be ignored. Lee circulated a memo to the management team in which he said that Goldcrest had to take immediate steps both to reduce the forecast deficit and to increase the available facilities.

To reduce the deficit, he listed the following measures:

1. Get the Australian tax deal confirmed as quickly as possible.
2. Secure Cinema Group's $5 million, which was now dependent on the Australian tax deal, by the end of June.
3. Ask Warner to pay their foreign distribution advances for *Revolution* while the film was still in production. The current arrangement was that the American advances would be paid during production but that the bulk of the foreign advances would be paid only on delivery of the finished film.
4. Ensure that Schuster paid his promised $4.5 million by July.
5. Secure at least 50 per cent third-party financing for *Horror Movie*, and ensure that US distribution terms involved payment during the course of production.
6. Delay or abandon the South African musical *Tembisa* (formerly known as *Dream Song*).

To increase Goldcrest's credit facilities, Lee proposed:

1. Securing up to $20 million from Credit Lyonnais by the end of June at the latest.
2. Increasing the Midland Bank facility to £12.5 million.
3. Approaching Noble Grossart or Rothschilds to organize bridging finance.

On the afternoon of 29 April Lee contacted Warner Bros., Chambers contacted Schuster and Norris telexed the Australian agent dealing with the Westpac fund, emphasizing the urgency of completing heads of agreement.

On 3 May Chambers flew to Rotterdam for talks with Frans Afman of Credit Lyonnais. He returned 'impressed and optimistic', and, on Monday, 7 May, the management meeting was told that 'it was hoped' that a Credit Lyonnais facility of $20–25 million would be agreed 'by the end of May to enable drawings in June'.

On 10 May Lee and Chambers met with Ted Harris, corporate finance director of Midland Bank, to inform him of the £12.4 million borrowing requirement, the overcost on *Revolution* and the plans for the Credit Lyonnais credit facility, which would replace the arrangement with the Midland itself. According to Chambers they received a 'sympathetic response', and Lee later recorded that Harris had indicated that, until such time as the Credit Lyonnais arrangements were in place, the Midland would consider financing Goldcrest's requirements 'on an overdraft basis'. Even by the most optimistic reading, however, Harris's assurances fell a long way short of actually promising to provide the bridge between Goldcrest's current credit limit and the £12.4 million required. For one thing, the bank insisted that the annual interest payable on its (or any other) loans should at no point exceed 40 per cent of Goldcrest's forecast pre-tax profits. On this count, Goldcrest had already reached the limit of its borrowing entitlement.

On 13 May Lee, Chambers, Norris and company secretary Robert Finney met to review the position. Finney summarized their conclusions in a memo circulated to the executive team on 16 May:

I note below points arising from the discussion immediately prior to the management meeting last Monday. James Lee, John Chambers, David Norris and I were present throughout that discussion.

John Chambers advised that the required charges in favour of Midland Bank were not yet executed and Goldcrest was in technical default. As previously reported, our cash flow forecast indicated peak borrowings in excess of the £10 million facility available, and default on the profit condition of the facility (net profit before interest and tax to equal or exceed 2½ times total group interest charges each year) was forecast for the year end.

Discussions with Credit Lyonnais had been held with a view to replacing the Midland facility, and their response was expected in several weeks. Clearly, a negative response would cause substantial problems and therefore alternatives had to be considered – in particular discussions with the First National Bank of Boston would be pursued, and the possibility of a Guinness Mahon-led consortium or even borrowings through Pearson were mentioned.

Even if Credit Lyonnais' ultimate response were positive, there was a problem in the interim and Goldcrest must be able to reassure the Midland that all practicable action was being taken. Specifically, Goldcrest could argue,

(a) cash flow requirements had been reduced by the deferral of the *Horror Movie* production into 1986, and,

(b) Goldcrest could take action to reduce overheads.

From this point on, Chambers was in daily contact with the Midland's man on the case, Mike Massey, and together they monitored all the cash flows in and out of the company with a view to keeping Goldcrest's borrowings within the permitted limits. To get an idea of how difficult this was to achieve, one only has to look at the cash-flow forecast for the first week of May, which showed Goldcrest's borrowing requirement increasing from £42,000 on 1 May to £4 million on 7 May. In the same period, Goldcrest's maximum permitted borrowings, as secured against signed contracts, amounted to £1.25 million. There was only one way out of this seemingly impossible contradiction: the withholding of payments.

Holding back cheques is a dangerous business. Not only is one open to charges of sharp practice, but one runs the risk of undermining confidence in the company. Some creditors, of course, will co-operate, and these can be told what is going on. Others, however, have to be left in ignorance and their angry protests ignored.

It is also an extremely complex business, requiring hours of late-night computations of payments and receipts due. And for every outgoing cheque held back from a creditor there is likely to be an equivalent incoming cheque being held back by a distributor who is playing the same game. Again, to insist on prompt payment, or even early payment, of distribution advances was likely to alert the industry to the company's predicament and perhaps cause long-term damage.

The task of supervising all this fell to Andy Parsons. It was he who organized the weekly cash advances to the films in production, authorized all expenditures and kept the daily bank balance. Outgoing cheques for *Revolution* and *The Mission* (other than for local payments in Colombia) were drawn up by the respective production accountants and then sent to Parsons for counter-signature and despatch to the creditors concerned.

'If we'd released everything as it was drawn we would have gone over the Midland credit limit without any question,' Parsons recalls. 'I was robbing Peter to pay Paul. It was horrendous, particularly when I'd got desk drawers full of cheques which couldn't be released and people screaming at me down the telephone. I think the maximum I had at any one time was about £1.3 million of cheques that I was sitting on. I simply didn't have the money to release them.'

This was not an emergency tactic adopted for a week or two. It started in May and went on until December. Parsons worked round the clock. His health and marriage suffered drastically.

The films, too, were badly hit. *The Mission*, being in a distant location and amongst people of a different language and culture, was clearly the most vulnerable. For four weeks, the supply of cash to the production suffered interruptions and delays, and Puttnam's accounts team had difficulty in paying local suppliers and crew. Part of the problem lay in the inefficiency of the means chosen – money went from London to Florida and from there to Cartagena, a process that took longer, and was less reliable, than had been expected – and partly it was a result of the production office itself supplying incorrect information as regards its cash requirements. But part of it, too, reflected the controls being put into effect by Parsons in London. 'Rightly or wrongly, we didn't necessarily advise him [Puttnam] that we were holding cheques,' remembers Parsons.

Parsons insists however, that *The Mission*'s Colombian operation was never interfered with; that he withheld only payments sent back to London for distribution in the UK. (The mostly British crew, for example, was paid in sterling in London, as were shippers, caterers, equipment suppliers and so on.)

'It was a timing thing and we thought we may get away with it without actually having to bother David Puttnam with it,' he explains. 'I think that's where we ran foul of him, because he thought information was being held from him. We did it in the best spirit. We weren't trying to be devious. We just didn't want to bother him with what was going on back at base while he was having all the problems out there.'

Such a deceit, of course, could not be maintained for long. Frustrated by the constant delays to his cash flow, and again facing the prospect of not being able to pay his bills at the end of the week, Puttnam, on 15 May, demanded not only that the banking arrangements be sorted out once and for all but that a $200,000 float be immediately put at his disposal in Colombia. Such a float, he said, would free him from all this aggravation. But this Goldcrest could not do.

'We were really getting to the stage that it was so finely tuned that even something like $50,000 extra was beginning to give us problems,' explains Parsons. 'To suddenly have to find this extra money to divert that way was impossible. *The Mission* money normally went out on a Friday, but the $200,000 had to be there overnight on the Wednesday. I hadn't got any dollars till Friday, until Warners had funded me. That's when David exploded. There wasn't the cash to meet the requirements on location.'

When Puttnam was told that the $200,000 would not be available until the end of the week, he decided to approach Warner Bros. direct. 'We kept getting these cockamamy excuses about why the money was late,' Puttnam remembers. 'For three weeks they lied to me. I got so desperate I called Bob Daly [Warner Bros.' chairman] and said, "I have got to have half, or maybe a quarter, of a million dollars, here in the bank available to me. I can't go through another week of scraping by and not paying bills." It ain't funny not paying bills in Colombia, I can tell you. So Bob says, "Well, that's fine. I don't mind. What I'll do is take it off your delivery payment." I said, "Fine, that will do." So he put the pro-forma to James Lee and said, "I'm going to send David some money. He needs some upfront." And James Lee went berserk. He said, "Don't send it, don't send it." He went absolutely berserk. I said, "Listen, I need the fucking money and if I can't get it off you I have to get if off someone else." It was all done at midnight: phone calls back and forth, back and forth. And he said, "How dare you let them [Warner Bros.] know we've got money troubles." I said, "James, *I* don't know we've got money troubles. What money troubles?" This was the first I knew of it.'

When the situation was explained to him, Puttnam's anger focused on *Revolution*'s £3 million overcost. Thus began a long-running, semi-public feud between Puttnam and the *Revolution* team of Winkler and Hudson (with whom Puttnam had long ago fallen out over the making of *Greystoke*).

'All my hysteria – public hysteria – about *Revolution* was only about what was being done to us,' Puttnam explains. 'You know what it's like with film crews. We knew every day what was going on on *Revolution*. Every single day a make-up girl or someone would say, "Oh, I was on the phone to my aunt, she's working on it . . ." We knew every day. And my argument was very simple: we were abroad, we were on budget, we were in a very dangerous place, and a very difficult place. I said. "I don't care what your problems are with *Revolution* – close the film down for all I care – but *don't* cut off our funds." '

Cash flow was only the most pressing of Puttnam's problems. Before the production had even started, Iain Smith had gone to great pains to investigate and accommodate Colombian labour laws and customs. He had hired specialist legal advisers, obtained all the necessary permissions from the relevant ministries and had arranged, wherever it was requested or required, for officials to approve or supervise the hiring of Colombian workers. Yet, only six weeks into the production, he was to report to Lieberson that 'certain individuals, encouraged by one lawyer in particular, have made complaints to the local labour office in Cartagena, saying that we have employed them on a permanent basis . . . and that on completion of their work we had reneged in not providing severance pay, holiday pay, pension, etc.'

This dispute was to drag on through May and June and at one stage even threatened to hold up the planned completion of work in Colombia in the first week of July. In the middle of negotiations between the production office and the Ministry of Labour, Smith, production supervisor Barrie Melrose, location manager Pamela Wells and props master Terry Wells were placed under a restriction order preventing them from leaving the country. In the end it was to be agreed that Goldcrest would meet 60 per cent of the workers' claims – a settlement that was to cost the company £100,000.

When Puttnam himself had first arrived on the location, he had summarized the state of play in the following letter to Lieberson:

Dear Sandy,

Since arriving here I must say that I have found more going right than going wrong, but there are two situations which bother me a great deal. The first I am discussing with Garth and is related to our ability to control the expenditure of the Special Effects Department, particularly as this impacts on the safety of the artists and the crew. I have never worked with this particular team before and it's going to be a struggle to understand what expenditure is really necessary and what is merely part of the old pals act.

I have already asked for Garth's advice and will keep you up to date.

The second is the impact of casting Robert de Niro and our ability to control personal expenses. I am sure this is something you are dealing with on a day to day level in King's Lynn, but it's certainly a subject of discussion for the board. Without doubt, as we discovered at the American Film Market, there are real advantages in the casting of 'big names'. However, sitting out here in Colombia, I am beginning to come across the equally real disadvantages.

First is the instinctive manner in which those departments which have to deal with him are understandably afraid and tend to overspend in order to be absolutely certain of meeting with his approval. This in turn also has an effect on Roland, and the net effect on the picture is that the focus is not necessarily consistently in the right place. Then there is the matter of cost. I have attached a schedule which shows you the add-on costs we have been forced to accommodate in the past month or so. All of which are outside our original expenses budget, and none of which on a major American movie would be regarded as unacceptable. I have to say that, in so far as I am concerned, they are! It is not just a question of de Niro himself, but the fact that the other artists, including Jeremy Irons, all look to receive similar treatment. The net effect of that particular syndrome is at present unquantifiable.

In essence, I would say that you should set the many advantages of having this quality of actor against a debit column amounting to some additional £100,000, in unavoidable but irrelevant expenditure. How am I supposed to treat this vis à vis the budget? Do we pay for it out of our overtime allowance or one of the other elements which clearly are used to underpin genuine screen value?

This is not a moan. It is a factual rundown of the situation on the ground, as opposed to the rather more mythological one which is liable to drift around the boardroom.

No doubt we will be talking on the telephone.

Yours as ever,

David

The attached schedule showed estimated expenses for De Niro, covering air fares, living allowance, hotel accommodation, telephone, meals, physiotherapist and fencing instructor, totalling £103,000, against a budget allowance of £43,000. Three weeks later, De Niro's agent, Harry Ufland, submitted further claims, none of which had been authorized or budgeted for. These personal expenses were not of great concern in themselves. What worried Puttnam was control – he is, probably of necessity, a control freak – and De Niro, the most powerful figure on the set, could easily throw the film off course. (Interestingly, both Roland

Joffe and Iain Smith have nothing but praise for De Niro and for the way he behaved on location. In their view, it was only after David Puttnam's arrival on the set that the problems with De Niro arose.)

Then, at the end of the fourth week of shooting, Roland Joffe collapsed on the set.

'It was a very unfortunate thing,' Joffe says. 'I had got flu and we were using a local doctor who in secret wanted to be a gynaecologist and, since I wasn't pregnant, didn't know how to treat me. And what he suggested as a remedy to get rid of my flu was to put on a T-shirt at night, turn the air conditioning off and sweat a lot. Which I did. But the water he gave me to drink wasn't putting back any minerals into my body. So, in fact, I just sweated out my minerals.'

Joffe plays down the seriousness of the incident. Nevertheless, he was in hospital for two days and had to take a further day off before he could go back to work. The production thus fell behind its already tight schedule and overages were inevitable.

Chapter Forty-six

Deeper into the Mire

Ilott: The dispute over the ending of the *Revolution* script had dragged on through the early weeks of shooting. In one version, the Kinksi character, Daisy, is killed, and the Pacino character, Tom Dobb, wanders aimlessly around battle-scarred New York. This was the ending preferred by Hudson, but not by Warner Bros. Warners wanted Daisy to live and for the ending to be upbeat. Indeed, one has the impression that Warners had all along wanted Daisy and Tom Dobb to fall in love and for them to live happily ever after. On 7 May, in the eighth week of what was supposed to have been a fourteen-week schedule, it was reported at a Goldcrest management meeting that Lieberson was again 'considering the final scenes and appropriate ending'.

What emerged, presumably as a compromise between the wishes of Hudson, Warner Bros. and Lieberson, was a new ending altogether. It was one that did not impress Chris Burt.

'It was a very expensive ending,' Burt explains. 'And I looked at it and said, "This is ridiculous. We have got all this pressure about money and now you are saying that the whole of New York is dancing and he's going through all these people – 2,000 people dancing in the streets – and suddenly he sees Daisy? It means getting all those streets back and dressing them, putting these extras in, and about four days to shoot it." It was crazy. I couldn't understand it. But that's what they wanted. It cost about £100,000 a day to shoot that; with all the bits and pieces, maybe more. Say half a million in all.'

Revolution duly moved back to King's Lynn, where the production designer and his team re-dressed the town. The first day's shooting of the final scene was to take place on 16 May. Michael Stoddart and his wife, accompanied by James Lee – Lieberson was away at the Cannes Film Festival – drove up from London for the occasion. In the car, Lee revealed to Stoddart that the visit had more than just a social purpose.

'I remember James saying that there were considerable arguments and we had to cut the costs and so on,' Stoddart recalls. 'We discussed it while driving over. He said, "Look, these are the problems. We are having a head-to-head with Winkler. I'm doing this and that because we are over budget and I'm really concerned about it." And I thought at the time that he handled it well. He was taking a fairly tough line and that seemed very sensible.'

In fact, there was even more to it than Stoddart knew, for Hudson and Winkler had their own plans for the visit. The script disputes – not just about the ending, but about nearly every scene – had spluttered on day by day. Welland's rewrites were submitted to Pacino, who, so one story goes, faxed them back to the original writer Robert Dillon for scrutiny. As often as not, Welland's amendments were rejected. Welland's work was also subject to examination by script editor Shawn Slovo. For example, 14 May found Slovo writing memos concerning the seventh revised version of scenes 1–19. It is not worth quoting her remarks except in the context of publishing the entire script, for unlike, say, the original reader's reports, which were general observations about the overall structure of the work, Slovo's notes are extremely detailed and technical. What they do tell us, however, is that, even at this late stage, basic matters such as the interpretation of the motives of major characters had not been settled. Hudson was determined to use Stoddart's and Lee's visit to establish once and for all that he, Hudson, had the final say on the script and that Welland was to be given free rein.

'Luckily, I had been forewarned that this was going to happen,' remembers Lee. 'So I called Sandy in Cannes and said, "You know, this is getting completely out of hand. What do you want to do about this?" To which he said, "James, you got us into this mess, you can get us out of it." I said, "Well, come on, what do you actually want me to do?" He said, "You seem to think you know what you're doing. You sort it out." '

The VIPs arrived on the set, were introduced to everybody and shown how everything worked. Lee was always a welcome visitor, for his enthusiasm was a great morale-booster. As Chris Burt recalls, 'When James came it was like a guy with a new train set. I mean it was amazing, he was so excited by it all. Which was bloody refreshing. His face used to beam with pleasure.'

Stoddart was impressed. 'I suppose like a naive chap who hasn't seen a film being made before I found it all very exciting,' he says. He was left in no doubt that the people working on the production fervently believed that, as he recalls, 'this was going to be a great movie'. By his own account, he gamely played the part of stern financier, although, as he admits, it didn't get him very far. 'I kept saying, "You're going over budget" and they kept on saying, "Yes." '

There was, however, what was from Hudson's and Winkler's point of view an enormously embarrassing problem: the great New York street scene couldn't be shot, for a key player was missing. Kinksi had flown to Rome.

'We had about 1,200 extras in costumes, with cattle, all kinds of props, jugglers, acrobats, fighters, everything for that ending scene, and Nastassia Kinski goes off to Rome,' says Winkler, still angered by the memory. 'She cost us about half a million bucks, just like that, gone. She was on call and decided to go to Rome. She didn't tell anybody. We couldn't reach her. And when she came back you couldn't criticize her, because if you said anything she might walk off the set. So you had to swallow your pride and not even complain about her.'

That evening, Lee, Stoddart and Stoddart's wife were invited to dine with Winkler, Hudson, Pacino and Sutherland. After dinner, the Stoddarts retired to the drawing room, there to be entertained by Donald Sutherland's stories. Pacino went to bed. Lee, Winkler and Hudson moved to the study to talk about the script. In Lee's recollection their discussion went on 'hour after hour'.

'I was up until about 3 o'clock in the morning, hammering away at Irwin Winkler and Hugh Hudson,' he recalls. 'I had to excruciatingly, painfully extract from them an agreement – which we scribbled out and the next day I had typed, and Hugh and Irwin signed – making it absolutely plain that there would be no further changes coming from Colin Welland unless, first, Sandy had approved them; second, Pacino had agreed; and, third, Garth Thomas had said there were no cost implications. It was absolutely bizarre, but this was the sort of atmosphere against which the crisis was being played out.'

Lee could have derived little satisfaction from securing Winkler's and Hudson's agreement to principles which had, after all, been laid down weeks before. Nor could he have entertained any illusions that his visit had achieved its main purpose: of having a 'head-to-head' with Winkler and putting the fear of God into Hudson. For, at the management meeting on the following Monday, 20 May, at which Lee gave his account of the agreement reached in King's Lynn, it was reported that 'Goldcrest's instructions' were still being 'largely ignored'.

'It was recognized', the minutes continue, 'that because many production costs were already committed there was limited scope for containing costs on the remainder of the film, but a determined stand must be maintained.'

The following week, Terry Semel visited London. He discussed matters with Lee, then went up to King's Lynn to see the production for himself. Although it did not matter to Warners what the film eventually cost, it did matter that the film should be finished, and that it should be good.

'I called Irwin. I met with him and I met with Hugh,' Semel recalls. 'And I asked Irwin, "Please, is there any chance that you can communicate to both sides?" He *had* to pull Hugh up short. He *had* to create some more savings, because they were in big trouble, they were *way* over budget. It was a classic case, also, of a movie that wasn't terribly well planned. They were changing things and changing the script while we were sitting there. They were going from 150 extras today to not knowing what they were going to do tomorrow.'

On his return to London, Semel had no new advice to give. He had seen it all happen before and had yet to find a way of dealing with it.

Lieberson, for his part, wanted nothing further to do with *Revolution*. When he returned from Cannes he announced that he would go to Colombia for five weeks to oversee *The Mission*, thereby allowing Puttnam to return to England for his daughter's wedding, and, from there, to go on to the Tokyo Film Festival.

On the weekend of 18–19 May 1985, Goldcrest moved from its home of the last two years, the cramped but serviceable offices in Holland Street, Kensington, to palatial new accommodation in Wardour Street, Soho. The timing of this move could not have been less fortunate.

There are two observations made about offices that are not less true for being commonplace. The first is that offices are amongst the most potent symbols of corporate self-image. The second is that comfortable, well-appointed and, most of all, impressive surroundings are as important to desk workers as are job titles or company cars. The office is not just the place where you do your work: it is an outward sign of your inner worth, in your own eyes and in the eyes of your peers. The arguments used in favour of the move to Wardour Street – that in Kensington the company had always been a bit isolated and that the growing staff required more space – were entirely reasonable. But of at least equal importance was the fact that the Holland Street offices were merely functional, fluorescent-lit and prosaically situated above a public library. James Lee wore a suit, beard and bow-tie. He wanted a suit, beard and bow-tie office: respectable, even grand, but with a hint of raffishness. The new prestige block at 180 Wardour Street, with its recessed lights, air conditioning, tree-filled, glass-domed, central atrium, tasteful matt paintwork and expensive detailing, in the midst of eternally down-at-heel Soho, with its sex shops, nude-encounter parlours, seedy pubs and restaurants, provided exactly that. Just as Eberts's Goldcrest had been truly at home on two floors of a Georgian house in Holland Park Avenue back in 1981, so Lee's Goldcrest had found its natural habitat in this Wardour Street oasis.

Unfortunately, the new offices cost a lot more than the old and, given that Goldcrest was in the middle of a cash crisis, the move looked unwise, to say the least.

In fairness to Lee, he had first proposed moving to Wardour Street back in June 1984. The plan had been approved, but was then shelved in favour of a reorganization of the Holland Street offices. It was soon realized, however, that the upheaval that would be caused by the decorators and designers would be more than Goldcrest could withstand. As chance would have it, the lease for 180 Wardour Street came back on the market shortly before Christmas 1984. The terms were reasonable, given the prestige nature of the accommodation, and Lee and Chambers immediately entered into negotiation with the agents. All this would have been put to the directors for approval at the February board meeting were it not for the fact that that meeting was cancelled for lack of a quorum. On 12 February, Lee circulated a memo to the directors, outlining the plan and asking for their comments. None was forthcoming. By the time of the March board meeting, at which the relocation *was* discussed, it was felt to be too late to stop it, although in fact contracts had not been signed and the board could have overruled Lee had it wished. The non-executive directors nevertheless believed that they had been presented with a *fait accompli*, and they were not pleased.

On the very day that the company moved into the new building, 20 May, Chambers presented yet another revised profit-and-loss forecast for the year. He was now anticipating a deficit of £500,000. The minutes of the management meeting at which he made this announcement tell us that the loss was 'mainly attributable to four events':

First, Showtime's refusal to pay the option price of $300,000 for the second series of *Robin of Sherwood* to which Goldcrest was already committed. The US pay-cable channel was prepared to pay only $100,000 an hour. Unfortunately, none of the alternative methods of US television distribution that were available to Goldcrest would yield even as much money as that. *Robin of Sherwood* was not a cheap product – the thirteen episodes were to cost Goldcrest £4 million – and at Showtime's new price there was very little chance that the series would break even. Lee proposed a compromise: Goldcrest would ask the equivalent of $176,000 an hour for the first six hours, with the remaining seven hours to be negotiated in the light of the ratings achieved by the first six. This was agreed, but only because the production was already under way. As one of the Goldcrest executives was said to have remarked at the time: 'If we can't make money out of *Robin*, what can we make money out of?' In the event, the thirteen episodes were to lose the company £2 million, which more than wiped out the surplus earned by the first series.

Second, the overrun on *Revolution*.

Third, the non-release of *Horror Movie* in 1985.

Fourth, the swing in Goldcrest's interest position from £0.6 million earned in 1984 to £0.6 million payable in 1985.

The minutes then list the actions that were to be taken 'to improve the 1985 out-turn over the forecast position':

1. Exploit available product to the maximum potential. So far as films were concerned, this meant primarily *Frog Prince*, *Mr Love* and *Smooth Talk* [the films then ready for release].
2. Consider selling Goldcrest's interest in certain television projects, such as documentaries.
3. Consider the potential for Australian finance similar to that on *The Mission*, for *Revolution* or other 1985 releases.
4. Attempt to minimize interest, for example by bringing forward the payment of funds by Schuster and Cinema Group.
5. Contain overheads.
6. Explore options for financing *Mandrake*, with a view in particular to minimizing Goldcrest's production finance exposure. The possibility of selling the project was mentioned briefly.
7. Seek an exclusive US distribution arrangement in return for a substantial contribution to Goldcrest's overheads.
8. Progress a major UK television sale of a package of Goldcrest product as soon as possible.

It may be unfair to examine this action-plan too closely, but the poverty of choice open to Lee and his team can hardly go unremarked. The price of 1984's production hiatus was clearly now being paid. Other than *The Killing Fields*, the theatrical release of which had now run its course, there were no major sources of revenue in sight. All the productions on the Goldcrest management-meeting agenda – *The Mission*, *Revolution*, *Absolute Beginners*, *A Room With a View*, *Horror Movie*, *Mandrake*, *Tembisa/Dream Song*, *Robin of Sherwood* and the clutch of still active television mini-series – were cash consumers, not, as yet, cash providers.

Meanwhile, the completion-guarantee deal with Film Finances Ltd (which had not been signed even though the two big films had already started production) had been dropped in favour of a deal with Entertainment Completions Inc. (ECI), from whom Norris had managed to secure marginally better terms. ECI, of course, insisted that *Revolution*'s overcost be included in the budget from which the completion liability and fee calculations were derived. Otherwise, the terms of the deal were much as before: Goldcrest would be responsible for a 10 per cent contingency and the first additional 10 per cent overcost, after which ECI was to be responsible for completion. The two companies would share the fees. The films included in the package were *The Mission, Revolution, A Room With a View* and *Absolute Beginners*.

Revolution, we know, was in grave difficulties. *The Mission* faced severe problems on location. *A Room With a View* had not yet started production, but, being in the safe hands of the very experienced Merchant–Ivory team, was not thought likely to prove troublesome. *Absolute Beginners* was about to start production and, being in the hands of the very inexperienced Woolley–Brown team, was already over budget and was to prove very troublesome indeed.

Everything about *Absolute Beginners* was difficult. A book that is short on drama and long on mood and style is not easily translated into a musical film, a form in which the British have anyway never been successful and of which even the Americans have become wary in recent years. The script was, according to one of those who worked on it, a monster: diffuse, episodic, overcrowded with characters and too long. The meetings that set out to deal with its problems are described by another participant as having been 'insane', often involving eight or ten people: a writer, Don MacPherson, say, or Richard Burridge; the director, Julien Temple; co-producers Steve Woolley and Chris Brown; Nik Powell from Palace, Al Clark and Robert Devereux from Virgin, Sandy Lieberson and Amanda Schiff from Goldcrest; Colin Young, principal of the National Film School and part-time consultant to Goldcrest; and any Orion person who happened to be in town. One legendary script meeting began in the Goldcrest boardroom at 6 p.m. and did not finish, several locations and many bottles later, until 4 o'clock the following afternoon. Thrown into these discussions were not only the opinions of those present, but dozens of notes and suggestions from script readers and from friends who knew the book or who had read one of the many versions of the screenplay. The loudest voices were those of producer Steve Woolley and director Julien Temple.

'Julien was saying, "*This* is the script, *this* is what I want to shoot," ' remembers Woolley. 'And I said, "There is no way we're going to shoot this; it would cost a fortune." By this stage, because now Don MacPherson wouldn't do anything without Julien, I had to bring in Chris Wicking to do the rewrites. With all the expansion for the Americans, all the incredible colour and all the Tashlinesque scenes, the script was limping all over the place. There was no thread. So Chris came in to do two things: to drive a thread through the script, and at the same time to reduce some of the scope of it.'

The script had to be approved by Goldcrest, Virgin and Orion before principal photography could start. It also had to be approved by Temple. But by the time Wicking had finished his work, Temple had gone to Rio to make a pop video with Mick Jagger. Woolley flew to Brazil, showed Temple the latest version of the script and secured his grudging approval. On his return to England, Woolley set about getting the film ready for production.

'Then Julien came back, launched himself into the film, got the casting together and *changed the script again,*' Woolley recalls. 'After that it was a fight between me and Julien, basically, which turned out to be no holds barred.'

Temple, says Woolley, 'was like a wounded, hurt artist'. For this, Woolley partly blames himself. 'In order to get a deal you really have to talk up a movie. You have to go into an office and talk a film through, sell it. And, of course, you say a lot of things that you mean, but you'd rather not say them with the director there. I'd rather not have Neil Jordan [director of *Company of Wolves*] sitting in while I'm telling somebody why I think Neil's a genius. But, because of the time pressures and the nature of the film and my lack of experience on a picture this big, Julien and I had to do this thing together. Which, coming on top of Julien's close association with lots of rock stars, meant that he was elevated into a very grand role as the director of this film. And I think he was seeing things in a very . . . the word "arrogance" is not fair. It was not that he was necessarily arrogant; it was just that he was uncompromising. There are two things you have to learn: every movie is a compromise and every movie is a collaboration. Julien didn't seem to get that. He wasn't prepared to compromise and he wasn't prepared to collaborate. I mean, even Stanley Kubrick has to stop somewhere.

'What Julien wanted to do was maintain *his* film. Having gone through all the shit he wanted to make *his* film. *The* movie.

'So he got all his mates to work on it. They were fantastic, great people, very talented. But not experienced. It was like *Company of Wolves* in a way: a lot of first-timers.

'Because of this, Goldcrest asked us to accept their nominated associate producer, David Wimbury. David Wimbury and Garth Thomas are the oldest of friends, and Garth encouraged us to take on David as the man who would look after Goldcrest's money. We agreed to it because we didn't think it was a bad idea. I like David a lot and I thought that his experience would help. But by appointing David the line to the floor became cloudy. Because my relationship with Chris Brown [co-producer] was that I was the producer in charge of the creative side and Chris was going to be the producer in charge of the practical side. But now we had David Wimbury between me and Chris, and David slightly usurped Chris's role.'

If the preparations were inauspicious, the actual making of the film, which (not counting the one-week shoot in January) started production on 3 June, was even worse.

'The bully boys in the industry will always tell you that if you stick to schedule you'll come in on budget,' says Woolley. 'But we had the wettest summer for years, and if the weather's no good you can't stick to schedule. The whole script called for sun. It was supposed to be the long hot summer, the heat sizzling down. So Julien couldn't help falling behind schedule. And I had the job of trying to re-order the script to get us back on schedule. So scenes that were previously longer would no longer be longer, or perhaps were not even going to be there at all. And the only way I could do that was with Julien's co-operation. I couldn't just walk in one day with the script and say, "Right, you've lost this, this and this." Theoretically I could, but in reality I couldn't.

'But Julien refused to co-operate in terms of cutting anything out of the script. He would say, "It's OK, don't worry, we'll make up the time, everything will be fine in the end."

'Having worked with Julien on the casting of the film I knew that there was only one way to deal with him, and that was to confront him with a proposal which would galvanize him into coming up with an alternative. So I made crass suggestions, knowing that if I said drop a particular scene he would more than likely come back and say, "No, I won't drop that scene, but I'll drop this scene." It was the only way, really, to get the thing going.

'From my point of view it was a struggle. The schedule was all the time falling apart. The film was going in and out of schedule, and not making any sense.'

This sounds all too familiar. A script that is overlong and unfocused, a wayward director, confusion over who exactly is the producer in charge, scheduling problems brought about by inclement weather and (although not mentioned by Woolley) pre-production overspending on sets, props and costumes: the stage was set for *Revolution Mark 2*.

Chapter Forty-seven

Rousing the Board

Ilott: Michael Stoddart had early on made it his practice to meet with John Chambers a few days before each board meeting, so that he could be briefed about the content and significance of the financial information that was to be put before the board. Goldcrest was an extraordinarily well-run company in this respect: every month the directors received bound copies of the board papers, which included sales reports, strategy papers, management reports, minutes, accounts and forecasts. These bound volumes were often three quarters of an inch thick, and within them the most detailed and extensive information was that provided by the accounts department. Cash-flow tables, income-and-expenditure forecasts, analyses of performance against budget, spread sheets of management accounts, bank balances: all the paraphernalia of proper financial reporting was included. Inevitably, it was not always easy to digest. The non-specialists on the board – Norris, Wooller, Puttnam, Attenborough, Whitehead, Lieberson and Mayer – could not be expected to draw their own conclusions from the data before them, and even the specialists, like Joll and Grossart, were often too busy to have had time to study it all in detail.

It was essential, therefore, that the financial information be summarized verbally at the meetings, a task that mainly fell to Lee, supported by Chambers. But accounting, of course, is no science, and were the board to rely wholly on Lee and Chambers it would hear only the management's interpretation of the state of the company's affairs. A second opinion was called for, and this was most often provided by Stoddart. Hence the monthly briefings, and hence, too, Stoddart's regular boardroom interventions by which he sought to draw attention away from Lee's habitually optimistic assessment of long-term opportunity towards, instead, such sources of anxiety as the rate of return, currency hedging and level of overheads.

Lee soon added himself to the Stoddart–Chambers briefing meetings, which became longer – sometimes lasting for two hours or more – and, while still predominantly concerned with finance, wider in scope, covering all aspects of the company's affairs.

As far as their attitudes to the theory and practice of business are concerned, Chambers and Lee could be said to be opposites: the former being problem-orientated and the latter being solution-orientated. This might have made for a good combination were it not for the fact that Lee, as well as being Chambers's boss, was much the more powerful personality. As a consequence, the briefing sessions became dominated by the discussion of Lee's solutions to the problems raised by Chambers's figures, rather than by a full consideration of the figures themselves. Inevitably, this characteristic carried over into the discussion at board level, where the executive directors, being Lee's subordinates, were obliged to endorse his views, and the non-executive directors, busy men with many other commitments, were only too pleased for him to do their thinking for them.

Reading through the board papers of 1984 and 1985, one is repeatedly struck by Lee's inadvertent tendency to pre-empt debate, putting forward closely argued solutions to problems that had yet to be closely investigated. Indeed, to be offered a range of options in one of Lee's strategy papers was akin to being asked to 'pick a card, any card' by a professional magician: as soon as you reach for it, you know that you are condemned to play by his rules to the end. This is not to say that Lee was ever anything other than honest and conscientious, but to point out that in his zeal to be a good leader he took all the initiative for himself.

Two days before the May board meeting, Lee, Chambers and Stoddart met at Stoddart's Temple Place office. The sudden downturn in the profit-and-loss forecast for the year and the continuing search for alternative banking arrangements were clearly the most pressing items on the agenda. As to the former, Lee had already set out a range of remedial policy options in his new strategy document, the '1985 Profit Improvement Programme', and it was on this that the discussion was focused. As to the latter, Stoddart was told that the Midland Bank was taking a supportive view and that discussions with Credit Lyonnais were well advanced. Some light-hearted exchanges concerning Lee's and Stoddart's visit to King's Lynn the previous week (a visit of which Chambers sternly disapproved) and an update on the progress of the films currently in production (A Room With a View had started shooting on locations in and around Florence), brought the meeting to its conclusion. It had been marked neither by controversy nor by any expression of alarm.

The following day, Chambers had further talks with Ted Harris and

Mike Massey at the Midland, from which it emerged that the bank could not be relied upon to support the company beyond the terms set out in the credit-facility agreement. The Midland had already transgressed those terms itself, for example by allowing the estimated interest payable to exceed 40 per cent of Goldcrest's estimated pre-tax profits. But it would guarantee neither to do more than that, nor even to continue doing as much as that, should Goldcrest's position deteriorate rather than improve. The bank, in other words, was giving clear notice that it would not refrain from bouncing Goldcrest's cheques. Chambers now believes that in doing this the Midland had an undeclared purpose in mind: to shock the Goldcrest shareholders into putting more money into the company.

The board meeting was to be held at 11 a.m. the next day, Thursday, 23 May. At 9 a.m. Norris and Chambers had a breakfast meeting at the Ritz with Angus Grossart. They handed him the following document:

The Reorganized Goldcrest – A Year On

At the time of the management crisis in February 1984 caused by the two-tier board structure, we expressed severe reservations about certain aspects of the Goldcrest operation, both present and future.

A. *The position in February 1984*

1. Television production and marketing:

It was obvious that the television operation was functioning badly and making no contribution to the profit of the Group, largely because of –

(a) the type of production we were getting into, e.g. large and small documentary series and made-for-television dramas with substantial deficit financing.

(b) the inadequacy of the management, in particular its inexperience of commercial and financial disciplines and marketing.

2. Film production:

We opposed the appointment of Sandy Lieberson as chief of production because we foresaw the introduction of a Hollywood-style operation involving greater emphasis and expenditure on the development of projects in-house. We anticipated that such a style would add considerably to our overheads, and to our incurring a high level of development write-offs.

3. The appointment of Don Cruickshank as deputy chief executive:

This appeared to us to be an unnecessary appointment at a high salary. After the removal of the Finance and Business Affairs functions from his control, the appointment appeared even less necessary.

4. Overheads:

The change in style (or philosophy) following Jake Eberts' departure resulted in a substantial increase in overheads. Jake and his two support staff were replaced by a chief executive with virtually no experience in the film and television industries, and a head of production with his new approach. The net result was to replace one well-paid executive and two junior staff with two highly (one very highly) paid executives, three junior executives, four secretaries and a chauffeur.

5. Pay-cable operation:

We were concerned about our involvement in this operation, about which we had never been consulted, and about the strain on the resources of Goldcrest, with the relative large sums to fund the development in its early stages.

B. *The present position*

After a year of operating Goldcrest following its corporate reorganization, it is useful to review the situation –

1. Television production and marketing:

The situation has worsened in the last year to a degree that knowledgeable insiders in the television industry regard the Goldcrest Television operation as sadly lacking. The satellite producer concept, which has now been abandoned, had proved disastrous, since, with the exception of Paul Knight, we were hiring people who had no experience of independent production, having led sheltered lives in either the BBC or in an independent television company. Late in 1984 we lost Steve Walsh to Consolidated Productions as a direct result of his frustration with the lack of leadership from the television department management. For the same reason we are likely to soon lose Paul Knight, who is the only bright spot in an otherwise depressing picture. To date, the television operation has turned in a substantial deficit, even before accounting for overheads both direct and indirect.

2. Film production:

This has developed as predicted. A department of two people has now become nine, with a cost in salary around £400,000 per annum. In addition, we have acquired a number of 'consultants', which has added a further £46,000 per annum. No projects are presently in production which have been developed by the in-house development team. In March 1985 we are making provisions in film development of about £200,000.

3. Appointment of Don Cruickshank:

The fact that Don Cruickshank left Goldcrest at under one month's notice to join Virgin and it was not felt necessary to replace him, speaks for itself.

4. Overheads:

These have shown a steep rise, and, while all staff are diligent and hard-working, there is much money and effort expended on unnecessary functions.

5. Pay-cable operation:

While Goldcrest's contribution is somewhat less than forecast, it is only because of the very slow development of the cable industry and prospects are bleak. A £300,000 contribution from Goldcrest during 1985 is an unacceptable burden in what is going to be a very lean year.

6. Cabinet responsibility:

Because of the need for the executive directors to show a united front at full board meetings, we have become involved in projects that had considerable opposition from some of the management team and were 'rammed' through by the chief executive, despite the reservations of other directors. These include *Mr Love, Frog Prince, Knights and Emeralds* and *Where Are You Going* [also known as *Smooth Talk, Fifteen*]. The last project, produced by Martin Rosen, was totally opposed by the chief of production.

7. Notwithstanding the above, there have been significant bright spots –

(a) Quality of our main feature programme – *Revolution, The Mission, Absolute Beginners, Horror Movie* – has been proven in the marketplace.

(b) Sandy Lieberson has tutored and encouraged Guy East, whose sales team is proving effective thanks to Sandy's leadership.

C. *The way ahead*

1. Television operation:

In spite of the recent policy rethink, whereby we will concentrate almost exclusively on developing/producing drama series and mini-series that are fully, or very nearly fully financed, and notwithstanding our development deals with ABC, NBC, BBC, etc, we both feel that we should completely close down our television operation. In our view, the alternative – to retain a single production executive, say Paul Knight, and a secretary, and to sub-license world-wide sales through third parties – means that we have no real function to offer independent producers or broadcasters and it will be but a short time before both realize that they can get along very well without us.

2. Film production:

(i) The future here is less clear cut. Some aspects are obvious:

(a) We must remain primary financiers of major feature films.

(b) We must capitalize on our newly won eminence in pre-sales.

(c) We must retain access on the best possible terms to our prime, North American, market.

(ii) The area that becomes more obscure is that in relation to development/production subject selection. The situation here is exacerbated by the uncertainty as to whether or not Sandy Lieberson will exercise his right to convert his deal to that of independent producer as of January 1, 1986. The indications are that he will do so (he has to make up his mind by the end of June) as it is no secret that he finds it virtually impossible to work with the chief executive. We feel that in many ways the exercise of his option will make future strategy easier as we both feel that we should abandon the in-house development facility and return to our old *modus operandi* whereby we offer finance from development through to production and delivery of product for film-makers of proven track records with scope for innovation.

3. Chief executive:

There is no doubting James's obvious intellectual talents, analytical abilities and courage. Nor is there any question but that he has learned a great deal very quickly and that we find him a good and supportive colleague. The problem remains, however, that in this, as in anything else, there is no substitute for experience and in-depth knowledge of the industry in which you operate, and this is lacking. It is also true, regrettably, that he antagonizes important figures in the industry with whom Goldcrest must maintain good relationships. This seems to arise from a lack of sensitivity to people and situations and, unfortunately, is a personal characteristic that is unlikely to change.

We both have a strong personal commitment to Goldcrest in particular and to the British film industry in general. We believe that Goldcrest's ability to weather the current storm, to survive and thrive is of importance not only to its shareholders but also to an independently financed British industry.

We believe we demonstrated this commitment and our loyalty to Goldcrest, not only in taking the strong stand that we did last February but also in our subsequent conduct. However, unless the urgent and necessary steps are implemented forthwith to streamline operations, to restore effective management and to restore our outside relationships, we have serious reservations about the future of the company and our position in it.

> John Chambers
> David Norris
> 22nd May 1985

This, of course, was the paper prepared at Attenborough's suggestion. It had gone through many drafts, becoming in the process, so the authors say, milder and more conciliatory in tone. In tone maybe, but not in substance, since it looked forward to the departure of Lee, Lieberson and Wooller, the closure of the television and development departments, the general reduction of overheads and the laying off of staff. Having written it, they decided to show it first to Angus Grossart because they judged him to be, in Chambers's words, 'very shrewd and very supportive; we felt he would understand'. Also, Grossart's reputation on the board was that of a hard-headed entrepreneurial banker, to whom the Jolls and Stoddarts were perhaps more likely to listen than to the no less shrewd but artistic and 'emotional' Attenborough. Attenborough anyway was already too strongly identified with the Norris–Chambers faction.

Grossart read the paper and, without making any comment himself, quizzed Norris and Chambers for half an hour or so. According to Chambers, he said that he 'understood our position but there was no way we could ditch Lee'. Grossart promised, nevertheless, to take up the matter with other non-executive directors.

The three men then made their way to the board meeting, which was to be held for the first time at the new offices in Wardour Street. Peter Mayer and David Puttnam were the only absentees.

The agenda of the meeting might have been drawn up specifically to support the case made in Norris's and Chambers's paper. The first item was a schedule of unrecouped development expenditure. Since 1980, Goldcrest had invested in 165 film and television projects. Of these, 37 (23 television productions and 14 feature films) had gone into production financed by Goldcrest, and one, *The Emerald Forest*, had been sold on. Of the remaining 127 projects, 32 were still in active development and 95 had been abandoned.

By far the most significant of the still active projects were *Mandrake* and *Horror Movie*, in which Goldcrest had invested £512,000 and £248,000 respectively. The others, 16 television projects and 14 films, ranged, in terms of money spent, from *The Blunderer* (£40,000) to *The*

Knights of the Round Table (£31). The outstanding advances paid to Enigma and the independent producers brought the total currently invested in development to £1.2 million.

As to the 95 abandoned projects, the numerical majority were in television, ranging from *Bodyline* (£37,000) and *Rock Family Trees* (£21,000) to *Hotel du Paradis* (£18). In money terms, however, the losses were more or less even, with television accounting for £505,000 and film £491,000. Earlier unrecouped advances to Enigma (£240,000) and the independent producers (£122,000) brought to £1.36 million the total that had been written off by the end of March 1985.

These figures caused considerable alarm. Grossart – who had, in effect, been briefed for this discussion at his breakfast with Norris and Chambers – wanted to know by what criteria all these investments had been made that so many had later been deemed unsuitable for production. He particularly questioned the usefulness of having had a large television department, six satellite producers and an ongoing relationship with Enigma Television if the bulk of what they had produced between them consisted of scores of abandoned projects. Lee, the minutes tell us, 'assured the board that the procedure for incurring development expenditure was strict and precise'. He stressed that there were 'limits on total development expenditure in any one year of £500,000, and on total net investment in development projects of £800,000'. The current level, he explained, was exceptional: 'if the figures for *Horror Movie*, now virtually in pre-production, and £205,000 of expenditure on the previous attempt to develop *Mandrake* in 1982–3 were excluded then total net development investment remained within these limits'. He believed that 'development write-offs would decrease, as, increasingly, expenditure was focused on projects targeted for production, or development partners such as Goldwyn were found who would bear a substantial portion of costs'.

There is no mention of it in the minutes, so it may be that none of the directors thought to point it out, but not one of the current films in, or about to go into, production – *The Mission* (developed by Ghia, Paramount and United Artists), *Revolution* (developed by Winkler and Warner Bros.), *A Room With a View* (developed by Merchant–Ivory) and *Absolute Beginners* (developed under the auspices of the National Film Development Fund) – had required development expenditure on Goldcrest's part.

The next item was Chambers's forecast of a £500,000 loss for the year. This caused quite a stir. 'Shareholders', the minutes tell us, 'would expect a clear explanation' of this 'substantial decline' and would want to know of 'the action being taken to remedy the situation'.

For the explanation, Lee referred them to his new '1985 Profit Improvement Programme'. This paper first set out a summary of the overall position:

	1983	1984	1985 budget	1985 forecast
Turnover £ million	12.4	14.0	17.6	14.3
Cost of sales	9.3	10.4	12.8	11.1
Gross profit	3.1	3.6	4.8	3.2
Overheads (operating expenses)	1.8	2.5	2.7	2.9
Operating profit	1.3	1.1	2.1	0.3
Interest	(1.3)	0.6	–	(0.6)
Profit/loss on exchange	–	0.2	–	–
Development write-offs	(0.2)	(0.3)	(0.4)	(0.2)
Pre-tax profit (loss)	(0.2)	1.6	1.7	(0.5)

The difference between the budgeted profit for 1985, £1.7 million, and the forecast loss, 0.5 million, was attributed by Lee to the following:

	Variance with budget £m
i. non-release of *Horror Movie*	(0.8)
ii. reduced profitability of *Robin of Sherwood*	(0.7)
iii. *Revolution* overcost	(0.4)
iv. interest on bank borrowing	(0.6)
v. increased overheads	(0.2)
vi. lower than expected losses on Premiere	0.1
vii. miscellaneous savings	0.3
Total variance	(2.3)

He picked out two of these points for special scrutiny. First, the £600,000 additional interest burden indicated an unbudgeted average annual borrowing requirement of £6.8 million. This, he said, was entirely the result of the increased budgets of *The Mission* and *Revolution* and the latter's overrun. Second, he noted that overheads, at £2.9 million (£200,000 over budget), now accounted for 20 per cent of turnover.

£ million	1983		1984		1985 budget		1985 forecast	
Turnover	12.4	100%	14.0	100%	17.6	100%	14.3	100%
Gross profit	3.1	25%	3.6	26%	4.8	27%	3.2	22%
Overheads	(1.8)	15%	(2.5)	18%	(2.7)	15%	(2.9)	20%
Operating profit	1.3	10%	1.1	8%	2.1	12%	0.3	2%

'Thus,' Lee concluded, 'our operating profit has got caught in a classic squeeze caused by inadequate turnover growth, declining gross margin and increasing expense ratio.'

In the discussion of this part of Lee's paper, it was pointed out that Solomon, Finger and Newman's valuation of the previous year had over-stated the worth of many projects. Write-offs on what were to have been profitable television films, and related unrecovered overhead payments to Enigma, for example, totalled £1.29 million. *The Far Pavilions*, instead of showing a surplus had required a provision of £60,000. *Dream One* had proved a disaster, and *Cal*, which had been expected to contribute over £1 million, actually showed a loss of about £120,000. Chambers had already accounted for many of these shortfalls in drawing up the 1985 budget, but even his latest projection included some revenue expectations that might have to be revised. It was agreed that a new valuation of the portfolio would be drafted in time for the company's Annual General Meeting on 12 July.

Lee concluded the explanatory section of his paper on an optimistic note. Some of the missing profits in 1985, he said, would turn up in later years, for part of Goldcrest's current problem lay in the phasing of its investments: just as in 1984 there had been a production hiatus, which had resulted in much-reduced revenues in 1985, so in 1985 there was a production boom, the benefits of which would be felt in 1986 and after. He devised the following table to demonstrate his point:

Contribution from film and television investments:

£ million	Films	Television	Combined
1983 and before	3.9	(0.7)	3.2
1984	3.9	0.2	4.1
1985	1.6	2.0	3.6
1986	5.8	0.8	6.6
1987 and after	6.3	2.0	8.3
Total	**21.5**	**4.3**	**25.8**

These figures represented not profits, but the forecast net revenues (i.e. the surplus of receipts over expenditure) before payment of over-heads, interest, tax and development write-offs, arising from all Goldcrest productions to date, including the current slate of films. The table clearly shows a dip in 1985 followed by a strong recovery in 1986 and after. If these figures were correct, then all Goldcrest had to do was get itself safely through the current year and invest wisely in the next.

Lee then demonstrated that longer-term changes to what he called 'the fundamental economic relationships that govern the business' were needed if Goldcrest was to show a consistent and healthy rate of profit in the future. He compared the present position with a set of ideal financial objectives:

	1985 Forecast	Financial objectives
Shareholders' funds	£30.0m	£30.0m
Gearing (borrowing as a percentage of shareholders' funds)	15%	50%
hence, Borrowing	£ 4.5m	£15.0m
Total capital employed	**£34.5m**	**£45.0m**
Capital turnover time	2.4 years	1.5 years
Annual turnover (total capital divided by turnover time)	£14.3m	£30.0m
Gross margin (gross profit as a percentage of turnover)	22%	33%
hence, Gross profit	**£ 3.2m**	**£10.0m**
Operating expenses (overheads)	(£ 2.9m)	(£ 2.5m)
Operating profit	**£ 0.3m**	**£ 7.5m**
Interest	(£ 0.5m)	(£ 1.5m)
Profit before tax	**(£ 0.2m)**	**£ 6.0m**
Return on shareholders' funds	negative	20%

To this table, he added the following commentary:

In a nutshell, we need to increase our gearing, improve our gross margin and reduce our overhead substantially if we are to achieve a 20 per cent return on our investment. You will see that at the moment our average borrowings to capital employed for the year are only 15 per cent. A higher rate of gearing, up to, say, 50 per cent, looks essential. Our capital turnover, that is the number of years it takes to turn investment into revenue, is just below 2½ years. The rate of recoupment needs to be increased significantly to about 1½ years. Incidentally, this is about average for the Hollywood majors. Our budgeted gross margin for the year was 27 per cent and our average for 1983 and 1984 was around 25 per cent. A gross margin of 33 per cent is needed on average. Operating expenses need to be contained at around the £2½ million level.

On this basis, and allowing for increased interest on the higher borrowings, a return of 20 per cent would be feasible.

It is by no means certain that these changes in our basic economic characteristics can be achieved. Nevertheless, over the next few weeks we will be studying a number of specific alternatives.

This, 'in a nutshell', is a good example both of Lee's theoretical and analytical strengths and of his tendency to dwell on optimistic, growth-orientated, long-term theoretical solutions to present problems, at the expense of the practical remedial measures that would take Goldcrest from its present predicament towards his ideal objectives. For his paper listed eight 'short-term profit improvement opportunities' – reworkings of the ideas discussed at the management meeting three days before – that amounted to little more than a combination of good intentions and good housekeeping:

1. The 'imaginative' marketing of *Mr Love, The Frog Prince* and *Knights and Emeralds* in the US, and a campaign to 'raise the attractiveness of these films in the international marketplace', with a view to improving on the forecast net contribution, from all three films, of only £62,000.
2. A 'massive' marketing campaign for *Revolution*, for which the latest forecast, taking into account the production's overcost, showed a net contribution of only £527,000. If the US rentals went as high as $35 million, Lee observed, 'then the 1985 contribution would be increased by an additional £1.1 million'.
3. A 'blitz' on sales of *Robin of Sherwood*, to 'raise additional gross revenues of $1 million in 1985 and net revenues of £220,000'.
4. The outright sale of a package of *First Loves* and other television films which had no further useful life in terms of short-term licensing.
5. A similar outright sale of a package of other television programmes, including *Gastank, How We Learned to Ski* and *The Wine Programme* – what Lee called the 'tail-end of thoroughly unattractive product' in the Goldcrest catalogue – from which no further licence revenue was expected.
6. The selling off of Goldcrest's equity interest in *The World: a Television History*, a project from which no revenue was expected in 1985.
7. A deal with Warner Television, whereby Warners would take over the marketing of Goldcrest's remaining television catalogue, thereby cutting Goldcrest's costs and improving its sales prospects.
8. A search for further tax deals, especially for *Revolution*.

There was little Goldcrest could do in respect of points one and two, since the marketing of these films was in the hands of distributors, chief among them Warner Bros., who had acquired them. Points three and six proved impossible and seven never happened. Points four and five, the packaging of the near-dormant television catalogue, were put into effect, but Goldcrest had to wait for more than a year for the deals to be closed. As for point eight, a tax deal was done, for *The Mission* rather than for *Revolution*, but not until April 1986.

The discussion of this part of Lee's paper introduced additional emergency measures to reduce overheads: no new staff, no salary increases, no first-class travel, reduction in the entertainment expenses of the sales team, and the sub-leasing of spare space in the new offices.

The whole package fell far short of the cost-cutting proposals contained in Norris's and Chambers's paper, just as Lee's analysis of Goldcrest's underlying problems was altogether less pessimistic than theirs. Whatever comfort the directors derived from this generally reassuring presentation would have been shortlived, for the third item on the agenda concerned the cash flow and banking position. The Midland's shock tactic was about to be put to the test.

'Mr Chambers', we are told, 'reported some difficulty in operating within the terms of Midland Bank's credit facility.'

The minutes continue:

The problem was aggravated by a substantial increase in Goldcrest's cash requirements due to the *Revolution* overage, and by the timing of Columbia's payments under the *Dream One* settlement. In addition, the increase in 1985 interest charges and reduction in profit would trigger one of the default provisions in the facility.

For some months, Mr Chambers had drawn attention to the inflexibility of the Midland facility. Successive finance reports had indicated deteriorating 1985 cash and profit positions, and the Group's peak borrowing requirement had been climbing towards the limit of Midland's facility. However, the present difficulties had only arisen since the sudden appearance of the *Revolution* overage in mid-April. Since February, discussions had been held with Credit Lyonnais, the First National Bank of Boston and, more recently, with European American Bank, with a view to securing more flexible borrowing facilities, and further meetings were being arranged. There was some confidence that Credit Lyonnais would offer to replace the Midland facility: a clear indication of this was expected within two weeks, and a formal offer before the end of June.

Meanwhile, the company was liaising with Midland's Corporate Finance Division on a daily basis, but it could not be assumed that Midland would cover the peak borrowing requirement. If additional finance were not found, Midland's certain refusal to allow Goldcrest to proceed with *Horror Movie* would compound other problems – for example, by significantly reducing 1986 profits.

The minutes, as ever, tend to put a tidy gloss on what was undoubtedly a far from tidy discussion. The last paragraph, however, conveys the essence of Chambers's report to the board: the Midland had given clear warning that it was not going to put up the funds needed to cover fully Goldcrest's existing commitments, let alone to cover new investments such as *Horror Movie*. The company had either to reduce the scale of its activities, which, since the three big films were already in production, was out of the question, make alternative banking arrangements and/or raise more money from its shareholders.

Stoddart erupted, demanding to know why it was that Chambers had given no indication either of the company's imminent cash exhaustion or of the Midland's new, tougher stance at the briefing session only two days before. That that meeting had been taken up with a discussion of Lee's profit-improvement plan, and that Chambers had not anyway spoken to the Midland until the following day, were not, it seems, excuses enough. Stoddart was joined by Grossart and Joll in the chorus of criticism that now rained down on Chambers's head. They were indignant, demanded explanations, wanted to know why they had not been kept informed.

All this was a bit hard on Chambers, given the voluminous information he had supplied to the directors each month, and given, too, that minuted discussions, many of which have been quoted here, had dealt at great length with the forecast cash shortfall, the search for third-party investors and so on. Perhaps the information supplied by Chambers was *too* detailed. Perhaps between what might be called Chambers's mania for minutiae and Lee's fondness for the grand plan there needed to be something else, a kind of medium-level tactical appraisal of Goldcrest's finances, such as might, for example, have been offered by Don Cruickshank. Joll, remember, once approvingly described Cruickshank as Lee's 'anchor' and 'brake', a function that he clearly felt was needed to balance the 'headstrong' chief executive.

'I think one of the problems with Goldcrest was that though John Chambers had experience and knowledge he didn't have the ability to stand up to James Lee when it came to crucial things,' Joll observes. 'You have to make yourself unpopular as a finance man sometimes, with your bosses and colleagues who want to do things, by saying "No, you can't do this"; by saying "Look, if we go on the way we're going we are going to run out of money." That's a finance director's first and only important duty. The one cardinal sin is for a company to run out of money. You *can't* go bust.'

At all events – and whether or not Chambers deserved the lambasting to which he was subjected – the Midland's plan had had something of its desired effect: the board had at last woken up to the crisis. The minutes tell us that

In view of the seriousness of the situation, the whole board were to be kept informed of developments, and Mr Lee and Mr Chambers would review the position with the chairman early in the following week. It was also agreed that both short-term profit problems and matters of overall strategy should be considered in greater detail.

For these purposes, a working party, comprising Stoddart, Chambers, Grossart, Joll and Lee, was to meet on 11 June to consider a 'detailed action plan for improved profitability'; the June board meeting would be convened at 8.30 a.m. to allow time for a full discussion of the matters raised by that working party; and a special strategy meeting of all the directors was to be convened on 18 July, at which Goldcrest's entire business plan would be subject to review.

The final substantive issue on the May board meeting agenda was *Revolution*. The directors were told that, although Goldcrest had appointed Garth Thomas to 'take action to prevent any further escalation in overage', his instructions were being 'widely ignored'. The previously agreed approach of 'seeking to contain' costs through 'tight Goldcrest supervision and numerous small cuts' was not working and Lieberson therefore recommended that the company 'formally exercise at once its full rights as completion guarantor to take over the production and place Garth Thomas in full and direct control, superseding the authority of the executive producer Chris Burt'. In this, he was supported by Attenborough and his recommendation, the minutes tell us, 'was endorsed by the executive directors and agreed by the whole board'.

After the meeting, Lee wrote to Winkler in the following vein:

The Board have asked me to make it absolutely clear to you and Hugh that the existing situation is intolerable.

The projected overshoot of £3.64 million, on a below-the-line budget of £8.9 million, has caused this company considerable financial difficulties . . . We have already had to delay the start of our next major production; we have withdrawn from another long-time commitment to a very attractive small film; and worse still I personally have been forced to ask one of our closest trading partners to agree to a rescheduling of one of our obligations . . .

For some time now Garth Thomas has been representing the joint completion guarantors, and in that capacity has made a number of suggestions both for specific areas of cost reduction, and for tighter controls over the use of resources, particularly cast and crowd (which together with the costs of travel and accommodation have accounted for almost £1.5 million of the overshoot). Garth's recommendations and instructions have been largely ignored.

In the circumstances, our completion guarantee partners have given us no option but to formalize Garth's position . . . The mission he has been given is to complete the remainder of the film as written, on schedule and on budget. He has *not* been required either to reduce the content of the script (although he will have serious concerns about scale), nor to attempt to 'claw back' what has already been lost.

. . . We do not take these steps with anything other than reluctance. Thank goodness we have never had to experience anything like this before, and I trust we shall never have to again.

(The 'next major production' was *Horror Movie*; the 'attractive small film' was *Tembisa/Dream Song*; and the 'close trading partner' was Warner Bros.)

Enclosed with this letter was the formal notification that Garth Thomas had been appointed to the picture full time, 'not only to represent us as primary financier, but also to represent and exercise all the powers and authority customarily vested in completion guarantors . . . In future, therefore, all heads of department, and any personnel working under them with authority to incur expenditure, will require the approval of Garth Thomas. Neither we, nor Entertainment Completions Inc., will be responsible for unauthorized expenditures.'

The first thing to be said about this action is, of course, that it was too late. The second is that, with Thomas now on *Revolution* full time, he would not be available to supervise *Absolute Beginners*.

In Rotterdam, meanwhile, Credit Lyonnais' Frans Afman was studying the Goldcrest figures and 'rubbing my eyes with disbelief . . . I looked at the books once, and I thought there was something wrong, either with the figures or with me,' he recalls. 'I thought maybe I had misunderstood something. So I left them for a day and then looked at them again. But they were still hopelessly out of line. It was obvious that the company was in deep trouble.'

Afman, perhaps the most experienced film banker in Europe, offers no opinion on what Goldcrest's best course of action would have been at the time. As far as his bank was concerned, its position as the potential source of a $20 million line of credit did not so much depend on Goldcrest's profitability as on the security it could offer against borrowings. The fact that Goldcrest numbered Pearson, Electra and other leading investment institutions among its shareholders was therefore of at least as much significance as its trading record. In other words, Credit Lyonnais was happy to continue negotiations with Chambers and Lee, but now did so in a sceptical rather than an optimistic frame of mind.

Chapter Forty-eight

At the Mercy of the Banks

Ilott: The day after the May board meeting, Andy Parsons drew up a schedule that showed that the company's borrowing requirement would increase from its current level of £3.7 million to £11 million by the end of June. Goldcrest had in hand £3.8 million worth of signed contracts, which, under the terms of the Midland facility, provided security for only £2.9 million of credit. The value of contracts still in negotiation, £9.2 million, would eventually provide security for a further £6.9 million of credit. However, the combined value of signed and unsigned contracts, £13 million, was not enough to cover the maximum requirement of £11 million, a figure which was anyway beyond the Midland's £10 million credit limit. Parsons's cheque-juggling routine could stem some of this outflow of cash, but not all of it, and certainly not for as long as was required to put in place alternative credit arrangements with Credit Lyonnais.

Lee had no choice, therefore, but to go on his hands and knees to Ted Harris at the Midland. He explained that the Goldcrest board was now fully aware of the problems, had formed a working party to investigate and make recommendations, and had scheduled a special meeting to review all aspects of the company's business strategy. Furthermore, Credit Lyonnais had indicated that it would soon make a proposal for a long-term credit facility.

Harris, doubtless gratified that his ultimatum had yielded such immediate results, and more than anything anxious that no obstacle should be put in the way of Credit Lyonnais' plan to take over Goldcrest's banking responsibilities, agreed not only to lend money against contracts that were not yet signed, but to allow Goldcrest, for a limited period, to borrow against 100 per cent of the value of such contracts rather than the 75 per cent previously agreed. It was thought that this new deal would see Goldcrest through to mid-June. But it did not answer the problem of what to do about the borrowing requirement above the £10 million limit.

On returning from his meeting with Harris, Lee was shocked to find that, as he noted at the time, 'very few of the unsigned sales are backed by any written evidence'. Confirmation of their existence relied on Guy East's say-so. Lee immediately called Harris, who, doubtless with severe misgivings, agreed that 'telexed confirmation would suffice, provided that the telex was followed immediately by a signed deal memorandum'. This information was included in a memo from Lee in which he asked Chambers to 'organize a major effort . . . to get all of the unsigned contracts turned into telex confirmation' as soon as possible. In the meantime, Lee added, 'the bank have agreed to honour all payments for this week'.

Lee also found time to write to the directors, expressing his fear that, 'because of lack of time, we gave inadequate consideration to the cash-flow situation at yesterday's meeting, and inadvertently created an impression of lack of control and crisis'. He reassured them that 'we are on top of the situation day by day and hour by hour. We have an excellent data base and cash-flow forecasting system, and the bank are privy to all of our financial information.' But, he added, 'there is a problem: we are projecting a peak borrowing requirement that is in excess of the limit of our facility'. Money was going to have to come from somewhere to fill the gap.

The next day, 25 May, Sandy Lieberson flew to Colombia to take over production chores on *The Mission*. He was to be away, and effectively out of touch, for four weeks.

On Monday, 27 May, the management meeting was informed that Terry Semel, while 'impressed' by the *Revolution* rushes, had expressed concern 'that the romantic scenes now being shot should match the quality of the battle scenes'. Four insurance claims had already been lodged on behalf of the production and a payment on account was expected from the insurers later in the week.

John Chambers, who had that morning returned from New York, where he had had discussions with European American Bank and Howard Schuster, reported that the Schuster investment in *Revolution* was 'not now expected until January 1986'. As the film was due to open before Christmas, Schuster would be able not only to view the completed film but to assess its first box-office returns before making his final commitment.

The management meeting heard, too, that the budget of *Absolute Beginners* was under severe pressure. The minutes record that, 'in view of concern to avoid the risk of a substantial overrun, Goldcrest had reiterated its determination that completion-guarantee rights would be exercised immediately if the estimated final cost rose above £6.3 million'.

After the meeting, Chambers, with the assistance of Guy East's sales staff, set to work contacting all the distributors with whom Goldcrest had outstanding agreements. Over the next few days, the telex machine was busy with return messages confirming details of films bought, advances agreed, licence periods and back-end terms.

In the evening, Norris and Chambers dined with Stoddart and Joll, who had earlier met with Grossart and who had now read Norris's and Chambers's paper, 'The Reorganized Goldcrest – A Year On'. Joll demanded to know if the real message of the document was that Norris and Chambers were once more threatening to quit; to which the answer was, according to Chambers, 'not if you do something about the crisis facing the company'. They then discussed television, development costs, Sandy Lieberson, the films in production, overheads and, most crucially, the role of James Lee. Chambers and Norris did not pull their punches, and even though Stoddart and Joll were not to be drawn into offering opinions of their own, it was clear that Lee's future was now to be the main item on the agenda of unofficial meetings such as this. Just as importantly, Norris and Chambers gave a full account of their discussions with Eberts. His name, too, was henceforth to be on everyone's lips.

On 29 May, Lee and Chambers flew to Rotterdam for talks with Michel Canny and Frans Afman of Credit Lyonnais. They agreed, subject to further scrutiny of the Goldcrest books and the approval of the bank's credit committee, that Credit Lyonnais would provide a two-and-a-half-year, $20 million line of credit, 50–70 per cent of which would be secured against contracts (at the rate of £1.33 of contract cover for ever £1 borrowed) and 50–30 per cent of which would be set against the net worth of the company, on the assets of which Credit Lyonnais would have first call. Credit Lyonnais would charge a 1.5 per cent arrangement fee ($300,000) and interest at 2 per cent over the bank base rate. The bank also agreed to make a $5 million short-term loan to *Revolution*.

When he got back to London, Lee wrote to Canny:

Dear Michel,

It was a pleasure to meet you. Thank you for the delightful hospitality, and particularly the very pleasant lunch in the sun. I was delighted to learn that you are enthusiastic about expanding your bank's activities in the entertainment sector, and it was nice to hear you say that Goldcrest was one of your prime target companies.

As you know, we need a new facility of at least $20 million to replace the existing Midland Bank facility of £10 million. Frans has confirmed that in principle this will be perfectly feasible, although, of course, it is still subject to completing his analysis and documentation and to the approval of the credit committee.

I fully understand that you would prefer the majority of this facility to be used in the form of project finance, with the remainder being applied to general balance sheet financing. I think we will need to separate the short and longer-term. In the short-term we will need a general facility, but over time I can see us using the facility more and more for specific project financing on individual films.

I am very impressed by Frans Afman, and believe that he and the rest of your team will be able to provide us with a very valuable corporate finance service for project financing. I would envisage a close relationship between us and the bank. We would consult Frans before deciding how to finance each film and consider his recommendations for the structure of each deal and the role that Credit Lyonnais Nederland might play.

So much for the future. In the meantime, I am delighted that you have agreed to lend $5 million to be recovered in first position out of our share of receipts from the film *Revolution*. This will help us with our immediate cash flow requirements and, very importantly, it will give the Midland Bank evidence that Credit Lyonnais Bank Nederland intend to take over the relationship.

We have agreed that Frans will complete the file by the end of next week and that, all being well, the new facility could be in place by the end of June.

Let me know as soon as possible when you will be visiting us and I will be delighted to take you to the location to meet Hugh Hudson the director and Al Pacino.

Kind regards,
   James G. Lee

Lee circulated copies of this letter to all board members. He further informed the company's executive directors that he had 'proposed to Cinema Group that they lend us $5 million as an interim measure, recoverable with interest in first position, and secured against [*The Mission*'s] foreign pre-sales'. Lee calculated that these two short-term loans, from Credit Lyonnais and Cinema Group, would bring Goldcrest's bank borrowing requirement down from £11.04 million to £4.34 million, a sum for which the company had enough sales contracts to provide cover. Goldcrest could thus weather the storm until such time as the new Credit Lyonnais facility was in place.

On 3 June, the latest *Absolute Beginners* forecast showed a final cost of £6.49 million. This figure, £190,000 over the most recently agreed budget, was not acceptable to Goldcrest. The script, timed at two hours and twenty minutes, was anyway still too long, and cuts, involving the elimination of whole scenes and the foreshortening of others, would have to be made to bring costs down to within the original limits.

The next day, Garth Thomas reported that the *Revolution* production team was now co-operating with his instructions and that 'controls on crowd, camera units and others' were being implemented. The production had fallen a further day behind, however, and 'script discussions between Pacino and Hudson continue to put pressure on the shooting schedule'. Thomas was now predicting a final overcost of £4.3 million, of which up to £1.5 million was covered by insurance claims. The insurers had now agreed to make an interim payment of £750,000. (This was the same sum, coincidentally, as the total of overdue unpaid bills that had just been unearthed in a search of the *Revolution* accounts. Further bills, mostly for hotel accommodation, could not be checked or approved as the relevant details had not been recorded.)

Warner Bros., meanwhile, had informed Goldcrest that the title *Revolution*, 'conjures up images of violence, war, death, Russia, etc.', and they wanted it changed.

Howard Schuster, alarmed by the *Revolution* overcosts, proposed new terms that would in effect guarantee him a profit on his proposed $3.5 million investment. There was no way that Goldcrest could agree to this, and Lee suggested that Cinema Group should now be approached with a view to replacing Schuster if need be.

Two days later, on 10 June, Norris flew to Oslo for talks with Viking. His aim was to secure a substantial investment in *Horror Movie* and to discuss a proposed investment pact, whereby Viking would become Goldcrest's long-term partner.

The following day, the working party – Stoddart, Chambers, Grossart, Joll and Lee – met to discuss the company's problems. Their only conclusion, however, was that everything depended on Credit Lyonnais.

Over the next few days, Lee visited the shareholders individually to reassure them that the company's affairs were not in as bad a state as might be inferred from the 1984 annual report, which had just been issued. He returned from this tour with, he said, a clear mandate (a) not to jeopardize the long-term prospects of the company for the sake of improving short-term profitability, and (b) to make the public flotation of the company in late 1987 his principal objective.

On 12 June, John Chambers sent details of the budget, sales contracts, completion-guarantee arrangements and profitability forecasts for *Revolution* to Frans Afman. In his covering letter, Chambers drew attention to inclusion in all these calculations of the $3.5 million investment from Howard Schuster, adding, presumably in the light of Schuster's latest and unwelcome proposals, that although 'the deal has now been agreed . . . as we all know we do not count the money until we actually receive it'. His revised profitability forecast for the film, taking into account the overcosts, showed a 'best-likely' contribution of £5.2 million, a 'worst-likely' loss of £4.5 million and a 'probable' contribution of only £450,000. This latter figure assumed that there would be no further overages, that the Schuster money came through, and that the film took US theatrical rentals of $25 million and gross receipts from the foreign markets of $8 million. In other words, *Revolution*, which everyone had *hoped* would be a very successful film, now *had* to be a very successful film if it was to break even.

On 17 June, Guy East, in his report-back from the Tokyo Film Festival, said that, 'despite considerable Japanese interest in *Revolution*, distributors there would not offer the asking price of $1.5 million until a substantial part of the film was available for viewing and was judged to have break-out potential'.

On the same day, the final-cost estimate for *Absolute Beginners* was put at £6.7 million. According to Garth Thomas, 'employment of the construction and wardrobe teams has been terminated, many scenes deleted and one set substantially reduced' in an effort to bring the final cost back down to £6.3 million. The real problem, however, was that a whole week needed to be taken out of the schedule if costs were to be brought into line.

On his return from Oslo, David Norris reported that Viking was preparing a prospectus to raise a substantial fund – as much as $25 million – for film production. Subject to terms, Viking would use this money to put up 50 per cent or more of the cost (net of US advances) of every Goldcrest film that had a budget of more than £5 million.

At their briefing session prior to the 20 June board meeting, Lee and Stoddart discussed an extraordinary proposal: that Goldcrest acquire a controlling interest in the US independent production and distribution company Orion. The idea came from America and had the backing of Warburg Pincus and Co., which controlled a substantial proportion of Orion share warrants. Orion had enormous prestige on account of the reputation, individually and collectively, of its principal officers, who had once formed the acclaimed management team at United Artists. However, their luck seemed to have run out at their new company, which, after its first release, the highly successful *First Blood*, in 1980, had had a string of flops, among them *The Bounty, Hotel New Hampshire, Harry & Son, Gorky Park, The Corsican Brothers* and *The Cotton Club*. In the first quarter of 1984, the company recorded net income of just $522,000 on a turnover of $51 million. Its balance sheet had been heavily reinforced by several public offerings – $36 million of equity in 1983 and $50 million of warrants and subordinated loan stock in 1984 – and by the outright sale of $20 million worth of films in its library to Time–Life. Orion's position had improved in 1985, with the release of *Desperately Seeking Susan, Code of Silence* and *Amadeus,* but its stock price continued to languish. For six months it had been no secret that the management was looking for a buyer.

Lee was all in favour of an Orion–Goldcrest combination. Goldcrest, he was to tell the management team, would 'benefit from Orion's strength in the American market during what, in the short term at least, is likely to be a difficult period for independent companies'; Orion's foreign-sales operations would 'further strengthen Goldcrest's position in the international market'; its financial resources 'will solve Goldcrest's capital problem'; and it had a television production and syndication arm that could 'help solve Goldcrest's difficulties in this area'.

Not the least of the attractions to Lee was that a Goldcrest–Orion merger would result in a 'genuine multinational but integrated film company controlled from the UK' – i.e. it would realize the dream that he and Puttnam had first had back in 1981. (Whether Orion saw the proposed merger in terms of a company 'controlled from the UK' is a moot point.)

Stoddart was sufficiently impressed to believe that the opportunity was 'worth pursuing further'. At this stage it was not clear how much a controlling interest in Orion, which had an annual turnover of about $180 million, would cost, nor where the money would come from.

At close of business on 19 June, Goldcrest's borrowing balance at the Midland was £8.5 million. The bank was monitoring the position daily to ensure that Goldcrest did not exceed its £10 million limit.

The June board meeting (the first that Puttnam had attended since March) was informed that a formal proposal from Credit Lyonnais was expected by 30 June. Credit Lyonnais was likely to provide the $5 million short-term loan for *Revolution* and a $15–20 million credit facility, divided between project finance ($5–10 million), general overdraft ($5 million), and an emergency reserve ($5 million). Without such a facility, the board was told, Goldcrest would be unable to go ahead with *Horror Movie,* or to enter into any other new investments, until revenues from the current pictures had replenished the company's coffers. Talks were also continuing with European American Bank, Guinness Mahon and First National Bank of Boston, but their interests were mainly in project finance and at this stage they were not considered viable alternatives to the proposed Credit Lyonnais facility.

As if to emphasize the urgency of the banking situation, John Chambers tabled a revised cash-flow projection which showed a borrowing requirement at the end of June – i.e. within ten days – of £12.2 million. This was £2.2 million more than the Midland Bank limit. Chambers expressed the view that the Midland, now desperate to get Goldcrest off its hands and willing to go to considerable lengths to facilitate the Credit Lyonnais takeover, would almost certainly allow Goldcrest the additional funds, but only if Credit Lyonnais' proposal had by then been received and accepted. The alternative was to press for the immediate advance of the proposed short-term loans from Credit Lyonnais and Cinema Group. Unfortunately, the terms now demanded by Credit Lyonnais and Cinema Group were such that they would in effect reduce Goldcrest's collateral for general borrowing by about $7 million, making Goldcrest dependent on the continued relaxation of the Midland's security requirements.

Joll, not surprisingly, was thoroughly alarmed by all this. He asked Chambers to call Afman at once to find out when the commitment letter in respect of Credit Lyonnais' short-term loan would be issued. He further proposed that should the likely date of that letter fall after the date on which the Midland borrowings were expected to exceed £10 million, then the Midland should be contacted immediately and asked for an extension to the facility. Should that be refused, then the shareholders present should make funds available in place of, or on the same terms as, the $5 million Cinema Group loan. This was agreed. Chambers left the meeting, but soon returned, having failed to get hold of either Afman or Michel Canny at Credit Lyonnais. It was decided that Joll, Lee and Chambers would discuss the matter further after the meeting.

The longer-term aspect of the cash-flow problem did not command much attention at the June board meeting, but in fact Chambers's new forecast painted a very clear, and alarming, picture of what was happening to the company. The forecast assumed that there would be no further overages on *Revolution*, that there would be no new productions other than *Horror Movie* and that the company would receive $5 million from Cinema Group in July, $3.5 million from Howard Schuster in January 1986 and a share of the $5.75 million thrown up by the Westpac leasing deal sometime thereafter. In summary, the resulting forecast was as in the table opposite.

The left-hand column, receipts, was an estimate of all the sales advances, distribution revenues, ancillary sales, VAT refunds, third-party investments and so on, coming into the company over the period. The timing of receipts was virtually impossible to predict accurately. The next column, payments, covered all the production costs, overheads, distribution expenses, interest charges and so on, going out of the company. The difference between the two was the net flow of cash, either in or out. The right-hand columns indicate the forecast level of Goldcrest's

£000	Receipts	Payments	Net inflow (outflow)	Opening balance	Closing balance
Jan./Mar. '85	3247	9707	(6460)	9350	2890
April	5272	8024	(2753)	2890	137
May	4042	6723	(2680)	137	(2543)
June	2840	12512	(9673)	(2543)	(12215)
Jan./Jun. '85	15401	36966	(21565)	9350	(12215)
July	7464	4926	2537	(12215)	(9678)
August	2428	4658	(2230)	(9678)	(11908)
September	3135	2180	955	(11908)	(10953)
October	2159	1831	328	(10953)	(10625)
November	2813	3942	(1130)	(10625)	(11755)
December	6134	3376	2758	(11755)	(8997)
total 1985	39533	57880	(18347)	9350	(8997)
January '86	4075	1752	2323	(8997)	(6674)
February	4944	1729	3215	(6674)	(3459)
March	2457	1371	1087	(3459)	(2372)
April	1488	1353	135	(2372)	(2238)
May	4042	1585	2457	(2238)	220
June	2467	1213	1254	220	1473
Jan./Jun. '86	19473	9003	10470	(8997)	1473

cash/borrowing balances. At the start of the period shown, Goldcrest had £9.35 million in the bank. By the end of June, borrowings would hit a peak of £12.215 million and it would not be until May 1986 that the company would again have a cash surplus.

We can best understand this forecast by breaking it down as in the graphs on pages 514–515.

These projections were, of course, full of uncertainties. On the revenue side, the Cinema Group and Schuster deals were not yet in place and there was no reliable basis, at this stage, for making a forecast as to the performance in the marketplace of *Revolution* or *Absolute Beginners*. On the payments side, there was no telling what the final cost would be of the films currently in production, since only *A Room With a View* seems to have been running on schedule. As for *Horror Movie*, it had been included on the assumption that it had an $8 million budget, 25 per cent of which was to be covered by a third-party investor. But neither the budget nor the investor was fixed.

Even leaving these uncertainties to one side, Goldcrest was left with an alarming borrowing profile (see graph on page 516).

While the company was certain to exceed the Midland credit limit, it was by no means certain to secure the Credit Lyonnais facility. And that,

RECEIPTS – sales revenue and third-party investments

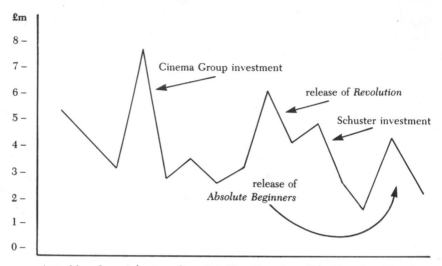

in essence, was the short-term cash-flow problem. Or it would have been, if the assumptions on which this table was based had been reliable, which they were not. Were Goldcrest to have taken out the contingent elements on the revenue side – Cinema Group's $5 million, Schuster's $3.5 million and Goldcrest's share of the $5.75 million expected to come from the Westpac leasing deal – they would have had to have added, according to Lee's own back-of-the-envelope calculations, about £4.2 million to the £9 million borrowings requirement at the end of 1985. Furthermore, the period of high-level borrowings would have had to be extended well into 1986, so that in June, at the end of the period shown, Goldcrest would still have had borrowings of about £6.4 million. It is true that these figures would have been manageable within the proposed Credit Lyonnais facility, but only at the expense of future investment capacity. And this, the longer-term aspect of the problem, was what was worrying Lee.

Put simply, Goldcrest's business plan, which envisaged a doubling of turnover, from £14 million to £30 million, through 1986 and 1987, depended on the outcome of the present negotiations with third-party investors and Credit Lyonnais. If the Cinema Group, Schuster and Westpac deals all came to fruition, and if the Credit Lyonnais facility

PAYMENTS – production costs, distribution expenses, overheads, etc.

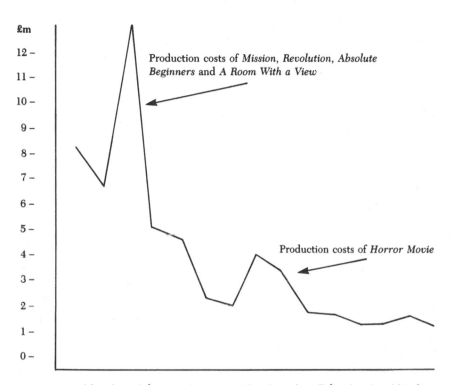

£m

Production costs of *Mission, Revolution, Absolute Beginners* and *A Room With a View*

Production costs of *Horror Movie*

Apr. May Jun. Jul. Aug. Sep. Oct. Nov. Dec. Jan. Feb. Mar. Apr. May Jun.

were to be agreed, then Goldcrest would have sufficient money available for the planned level of investment in 1986. If the third-party investors did not come through, then the shortfall in revenue would so increase the borrowing requirement as to use up the best part of Credit Lyonnais' $20 million, leaving little for new investment. If neither the third-party investors nor Credit Lyonnais came through, then Goldcrest would have no money for new investment at all.

Lee was already working on a study of investment capacity along these lines. For the present, he noted Goldcrest's extreme vulnerability. The very jaggedness of the revenue and expenditure graphs shown here

BORROWING REQUIREMENT

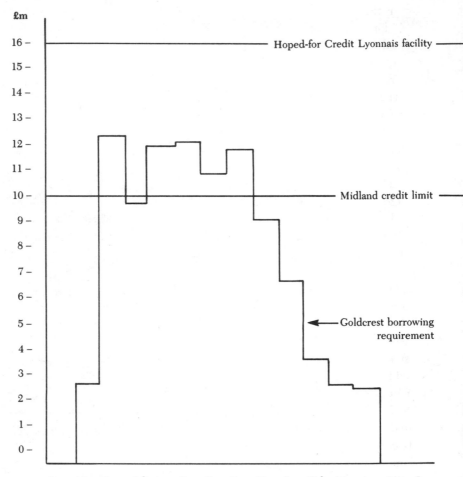

demonstrates the difficulty of trying to impose order and planning on a hit-based industry that has high unit costs.

The last item on the agenda of the June board meeting was the Orion merger proposal. Norris and Chambers were strongly opposed: a plan for a multinational, multi-media entertainment company was the last thing that they wanted to discuss in the midst of the present crisis. Stoddart spoke in its favour, 'in view of the doubts as to the viability of Goldcrest as at present capitalized'. He suggested, however, that 'for the time being, the efforts of Goldcrest's management should be concentrated on resolving its short-term cash difficulties'. The matter was left at that.

After the meeting, Lee telexed Michel Canny at Credit Lyonnais, asking for confirmation that project financing for *Revolution* and the proposal for the general facility would be received by the end of the month.

There was no reply.

At the close of the day's business on 21 June, Goldcrest had drawn down £8.7 million of its credit facility. The company had £12.9 million worth of telexed sales contracts to hand, which, on the basis of the 100 per cent rule, would have provided enough cover for its peak borrowing requirement were it not for the Midland's £10 million limit.

On 24 June, Lee spoke to Afman, who promised to advise 'by Wednesday' (26 June) whether the $5 million loan for *Revolution* would be offered. If so, the funds would be available 'very shortly thereafter'. If Credit Lyonnais refused the *Revolution* loan then it had to be assumed that the general credit facility would also be refused.

Revolution had now fallen fourteen days behind schedule. The projected overage, including that part covered by insurance claims, was £4.8 million – i.e. actual costs were running at 153 per cent of the below-the-line budget.

In Colombia, Puttnam requested that the shooting schedule for *The Mission* be extended. This was agreed. A further $250,000 had to be added to its estimated final cost, which was currently running at £750,000 over budget.

On 25 June, Lee circulated two memos. The first presented his now more detailed analysis of the 20 June cash-flow forecast, looking especially at its consequences for future investment. He demonstrated that 'with a £15 million borrowing facility and success with Schuster and Ozfilm [Westpac], we could make new commitments of around £15 million by the middle of 1986. With the Norwegian financing [Viking's proposed $25 million fund] in place this would be closer to £30 million. If either Schuster or Ozfilm fall out, or if we fail to get our borrowing limit raised, our investment capacity is around £6 to £8 million. If both Schuster/Ozfilm investments fail, and we do not get a higher bank borrowing limit, then we have no financial capacity.' From this he concluded that Goldcrest 'cannot go ahead with *Horror Movie*, or any other new investment, until the new Credit Lyonnais facility is in place or both the Schuster and Westpac deals are confirmed'.

The second memo concerned what Lee called 'the equity gap'. Taking the same cash-flow forecast, but removing *Horror Movie* from the expenditure side and Cinema Group from the income side, he arrived at the following schedule:

£ million	June	July	Aug.	Sept.	Oct.	Nov.	Dec.
Borrowing requirement	(12.2)	(13.5)	(15.7)	(15.0)	(14.3)	(15.2)	(12.4)
Pre-sale contracts	12.5	12.4	10.8	10.1	9.8	9.8	8.3
Equity gap	–	1.1	4.9	4.9	4.5	5.4	4.1

We had originally planned to fill this equity gap through the Schuster investment in *Revolution* and the Cinema Group equity investment in *The Mission*. These two deals together would have provided $9.5 million, or £7.3 million. Thus, they would close the equity gap. In the event, the Schuster investment has been reduced (from $5 to $3.5 million) and delayed until January 1986, and the Cinema Group investment will remain in the form of a loan (i.e. using up our coverage) until David Norris has settled the Australian tax deal. Our principal plan for closing the gap in the short-term is an overdraft facility from Credit Lyonnais. As a short-term measure we hope to borrow from Credit Lyonnais against the Schuster equity investment to be received next year. In addition, David Norris is to pursue the Australian tax deal with the utmost urgency with a view to securing either Cinema Group or Viking as equity investors in *The Mission*. These events are mainly stopgap measures however. It is becoming apparent that we are under-capitalized for our planned level of operation. Either a new equity issue or some more permanent form of long-term debt is needed.

Four points. First, this was surely a belated realization of what had been apparent for most of the year. Second, from the beginning, the capitalization of the company had been known and fixed; its level of operations had not. So, rather than use the solution-begging formulation 'we are under-capitalized for our planned level of operation', Lee would have been more accurate had he said 'our planned level of operation is too ambitious for our capitalization'. This is an important distinction, for the form of words used by Lee admitted of no blame, whereas, and this is the third point, Lee, as he must by now have realized, was clearly guilty of mismanagement. He had run the company into a corner. (There are those on the board, not just Norris and Chambers, who were themselves coming to this conclusion.) Fourth, Frans Afman had studied these same figures and his already gloomy assessment of the company's prospects had been reinforced. What prevented him from withdrawing from negotiations altogether was the possibility that *The Mission, Revolution* or *Absolute Beginners* might be hugely successful – Goldcrest had an enviable track record, after all.

On 26 June, Afman failed to turn up as arranged at the Goldcrest offices. Instead he called Lee and proposed a trial scheme, in the course of which Credit Lyonnais would have the opportunity to 'become more familiar with the company and its management'. His plan was that a credit facility of up to £16 million, £10 million of which would be secured against contracts and £6 million of which would be in the form of an overdraft facility, would be made available, shared equally, as regards the amount, risk and security, between Credit Lyonnais and the Midland Bank. At the end of, say, twelve months, Credit Lyonnais would have the option to take over the entire facility itself and Midland would have the option to withdraw. In either case, six months' notice would have to be given. In the meantime, subject to confirmation by its credit committee, Credit Lyonnais would advance a $4 million loan (for some reason reduced from $5 million) to *Revolution*, secured in first position against Goldcrest's share of all receipts.

This was a major revision of the terms that had been previously agreed and it indicated the very considerable doubts that Credit Lyonnais now had about lending money to Goldcrest. Lee took the matter back to his management committee for discussion. They agreed that, while the proposal was not what they had been expecting, they had no alternative but to pursue it. Its acceptance, however, depended on the agreement of the Midland, not only in respect of the joint facility but also in respect of the security that had to be released to cover Credit Lyonnais' $4 million short-term loan.

The next day, Lee wrote to Ted Harris at the Midland, outlining Credit Lyonnais' plan. His letter concluded:

I believe that this is an attractive and reasonable proposal. I realize that it is not what you had been led to expect. Nevertheless, I hope that the Midland will decide to go along with this interim measure. From your point of view, you would reduce your overall exposure from £10 million to £8 million. From our point of view, an arrangement of this size and mix would see us through the next three-month peak borrowing requirement . . .

Later that morning, Lee and Chambers visited Harris to discuss the matter further. Harris agreed to give them an answer within twenty-four hours. He proposed that, in any event, Goldcrest, Credit Lyonnais, the Midland and the Midland's merchant-banking division, Samuel Montagu, should get together on 4 July for an exploratory discussion.

After lunch, Lee received the following telex:

In order to enable our bank to make a tentative commitment on the proposed facility of $4 million [for *Revolution*], you are kindly requested to supply us with the following documents:
  1. The various Warner agreements
  2. The completion guarantee
  3. Cost to date, cost to finish and the shooting schedule
  4. Insurance policies, including the claims

5. The Viking agreements, including recoupment.

. . . I will try to obtain board approval tomorrow. As you will undoubtly appreciate, the bank's commitment will be subject to legal documentation.

Best regards,

Frans Afman

Lee noted his own disappointment 'that things are moving so desperately slowly'. He had only two days left in which to secure the funds to meet Goldcrest's cash requirement.

The next day Ted Harris called Lee to say that the Midland was not interested in sharing banking chores with Credit Lyonnais. The Midland, he said, had all along expected to be replaced completely as far as Goldcrest's credit facilities were concerned, and it had relaxed its lending rules on the understanding that such an arrangement was in the offing. Since that was now not the case, the Midland would not allow any further draw-down of the credit facility, and it expected Goldcrest to take immediate steps to reduce its borrowings to a level commensurate with the original rules, in particular that there be £1 in sales contracts to cover every 75 pence borrowed. As for the $4 million loan, there was no possibility of the Midland's releasing its own security to cover Credit Lyonnais.

Goldcrest had come to a stop. It could not meet its immediate borrowing requirement of £12.2 million. It could not cover its coming week's expenses. It could not issue cheques.

16 The Gang of Four. (*left to right*) David Puttnam, Richard Attenborough, Jake Eberts and James Lee.

17 (*top*) Sandy Lieberson, the new head of production, flanked by David
Puttnam and Richard Attenborough.

18 Finance director John Chambers with his wife Pat and director of business
affairs David Norris with his wife Rosemary at the première of *Another Country*
– in the midst of the management crisis that paralysed the company in March
1984.

19 Producer Irwin Winkler with director Hugh Hudson on the set of
Revolution.

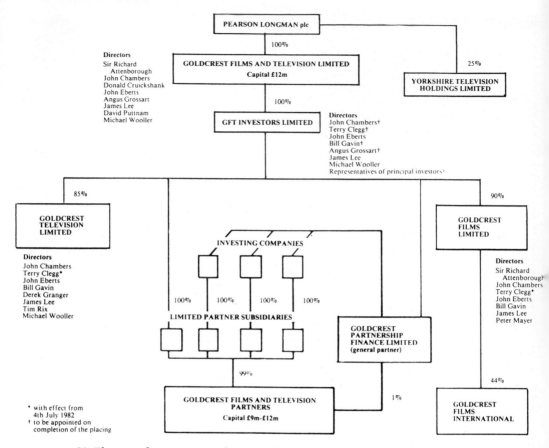

PEARSON LONGMAN plc

100%

Directors
Sir Richard
  Attenborough
John Chambers
Donald Cruickshank
John Eberts
Angus Grossart
James Lee
David Puttnam
Michael Wooller

GOLDCREST FILMS AND TELEVISION LIMITED
Capital £12m

25%

YORKSHIRE TELEVISION HOLDINGS LIMITED

100%

GFT INVESTORS LIMITED

Directors
John Chambers†
Terry Clegg†
John Eberts
Bill Gavin†
Angus Grossart†
James Lee
Michael Wooller
Representatives of principal investors†

85%

GOLDCREST TELEVISION LIMITED

Directors
John Chambers
Terry Clegg*
John Eberts
Bill Gavin
Derek Granger
James Lee
Tim Rix
Michael Wooller

90%

GOLDCREST FILMS LIMITED

Directors
Sir Richard
  Attenborough
John Chambers
Terry Clegg*
John Eberts
Bill Gavin
James Lee
Peter Mayer

INVESTING COMPANIES

100% 100% 100% 100%

LIMITED PARTNER SUBSIDIARIES

GOLDCREST PARTNERSHIP FINANCE LIMITED
(general partner)

99%

* with effect from
  4th July 1982
† to be appointed on
  completion of the placing

GOLDCREST FILMS AND TELEVISION PARTNERS
Capital £9m-£12m

1%

44%

GOLDCREST FILMS INTERNATIONAL

20 The complex structure of partnerships, cross-holdings and subsidiaries that made the administration of Goldcrest a nightmare prior to formation of Goldcrest Holdings in 1984.

21 (*left*) Embassy Pictures' boss, Jerry Perenchio.

22 (*right*) Michael Stoddart.

23 (*top*) In December 1983, Alan
Parker didn't believe in a Goldcrest
without Eberts.

24 Barry Fantoni's view – a cartoon
that appeared in *The Times*.

25 (*Opposite*), Alan Parker's view of
Eberts's return to Goldcrest in 1985.

The Alan Parker Film Company, London, England

Aug '85

BIG JAKE RETURNS TO CLEAN UP TOWN.

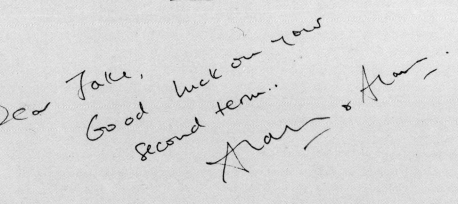

Dear Jake,
Good luck on your
second term..
Alan & Alan.

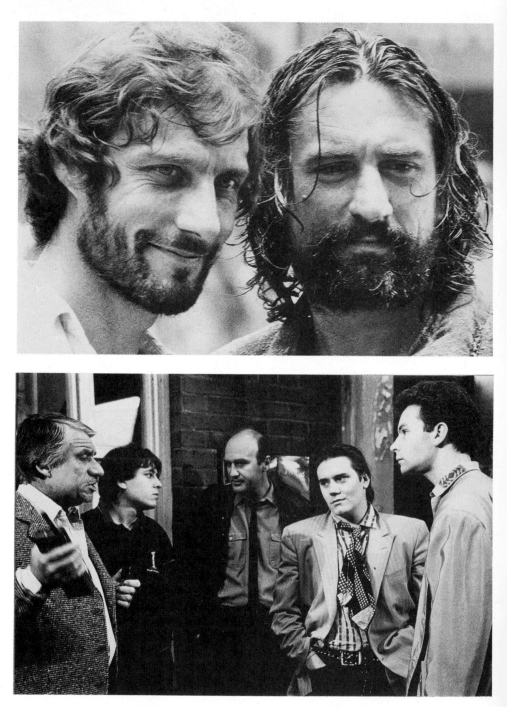

26 Roland Joffe and Robert De Niro on the set of *The Mission*.

27 (L to R) First assistant Ray Corbett and the production manager Peter Kohn discuss production problems with producers Chris Brown and Stephen Woolley and director Julien Temple at the Shepperton Studios set of *Absolute Beginners*.

Chapter Forty-nine
'How Did We Get into this Mess?'

Ilott: Lee, Chambers and Norris went straight to the Pearson offices in Millbank Tower. Having informed Pearson of the Midland Bank's decision to reject the Credit Lyonnais proposal, Lee had to explain, first, that Goldcrest's cash requirement in the coming week was forecast to be more than £1 million – there was no money to cover this; second, that that part of the company's short-term borrowing requirement that could not be met within the original terms of the Midland facility was forecast to be about £6 million – there was now no source of credit on this scale in sight; and, third, that, in the long term, Goldcrest's investment capacity depended on the successful conclusion of the Westpac, Schuster and Viking deals, and the performance of *Revolution* in the marketplace – factors over which the company had little or no control. Goldcrest had to be refinanced.

Pearson – in the persons of Joll, Blakenham and managing director John Hale – agreed to make an immediate £1 million loan, on condition that Goldcrest's accounts, and in particular its cash-flow forecasts, be henceforth subject to the scrutiny of an independent auditor.

Pearson also agreed to hold talks with Electra and Noble Grossart, with a view to providing a three-month loan that would give Goldcrest breathing space in which to reconstruct its balance sheet by whatever means – selling off assets, accelerating the licensing of rights in the ancillary markets, merger with Orion – that Lee could devise.

It appears that the Pearson directors were far from unanimous in deciding to support Goldcrest in this way. Pearson, after all, had long been looking for a way out of Goldcrest altogether. Even Joll and Blakenham, Goldcrest's staunchest supporters on the Pearson board, were apprehensive about the level of risk to which they had been exposed. Their nervousness was increased when, later that same day, Lieberson formally gave notice of his intention to step down as head of production. This announcement, which had been left until the last possible moment, came as no surprise to Lee, Norris or Chambers, all of whom, in one way or another, welcomed it, but Joll and his colleagues were stunned: Lieberson's decision to quit in mid-term could not be interpreted as anything other than a declaration of no confidence in the company by its most expensive and, in film terms, most experienced executive.

Over the weekend, while other members of the Goldcrest team were entertained at Wimbledon by Australian tycoon Kerry Packer, Stoddart, Joll and Lee held rescue talks. Stoddart called Angus Grossart in Portugal and asked him to cut short his holiday to attend an emergency meeting of shareholders on Tuesday, 2 July. Stoddart then devised the following plan:

1. Goldcrest would issue six million shares of convertible unsecured loan stock to existing shareholders on a one-for-six rights basis.
2. Each share of convertible loan stock would carry a warrant to purchase one ordinary share at 75 pence.
3. The loan-stock offer would be underwritten by Pearson, Electra and Noble Grossart, in proportion to their existing holdings.

Translated into plainer language, this meant that Goldcrest's existing investors would be asked to buy new shares in the company at the ratio of one such share for every six they currently held. These new shares would be in the form of loan stock – i.e. they would earn interest and they would be redeemed on a certain date – and, although they would not be secured against the assets of the company, they would be convertible, which meant that they could be exchanged for ordinary shares at any time at a fixed price. To make the offer more attractive still, warrants were to be issued giving the new loan-stock holders the right to buy further new shares at a price of 75 pence.

Those shareholders who took up this offer would be banking on an improvement in the company's fortunes of sufficient magnitude to push up the value of Goldcrest shares, thereby making the conversion of the loan stock and the exercise of the warrants profitable. Those shareholders, on the other hand, who did not take up the offer would see the value of their current shareholdings diluted upon the conversion of the loan stock, and diluted further upon the exercise of the warrants. Thus, the only reason for not taking up the issue (other than shortage of funds) was that the shareholders in question were of the opinion that the company's prospects would not improve.

To ensure the success of the offering, the three major shareholders, Pearson, Electra and Noble Grossart, were prepared to purchase all the unsold loan stock – i.e. underwrite the issue – themselves.

4. The three underwriters would begin to advance funds against the loan-stock offering by the end of the week – i.e. they would make the £6 million available immediately.

5. On the basis of this recapitalization, the Midland, via its merchant-banking division, Samuel Montagu, would be asked to increase its loan facility from £10 to £12 million.

In the meantime, the independent auditors appointed by Pearson, Deloitte Haskins and Sells, in collaboration with Pearson's merchant bank, Lazard, would scrutinize Goldcrest's books to ascertain that the £8 million (£6 million loan stock and £2 million additional credit) would be enough to cover the company's requirements for the coming period, *on the assumption that the Schuster, Cinema Group and Westpac investments did not materialize.* Goldcrest's lawyers, Freshfields, in collaboration with Noble Grossart, would draw up the offering memorandum.

All these arrangements were to be confirmed by Friday, 5 July.

At the management meeting on 1 July, it was reported that 'further confrontation' on the set of *Revolution* appeared 'inevitable' as a result of the 'limitation being imposed on the number of shooting days left, and Goldcrest's insistence on the Norwegian shoot'. A new schedule, based on a completion date of 2 August, was being drawn up for discussion with Hudson and Winkler. If they failed to co-operate, they would 'need to be fired'. Lee would warn Terry Semel of this. Garth Thomas expressed the opinion that the reluctance to film in Norway came not from Hudson but from Winkler, who was using the issue 'to press for part-payment' of his deferred fee. (Winkler's fee, it should be noted, was fourth in line of recoupment, after the recovery of the budgeted cost of production, the completion costs and the balance of Hudson's fee. If the picture failed to generate enough income to cover these, Winkler would not be paid.) Warner Bros. was to be asked to make an offer for distribution rights in Germany and Japan, the two remaining unsold territories. The estimated final cost of the film, after recovery of insurance claims, was now £19.1 million ($23 million).

The latest cost forecast for *Absolute Beginners*, three weeks into principal photography, showed an overage of £900,000. This was attributed to 'overcasting, bad costing of sets, and poor organization and budgeting on costumes'. Garth Thomas reported that there was 'no realistic possibility' of completing the film for £6.3 million. The overcost would push up Goldcrest's cash requirement by at least £300,000.

In Colombia, meanwhile, David Puttnam had signed a cost statement at the end of *The Mission*'s eleventh week that showed an overage of £930,000. This took the production £180,000 over its contingency. In a note to Lee and Lieberson, he said: 'the increase . . . reflects additional running costs during our final week in Colombia; includes a budget provision for a two-day studio shoot in London in September; and provides for the cost of a helicopter at Iguazu which had previously been unavailable to us and which will significantly improve our speed of operation'.

An $8 million budget for *Horror Movie* had been submitted, but the film now had no chance of going into production unless 20th Century–Fox put up 50 per cent of the cost in advance, and the remaining 50 per cent was shared between Viking and Cinema Group (or other third parties). Goldcrest's resources would not stretch beyond the development and pre-production costs that had already been incurred. Nor, the minutes of the management meeting tell us, 'in the light of recent experience', would Goldcrest 'bear any part of the completion risk'.

After the management meeting, Lee, who had again been working on the cash-flow forecasts, sent Norris and Chambers a memo in which he predicted that the end-of-year borrowing requirement could go as high as £17 million. Goldcrest would have contract cover for only £8 million of this. Lee based his calculation on lower than expected revenues from *The Killing Fields*, David Puttnam's three low-budget films and a clutch of television productions (total, £2 million); still higher costs on *Revolution*, *The Mission* and *Absolute Beginners* (a further £2 million); and the failure of the hoped-for third-party investors (£4 million). Deloitte was to come up with its own calculation of the maximum borrowing figure by Wednesday, 3 July.

Lee then spoke to Ted Harris, a conversation which he recounted in another memo to Chambers and Norris:

Ted Harris has discussed the possibility of a £12 million loan package with John Evangelides at Samuel Montagu. They will not be in a position to respond until they have seen Deloitte's analysis and also the terms of the shareholders' offer. In the meantime, the Midland have agreed to a lending limit of £9.5 million for the week. Prior to the advance to *Revolution* the balance was standing at £8.8 million, after taking account of the Pearson injection of £1 million and all payments to date. I have given my word to Ted Harris that we will not allow the balance to go beyond the £9.5 million under any circumstances. I have agreed to meet John Evangelides as soon as possible, and will take David Norris with me.

The next day, Robert Finney, company secretary, gave notice of an emergency holdings-board meeting to be held on Friday, 5 July.

At lunchtime, Lee met with Stoddart, Joll and Grossart, to discuss the proposed rescue plan. On his return to Wardour Street, he summarized their conclusions:

At today's meeting with the shareholders at Millbank the following proposal was hammered out.

1. Subject to the other conditions, Pearson, Noble Grossart and Electra will make available £6.1 million to the company on Friday afternoon.

2. The advance is a facility conditional on the company (a) using its best endeavours to implement a new capital issue, and (b) completing negotiations with the Midland Bank to raise the loan facility to £12 million.

3. In addition, the advance will be conditional on directors of the company being able to verify that the issue will provide sufficient working capital to meet immediate commitments. Advice to be taken from Deloittes.

4. The capital reconstruction will have the following features:

(a) 6.1 million units of £1 five-year 10 per cent convertible subordinated loan stock. The loan stock will be convertible into 12.2 million ordinary shares at 50 pence.

(b) 6.1 million warrants to purchase shares at 75 pence each.

(c) Conversion of loan stock will be required either on sale or on refinancing.

5. By the end of the week we must get an agreement in principle from Samuel Montagu and Midland Bank that they will provide a £12 million project financing facility on terms acceptable to the company.

6. The issue will be underwritten by Pearson, Electra and Noble Grossart in proportions to be agreed. The underwriting fee will be 1½ per cent.

7. The advance will bear interest at 1½ per cent over the Midland base rate (or on the same terms as the current Midland lending).

In addition, it was agreed that:

1. Angus Grossart would contact the Edinburgh shareholders over the next two days to get an indication of interest and decide whether the warrants were necessary.

2. The company would prepare a circular to shareholders explaining the situation and the offer to be released on Monday in time for the Annual General Meeting.

3. The documentation would be prepared by Mr Bell of Ashurst, Morris and Crisp, and Charles ap Simon [of Freshfields] would respond on behalf of the company.

4. The company would be presented with a firm proposal at a special board meeting to be held on Friday morning.

('£1 five-year 10 per cent convertible subordinated loan stock' is loan stock that earns 10 per cent interest a year, is to be repaid after five years, can be converted within that time to ordinary shares at the rate of one unit of loan stock to two ordinary shares at 50 pence each [i.e. half the price paid at the time of the 1984 reorganization], and that is subordinate to all the other obligations of the company in terms of interest payment and eventual redemption. For every one such unit of loan stock bought, shareholders would also receive a warrant to buy a further ordinary share at a price of 75 pence.)

In preparation for the Friday board meeting, Lee circulated the following document:

Refinancing

We shall be meeting on Friday morning to consider a proposal to raise £6 million of additional capital from our existing shareholders – the financing to be underwritten by Pearson, Electra and Noble Grossart. In addition, we will be asking the Midland Bank to raise our credit limit from £10 million to £12 million. These two actions will raise our available capital by £8 million.

At Friday's meeting, among other things, we will need to address three questions.

1. Why do we need as much as £8 million additional capital?
2. Will £8 million enable us to complete the committed production programme?
3. What financial capacity will exist to support the 1986 new production programme for 1987 release?

This paper addresses each of these three questions in turn.

How did we get where we are?

[The schedule] attached gives you an analysis of the three major productions, *Revolution, Mission* and *Absolute Beginners*. At the beginning of the year we planned for budgets of £32.3 million for the three films. We were looking for £9.3 million of third party investment, making the Goldcrest investment £23 million. £6.3 million of the £9.3 million of third party investment was committed. We were still looking for an equity investor in *The Mission*.

We then committed to higher budgets for two of the three films. The *Revolution* budget was raised from £11.5 million to £14.6 million to accommodate the star cast and an adjustment below-the-line. The *Mission* budget was raised from £14.8 million to £16.0 million, mostly to increase the below-the-line, but also to accommodate Robert De Niro. These two decisions raised the gross level of film investment by £4.3 million.

As part of our decision to increase the budgets of the two films, we set out to raise additional third party investment to cover the increase. You will see from [the schedule] that we put in place a deal to raise £3.5 million for *Revolution* through Schuster, and £3.9 million from Cinema Group. Assuming that these two placements had been achieved, the net level of Goldcrest investment would not have changed.

It is worth noting that as a result of the star casting the pre-sale potential of the films rose substantially.

In addition, we began discussions with alternative banks – Boston, Credit Lyonnais, European American Bank and later Guinness Mahon and Samuel Montagu – to raise the facility from £10 million fully secured to $20–25 million on a part-secured basis.

By the time of the June cash flow, *Revolution* was £2.5 million over budget and *The Mission* was showing overage as well. The cash flow was done on the basis that overages of £4.1 million were being suffered. At the same time, Schuster had reduced the size of the investment in *Revolution*, so our net Goldcrest investment had risen by £4.8 million.

The latest forecast shows that *Revolution* could cost £18.3 million. *The Mission* is still well within a 10 per cent contingency, and the Goldcrest investment is therefore £6.2 million above business plan levels. This £6.2 million explains the need for the additional £8 million permanent capital.

Is £8 million enough?

I have attempted to analyse the downside risk. First, [in the schedule] the last column, labelled 'downside risk', assumes that *Revolution* goes all the way up to the point of investment by Entertainment Completions Inc.; that *The Mission* uses its full 10 per cent contingency; and that *Absolute Beginners* goes £1 million over the budget of £6 million.

I have also assumed that the Schuster investment could fall through, since we know that Schuster has failed on other occasions, and the higher cost obviously makes the investment less attractive to his investors.

On this basis, our financing requirement for these three films alone could be more than £10 million above business plan. The business plan had a peak borrowing of £6 million.

Deloittes will analyse the risk associated with the cash flow. At the year end, borrowing is shown at £9 million. Assuming that up to £2 million of revenue inflows are uncertain, and that the final cost could rise by £2.8 million, then the year end borrowing would rise to £13.8 million – well within our capacity. However, if we failed to get £4 million of new equity into *Mission*, then the borrowing requirements would come very near the £18 million limit.

Thus, we conclude that the £8 million additional capital is just sufficient, with little margin.

What can we do in 1986?

We already have the 1986 release plan well covered.

Under different circumstances we would have been looking for a programme of five films with a gross investment cost of, say, £40 million, for release in 1987, to be produced in the second half of 1986 and the beginning of 1987. On the assumption that half of this investment is covered by US advances and a quarter is covered by equity from the Viking Fund, this programme would imply a financing requirement of £10 million from our own balance sheet.

Our projected cash by the middle of 1986 is a positive balance of £1.5 million. But this includes a number of areas of uncertainty, as follows:

Schuster	£ 2.7 million
Australian tax deal	£ 4.5 million
Overruns	£ 2.8 million
Total uncertainty	**£10.0 million**

Thus, our mid-year balance might be £8.5 million overdrawn, leaving us with capacity within our £18 million limit of £9.5 million – less than is required to finance the operating plan.

If, in addition, we fail to get a £4 million equity investment in *The Mission* from some source before the middle of next year, then the overdraft would be £12.5 million and the capacity to finance new production severely restricted.

It is therefore essential that we secure this equity investment as a matter of urgency and before any new commitments can be made.

Conclusions

On balance, therefore, we can conclude that £8 million is needed, but that it will only just be sufficient to deal with the immediate risks, and will leave us short of capacity to support the 1986 operating plan.

James

The attached schedule, here slightly abbreviated, was as follows:

Major film-investment programme:

£ million	Business plan	Agreed operating budgets	Lastest forecast	Downside risk
Revolution	(11.5)	(14.6)	(18.3)	(19.0)
Mission	(14.8)	(16.0)	(16.9)	(17.5)
Absolute Beginners	(6.0)	(6.0)	(6.9)	(7.0)
Film investment	**(32.3)**	**(36.6)**	**(42.1)**	**(43.5)**
Viking	3.3	3.2	3.2	3.2
Schuster	–	3.5	2.7	–
Cinema Group	3.0	3.9	3.9	3.9
Virgin/Palace	3.0	3.0	3.1	3.1
Total third-parties	**9.3**	**13.6**	**12.9**	**10.2**
Warner advances	7.1	7.1	8.7	8.7
Pre-sales	6.0	9.8	10.7	10.7
Total cover	**22.4**	**30.5**	**32.3**	**29.6**
Goldcrest exposure	**(9.9)**	**(6.1)**	**(9.8)**	**(13.9)**

Lee's paper calls for some examination. To the first question, 'How did we get where we are?', he provides only a description, not an explanation, of what has happened to the company. He says that the budgets of the films have increased; that the films have since run over budget; that the looked-for third-party investors have either failed to turn up or are now in doubt; and that attempts to arrange a larger and more flexible credit facility have met with failure. As result, he concludes, 'Goldcrest investment is . . . £6.2 million above business plan levels. This £6.2 million explains the need for the additional £8 million of permanent capital.'

This surely won't do. The increases in the budgets of the two big films did not happen by chance: they were proposed, discussed and agreed. The third-party investors did not suddenly drop out, for, apart from Viking, they were never in, and they should not have been included in

any but the most speculative calculations. The same was true of the
hoped-for credit arrangements. The only elements in Lee's presentation
that could be said to lie outside his immediate control were the costs of
the films themselves. Between them, and net of insurance claims, these
were running at about £4 million over budget. A £4 million budget
overage could not bring a healthy £35 million company to its knees. The
problem with Goldcrest was that it wasn't healthy.

The nature of its affliction can be diagnosed with the help of the
investment rules laid down first by the GFI board, of which Lee had
been chairman, and then by Lee himself at the September 1984 board
meeting. The GFI rules were: first, that there be a maximum exposure
in any one project; second, that investments be spread across a wide
portfolio; and third, that Goldcrest's equity be covered as far as possible
by pre-sales. Lee's rules were, in addition: first, that Goldcrest should
follow talent, not themes; second, that the company should 'deliberately
favour' distinctive rather than mainstream projects; third, that negotiations should always be conducted from a position of strength, by
relying on projects developed in-house, the distribution terms of which
Goldcrest could dictate itself; fourth, that investments should be spread
across a wide spectrum of film types, appealing to both mass-market and
specialist audiences; fifth, that the market for each project should be
clearly identified, and decisions as to budget, distributor and marketing
campaign made accordingly; sixth, that too great a dependence on any
one distributor should be avoided; seventh, that in dealing with a major
studio, foreign rights should always be retained by Goldcrest, for sale on
a territory-by-territory basis; eighth, that risks should be 'taken intelligently', being careful to avoid projects that have little sales potential;
and ninth, that Goldcrest should keep within capacity. As to this last
point, Lee had been very firm. 'A film company that lives beyond its
means inevitably gets into trouble,' he had said.

It is on the first two points in the GFI rules that Goldcrest had come
most adrift as far as risk and profitability were concerned. It was on the
last point in Lee's rules that it had run aground on cash flow.

These rules having been broken, it hardly mattered that *Revolution*
had gone so far over budget. For if there was no margin within which
to manoeuvre, then whatever went wrong – the lower than expected
revenues from television product, Showtime's $100,000 per hour offer
for *Robin of Sherwood*, the spiralling overhead costs, the cable losses –
would cause disproportionate damage. If a number of things – i.e. all the
above – went wrong at the same time, it was no good pointing the finger
of blame at this one or that. *Revolution*'s overage could be blamed only

for the damage, if any, that it did to *Revolution*'s profitability. Nothing else. Hudson and Winkler had absolutely no responsibility for Goldcrest's general financial condition. That is not to say that having gone over budget in the manner and for the reasons that they did, they should not have been penalized. It is merely to say that their responsibility began and ended with the film itself.

The second question Lee asks in his paper is, 'Is £8 million enough?' Here, for the first time, he begins to look over the shoulder of Chambers's 'worst-likely' forecasts to see what lies beyond. And yet the right-hand column in the above schedule, downside risk, still falls some way short of a 'worst-possible' forecast. For, as Lee himself explained, the £13.9 million bottom-line figure was arrived at on the assumption that the Cinema Group investment would come through, that *The Mission* would stay within contingency and that *Absolute Beginners* would go over by no more than £1 million. If it had been assumed, on the contrary, that the Cinema Group investment (£3.9 million) wouldn't come through, that *The Mission* and *Absolute Beginners* would consume both the 10 per cent contingencies and the 10 per cent completion overrides for which Goldcrest was responsible (a further £3 million), then the bottom-line downside-risk figure would have been £20.8 million. To this could have been added Goldcrest's overhead fees and other deferments in respect of all three films (at least £2.5 million), bringing the total to £23.3 million. This would have been the true downside figure in respect of the information included in the schedule. (Not included in the schedule, of course, were expenditures and receipts in other areas, notably television.)

And with what expectation had Goldcrest undertaken this level of risk? Chambers's most recent profitability forecasts for the three films showed an aggregate 'probable' contribution of £6 million. Goldcrest, in other words, had invested £35 million, in expectation of a 'probable' net return of £6 million, but at risk of losing £23 million. Three throws of the dice. The company had wandered a long way from the investment rules by which it was supposed to have been governed.

On the afternoon of 3 July, Lee received a strangely worded telex from Canny and Afman at Credit Lyonnais. First, they reiterated the terms of the credit facility that had been discussed on 29 May and verbally offered to Goldcrest on 26 June. Only this time there is no mention of a trial period or of sharing the facility with the Midland. Then they reminded Lee that, as an interim measure, they had been prepared to make an immediate loan to *Revolution*. They complained that this offer had been rejected. 'All we asked for were a number of signed documents,' they said. 'Unfortunately, some of these documents were not available. Nonetheless, we indicated to you on 28 June that we would be prepared to make available $4 million immediately in anticipation of the required documentation. This offer was apparently not acceptable to Goldcrest and their bankers, the Midland Bank.' The telex ended on what appears to be a note of regret: 'Please understand that [we] are very committed to the motion picture industry and that we would have been delighted to enter into a relationship with Goldcrest. Although we try to be an innovative and flexible bank, we have to adhere to certain minimum requirements and standard procedures. Should you wish to avail yourselves of our advice and consult, please do not hesitate to call us.'

Lee, puzzled, replied as follows:

Dear Michel and Frans,
  Thank you for your telex . . . which was most welcome. It needs clarification. You state that 'this offer was apparently not acceptable to Goldcrest and their bankers, the Midland Bank'. This offer would have been very acceptable to both Goldcrest and our bankers. Last week Frans informed us that Credit Lyonnais would only offer this facility if it were to be shared equally in all respects with the Midland Bank. It was that condition that was unacceptable to the Midland. If we are to understand from your telex that Credit Lyonnais are still prepared to consider advancing $20 million along the lines indicated in your telex, then it is well worth renewing discussions as a matter of urgency.
  . . . Could you please call or telex tomorrow, indicating whether your proposal still carries the condition that the Midland must share the facility.
  Kind regards, James.

On 4 July, Goldcrest company secretary Robert Finney circulated the agenda for the emergency board meeting. With it was Deloitte's cash-flow report. This report painted a rather worse picture than that which had so alarmed the shareholders at the June meeting, for, according to Deloitte, even with the injection of £6 million of new shareholders' capital, Goldcrest's borrowings would not only remain in the range of £8–12 million in the period July–December 1985, but would continue at a high level into the summer of 1986.

Deloitte concluded their report by saying:

. . . A total of £18 million borrowing facilities (£6 million loan stock and £12 million bank credit), although prima facie adequate, even allowing for some slippage on receipt of revenues and for additional interest, leave little margin for further contingencies given the significance of many of the amounts involved . . . [And] there is a significant shortfall in cover if the secured portion of borrowings remains at the present level of £10 million. Renegotiated facilities will need to have a secured portion at a lower level.

With forecast borrowings continuing at high levels well into 1986, and given proposed facilities of £18 million, it would appear that no more commitments can be given to new productions unless the production costs are virtually wholly financed by firm contracts from distributors or co-investors.

The message was clear: even with £6 million from the shareholders and an increased line of credit from the bank, Goldcrest would be effectively out of action until the current films produced sufficient income to reduce the debt and generate new investment capacity. A production hiatus, such as that experienced in 1984, the dire consequences of which were now crippling the company, was thus in prospect for the best part of 1986.

What were the shareholders to make of all this? For Lyn Hopkins of the Post Office Staff Superannuation Fund and Paul Whitney of the National Coal Board Pension Fund, and for fund managers in the offices of Coral Leisure Group, London & Manchester Assurance Company, Ashdown Investment Trust, Trans-Oceanic Investment Trust, Sand Aire Investment Company, the Scottish Investment Trust, Standard Life, Legal & General, Atlantic Assets Trust and the Murray Johnstone Group, the case called for hard thinking. If they bought the loan stock, they stood a good chance of throwing good money after bad. If they did not, and the company's fortunes improved, they would find themselves with significantly smaller shareholdings in a profitable company that planned soon to go public.

Chapter Fifty

Desperate Measures

Ilott: The emergency meeting of the holdings board started at 8.30 a.m. on 5 July. Stoddart was in the chair and all the directors were present except for Grossart, Puttnam and Attenborough. Grossart participated by telephone, and Lee tabled notes of earlier conversations with Puttnam and Attenborough, 'in which they expressed confidence that the management and the board's financial advisers would act in the best interests of the company in resolving its financial difficulties'. Both men, said Lee, had 'expressed concern that sufficient finance be raised not only to complete existing productions but to support further productions in 1986'.

Representatives of Freshfields, Deloitte and Ashurst Morris Crisp and Co. (the firm that was to draw up the documentation for the loan-stock rights issue) brought the number of those present to fifteen. As noted in the minutes, they were gathered together 'to agree upon action to resolve the severe cash-flow shortage in the group . . . to review the cash-flow forecasts . . . and to consider detailed fund-raising proposals devised by the chairman'.

Stoddart explained the terms of the offer by Pearson, Electra and Noble Grossart to lend the company £4 million, £1.76 million and £340,000 respectively. These loans, totalling £6.1 million and granted for three months, would earn interest at a rate of 1.25 per cent above the bank base rate, and were offered against a commitment by the three shareholders to underwrite a loan-stock issue of the same value. This issue, as we have seen, would give subscribers not only stock convertible at the rate of one £1-unit of loan stock to two ordinary shares, but additional warrants to purchase further shares at the fixed price of 75 pence.

Commenting on these terms, Stoddart said that they were 'reasonable and appropriate in the circumstances', since Goldcrest was 'relying on a small group of shareholders to put additional funds at risk to rescue the company'. He recognized, however, that the issue of loan stock and warrants on these terms would significantly dilute the existing sharehol-dings and could be construed as detrimental to the interests of those shareholders who did not take up the offer. Lee himself had drawn up a table which showed that the existing shareholdings would be diluted by as much as 22 per cent should the loan stock be converted and the warrants exercised.

It was Grossart's opinion that this degree of dilution was too great, and he reported that the Scottish shareholders with whom he had con-sulted were not happy with it. Nevertheless, he believed that the com-pany's predicament was so serious, and its capital requirements so urgent, that, in the absence of any other proposal, Goldcrest had no choice but to accept the offer. Pearson, Electra and Noble Grossart, he pointed out, did not intend to profit from the offering as such. On the contrary, their new money would be very much at risk. They would derive benefit only if the company's fortunes revived.

Joll observed that there was anyway 'scope for some adjustment of the proposed underwriting commitment', and that 'the opportunity exists to arrange the rights issue on more favourable terms', or even to arrange 'alternative finance', so long as the £6.1 million loan was repaid at the end of its three-month term. The decision to be made at the meeting, in other words, concerned the loan only: the rights issue was merely the one means of repaying that loan that had thus far been tabled for the directors' consideration.

On this basis, and after further consideration of the Deloitte cash-flow report, the meeting agreed that the offer of the loans be accepted on the terms proposed and that an Extraordinary General Meeting be called to approve the proposed rights issue. The loans would be put in place after the present meeting, to allow an initial draw-down of £1.5 million before the end of the day.

Michael Stoddart left the room to call a senior executive at the Midland Bank. He returned to report that the Midland would consider a £12 million facility at its credit committee meeting on Tuesday, 9 July. Stod-dart was 'reasonably confident' that it would be approved.

Before the emergency board meeting closed, Charles ap Simon, of Freshfields, warned the directors of the legal consequences of fraudulent trading (i.e. continuing to trade while in the knowledge that the company had insufficient funds to meet its obligations), for which they, as directors, would be held personally accountable.

During the course of the meeting, Lee had been handed a telex from Frans Afman:

Dear James,

Pursuant to our telephone conversation of July 4, 1985, I talked to Michel Canny regarding a possible meeting with Midland. Unfortunately, due to the holiday period, he has no possibility to go to London. May I suggest that I call Midland Bank today. Please advise me whom I should approach.

As regards the initial facility of $4 million, I believe that our bank has not changed its position. I have instructed [our lawyers] Denton Hall and Burgin to proceed with the documentation.

Finally I did mention to my board that Goldcrest is preparing a rights issue of £6 million, which is very good news indeed.

During my four weeks' stay in Los Angeles, Ria Janke and Henk Altink will do the necessary follow up.

Best regards, Frans J. Afman

This message was almost as cryptic as the last.

As soon as the meeting was over Lee wrote to Michel Canny, confirming that the rights issue was to go ahead and adding:

. . . we believe it is the intention of the Midland to ask Samuel Montagu to lead a project to provide a larger and more appropriate debt financing facility. I have been in contact with John Evangelides of Samuel Montagu and he is aware of your continued interest in serving our company. We now have time to do things in a slightly more relaxed fashion. Frans is off on one of his trips again. He tells me that he will not be back until the beginning of August. By the time that John Evangelides has decided to accept the project management role and prepared a plan of action, Frans should be back. Thank you for your continued interest in working with our company.

He then wrote to Ted Harris:

Dear Ted,

I am pleased to say that the Goldcrest board has agreed to accept a loan of £6.1 million from our three major shareholders . . . Agreement was reached at lunchtime today . . . and funds are now being drawn down.

. . . I met Mike Massey on Thursday with James Joll. We made a formal request for the Midland Group to increase our borrowing facility from £10 million to £12 million. In the light of the Deloittes report we feel that the balance of this facility should be £7 million secured by distribution contracts of no more than 133 per cent of the advances made by the bank, and the remaining £5 million should be loaned against the net worth of the company. Once you have had a chance to study the Deloittes report, you will see that a £12 million facility on a fully secured basis would not meet our immediate financing requirements.

I recognize that you must complete your investigation and go through the necessary processes within the bank. However, we do need a quick decision. We cannot implement the rights issue until the facility is agreed.

As soon as this minimum facility is in place, then I would suggest that we work together with Samuel Montagu under more relaxed circumstances to design a more appropriate long-term method of debt financing; which would then replace the Midland £12 million facility.

... Thank you for your continued help and support ...
James G. Lee

Lee enclosed copies of the letters to Canny and Harris with another letter, this time to John Evangelides, in which he remarked: 'There seems to be considerable goodwill on the part of Credit Lyonnais, despite recent circumstances. You have said that you are happy to work closely with Frans Afman. I am sure he will recognize the need to work under your leadership.'

On 8 July, Lee received the following telex from Frans Afman:

I did call Mr Massey of Midland Bank last Friday afternoon. He gave me the impression that Midland wants to arrange a financial package in conjunction with Samuel Montagu. Apparently they are not interested in talking to us within the near future.
Best regards, Frans

At the management meeting that morning it was decided that no press release would be issued in connection with the raising of the £6 million of new capital. Goldcrest's public position was that the company was now 'fully capitalized after a temporary difficulty arising from the *Revolution* overage'. In the same spirit, executives were warned of 'the need to avoid discussing with outsiders the difficulties and discord' that had plagued *Revolution*. 'Goldcrest', the minutes of the meeting record, 'must ensure that the prospects for what would be a spectacular, high quality film were not prejudiced by rumour and bad publicity.'

On 10 July, the London editor of the *Hollywood Reporter*, Chris Goodwin, obtained confirmation that Lieberson was to stand down as head of production at the end of the year. Goodwin wrote an 850-word piece that managed to include all the salient points of the Goldcrest crisis: that *Revolution* had gone 'drastically over budget'; that the company was 'overstretched' financially and had had to resort to 'additional borrowing'; and that it was 'likely to slip back into loss during the current year'. He noted that Lieberson's decision came mid-way through the second year of his three-year contract, and he observed that this was consistent with reports that Lieberson and Lee had had 'serious differences'. In all this, Goodwin was merely putting on record rumours that had long been rife in Wardour Street. But he led his story with an item that was news to everyone other than Lee: Lieberson was not to be replaced.

Goodwin's story appeared first in Hollywood, but it was faxed across the world within hours. Guy East had a copy waiting for him on his desk when he got into work. So did the British national showbiz and media writers and film-trade journalists. Over the next few days, similar stories were to appear in *Variety*, *Screen International* and the *Sunday Times*. None of them had anything substantive to add to Goodwin's account, but all the journalists concerned were aware that there was a major story in there somewhere, the key to which was in the meaning of Lee's reported remark that Lieberson was not to be replaced.

On 11 July the Midland made a formal offer of a £12 million credit facility, on the following conditions: (a) that the interest payments and the eventual redemption of the £12 million take precedence over the servicing and redemption of the £6 million shareholders' loan; (b) that the whole £12 million be repayable after three months; (c) that amounts above the existing temporary credit limit of £9.5 million could be drawn down only when the £6 million shareholders' loan had been exhausted; and (d) that £9.98 million of the £12 million facility must be secured against contracts.

These terms could not be met. For one thing, a £12 million loan facility that was available only for three months would make it virtually impossible to put together a meaningful rights issue: who would invest in a company that was in imminent danger of having the rug pulled out from under it by the bank? Lee would have to have further talks with the Midland and with Pearson. In the meantime, the Goldcrest management team would redouble its efforts to arrange a larger and more flexible facility with either Samuel Montagu or Guinness Mahon.

The next day, 12 July, the Goldcrest Annual General Meeting, falling unhappily in the midst of the present crisis, attracted thirteen shareholders' representatives, six other directors (including Puttnam but not Attenborough) and eight advisers and other participants. It began at 12.05 p.m. with the report and accounts for 1984, which were accepted without discussion, then moved on to the re-election of directors and re-appointment of auditors. The formal business having thus been concluded within the first five minutes, Stoddart reported on two items of other business: Lieberson's departure and the cash-flow crisis. Of the former, Stoddart noted merely that the company 'looks forward to a fruitful relationship with Mr Lieberson in his role as independent producer'. Of the latter, he promised an explanation in a circular, 'giving a full account of the background to the difficulties, detailing the terms of the proposed rights issue and calling an extraordinary general meeting to increase the share capital of the company and alter the borrowing powers in its articles'. Stoddart promised that this circular would be posted to shareholders 'within the next few weeks'. He ruled that, 'since a number of shareholders are not represented at the present meeting' and the matter was anyway to be fully discussed at the EGM, it would be 'inappropriate to discuss the difficulties and the rights-issue proposals at this stage'.

Two questions were then put from the floor. The first asked for 'some indication of the company's profitability in the medium term'. No answer to this was forthcoming. Instead, Lee, while acknowledging that the prospects for 1985 looked bleak, reiterated that the target gross-profit margin in the future was '25–30 per cent, which should result in a 10 per cent return to shareholders'. The second question, put by Roger Brooke (Lee's predecessor at Pearson Longman and the man who had put the first money into both *Watership Down* and the original Goldcrest development fund), asked for an account of current activity in television. The answer came from Wooller, who outlined the new emphasis on 'international productions targeted primarily at the US market'. Lee's only contribution was to observe that Goldcrest 'expects shortly to make an important announcement regarding its future strategy in television production'.

There were no further questions and the meeting was closed. It had lasted all of thirty minutes.

Variety and the *Hollywood Reporter* had that day carried stories claiming that *Horror Movie* had been abandoned. Lee issued a denial.

At the end of the day, Lee gave copies of the first draft of a major review of Goldcrest's business strategy to Puttnam, Norris and Chambers. He had prepared it for the meeting to be held on 18 July. It is an extraordinarily comprehensive and complex document, in which Lee analyses what had gone wrong with the company. Set out across eight double-width spread-sheets, it lists, down the left-hand margin, five major areas of activity – production, development, distribution, finance and production control – which are then subdivided into twenty-three decision-making categories. For example, under the major heading 'Production' are listed: (i) preferred film type; (ii) optimum budget levels; (iii) production-programme mix; (iv) level of output; and (v) choice of film-makers. Across the width of the page, each of these categories is then considered from the point of view of the existing strategy, the rationale for that strategy, the problems arising from that strategy and the alternatives to that strategy, before concluding with Lee's recommendations.

In all, there are twenty-four such recommendations, of which eight call for no change, six call for changes of emphasis only and ten call for wholly new policies. These recommendations were not all of equal importance, of course. The main ones, in the order in which they appear in Lee's paper, can be summarized as follows:

That there be no change in Goldcrest's policy of producing 'high-profile special-interest films' rather than mass-market, youth-orientated or exploitation movies; that, while the company should in future 'avoid budgets in excess of $15 million', more emphasis should be given to major titles at the expense of low-budget 'classics'; that output should remain at between four and eight films a year; that the in-house development operation should be abandoned in favour of a return to the old policy of working with established producers, who would, in turn, act as 'godfathers' to new talent; that Goldcrest should experiment with further 'first-look' development deals along the lines of the existing contracts with Lieberson and Puttnam; that, instead of appointing a new head of production, the chief executive, advised by Puttnam and Lieberson and supported by a small script-reading staff, should deal directly with producers himself; that, in dealing with the US, higher advances should be sought, even at the expense of good back-end terms, whenever this was deemed appropriate (i.e. whenever the company had less than complete faith in the project in question); that East's foreign-sales operation should be bolstered by the acquisition of third-party pick-ups, as this was 'a key factor for our continued existence against world competition'; that Goldcrest should 'promote the formation of linked pools of capital' in Europe (such as was envisaged in the proposed relationship with Viking), Australia (with Roadshow) and the US (possibly with Orion or one of the other independent distributors); that a team of experienced producers – what Lee called a 'pool of heavies' – should be recruited to oversee the physical production of Goldcrest films, to ensure that the Revolution débâcle was not repeated; that, for the same reason, a special accounts team should be set up to deal solely with the financial control of current productions; that henceforward the company should 'obtain full completion guarantees from third parties in all instances'; and, finally, that every budget should include a 10 per cent contingency at the outset.

Puttnam, Norris and Chambers instantly focused on the one controversial item on this list: the proposal that the chief executive take responsibility for creative decisions. To this they were adamantly opposed, principally because, in their view, Lee had had too much power all along and had exercised it unwisely. Furthermore, he was not, in their opinion, a suitable person to take creative decisions.

On 15 July, the management meeting was told that principal photography on Revolution would now finish on 5 August, twenty weeks after the start and five weeks over the original schedule. The latest final cost estimate projected a budget overage of £5.2 million, of which £1.5 million was almost certain to be recovered from the insurers. There was still a risk of further overages in post-production, for the task of getting the film ready for release by Christmas had been made more difficult by the delayed completion of photography. A February/March UK release was now in prospect as no major West End cinema could be found to take the film in the Christmas period.

Absolute Beginners' producer, Steve Woolley, was reported to have 'kept photography on schedule by deleting many scenes from the script'. However, further substantial cuts were required if the film was to come in at under two hours.

The management meeting was also told that the Westpac tax deal looked 'increasingly uncertain'. The Cinema Group investment in *The Mission* had become dependent on the cover provided by the Westpac deal, and Harry Gould was now to be informed that 'unless Cinema Group [is] prepared to commit to an equity investment unconditional upon the Australian tax deal, Goldcrest must seek alternative equity investment in the picture'.

After the management meeting, Lee and Chambers met with John Evangelides of Samuel Montagu to press for a £16 million credit facility. Evangelides, having ploughed through the Goldcrest documentation over the past several days, was willing to enter into serious negotiation. But he laid down the following conditions: that there would be full completion guarantees on all Goldcrest productions; that interest on the facility would be at least 2 per cent above the bank base rate; that the arrangement fee charged by Samuel Montagu would be 1.5 per cent of the amount of the total facility; that security for the greater part of the loan would have to be provided at a rate of £1.25 in sales contracts for every £1 borrowed; and that some unsecured lending would be allowed, but according to a formula that related the level of such borrowing to the projected cash flows of the company.

Lee and Chambers returned to the office to work out the implications of this. Further discussions would be held with Pearson.

The following day, in Wooller's absence, four members of the television department were given notice. The entire staff were shocked and distraught. The redundancies had not been preceded by a meeting or any other attempt to explain why they were necessary, and this added to the staff's distress. Fairly or otherwise, Lee was blamed for his clumsy handling of the matter.

In fact, a few days earlier Lee had informed Wooller that Goldcrest was to enter a joint venture with Warner Television that would enable the company to abandon its existing and costly television production and distribution activities. In future, Lee said, Goldcrest would confine itself to investing in a small number of major mini-series, with Warner Bros. taking responsibility for most of the creative and marketing chores. This effective closure of the television department had apparently already been discussed with Philip Whitehead and David Puttnam, the board members most concerned, as well as with Joll, Blakenham and Stoddart. Lee offered Wooller the choice of either becoming an independent producer with the company, for a period of, say, eighteen months, or accepting a redundancy package. Wooller, who, although he had long expected the axe to fall, was profoundly shocked, opted for the latter. He received £85,000 compensation and left the company in August 1985.

On 18 July, the board convened for the long-awaited strategy review.

Chapter Fifty-one

Showdown

Ilott: The 18 July meeting was bound to witness a showdown. Not that this had been its intended purpose. When it had first been mooted, at the May board meeting, it had been expected to provide an opportunity for a wide-ranging discussion of Goldcrest's activities, in the light not only of the cash-flow crisis but of some of the operating difficulties encountered in television, in the management of *Revolution*, in the level of development write-offs, in the failure of the satellite-producer relationships and in the costly completion-guarantee policy. But developments since May – the dissemination of Norris's and Chambers's paper among the non-executive directors, the cash crisis and Lieberson's decision to stand down – had changed the picture dramatically, and the meeting, instead of being merely a forum for such an open-ended exchange of views, looked likely to become the occasion for a critical examination of Lee's leadership. His own strategy paper, spelling out, error by error, the shortcomings of Goldcrest's present policies, provided the ideal text for this purpose. And within that paper, the real point of contention – the issue which guaranteed that the debate would focus on Lee's perceived personal shortcomings in such a way as to make subsequent reconciliation unlikely – was his insistence on taking over as head of production.

Puttnam, who knew that if the proposal were not withdrawn he would have to speak out against it himself, approached Lee directly. 'I told James exactly what was happening,' he remembers. 'I told him a week before the board meeting, and a day before the board meeting and the day of the board meeting, and I have never understood why he didn't believe me. I said, "James you are going to get done in. If you pursue your Margaret Thatcher arrogance you are going to get done in."'

Chambers, too, tried to persuade Lee to drop the idea: 'He had discussed it with David [Norris] and me, and we tried to head him off. We were saying, "There is no way it's going to be accepted. You just don't have the sympathy of, or empathy with, the creative community, and there's no way you're going to get away with this. If you go along that route you're going to build up trouble for yourself." '

Norris confirms that he warned Lee that the proposal was 'wrong and it won't fly'.

But Lee refused to remove the offending paragraph from the document.

Attenborough offers three explanations for Lee's obduracy. The first is that Lieberson's decision to step down had presented Lee with an opportunity that was simply too good to miss. In Attenborough's opinion, Lee 'was absolutely besotted by the possibility of doing that job . . . seduced totally by the excitement [of it]'. The second is that Lieberson's decision left Lee, for the first time and to his considerable relief, in undisputed command of the company. It was a position that he did not intend to relinquish. 'I think he knew, probably, that to merely continue on the existing terms was not what he wanted,' Attenborough explains. 'The preservation of his chief-executive position was not all that important to him. He wanted to go for the whole hog . . . I mean, Goldcrest was Jake's. Goldcrest forever would be Jake's. And James wanted it to be his. And he wanted it to be seen to be his.'

Attenborough's third explanation is that the proposal ranked as a test of confidence, so that, should Lee fail to win the day, he would have adequate grounds on which to make what Attenborough calls 'an exit with dignity' from the company.

All three elements are evident in the explanation put forward by Lee himself.

'I proposed that only one person be in charge of production, because of the confusion of roles and the way we had all been manipulated [on *Revolution*],' he says. 'We were all being played off against each other. Norris was being played off against Sandy, and John Chambers's number two, Andy Parsons, was being played off against Garth Thomas. We were getting Garth being quoted to Andy Parsons that he had agreed certain things, only to find that it wasn't true. We shouldn't have been in a position to be exploited like that. That's why I proposed that we no longer have a head of production at all . . . and that the chief executive of the company, which was me, would have a direct control over the affairs of each production. But backed up by two things: one was the "pool of heavies", to be there available to be brought in . . . like the fire-fighter Red Adair; and, secondly, on the development front we would go back to the idea of having a small group of producers under contract who would develop projects under their wing.

'I mean, by that time I had really had a bellyful. It was difficult enough trying to run the company under the prevailing conditions; but when you have to be fighting battles externally and internally at the same time, there is no point in going on.

'My attitude, which was quite belligerent actually – I really took the initiative, I was probably encouraged to do it, but the initiative remained with myself right to the end – was "I have just about had a bellyful of this." I had a wonderful vision which I was trying to fulfil, and it was becoming very clear to me, day by day, that, even if we got through the immediate crisis . . . it wasn't going to work out with that team. And therefore I had to pursue what the Americans call a "shit-or-bust" strategy. I deliberately went into that meeting in that frame of mind.'

Lee's reference to Goldcrest's not working out 'with that team' can be taken to indicate his dissatisfaction with the board as well as with his management colleagues. He had plans, he says, once his strategic policy review had been accepted, to 'tackle the role of the non-executive directors'.

'It was my doing rather than Jake's to have film-makers on the board,' he explains. 'And I think Jake was right and I was wrong on that . . . It was a sort of nice sixties idea that there was a consensus between the money and the talent, and that we all at the end of the day had common interests. Of course, it wasn't true. It never was true. I am not in any way suggesting that the non-executive directors used their position to pursue their self-interest. I don't think that was the case. I think, however, that their own interests and their point of view did contaminate to a great extent their view of the business and their view of what we should do, and therefore we couldn't really get objective advice from them. So I would have . . . probably turned the board into a purely business one, and then tried to re-create relationships with the producers in another way.'

Thus, in Lee's longer-term plan, Puttnam, Attenborough and White-head would have been removed from the board at the same time as Lee himself took over the chief creative as well as the chief executive role in the company. It will be recalled that Lee already styled himself chairman of Goldcrest. He would not be satisfied, it seems, until all power had been concentrated in his hands.

The full scope of these proposals was not known, of course, at the time of the meeting. Indeed, not all of his necessary reforms were known even to Lee himself: when, in the midst of the meeting, he discovered the extent of Norris's and Chambers's opposition to him, he decided that they, too, would have to go. This was despite the fact that in his original plan Norris and Chambers were to have become joint managing directors

of the company with responsibility for legal, business affairs and production (Norris) and finance, administration and sales (Chambers).

What was known, and understood, was that if Lee got his way on the
production issue it would be impossible to hold him in check thereafter.
Thus, when he declined to take the offending paragraph out of his
paper, the non-executive directors – principally Puttnam, Attenborough,
Grossart and Joll – concluded that a showdown was inevitable. It was a
prospect that, by now, they faced with equanimity.

'My own feeling was that the moment we put up the rescue money . . .
James would have to go,' comments Joll. 'Just when and how he went
was perhaps not clear, but it seemed to me that, having brought the
company to this pass . . . he would have to go.'

There were, however, two questions that caused the non-executive
directors some concern. First, would Norris and Chambers speak against
Lee? If they did, then the rest of the executives and staff would probably
follow their example. If they didn't, the non-executive directors – since
it was they who would have to lead the attack on Lee – would be left in
an awkward position. Second, who would take Lee's place? Or rather,
since there was only one possible candidate, would Eberts come back?
Attenborough seems to have been deputed to find answers to both
questions. First he called Chambers.

'Dickie said, "As you know, there have been a lot of meetings of the
non-executive directors just recently . . . ," ' Chambers recalls. 'I said,
"No, I don't know, but I'm not surprised." He said that they had thought
about it and they had decided that Lee really must go and they would
bring Jake back, and so on. "But", Dickie said, "a problem has arisen
and I have been asked to call you about it. Puttnam says that, if it came
to the push, you and David [Norris] would not speak against James in a
board meeting." I said, "Well, that's a bit unfair. We were prepared to
quit our jobs on that very thing at a board meeting. You can't get a more
forthright manner of expressing your opinion than that." So he said,
"Well, yes, I agree, but that's what concerns David [Puttnam]." I said,
"Well, I can only speak for me; I can't speak for David [Norris], but I'm
sure he would agree that we will give whatever support you need." '

Attenborough then called Eberts.

Eberts: Dickie's call was only the latest of many conversations with
Goldcrest people over that two- or three-month period. I had had dinner
on at least one occasion with Michael Stoddart, who is a friend as well
as a founding shareholder in Allied. I had often seen Dickie, of course.
And I think I met up with David Norris and John Chambers once or

twice more. So I had a fair idea that things were going badly at Goldcrest. Just how badly I didn't realize until the last weekend of June, when I was at Wimbledon as a guest of Kerry Packer's Australian television company, Channel Nine. Most of the Goldcrest people were there, but not James.

I said to Mike Wooller, 'James should be here. After all, Channel Nine's an important customer of yours.'

And Mike said, 'Oh, Jesus, we've got a very serious problem – a crisis in the company. James is having to put together an emergency fund-raising.'

It was the first I knew of the financial crisis in the company. Until that point I had thought that the problems were to do with staffing, overheads and personality clashes.

About a week later – this would have been after the first discussion of the loan-stock rights issue – I got a call from Michael Stoddart, confirming that Goldcrest was indeed in a deep financial crisis: there was no cash in the bank, the films were over budget and not properly covered by completion guarantees and there were grave doubts about the long-term viability of the company.

Michael said, 'Look, things are very shaky and I am very concerned. I don't know what is going to happen, but I would like to know whether you would be prepared to help.'

I said that there was not much that I could do. I was committed to Allied for five years. I was committed to Warner Bros. for three years. And anyway, I couldn't come back into the company while James was there unless he invited me himself. I did not want to get involved in a palace *coup* against James. I had no quarrel with him.

I said, 'If you choose to get rid of James, then fine, I'll be happy to talk about what I might be able to do for you. But I don't want the fact that I'm saying that to become an excuse for throwing him out. I'll help, but only as a last resort.'

I recounted this conversation to Fiona. She was adamant that I should have nothing to do with Goldcrest. She remembered all too well the seven-day working weeks, the twelve-hour days, the late-night and early-morning telephone calls. The last year at Goldcrest and the entire fourteen months at Embassy had been very unpleasant for her, and she wanted nothing more to do with that kind of life.

I didn't want to go back to that kind of life either. But Goldcrest was Goldcrest. I knew, deep down, that I wouldn't leave it in the lurch.

Then, about ten days later – this would have been, I suppose, more or less on the eve of the 18 July meeting – I got the call from Dickie.

There was going to be a showdown with James. He didn't know what the outcome would be, but he did want to know, in the event that James left, if I would come back. I told him what I had told Michael: that I would talk about it, no more than that. I did not want to be used as a reason to get rid of James.

Ilott: There had not been so crucial a meeting in the history of Goldcrest since the famous Pearson lunch in February 1981, at which Lee managed to secure the $4 million to replace the Patel investment in *Gandhi*. If Lee's strategy review were now adopted in its entirety then Goldcrest would be radically refashioned according to his plan. If his review were rejected, he would have little choice but to resign and the company would have to be even more radically refashioned without him. Both sides knew that, whatever else was discussed at the meeting, or however much time was spent on the other twenty-three recommendations in Lee's document, it was the paragraph relating to Lieberson's successor as head of production that would provide the platform on which the real issue – Lee's leadership – would be thrashed out.

'I was not at all confident that I was going to win the day,' Lee recalls. 'But I was in the sort of frame of mind to say, "Well, there isn't any point in winning it any other way." If I was compromised, or if somehow or other we fudged all this, all that was going to happen was that we were going to get through this particular crisis and it would go on and on. Therefore, I had better say, absolutely clearly, what I wanted to do, and the conditions under which I wanted to do it.'

It was having thus fashioned what David Norris calls a 'noose with which to hang himself', that Lee entered the meeting.

Proceedings commenced at 9 a.m. As the meeting was to be devoted solely to a review of strategy, it had been decided that head of sales, Guy East, and the executive in charge of production, Garth Thomas, neither of whom was a director, should attend. They brought to thirteen the number of people seated around the baize-covered table in the boardroom of the plush Wardour Street offices: Stoddart, in the chair, Attenborough, Chambers, Joll, Lee, Lieberson, Norris, Puttnam, White-head, Wooller, East, Thomas and the company secretary, Robert Finney. Only Angus Grossart and Peter Mayer were absent. The agenda, which had been deliberately structured to allow a wide-ranging debate, listed such broad topics as investment policy, management and decision-making, rate of return, capital requirements and cost structure. Five papers had previously been circulated: Lee's production-strategy review; an abstract of the 1986 financial objectives; and three short documents dealing with return on investment, capitalization and overheads. Philip Whitehead asked that television be added as a separate item for discussion.

On the following pages are long extracts from the minutes of the meeting. These minutes provide the only reliable account of an event that is not only a distant memory for most of its participants but that was so charged with emotion at the time, and so dramatic in its outcome, that it has subsequently proved vulnerable to imaginative, and inaccurate, recall. Few of those present now agree on what happened or who said what to whom, in what context and to what effect. Suffice to say that in every case the memory of the event serves to present the participant's own contribution in the best possible light.

The meeting seems to have fallen into four phases. The first, a dispassionate discussion of many of the strategic issues of the day, is described by David Norris as having been 'a kind of formal dance, a polite ritual'. The second, which dealt with a host of criticisms – put by the executive as well as the non-executive directors – of the Lee regime, is described by Lee as having been 'the most awful sort of rabble'. The two stages together took up three hours or so. Over that period the debate certainly became heated, but still the main point of contention – Lieberson's replacement as head of production – had not been broached.

'All through the morning it was like Alice in Wonderland,' says Norris. 'You were waiting and waiting and you knew that nobody was actually grasping it. I wasn't going to light the touchpaper. It was intriguing to see who would.'

The task fell to Puttnam, who, while trying to contain his remarks within the bounds of an impersonal discourse on management philosophy, could not help but launch a painful dissection of those shortcomings in Lee's character that made him, in the opinion of his colleagues, an unsuitable candidate for Lieberson's job. In this, Puttnam was backed up by Lieberson, Attenborough and, to a lesser degree, Norris and Chambers. This third stage took the proceedings through to the lunchtime adjournment. Lunch itself counts as the fourth, and most dramatic episode, in a traumatic day.

'It was an impossible meeting,' remembers Lee. 'There was no attempt whatsoever to impose any structure or rigour . . . The trouble is I don't think he [Stoddart] knew what was going to happen when he took the lid off. In effect, what I had been trying to hold together, under difficult conditions, and what I was sitting on top of, was a volcano. And he literally came in and used that meeting to open up the vent. And it just poured out on to the table. In the course of four hours, everybody's gripes – "We should never have made this film . . .", "If only somebody had listened to me . . .", "We shouldn't have gone into this business . . ." – just sort of welled up.'

Stoddart opened the meeting by addressing the points raised in the paper called 'Return on Investment'.

The paper . . . indicated a long-run rate of return of 8–10 per cent. The chairman considered this inadequate and suggested a number of options for the company's future structure or capitalization:
(i) apart from the £6 million rights issue, make no change in capitalization or overhead structure. The chairman considered this option impractical;
(ii) reduce overheads drastically (to a level covered by revenues from existing product) and invest Goldcrest capital in a broad spread of product, syndicating the vast majority of the investment in each project. It was pointed out that the inability to maintain leverage against third parties in the long-term limited the potential of this method of operation. This role of passive investor, along the lines of Goldcrest's investment partnerships in earlier years, was rejected as no longer constituting a viable option;
(iii) pursue a merger with Orion, along the lines discussed at the board's June meeting – this, too, might well be impractical. Mr Puttnam indicated that he felt committed to Warners: a Goldcrest merger with Orion would place in doubt the nature of his future relationship with Goldcrest;
(iv) seek a substantial capital injection from a non-City source – since it seemed to be unlikely that further City funds could be obtained at present.
It was argued that a high rate of return in the short to medium-term was a misguided objective and probably unobtainable. Goldcrest was building a valuable library of product which would continue to generate revenues for many years, but the company's balance sheet did not reflect this. Nevertheless, the chairman believed that City institutions were unlikely to invest further in the company until it had produced a proven record of profitability. Mr Lieberson believed that the nature of the business virtually precluded consistent profitability and suggested that the company aim for flotation in the United States, where he understood that this was considered less important than the UK.

Perhaps deciding that this discussion, focusing as it did on the company's future capitalization and cost structure, should have come last rather than first, Stoddart then changed tack, deciding that 'long-term strategic issues should be clearly distinguished from the immediate financial difficulties', and proposing that 'it might be constructive to examine the present difficulties' first. The ensuing, and much more lively, debate, which focused on 'a number of shortcomings in the management of the business and in decision-making procedures', and which seems to have involved almost everybody at the meeting, came to the following conclusions:

1. *Third party investment*
Syndication to unidentified third parties should never be relied upon: third-party

investment should be regarded as a desirable but not an essential objective. Mr Chambers stated that, in January 1985, the company's cash flow forecast had indicated that it could not fund both *Revolution* and *The Mission* within its proposed production programme without additional resources: in the event, the failure to complete third-party investments by June had been one of the major causes of the present cash flow difficulties. The attraction of the new Viking fund in Norway was its ability to commit finance at an early stage of development/pre-production. Such finance should not reduce the pressure on Goldcrest to select projects likely to generate an adequate investment return.

2. *Consultation*

Greater use should be made of the expertise of film-makers on the board: the consultative meetings between the executive board and Sir Richard Attenborough and David Puttnam, first proposed at the time of the 1985 reorganization, would be introduced. Consultation was particularly important before any production commitment was made.

3. *Board's authority*

The board should be more closely involved in the important business decisions, particularly in connection with the commitment of production finance.

Clear guidelines for the reference of decisions to the board were required. Concern was expressed specifically at the failure to raise with the board (i) the importance of third-party investment in *Revolution* and *The Mission*, and (ii) completion-guarantee arrangements.

4. *Production decision-making*

(a) Timing:

Pre-production had often been well-advanced, and on occasion principal photography had commenced, before detailed budgets, schedules, casting etc. had been in place. Consequently, many important decisions had been taken under extreme pressure, in the context of an already heavy financial commitment. This was particularly the case with *Revolution*, where it could be argued that Goldcrest was in effect drawn into the production on false assumptions about costs and profitability.

Goldcrest could not insist on all elements being in place before committing production finance, unless it became a passive investor like Cinema Group. Nevertheless, many key elements could and should be resolved in advance, so long as the company was prepared to incur potentially large development write-offs.

(b) Financial and other factors:

Because Goldcrest's exposure on each project was significant in relation to its total capital, individual investment decisions were often critical to the company's future. Such decisions, and the scheduling of the films concerned, should not be taken to fit short-run financial objectives, e.g. to fall in a release schedule designed to earn corporate profits in a particular year.

While success for any one project was never assured, Mr East believed it was possible to determine which projects had little or no potential. Mr Chambers argued that Goldcrest should avoid involvement in such projects, and not be drawn by speculative, extraneous benefits. The process of production finance decision-making and the factors relevant to the decisions were considered in the context of the commitment to the Enigma–Goldcrest–Warner three-film package (*Frog Prince, Mr Love* and *Knights & Emeralds*), which appeared to have caused some controversy among Goldcrest's executive directors.

(c) Structure and process:

In addition to a need for greater involvement of the board in production decision-making, substantial improvements in the decision-making structure and process were required at operating company level. Although problems were aired in discussion at management meetings, greater consensus and cohesion amongst executive directors was essential if the company was to function effectively.

5. *Net profit participation*

Net profit participations should never be relied upon to motivate talent towards corporate objectives: because few films generated significant net profits, such participations rarely persuaded talent to abandon individual objectives.

6. *Policy approach*

The policies with regard to film development, finance, production and distribution had been discussed by the board in fairly abstract terms. There was a need for the board to define detailed parameters within which the various decisions on individual productions should be taken.

7. *Communication*

The lack of effective communication among executive directors and between them and the board appeared to be one of the most severe problems in the company. It was questioned whether departments were too insular and respective responsibilities defined with sufficient clarity.

8. *People management*

The success of a film business was particularly dependent on the people employed in it, and the overall management of Goldcrest's team was severely criticized. The communication and demarcation problems referred to were partly responsible for this.

9. *Capital and cost structure*

It was doubted whether the scale of existing activity was sufficient to bear the present overhead structure. Changes in that structure, and strategies to increase the level of activity, should be considered.

Doubtless there are many useful lessons in all this for the budding film financier. Some of the observations, especially those of a general nature – e.g. never rely on unidentified third parties, make investment decisions according to no other criteria than the likely profitability of the projects in question, and don't look to profit participations to motivate talent towards corporate objectives – were indeed well made. But one does not have to be an apologist for Lee to realize that, in both substance and tone – detectable even through the soft-focus gauze of Robert Finney's minutes – others of these observations, especially the detailed criticisms, were selective and self-serving on the part of the board.

That 'greater use should be made of the expertise of film-makers on the board' was, in the circumstances, a redundant observation. Of the fifteen board meetings held since Lee took over from Eberts, Puttnam and Attenborough had each attended six. (Attenborough, in fact, had managed to attend only one of the last ten.) They had both been present at the same board meeting on only two occasions. In the entire period of their association with Goldcrest they had each spent at least as much time out of the country as in. Neither had been available at the time the production programme had been drawn up by Lieberson and Lee, and it is doubtful, given their self-imposed rule of never commenting on projects other than their own, that they would have had much to say about it if they had been. It is impossible to fathom how Lieberson, in the case of *Revolution*, was anyway supposed to consult Puttnam, who had been a sworn enemy of Hudson since they fell out over *Greystoke*, or Attenborough, who not only had a project, *Tom Paine*, that had had to be shelved the day that *Revolution* got the go-ahead, but who had even been offered a part in Hudson's film, without leaving them open to charges of conflict of interest.

That the board should now want to be 'more closely involved in the important business decisions', when the directors were every month presented with as complete a package of information on all the aspects of the company's affairs as they could wish for, stands, surely, as an indictment of their own feebleness rather than any supposed obstruction on the management's part. Attenborough, for example, confesses to having never read the September 1984 board papers, which contained all the information pertaining to the fateful decision to invest in the current slate of films. He even admits to having not read the papers for this very 18 July meeting. They were sent. He received them. He just didn't read them. He didn't have time. How many of the non-executive directors, one wonders, *did* read the board papers?

As for the supposed 'failure to raise with the board (i) the importance of third party investment . . . and (ii) completion guarantee arrangements', one has only to refer to the minutes, many of them already quoted here, at which these matters were discussed *ad nauseam*. The only significant decision that was made without the proper authorization of the board was the move from Holland Street to Wardour Street. In that case, as we have seen, there were extenuating circumstances, in that the board meeting at which the matter should have been discussed had been abandoned for want of a quorum. The directors had anyway been clearly warned of the move by letter three months before the event: had any of them wanted to, they could have intervened.

That 'many decisions had been taken under extreme pressure' was certainly true. But that the focus of this criticism should be on *Revolution*, rather than *The Mission*, was unfair. The only thing that had gone wrong with *Revolution* was that it had gone over budget. That cannot be counted a 'false assumption about cost', since it was always understood that staying on budget was going to be *Revolution*'s biggest problem. Nor did it have anything to do with the timing of decisions or even with the general calibre of management (Warner Bros.' experienced management had endured far worse with Hudson on *Greystoke*, and worse again with Winkler on *The Right Stuff*). Every increment in *Revolution*'s cost and every revision of its forecast profitability had been presented to the directors and, where appropriate, put to the vote. The single biggest increase in the film's budgeted cost, the casting of Pacino, was not decided upon by Winkler, or Hudson, or Lee, or even Lieberson, but by the full board. The two votes against were not Grossart's and Joll's, but Norris's and Chambers's. In the case of *The Mission*, on the other hand, the budget went up in stages and at each stage there was a high price to be paid for pulling out. About *The Mission* it could be said that the board had been 'drawn into the production on false assumptions about cost'.

There is no doubt that much of the blame for Goldcrest's problems can be laid at Lee's door. There is equally no doubt that the Goldcrest executives were ineffective in containing him, though whether this can be counted a criticism, since they were his subordinates, is open to question. But what is distressing about the 18 July meeting is that the finger of blame was pointed only at the management. There is nowhere a hint of self-criticism on the part of the non-executive directors. Nor, beyond a blushing 'Gosh, I've learnt my lesson and won't do that again,' was there any such hint in their later interviews. The board put Lee in, kept him in, ignored the numerous management protests about his policies and style of work, and then, when he ran the company into a corner, rounded on him and claimed to have been misinformed and stampeded into making wrong decisions.

'I have never in my whole life felt so incensed and so helpless at the same time, as sitting in that meeting,' Lee recalls. 'I had got used to controlling meetings, [and] therefore it was difficult to become a sideliner on the thing, which is what I was virtually turned into. To sit and listen to this and not be able to intervene was absolutely appalling.'

So the meeting moved towards stage three. First, however, Philip Whitehead's request, that television get a hearing, had to be dealt with. Wooller argued that the proposed reorganization of Goldcrest's television operation was 'ill considered and shortsighted' and he maintained that 'the poor financial performance of *The Far Pavilions* and television films was attributable to misguided attempts to exploit them theatrically'. The decision to pass distribution responsibility to Warners, he said, would be to 'forfeit' the 'long-term potential' of the catalogue. Lee, in reply, cited the dismal record of past television programming and pointed to the current difficulties that the company was experiencing 'in securing US commitments to *Robin of Sherwood, Cry Freedom* [not Richard Attenborough's Biko film, which was later entitled *Cry Freedom*, but a television documentary on the 1956 Hungarian uprising] and *Triads*'. He thus supported his argument 'that closer relationships were necessary in the US market'. The board was clearly of a mind to back Lee on this question, but nevertheless rapped him across the knuckles for his conduct in the matter.

There was widespread criticism of the handling of the resulting redundancies in the television department. Mr Whitehead had understood that no action would be taken in advance of the present meeting. Mr Lee explained that the remaining members of the board had approved the action in principle and, in view of the pressing need to reduce overhead expenditure, he had implemented the redundancies without delay. Discussion of this matter re-affirmed the board's conclusion as to the severity of the structural, management and communication problems in the company and it was considered that these must be tackled before further finance were sought.

Then, at last, the question of Lieberson's replacement as head of production was raised. By now the meeting had become heated and tense. The first to speak was Lee.

Mr Lee regretted Mr Lieberson's decision to become an independent producer instead of continuing as Goldcrest's chief of production. However, in his strategy review paper, Mr Lee proposed that no new chief of production be appointed when Mr Lieberson relinquished that post at the end of 1985. He advanced the following arguments in support of this proposal:
1. Goldcrest could not afford a new chief of production in addition to the costs of Mr Lieberson's independent producer's agreement – to finance a production department costing £500,000 per year required a significant increase in the rate of return on individual film projects;
2. There was no suitable candidate in the UK, and to secure a suitably experienced executive from the US would be prohibitively expensive;
3. Producers on Goldcrest projects should be clearly accountable to the company, but, he believed, the existence of a chief of production had interfered with this;
4. Goldcrest could be an effective production and sales organization if the following elements were in place:
    (a) *Source of product* – given Goldcrest's contacts with the best British film directors and producers, and the widespread awareness of its production capability and strong sales team, a chief of production was not required to attract and secure production opportunities;
    (b) *Production control* – the appointment of an experienced production

accountant to Goldcrest's staff would re-enforce Garth Thomas' effectiveness in monitoring and controlling production;

(c) *Sales team* – Goldcrest had a first class sales team and the necessary technical support staff;

5. With a small development team, and access to advice from experienced film-makers such as Sir Richard Attenborough and Messrs Puttnam and Lieberson, Goldcrest could analyse and progress projects to the production stage;

6. The director of business affairs should negotiate the key deals on individual productions, such as agreements with the producer, director and US distributor.

Puttnam, supported by Attenborough, Norris and Chambers, led the replies:

Several members of the board argued that this analysis ignored the personal element in relationships with individual film-makers. Producers and directors expected their contact with Goldcrest to be with an executive who (i) commanded respect; (ii) had substantial decision-making authority; (iii) had empathy with themselves as film makers; and (iv) would instinctively understand their problems. It was suggested that the chief of production should have sole responsibility for contact with film makers, and that his role was more crucial to the organization than that of the chief executive.

Lieberson then added his remarks, with, according to Stoddart, devastating effect:

Mr Lieberson stated that his decision to exercise his option to become an independent producer arose from fundamental philosophical differences between himself and Mr Lee as to the demarcation of their respective responsibilities. He believed that, primarily through the actions of Mr Lee, his responsibilities had been eroded and his authority curtailed and undermined: he specified several instances of this in connection with the *Revolution* project, which he believed had contributed significantly to subsequent difficulties with that production.

Lee could not let this pass. Many of the difficulties referred to, he said, 'were the result of misunderstandings arising from a lack of full and clear communication by Mr Lieberson to other members of Goldcrest's management team . . .'

In expressing this view Lee undoubtedly enjoyed the sympathy of many of those present. Lieberson was not much respected within Goldcrest. He was judged unpredictable ('quite frankly, on any two days of the week you would get totally different responses to the same question, in the same set of circumstances' – Norris); 'maddeningly' indecisive (Joll); 'unwilling to give clear instructions' (in-house solicitor Peter Coles); and so detached – never becoming one of the team, indeed never seeming fully to associate himself with Goldcrest at all – that his contributions at management meetings had the flavour of 'pronouncements' (Chambers), while on the board 'he just sat there and pontificated' (Stoddart).

'Sandy', says Norris, 'was a great fence-sitter, and didn't like to be the one who said, "Right, that's it, this is what we do." He would always "advise". "My advice to you would be . . .": it was always couched in those terms.'

The board, however, was in no mood to examine the shortcomings of anyone other than Lee: the order of the day, as by now everyone must have realized, was to secure his resignation.

Official minutes are, of course, no great guide to the emotional tenor of a meeting such as this. Nevertheless, one can fairly imagine the mood in the room. While Chambers talks of the 'furore' and Stoddart of 'vociferous argument', a more common assessment is well expressed by Puttnam's remark, made immediately after the meeting, that it had been 'odd but not hostile'. Adrenalin was pumping and the frustrations that had built up over fourteen months were loosed across the table, but Lee was humbled rather than trounced.

The minutes continue:

After further discussion the board concluded that it was essential to appoint someone to fulfil the role of head of production, almost irrespective of cost. However, the responsibility and authority attaching to the position needed to be clearly defined – especially as regards its relationship to the position of chief executive. The decision to appoint a new head of production would have significant implications for the group's capital structure and operations and appropriate account would have to be taken of these.

Mr Puttnam suggested that a head of production should have wide authority and discretion to run the production element of the business within overall financial parameters fixed at the outset; within these parameters he should be accountable only to the board.

Puttnam's insistence that not only should a head of production other than Lee be appointed, but that he or she should have, in effect, greater power than the chief executive, could hardly have been a more calculated provocation: there was no way that Lee could accept it.

The meeting now had to be called to a halt before things were said that would later be regretted. Fortunately, it was well past the time allocated for lunch, and Stoddart was able to declare an adjournment.

Sandwiches, bread and cheese, salads, wine and mineral water were served in the boardroom. There was little conversation: Norris recalls that lunch was eaten 'in a state of suspended animation', while Wooller remembers, 'there was nothing to say . . . we were all pretty shell-shocked'.

Stoddart and Lee withdrew to the latter's office. According to his own recollection, Lee said, ' "Look, this is absolutely a shambles. There is no way we can go on with this. The issues in my mind are absolutely clear now: you either want us to do this, to have the company run with me, in which case you have to do it my way – and now, I fear, having gone through this morning with my people, I'm going to have to make some changes – or you don't. But I cannot go on running this company and not being given sufficient hand to do it. And what I can't do" – and once again we were heading towards trying to raise some capital in the form of the emergency money – "is go to the City and say that I'm a graduate of the Harvard Business School and that we can apply disciplined management to an unruly industry and that's why [they] should have faith in us, when we've got this sort of shambles here. And, therefore, if you are going to expect me to raise the money in the City, it had better be done my way." '

Lee continues: 'So this ghastly conversation took place, and, not at all to my surprise, I was told that he wasn't in a position to give me that assurance then, and that the non-executive directors would have to be consulted – which was absolutely the correct procedure.'

The non-executive directors – Attenborough, Puttnam, Stoddart, Joll and Whitehead – withdrew to an adjacent office to have a conference of their own.

'There was no debate,' Attenborough recalls. 'There wasn't a single person who was prepared to advocate James staying. I mean, I think James got the feeling that the hatchets were reached for with delight and plunged into his back, but if he had given grounds for the retention of the status quo I don't think anybody would have been saying "James must go." But the fact that it was an ultimatum – he made it absolutely clear that we either accepted his management plan, which resulted in his being head of production as well as leader of the company, or he wasn't going to stay – I don't think anybody had any hesitation whatsoever.'

Joll remembers: 'It [had] become clear during the course of the meeting that something had to give. James said, "Either I have total control of production or it's not going to work." His executives were against him, and he saw it as him or them. And the thought of him, as it were, saying that he was going to do it all by himself, and that he didn't need any help, in the circumstances of having run out of money . . . for which he was clearly responsible – OK, John Chambers should have said "Over my dead body" or something, but James was clearly the responsible person – and for James to say, "It's either me or them." Well, Jesus, it had to be them. The idea of James running that business on his own, with Norris and Chambers and everyone else swept aside, didn't bear thinking about.'

Lee, meanwhile, had returned to the boardroom, there to put a question to his fellow executives.

'He said, "Look, I have had a hard time . . . It looks like I'm going to be asked to resign. Obviously there are problems with the company. The issue of the head of production, that is only part of the thing. But I want to get a feel from you guys as to whether you want me to stay or not," ' recalls Chambers. 'And he sort of went round the table on us.'

East confirms that Lee 'asked each executive, one by one, face to face, something like, "Do you have confidence in me to run Goldcrest?" Which meant that you had to categorically answer yes or no. I respected him for standing up and doing that.'

In Chambers's recollection only he and Norris were unequivocal in saying no. East thinks that, other than himself, everyone said no. It hardly matters, for as Chambers points out, 'it didn't make any difference what we thought at the end of the day. What mattered was what those guys in the other room were thinking.'

'Those guys' did not see fit to consult the executives at all.

Lee left the boardroom without, apparently, having made any decision. Stoddart emerged from the meeting of the non-executives, and the two men again conferred in Lee's office.

'James said to me, "Do you think I ought to resign?" ' Stoddart remembers. 'I said, "At the end of the day, you've got to. I really think you should." And James said, "Will you protect my position?" And I said, "I will protect it as long as it's fair." '

Lee then left the building, presumably to think over the matter on his own, while Stoddart returned to the boardroom and, without explanation, declared the meeting closed. The executives were, in Chambers's words, 'aghast and furious', for the issue of Lee's mooted resignation was left hanging in the air.

It was Attenborough, apparently, who at some point in the afternoon let it be known that Lee had tendered his resignation. The executives then 'sat there for hours afterwards', according to Chambers, 'just mulling things over', letting the adrenalin run down. 'There was a frank exchange of views between people – not in a personal, unpleasant way, but . . . laying everything open. It seemed like a good time to do it.'

It would seem that Stoddart had meanwhile consulted with Blakenham and Joll, and by telephone with the absent Grossart. He returned to Wardour Street later in the afternoon. He confirmed that Lee had offered his resignation, which had been accepted, and he asked the management team if they had any objection to Eberts being invited to take Lee's place. There being no such objection, he undertook to approach Eberts formally later in the day. In the meantime, and pending the drafting of a press release announcing Lee's departure, the executives were to say nothing.

Eberts: Our farm in Canada, on a hill overlooking Lake Massawippi on the border between Quebec and Vermont, had become increasingly important to me over the years, to the point that, by the early 1980s, I began to feel that it was our real home. We bought some horses and I decided to build a barn. I designed it myself and, with the help of a couple of local men, felled our own trees for the timber, laid the foundations, mixed the concrete and hammered in the nails. I was – I am – very proud of this barn.

On the afternoon of 18 July 1985, I was working in the barn. Whoever was helping that day was off on an errand somewhere and I was on my own. I was standing on a ladder fixing a roof truss. As usual, I carried a mobile telephone in my belt and, just as I was reaching up to nail the piece into place, the phone rang. Holding the truss now with one hand, I took the phone from my belt with the other. It was Michael Stoddart, calling me from the Savoy, where he was having dinner.

He told me that they had had a board meeting that day, that James had resigned and that they were eager to know whether I would be prepared to come back. He took pains to make it clear that this was not an informal enquiry, as his previous calls had been, but a formal invitation, sanctioned by the board and the management. My first reaction was not too enthusiastic, and he spent the best part of half an hour persuading me that not only was I the only person who could do the job, but that all my requirements about the degree of my commitment and so on, would be met. As I listened, the truss was getting heavier in my hand.

Finally I said, 'Well, it depends entirely on what you want me to do. In principle, I'm prepared to help, but I can't make any commitments which could conflict with my deals with Warner Bros. or with Allied.'

Michael, being a major prospective shareholder in Allied, assured me that he could see no problem: all we had to do was work out a contract that would suit all parties. So, under the combined weight of his arguments and the truss in my hand, I said, 'OK, the answer is "yes, if": yes I will come back, if the contractual obligations can all be met.'

I climbed down from the ladder, massaged my aching arm, and went to the house to tell Fiona the bad news. She thought I was crazy. I tried to reassure her, and myself, that it would be only a temporary job, until

Goldcrest was put back on an even keel, and it wouldn't even be full time. As I saw it, I only had to see the films finished, keep the bank happy and restore staff morale. After that, we'd see. Fiona wasn't convinced and, as I listened to her, neither was I. In fact, I wasn't at all sure why I had said yes to Michael Stoddart. I was flattered by his entreaties, of course. And I had a tremendously strong sentimental association with the company. But by any other yardstick I was crazy even to think about going back.

Ilott: Lee went home that night 'extraordinarily relieved'.

'I don't mean that I wanted out of it,' he explains, 'because to this day I loathe the fact that I'm not still there. But I felt relieved because I think any solution other than an outright "yes" would have been disastrous.'

Relieved he may have been, but his self-esteem had clearly suffered a tremendous blow. As Chambers recalls, when Lee came into the office the next morning, 'he was obviously pretty dazed'.

'I was actually with David [Norris] at the time,' Chambers recalls. 'James would usually come in and say hello, but he walked straight past us, looking over the left. I said to David, "We'd better go in and have a chat with him." We went into his office and sat down. He was very upset, chastened and subdued. I said, "Well, all we want to say is, I know we said some hard things yesterday, but it was nothing personal. It is just that we think this is the only way forward for the company." He said, "Well, you guys certainly didn't do me any favours." Then there was all this stuff about Puttnam. Puttnam was his great friend, and he was upset that Puttnam, whom he had championed all the way along, had turned against him at the end of the day. Then that was it. He cleaned out all his stuff, attended to a few last things and left.'

One of the 'few last things' Lee did before leaving was write the following letter to Chambers:

Dear John,

Goldcrest is a business. A company exists to make an acceptable return on investment for its shareholders – whether it works in the arts, the sciences or any other trade.

This company exists by making films. It makes profits from films by working in partnership with film-makers. Sometimes the relationship between the film-maker and the company rests on mutual interest. More often, the interests of the two are different.

The art of good management in any creative enterprise is to balance the creative interests with the financial – that is 'art' and 'brass'.

The man who runs Goldcrest must be very sensitive to both sets of interests, but at the end of the day it is the shareholders' interests that are paramount.

This is why I believe that Goldcrest needs both a chief executive and a head of production. The chief executive represents the financial interests, and, to a greater extent, the head of production represents the creative. In this way, the inevitable tensions between the two are represented by two separate individuals. The ultimate power rests with the individual who represents the shareholders' interests.

I believe that Goldcrest needs a head of production. I asked Sandy to stay and to continue to play that role. When he declined the only reason I decided not to replace him was in the interests of cost. Thus, our difference of opinions rests not on the question of whether or not there should be a head of production, but on the question of the extent of delegation to the head of production. The press release speaks of appointing a head of production 'with very considerable delegated responsibilities'. I disagree.

It is naive to imagine that there is a distinction between creative decisions, on the one hand, and business and financial decisions on the other. Every so called creative decision has a financial impact. Some more than others. It is for this reason I have insisted, and continue to insist, that the major decisions concerning any production are made by the chief executive and not the head of production. Sandy and I have had many debates and clashes over this, but he understands my point of view.

When the board decided that it was necessary to have a chief of production with considerable delegated responsibilities I resisted.

Such a serious step as my resignation must be based on a fundamental issue. There is no more fundamental issue than this.

I think Goldcrest was placed in a very strong position. If we had played our cards right the renaissance of the British film industry could have been assured. I now fear for the future, although I wish all of you well, and the best of luck.

Kind regards,

James

Lee was to receive compensation of £185,000 and the gift of his company car. The press release to which he refers in his letter was issued by the Goldcrest board at 5 p.m. that afternoon. It reads as follows:

Following the decision by Mr Sandy Lieberson to exercise the option in his contract to become an independent producer with effect from 1st January 1986, the board of Goldcrest Films and Television (Holdings) Limited has been reviewing the organizational structure of the business.

It is the unanimous opinion of the board, with the exception of Mr James Lee, the chief executive, that a new head of production should be appointed with very considerable delegated responsibilities.

Accordingly, Mr Lee has tendered his resignation to the board and it has been accepted with regret.

A further announcement will be made in due course.

The *Observer* ('Goldcrest Cash Blow'), the *Sunday Times* ('Why Lee Quit Goldcrest'), the *Financial Times* ('Resignation Increases Goldcrest

Uncertainty'), the *Hollywood Reporter* ('Lee Exits CEO Post of Goldcrest Films'), *Variety* ('Goldcrest Pix Chairman Lee Leaves Position') and *Screen International* ('Goldcrest Faces Difficult Future') had a field day. All reported the cash-flow crisis, the budget overruns, the closure of the television department (which, according to the mistaken view of many of the reports, had been the only profitable part of the company) and the clashes between Lieberson and Lee. *Screen International*, in a long and substantially accurate account of the differences between the board and Lee that had led to the latter's departure, strongly tipped Eberts to return as chief executive, adding, 'ironically, if Eberts does take the job he will certainly not want a head of production. He can do that job himself.'

Chapter Fifty-two

'How Could I Refuse?'

'We will soon be in a better position than at any time in the last two years.' – Sir Richard Attenborough, August 1985

Eberts: Six weeks elapsed between James's departure and my arrival in the Goldcrest offices. In that time, a lot of contradictions had to be resolved: between me, Allied, Warner Bros. and Goldcrest, as well as between me and my better judgement.

In the first place, I had very strong second thoughts about coming back. I had finalized the terms of my relationship with Warner Bros., I had firm commitments from the major Allied shareholders and I had verbal agreements with five or six of the film-makers with whom I hoped to be associated. In addition, I had money in the bank. Everything, in other words, was looking good: why spoil it by immersing myself in the Goldcrest cauldron? In the second place, everyone I spoke to advised me against it. Irene Lyons, my long-time personal assistant, wrote a memo to the effect that if I went back I would be doing no favours to anybody, least of all myself. She did not openly threaten to resign, but I could read between the lines that at the first sign of trouble that was exactly what she would do. My friend and unofficial career counsellor Marty Baum said to me, 'Don't do it, because you can't win: if it goes under you'll be blamed, and if it succeeds you won't be given the credit for it.' His was a very cut-and-dried Hollywood-agent view that took no account of loyalties, personal ties or pride. But that doesn't mean it was wrong. It was a view that was echoed by all my friends in the business, with the exception, of course, of my former colleagues at Goldcrest.

I had long conversations with Dickie, David Puttnam, David Norris, John Chambers and Angus Grossart, in which I expressed my doubts and they sought to persuade me that there were no obstacles to my return that couldn't easily be surmounted. I did not want to work full time? – no problem, they'd made it part time. I did not want to run the business day to day? – leave it to Norris and Chambers. I would want to return to Allied just as soon as Goldcrest had weathered the storm? – they would settle for a short-term contract.

The most persuasive of them, of course, was Dickie. He played on my deeper feelings. Goldcrest was my baby, after all. I had spent seven years of my life building it up and I was proud of it. It was important to me. I knew that we had a lot of luck, but I also knew that we had used that luck to our best advantage. I just couldn't imagine all that effort going down the drain. Dickie teased all these emotions to the surface. He knew, too, that I still had good relationships with the Goldcrest shareholders (Pearson, Electra and Noble Grossart had always behaved well, and I was personally on excellent terms with Michael Stoddart and Angus Grossart, while enjoying cordial, if not so close, relationships with Michael Blakenham and James Joll) and he was able to contrast that with the situation that I had left behind at Embassy.

Furthermore, Dickie was full of an irresistible sense of mission: to save Goldcrest, to save the British film industry, to save all that we held dear, to make the world a better place for our children, etc. He tends to see things in rather grand terms. He cajoled, encouraged, pleaded, begged, reasoned, exhorted and flattered me, while, at the same time, imploring me to consider the damage that would be done if I didn't come back and Goldcrest went under. If we didn't save the company, he and I, there would soon be no British film business left.

How could I refuse? Dickie had created the greatest success of my career, *Gandhi*, and he was the man I felt close to above all the others at Goldcrest. When someone you like that much asks you to do them a favour, you do it. You don't ask yourself why.

I had no idea, and Dickie had no idea, just how bad the problems were. Not a clue. I thought that it was going to be a part-time job, leaving plenty of time for Allied. That's how I sold it to the Allied shareholders and to Warner Bros., both of whom could reasonably have expected me to honour my obligations to them to the exclusion of all else.

Terry Semel was very relaxed about it. He already thought of Goldcrest as his European production arm and he wanted to see the situation stabilized and *Revolution* and *The Mission* finished. I don't think he ever anticipated any serious problem about my working for Goldcrest as well as for Allied; indeed, he probably saw advantages to it. More than that, he is a very understanding man. He recognizes, and respects, passion and commitment.

I had a much tougher time, however, with the Allied shareholders.

They were not at all happy about my going back to Goldcrest. It took weeks of negotiation before finally we settled on a formula whereby, in exchange for sharing my services with Goldcrest, Allied and I would have options to buy 10 per cent of Goldcrest's equity at 65 pence a share. This was 15 pence more than the conversion price of the loan stock but it still represented a 35 per cent discount on the value of the shares the last time capital was raised. It indicated, incidentally, that we valued the company at roughly £25 million – i.e. we expected a write-off of about £6 million to add to the £3.9 million accumulated losses from previous years. In fact, Dickie, who, shortly after James's resignation, had very generously agreed to become chairman of the operating company in order to provide temporary leadership, had his own accountants go through the books with John Chambers. He wanted to be assured that he wasn't going to preside over a débâcle. His accountants had come to much the same conclusion as we had: that Goldcrest would have to write off £6–8 million, most of it unrecovered expenditure in television, the low-budget films and budget overruns on *Revolution* and *Absolute Beginners*. The figures did not include bank interest charges, nor did we have any way of telling how successful or otherwise the three big films were going to be, or even how much money would be needed to complete them, but we were satisfied that the estimate was fairly reliable.

A £6 million write-off would value the company at about 75 pence a share. From Allied's point of view, therefore, the 65-pence options, although they could not be exercised until March 1987, represented a reasonable inducement. Furthermore, I was able to persuade the Allied shareholders that there was considerable synergy between the two companies, Allied having the projects and film-makers and Goldcrest having the foreign sales, production and back-office expertise. And both, of course, had very close relationships with Warner Bros.

But I had no sooner secured Allied and Warners' co-operation, than John Chambers, David Norris and the Goldcrest board decided that they were not happy after all. They could not come to terms with what they perceived to be a conflict of interest between Allied and Goldcrest. Indeed, having begged me to come back, and knowing that I was already committed to Allied and Warners, Goldcrest put all manner of obstacles in the path of reaching an agreement. It was very frustrating, especially as we wasted an awful lot of time talking about my deal and the Allied–Goldcrest relationship when we should have been tackling the problems of the company.

Ilott: Whether or not they should have devoted so much time and energy to the question, the Goldcrest board did have genuine reason to be worried that the Allied tail, as they saw it, might end up wagging the Goldcrest dog. At two late-night meetings in the week following Lee's resignation, fears were expressed that the proposal, put by Eberts, that Goldcrest should cease development activity altogether and leave the choice and packaging of projects to Allied – a re-working of the plan that he had first put to Lee back in April – would make the company dependent on Allied long after its present financial troubles had been overcome. Consequently, the board passed a resolution that Goldcrest 'must continue to be a creative organization with the capacity to provide seed money and be involved at all stages of development and pre-production'. That resolution, however, guaranteed that there would be a conflict of interest between Allied, the sole business of which was development and packaging, and Goldcrest. Both companies were to be headed by Eberts, but which one of them would have prior claim to develop, for example, Richard Attenborough's next production, *Cry Freedom*? Attenborough had been one of the first film-makers to reach agreement with Allied, which stood to earn substantial fees and profit participations were it to develop and package the project. But Attenborough was equally keen that Goldcrest should have a stake in it. When he discussed the film with Eberts was he talking to Eberts/Allied or to Eberts/Goldcrest? As long as Allied and Goldcrest were deemed to be working in the same field, such conflicts of interest were bound to arise, and the attempts to find a formula that would avoid, or accommodate, them dogged the settlement of Eberts's contract.

Peter Mayer, a non-executive director of Goldcrest, suggested that the two companies could share the development function, but it was pointed out that it would be invidious for either to have to invest in the other's projects, and more invidious still for the one to have to submit its choices to the other for approval. David Norris proposed, instead, that Eberts should produce a list of film-makers with whom he would have reached agreement by 31 December 1985. All projects produced by or associated with these film-makers, for an initial period of, say, twelve months, would be Allied's. The rest would be open to joint development, according to the wishes of the respective parties. Eberts, reluctantly, agreed to draw up such a list.

Similar anxieties arose concerning the allocation of Eberts's time between Goldcrest and Allied. About this, nothing concrete could be done, beyond saying that he would devote as much effort to each company as proved necessary for the proper conduct of its affairs. As a rule of thumb, it was understood that this would require him to give not less than 60 per cent of his time to Goldcrest, at least for the first year. (In the event, for the first nine months at least he was to work non-stop for Goldcrest.)

The board also wanted assurances that Eberts would protect the company's strategic position: that he would steer a course that would not only see Goldcrest through its present troubles but would leave it equipped to carry on its development, production and distribution activities in the future. Again, there was little that could be done about this, beyond agreeing with Stoddart's suggestion that Eberts should have a free hand in the first year, and that any policy directives, other than the stated intention of spreading Goldcrest's risks 'through limited investments in many productions and occasional distribution pick-ups', and working 'exclusively with film-makers of proven talent', would await a strategy review in the autumn of 1986.

The protracted discussion of these questions undoubtedly caused irritation and inconvenience to Eberts and Allied, who, after all, had not sought to be put in this position. But such a discussion was perfectly proper, the more so as the Goldcrest board was now acutely conscious of its poor record in protecting the interests of its shareholders.

Eberts: It may have been perfectly proper, but it was not appropriate at that time and it drove me nuts. Allied Filmmakers was set up in order to provide development financing for a limited number of film-makers: ten, maybe fifteen. Those film-makers naturally consisted largely of people with whom I had done business while I was at Goldcrest. They were the people I knew best. That was why I offered a deal to Goldcrest in the first place when I went to see James. As far as I could see, far from there being a conflict of interest, there was an identity of interests. The Goldcrest board, however, wanted to have an iron-clad guarantee that there was no way that Allied could benefit from a relationship that I had developed, or was likely to develop, while working for Goldcrest. There was a sneaking feeling that I would run off with the crown jewels. It was crazy. There were no crown jewels. It was punitive towards Allied while not the least helpful to Goldcrest. They imposed upon me a list of people for whose services Goldcrest would not compete with Allied. Anyone else was supposed to be fair game for the two companies equally. All this at a time when Goldcrest had less than no money and was in no position to compete for talent with anybody. They kept talking about 'when Goldcrest gets back on its feet again', thinking that within twelve months the company would be flush with cash and back in the business of developing and producing pictures, and that if I had already snapped up all the best film-makers under the Allied umbrella there would be no one left for Goldcrest to work with.

Such a problem existed only in theory. A conflict of interest could not be said to exist unless Goldcrest had the money to put up, had the talent within the company actually to develop and package projects, and had found film-makers who would rather work with Goldcrest than with Allied. None of these criteria could be met.

For three months, the question of conflicts of interest occupied more time and effort on the part of board members, lawyers, myself and the shareholders of Allied than did the business of getting Goldcrest out of the hole. What aggravated me most of all was that the Goldcrest directors were very anxious to have me run the company but they did not want to accommodate any of the problems associated with my other, and prior, commitments. Indeed, at times they were in danger of overlooking the great advantage that Goldcrest, a penniless bureaucracy, would gain from its association with Allied, a freshly capitalized development fund that could provide a stream of product to feed into the Goldcrest sales machine. At one point I said, 'Gentlemen, since you're so concerned about the disadvantages of appointing me, it may be better that we drop the whole idea. I'll step down. But you should know that in my opinion there is no conflict. I'm an honest man. You're honest men. If a problem arises, we'll talk about it. Let's not get our knickers in a twist about devising a cast-iron, problem-proof contract. It doesn't exist. All we're doing is wasting precious time, when what we should be doing is concentrating on how to keep the company alive.' This constant wrangling by the board over non-substantive issues should have given me a better understanding of how the company got into the mess it was in – and the problems I was to encounter convincing the same board how to get out of it.

I did, nevertheless, provide the list of Allied film-makers as requested. It included Richard Attenborough, Alan Marshall, Alan Parker, John Boorman, Roland Joffe, Michael Douglas, Peter Weir, Bill Forsyth, Jerome Hellman, Sean Connery, Michael Apted, Hugh Hudson, Pat O'Connor, Peter Yates and Iain Smith. None of the proposed relationships, whereby Allied would pay for script development and, if necessary, contribute to the film-makers' overheads, was to be exclusive – it was only between Allied and Goldcrest that a prior claim of access had to be laid down, and even that, of course, was subject to the film-maker's preference.

There was a huge fuss that my list was so long. This led to more arguments. Eventually a final list, agreed between the shareholders of

Allied and Goldcrest, was drawn up. It excluded Apted, Smith and O'Connor but added Alan Pakula, giving thirteen film-makers in total. A time limit, to 1 June 1986, was imposed on Allied's prior access to their services. (It has to be said that, for all the hours of talk, the thousands of pounds of legal fees and the ill-feeling generated by this discussion, the question of conflict of interest arose only once, when David Puttnam objected to the inclusion of Roland Joffe's name on the list on the ground that he had already reached an understanding with the director for a film called *The Manhattan Project*. I said that I could see no problem; that if David and Roland wanted to make the film with Goldcrest and Warner Bros. that was fine by me. In the event, neither Puttnam, Goldcrest, Warners nor Allied had anything further to do with the project, which was renamed *Fat Man and Little Boy* and produced by Paramount.)

Other conditions to which I agreed were that, in my capacity as chief executive, I would not vote on any investment proposal involving an Allied project, and that Goldcrest would have the right to invest in any Allied project not fully financed by Warner Bros.

My salary was sufficient to be serious, yet modest enough to indicate that my commitment was neither full time nor permanent. In addition, Goldcrest provided me with office space for Allied, a car and medical insurance. I had access to the usual office services but paid my own secretarial help. In fact, my secretary was employed by Allied, not Goldcrest, even though she worked on behalf of both companies. My expenses were to be divided between Warner Bros., which covered the bulk of my Allied overheads, and Goldcrest, which paid only those travel expenses directly related to Goldcrest business.

Since I was in fact to work for Goldcrest full time, and since my non-travel expenses were to come to considerably more than my annual salary, Goldcrest had, in effect, secured my services for nothing. The true upside for me was my allocation – 70 per cent – of the stock options granted to Allied. If the value of Goldcrest stayed at about 75 pence a share, then, provided that I had the cash to exercise my options, and could find a buyer once those options had been converted – all of which was hedged about with detailed conditions and provisos – I could make a paper profit of up to £270,000. If the share price increased to 85 pence, I could make a paper profit of up to £500,000. Thus, if I succeeded in shepherding Goldcrest through its present troubles, and if the three big films currently in production and post-production performed well, and if I so managed things thereafter that the company was well placed to make fresh investments in the future, then I would do very well. And so would the Goldcrest shareholders. These were big 'ifs', of course, but it was just such a performance-related package that I wanted. I was not coming back to Goldcrest as a career executive but as a short-term company doctor whose reward had to be based upon results. It should be noted, while on this subject, that Dickie and David Puttnam generously surrendered half their own share options to facilitate these arrangements.

The remaining sticking-point was how long I would stay. They wanted me to commit to two years. I wanted to commit to one year. We made a compromise: eighteen months. I was not wild about staying for eighteen months. I hadn't even been wild about the prospect of staying for twelve months. But I was persuaded that it would take six months to find out what the problems were and twelve months to put them right – if they could be put right. So the contract was to run to 1 March 1987.

Before making a final commitment, I had to view the films in production and visit the Midland Bank.

I saw *Revolution* first, on an editing machine rather than a big screen, which was unfortunate. I did not see any dramatic scenes involving the principal actors. All I saw was action sequences, and they looked very good. I then went out to Shepperton and saw the opening sequence of *Absolute Beginners*, which was well shot and looked encouraging. I went on to the set and said hello to a few people, had a chat with David Bowie and gleaned what I could about the state of the production. The news regarding the budget was not encouraging. I saw about an hour's footage of *The Mission* last and thought it by far the best. I sent David Puttnam a telegram saying, 'Thank you for saving Goldcrest.' It wasn't meant entirely seriously but the remark stuck, and was to become something of a burden to both David Puttnam and Roland Joffe later on.

Then there were *Knights and Emeralds*, *Mr Love*, *The Frog Prince*, *Smooth Talk*, *Dance With a Stranger* and *A Room With a View*. The first three were completely unsuitable for the world theatrical markets and made no money at all. Two of them were never even released. They were television movies. *Smooth Talk*, on the other hand, was a bit of a sleeper. Not much was expected of this film, and there was little fuss when it opened, but it actually went on to do quite well. We made about £120,000 from the film – not enough, unfortunately, to make any difference to our cash flow.

I had turned down *Dance With a Stranger* before I left Goldcrest in 1983. The finished product, I am glad to say, was a very good film, but, like *Smooth Talk*, much too small to make any impact on our finances. We had invested only £250,000 and made a profit of about £100,000. That £100,000 did not arrive all at once in the form of a big cheque. Being mostly comprised of our net-profit share, it was paid out only after the film had reached break-even and then in dribs and drabs. By September 1987, for example, our cash surplus on the film had reached only £32,000.

I had been completely wrong about *A Room With a View* on several occasions. The project had been brought to me before I left Goldcrest and I had turned it down, not once but twice. Even when I saw the finished film, at its opening in New York, I thought it had no chance commercially. In fact, it was to take about $12 million rentals in the US – a remarkable figure for a film that had cost £2.3 million. *The Killing Fields*, by way of comparison, had cost £11 million and had taken $16 million US rentals. But our share of *A Room With a View*, like our share of *Dance With a Stranger*, was quite small – we put up £475,000 – and our eventual return, £1.4 million, while representing a handsome rate of profit, was again just not a big enough sum to make an impact on our cash flow. The film's main benefit to us was that it added lustre to our name, helped to maintain our high profile in the foreign markets and, not least, earned us some welcome sales commissions.

My overall assessment of the slate of films, then, was fairly positive. The big ones seemed OK, the small ones didn't much matter. Certainly I could see no cause for despondency.

The bank visit, too, was reassuring. While Ted Harris and Mike Massey were clearly very anxious, they had decided that it was in their best interest to keep the company afloat, at least until either the major films had been released and the production costs recouped or another bank syndicate had taken over the debt burden. Accordingly, they had agreed to increase the line of credit from £10 to £12 million. They were, as John Chambers and Andy Parsons would confirm, very co-operative and helpful to us.

Ilott: Eberts's return to Goldcrest was announced on 13 August. The press, as well as the Goldcrest staff, greeted him almost as a redeemer. Indeed, his earlier regime, lauded to the skies at the time, now began to assume Camelot-like status: a golden age to contrast with the Lee administration, upon which was heaped all the blame for the company's present problems. Eberts himself was aware of the dangers inherent in all this – the expectations being attached to his appointment, both inside and outside the company, were in many cases wholly unrealistic – and in interviews given to the *Sunday Times, Screen International* and the *Financial Times*, among others, he was careful not to knock Lee and not to make predictions.

Chapter Fifty-three

Picking up the Pieces

Eberts: I called a meeting of the staff on my first full day back in the office. Morale had hit a low point at the time of James's resignation and I think everyone was just greatly relieved that someone was coming in to take over. Anyone would have been welcome. I reassured them that I had seen the footage of the films, that I had talked to the bank and that I was hopeful that the company would eventually emerge in good shape. I had to warn them, however, that in the short term costs would have to be cut and that would undoubtedly entail redundancies. What I said was not news – the staff did not need me to tell them that the company was in trouble – and it was accepted with good humour. In fact, I would say that the mood among the employees at that time was determined and optimistic. Among the senior executives, which in effect meant John Chambers and David Norris, the mood was very upbeat. It was as if James's resignation had been some kind of catharsis.

My first days in the office were practically round the clock. It was night and day, catching up, talking to the bank, shareholders, management and individual members of staff. Meeting followed meeting followed meeting. I studied reams of paper. John Chambers, David Norris, Andy Parsons, Sandy Lieberson, Garth Thomas and Guy East briefed me about their respective areas in detail. After about three weeks of this immersion in the world of Goldcrest, I was forced to concede that the situation was rather worse than I had thought.

In particular, the big films were not as promising, and were plagued by many more problems, than I had realized. My first priority was to get them finished, as quickly and as cheaply as possible, in order to meet the contracted delivery dates.

Absolute Beginners was weeks behind schedule. It was amateurland. The production team didn't know what they were doing. There was no way that we could begin to plan the post-production schedule, let alone think about delivering the picture on the due date of 30 January 1986,. because the whole project was out of control.

The picture had had problems from the beginning, with overcosts in set-building and costumes. At 160 pages, the script was far too long. They seemed to be cutting it while they were going along. Then they came up against the atrocious summer weather, which entailed a lot of rescheduling, which in turn did not help to calm the already high state of tension that existed between various members of the production team. Julien Temple was going one way, Steve Woolley and Chris Brown another, while David Wimbury and Garth Thomas were straining at the reins trying to keep the film on the right track.

The production had got into really serious difficulties in the period between James's departure and my arrival. The budget had been drawn up when the pound stood at $1.06, which meant that the $2.5 million contract with Orion covered about 40 per cent of the estimated costs, with foreign-sales contracts covering another 50 per cent. During the course of filming, however, the pound went from $1.06 to $1.56, thereby reducing Orion's contribution, which wasn't payable until the film was delivered, to something less than 30 per cent. So instead of 90 per cent of the cost being covered by the Orion deal and foreign pre-sales, the proportion went down steadily towards 60 per cent. Then, in mid-July, it was realized that the picture was seriously over budget: by the time I got there it was about £1.4 million over, giving us a final projected cost of at least £7.6 million. The film would have to perform outstandingly at the box office for it to cover the gap. On top of all that, our co-guarantors, Entertainment Completions Inc., refused to pay their share of the overcost. They claimed that the picture had gone over budget only because of what they called 'enhancements' – changes to the script, schedule or other costs that we had approved. This was not true.

Every week the estimated final cost of the picture went up – it eventually came in at £8.4 million, which, being an overage of about 30 per cent, put it ahead of even *Revolution*, the overage of which was about 20 per cent – and every week the likely delivery date receded further into the distance.

Temple, Woolley and Brown were still shooting, building sets they hadn't originally planned to build, adding musical numbers they hadn't originally planned to shoot, not realizing that they had already shot so much footage that they were likely to end up with a three-and-a-half or four-hour first assembly for a film which was supposed to run to two hours maximum. Every film has to be cut, but you shouldn't have to cut whole sequences. You shouldn't shoot sequences that you'll never use.

If each day costs $100,000 and you are five weeks over, you are talking about $2.5 million in additional shooting costs. It is a complete waste of money if you then have to cut out large chunks of that material. A lot of footage was shot that never appeared on the screen. Hugh Hudson, who was roundly criticized for being profligate on *Revolution*, did not shoot anything that wasn't used. The first assembly of *Revolution* came out at about ten minutes longer than the final cut.

So we were in deep trouble on *Absolute Beginners*. The currency risk wasn't covered, costs had soared and we were on the line for the completion guarantee. No one on the Goldcrest staff, not even Garth Thomas, who had the *Revolution* post-production to attend to at the same time, seemed able to grab hold of this film and wrench it around in order to deliver a product which was akin to the film promised to our distributors. It was our contractual right, once the film was over schedule and over budget, to protect our position in whatever manner we thought fit. So I decided that we were going to have to bring in our own man. That man was Alan Marshall.

Alan Marshall is probably the best production person in the business. He is very experienced, very tough and very shrewd, artistically as well as commercially. He has made films in all kinds of circumstances, in the UK, in the US, in Third World countries, on location and in the studio, and in every case the production has been tightly controlled. If anyone can bring a wayward film back into line, he can. Moreover, he started life as an editor and the main problem on *Absolute Beginners* was not now in the shooting, which was almost finished, but in making sense of the mess of footage.

So I prevailed upon Alan, using the pressure of old friendship, to give us a hand. Together we viewed a three-hour assembly one afternoon in a screening room just off Soho Square. He came out shaking his head. But, I think out of loyalty to Goldcrest – we had, after all, put up the money for *Another Country*, which was a very successful and personally satisfying picture for him – he agreed to do it. It was a generous gesture on his part, because whatever he did with *Absolute Beginners* it was not going to emerge as any kind of masterpiece and it was unlikely to add any lustre to his reputation.

I agreed to pay him £50,000. There were objections on the part of members of the Goldcrest staff, and more especially on the part of the production team, because I was eventually going to charge that fee to the budget of the film. But I couldn't waste time on contractual niceties at that stage. We were in terrible shape, there were thousands of feet of excess footage and the film looked likely to run to about four hours. Given the problems, £50,000 was cheap.

The production team undoubtedly suffered bruised egos when Alan was first appointed, but they quickly got used to the idea. Although my decision was cut and dried – it was not a matter for discussion – it was not implemented in an unfriendly way.

Alan hired a couple of editors. For about six weeks they slaved away. Every week I would go and look at the footage, and every week I could see some improvement. But there was no way we were going to be able to deliver a commercial picture. The film-makers had made many mistakes and rudimentary aspects of film-making, such as continuity, had been disregarded. But the real problem was the lack of a storyline. There were bits and pieces. There were vignettes. There were individual scenes. There were touches of music and touches of action, some of it wonderfully shot. But there was no story to hold all the pieces together. That was not Julien Temple's fault directly. It was the script's fault – it just wasn't coherent, and responsibility for that must be shared between the production team, Virgin, Orion and Goldcrest. Furthermore the acting was lamentable. I don't think I have ever seen worse acting in a major British film.

There was nothing in the picture to which you could attach hope. You couldn't say, 'Yes, it's terrible, but it has great music', or 'Yes, but it's got wonderful performances', or 'Yes, but you really care about the characters', or 'Yes, but there's some great dance numbers'. The music, the performances, the characters and the dance numbers added up to one of the least attractive films of the decade.

As for the once loudly trumpeted notion of boldly breaking the rules and making a picture that the kids would flock to, that was just a lot of hot air. Anyone who believed all that was either vain or naive. The reality was that Alan Marshall had a terrible struggle just to put together something that resembled a feature film.

The worst part for me was that I had to lie through my teeth about what I thought of it. I had to say to the staff, to the press, to anyone who asked, 'I think we have a great film here.' What else could I say? You kill a film stone dead if you tell people it's bad. You have to talk it up, give it a chance. You justify this to yourself easily enough by saying, 'Well, maybe I'm wrong. Maybe the kids will love it. Maybe I'm out of touch, or too old, or just can't see it. Maybe I've got no taste at all.' You have been wrong before. Over the years I had turned down several projects which later proved to be successful movies. But in my heart of hearts I knew that we did not have a great film here. We had a turkey.

And while I could lie to the press, and lie to the staff, and even lie to Alan Marshall, I could not lie to our partners. I certainly could not lie to Orion, who, the minute they saw the picture, would know exactly how bad it was. So I kept them away from it, and when Mike Medavoy (Orion's head of production) asked me, I would say, 'Well, I must confess that I've seen the footage and I'm not able to tell you whether the film's good or bad. It's certainly not in the kind of shape that I'd like to show you now.'

One reason for hiding it from them was that, as they were going to see it anyway, it was as well to wait for the best possible version to be available. Another was that we were in danger of missing the delivery date. If a distributor wants to stick to the letter of a contract, he can refuse to accept a film that is late. And while this is a rare occurrence, it is much more likely to happen if they have seen the film in question and decided they don't want it. This was a real consideration in the case of both *Revolution* and *Absolute Beginners*.

On *Revolution*, I didn't doubt that Warner Bros. would pay up, because they had played a fairly significant role in the scripting and casting of the picture. Furthermore, we had a very close relationship with them. I could get down on my knees to Terry Semel and say, 'Terry, don't do this to us', and he wouldn't do it. But there were plenty of foreign distributors to whom we were not so close.

In the case of *Absolute Beginners*, I had severe doubts. While Orion didn't have much at stake in *Absolute Beginners* the company desperately needed to be associated with successes rather than failures. If I had been Orion, and I had seen this picture, and if the picture had not met the delivery date, I would have been sorely tempted to refuse it. As for the foreign markets, I told Guy East that I did not want to stick any of our regular distributors with a picture that was unreleasable. If we couldn't deliver a first-class film then we shouldn't force it on them, not if we were going to be in business for years to come. (In fact, none of our customers reneged. One of them even thought *Absolute Beginners* was quite good.)

At the end of the day, and despite all the efforts of Alan Marshall and his team, the film was not only late but so bad that it made me squirm. My one hope was that my kids would like it. I brought home a video copy of the first cut, which had everything on it except the title song. (That song, in my opinion, was the only good feature of the whole film.) Now, my kids will watch anything, but they couldn't watch this. Nor could their friends.

The major problems on *Revolution* were all over by the time I arrived back. The picture had finished shooting and they were in post-production. There were no great difficulties in assembling or cutting the material, except that the editors might have to deal with eleven or twelve near-identical takes of the same scene. But there were two other problems which did bear directly on the editors' work. The first was that the film needed a stronger dramatic line, and Hugh toyed with the idea of adding narration to clarify the action and to give context to the relationship between Kinski and Pacino. His plans, however, fell foul both of Warners' opposition – they thought it was a lousy idea – and of the second problem, which was to get the film finished in time for a pre-Christmas release.

The big debate within Goldcrest was, 'Should we continue at this hell-for-leather speed to finish the picture, or should we lay off and give the film-makers six more months to work on it?' I think everyone now realized that it had been nonsense to start a picture of this size in March with the expectation of delivery by early December. To start any picture in March for delivery in December is nearly impossible under the best of circumstances. And these had been far from the best of circumstances. By comparison, *The Mission*, which started four weeks after *Revolution*, was not delivered until 30 June 1986.

But while Hugh was concerned about the coherence of the story, neither he nor Irwin was remotely interested in taking more time. They wanted to finish the picture, perhaps because they were just tired of it and wanted to get it out of their hair, or because they wanted to make sure it qualified for the Oscars, or because they felt they had a commitment to Warner Bros. which they could not break. Whatever the reason, they did not want to prolong the post-production period.

My own view was that there was nothing to be gained by delay. I did not think that the film could be improved in any particular way. There was no footage on the floor that could be put back in. Hugh had shot what was in the script, and if the script was incoherent it was a bit late to be tinkering with it now. Only Sandy Lieberson, who constantly counselled delay, felt that the film could be improved. It seemed to me that Sandy was simply unaware of what the picture looked like. I think you can always say that by delaying you can get a better cut, or a better score, or a better whatever it is that you want to get. But there has to be the possibility of a really quite significant improvement to justify that kind of delay. No such thing was in prospect in this case.

So the consensus was that the sooner it was finished the better. We put teams of editors and assistants on it, adding further to the cost, and they worked night and day to produce a cut that we could show to Warner Bros.

The result was not great. You could not avoid the fact that the picture had no story and there was no relationship between the two leads. But at this stage there was still no score and no sound effects: no booming cannons, no clashes and screams in battle. It just had the wild track, the sound actually recorded on the set. So there was no way I could really feel the emotion of it. I thought that once the dubbed and mixed soundtrack had been added the picture would be much better. My view was shared by Warner Bros., to whom we screened the assembly in New York a few weeks later. They felt that it wasn't so bad, and that a big sound track would greatly enhance it.

There were also two or three key sequences which still had not been edited. One of them was an awful scene between Pacino and his son, when the boy's feet are being cauterized. Others were scenes between Pacino and Kinski. And they had not yet decided the order of the scenes at the beginning of the picture: they were experimenting with various assemblies that would either increase or decrease the importance of the relationship between Kinski and Pacino.

So all these things remained to be done, and we were optimistically saying, 'Well, it's not so good now, but when the score's added and the effects, and the opening sequences are sorted out, and the big emotional scenes between Pacino and Kinski are added, it'll be much better.' To our astonishment, when all this was accomplished the finished film was worse. The picture fell completely flat.

The only thing that saved *Revolution* was that it was spectacular to look at and some of the battle scenes were breathtaking. Also, I felt that in foreign territories it might not play too badly. The one thing I couldn't stand was Al Pacino's accent, and the mixture of accents between Pacino, Sutherland and Kinski. When the film was dubbed into Spanish, Italian or German then at least the accents would be consistent and some of the dialogue might be easier to hear.

The Mission was still shooting in Argentina when I arrived back at Goldcrest, and I did not see or talk to David Puttnam or Roland Joffe until some weeks later. But they had sent to London a two-hour assembly. It didn't include any of the waterfall sequences, which were very spectacular, but it was beautifully shot and beautifully acted. My doubts about it centred, as in the case of *Absolute Beginners* and *Revolution*, on the script. It just wasn't coherent. Even today, after I have seen the film maybe six or eight times in its final form, I still don't feel that it is absolutely clear what is going on. Most people do not know, after seeing the picture once, what it is all about. They cannot explain to you in simple terms what the story is. To me, that meant problems at the box office. My second reaction was that Robert De Niro was out of place. He is a wonderful actor, but I don't think you can put an actor like that, who has always played contemporary roles, into a situation where he is not playing what the audience expects of him. I just never could believe that he was a seventeenth-century priest, any more than I could accept Al Pacino as an eighteenth-century migrant trapper in *Revolution* or than I would have accepted Dustin Hoffman as Gandhi.

On a practical production level, however, there were no problems with *The Mission* at all. David Puttnam and Iain Smith were, as always, impeccable. There had been an argument about whether they were over budget, on budget or below budget – it raged fiercely for a few weeks for reasons that I have never been able to fathom – but by the time I got there that had mostly passed. I was told that the picture was going to cost £17 million in cash and it cost £17 million. I had no time, and less interest, to go back through all the business about what the first budget was; it had no bearing on the problems facing the company.

The films, then, on looking at them again, were not as promising as I had first thought.

My second priority was to get to grips with the overheads. When I had left Goldcrest for Embassy, in December 1983, our office costs had been running at about £1.7 million a year and we had employed forty-one people. There had been a huge debate about this at the time. We had all felt that the costs were out of line. I was therefore at a loss to understand why it was that overheads were now running at £3 million a year and we were employing nearly sixty people.

Here is a simple comparison between 1983 and 1985:

	1983	1985	Increase
Turnover	£12.4m	£16m	29%
Maximum staff employed	41	55	34%
Total investments	£23.4m	£35m	49%
Overheads	£1.7m	£3m	76%
Overheads as a percentage of turnover	14%	19%	5%

These 1985 figures are culled from the 1985 annual report. As a general rule, if your investments increase by 49 per cent, then your turnover should increase by at least as much, and your overheads, as a proportion of your turnover, should therefore decrease markedly. Goldcrest had gone in the opposite direction. In spite of the enormous increase in investments (49 per cent), the percentage increase in overheads (76 per cent) was much greater.

I knew that we had to get rid of an awful lot of people. Fortunately for me, this task had already been put in train following the decision to release Mike Wooller and cut back the television department. The entire television division, six people, had to go. Next was Sandy's department of nine people. Since there was no chance of Goldcrest's developing new projects in the foreseeable future, I had no use for them. I then had a shock when I discovered that David Norris had a team of seven and that John Chambers had a finance team of ten, with a further eight people working in administration. This was far too many and some of them had to go. The only area that I didn't worry about was sales, where Guy East had a team of twelve. Guy's was the only income-producing area of the business and, far from cutting it back, I was more likely to build it up. At very low cost, we could expand in foreign sales by picking up third-party product; the sales commissions we earned would contribute to our general overheads.

By the end of September, I had pretty well made up my mind who had to go. They were all first-class people and they all, every single one, either found a job themselves or we were able to find a job for them – a tribute to the high quality of the Goldcrest staff. No one was actually put out on the street. We were very fair in our redundancy payments and there were no complaints on that score. By the second week of October we were down to forty-three employees. By the end of the year we were down to thirty-two, and by mid-1986 we were down to twenty-seven.

All these redundancies cost money in the short term and, in the context of the cash-balancing act that was driving Andy Parsons in the direction of an early grave, they had a seriously negative effect on our immediate financial position. But they were unavoidable.

The biggest single immediate cash saving was the disposal of the office space, which was costing us about £500,000 a year to run. The offices were a joke. They were far too grand for our needs. Indeed, I was so embarrassed by them that on one occasion, when we had arranged to meet our bankers in my office, I brought two spare desks into the room, just to fill it up and make it seem less ostentatious. When the bank people came round, I said, 'Oh, and this is Dickie's desk, that's my desk and that's my secretary's desk', just to make it look as if it was filled with people. In fact, neither my secretary nor Dickie ever worked in the office.

We employed agents to dispose of the lease for us and to look for alternative accommodation. It took a long while to come up with something suitable, but we did eventually move to smaller, cheaper premises just around the corner in Noel Street, and we got a very good price for the Wardour Street lease.

Another area of savings was in development. There were three projects in particular, *Tembisa* (formerly *Dream Song*), *Horror Movie* and *Mandrake*, that had to be written off. The first one I wrote off immediately. *Tembisa* was a small-scale production, the financing of which was more complicated than even *Gandhi's* had been, and the production of which would have caused us endless headaches. Nor, in creative terms, was it a Goldcrest type of project. Even if we had had money in the bank I would have dropped it. *Horror Movie* had been around for more than a year and had been flogged to death. The script had been through many revisions without noticeable improvement and the studios just were not interested. There came a point at which you couldn't fool yourself any longer. It had to be written off. *Mandrake* was a project that I had always liked and on which we had spent a good bit of money back in 1983. I now spent more time on it, thinking it might be the major project in hand once the company was back on its feet. I got an extension on the option and touted it around Hollywood. I did everything I could within the limits, of both time and money, that we could afford. But there were no takers. The problem was that, from Hollywood's point of view, the idea was good but it had the wrong script, the wrong director and the wrong producer. After six or eight months, I was left with no choice but to write it off. Between them, *Mandrake* and *Horror Movie* siphoned off nearly £1 million of Goldcrest's money and used up enormous amounts of energy and back-office services.

At the end of August, Deloitte had prepared a revised sixteen-month cash-flow report which showed that, even with the addition of the shareholders' loan of £6.1 million and the extension of the Midland facility from £10 million to £12 million, Goldcrest could not meet its forecast commitments.

Deloitte's calculations were based on much more conservative assumptions than their previous reports and they had taken into account the likely late delivery of *Absolute Beginners*, the overcosts incurred in the editing of *Revolution* and the decision to hold back the release of *The Mission* until the autumn of 1986. (The extended shoot in Argentina had led to difficulties in securing alternative dates for editing and dubbing. As a consequence the film would not be ready for a spring release, and it was then thought wise to delay the opening until the big summer pictures had run their course.) The resulting forecast showed a maximum borrowing requirement of £13.4 million.

This was an awful burden. Even before thinking about raising new finance or putting in place new credit facilities, we needed at least an extra £1.5 million just to bring the forecast peak borrowing back down below the £12 million Midland limit. It was therefore agreed to increase the loan-stock offer from £6.1 to £7.6 million, the additional money being partly underwritten by one of our smaller shareholders. It was unlikely, however, that a rights issue document would be ready until mid-October, which in turn meant that the money would not be raised until November. In the meantime, Andy Parsons was put under extreme pressure to manipulate the outflow of cash through September and October in order to keep us under the limit. Likewise, Guy East and his team devoted themselves to chasing up debtors and seeking pre-payment from some of our closer customers.

For my part, I flew to the States for meetings with Orion and Warner Bros., from whom I hoped to secure additional advances totalling $1.5–2 million. In each case I said, 'Look, we're out of money. We're not going to be able to meet our obligations. The company's rapidly losing credibility with the distributors in the foreign markets. The banks are telling us that we have exhausted our line of credit, and unless we are able either to raise some more equity or get better terms from you on the pictures, we're going to be in deep trouble.'

I got no sympathy from either of them. As Terry Semel said, he has a board of directors too, and he has to explain his actions and justify his risks the same as anyone else does. If his best friend came along and said, 'Look, I need to borrow from you personally to take care of a problem', he would lend it to him in a flash. But if someone who is running a company, no matter that he is also a good friend, comes along and says, 'Look, my company needs money from Warner Bros.,' then, whatever Terry's personal feelings might be, he would have to consider it strictly in terms of the risk:reward ratio as far as Warner Bros. was concerned. And there were no rewards that I could add to what Warners already had.

Orion was a slightly different case, because not only did they have little or no exposure on *Absolute Beginners*, their $2.5 million being covered by their output deal with HBO, but they knew that they would receive substantial payments from Vestron, which had acquired US video rights. Part of Vestron's payments would have to be reimbursed to us. What I was asking of Orion, therefore, was no more than that they should anticipate those payments and give us our share in advance. We would discount it and effectively pay them interest on it. We would thus increase our immediate cash flow without in any way increasing their risk. But they refused to do it. They would not even consider it. I felt they behaved in a most unfriendly manner.

In their defence, there may have been an element of scepticism about the film itself: Mike Medavoy may have been made suspicious by my constant stalling. Furthermore, for all I know Orion may have had cash-flow problems of their own.

I came back from America empty-handed. But I was not downcast. In fact, I was enjoying myself. I disliked some of the things I had to do, like getting rid of people. And I certainly disliked the idea of spending so much time on Goldcrest that I had no time left for Allied. (In what seemed like spare moments, I rushed off to Oslo, or France, or Jersey, trying to put the finishing touches to the Allied fund.) But overall, and maybe because it was such a contrast to my time at Embassy, I enjoyed those first few months enormously. It was just a whirlwind of activity.

What's more, in a way I was proud to be doing what I was doing. Getting Goldcrest out of the hole had become a campaign, a crusade. And that kind of feeling spread. The company's problems had by now been well publicized – the members of the board and the senior managers were not famous for their discretion when it came to talking to the press – and a lot of people came forward to help. They said, 'What the hell: here's someone who is prepared to take a year, or two years, out of his life for this. Let's see if we can't give him a hand.' The co-operation we had from some of our customers and suppliers, and the offers of assistance from colleagues in the British film industry were heartwarming. We even had an exceptionally generous offer of free accommodation from the leading British facilities company, Samuelson. Even Fiona was placated. We had dinner one night with Dickie, who weaved his magic on her and explained how the British Empire was about to sink if Goldcrest wasn't saved. If not quite won over to the cause, she was at least reconciled to seeing it through.

My relationships with my colleagues, however, were not always smooth. I think they had expected me to be just the same as I had been before, and for Goldcrest somehow to go back in time. But, of course, that could never have been the case. I had changed, and Goldcrest had changed.

In the first place, the Goldcrest executives had become accustomed to endless meetings: management meetings, compensation-committee meetings, fund-raising-committee meetings, production meetings, sales meetings. They had meetings all day, every day. I could never get anyone on the phone: they were always in a meeting somewhere. I would call from LA, from the airport, from home, from the car, from the office across the hall. They would have to call me back. That's OK for the head of a studio. If I call Terry Semel I don't expect to get him on the phone just like that. I speak to his secretary, and she says, 'He'll be free between 10.30 and 10.45 and he'll call you then.' Or she'll ask me to call him at such-and-such a number and such-and-such a time. He's the head of the studio and incredibly busy, and that's normal, courteous behaviour on his part. But I couldn't get Joe Bloggs at Goldcrest. They were all in meetings.

Of course there's a need for lots of meetings, but they should be informal and they should involve only those people who have to make the decision in question. And they shouldn't last more than a few minutes. Other than that you have a management meeting once a week and a board meeting once a month. Once you start having round-table discussions two or three times a week, or every day, then the meetings themselves quickly become the agenda for other meetings. The dog starts to chase its own tail. When I had been at Goldcrest before, we had very few formal meetings, perhaps too few. But I would sit down with Bill Gavin and say, 'Bill, what shall we do about this?' We would talk about whatever it was, he would tell me what he thought we should do, we would come up with a solution and that was it. Total time elapsed – maybe ten minutes. Now Goldcrest had become a kind of collegiate management team.

Second, everyone was absolutely scared stiff of losing his or her job. From having had assets of £30 million and £10 million cash in the bank, Goldcrest was now, one year later, £12 million in debt and without the means of paying it off. The company even had to be bailed out by its leading shareholders to the tune of £6.1 million. That's an incredible change of fortune. The company had made errors. The staff had seen their films go over budget. They had seen the company's name bandied about in all the papers: every day you would read an article telling the world that Goldcrest was going down the tube. Naturally, this made them very, very nervous. They had lost their confidence. They were under tremendous strain.

Of course, I wasn't suffering from any of this. None of the press criticism was aimed at me. I could afford, for example, to take an impartial view of the merits or otherwise of Hugh Hudson's version of events on *Revolution*. Because I was fresh and just wanted to clear away the junk and sort out the mess, I was perhaps not always as sympathetic as I might have been towards the feelings of my colleagues. Certainly I was aware of the fact that, once the euphoria of the first two or three weeks had worn off, an element of disillusionment among the senior staff began to creep in. The realization dawned that I wasn't a miracle worker and that we couldn't turn back the clock. I have been told since that I was much harder, tougher, the second time round. Maybe. I certainly saw the problems very differently from the way my colleagues saw them. I was, after all, undoing much of the work that they had done over the last year or so. Furthermore, they were in it emotionally up to their eyeballs. I was much more detached.

But I was still single-minded. I was determined to get the company back on its feet, and quickly. I had no intention of staying more than the eighteen months I had promised.

By the end of September 1985, I had a grip on the problems. The films were in hand. Costs were being cut back. I had written off everything in development except *Mandrake*. We were well advanced in raising credit facilities. The rights issue, which would repay the £6.1 million share-holders' loan and give us a £1.5 million cushion to cover our expected bank borrowing, was going ahead as planned. All this was to the good. On the other hand, I had failed to get money out of Orion and Warner Bros. and our financial position was deteriorating week by week.

Thus, a month or so into the job, I turned all my attention to my third, and from now on virtually my only, priority: raising new money.

Chapter Fifty-four

The Search for Partners

Eberts: We already had $15 million of project finance promised by four investors, Viking, Schuster, Westpac and Cinema Group, whose money was specifically earmarked for investment in our three big films. The deals had been in the pipeline for months and we were no nearer to closing them than we had been at the beginning of the year. If they all came through, our short-term cash position would certainly be made a lot easier. The problem was that we had no control over the matter. Viking was raising a fund. Schuster was raising a fund. The Cinema Group investment depended on the participation of Westpac, and Westpac had to get clearance from the Australian tax authorities. All we could do was hope.

One of the Viking men in Norway (let's call him Olaf Olafsson) who had helped get together $4 million to invest in *Revolution*, had grandoise plans to raise tens of millions of dollars for investment in mainstream, commercial films. Naturally, every hustler in Hollywood and New York heard about this and headed for Oslo. It was like a convention of schlockmeisters up there that autumn. They were all hoping to pick up some of the fabled money that was to be raised by Mr Olafsson. But Olafsson, who was completely infatuated with show business, had absolutely no concept of how hard it is to raise money for film investment. His biggest mistake was to have helped to raise the $4 million for *Revolution* in the first place. It gave him the impression that he was a mogul and that he would be able to raise substantial amounts of money for other films. He kept talking about putting millions into *Absolute Beginners* and *The Mission*. I don't believe he ever had the remotest chance of raising all that money.

In November, Dickie was doing a publicity tour for *A Chorus Line* and one of the stops on his itinerary was Oslo. He arrived at his hotel late one afternoon and went up to his room to have a bath and get ready for the black-tie charity première. While he was in his bath, the telephone rang. His wife, Sheila, took the call. It was Olaf Olafsson to say that it was a matter of life and death that he speak to Sir Richard. Sheila said that unfortunately he was not available. But Olaf insisted that Dickie come to the phone. So Dickie got out of the bath and took the call. Olaf said, 'You don't know me, but I know that you're the chairman of Goldcrest Films and what I have to ask of you is a matter of life or death for the company.'

He went on, 'I'm the gentleman who was able to arrange the $4 million investment in *Revolution*, and I'm about to raise a great deal more money for *The Mission* and *Absolute Beginners*. I've told all my investors who are gathered with me in a suite right below yours, that you're a very good friend of mine. Part of my sales pitch to them is based on the fact that I have a close personal relationship with you. Of course, now that they've learned from press reports that you're in Oslo, they all want to meet you. And I've had to agree to arrange it. So I would like you to come downstairs and say hello. But, since you and I have never met, you'll have to pretend that you know me.'

So there was Dickie, sitting with the telephone in his hand, wrapped in a towel, dripping wet, wondering if he was talking to a fruitcake. He had heard Olaf's name, of course, because in the board meetings the money Viking was supposed to be bringing in had been discussed often and at length.

Dickie attempted to protest, pleading lack of time and saying that he did not want to be involved in this kind of charade. But Olaf, being a salesman, was very insistent and managed to convince Dickie to cooperate with his preposterous plan – saying something to the effect that 'if you do this we can save Goldcrest together'. These were the magic words, so Dickie agreed to come downstairs as soon as he was dressed.

Olaf, much relieved, then said, 'Since you don't know what I look like, and since you're supposed to know me well and we're the best of friends, I'll come up to you as soon as you enter the room. I'm tall, dark-haired and thin, and I'm wearing a dark-blue suit, white shirt and blue tie, so you'll recognize me. We will meet and shake hands warmly.'

Dickie, of course, is completely theatrical in his approach to a greeting. He doesn't shake hands with anyone he likes, or is supposed to like: he embraces them and calls them 'darling'.

So he got dressed, went downstairs and knocked on the door. It opened and standing right there in front of him, smiling, was a tall, thin gentleman, wearing a dark-blue suit, white shirt and blue tie. Dickie embraced him with a beaming smile and said, 'Hello, darling, wonderful to see you.' It was, of course, the wrong man. The room was full of tall, thin men wearing dark-blue suits; this one just happened to be nearest the door when Dickie knocked. The man recoiled in embarrassment and Dickie, without so much as a flicker of hesitation – he was into the act and wasn't going to be defeated – glanced round the room, made eye-contact with the right man and waltzed over, embracing Olaf like a long-lost friend and persuading this roomful of staid investors that the two of them were the closest and bestest buddies in the world.

The way he tells the story, it is clear that Dickie enjoyed every minute of the performance. He is, it should never be forgotten, first and foremost an actor.

Olaf, on the other hand, was first and foremost a salesman. I made three or four trips to Oslo, we had endless meetings in London, and we exchanged telexes and confirmations that the money had been, or was about to be, raised. Poor David Norris went back and forth to Norway a dozen times with a briefcase bulging with documents, charts, diagrams, deal structures, etc. But Olaf did not raise the money. He raised some, but nothing like the figure he had boasted of, and not enough to put any of it into our films.

In my frustration, I finally wrote him a letter in which I said, 'Go back to your playpen and find some other toys to play with. We're in serious trouble, and because of your preposterous promises and constant lies you've wasted the most valuable and most finite of our resources – our time.' In my opinion, the man never had a chance of raising that money. David Norris to this day gives him the benefit of the doubt.

Cinema Group did have funds. It was a privately owned film-investment company which, among other things, had put some money into three Paramount films. The one they didn't want but had to take as part of the Paramount package was *Flashdance*, which, of course, was the one on which they ended up making the most profit. So they had money and they knew the business. But I don't think they were ever serious about investing in our films. They were talking and dancing around, but they never had any intention of taking a risk.

Howard Schuster was more serious, but he did not yet have the money. Howard is a broker who raises funds from private investors for investment in films, primarily in return for tax benefits. He had raised a lot of money in this manner in the past and, although the tax laws were changing and becoming less attractive to film investors, there was still some benefit to be achieved. But Howard was having great difficulty putting together the finance for *Revolution*. He didn't admit this to us at the time, but I knew from other sources that this was the case.

As for Westpac, we were soon advised that this deal was very unlikely to get approval from the Australian tax authorities.

So, of the four known sources of project finance, not one could be relied upon to come up with the promised funds. There were other potential investors, but all three productions were now so close to being finished that the terms demanded by new investors were often punitive: essentially, they wanted to be last in and first out.

Vestron, an American-based video company, talked of a deal whereby they would put up 30 per cent of the budget of any future production, plus a contribution of $5–7 million towards the print and advertising costs of the US theatrical release, in exchange for worldwide video rights. Such a deal, however, would mean Goldcrest's committing 70 per cent of the budget and surrendering control of script and cast. Vestron would get high-quality films, without any of the headaches involved in actually having to produce them themselves, and they would recoup their investment directly out of worldwide video revenues, all of which, of course, would be cross-collateralized. Silver Screen, led by my old friend and IFI colleague Roland Betts, discussed an idea to put up 60 per cent of the budget, as well as print and ad. finance, in exchange for US video, pay-cable and syndication rights to three pictures. The same objections applied.

My discussions with Warner Bros. had not secured any further advances for *Revolution* or *The Mission*, but the studio did offer an advance of $5 million for the residual US rights to *The Killing Fields*. This would not be new money as such, since we had planned to receive income from the exploitation of those rights anyway; nor was it the cheapest money – a fact that David Puttnam would have to weigh up before deciding whether to give his approval to the deal – since Warners, in making an advance against future income, would naturally want a substantial discount. But it was money now rather than money later. I asked them to keep the offer open until January, to which they agreed. The immediate benefit of the Warner proposal was that the Midland accepted it as security for about £1 million of credit.

At about the same time, David Puttnam offered to buy back the *First Love* series outright. I am sure he saw it as a worthwhile investment from his point of view, but his principal motive was undoubtedly to help raise money for Goldcrest. In the same spirit, he had already decided to forgo, or refund, about £100,000 of the overhead contribution that Goldcrest was supposed to pay Enigma. David has his critics – successful people always do – but no one has ever accused him of being either mean or avaricious. The figure he had in mind for the purchase of the

First Loves was about $900,000. This was certainly worthy of consideration. Unfortunately, taking the *First Loves* out of the catalogue was likely to do us more harm than good, and our discussions on the subject did not get very far.

All these potential sources had to be followed up, but none of them was close to what I wanted: $4 million here, $1.5 million there, $3 million somewhere else, all of it heavily secured against distribution contracts or other forms of revenue, was not the kind of money that we needed. We needed large amounts of fresh equity.

If we didn't get fresh equity, the company would have no long-term future. And if the company had no long-term future, we could not go ahead with the loan-stock offer, for it is illegal as well as immoral knowingly to raise money for an insolvent company. At a meeting held on 25 September, while I was in America, Michael Stoddart, James Joll, David Norris and John Chambers decided that Goldcrest had to have 'reasonable prospects' of raising at least £4 million by the end of the year, and further funds early in 1986, for the loan-stock offer to proceed. If there was any doubt about our ability to raise that money then the loan-stock offer would have to be suspended, which, in effect, would lead to the winding up of the company. When I returned from America, on 1 October, Norris, Chambers and I decided that there was no way that we could *guarantee* that such an amount of money would be secured. At the same time we were unable to countenance the winding up of the company when the three big films had yet to be released. Either the loan-stock offer would have to be increased from £7.6 to £12 million – giving us the £4 million we needed – or the rights issue circular would have to contain a clear warning of the consequences of failing to raise such an amount from other sources. The first option was unlikely to meet with success: our soundings among the shareholders were not encouraging even as regards the £7.6 million; it was certain that no one would underwrite £12 million. So it had to be the second option: the shareholders would be invited to subscribe to the loan-stock issue on the understanding that, in so doing, they were not necessarily securing the long-term future of the company. It was not the most helpful note to add to a money-raising prospectus.

Ilott: On 18 October, the rights-issue document was circulated to shareholders. On its first page, in bold capital letters, was the following warning:

SHAREHOLDERS SHOULD READ CAREFULLY THE SECTION IN THIS DOCUMENT HEADED 'CURRENT FINANCIAL POSITION' BEFORE

DECIDING WHETHER TO APPLY FOR STOCK UNDER THE PROPOSED RIGHTS ISSUE

The conclusion of the section in question, also printed in bold type, informed the shareholders that

If Midland Bank does not extend Goldcrest's existing overdraft facilities beyond 31st December 1985 and alternative finance is not obtained, Goldcrest will probably have to cease trading . . . Although Goldcrest's borrowing requirements over the next twelve months are projected to continue within Midland Bank's existing £12 million limit, the present security arrangements would not allow Goldcrest to draw down the funds it expects to require from the end of December 1985. The projected shortfall in security is £0.5 million in January 1986, rising to £2.5 million in March 1986 and continuing to rise thereafter. Accordingly, even if Midland Bank extends its facility on current terms, Goldcrest will require additional security . . . It is therefore essential that Goldcrest raises considerable additional third party finance . . .

The reason that Goldcrest's collateral was likely to diminish from December onwards was that, as each film was delivered, so Goldcrest would be in receipt of the relevant distribution advances, and the contracts pertaining to those advances would no longer be available to offer as security to the bank.

As the rights-issue document also included a brutally frank account of the origins of the company's present financial crisis, it is little wonder that the majority of shareholders were not keen to participate. The issue closed on 19 November, with £2.6 million of unsubscribed stock falling to the underwriters. Pearson took 55 per cent of the issue, Electra 25 per cent and Noble Grossart 5 per cent (total, 85 per cent), against their holdings of ordinary shares of 41 per cent, 5.5 per cent and 2.8 per cent respectively (total, 49 per cent). Of the other nineteen shareholders, only seven took up the loan-stock offer. The biggest vote of no confidence came from the National Coal Board Pension Fund, which, with 10 per cent of the ordinary stock, was the second biggest shareholder in the company. The NCBPF had recently been granted a seat on the board (as an inducement to subscribe to the loan-stock offer as much as anything else) and its representative, Paul Whitney, was, by all accounts, keen to support the company. But Whitney was overruled by the NCBPF trustees who voted against the investment.

The outcome of the rights issue was, naturally, thought to be very disappointing, and much blame was attached to the depressing tone of the offer document.

Eberts: It was worse than disappointing. It was a hammer-blow. How could we go to new investors and invite them to put money into the company if most of our own shareholders did not think the risk worthwhile? From the day the rights issue closed, I felt that Goldcrest was never going to get back on its feet. Everything now depended on the unreleased films, and those who, like me, had seen the footage, shared my view that the films were not going to perform. This was not something we ever discussed openly, but privately I think we were all of the same mind.

Two days before the offer closed we had held sneak previews of *Revolution* in Long Island. The results were very depressing.

Sneak previews, or test screenings, are arranged once the director has completed his cut. They give everyone concerned the opportunity to see the film from a completely fresh viewpoint. After all the trials and tribulations of developing, packaging, making and editing a picture, most of the participants are punch-drunk: they have no objectivity left. Furthermore, a finished film, especially one that is felt to be unsatisfactory, can easily become a battleground between the film-makers, the investors, the distributors and the production company: each has an opinion about the final form it should take. Useful arbiters in all this are members of the public, who come to the picture without preconceptions. They are very carefully chosen, by specialists who work in this field, to be as much like an average or target audience as possible. In fact, you can have several previews, each one with a different audience mix, out of which you might be better able to identify what your core audience is and why they are attracted to the picture. This information is then used by the marketing and publicity people who are going to release the film.

Each member of the target audience is given a questionnaire to fill out once the screening is over. There are two or three things you look for on the preview cards. The first is the audience's general assessment: is the film excellent, extremely good, very good, good, fair or poor? If you get more than 75 per cent in the categories excellent/very good then you are on the way to success. *Revolution* scored less than 40 per cent.

You then look at the answers to the question: 'Would you recommend this picture to your friends?' This gives you an idea of how strong the word-of-mouth is going to be. There is often a big discrepancy between the general assessment and the recommend figures. In the first place, one's enjoyment of a picture depends on one's state of mind, the comfort of the cinema, and audience atmosphere and so on. Indeed, the very fact of being invited to a sneak preview can enhance the experience for many people. But when it comes to recommending it to friends, the audience is inclined to think more objectively and more critically. Second, sometimes a film is so horrific, or so devastating, that the audience, although it may have been much moved by the picture, does not want to recommend it to friends (*The Killing Fields* had been a case in point). Allowing for these factors, if you get a 60 per cent recommend figure, then you're in good shape. *Revolution* got about 13 per cent.

Other things you learn from the questionnaires are what the audience thought of certain members of the cast, or certain aspects of the story. You also invite them to identify the overall weaknesses of the film, for which purpose you can either suggest options from which they can choose, or you can just leave a space for them to write in whatever they want. Their opinions are invariably extremely helpful – as we saw earlier, for example, in the case of subtitling *The Emerald Forest*.

You also invite the audience to tell you what they most like about the picture. In the case of *Revolution* there was very little that they liked. The action scenes and the photography were good, but other than that all the comments we had were negative. Most of the audience simply could not understand what an Italian-American from Brooklyn (Al Pacino) was doing in the movie. Historically, it *is* possible that someone like the man that Al Pacino plays would have had a Brooklyn accent. But the audience just couldn't accept it. As cinema, it was not acceptable. Nor could they get to grips with the Kinski character, and they found some of the gory scenes too upsetting.

With so many objections, and so few good comments, and with such a low recommend figure, the film was clearly in trouble. Worse, at a focus-group discussion after one of the screenings, at which about twenty members of the audience were asked more detailed questions, it was clear that no one had any suggestions about how to make the picture better. At these gatherings people usually say, 'Why don't you try this?' or 'That scene is too long, and if you cut out so-and-so I would have liked it more.' Whether their comments are of any practical consequence doesn't matter much: they give you general pointers towards ways of improving the film. But in this case there was just a blank: they felt that the picture just didn't work.

Sandy again counselled delay. But there was no going back at that stage. I did not feel that there was any hope that a delay would improve the film. We had spent a lot of time and effort getting the picture ready for a pre-Christmas release and it would open come what may. The only concession we made – and we had no choice in the matter, since there had to be further editing changes – was to put the opening date back from 13 to 25 December, the last day on which the film could open and still be eligible for the 1985 Academy Awards.

Chapter Fifty-five

A Trail of Frustration

Eberts: Meanwhile, the financial position of the company continued to deteriorate. John Chambers and I would visit the bank twice a week. At every such visit we were only able to report worse news than before. I had to take a brutal view of the company's situation, which I could afford to do as I could always deny any responsibility for the mess we were in. It was easier for me to be objective than for the rest of the management team. At my insistence we began to be more realistic in our assessment of Goldcrest's future position. For example, on 10 October John revised his contribution forecast for *Revolution* from a 'probable' surplus of £450,000 to a 'probable' deficit of £2.1 million. That figure could be achieved only if the film performed exceptionally well at the box office, taking US rentals of $25 million and foreign rentals of $14 million. It also assumed that Howard Schuster would be an investor. If the film did not perform so well, and if Howard Schuster failed to come up with the money, then we were looking at a 'likely' loss in excess of £8 million. In other words, we had a whole team of people working day and night to finish a film that we knew would almost certainly lose money, possibly a lot of money. This was a very dispiriting prospect. John Chambers also produced an end-of-year profit-and-loss forecast that showed an overall pre-tax deficit for the company of £4.5 million, to which had to be added further television write-offs and any *Revolution* deficit in excess of £2.1 million. At a guess, therefore, we were looking at a trading loss in 1985 of £7–8 million.

Andy Parsons was working day and night to keep our borrowing below the £12 million limit, while John and his team were on the phone twelve or fourteen hours a day calling up customers and begging them to get their money in on time. At one point, we were owed about £2.2 million by the VAT people. We were desperate to get that money and John harried them to pay up. He succeeded in the end, and I think Goldcrest must hold the speed record for forcing a rebate out of the tax authorities.

At the same time, Guy East was selling off as many television and film projects from the library as he could. He went through the list, going right back to such clinkers as *An Unsuitable Job for a Woman* and *Red Monarch*, looking for rights that hadn't been sold. A significant chunk of the television library, for example, went to sales agent Richard Price Television Associates, who paid us an advance of £500,000. We felt they would do a much better job than we could in the television markets, as was subsequently proved: they quickly recouped their advance and thereafter paid us 65 per cent of all revenues. Cheques came in regularly. In the midst of all this, we were preparing to sue Entertainment Completions Inc. for reneging on our completion guarantee deal for *Absolute Beginners*. About £1.3 million was involved – again, money which we urgently needed.

With Goldcrest's problems splashed across the business pages of the newspapers every week, all kinds of people, from wool merchants in the English Midlands to wealthy individuals in the south of France, approached us with offers of money. The film business attracts time-wasters in greater numbers than any other business with which I have been associated. People with money, when they hear that you're looking for funds, will string you along and delude themselves with their own promises. Successful entrepreneur who are involved in completely unrelated industries suddenly get struck by showbiz. They want to be film producers. They are not quite sure what the job entails, but they have an inkling that it will make them very powerful and very glamorous and might even give them the right to sleep with the leading lady. In fact, most 'potential' film investors are not potential investors at all. They are bullshit artists who like to be seen with movie people and to boast to their friends at dinner parties about how they are investing in so-and-so's new production. When it comes to putting up hard cash, 99 per cent of these people bow out.

Even of the serious investors, only a minority really know what they are talking about. In ideal circumstances, they are the ones to deal with. Forget the rest. The circumstances in which we found ourselves towards the end of 1985 were, however, far from ideal. In fact, it eventually got to the point that I would talk to anybody.

Two examples illustrate the frustrations and time-wasting that can be involved when you leave your door wide open.

The first occurred in early 1986. A man whom we shall call Robert Smith operated as a financial consultant for clients who were mainly interested in tax-shelter deals. At that time we had a number of films, chief among them *Absolute Beginners* and *The Mission*, which, being

British, could attract some tax benefits for UK investors. Hence Smith's interest.

He was an interesting character, to say the least. He would sit there with a briefcase on his lap. In it was a portable computer and a telephone. That telephone could be relied upon to ring at the most inappropriate, and crucial, moments in any meeting. He would open the case, pick up the phone and whisper into it arcane and cryptic messages, some of them in code, and then hang up. It was not a performance that inspired confidence.

He made a proposal whereby his client would acquire either *Absolute Beginners* or *The Mission*, or both, lease them back to us and give us a share of the tax benefits. The amount of cash involved was several million pounds and, in spite of overwhelming scepticism on the part of the board that Smith was for real, I pursued it avidly – for weeks. We had frantic meetings, sometimes through the night, trying to put a package together that would satisfy both Goldcrest and Smith's client, a British company that he refused to identify. Because of the air of mystery which generally surrounded him, and the confused nature of our discussions – every time we met he would amend the proposal – it was very hard to figure out what Smith was actually doing. The anonymity of his client added to our unease.

In the event it turned out that the client in question was a major bank. We had done a tax deal with this bank some years before, so we knew them pretty well. In fact, we knew them well enough not to need an intermediary like Smith. However, he had introduced the proposal, it was his deal, so we had to stick with him. At least we had the comfort of knowing that the client was not only for real but had some expertise in this area.

We had insisted in all our negotiations that no Goldcrest shareholder should be required to guarantee the tax benefits of a third-party investor. Such guarantees, or indemnities, are common in the tax-shelter business, but the Goldcrest shareholders, Pearson and Electra in particular, wanted to avoid taking on board what could be a substantial and long-term liability. This point had been made abundantly clear to Smith on several occasions and he assured us that no such indemnity would be required.

The negotiations continued, and with each new amendment the possible excess cash thrown up by the deal increased. At one point we were expecting £3.8 million 'free cash'. I never really understood where all this money was coming from, and Smith's excitement and general incoherence made it difficult for me to pin him down. My colleagues, and John Chambers in particular, thought I was crazy to spend time on it.

As far as they were concerned, Smith was just another time-waster. He was certainly greedy, demanding a fee of £500,000 for his services. We offered him half that.

One day, when our negotiations were supposedly drawing to a close, Smith appeared in the office and casually said that, notwithstanding his previous assurances, he did in fact need Pearson to guarantee the deal. That was the end of that. A complete waste of months of effort and energy. It left an extremely bad taste in the mouths of those involved. On our side there was nothing but disgust and dismay. None of our leading shareholders, and certainly none of our executive team, would ever contemplate taking a phone call from Robert Smith again.

The second such incident occurred much later, when our need for funds had become desperate. I had a telephone call from a lawyer in San Francisco. Since I have succeeded in blotting his name from my memory, we'll call him John Grey. He said, 'You don't know me, but I know you and I know of Goldcrest's reputation. I also know that you need money. I have a client who has a lot of money and he'd like to invest some of it in the film business. He'd like to come and see you.'

'Well,' I said, 'that's very interesting. Could you tell me something about this person?'

He said, 'Well, I can't tell you much. He's from a very rich family and if you agree to see him I'll call him right now and get permission to reveal his identity.'

'Fine,' I said.

He called back about five minutes later: 'I'm sorry I can't tell you his name but I can reveal that he is from a very prominent Middle Eastern family. If you're interested in talking to him, he can be at your office in half an hour. He can then give you further details himself.'

'Fine,' I said.

'Oh, and can you make sure that there is a place to park his Rolls-Royce?'

'Fine,' I said. 'But since I don't know his name, or his nationality or even what he looks like, how will I know it's him?'

I was told not to worry, he would introduce himself as 'John Grey's client'.

At that time we were in the midst of moving from Wardour Street to our new offices round the corner in Noel Street. The grand Wardour Street offices therefore had a half-empty look. The walls were bare, boxes were on the top of desks, rolls of film posters stood in corners and paper was strewn across the corridors. In the space of twenty minutes, Andy Parsons, myself and one or two other staff who happened to be available, tidied the place up and fixed some posters back on the walls: it is no bad thing for a prospective investor to be greeted by big glossy spreads of *Gandhi, The Killing Fields, The Mission* and *Chariots of Fire*. I had just settled myself back at my desk when the receptionist announced that 'Mr John Grey's client' had arrived.

He was very young, very small and nervous. He was smoking when he arrived and chain-smoked throughout our meeting. His fingers were stained with nicotine. I welcomed him at the reception area and walked with him back to my office, making sure that he took note of the film posters that had been put up only minutes before his arrival. He recognized them all and seemed to be suitably impressed. No sooner had we sat down than he said, 'If I gave you £100 million, what would you do with it?'

'Well, I can't answer that question off the top of my head,' I replied. 'I'd have to think about it very carefully. My first reaction is that I don't know that I could spend £100 million. It's hard to put that much money to work in this business. If you said £50 million, and gave me a couple of days, or a week, to think about it, I might come up with a proposal.'

'How about buying a film studio?' he asked.

'Frankly,' I said, 'it's not the kind of thing which makes that much sense these days. Even in the States, where there is a very active film and television business, studios are not thought to be a very good investment. It's like owning a warehouse. If you have the goods to fill the warehouse, it's OK. But you can't always guarantee that you will have the goods. Whether the warehouse is full or empty the costs of mortgage and maintenance are just the same. Anyway, studio-ownership is not the kind of thing we're into. We have no expertise applicable to that area. What we do is make films.'

He said, 'OK, why don't you come up with a plan to spend this £100 million on films? Because I'd like to give it to you.'

Again I said, 'I don't think I can do that. I don't think I can devise a way of spending £100 million. There just aren't that many good projects around. You would have to be prepared to go beyond the basic production business. If you'd like to own a television station or perhaps take a share of an American distribution company, it should be possible.'

'Well,' he said, 'you come up with a plan and we'll talk about it.'

I said, 'Before I'd go to the trouble of doing that I'd like to know who you are and where the money's coming from.'

After some hesitation he told me that he was His Royal Highness Prince Ali Al Kaled, son of the ruler of a Middle-Eastern country. Now it was my turn to be impressed.

I said, 'Well, that sounds fine to me. I'm very happy to have met you.'

He rose from his chair, apologized for having to rush off – he said that he was on his way to Oxford to attend some lecture or other – and gave me the contact number of his representative in Richmond. Then he left. I never saw him again. Every day for about a month I called the number he gave me. I called John Grey. But I got replies from neither of them.

Ilott: Not all the unsolicited approaches were so nonsensical. In the first week of October 1985, an Australian group, UAA, approached Goldcrest with a view to merging the two companies. UAA was a tax-shelter fund with which David Norris had done business five or six years earlier, in the days when he was a partner at the law firm of Denton, Hall & Burgin. He had kept in touch with them ever since. They had considerable experience of movie investment, putting money into a number of major studio pictures, and they had been successful. However, the company had become enmeshed in a protracted dispute with the Australian tax authorities, as a result of which it had had to reorganize and transfer much of its money to America. This restructured American company found itself in the position of having a considerable future cash flow, some $30 million, all of it receivable in the period 1985–9, but no business to put the money into. Goldcrest had a business, but no cash flow. It seemed an ideal combination, the more so as Goldcrest had something else that UAA needed: management. Many of the problems that had beset the Australian fund, and which were later to cause havoc in the American company, arose from a lack of expert management. As David Norris puts it, 'They wanted to buy Jake, John, Guy and myself as well as the Goldcrest name.'

Two UAA executives arrived in London on the afternoon of Friday, 4 October. Eberts being at that time back in America trying to raise money, the UAA team met with Norris and Chambers, and the four of them, with the knowledge of the Goldcrest board, spent most of the weekend, from Friday evening to midday Monday, going through the company's books. Chambers and Norris gave them access to everything: cash-flow forecasts, accounts, sales projections, board- and management-meeting minutes, board papers, production contracts and bank statements. There was to be a Goldcrest board meeting on the Monday afternoon and by Monday lunchtime, after seventy hours' concentrated work, the two UAA executives produced a proposal which was put, initially, to Goldcrest board member Angus Grossart.

The UAA plan was to isolate *Revolution, The Mission* and *Absolute Beginners*, since there was no way that a price could be put on them, and to give the existing shareholders, penny for penny, everything that those films earned from distribution. For the rest of the company, UAA offered the equivalent of 25 pence per share. UAA would take a controlling interest, leaving the existing shareholders with 20–25 per cent of the merged company, into which UAA would then pump a substantial tranche of new capital.

The 25 pence offer valued the rump of the company at about £7 million, which, when added to the book value of the three films (i.e. discounting pre-sales and third-party investors) of about £15 million, brought the total to £20–22 million, which was on a par with the company's own estimate of its value. But the Goldcrest board, and Grossart in particular, did not see it that way. The company was in the midst of a loan-stock rights issue which had a conversion price, 50 pence, that was supposed to make it very attractive to investors. UAA's offer of 25 pence, never mind that the major films were excluded, was felt to be unacceptable. That the offer was typed out on a single sheet of plain paper – the UAA executives had not brought headed paper with them and had to make do with what they could find in the Goldcrest offices – added to the impression that these were not people to be taken seriously. Furthermore, Grossart believed that UAA had vastly overestimated its own worth. He had perused the UAA papers – reorganization documents, accounts, letters of confirmation from banks and so on – and was not impressed. According to Norris, he 'gave them [the UAA executives] twenty minutes and treated them like colonial country cousins. I like Angus, but I could not forgive anybody who would let people fly 12,000 miles, spend the entire weekend, more or less day and night, making an evaluation of the company – which, incidentally, turned out to be extremely accurate – and then dismiss them as if they were making a derisory off-the-cuff offer.'

The board, at its meeting later in the day, endorsed Grossart's rejection of the UAA proposal. Nothing remotely as good was ever to be offered to Goldcrest again.

Norris was very upset by this episode, and it added to his growing frustration at the direction being taken by the company. Indeed, of all the Goldcrest executives, Norris was the most disappointed at the turn events had taken since Eberts had come back. He felt that the company had been run down too quickly; he was very unhappy about the conflict of interest between Allied and Goldcrest; he had had to sack most of his own staff; and he faced the prospect of caretaking the company into decline. He had already proposed a part-time arrangement for himself that would save Goldcrest a considerable amount of money, in terms of his salary, secretarial help and office expenses, but it had met with little enthusiasm on the part of Eberts. Within two weeks of the rejection of UAA's offer he gave notice that he would leave at the end of the year. He was undecided whether to stay in the film business or go back to law.

Eberts: While I was sympathetic to the UAA proposal – and I took their offer completely seriously – I was far from being convinced by it. I felt that the kinds of films they were interested in, and the sort of company they wanted to operate, was quite different from the one that I had in mind and the one that the board had in mind. Goldcrest had a track record, a name, priceless goodwill with its customers and prestige within the industry. UAA had nothing. It was an agglomeration of tax-shelter funds. And while it is true that we never did get as good an offer again, it is also true that the subsequent history of UAA was so disastrous that we were probably lucky not to have gone into business with them.

As for David's resignation, he had built up quite a large staff and he was naturally very loyal to them. I think he was dreadfully disappointed that it all had to be dismantled. In fact, he didn't fire anyone himself. I had to do it. He was disappointed too that, for as far into the future as we could see, the excitement was over: from here on it was just a long haul of routine, defensive management. Goldcrest, in other words, was not going to be the company that he had set his heart on. Most of all, he was very tired. Like John Chambers, indeed like most people at Goldcrest, David had a phenomenal capacity for work. But it had taken its toll. The Viking affair, the endless negotiations with Westpac and with Cinema Group: these things had consumed months of his time and energy to no purpose. You can't go on doing that kind of thing without losing your enthusiasm.

David's offer of a part-time consultancy arrangement did not interest me for the simple reason that I wanted a full-time legal workhorse and such a person already existed in David's assistant, Peter Coles. In addition, I did not want to encourage David to stay with a company which I felt might, just might, have no chance of survival. So I said to David, 'No, you have an opportunity to go off and do your own thing. Go off and do it. Hanging around here won't do you any good, and it's not really what I need.' So we parted company.

With Mike Wooller, Bill Gavin, Terry Clegg and David Norris gone, only myself and John Chambers were left from the original Goldcrest executive team.

Chapter Fifty-six

The February Deadline

Eberts: I had set myself a target of $20–25 million of new equity, which was what we needed if there was to be any prospect of making investments in the coming year. And I gave myself a deadline – 1 February 1986 – by which to raise it. If I couldn't get the money by that time, I probably never could. In the US, I had spoken to a range of financiers and brokers. My first calls were to Interscope in Los Angeles, a development-financing company that brought projects to the major studios, and Boston Ventures, a major media-investment fund. I knew both companies fairly well and I felt that they might have an interest in getting involved in the foreign-sales business. Both companies, however, turned me down.

I had long talks with Coca-Cola. We discussed financing a $25 million recapitalization of Goldcrest and then merging it with Embassy Home Entertainment (EHE), their video-distribution subsidiary. With the recapitalized Goldcrest having a net worth of about $50 million and EHE being valued at about $100 million, our shareholders would end up owning about 20 per cent of the joint enterprise. Coke wanted to have a 33–40 per cent interest, with the rest spread amongst the other EHE shareholders, chief among them being EHE founder and chief executive, Andre Blay. The plan suited me because, as I saw it, the video business, which was already very nearly as big as the theatrical business and likely to get bigger, was of increasing importance to us as independent producers. Video companies were prepared to put up considerable amounts of cash for good-quality pictures. Indeed, they were locked in such a desperate competition for product that we could actually get bigger advances against video rights in North America than we could for theatrical rights. So here was an obvious match: we needed the money and they needed the pictures. The merged company would have a substantial production and foreign-sales division in Goldcrest, and a substantial video outlet in EHE. On paper at least it was a very good idea.

But we never got very far with it, because, at the same time as we were discussing this, Coke was entering into negotiations to sell EHE to Andre Blay. We could have tried to consummate the deal subsequently but Coke then decided not to sell to Andre but to sell to another company, Nelson Entertainment. And the head of Nelson, Barry Spikings, the former joint managing director of EMI Films in London, knew full well that he could build up his own foreign-sales company a lot more cheaply than by entering into a merger with Goldcrest.

I also had talks with Rust Ventures, who were interested in investing up to $3 million and acting as a focus for other American investors. They had a few people in mind and talked of bringing as much as $10 million into the company, in the form of low-yield loan stock, convertible at 65 pence. Rust, however, wanted to isolate this investment from our past losses, which would involve a restructuring of Goldcrest's business in a way that would be likely to jeopardize our other fund-raising efforts.

Hachette, a major French publishing house and one of the leading shareholders in Allied, expressed interest in Goldcrest and talked about putting up £25 million at 65 pence a share, plus warrants. This would have given them about a 40 per cent stake in the company. But the deal fell foul of two obstacles. First, to my amazement the Goldcrest shareholders were very unwilling to surrender so much of the company for what they thought was too low a price. (None of the big films had been released and there was no reason, for the board at least, to expect them to be anything other than successful.) Second, although Hachette expressed a lot of interest, they never really came to grips with the matter. For example, they didn't spend enough time studying the documentation. To do a proper study of our documentation would take about three weeks and would involve numerous exchanges with us to have this or that figure explained. But Hachette never did that. They kept on saying that they were very keen, but they never did the work required and they never asked detailed questions, so it soon became apparent that their interest was not for real.

A leading Wall Street investment bank, Allen and Co., was interested in handling an investment package on our behalf. They are very knowledgeable about the business, having been involved in many deals with Tri-Star and Columbia Pictures, of which they were, for a long time, major shareholders. But it turned out that Allen and Co. wanted only to put us together with one of their clients, either PSO/Delphi or Columbia Pictures. They never made a proposal for us to raise money on our own.

Two other New York investment banks, however, did offer to make proposals. Wertheim and Co. suggested a private placing in the US, with a view to raising $25 million in ordinary share capital at a price that assumed a net book value of the company of not less than £20 million, which was pretty much our current estimate. And Merrill Lynch suggested much the same. I couldn't deal with both, of course, but either one could have been integrated with the Rust proposal.

I chose Wertheim. They were very knowledgeable about the business, having been one of the principal investors in Orion. They were also very close to Michael Stoddart and Electra, with whom they had a number of joint investments. Two of their entertainment industry analysts, David Londoner and Francine Bloom, were held in particularly high regard (they regularly issued informative and accurate research reports on Disney, Paramount, Warner Bros. and the US television networks). They were very aggressive, hard working and well connected. And they were keen to do a deal. Merrill Lynch were good, too, but Wertheim just seemed more confident.

I met with them about five times. Our discussions were a joy. I didn't have to explain distribution deals, gross participation, completion guarantees or any of the intricacies of film finance. They knew all about these things. Nor did I have to labour too long in explaining our problems and how they had come about. They grasped the details of the situation very quickly. By the end of our discussions they had agreed to try to raise $25 million of new equity, at a price of 65 pence a share, on a 'best-efforts' basis – i.e. they did not guarantee it, and they would not underwrite it, but they would give it their best shot. They had twenty investors in mind and intended issuing a prospectus by mid-December. They gave me a letter to this effect, and I headed back to London in triumph. To have a major Wall Street house backing our team was a tremendous boost.

I took an overnight flight, arriving at Heathrow first thing in the morning. I went straight from the airport to Wardour Street, just in time for the November board meeting. I strode in waving this piece of paper, like Chamberlain announcing 'peace in our time'.

Unfortunately, the news that greeted me was not good: the balance sheet was even worse than the deliberately downbeat picture I had painted in New York. By far the greater part of the net worth of the company was invested in three big pictures and, as each week went by and our estimates of the value of the rest of the company went down, so the significance of these pictures increased. No one in their right mind was going to invest equity in a company whose entire fortunes were riding on three unreleased pictures. Our potential investors had nothing to lose, and everything to gain, by waiting. By the same token, the attitude of our shareholders was that we should not surrender control of the company now, at a price of 65 pence or less, when *Revolution*, *Absolute Beginners* and *The Mission* – any or all of which could be monster hits – had yet to prove themselves. From the board's point of view, this was not the ideal time to be raising new money. I thought the board was being completely unrealistic. They were still living in the glorious past and seemed unable to grasp the fact that we were in *very* deep trouble.

Wertheim tried their best, but within a month they reported that they could not raise the money on the agreed terms. If a leading entertainment-industry investor could be found (Rust by this time had dropped out), and a price of 45 pence fixed, then they might try again, but only after the results of *Revolution* were known and even then with a lower subscription target than $25 million. An offer price of 45 pence, of course, posed a bit of a problem, since we had just raised loan stock that had a conversion price of 50 pence.

I undertook to speak personally to all the people on Wertheim's list. Wertheim were right: no one was interested. At the December board meeting we agreed that there was no point in pressing Wertheim to proceed.

But if Wertheim couldn't do it, who could? And even if we could find someone else to do it, would they do it on terms that the board would accept? We were already perilously close to giving the company away.

Thus, by mid-December 1985, after four months of chasing up every possible lead, we had to face the fact that we were not going to be able to raise money from the investment community in the United States nor, following the relative failure of the loan-stock issue, from the investment community in the UK. Our remaining hope was that we might still find a merger partner – someone in the industry to whom our name and reputation were worth more than our asset value.

The Orion proposal, which pre-dated my return to Goldcrest, had died once our financial problems had become known. The same was true of the proposed joint venture with Warner Television. Embassy Home Entertainment, as we have seen, had come and gone, as had UAA. I sought out other possible partners.

A British video company, Heron, might have made a match for us in much the same way as EHE. Gerald Ronson, the Heron boss, was someone I had known for a long time and whom I much admired. Heron was exclusively involved in home video and had no interest in production, foreign sales or theatrical distribution. It was, therefore, in a comparatively weak market position. Goldcrest could provide not only first-class product, which every video distributor then desperately needed, but many of the other services that Heron lacked. But Gerald wasn't keen. In fact, I am not sure that at that time he was even keen to go much further in the video business. Also, Gerald is not one for overpaying for an asset – he invariably buys at a heavy discount – and he had his doubts about the value of what I was proposing. We had a lot of very interesting meetings, but we never actually got anywhere.

Another British company, ITC, was considering making a bid for Gold-crest. ITC had a big library of both film and television product, but, following the takeover by Robert Holmes à Court, it was in a state of disarray. The company presented a very confused image to the industry and had actually dropped out of production. Goldcrest, which had prob-ably the highest profile of any film company outside the Hollywood majors, and which had a display cabinet full of Oscars, was thus a very attractive partner. A merger would put ITC back on centre stage. But, like Gerald Ronson, Robert Holmes à Court had built his reputation and his empire on the principle of buying cheap. He didn't like to pay the market price for assets and was only interested if we were prepared more or less to give the company away.

At about this time, towards the end of 1985, David Puttnam had suggested that we might sell off a package of television films, including the *First Loves*, to Michael Green's company, Carlton Communications. I followed up this idea but Michael would not even consider our asking price. He had hired Bill Gavin as his consultant and Bill had made an esti-mate of the value of those assets which was a great deal lower than ours.

Partly prompted by David, who is an old friend of his, Michael Green did, however, show some interest in buying into the company. This was a very promising development, as Carlton was in every way compatible with Goldcrest. It was a well-run, very profitable and rapidly expanding company that had its roots in the stable and profitable, if less glamorous, business of television production facilities, equipment and related ser-vices. Michael is an outstanding entrepreneur and, of all the people I talked to at that time, he was the only one with whom I would really have enjoyed working. I knew that he would see in Goldcrest not just a library of pictures that he could pick up cheaply, but an opportunity for growth in the feature-film area. The proposal came unstuck, however, on his insistence that I commit myself personally to a five-year, full-time contract. If he was going to build up the business, he said, he wanted the Goldcrest management team to stay in place and me to lead it.

Michael suggested he could give me enough stock options to make me a wealthy man, but I knew myself well enough by this time to know that I couldn't do it. For one thing, I had Allied and I had my relationship with Warner Bros. But even if I had had nothing to fall back on, I could not devote five years of my life to building an empire for Michael Green. I was no good at building empires for people. I was through with empires. No amount of money or stock options could change that fact.

The failure of these talks led to some strong exchanges between me and David Puttnam, who was very disappointed, even angry, that I had proved uncooperative. His remarks were reminiscent of his earlier comments, back in December 1983, about my 'failure' to 'raise my game' and my unwillingness to 'play the part of chief executive'. From Goldcrest's point of view he may have been right. But I can only reiterate that when the board had begged me to come back they had known exactly what they were getting. I had quite clearly explained my level of commitment, and they had accepted it. In the four or five months since then, all the concessions had come from my side: far from spending 60 per cent of my time on Goldcrest, I spent 100 per cent – ten or twelve hours a day, seven days a week. I would go that far, but I would not go further. I certainly couldn't contemplate a five-year commitment that would require me to abandon Allied.

Other potential merger partners in, or on the fringes of, the industry included Virgin, Saatchi & Saatchi and First Leisure, but none of them came close to making an acceptable offer.

With the collapse of our hopes of raising new equity, and with the failure of our attempts to find a merger partner we were left with very little but our own resources to fall back on. We had two income-generating areas within Goldcrest: the library and the sales department. To sell the library would be tantamount to closing down the company, something which we were not yet ready to contemplate, least of all with three big films still awaiting release. The sales division, however, did suggest a way in which we might yet lift ourselves out of the hole. I had the idea of splitting it off from the rest of the company and capitalizing it separately.

The problem we had come across time and again with prospective investors was that any new equity would be soaked up by our debts. If we could keep the sales company debt-free and then recapitalize it, and then make a fee arrangement between the sales operation and the rest of Goldcrest, sufficient income might be generated to service the debt burden and cover our much-reduced overheads until some other major source of funds – a merger, a big box-office success or a new investor – came our way. This idea met with some opposition. It was rightly pointed out that if we were to remove the most significant income-generating area of the business, our hopes of raising new money for the rest of Goldcrest would effectively be dashed. But of course my idea was really based on the premise that we were *not* going to be able to raise new money for the rest of the business. We had tried every avenue and we had come up with nothing. The board, however, lived in hope that once the films were released and generated substantial rentals, our financial position would improve sufficiently to make the company a much more attractive proposition for an investor. So the sales-company idea was, for the moment at least, put to one side.

Variations on the theme, however, kept suggesting themselves. During the course of a visit to Hollywood I had discussions with a number of independent production companies, chief among them Lorimar, King's Road and PSO. We talked about the possibility of setting up a co-operative US distribution venture, headed by Lorimar, into which Goldcrest would channel all its product. With our own four or five films a year, plus pick-ups from other producers, we might have been able to supply as much as one third of the films needed for such an operation. It would have meant not only by-passing, but competing with, the majors, which would have been a fairly bold step to take. But it would have had the great benefits not only of giving us earlier access to the box-office dollar, and a bigger share of that dollar, but of guaranteeing the distribution of our films. On the strength of such a guarantee we could raise additional production finance. An extension of this idea was that Lorimar, King's Road and PSO should channel all their foreign distribution through another co-operative venture that would be led by us.

But as great as the paper advantages of such schemes were the practical problems. My personal vision was that King's Road and Goldcrest should merge into Lorimar, which was a much bigger company than either of us. Lorimar's business was primarily in television, and it had a very weak feature-film division. But Goldcrest had nothing to offer in the way of capital, and Lorimar and King's Road were so busy making other plans that our discussions never got very far. In the end they each decided to go into distribution on their own. The result was, perhaps predictably, a bad move for both companies. Within three years, Lorimar was to find itself in deep trouble. It was eventually acquired by Warner Bros. King's Road is, at the time of writing, teetering on the brink of bankruptcy. As for PSO, it soon entered a financial quagmire from which it was never to emerge.

On another occasion we had talks with a London-based foreign-sales company, J&M, with a view to cutting our costs by sharing our back-office services. But it was never a very serious proposal and I don't think they were any more keen than we were. They operated a completely different kind of operation from ours: different kinds of films, different customers, different film-makers, different corporate approach. The discussions never got beyond the 'wouldn't it be great if . . .' stage.

On 17 October 1985, Guy East had hosted a series of screenings of trailers, rough-cuts, assemblies and finished prints of all our current productions for about 150 foreign distributors, among them our two dozen or so best customers, who were in London prior to the Milan film market. The general reaction to the three big films had been very favourable and had given us much encouragement. At Milan itself, Guy was able to offer, in addition, Allied's first project, *The Name of the Rose*, produced by Bernd Eichinger. I had arranged the US financing and distribution for the film with Fox and Embassy. Bernd did not need a substantial cash advance for foreign sales, as he had already covered his production costs and the film was about to start shooting, so I was able to persuade him that, although we couldn't put up any money, we would do the best possible sales job for him and we would do it quickly. In fact, Bernd was very generous to us. He could easily have taken the picture elsewhere and got a good advance for it. The prices Guy managed to get were excellent – in Milan he did $1.1 million worth of sales for that one film – and Bernd was more than satisfied.

Ilott: On his way from the Milan film market to New York, Eberts gave an interview to *Screen International* in which he said, 'I have three priorities: cash, cash and cash.' Not for the first time, he referred to the self-imposed February deadline, indicating that if new money was not raised by that time Goldcrest might have to be wound up. In London, he gave a much longer interview to the influential listings magazine *Time Out*. As he has himself described, Eberts felt no responsibility for the mistakes of the Lee regime; nor did he intend to stay once Goldcrest had been put back on a sound footing. He was therefore probably able to speak more candidly than anyone else in the company. In the *Time Out* interview he did his best to provide frank, no-nonsense replies to the questions put to him. In so doing, he gave the writer plenty of quotable material that was critical of the Lee administration, bemoaned the burden of excessive overheads and debts, and warned of possible catastrophe.

'If this figure here', Eberts was quoted as saying, pointing to a column of figures on his desk, 'doesn't match this figure here by December, then that's it, we fold. Of course, it's unthinkable. But we are a company, like any other manufacturer of shoes or ice-creams. We could go under.'

The *Time Out* interview was published as part of a six-page special report in the magazine's 7 November edition. It was headlined, 'Goldcrest's Gamble: will Absolute Beginners, Revolution and The Mission break British Cinema?' Looking at *Revolution* in particular, *Time Out* assured its readers that, 'according to most reports', the film 'has already exceeded its £16 million budget by about a further £6 million', and it suggested a comparison, in what it called the 'ultimate bastard on the set' stakes, between Hugh Hudson, Michael Cimino and Stanley Kubrick.

Cimino, of course, was the man who had made *Heaven's Gate*, the failure of which had led to the demise of United Artists, and there were sufficient similarities between that film and *Revolution* for the two to be linked. The personality clashes on set, the scheduling problems, the supposed profligacy of Hugh Hudson in directing the film and of Irwin Winkler in providing for his own creature comforts while producing it: all this was easily picked up from the Wardour Street rumour mill.

The *Time Out* feature caused great pain within the Goldcrest camp. At the board meeting of 21 November, Angus Grossart blamed the poor response to Goldcrest's fund-raising efforts on 'adverse publicity', and Lieberson complained that 'so much attention has been focused upon the prospects for the three major pictures that any disappointment with *Revolution* could severely damage the other pictures and Goldcrest's business as a whole'. (He said this, of course, knowing that the dice were loaded against the company. That the press could smell blood was bad: that *Revolution* was about to provide the stuff in buckets was worse.)

Blame for the bad publicity was placed principally on Eberts. The board asked him to be more discreet when talking to journalists in future, and suggested to all directors that a more upbeat presentation of Goldcrest's affairs would not go amiss.

Another altercation between the board and Eberts concerned clauses in Winkler's and Hudson's contracts that reduced their profit points in proportion to the *Revolution* overcosts. Eberts had agreed to abide by Lee's reported decision to waive these penalties. The board was outraged.

Then there was the problem of the seemingly endless Allied–Goldcrest deal negotiations. On 8 November, the Allied shareholders went so far as to threaten to withdraw Eberts's services if this matter was not brought to a speedy conclusion. It would have been hard to take such a threat seriously, since Eberts and Stoddart were themselves major shareholders in Allied, but the point had been made.

Eberts: There was no ill-feeling between me and the board, but I think both sides at times felt a certain exasperation. That's bound to happen when an enterprise is in a downward, rather than an upward, spiral. I had no time for the more formal, constitutional procedures in which I felt the board indulged, and they perhaps had their noses put out of joint by my individualistic style. I may well have been wrong when it came to talking to journalists, although in mitigation I would have to say that Goldcrest enjoyed unusually close relations with the press. Dickie Attenborough and David Puttnam were very high-profile people in the UK, and Goldcrest was a household name. We had used the press to our great advantage over a period of five or six years. It was hard to break that habit.

The Hudson–Winkler affair, though, was just ridiculous. To spend time discussing the overcost penalties in their contracts was academic. First of all, Winkler had deferred all his fee, and Hudson half his, to make the picture. The balance was meant to be paid out of revenues, but not until the film had recouped its investment. Thus, they were supposed to have had a strong incentive to keep the costs of the film down. Just to make doubly sure, a further clause stated that their shares of the net profits would be penalised if the film went over budget. Both aspects of the contracts were in dispute – according to Winkler and Hudson, James Lee had agreed not to impose the overcost penalties – and the matter hinged on the definition of break-even. We had to determine what the budget was, what the overage was and what part of the overage was excess – i.e. the responsibility of the film-makers – and what part was incremental – i.e. incurred with our approval. And what it came down to was, would the picture move into profit with net receipts of £17 million or £19 million? The argument was so preposterously academic that I said, 'Gentlemen, it makes no difference. Let's not waste time arguing for weeks on end about who's to blame, and what should and shouldn't be included in the budget. This film hasn't the remotest chance of recouping £17 million and going into profit. Forget it. James Lee agreed to drop the penalty clause and I've undertaken to abide by his decision. Don't waste my time and everyone else's time, lawyers' fees and God knows what on a matter which is of no practical consequence.'

But the board would not have it. They were adamant that we had to settle the issue right there and then, because they were damned if they were going to let Hudson and Winkler even technically be eligible to get the balance of their fees, let alone a share of the profits. They wanted to make sure that the whole world knew that the picture had gone over budget and that Hudson and Winkler were to blame. It was crazy. Where people got the time, energy and interest to waste on these things, I don't know. The matter was put to the vote in my absence, and I was overruled.

According to the minutes of the meeting in question, Hudson and Winkler were to be told of the decision 'at an appropriate time after the release of the picture'.

I began to experience an enormous sense of frustration at the board's apparent insistence on form over substance, and their refusal to recognize that the company was in deep financial trouble. They had rejected injections of capital because the prices were too low, they had shelved the sales-company idea and they persisted in naive hopes that the three unreleased films, particularly *Revolution*, were going to save the day. These hopes seemed to have blinded the board to the realities of the situation. Either that, or, as I began to suspect, they had not been blinded at all but were only too aware of the extent of their mismanagement; they were simply hoping that their past errors would somehow be put right by miraculous box-office receipts. If it happened it would not be the first time that mismanagement in the movie business had been covered up by last-minutè success.

Chapter Fifty-seven

The Killer Blow

Ilott: On 25 December 1985, *Revolution* opened in New York to some of the worst notices in living memory. 'Why *Revolution* Is Revolting' moaned the headline on Vincent Canby's thoughtful but depressing, and, from Goldcrest's point of view, depressingly influential, review. Canby set the tone: '. . . watching *Revolution* is like visiting a museum' (*Variety*); 'almost as big a débâcle as *Heaven's Gate*' (*LA Herald*); 'utterly and fatally devoid of a story' (*LA Times*); 'one of the worst films ever made' (TV pundit Robert Osborne); 'easily one of the worst movies of the year' (*LA Daily News*); 'dingily photographed with the compositional eye of an earthworm' (*Toronto Globe and Mail*); 'a chaotic two-hour, four-minute mess' (*Time*); 'the most hilariously maladroit historical pageant since King David – this movie is nuts' (*Village Voice*); 'dull and long-winded' (*Christian Science Monitor*); 'if Al Pacino's accent doesn't put you off, wait till you hear the screams during the ten-minute infected-foot cauterizing scene. Not the patient's screams – yours' (*USA Today*). For every half-heartedly favourable notice there were a dozen of these excoriations.

There was much defensive talk in the Goldcrest–Hudson camp about Americans being prejudiced against the film because they didn't approve of an Englishman having made it, or because they didn't like the spotlight being trained on the grimy side of the most glorious episode of their history, or because they were still smarting from Colin Welland's triumphant cry, 'The British are coming!' at the 1982 Oscar ceremonies. It is more likely, however, that they just didn't like the film.

Revolution took a respectable $96,000 from four screens in its first six days. But that just soaked up the cinema buffs who would check out a Hugh Hudson movie whether it was good or bad. Thereafter the release was a catastrophe. Warner Bros. at first reduced their planned nationwide opening from 1,200 prints to less than 800, and then opted for a concentrated 60-print trial release in the San Diego area, backed by television advertising. It was a disaster. By the third weekend, takings per cinema were so low that the film, which had hardly had a chance to open wide, was already being withdrawn. Warner Bros. predicted total US rentals of $3–4 million. (In fact, the film was to generate less than $1 million rentals.) Howard Schuster withdrew his promise of funds – his investors, he said, would baulk at putting money into a known failure – and Goldcrest, facing an outcome much worse than even Chambers's 'worst-likely' calculations, now faced a certain loss of almost £10 million on the picture. In addition, there would be pressure from foreign distributors to renegotiate their advances at the forthcoming American Film Market, and Goldcrest could expect no more than distress-sale prices for the still unsold territories of Germany and Japan.

Eberts: My only hope was that, in spite of the reviews, there would be enough interest in the picture to ensure big video-cassette sales, respectable prices in pay-cable and maybe even a network deal. But the news just got worse and worse. When a film opens badly and then plunges in the second week, there is nothing you can do to save it. No matter how much is spent on advertising and no matter how hard you promote it, if takings drop 50 per cent on the second weekend, and a further 50 per cent on the third weekend, as happened to *Revolution*, then that's it, it's over. With all the ancillary sales tied to the theatrical performance you can say goodbye to the video, cable and television money too. Much worse than the budget overrun was *Revolution*'s failure at the box office.

Hugh was heavily criticized for opting out of the round of press interviews and personal appearances that usually accompany a major release. But it's a rare director who would submit himself to public scrutiny in the face of certain failure. Indeed, the people you see on chat shows after a movie opens are only ever promoting films that are already known to be, or expected to be, successful. Dickie had thrown himself into a full-blooded promotional rescue of *A Chorus Line* after it had been trashed by the American critics, and he won much praise in the industry for doing so. But Dickie is something of a special case He is a promoter's dream – never giving up, working tirelessly for his film. Where *Revolution* was concerned you couldn't see Al Pacino, Nastassia Kinski, Hugh Hudson or Irwin Winkler for dust.

Hugh had been so psychologically battered by the pressure put on him to finish the film, and so shattered by the reviews, that he was simply not in a fit mental state to go out and face the public. He just couldn't do it. And he can't be blamed for that. You have to remember that, in making the film, Hugh had to work with a combination of Irwin Winkler, Chris Burt, Sandy Lieberson and Garth Thomas. Whatever their respective merits, these men were not going to give Hugh the service that he needed on a film of that size. What he needed was an Alan Marshall figure, or what Roland Joffe had: David Puttnam and Iain Smith, at that time arguably the best production team around. Maybe Hugh brought the situation upon himself – I don't know. But the fact is that he was mentally destroyed by December. He was a mess. He was exhausted. It took him the best part of a year to recover from *Revolution*.

His critics in the press have no idea how hard film-making is. On the one hand, they adore the *auteur* who struggles for his true vision against all the odds, and especially against the financial imperatives of his backers. On the other, they lambast the irresponsible and profligate megalomaniac whose film goes 'wildly' over budget. Not that they stick their necks out and make such a judgement off their own bat. They wait until the public has given its verdict: if the film is a success, the director is an *auteur*, as Hugh was after *Chariots*; if the film is a failure, he's a megalomaniac, as Hugh was after *Revolution*.

After a suitable time has elapsed, say ten or twenty years, the judgement might be reversed, so that the profligate director of the costly, and commercially unsuccessful, film is suddenly revealed as having been an *auteur* all along. Thus, Michael Cimino, whose *Heaven's Gate* was laughed off the screen in 1980, has since become a cult figure among art-house filmgoers.

On 6 January 1986, in the midst of the *Revolution* débâcle, we held sneak previews of *Absolute Beginners* in LA. The subsequent report informed us that there had been 'an unusually high walk-out rate', but that there had been a 'favourable response from those who stayed'. More than twenty cuts to the film and various improvements to the soundtrack had to be completed in time for further previews, on the East Coast, later in the month. Not only was I depressed about the quality of the film, which I thought was execrable, but I was nervous that, if each preview threw up a dozen or so changes, we could find ourselves slipping far past our delivery date. Orion, who had now seen the film and decided to stand by it, might conclude, as Warners had done in the case of *The Mission*, that it would be better served by an autumn opening. Our cash flow would not stretch that far.

We had by now really shot our bolt. In five months, all our efforts had got us precisely nowhere. And the first of our three throws of the dice, *Revolution*, had proved to be a complete loser. The 1 February deadline that I had set myself was approaching and I had failed to raise new money. The minutes of the management meeting of 13 January record

the general opinion that 'in view of *Revolution*'s disappointing performance and the withdrawal of third-party investments, it was unlikely that
the company could repay its bank borrowings within the foreseeable
future'. This was it. We were at, or very near, the end of the line.

Curiously, I still had great difficulty persuading the shareholders on
the board to take the crisis seriously. They seemed to want to blot out
the bad news in the hope that it would soon turn good. They were kept
informed about the situation but the message just didn't seem to get
through. I would say, 'Gentlemen, I think we're on the verge of bankruptcy. We're in danger of contravening the Companies Act by continuing to trade while insolvent. Unless something happens very quickly
we're going to have to wrap it up.' And the response was, 'Oh, we'll get
money in from the VAT people', or 'Don't worry, ECI will soon pay what
they owe on the completion guarantees', or 'Perhaps *Absolute Beginners*
will do well after all'. There was no urgency to their deliberations. There
was a sense that, well, somehow we could muddle through. I kept saying
to myself, 'Maybe I'm not making myself clear. Maybe they're just not
focusing on it and it needs me to present it in some other way.' At other
times I'd think, 'Maybe I'm wrong, maybe the situation isn't so bad after
all.'

Looking back, I realize that, as far as the shareholders were concerned,
Goldcrest was just one of their many interests, and a very small one at
that. When Goldcrest was on the way up, they attended to it assiduously
in the hope that it would become a significant business for them. When
it was on the way down, however, they found their time taken up with
other, bigger or more promising investments. They would do their duty
by Goldcrest, but if, as I kept predicting, it was going to go down the
tube anyway, then they were not going to waste time on it. Still less
were they of a mind to put more money in – the response to the loan-
stock offer had proved that. (At one time, Pearson were prepared to
invest further money themselves, but could not do so unless the other
shareholders did the same, for Pearson had to avoid taking their stake
beyond the point, 50 per cent, at which they would have to account for
their share of Goldcrest's losses in their accounts.)

It is in this context that I can now see that Michael Stoddart's role in
1986–7 was little short of heroic. There was nothing in it for him –
Goldcrest accounted for less than 1 per cent of his portfolio of investments
– yet he plugged away, attending meeting after meeting and dealing with
all manner of problems. In fact, when he offered, as a cost-cutting gesture,
to halve his director's fee of £15,000 a year, we refused, on the grounds

that he, more than anyone, deserved the money for the work he was putting in.

Early in 1986, I requested a meeting with our three leading shareholders' representatives, Michael Stoddart, James Joll and Angus Grossart. I wanted to present the company's predicament to them in the plainest possible terms and put before them my plan to split off and separately capitalize the sales department. This was, as far as I was concerned, Goldcrest's last hope.

Partly in preparation for this plan, I had, on 4 December, recommended that Guy East be made a director of the company and that his salary be increased from £43,000 to £65,000 a year. This was a substantial jump in earnings and came at a time when the company was doing everything possible to cut costs. Moreover, it put him on a par with John Chambers, who was his senior, by a significant margin, in both age and experience. There was therefore, predictably, considerable opposition to the proposal and I had quite a fight on my hands to get it approved. Certain members of the management team tended towards the view that everyone should be paid the same, with increments being awarded only for experience or long service. The idea was that we were all of equal worth: Guy was the salesman and made the deals, but someone else had to translate those deals into contracts, which was just as important. The trouble with this approach is that it ignores the market. There were then very few experienced and capable salesmen in the film business, and Guy was one of them. As soon as it had become known that Goldcrest was in trouble, he had started getting offers from other film companies, some of whom were prepared to pay more than double his Goldcrest salary.

If we lost Guy I would have a terrible job trying to replace him. Back-office staff were easier to come by. I am not saying that I could just go out and hire people of the calibre of John Chambers or David Norris. Nor am I denying that John in particular, by virtue of his extraordinarily detailed knowledge of Goldcrest's affairs, was anything but crucial to the company. If we lost him, we were sure to suffer. But, as a general rule, I could recruit a competent finance man at short notice, just as I could use Peter Coles to take over from David Norris. Competence in the back office is what gets you by. When it comes to salesmen, however, competence of itself is not enough. In fact, a competent salesman is no salesman at all. There has to be something else: personality, flair, a nose for a deal, and, most of all, the ability to be both tough in negotiation and popular with the customers. Guy had charisma and an excellent manner. He was well liked in the business. He was fluent in a number of languages, had a legal training that stood him in good stead in contract negotiations, and by now he had a lot of experience. So my view was that we had to pay Guy enough money, and give him enough status, to secure his services in the long term. This was all the more important, of course, in the light of the fact that he was the linchpin in the sales-company plan.

The idea was to set up Guy in a separate company with its own capital and staff, isolated from the rest of the company and unburdened by the debts and other problems with which John Chambers and his team were battling. Guy would acquire sales rights to third-party product and, from the commissions earned, pay a service fee to Goldcrest for the use of office space and back-office facilities. Guy's chief source of product would, of course, be Goldcrest itself.

All this was discussed in outline – a detailed proposal would take time to prepare – at my meeting with James Joll, Michael Stoddart and Angus Grossart on 14 January. In principle, they approved the plan, and they decided that it should be put before an emergency shareholders' meeting on 29 January. It would also be the main item for discussion at the intervening board meeting on 23 January.

As far as I was concerned, these meetings were to be make or break for Goldcrest.

Chapter Fifty-eight

Rallying to the Flag

'I'm bitter and very angry. I have put ten years of my life into this company. It's tragic to find all that work wasted and the company in tatters. The bank, Pearson and the board have put up with shit I wouldn't have put up with for 30 seconds. Who do I blame? I blame people whose priorities are different from ours, people who want to get rich, want to make a name for themselves, and who have no sense of responsibility for the British film industry. The chain of mutual responsibility between writers, producers and artists has been broken, and what's been done at Goldcrest has been done to all of us. No winner comes out of this. It is interesting that James [Lee] lost his job and lost his credibility. Likewise, Sandy Lieberson. But Irwin Winkler and Hugh Hudson will go on and make more films. It doesn't seem right. I'm sorry that we're picking over the bones of a single movie, but I'm afraid that with that movie goes the City's confidence in Goldcrest and the film industry as a whole. Had Revolution been even moderately OK and on budget none of this would ever have happened. Goldcrest would have seen its way through.' – David Puttnam, interviewed by Terry Ilott, 20 January 1986

'The irony and the tragedy is that Jake and I came into a predetermined situation. The pictures were already made and had already gone over budget. That was not of our making. We inherited the crisis from James Lee, who, as chairman and chief executive, must accept responsibility. Likewise, Sandy, as head of production, must bear some responsibility.' – Richard Attenborough, interviewed by Terry Ilott, 21 January 1986

'All that's happened is that Hudson ran over and Julien Temple ran over and Goldcrest didn't have the resources to deal with that.' – James Lee, interviewed by Terry Ilott, 23 January 1986

Eberts: The disastrous release of Revolution in the United States had produced an avalanche of press comment, both in the trades and in the British national newspapers. Even television news programmes took an interest. With reporters calling our offices all through the day, it was inevitable that news of the emergency shareholders' meeting would soon get out. 'Showdown Is In Offing for Goldcrest Pix', announced *Variety* on 17 January. Two days later, the *Sunday Times* ran a major feature on Goldcrest's problems under the headine, 'Is This the Final Cut?' The information in this article was remarkably accurate and could have come only from someone inside the company.

Again, complaints were heard within the company about those who had 'leaked' sensitive information to the press. But as far as I could tell, it was the very people who objected most strongly who had now become the willing conduits of information. As the quote that opens this chapter amply demonstrates, David Puttnam in his anguish was as willing to open his heart to a reporter as anyone. Film is a very high-profile industry. It commands much greater attention, even on the business pages, than its size or economic significance can justify. Hollywood employs only about 80,000 people, but Hollywood – the industry, not the movies – gets at least three times the press coverage that the vastly bigger and more important Californian aerospace industry gets. Goldcrest, the flagship of the British film industry, never employed more than fifty-five people, yet the names Puttnam, Attenborough, Eberts and Lee had appeared dozens of times, in all kinds of publications, in connection with the company's business affairs. Dickie, of course, is famous in his own right, and David is too. But the fascination of the press for our business did not depend entirely on them. It was remarkable and out of all proportion to our importance.

All this attention meant that we each knew journalists with whom we kept in more or less regular contact. And, on one level, we had to: if we did not put out accurate information, they would write something inaccurate and, in the process, probably do far more damage to the company. I had a particularly good relationship with Raymond Snoddy at the *Financial Times*. Ray was a meticulous reporter. He was well informed and very bright. His coverage of Goldcrest's affairs over the years, indeed his coverage of the entertainment business as a whole, was always reliable. On 20 January he called me. He had somehow managed to acquire detailed information regarding our financial situation and the critical nature of our problems. He wanted my confirmation and comments. As he recounted our troubles one by one, it occurred to me that it might be a good thing to be more than usually forthcoming in my reply.

My fear was that the 23 January board meeting and the shareholders' meeting that was to follow would come to no particular conclusion. This would be the worst thing that could happen to Goldcrest. In my opinion, the situation was so grave that it required a clear-cut response. The 23 January board meeting *had* to be do-or-die. The company *had* to be faced with an unequivocal choice: either we kept going, or we packed our tents. If we kept going, then we would probably have to act on the idea of dividing the company in two, capitalizing the sales division separately. But even if we did not do that – and at this stage we had not gone into it in sufficient detail even to know if it were possible – we would have to give some assurances to the staff, and to Guy East and John Chambers in particular, that it was worth their while to stay on board. It was with this in mind that I confirmed to Ray Snoddy that his information was correct. I knew that if the *Financial Times* ran a story that set out the stark choices facing Goldcrest, and if that story put the spotlight clearly on the board, then the non-executive directors would feel obliged to 'answer' the piece by acting decisively.

Ray's story appeared the next morning, 21 January, and, from my point of view, it was a complete success. Headlined, 'Future of Goldcrest in the Balance', it was no more than an accurate statement of the facts. But it was apocalyptic enough in tone to make it unlikely that the board would duck the issues.

Ilott: Snoddy's was not the only story to appear that day. Indeed, it would seem that Eberts was not the only Goldcrest executive to have spoken to a journalist with more than the usual candour. The *Hollywood Reporter* ran a long front-page piece under the headline, 'Goldcrest Board to Address Future'. It was filed by the paper's London bureau chief, Chris Goodwin, who, along with Sue Summers at the *Sunday Times*, was probably the best-informed reporter working on the story. Goodwin noted that Goldcrest had a choice: either to close down or to become a sales company. In the latter event, he said, 'it is difficult to see that Jake Eberts would wish to continue in his present capacity'. This remark, the first suggestion in print that Eberts might drift out of Goldcrest, was right by instinct but wrong in expression. It wasn't so much that Eberts would not wish to continue in a sales-only company, but that the setting up of such a company, to which he was now giving a great deal of his attention, would provide him with a welcome way out of Goldcrest. More than that, a sales company, in order to secure a line of product, would most likely enter into a relationship with Allied, thereby realizing the Goldcrest shareholders' earlier fear that the product-generating tail, Allied, would end up wagging the product-selling dog, Goldcrest.

Like Snoddy, Goodwin noted that Goldcrest's tribulations were likely to have a severely damaging effect on City attitudes to film investment – a refrain that was to be heard up and down Wardour Street for years to come.

The next day, *Variety*, following up Goodwin's report, and displaying its famously idiosyncratic usage of the English language, headlined its story, 'Brit Goldcrest's financial crisis on the rise with pallid Revolution; say Eberts put up for-sale sign'. And in London, *The Times*, reproducing much of Snoddy's account, stated, 'Financial Crisis Puts Goldcrest's Future in Balance'. After that the floodgates were opened, and the next morning, the morning of the board meeting itself, more or less accurate stories appeared in the quality and tabloid press, the trades and on national radio. In one way or another they all announced that this was it: that the fate of Britain's bravest and most glorious film company, the company that had challenged Hollywood on its own turf and won, was to be decided at what they all called an 'emergency meeting' of the board. The coverage whet the appetite of the public and guaranteed that there would be huge interest in the outcome of the day's proceedings. As Goldcrest staff arrived at the Wardour Street offices, television crews were setting up their equipment on the pavement outside. Eberts's plan had worked rather better than he could have expected.

Eberts: I had a parking space in the basement of our office building, so I drove round the back, went down in the car lift and came up the internal staircase in order to avoid having to go through the lobby. Of course, Dickie came through the lobby as he always did, as did David Puttnam. They got caught in the scrum of newsmen and were besieged with questions.

The meeting started at about 10.30 a.m. All the directors, including the newly elected Guy East, were in attendance. There was an atmosphere of great expectation, largely engendered by the press interest. I think the board finally realized that decision day had arrived.

Proceedings began with brief updates on the disposal of the office lease, *Revolution*'s latest box-office figures (the film had already been withdrawn in New York), my vain attempts to terminate or amend our independent production deal with Sandy Lieberson (we were obliged to pay him a $300,000 advance against fees and up to $150,000 as a contribution towards his overheads), the dispute with ECI, and the previews of *Absolute Beginners* (Orion had dramatically reduced the scope of the planned US release), all of which took no more than a few minutes.

John Chambers then reported on the current cash-flow position. With lower than expected receipts from *Revolution*, the withdrawal of the promised Schuster funds and the failure of the Viking investments (Viking had raised only half the money expected and we had been informed that the promised £1.5 million investments in both *Absolute Beginners* and *The Mission* would not be forthcoming), we faced a borrowing requirement significantly in excess of the Midland's £12 million limit. Moreover, we had in prospect sufficient contracts to secure, at best, £10.8 million of credit.

I then outlined the steps we had taken over the preceding months to try to alleviate our situation. The management team had given highest priority to five potential sources of funds: a buyer, merger partner or other form of new equity investment; disposal of whatever disposable assets still remained in the company; accelerated exploitation of ancillary rights; third-party project investment; and maximization of the use of tax losses, write-offs and capital allowances.

As regards the first of these, Wertheim had now come up with a plan to raise £4–8 million of equity finance on a 'distress basis'. Unfortunately, the terms they required were, as was to be expected, punitive. UAA, presumably because they were having no luck finding an alternative vehicle for their money, had come back to say that they were still interested in a merger. This was something that we would follow up. As for asset sales, Dickie and I had that morning had an exploratory breakfast meeting with Rank to discuss the disposal of all our unsold film rights. Michael Green at Carlton Communications was expected to come up with another proposal for the television films. And Warner Bros. were preparing an offer for the residual rights to *The Mission* in those territories for which they already had theatrical distribution. Guy East reported that we still had a substantial portfolio of unsold television licences – including rights to many of the feature films, the *First Loves* and *Robin of Sherwood* – which could be packaged on a territory-by-territory basis. Discussions were already under way with broadcasters in Scandinavia, from whom we hoped to receive more than $400,000 and in the UK, where Guy was offering a package to the BBC for £2.5 million.

John Chambers reported on our project-financing efforts: Centrespur, a film-finance broking house, had a client that was interested in doing a tax deal on *The Mission*, from which the benefit to us might be £2 million; a Scandinavian financier, Bertil Ohlsson, was considering a $1 million investment in the same film; and two television distributors had made offers of advances, worth as much as £600,000, for the sales rights to *Robin of Sherwood*.

John also explained the rather arcane business of capital allowances, group tax losses and the carried-forward losses from the pre-1984 limited partnerships, all of which had been surrendered to Pearson to be set against its own tax liabilities. Once all the sums had been worked out, Pearson would reimburse Goldcrest a proportion of the money thus saved. Losses of £6 million would net us £1.74 million. Losses of £3 million would net us £870,000. If a suitable figure could not be agreed, or if some insurmountable technical obstacle were encountered, then, since Pearson had not yet utilized the losses, they could be offered as an inducement to a potential investor in the company. Such an investor, however, would have to own 75 per cent of the company to be eligible to use the losses against tax.

And that was it. Did it present a sufficiently encouraging picture for the shareholders to want to continue, I asked. If it did, we could move on to the next item on the agenda: the sales-company proposal. If it didn't, we could begin the process of winding up our affairs.

I stated that no purpose would be served by liquidating the company when two major films had yet to go into distribution. We had reached what must surely be the lowest point in our fortunes, and a steady, if slow, improvement might be expected from here on. (John Chambers had prepared forecasts that showed that a modest improvement was likely, regardless of the performance of *Absolute Beginners*, from March or April onwards.) I added that our great assets – our name and reputation – might yet attract a hitherto unidentified redeemer. In short, we should carry on.

I did not ask for more money, because I knew I could not get it. Nor did I expect the commitment to be open-ended. What I asked for was a twelve-month lease of life. In that time, we would have received the bulk of whatever we were to receive on our film investments, including *The Mission*; we would have stabilized the company; and we would be able to go back to the market with a much clearer estimate of Goldcrest's worth.

An impassioned, dramatic and emotional debate, by turns reflective and rousing, ensued. Dickie spoke brilliantly and wept copious tears. David Puttnam, equally forceful if not as emotional, made a strong case for standing by our responsibilities to the British film industry as a whole. He pleaded with the shareholders to maintain the name of Goldcrest, at least until *The Mission* had been released. He predicted, also, that Goldcrest's portfolio – we had by now invested in twenty-four feature films, twelve television films, seven television drama series and eight documentary series – would so increase in value, with the advent of cable and satellite and the deregulation of markets, that it would more than pay back whatever losses were incurred in the coming year. Guy East, too, made a tear-laden speech, pleading for his own position, and that of his staff, to be made secure and begging to be given time to generate enough revenues from third-party product to pay off our debts. John Chambers, less vocal perhaps, and certainly less effusive, was no less impressive in his commitment to pulling the company through. For myself, at the start I was as cool-headed as could be, in spite of my inner anxiety. But even I was moved by the eloquence of the speeches, especially Dickie's.

The non-executive directors were, in a sense, cast in the role of devil's advocates, focusing on the problems and contradictions in our arguments. And while they personally may have been in sympathy with our point of view, they were themselves under considerable pressure. They had to take a lot of heat from their own boards of directors for having allowed the situation to go so badly wrong. It was not as if the Goldcrest board had been an inactive board. On the contrary, it had been very active. They all say now that they did not know much about the film business, and that they did not properly grasp what was going on, but the fact is, and it is recorded in the minutes, that a lot of basic operating questions were brought to them for decision. The choice of investments, the completion-guarantee policy, even the casting of Al Pacino, were matters which were decided, not rubber-stamped, at board level. It would have been very hard for James Joll's or Michael Stoddart's colleagues to understand how they could have presided over the investment, in a two-year period, of £34 million of cash, £12 million of bank credit and a further £7.6 million of loan stock without knowing much about the film business.

The press leaks and the media forecasts of our imminent demise, combined with the stirring pleas from the executives and film-makers on the board, finally had their effect. The shareholders gave a clear assurance that they would back Goldcrest for another year at least, that jobs would be secure and that they would support our attempts to set up an independent sales company. Thus, at the end of three hours of passionate discussion, we knew that we had at least a year in which to put the company back on a sound footing.

The question now was how to communicate our resolve to the hordes of newsmen waiting impatiently outside, and, through them, to the industry itself. As Guy pointed out, the speculation about Goldcrest's future had led to a suspension of confidence amongst our suppliers and customers.

Our advertising agency, for example, would do work for us only if we paid in advance.

Screen International had a press deadline of 4 p.m. and I was very anxious that a good, upbeat story should appear on its front page the next morning. Everyone in Wardour Street would be looking out for it. With the board's permission, I had already arranged to speak to *Screen* at some point early in the afternoon. I also had a list of numbers to call back: *Variety*, the *Hollywood Reporter*, the *Sunday Times* and others. We decided that time would be set aside for me to make my calls to the press and for David and Dickie to go down to the lobby and answer questions from the assembled television journalists. A press release would be drawn up by myself, James Joll and Philip Whitehead during the lunchtime adjournment.

It read as follows:

The board of Goldcrest Films and Television (Holdings) Limited held its regular monthly board meeting this morning. The company has been known to be operating under tight financial constraints since last summer and reviewed its situation, especially in the light of the disappointing results in the US of *Revolution*. It has kept its bankers fully informed at all times and continues to enjoy their support and to operate within agreed facilities.

In view of misleading speculation regarding costs of the company's major films, the board thought it appropriate to release the relevant details concerning these films, as follows:

	Budget	Cost
Revolution (£million)	16.0	19.0
The Mission	17.5	16.8
Absolute Beginners	6.6	8.4
A Room With a View	2.4	2.3
	42.5	**46.5**

The budgets for these films, drawn up according to industry practice, include completion fees (less rebates, where applicable) and a 10 per cent contingency on direct cost.

Looking to the future, the board today unanimously adopted the following strategy:

1. Continued active participation in the British film industry with an ongoing commitment to feature film production;

2. Expansion of its successful international sales and marketing operation;

3. Accelerated licensing of the company's existing film and television portfolio in order to reduce interest charges; and,

4. Further reductions in operating overheads, with particular emphasis on office relocation.

In addition to *Revolution* Goldcrest has eight other films either in or going into worldwide release this year and other considerable assets to exploit. The board affirmed its confidence in the quality and commercial potential of these forthcoming releases, including *Absolute Beginners, The Mission, A Room with a View* and *The Name of the Rose.*

The budget figures had been rounded up, so that, while the main points of comparison were correct, the details were a little awry. For one thing, *The Mission* wasn't finished yet, so the figure of £16.8 million was an estimate, albeit a very accurate one. For another, *Revolution* had never had a contingency allowance in its budget, so the £3 million overage was an understatement. That we chose to release the figures at all, an extremely unusual, not to say unprecedented, step for a film company, was entirely due to my desire to mollify David Puttnam. He was fed up – steaming with rage would be a better description – at the constant speculation in the press about *Mission* overages. This was not a matter that, hitherto, had concerned me at all. There had been specific overages – £100,000 to settle the Colombian labour dispute, £206,000 for the extended shoot in Argentina, £70,000 for unapproved expenses incurred by Robert De Niro. Some of this additional expenditure had been absorbed by a favourable shift in exchange rates. For example, the final cost statements showed a saving of £563,000 in the fixed above-the-line expenditure, much of which was payable in dollars. The total item-by-item below-the-line cost, on the other hand, showed an overage of £1.9 million. Taking the contingency allowance into account, this left *The Mission* £395,000 over its agreed operating budget, but well within the budget devised for completion-fee purposes. The true total cost, including Goldcrest's deferred overheads, the full contingency allowances and rebated completion fees, was £18.2 million, against a budget of £18.5, a saving of about £300,000. The correspondence on this subject was voluminous (and, now that I have written this, is likely to get more voluminous still) and reflects the fact that David's reputation is worth more to him than gold. He was especially anxious that *The Mission* and its production team should not be tarred with the same brush as *Revolution* and *Absolute Beginners.*

I made my various calls to the press, and in each case put a very upbeat gloss on the story: the board was backing us all the way, soon we would bring down the debt, *Absolute Beginners* and *The Mission* were going to be great, and so on. Dickie and David did the same downstairs in the lobby. Interestingly, the trades were very happy with the story and gave it massive and positive coverage, but among the nationals, and especially on the part of the television news organizations, there was considerable disappointment. 'Goldcrest Goes Under' would have been a great story. 'Goldcrest Carries On' was not. I have since been informed that three special features, on Channel 4 News, ITN and BBC's *Newsnight* were cancelled the minute the press release went out. Our news was not bad enough.

The meeting reconvened at about 5 o'clock and went on into the evening. The chief remaining item on the agenda was the sales-company proposal, which was discussed at considerable length.

By the end of it all I was exhausted. With twelve people gathered around a table, talking and arguing, fighting and crying, breaking for lunch, having cups of coffee, taking messages and dealing with the bank and the press, the time had flown by. The meeting had lasted nine hours. Even then, we continued the discussion in groups, in the boardroom, in our respective offices or over dinner. In those days, indeed throughout the history of Goldcrest, a twelve-hour day was the norm, but even for us a nine-hour meeting was something exceptional.

The next morning my desk had all but disappeared under a stack of newspapers: 'There Is No Crisis, says Goldcrest Films Boss' (*Daily Mail*); 'Goldcrest Denies Film Crisis' (*The Times*); 'Goldcrest Sales Campaign' (*Guardian*); '*Gandhi* Film Company in Cash Battle' (*Daily Express*); 'Film Company To Scale Down Production' (*Daily Telegraph*); and 'Goldcrest "Problems Exaggerated" ' (*Financial Times*). *Screen International*, under the headline 'Business As Usual As Goldcrest Board Backs Eberts' Survival Plan', ran the story on the front page, noting, rightly, that the four-point survival plan amounted to 'little more than hanging out a "we are still in business" sign'.

I was pleased with the general tone of the coverage: the press was no longer salivating at the prospect of our demise, and I expected that the story would soon be downgraded, or dropped altogether.

There was, however, to be one further sweep of the media spotlight before things did indeed quieten down.

On 29 January, we held the emergency shareholders' meeting. We outlined the position of the company and put to them, for their approval, the decisions of the previous week's board meeting. There was no problem and approval was duly granted. However, John Chambers had by now worked out a draft profit-and-loss account for 1985 and this had been tabled at the meeting. Somehow its most salient points, including an absolutely staggering estimated loss for the company, found their way into the press.

Ilott: The preliminary figures that Chambers put before the shareholders on 29 January did not differ significantly from the final figures given in the audited accounts eventually published on 14 April. These show a loss for the year of not £7 or £8 million as had been predicted as recently as November, *but just over £20 million.*

Profit and loss account	1983	1984	1985
Turnover £000	12,402	13,990	16,081
Direst costs and amortization	(9,338)	(10,350)	(32,041)
Gross profit/(loss)	3,064	3,640	(15,960)
Operating expenses	(1,741)	(2,501)	(2,978)
Operating profit/(loss)	1,323	1,139	(18,938)
Associated companies, non-film write-offs,			
currency exchanges, etc.	(198)	(127)	(669)
Profit/(loss) before interest	1,125	1,012	(19,607)
Interest receivable	148	699	334
Interest payable	(1,444)	(97)	(1,360)
Pre-tax profit/(loss)	(171)	1,614	(20,633)
Taxation	(864)	(30)	894
Profit/(loss) after tax	(1,035)	1,584	(19,739)
Extraordinary items	–	40	(369)
Retained profit/(loss)	(1,035)	1,624	(20,108)

The losses comprised £10 million written down against *Revolution,* £4.8 million against miscellaneous television projects (bringing the total

Balance sheet			
	1983	1984	1985
Assets: £000			
office equipment, motor cars, etc.	138	192	142
associated companies (mainly cable TV)	383	227	10
films/TV in distribution	5,388	14,508	11,455
films/TV in production	10,477	3,760	15,012
films/TV in development	724	862	644
Total fixed assets	17,110	19,549	27,263
current assets/(liabilities)	673	10,472	(10,521)
	17,783	30,021	16,742
Liabilities:			
creditors (including loan-stock holders)	(307)	(545)	(7,783)
deferred taxation	(616)	(273)	(143)
Net assets	16,860	29,203	8,816
made up of,			
share capital and other reserves	22,407	33,119	32,846
accumulated losses	(5,547)	(3,916)	(24,030)
	16,860	29,203	8,816

television write-off to date to £7.2 million), about £500,000 against *The Frog Prince* and various development projects, and roughly £400,000 against the losses of the cable venture, Premiere. To that were added the £3 million overheads, a deficit of about £300,000 on currency exchanges, £1 million net bank interest and £370,000 of redundancy payments.

As the balance sheet on the previous page shows, Goldcrest was now worth £8.8 million.

The important debits to note in the balance sheet are the £10.5 million of current liabilities, most of which was accounted for by bank borrowings of £11.4 million, and the £7.78 million owed to creditors, most of which was accounted for by the £7.65 million of loan stock. Both items were interest-bearing, hence the £1.3 million of interest payable. The two major credits were the value of the assets then (i.e. at 31 December 1985) in distribution, £11.5 million, and the value of the assets then in production, £15 million. The former figure was the residual book value of Goldcrest's entire catalogue. It would have included, for example, the television, cable and satellite rights in various territories to *The Killing Fields* and *Revolution*, and income yet to be received from the distribution of such films as *Dance With a Stranger*. The latter figure was the book value of *A Room With a View*, *Absolute Beginners*, *Mr Love*, *Knights and Emeralds* and *The Mission* – the five films yet to be released – upon which Goldcrest's future prosperity mainly depended. All but £9.7 million of this sum was covered by pre-sales, guarantees and other advances. But that £9.7 million was the big unknown on the balance sheet, and one which any cautious prospective investor would wish to discount. If the five films realized more than their £15 million aggregate book value, then the net worth of the company would be increased. If they failed to realize their full book value, the worth of the company would be diminished. If they were to realize about half their book value (£7.5 million) or less, the company, worth only £8.8 million and with projected overheads in 1986 of £1.3 million, would be wiped out.

It was with this in mind that the auditors, Deloitte Haskins and Sells, added a note to accounts saying that 'until worldwide release, neither we nor the directors are able to assess with certainty the ultimate commercial success of the films and accordingly whether the amount [the book value of the five films] is fairly stated'. Deloitte also drew attention to the fact that the viability of Goldcrest as a going concern depended 'on the group's bankers continuing to provide their present overdraft facilities and on the group obtaining sufficient funds from other sources'. Taking all this into account, they concluded, 'we are unable to form an opinion as to whether the financial statements give a true and fair view of the state of affairs of the company'. The £8.8 million, in other words, was not, in the opinion of the auditors, a reliable estimate of the company's worth.

They were right to be cautious.

'Goldcrest Writes Off £20 Million' announced the *Guardian*. 'Shareholders Could Face £20 Million Write-off In Goldcrest Rescue' declared *Screen International*.

Wardour Street was stunned by the scale of the losses.

On 30 January, *Revolution* opened in the UK to reviews that were almost as unkind as those in America: '[the film's] storyline often appears confused and fractured and its script at times almost laughably one-dimensional' (*Guardian*); 'an undigested mess' (*Evening Standard*); 'quite simply, it's dull' (*Daily Express*). The following week, it got the same reception in Australia; Roadshow, the Australian distributor, described the release as 'disastrous'. In France and Spain, though, *Revolution* was doing quite well. In both territories the film had been released in dubbed versions, thereby concealing the actors' disconsonant accents.

Chapter Fifty-nine

Staying Afloat

'The trouble they're in, they're going to work twice as hard to make these films successful.' – Alan Kaupe, UK head of Embassy Home Entertainment, on his decision to entrust the foreign distribution of two EHE pictures to Goldcrest's sales team

Eberts: For the first four months of 1986 we were struggling just to stay afloat. We had not raised any new money or found a merger partner, *Revolution* had been a catastrophe and the board's decision to back us for another year would not mean anything in practical terms until we had properly drafted the sales-company proposal. This latter task was extraordinarily complex, involving a restructure of the existing company, a reorganization of the staff, a reallocation of resources and liabilities and a fresh capitalization of the new sales entity. Had we been able to start from scratch, there would have been no problem. But we had to reconcile the needs of the new sales company and its investors, whoever they might be, with the needs of the existing company and with the ongoing obligations of the Goldcrest shareholders. We had to do all this within the constraints not only of company law, but of the interests and desires of the staff, shareholders, our trading partners and the film-makers who had profit participations in the films in the library. All of this at a time when we were working flat out to keep the company from going under. It was to take months.

My principal concern, meanwhile, was to ensure that our remaining pictures got the best possible release. The first of them was *A Room With a View*, which opened in New York in March to ecstatic reviews and, against all my predictions, excellent business. When it opened in London it went straight into the top ten box-office charts and stayed there for fifty-two weeks – an all-time record. But, as I have explained, we just did not have enough money in *A Room With a View* for its success to be meaningful to our finances. Much more important were

Absolute Beginners, which was to open on 4 April, and *The Mission*, which was to open in October. We had almost £17 million invested in *The Mission* and, if it proved to be a big success, it could transform the fortunes of the company. John Chambers's 'best-likely' forecast, for example, showed a net contribution to Goldcrest of £9 million, which would be enough for us to reduce the bank debt and to finance significant new investments in 1987. To reach that figure, however, *The Mission* would have to achieve US rentals of about $40 million, on a par with, for example, *Out of Africa*.

Early in February the first cut of *The Mission* was ready and we held previews in Reading, Berkshire. The ratings were as follows:

Excellent	–	43 per cent
Good	–	34 per cent
Fair	–	20 per cent
Poor	–	3 per cent

The walk-out rate, 2 per cent, was low. But the recommendation rate was low, too, a fact that David Puttnam did his best to rationalize by pointing to the example of *The Killing Fields*, the previews of which had produced much the same results. In fact, David was confident that *The Mission* would do at least as well as that earlier film. This was no great comfort to us, since *The Killing Fields* had taken US rentals of only $16 million. If *The Mission* did the same, we would lose a lot of money.

My own reaction to the completed film was quite favourable, but not as favourable as I had hoped it would be. One of my weaknesses is that I don't like long films. I don't like anything over two hours. When I had seen an earlier assembly of *The Mission*, without the waterfall sequences, it ran to about that length and I thought it was OK. The waterfalls added plenty of spectacle and majesty but they also added thirty minutes, without, as far as I could see, doing much for the story. It really was too long, and it worried me.

At the end of March, the Oscar ceremonies were marked, as far as we were concerned, by our absence. It was the first time since 1982 that no Goldcrest film had figured in the awards or nominations. A run of four consecutive years with Best Picture nominations had come to an end.

The following week, *Absolute Beginners* opened in London. It was distributed by Palace Pictures, who mounted an extraordinary promotional campaign on its behalf. Indeed, probably no film has been so over-promoted in the history of the British film business. The expectations of the audience were raised to such heights that the picture could only suffer by comparison. It was nothing like the film people had been led to expect. If they had come across it by chance they might actually have enjoyed it and it might have built up a following. But the hype and hullabaloo and exaggeration that preceded the opening guaranteed that, even if it had been twice as good as it was, it would have failed. You cannot sell a film as something that it is not. You cannot sell a film on the strength of promotion if the promotion does not truly represent what the film is all about. If you do, the audience, so full of expectations going in, comes away bitterly disappointed. And a disappointed audience is one that bad-mouths a film.

Absolute Beginners, which had been a textbook case of how not to make a movie, now proved a textbook case of how not to market one. It was overblown, the publicity was endless. You couldn't pick up a news-paper or magazine, or listen to the radio or turn on the television, without having *Absolute Beginners* thrown at you.

And some of it was in bad taste. I thought the way they treated the leading actress, Patsy Kensit, was dreadful. I felt very sorry for her. She said things, or she was made to say things, which were obnoxious: how she wanted to be a major star, how this was the only thing in her life and so on. You were sick to death of Patsy Kensit by the time the film opened. I think the audiences went into the picture actively disliking her. They were saying, 'God, let's not hear one more word about this seventeen-year-old bore. We've heard all that we want to hear from her.' And they came out of the cinema with their prejudices confirmed and they told their friends not to bother.

Palace spent £500,000 on prints, ads. and promotion. In the UK market at that time, that was a lot of money. They generated, in return, about £500,000 in rentals. In other words, it was a trade-off: Palace's expendi-ture on promotion was as good as buying the tickets themselves. They may have got something back from video and television, but if they broke even overall they were lucky. We lost a fortune: we had invested £5 million and we wrote off £3.2 million. Virgin also lost, although not as heavily as we did. In the States, the film was a catastrophe, taking rentals of less than $300,000. I am sure that, even though they had ancillary deals with HBO and Vestron, Orion, too, after accounting for prints and ads., would have lost money on it.

The whole exercise had been a disaster. At every stage, from the original conception, through the script, the pre-production, production and post-production, to the marketing and distribution, *Absolute Begin-ners* was an object lesson in how not to produce a movie.

All our hopes now rested on *The Mission*.

The beginning of May found us in Cannes, where I invited the trade press to a small reception at which I announced, for the first time publicly, a list of Allied's film-makers and investments. Allied had been in semi-limbo all this while, and I wanted to remind the industry that it was still in business, had money and had relationships with film-makers of the highest repute. I was working on five or six projects at that time, including *Biko* (*Cry Freedom*) with Dickie Attenborough, *City of Joy* with Roland Joffe, *Hope and Glory* with John Boorman and *Spring Moon* with Alan Pakula. In addition, I was contributing to the overheads of Alan Parker and Alan Marshall, from whom I expected other projects in due course.

The news about Allied received excellent coverage in the trades, and the upbeat tone of my comments spilled over, very helpfully, into the journalists' various comments about Goldcrest. But the main story at Cannes was that *The Mission* won the Festival's big prize, the Palme d'Or.

There had been great controversy about entering *The Mission* for Cannes. (Properly speaking, one doesn't enter or offer a film: one responds to the Festival's invitation.) Fernando Ghia, the originator of the project and co-producer with David Puttnam, had been adamantly and publicly opposed to it, both before and after the event. Roland Joffe and David, on the other hand, were all for it. My view was that, unless we had a very strong reason to do otherwise, we should go along with what the film-makers wanted. Of course, if I thought that a film-maker was making a clear-cut, categorical error, I would object. But in this case I had no strong feelings either way about Cannes and the film-makers in question were not the kind of people whose judgement I would call into question. David Puttnam has a real feel for the value of things like festivals. Fernando, on the other hand, did not have that kind of expertise. So when it came down to siding either with Fernando or with Puttnam and Joffe, I chose the latter.

The arguments for going to Cannes are that it gives your picture exposure (there are 3,000 journalists there, including all the major film critics, show-business editors and entertainment columnists from around the world); it gives you a platform from which to launch a European release; and, should you win a prize, it gives you and the film additional prestige. The arguments against going to Cannes are that, if you enter a competitive section, you stand a good chance of losing; that Cannes will give your film art-house connotations that could be a serious disadvantage at the US box office; and that, unlike, say, the Oscars, even if you do win a prize, it means nothing to the cinema-going public.

David and Roland just wanted to put *The Mission* on the map. They had finished it in early May but it wasn't to be released until October, so they were just itching to put it in front of an audience. They won the prize, so in that sense they were vindicated in their decision. But, as Fernando predicted, the Palme d'Or meant nothing at the box office.

On our return from Cannes we learned that the efforts of Guy East, John Chambers, Peter Coles and Andy Parsons were beginning to bear fruit. We got a tax deal for *The Mission* which threw up about £2 million of 'free cash'. We closed the deal with Richard Price Television for distribution rights to *Robin of Sherwood*, and received an advance of £500,000. Channel 4 put up £250,000 for re-run rights to a package of films. The BBC paid £1.2 million for television rights to *The Mission*, *The Killing Fields*, *Revolution*, *Smooth Talk*, *Enigma* and *Dream One*. We settled the group tax-relief deal with Pearson, and received £1.7 million. We got our VAT refund of £2.2 million. And the much-discussed Scandinavian television package brought in £473,000.

In addition, the release of *Absolute Beginners*, *A Room With a View* and *Mr Love* had triggered the payment of distribution advances. This money, of course, had already been discounted, but the cash inflow was welcome nevertheless. Like all the other receipts, it went straight to the bank to reduce the debt.

All this income served to relieve us of the pressure of imminent collapse. From here on, we were able to operate in conditions of relative stability.

I use the word relative advisedly, for we were far from being out of the woods. The £3.2 million write-off against *Absolute Beginners* had been a tremendous blow. We had earlier written off £160,000 against *Mr Love*; a further sum against our cable-television venture, Premiere, from which we had at last extricated ourselves; £600,000 against *Mandrake*, which by now I had had to concede was never going to get off the ground; and a similar sum against *Robin of Sherwood*, the second series of which had proved much more expensive, and much less lucrative, than had been expected. Thus, while we had brought the level of our borrowing down, it was still running at about £8 million. We had reduced our annual overheads, but still they consumed about £1.3 million. The staff had been cut by half, but that still left us with twenty-six people.

At the end of June 1986, John Chambers produced draft accounts that showed a loss of £6.2 million in the first six months of the year. The net worth of the company thus fell to £2.8 million, or roughly 8 pence per share. Given our doubts about the commercial viability of *The Mission*, we had to face the fact that there might be nothing left at all by the end of the year.

Our only lifeline was the sales-company proposal.

Following the make-or-break January board meeting, Guy had presented the board with a choice: either expand the sales division, from twelve to as many as twenty staff, and run down the rest of the company, thus quickly transforming Goldcrest into a sales-only enterprise; or split off six members of the sales team and establish them as a separately funded and self-sufficient company, to which other Goldcrest staff would be transferred over a period of, say, two years, until eventually the existing company would be wound up. The main difference between these two proposals was that the first would initially have been expensive, requiring some form of recapitalization of the debt-ridden Goldcrest – a prospect so unlikely that it wasn't worth discussing – whereas the second proposal would require capitalization only of a new, debt-free entity. Also, whereas Goldcrest's sales and marketing budget for 1986 was set at £550,000, Guy was forecasting overheads of only £250,000 for his new slim-line operation. To put this into perspective, in 1985 Guy's team had achieved sales of $18.5 million. Had his team been constituted as a separate company, it would have earned between $1.85 million (10 per cent) and $2.8 million (15 per cent) commission on those sales.

The board had agreed in principle to the second option. The new sales company would represent the Goldcrest catalogue, while Goldcrest would provide office space and administrative back-up. The commission that the sales company would earn from the catalogue sales would be more or less matched by the fee that Goldcrest would be entitled to charge for its office services. Thus, Goldcrest would continue to receive sales income while being free of the overhead burden of the sales and marketing operation (at that time, about one third of our total operating costs). For its part, the sales company would have covered all its back-office expenses from sales of the Goldcrest product and would be free to use its new capital to put up guarantees or advances for product from third parties. It was from the exploitation of this third-party product that it would generate profits.

At Cannes these ideas had been developed a stage further, partly as a result of negotiations I had with Andre Blay, who at that time was still running Embassy Home Entertainment. I had been trying to get Andre to finance the production of John Boorman's film *Hope and Glory*. If he put up $6 million for the video rights, we, Goldcrest, would put up $2.6 million as a guarantee against foreign sales. Together we would cover the cost of the picture. Only, of course, we did not have $2.6 million. However, Allied had developed this film with John Boorman, and it was very much in Allied's interest that it should go into production. Allied could itself contribute part of the money. Thus was born the idea of a third company, Goldcrest Allied Guarantees Ltd.

GAGL, as it was known, would be a separate pool of capital, financed by Allied, Pearson, Electra, Noble Grossart and whoever else we could get to take an interest, the sole business of which would be to put up guarantees against foreign rights. We were thinking in terms of raising $3 million, which sum would be backed up by a line of credit from Credit Lyonnais (Frans Afman was keen) of $6 or $7 million. With a total of $9 or $10 million to spend, we could easily put up guarantees for four or five pictures a year. These would be sold in the foreign markets by Guy's new sales company.

It was the draft proposals for the sales company and GAGL that now occupied our attention.

Ilott: All the parties concerned thought that the Goldcrest/New Sales Company/GAGL arrangement was excellent. But they haggled for weeks over exactly how much money each should put up and what shares they should get in exchange. Eberts proposed that Allied should invest $500,000 in GAGL for a 12 per cent equity interest and a further carried interest of 25 per cent. His argument was simple: he had been drawn back into Goldcrest on the basis of 65 pence share options, while the shares, through no fault of his, were now worth 8 pence and going down. In respect of that alone, Allied, he said, should be granted a compensatory carried interest. In addition, of course, GAGL was going to benefit enormously from his unpaid services and from the product, such as *The Name of the Rose* and *Hope and Glory*, that Allied provided.

But the Goldcrest shareholders would have none of it. They proposed that Allied should have a carried interest in GAGL of no more than 15 per cent.

A further complication was that Eberts insisted that GAGL should have the option to acquire the new sales company, to be known as Goldcrest Distributors Ltd, at a price equal to its net book value after a period of three years. The Goldcrest shareholders felt that for the tail to wag the dog was bad enough but for the tail to own most of the dog was going too far. They insisted, on the contrary, that Goldcrest Distributors should own 75 per cent of GAGL and that there be no option-to-buy arrangement.

A third complication arose from the conflict of interest between Eberts's roles in Allied, which was to be the supplier of product, and in Goldcrest, which was to be a user of product, and hence, in a sense, Allied's customer.

Eberts: The arguments went on and on. We started the discussion of this matter in June and we were still discussing it in October. As usual, the board simply could not make a decision. Throughout that time Goldcrest had to keep paying its bills. That it did so is a tribute largely to the earning power of the library (*Gandhi*, for example, continued to make money for the company), and also to the success of Guy East's policy of picking up third-party product for sale in the international markets. Ever since *The Name of the Rose*, which he had sold at the Milan film market and from which he had earned substantial fees, Guy had been looking for suitable films to represent. During the course of 1986, he acquired rights to *Half Moon Street* and *Sid and Nancy* (from Embassy Home Entertainment), *Maurice* (from the Merchant–Ivory team that made *A Room With a View*), *White Mischief*, *Hope and Glory*, *Fire and Ice*, *A Man In Love*, *Matewan* and *Maschenka*. All these films not only generated welcome revenues, but they were proof that an autonomous sales company could thrive in association with Goldcrest.

It was a proof that was not needed, since the board was persuaded of the soundness of our plan. What was needed was a greater sense of urgency to get that plan into action. We all had our doubts about Goldcrest's long-term viability and, from the point of view of our purely selfish interests, we each had to be thinking of alternative arrangements. At the end of June, David Puttnam resigned from the Goldcrest board to take up the top motion-picture job at Columbia Pictures. In July, John Chambers proposed a cost-saving arrangement whereby he resigned from the company and became instead an outside consultant. (I rejected the proposal.) In September, Dickie went off to film *Cry Freedom* in Zimbabwe. Guy was all the time torn by conflicts between his loyalty to Goldcrest and the spectacular offers he was getting from elsewhere. For my part, I now had five projects in development at Allied. It was more than enough work to occupy me. All of us, in other words, had half an eye, at least, on other things. It was in this context that the arguments over the sales-company proposal were so vexing.

By September 1986, I had become so fed up with it all that I proposed that Allied should withdraw from GAGL, which would be financed solely by the Goldcrest shareholders and/or other investors. At the same time, I announced that I would cease to play an executive role at Goldcrest.

There was no reason for me to stay. Indeed, there were good reasons for me to go. As I saw it, John Chambers would run Goldcrest Films and Television Ltd, which would look after the administration of existing product, and Guy would run Goldcrest Distributors Ltd, which would represent both the Goldcrest catalogue and the third-party product acquired with GAGL's money. As GAGL was just a fund with neither staff nor overheads, Guy would run that too. Allied, to which I would move full time, would then enter into a relationship with Goldcrest, whereby Goldcrest would pay Allied an annual fee in exchange for a second look, after Warner Bros., at all Allied projects. In practice, because of the close relationships between Goldcrest, Warners and Allied, this would mean that Goldcrest would secure the foreign-sales rights to virtually all the Allied films. This was precisely the arrangement I had proposed to James Lee eighteen months earlier.

The benefits of my scheme were that it would sort out once and for all the supposed conflict of interest between Allied and Goldcrest, while allowing both companies to get on with the businesses that they knew best. At the same time, it gave us a very close working relationship which, as well as being mutually beneficial, would reassure the Goldcrest shareholders and the bank.

All this was discussed with Michael Stoddart on 23 September 1986. He and I eventually agreed:

1. that I would cease to be chief executive and would become instead non-executive deputy chairman of Goldcrest,
2. that Goldcrest's payment to Allied would be in the form of an advance,
3. that this advance would be recouped from a 10 per cent override that Allied would earn on all sales commissions earned by Goldcrest, and,
4. that any part of the advance still outstanding would be recouped from production fees earned by Allied in excess of the amounts payable to Warner Bros.

All this was confirmed at the 25 September board meeting. At the end of November 1986, I stepped down as Goldcrest's chief executive for the second time.

I had done the job for fourteen months and I had given it my best. I would never have taken it on had I known the true state of the company, but that is not to say that I was dissatisfied with what I had achieved. We had done everything possible to save the company. Nothing could have prevented the disastrous performances of *Revolution* and *Absolute Beginners*. Nothing more could have been done, by myself or the management, in the matter of raising money or looking for merger partners. Goldcrest was now trading on a stable basis, and had in hand a plan for renewal. Since part of that plan involved a relationship with Allied, and since as long as I worked for both companies we were going to be faced with the intractable problem of conflicts of interests, it was in everyone's best interest for me to stand down as chief executive. I would better serve the company by supplying it with a stream of high-quality films from Allied.

Whether or not the sales proposal, and the division of Goldcrest into two companies, would ever have come about, we will never know, for we were suddenly faced with an unexpected and very welcome intervention by an American property developer by the name of Earle Mack.

Chapter Sixty

Bids and Bidders

Eberts: John Chambers had been introduced to Earle Mack in New York in the second week of September 1986. The go-between was Sid Finger, a specialist film auditor and producers' representative. Sid is an old friend of mine and one-time board member of IFI. He was the man who had prepared the valuation of Goldcrest's portfolio back in 1983. He had also audited, on our behalf, Embassy's distribution accounts for *Escape from New York* and *The Howling*. Sid is soft-spoken and low-key, but utterly professional and as hard as nails. He was now, amongst other things, a consultant to Mack. Sid had informed John that his client was looking for a suitable entrée into the entertainment business. Goldcrest, he felt, might be the ideal vehicle. So John met Mack and came back to London singing his praises. Mack was rich, smart and classy. He was forty-seven years old, a real-estate tycoon, anglophile, breeder of racehorses, and board member of several cultural institutions in New York. He wasn't interested in asset-stripping or buying up tax losses. He could see the value of Goldcrest's name and reputation and was interested in putting money in to rebuild the business.

On 1 October I met Mack myself. I, too, was impressed. He was not in any way connected with the film industry, although he had made two or three highly regarded small films on his own account some years before, but he grasped the details very easily. He was certainly a good businessman and had no trouble at all in making an assessment of Goldcrest's present condition and future prospects. Two days after our meeting he made an outline offer in writing.

Earle's proposal was that he would leave the existing shareholdings as they were: he was not going to offer money to buy anybody out. As for how and to what degree the loan-stock holders would take precedence over the rest, he would leave that for the Goldcrest shareholders themselves to decide. He was not offering money for the loan stock either. He would also leave *The Mission* to one side, so that all income generated by it would be shared among the existing shareholders. What he would do was put about £6 million of new cash into the company in exchange for an 85 per cent shareholding. The existing shareholders, in other words, would see their combined holdings reduced to a mere 15 per cent share. But instead of having 100 per cent of a company worth, at best, £2.8 million, including *The Mission*, they would have 15 per cent of a company worth, say £8 million and they would still have *The Mission*. The proposal was very much more complicated than that in its details, but in outline it was fairly simple. The important point to grasp is that Mack's deal was so structured that it guaranteed the future of the company. We would have £6 million for new investment. This was a simpler and more attractive proposal than the sales company/GAGL idea, which did not interest Earle at all.

The first reaction of the shareholders was to say, 'Well, that's not a very good deal.' Hell, it was the *only* deal. We had had one previous firm offer, from UAA, and that had been thrown out after cursory consideration. A year had passed without so much as a nibble of interest on the part of anybody. In that time, the value of the company had tumbled so much that it made the UAA offer look generous in retrospect. But the shareholders hummed and haa'd, hoping, I think, that *The Mission* would be such a smash that Mr Mack's money would not be needed.

They did not have to wait long to find out.

The Mission opened on 4 October in Paris and Madrid. At first it did very well and we were able to take ads. in the trades congratulating the film-makers on their success. On 30 October, the film opened in London, again to pretty good business. But Paris, London, and Madrid were not the markets that interested us. On 7 November 1986, it opened in New York. For a couple of weeks it did well on limited release in showcase cinemas, but when it went wide it simply failed to attract an audience. By the end of its US run it had taken rentals of only $8.3 million. By comparison with *Revolution* and *Absolute Beginners* that was pretty good, and it was on a par with, for example, *Missing* (1982, $7.9 million), *Gorky Park* (1983, $8 million) and *Mosquito Coast* (1986, $7.7 million). But none of those comparisons had any meaning. The real meaning of rentals of $8.3 million was that we had to take a write-off of £3 million. Far from saving the company, *The Mission* had delivered the *coup de grâce*. Its losses brought our total deficit for the year to £9.3 million, leaving the company with a negative net worth (i.e. we were insolvent) of £450,000.

Profit and loss account	1983	1984	1985	1986
Turnover £000	12,402	13,990	16,081	15,998
direct costs and amortization	(9,338)	(10,350)	(32,041)	(23,842)
Gross profit/(loss)	3,064	3,640	(15,960)	(7,844)
operating expenses	(1,741)	(2,501)	(2,978)	(1,785)
Operating profit/(loss)	1,323	1,139	(18,938)	(9,629)
Associated companies,				
currency exchanges, etc.	(198)	(127)	(669)	190
Profit/(loss) before interest	1,125	1,012	(19,607)	(9,439)
interest receivable	148	699	334	124
interest payable	(1,444)	(97)	(1,360)	(1,620)
Pre-tax profit/(loss)	(171)	1,614	(20,633)	(10,935)
Taxation	(864)	(30)	894	1,229
Profit/(loss) after tax	(1,035)	1,584	(19,739)	(9,706)
Extraordinary items	–	40	(369)	370
Retained profit/(loss)	**(1,035)**	**1,624**	**(20,108)**	**(9,336)**

Balance sheet	1983	1984	1985	1986
Assets: £000				
office equipment, etc.	138	192	142	60
associated companies	383	227	10	40
films/TV in distribution	5,388	14,508	11,455	12,229
films/TV in production	10,477	3,760	15,012	–
films/TV in development	724	862	644	–
Total fixed assets	**17,110**	**19,549**	**27,263**	**12,329**
current assets/(liabilities)	673	10,472	(10,521)	(4,454)
	17,783	30,021	16,742	7,875
Liabilities:				
creditors (inc. loan stock)	(307)	(545)	(7,783)	(7,687)
deferred taxation	(616)	(273)	(143)	(638)
Net assets/(liabilities)	**16,860**	**29,203**	**8,816**	**(450)**
made up of,				
share capital and other reserves	22,407	33,119	32,846	32,846
accumulated losses	(5,547)	(3,916)	(24,030)	(33,296)
	16,860	**29,203**	**8,816**	**(450)**

To quote from a circular issued by the board at the time:

While Goldcrest remains able at the moment to meet its commitments as they fall due, these accounts show that, without a significant financial injection, the company is technically insolvent and will not be able to continue in business. In the event of liquidation, the existing ordinary shares would be of no value and it is likely that there would also be a substantial deficit as regards the existing loan stock.

All of a sudden, the Mack offer looked very reasonable.

Negotiations were entered into with Mack in earnest and reached fruition with the signing of a heads of agreement in January 1987. Pearson, Electra and Noble Grossart were signatories to this agreement, so it enjoyed the support of very nearly a majority of shares. But since the Mack proposal required a major capital reconstruction, it would, according to our articles of association, have to command the support, not of 51 per cent but 75 per cent of the voting stock. One of the terms of the heads of agreement was that we would use our 'best efforts' to secure the support of the remaining shareholders.

As soon as news of this deal hit the trades, we received counter-bids from Hemdale and Brent Walker, and indications of interest from Virgin and others. It was incredible. We had been on the block for months and no one had shown a glimmer of interest. Since September 1985, I had approached every single source of funds, including all the other worthwhile independent companies that I could think of. Nothing. But it often happens that when the ugly girl is finally asked to dance, all the other guys in the hall jump up and want to dance with her too. That's what happened to Goldcrest. We had fourteen or fifteen enquiries in the space of a few weeks, but did not respond to any of them. We couldn't. We were bound by our 'best-efforts' agreement with Mack, an agreement which was not only legally, but morally binding.

A number of our smaller shareholders took great exception to this. It was not that they approved or otherwise of the Mack deal; it was that they disapproved, on principle, of not being able to consider whatever else was on the table. Not that there was much else on the table: pretty soon most of the interest died down and it was just Mack, Hemdale and Brent Walker, the latter operating through a joint venture with one of our existing shareholders under the name Masterman. On 20 February, Masterman made a formal offer. This was followed, on 25 February, by a formal offer from Hemdale. There then began the most bizarre episode in Goldcrest's history, at the end of which we sold the company to the wrong bidder.

First it is important to understand what was at stake. Goldcrest was a name, a marque, of the highest quality. Our shareholders were blue-chip companies, our films were Oscar winners, our reputation for honest dealing was unquestioned. These were, and still are, uncommon qualities in the independent film world. They were qualities that were shared by Earle Mack. It was our reputation that had first attracted him. His plan was to ignore our losses and mistakes, and to build on our undoubted strengths. Furthermore, he had every intention of honouring the deal that had been agreed between Allied and Goldcrest.

Masterman was a different prospect altogether. They were bidding for: (a) a library of twenty-four films and nearly 100 hours of television; (b) net forward income of £9–11 million (i.e. the long-term forecast Goldcrest share of revenues to be received from the exploitation of that library); (c) accumulated losses of £33 million that could be set against their own tax liabilities; and (d) the name. In that order. The main point was that Masterman could give no guarantee that they would protect the independence, good name or reputation of Goldcrest, nor that they even intended to keep the company going. Brent Walker's activities in the film business had included video and film distribution as well as film and television production, but the kind of product in which they had hitherto shown an interest – they had invested in *Loophole*, *Return of the Soldiers*, a series of Gilbert and Sullivan operas and two Joan Collins pictures, *The Bitch* and *The Stud* – was not compatible with the kind of product financed by Goldcrest. Furthermore, it was most unlikely that they would want to honour the deal between Allied and Goldcrest. They were interested only in snapping up some cheap assets.

The same was true, point for point, about Hemdale. The only difference between Hemdale and Masterman was that Hemdale, although nominally a British company, was based in LA and had a US theatrical distribution operation.

However, unlike Earle Mack, both Masterman and Hemdale were prepared to buy out the existing shareholders. Masterman offered 6 pence a share, or the equivalent in Masterman loan stock and warrants, for all the ordinary Goldcrest shares, plus 36 pence a share, or the equivalent in Masterman loan stock and warrants, for the Goldcrest loan stock. The combined outright cash value of this bid was £4.9 million. Hemdale, whose bid was complicated by a pledge to subscribe new loan stock and guarantee a loan facility, offered 3.5 pence for the ordinary shares, and just under 5 pence a share for the loan stock. The outright cash value of this bid was just under £2 million. For any Goldcrest shareholder wanting to get out, the Masterman offer was clearly preferable to the offer made by Hemdale, and both were better than Mack, who wasn't buying anybody out at all but merely putting fresh money into the company.

On 2 March 1987, an extraordinary general meeting of the Goldcrest shareholders agreed that, given the nature of the heads of agreement signed with Mack, the Mack deal should be put to the shareholders first. If it was accepted, then so be it. If it wasn't, then the company would be absolved from its obligations to Mack and would invite bids from all-comers. The vote on the Mack deal was set for 3 July 1987.

Sold

Ilott: Earle Mack's intervention and the shelving of the GAGL proposal had thrown the Goldcrest management into some confusion. On stepping down as chief executive, Eberts's plan had been that Chambers and East would be managing directors of sister companies. Now that Goldcrest wasn't to be split, there was need for only one leader. Eberts favoured East, on the grounds that, for the foreseeable future, Goldcrest would be a sales-led company. He also argued that East had the front-office experience and a wide range of contacts in the industry. Chambers, however, would not work under East, whom he regarded as a competent but relatively inexperienced salesman who had no knowledge or understanding of how to run a business. Mack favoured Chambers, in whom he saw a professional manager who spoke a business language that he, Mack, understood. But East would not work under Chambers.

In April 1987, just after the Oscar ceremonies at which *Room With a View* won three awards and *The Mission* one (bringing Goldcrest's remarkable tally to nineteen Academy Awards in six years), East solved the problem by resigning to join an American company, Carolco. This loss was a tremendous blow to Goldcrest's prestige, especially among international distributors. Chambers had a wealth of experience in running film companies, but no one outside Wardour Street knew who he was.

On 11 June 1987, Chambers was duly appointed Goldcrest's managing director. He immediately set about drumming up support for the Mack deal among the shareholders. Indeed, it would be no exaggeration to say that Chambers set his whole heart on Mack's success.

Hemdale and Masterman however, were also canvassing support.

Eberts: It was not just John who wanted Mack to succeed. We all did. Dickie, myself, the management and staff, Pearson, Electra, Angus Grossart: all the stalwarts of Goldcrest wanted Mack's offer to be accepted. It did not put money straight into the pockets of the share-holders, in the way that the Masterman and Hemdale deals would do, but it did put money into the company, and it guaranteed that Goldcrest would have a future.

At one point, 74 per cent of the votes seemed likely to favour Mack, 17 per cent to oppose him and 9 per cent to be undecided. For his offer to be accepted we had to secure 75 per cent of the total. So we worked feverishly to find a shareholder somewhere who would commit that missing percentage point. We failed. On 3 July 1987, Mack's offer received 74.39588 per cent of the votes and therefore fell short of the necessary 75 per cent majority by a margin of 0.6 per cent. This was the bitterest blow of all for us at Goldcrest. We had kept the leaking ship afloat for two years and at last we had found a saviour, an investor who understood and appreciated what Goldcrest was all about. To have reached agreement with Mack, and for that agreement to have been endorsed by Electra, Pearson and Noble Grossart, and for their endorse-ment, in turn, to have been backed by more than 74 per cent of the votes, only to have the whole thing lost on the votes of six or eight shareholders who between them accounted for less than 26 per cent of the stock, was as much as we could bear.

Theoretically, Mack's offer stayed on the table – indeed, he offered to match the Masterman offer for all those shareholders who were not signatories to the original heads of agreement – but there was no chance that, having been rejected once, it would be accepted the second time. The 75 per cent rule ensured that the majority would now vote with the minority just to ensure that there was a clear outcome. This logic may seem perverse, but it has to be borne in mind that there *had* to be an injection of money for the company to survive. It was technically insol-vent. If neither Hemdale, nor Mack, nor Masterman, nor any other bidder could command the support of the shareholders, Goldcrest would collapse. After the failure of *The Mission*, not even the sales-company idea could be resuscitated.

We invited tenders from all-comers and gave them until 14 August to enter their bids. Bundles of documentation were despatched to more than a dozen parties who declared themselves interested, but, in the event, none of them made an offer. Even Hemdale dropped out. We were left with Masterman. On 20 August the board decided to recommend the Masterman bid to the shareholders. Although I had been strongly in favour of the Mack offer, and had nothing at all to gain from Masterman, I too voted for this recommendation. John Chambers could not bring himself to do it. He abstained. I think he was wrong. To abstain was merely to cock a snook at Masterman; it didn't help Goldcrest at all.

On 22 September 1987, Masterman's offer document, with the board's recommendation, was issued to shareholders, who were given until 13 October to register their votes. The offer was duly accepted in respect of 87 per cent of the ordinary stock and 95 per cent of the loan stock. The hold-outs were those, like Mike Wooller (who still owned a share of Goldcrest), who would not vote for Masterman on principle.

All this had to be put formally to an extraordinary general meeting which was held on 15 October. It was Goldcrest's last gathering. Two outside shareholders – i.e. non-board members – attended. One of them represented Ensign Trust, which was Brent Walker's partner in Masterman. The other was Lyn Hopkins from the Post Office Staff Superannuation Fund, a strong supporter of the Mack deal and one of the first people to have put money into Goldcrest all those years before. No one else showed up. The meeting took about three minutes. Half a dozen resolutions, all of them concerning the transfer of ownership of stock, options and warrants, were put and duly carried. And that was it. End of meeting. End of Goldcrest.

I cried. It was a very sad day. I had a hard time leaving the room. I wanted to continue the meeting somehow, prolong Goldcrest's life for two or three minutes more by having conversations with people. It seemed so preposterous that it should have come to this. So unnecessary. £34 million down the drain. A decade in our lives. And to have sold out to Masterman after 74 per cent of the shares had been voted in favour of Mack. It was absurd. Such an end called for ceremonial, or even a wake. But we were already saying our goodbyes.

I left the room, and in that minute I was thinking about the next thing, about Allied and about setting up a new Goldcrest in some way.

Postscript

Ilott: Masterman took over the reins of Goldcrest on 16 October 1987. Although Masterman would have been happy to have them stay, four Goldcrest staff resigned immediately and others followed soon after. John Chambers, a bitterly disappointed and exhausted man, quit in November to make way for a new management team, led by John Quested and Don Andersen. Quested and Andersen were cut of a very different cloth from the likes of Eberts, Chambers, Norris, Wooller, Gavin or Clegg, and they did not find ready acceptance with the staff. Within a year, only one of the old Goldcrest employees remained. As expected, Brent Walker's other film and television operations were merged into the company, which, although it kept the name and the library, was Goldcrest no longer.

After a long period of apparent inactivity, the new Goldcrest made a series of acquisitions and production deals. It bought Elstree studios (home of the *Indiana Jones* series), a sound studio, the Roger Cherrill post-production house and the Cherry Video facilities house. It entered into a $44 million deal with Sullivan Bluth Productions (makers of *An American Tail*) for the production of three feature-length animated films. And it put four of its own projects, *Killing Time, Black Rainbow, Golden Glory* and *Madame Solario*, into development. By the middle of 1989, Goldcrest comprised four divisions: production, sales, communications (the company has interests in cable television) and facilities (the studios).

In all this activity, Brent Walker acted for the new Goldcrest in much the same way as Pearson had acted for the old: as banker, guarantor and lender of last resort. And just as Pearson had been keen to have Goldcrest established as a separate company in 1984, so Brent Walker was soon to be looking for ways that the new-look Goldcrest could be floated off as a fully independent entity, taking the Brent Walker film and television library with it. By the end of 1989 a management buy-out was being planned. A price tag of £90 million has been put on the company, which now has fifteen more staff than it had at the time of the takeover.

The new Goldcrest is profitable. The library has generated considerable income and the new administration's first two releases, *All Dogs Go to Heaven*, directed by Don Bluth, and *Black Rainbow*, directed by Mike Hodges, have been well received. But it is no longer the flagship of the British industry, cannot boast board members of the calibre of Puttnam and Attenborough and is unlikely, at least for the foreseeable future, to figure in the lists of Academy Award winners. And, again unlike the old Goldcrest, it keeps a very low profile in Wardour Street.

John Chambers founded his own company, Golden Square Films, in January 1988. He intended this company to emulate the successes, while avoiding the failures, of the old Goldcrest. In the summer of 1989, he shelved the idea and joined John Heyman's World Film Services. David Norris went back into law, with a partnership specializing in entertainment business. He was soon again trying his hand at independent production. Bill Gavin slowly built up his own sales company, Gavin Films, which has weathered the storms that have buffeted the independent film industry in the last three years. James Lee worked for a year with a consortium which eventually failed to secure a satellite television franchise from the British government. He then went back to management consultancy with the Boston Consulting Group. (One of the companies that did win a satellite franchise, British Satellite Broadcasting, is heavily backed by Pearson.)

Michael Stoddart, still at Electra, soon found himself embroiled in what must have seemed like a case of *déjà vu:* another boardroom battle, this time at the Next retail group, in the course of which the founder and inspiration of the company, George Davies, was forced to resign and Stoddart himself took the chair.

David Puttnam endured what has to be described as a disastrous year at Columbia before quitting to return to independent production. His company, Enigma, again has a relationship with Warner Bros. Don Cruickshank did not last long at Virgin, the public flotation of which proved to be a costly embarrassment to all concerned. Mike Wooller found himself running the feature-film division of Granada Television. This did not last long, nor was it considered to have been a conspicuous success. Sandy Lieberson resumed the life of an independent producer before taking up the job of head of international production for his old friend Alan Ladd at Pathé (formerly the Cannon Group).

Guy East was soon out of Carolco and set himself up in his own company, Majestic Films, primarily selling films developed or financed by Jake Eberts's company, Allied Filmmakers. Garth Thomas, like his predecessor Terry Clegg, went back to freelance producing. Richard Attenborough made the much-acclaimed, but financially unsuccessful, *Cry Freedom*, and is now working on two long-cherished projects, *Tom Paine* and *Charlie Chaplin* (the former being developed with Eberts). Hugh Hudson's first film since Revolution, *Lost Angels*, was shown to a decidedly mute response at Cannes in 1989.

Junior Goldcrest employees are to be found in offices up and down Wardour Street, in the Groucho Club or the brasserie of L'Escargot. They form a clan of the living dead: unable quite to shake off the memory of what were golden days, and equally unable to establish new lives for themselves in an industry that has dwindled drastically since the real Goldcrest left the scene.

Indeed, the Goldcrest legacy is mixed. On the one hand, the company can boast of having been involved in films which received forty Academy Award nominations and nineteen Academy Awards (Oscars) in the space of six years. This achievement, unequalled by any other independent company, stamped the mark of quality and international acceptance on what was undoubtedly a renaissance of British film-making. That renaissance itself was fuelled by Goldcrest's money. Between 1980 and 1987, the company invested £90 million in British film and television productions. Those productions, in turn, launched the careers of a host of new British talent.

On the other hand, Goldcrest's sudden collapse was followed by an immediate withdrawal of virtually all City investment in independent film and television production. To this day, it is almost impossible for a British producer to raise finance within Britain. Indeed, it is virtually impossible to raise finance from outside the entertainment industry itself. This has meant that leading figures in the UK such as David Puttnam, Richard Attenborough, Alan Parker and Hugh Hudson now have to rely principally on the funds of American studios, which, naturally, demand approval rights of the creative elements in any film package. To what degree, for example, a Puttnam film such as *Memphis Belle*, which tells the story of a wartime American bomber crew based in England, can be called British is open to question.

Does this matter? To anyone who cares about films and thinks that they have something to contribute to our understanding and enjoyment of ourselves, the answer has to be yes. For a film culture, like any other, thrives on diversity and depth of experience. For British film-makers to find themselves making only American films with American subjects is as great a loss to the American public as it is to the public in Britain.

This touches on what is perhaps the truly sad element in the Goldcrest story. The loss of Goldcrest has meant that, once again, British film-makers have no home, no source of reliable and regular employment out of which a coherent body of work can emerge. Without such a body of work there is no tradition, no canon, no accumulation of skills on which to draw. And the skills that are lacking are not just creative ones, but the entrepreneurial, administrative and management skills without which the creative voices will never be heard. Ealing, London Films, the production arms of Rank and EMI, and now Goldcrest have flickered into brilliant light only to flicker out again leaving nothing but shadows.

It has to be said that Goldcrest's demise was not an isolated event. PSO, Atlantic Entertainment, the Cannon Group, De Laurentiis Entertainment, New World Pictures, King's Road, Empire: a host of independent companies faltered or ran aground in the late 1980s. The equation of independent film financing, which had worked very much in favour of independent producers in the late 1970s, began to work very much against them as soon as the supply of product, fuelled by the huge influx of money in the period 1980–4, exceeded the demand. It was the US majors, who had suffered at the hands of the independents in 1982, who were able to pick up the pieces and re-establish, with even greater authority, their hold over the industry. By 1989, the independent sector lay in ruins and the studios announced the biggest takings in their history. In this context, the question arises, would Goldcrest have foundered in any event? Or, to put it another way, would Eberts have done any better than Lee had he not left the company at the end of 1983?

Eberts's legacy to Lee had been a small accumulated deficit, a magnificent library, an enthusiastic, expert but ever-growing staff and three major projects, *Mandrake*, *The Mosquito Coast* and *The Emerald Forest*. *Mandrake*, as we know, soaked up a great deal more money under the Lee regime before it was written off with a loss to Goldcrest of about £600,000. *The Mosquito Coast*, which was eventually made under the auspices of the Saul Zaentz Company (with the downbeat ending unchanged), proved a financial failure, taking US rentals of only $7.7 million. *The Emerald Forest* turned a profit.

Evidence from the company minutes dating from before Eberts first left Goldcrest, and Richard Attenborough's recall of conversations the two men had in New York, provide strong support for Eberts's claim that he would not have made *Absolute Beginners*, *A Room With a View*, *Dance With a Stranger*, *The Mission* or *Revolution*.

Eberts: After Goldcrest, I concentrated exclusively on Allied. The entire staff consists of me and my assistant, Irene Lyons. We work out of one small room in Mayfair – even smaller than Goldcrest's first office back in 1977. The film-makers with whom Allied has worked in the last three years include Dickie Attenborough, John Boorman, Alan Pakula, Hugh Hudson, Terry Gilliam, Jean-Jacques Annaud, Bernd Eichinger, Roland Joffe, Kevin Costner, Bruce Beresford, Peter Bogdanovich, Richard Lester and Richard Williams: all major film-makers of international acclaim. The company has already been involved in the production of fourteen films, including *The Name of the Rose, Hope and Glory, Me and Him, Baron Munchausen, Last Exit to Brooklyn, Driving Miss Daisy, Where the Heart Is, Texasville, Dances with Wolves, City of Joy, Get Back* and *The Thief and the Cobbler*. At the time of writing, seven of these are still in production. We have seven other projects in development, each of which has a major film-maker attached.

The record, from a creative point of view, is excellent. *Baron Munchausen, Hope and Glory* and *Driving Miss Daisy* together received eighteen Oscar nominations. Financially, Allied has been far more successful than Goldcrest ever was, even though Allied's total subscribed capital is only $5 million. *The Name of the Rose* was one of the biggest critical and commercial successes of the 1980s. It did poorly in its US release, but it took over $100 million in box office receipts in the international markets.

But this record does not necessarily mean that I would have managed Goldcrest's affairs any better than James did. It was when he and I were working together, after all, as chairman and chief executive respectively, that the company's growth got out of hand. We should never have been involved in television, and that we did so was partly my fault. We should not have built up such a large head office, covering legal, business affairs, finance and administration, nor should we have been involved in extraneous activities like cable, video and magazine publishing. These initiatives came mainly from James, but I share some of the blame – if only for not objecting to them more strongly. We should have got involved, as we did, in foreign sales, and for that I take some credit. It was the sales operation that kept Goldcrest going through 1986 and 1987, and foreign sales have fuelled Allied's success.

But my Allied record does point to the major cause of Goldcrest's demise. Goldcrest's fortunes hinged on the choice of film investments. The production programme entered into by Goldcrest in 1985 was wrong on every count. In almost every case, the scripts were not good, and were known to be so. All the films were too expensive, and were known to be too expensive. Too much risk was spread across too few productions.

Two of the production teams were unreliable. James and his colleagues must take the blame for the fact that, in spite of all these things being known, they allowed that production programme to go ahead. It was primarily on the failure of that programme, and not on the changing conditions in the marketplace and the burdensome overheads, that Goldcrest foundered.

Appendix I

Goldcrest Film and Television Investments

Profit-and-loss summary at 30 September 1987, immediately preceding the sale of the company to Masterman:

	Goldcrest's share of investment	Share of revenues	Cash surplus/ (deficit)	Book value	Contribution/ (deficit)
Feature films £000	63,341	50,275	(13,066)	6,636	(6,430)
Television features	5,443	4,050	(1,393)	797	(596)
Television drama series	13,553	10,613	(2,940)	(263)	(3,203)
Documentaries, etc.	5,485	1,809	(3,676)	557	(3,119)
Total	**87,822**	**66,747**	**(21,075)**	**7,727**	**(13,348)**

As the £7.7 million book value testifies, there was considerable revenue-earning life left in these investments at the time of the Brent Walker/Masterman takeover. The following long-term forecast shows what Masterman expected to happen (and what by and large did happen) in the years after 1987:

Long-term profit-and-loss forecast, by project:

£000	Goldcrest's share of investment	Goldcrest's share of revenues	Contribution/ (deficit)
Feature films			
Absolute Beginners	4,680	1,859	(2,821)
Another Country	735	858	123
Cal	396	278	(118)
Chariots of Fire	–	864	864
Dance With a Stranger	253	361	108
Dream One	2,099	1,482	(617)
The Dresser	1,456	1,744	288
Enigma	985	355	(630)
Escape from New York	720	1,392	672
The Frog Prince	896	334	(562)
Gandhi	5,076	11,461	6,385
Hope and Glory	1,288	1,665	377
The Howling	145	396	251
The Killing Fields	8,419	10,664	2,245

£000	Goldcrest's share of investment	Goldcrest's share of revenues	Contribution/ (deficit)
Knights and Emeralds	1,113	340	(773)
Local Hero	2,551	3,290	739
The Mission	15,130	12,250	(2,880)
Mr Love	486	330	(156)
The Plague Dogs	903	308	(595)
Revolution	15,603	5,987	(9,616)
A Room With a View	460	1,901	1,441
Smooth Talk	516	635	119
Unsuitable Job for a Woman	316	196	(120)
White Mischief	1,300	1,633	333
Sub-total – feature films	**65,526**	**60,583**	**(4,943)**
Television features			
Arthur's Hallowed Ground	319	265	(54)
Dark Enemy	10	–	(10)
Experience Preferred	480	728	248
Forever Young	420	514	94
The Ploughman's Lunch	398	271	(127)
P'Tang Yang Kipperbang	378	749	371
Red Monarch	553	292	(261)
Runners	721	401	(320)
Secrets	461	620	159
Sharma and Beyond	504	340	(164)
Those Glory, Glory Days	556	313	(243)
The Big Surprise/Winter Flight	581	388	(193)
Sub-total – television features	**5,381**	**4,881**	**(500)**
Television drama series			
Concealed Enemies	558	545	(13)
The Far Pavilions	6,755	4,755	(2,000)
Robin of Sherwood 1–6	1,289	1,683	394
Robin of Sherwood 7–13	1,944	2,408	464
Robin of Sherwood 14–26	4,035	1,964	(2,071)
Three Sovereigns	149	219	70
Tottie	25	6	(19)
Sub-total – television drama series	**14,755**	**11,580**	**(3,175)**
Television documentary series, etc.			
Assignment Adventure	1,300	755	(545)
Gastank	196	173	(23)
How We Learned to Ski	150	72	(78)
The Living Body	2,650	995	(1,655)
The Magic Planet	105	22	(83)
Shakespeare's Sonnets	307	83	(224)
The Wine Programme	257	106	(151)
The World: a TV History	508	148	(360)
Sub-total – documentaries	**5,473**	**2,354**	**(3,119)**
Grand Total	**91,135**	**79,398**	**(11,737)**

Variance between actual performance at 30 September 1987 and long-term forecast:

£000	30.9.87	Forecast	Variance
Goldcrest share of investments	87,822	91,135	+ 3,313
Goldcrest share of revenues	66,747	79,398	+10,651
Forecast surplus of future revenues over future investment			7,338

The price Masterman paid for Goldcrest was £4.9 million in cash, Masterman stock and warrants. Masterman had to honour forward commitments in support of Goldcrest's current investments of £3.3 million, making a total outlay of £8.2 million. In exchange, Masterman received a virtually guaranteed cash inflow of £10.6 million, the name and reputation of Goldcrest and the copyright of the titles in the Goldcrest library. By any reckoning this library is very valuable. Masterman did a very good deal.

Appendix II

US Rentals, 1981–7, for Goldcrest Films and Comparable Releases

1981	$ million	
On Golden Pond	61.2	
Chariots of Fire	**30.6**	4 Oscars
Four Seasons	27.1	
Reds	21.0	
Taps	20.5	
Absence of Malice	19.7	
Outland	10.0	
Ragtime	10.0	
S.O.B.	6.2	
Rich and Famous	5.5	
Atlantic City	5.0	

1982		
Tootsie	96.2	
An Officer and a Gentleman	55.2	
The Verdict	26.6	
Gandhi	**25.0**	8 Oscars
Best Friends	19.0	
Bladerunner	14.9	
Sophie's Choice	14.2	
Pink Floyd: The Wall	9.1	
Missing	7.9	
My Favorite Year	7.1	

1983		
Terms of Endearment	50.3	
The Big Chill	24.3	
Yentl	19.7	
Silkwood	17.8	
The Right Stuff	10.4	
Gorky Park	8.0	
Educating Rita	5.7	
Local Hero	**3.0**	
Another Country	**1.5**	

1984		
The Natural	25.0	
Amadeus	22.8	
The Killing Fields	**15.9**	3 Oscars

A Passage to India	13.8	
Falling in Love	5.8	
The River	5.1	
The Dresser	**2.5**	

1985

The Color Purple	47.9	
Out of Africa	43.1	
Witness	28.5	
The Emerald Forest	**10.7**	
1984	4.4	

1986

Platoon	69.7	
Legal Eagles	27.7	
Peggy Sue Got Married	16.8	
A Room With a View	**12.0**	3 Oscars
Hoosiers	11.6	
The Mission	**8.3**	1 Oscar
The Mosquito Coast	7.7	
Revolution	1.0	
Absolute Beginners	0.3	

1987

Moonstruck	34.4	
Wall Street	20.2	
The Last Emperor	18.8	
Nuts	14.1	
Hope and Glory	4.3	

In addition to the nineteen Oscars listed above, Goldcrest film and television productions received a host of international awards and prizes, including more than fifty BAFTAs, the British Oscars.

Index

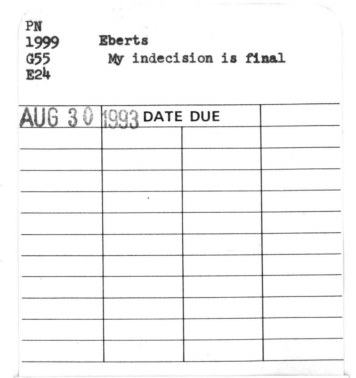